Data Structures using C

Third Edition

Reema Thareja
Assistant Professor
Department of Computer Science
Shyama Prasad Mukherji College for Women
University of Delhi

OXFORD
UNIVERSITY PRESS

OXFORD
UNIVERSITY PRESS

Oxford University Press is a department of the University of Oxford. It furthers the University's objective of excellence in research, scholarship, and education by publishing worldwide. Oxford is a registered trade mark of Oxford University Press in the UK and in certain other countries.

Published in India by
Oxford University Press
22 Workspace, 2nd Floor, 1/22 Asaf Ali Road, New Delhi 110002

First Edition published in 2011
Third Edition published in 2023
Fourth impression 2025

ISBN-13: 978-93-5497-719-0
ISBN-10: 93-5497-719-7

eISBN-13: 978-93-5497-858-6
eISBN-10: 93-5497-858-4

Typeset in Times New Roman
by Ideal, New Delhi
Printed in India by Thomson Press India Private Limited

For product information and current price, please visit www.india.oup.com

I dedicate this book to my family
and
my uncle Mr B.L. Theraja

Preface

Data structures are the backbone of any computer program. They enable efficient data storage, retrieval, and manipulation, allowing programs to process large amounts of information quickly and effectively. In today's world, where data is ubiquitous and the need for speed and accuracy is paramount, a thorough understanding of data structures is essential for every programmer.

This book, *Data Structures using C*, is designed to provide a comprehensive introduction to the fundamental concepts of data structures and their implementation in C programming language. The book is aimed at students, professionals, and anyone interested in computer science, who want to learn about data structures in a practical and easy-to-understand way.

The book starts by introducing the basic concepts of data structures, including arrays, linked lists, and stacks, and gradually builds upon them to cover more advanced topics like trees and graphs. Each chapter includes examples and exercises that help readers gain a deeper understanding of the concepts and their applications.

Throughout the book, the author emphasizes the importance of good programming practices and provides readers with numerous tips and tricks to help them write efficient and error-free codes. The author's experience as a programmer and educator shines through in the book, making it an invaluable resource for both beginners and experienced programmers.

In conclusion, *Data Structures using C* is a must-have for anyone looking to master data structures and their applications. We hope that this book will provide readers with a solid foundation in data structures and inspire them to create innovative and efficient software solutions.

New to the Third Edition

Based on the suggestions from students and faculty members, this edition has been updated and revised to increase the clarity of presentation where required. Some of the prominent changes are as follows:

- Sections on best practices to be followed while writing a C program, need and selection of a data structure
- Updated chapters to demonstrate real-world applications of data structures
- Appendices on code optimization techniques and case studies
- Practical implementation of the algorithms using tested C programs
- Objective type questions to enhance the analytical ability of the students

Content and Coverage

This book is organized into 16 chapters.

Chapter 1, Introduction to C provides a review of basic C constructs which helps readers to familiarize themselves with basic C syntax and concepts that will be used to write programs in this book.

Chapter 2, Introduction to Data Strctures and Algorithms introduces data structures and algorithms which serve as building blocks for creating efficient programs. The chapter explains how to calculate the time complexity which is a key concept for evaluating the performance of algorithms.

From *Chapter 3* onwards, every chapter discusses individual data structures in detail.

Chapter 3, Arrays provides a detailed explanation of arrays that includes one-dimensional, two-dimensional, and multi-dimensional arrays. The operations that can be performed on such arrays are also explained.

Chapter 4, Strings discusses the concept of strings which are also known as character arrays. The chapter not only focuses on reading and writing strings but also explains various operations that can be used to manipulate the character arrays.

Chapter 5, Structures and Unions deals with structures and unions. A structure is a collection of related data items of different types which is used for implementing other data structures such as linked lists, trees, graphs, etc. We will also read about unions which is also a collection of variables of different data types, except that in case of unions, we can only store information in one field at any one time.

Chapter 6, Linked Lists discusses different types of linked lists such as singly linked lists, doubly linked lists, circular linked lists, doubly circular linked lists, header linked lists, and multi-linked lists. Linked list is a preferred data structure when it is required to allocate memory dynamically.

Chapter 7, Stacks focuses on the concept of last-in, first-out (LIFO) data structure called stacks. The chapter also shows the practical implementation of these data structures using arrays as well as linked lists. It also shows how stacks can be used for the evaluation of arithmetic expressions.

Chapter 8, Queues deals with the concept of first-in, first-out (FIFO) data structure called queues. The chapter also provides the real-world applications of queues.

Chapter 9, Trees focuses on binary trees, their traversal schemes and representation in memory. The chapter also discusses expression trees, tournament trees, and Huffman trees, all of which are variants of simple binary trees.

Chapter 10,Efficient Binary Trees broadens the discussion on trees taken up in *Chapter 9* by going one step ahead and discussing efficient binary trees. The chapter discusses binary search trees, threaded binary trees, AVL trees, red-black trees, and splay trees.

Chapter 11, *Multi-way Search Trees* explores trees which can have more than one key value in a single node, such as M-way search trees, B trees, B+ trees, tries, and 2-3 trees.

Chapter 12, Heaps discusses three types of heaps—binary heaps, binomial heaps, and Fibonacci heaps. The chapter not only explains the operations on these data structures but also makes a comparison, thereby highlighting the key features of each structure.

Chapter 13, Graphs contains a detailed explanation of non-linear data structure called graphs. It discusses the memory representation, traversal schemes, and applications of graphs in the real world.

Chapter 14, Searching and Sorting covers two of the most common operations in computer science, i.e. searching and sorting a list of values. It gives the technique, complexity, and program for different searching and sorting techniques.

Chapter 15, Hashing and Collision deals with different methods of hashing and techniques to resolve collisions.

Chapter 16, the last chapter of the book, *Files and Their Organization*, discusses the concept related to file organization. It explains the different ways in which files can be organized on the hard disk and the indexing techniques that can be used for fast retrieval of data.

The book also provides a set of seven appendices.

Appendix A introduces the concept of dynamic memory allocation in C programs.

Appendix B provides a brief discussion of garbage collection technique which is used for automatic memory management.

Appendix C explains backtracking which is a recursive algorithm that uses stacks.

Appendix D includes two C programs which show how to read and write binary files.

Appendix E includes a C program which shows how to sort a list of numbers using address calculation sort.

Appendix F discusses optimization techniques used to transform a program.

Appendix G provides chapter-wise answers to all the objective questions.

Acknowledgements

The writing of this textbook was a mammoth task for which a lot of help was required from many people. Fortunately, I have had wholehearted support of my family, friends, and fellow members of the teaching staff and students at Shyama Prasad Mukherji College, New Delhi.

My special thanks would always go to my parents, Mr Janak Raj Thareja and Mrs Usha Thareja, and my siblings, Pallav, Kimi, and Rashi, who were a source of abiding inspiration and divine blessings for me. I am especially thankful to my son, Goransh, who has been very patient and cooperative in letting me realize my dreams. My sincere thanks go to my uncle, Mr B.L. Theraja, for his inspiration and guidance in writing this book. I also want to thank Rashi Agarwal, Kanika Khatri, Khushi Tyagi and Priyanka Mehta for providing their valuable inputs for bringing out the revised edition.

Last but not the least, I would like to thank the editorial team at Oxford University Press, India for their help and support over the past few years. Comments and suggestions for the improvement of the book are welcome. Please send them to me at reemathareja@gmail.com.

Reema Thareja

Brief Contents

Detailed Contents

CHAPTER 1

Introduction to C

LEARNING OBJECTIVE

This book deals with the study of data structures through C. Before going into a detailed analysis of data structures, it would be useful to familiarize ourselves with the basic knowledge of programming in C. Therefore, in this chapter we will learn about the various constructs of C such as identifiers and keywords, data types, constants, variables, input and output functions, operators, control statements, functions, and pointers.

1.1 INTRODUCTION

The programming language 'C' was developed in the early 1970s by Dennis Ritchie at Bell Laboratories. Although C was initially developed for writing system software, today it has become such a popular language that a variety of software programs are written using this language. The greatest advantage of using C for programming is that it can be easily used on different types of computers. Many other programming languages such as C++ and Java are also based on C which means that you will be able to learn them easily in the future. Today, C is widely used with the UNIX operating system.

Structure of a C Program

A C program contains one or more functions, where a function is defined as a group of statements that perform a well-defined task. Figure 1.1 shows the structure of a C program. The statements in a function are written in a logical sequence to perform a specific task. The `main()` function is the most important function and is a part of every C program. Rather, the execution of a C program begins with this function.

From the structure given in Fig. 1.1, we can conclude that a C program can have any number of functions depending on the tasks that have to be performed, and each function can have any number of statements arranged according to specific meaningful sequence. Note that programmers can choose any name for functions. It is not mandatory to write Function1, Function2, etc., with an exception that every program must contain one function that has its name as `main()`.

1.2 IDENTIFIERS AND KEYWORDS

Every word in a C program is either an identifier or a keyword.

Identifiers

Identifiers are basically names given to program elements such as variables, arrays, and functions. They are formed by using a sequence of letters (both uppercase and lowercase), numerals, and underscores. Following are the rules for forming identifier names:

- Identifiers cannot include any special characters or punctuation marks (like #, $, ^, ?, ., etc.) except the underscore "_".

```
main()
{
        Statement 1;
        Statement 2;
        ...........
        ...........
        Statement N;
}
Function1()
{
        Statement 1;
        Statement 2;
        ...........
        ...........
        Statement N;
}
Function2()
{
        Statement 1;
        Statement 2;
        ...........
        ...........
        Statement N;
}
...................
...................
FunctionN()
{
        Statement 1;
        Statement 2;
        ...........
        ...........
        Statement N;
}
```

Figure 1.1 Structure of a C program

- There cannot be two successive underscores.
- Keywords cannot be used as identifiers.
- The case of alphabetic characters that form the identifier name is significant. For example, 'FIRST' is different from 'first' and 'First'.
- Identifiers must begin with a letter or an underscore. However, use of underscore as the first character must be avoided because several complier-defined identifiers in the standard C library have underscore as their first character. So, inadvertently duplicated names may cause definition conflicts.
- Identifiers can be of any reasonable length. They should not contain more than 31 characters. (They can actually be longer than 31, but the compiler looks at only the first 31 characters of the name.)

Keywords

Like every computer language, C has a set of reserved words often known as keywords that cannot be used as an identifier. All keywords are basically a sequence of characters that have a fixed meaning. By convention, all keywords must be written in lower case letters. Table 1.1 contains the list of keywords in C.

1.3 BASIC DATA TYPES

Data type determines the set of values that a data item can take and the operations that can be performed on the item. C language provides four basic data types. Table 1.2 lists the data types, their size, range, and usage for a C programmer.

The `char` data type is of one byte and is used to store single characters. Note that C does not provide any data type for storing text. This is because text is made up of individual characters.You might have been surprised to see that the range of `char` is given as –128 to 127. `char` is supposed to store characters not numbers, so why this range? The answer is that in the memory, characters are stored in their ASCII codes. For example, the character 'A' has the ASCII code of 65. In memory we will not store 'A' but 65 (in binary number format).

Table 1.1 Keywords in C language

auto	break	case	char	const	continue	default	do
double	else	enum	extern	float	for	goto	if
int	long	register	return	short	signed	sizeof	static
struct	switch	typedef	union	unsigned	void	volatile	while

Table 1.2 Basic data types in C

Data Type	Size in Bytes	Range	Use
char	1	-128 to 127	To store characters
int	2	-32768 to 32767	To store integer numbers
float	4	3.4E-38 to 3.4E+38	To store floating point numbers
double	8	1.7E-308 to 1.7E+308	To store big floating point numbers

In addition, C also supports four modifiers—two sign specifiers (`signed` and `unsigned`) and two size specifiers (`short` and `long`). Table 1.3 shows the variants of basic data types.

Table 1.3 Basic data types and their variants

Data Type	Size in Bytes	Range
char	1	-128 to 127
unsigned char	1	0 to 255
signed char	1	-128 to 127
int	2	-32768 to 32767
unsigned int	2	0 to 65535
signed int	2	-32768 to 32767
short int	2	-32768 to 32767
unsigned short int	2	0 to 65535
signed short int	2	-32768 to 32767
long int	4	-2147483648 to 2147483647
unsigned long int	4	0 to 4294967295
signed long int	4	-2147483648 to 2147483647
float	4	3.4E-38 to 3.4E+38
double	8	1.7E-308 to 1.7E+308
long double	10	3.4E-4932 to 1.1E+4932

Note When the basic data type is omitted from a declaration, then automatically type `int` is assumed. For example,

```
long var;    //int is implied
```

While the smaller data types take less memory, the larger data types incur a performance penalty. Although the data type we use for our variables does not have a big impact on the speed or memory usage of the application, we should always try to use `int` unless there is a need to use any other data type.

1.4 VARIABLES AND CONSTANTS

A variable is defined as a meaningful name given to a data storage location in the computer memory. When using a variable, we actually refer to the address of the memory where the data is stored. C language supports two basic kinds of variables.

Numeric Variables

Numeric variables can be used to store either integer values or floating point values. Modifiers like `short`, `long`, `signed`, and `unsigned` can also be used with numeric variables. The difference between signed and unsigned numeric variables is that signed variables can be either negative or positive but unsigned variables can only be positive. Therefore, by using an unsigned variable we can increase the maximum positive range. When we omit the `signed/unsigned` modifier, C language automatically makes it a signed variable. To declare an unsigned variable, the `unsigned` modifier must be explicitly added during the declaration of the variable.

Character Variables

Character variables are just single characters enclosed within single quotes. These characters could be any character from the ASCII character set—letters ('a', 'A'), numerals ('2'), or special characters ('&').

Declaring Variables

To declare a variable, specify the data type of the variable followed by its name. The data type indicates the kind of values that the variable can store. Variable names should always be meaningful and must reflect the purpose of their usage in the program. In C, variable declaration always ends with a semi-colon. For example,

```
int emp_num;
float salary;
char grade;
double balance_amount;
unsigned short int acc_no;
```

In C, variables can be declared at any place in the program but two things must be kept in mind. First, variables should be declared before using them. Second, variables should be declared closest to their first point of use so that the source code is easier to maintain.

Initializing Variables

While declaring the variables, we can also initialize them with some value. For example,

```
int emp_num = 7;
float salary = 9800.99
char grade = 'A';
double balance_amount = 100000000;
```

Constants

Constants are identifiers whose values do not change. While values of variables can be changed at any time, values of constants can never be changed. Constants are used to define fixed values like *pi* or the charge on an electron so that their value does not get changed in the program even by mistake.

Declaring Constants

To declare a constant, precede the normal variable declaration with `const` keyword and assign it a value.

```
const float pi = 3.14;
```

1.5 WRITING THE FIRST C PROGRAM

To write a C program, we first need to write the code. For that, open a text editor. If you are a Windows user, you may use Notepad and if you prefer working on UNIX/Linux, you can use `emac` or `vi`. Once the text editor is opened on your screen, type the following statements:

```
int main()
{
    printf("\n Welcome to the world of C ");// prints the message on the screen
    return 0;// returns a value 0 to the operating system
}
```

After writing the code, select the directory of your choice and save the file as `first.c`.

`#include <stdio.h>` This is the first statement in our code that includes a file called `stdio.h`. This file has some in-built functions. By simply including this file in our code, we can use these functions directly. `stdio` basically stands for Standard Input/Output, which means it has functions for input and output of data like reading values from the keyboard and printing the results on the screen.

`int main()` Every C program `contains` a `main()` function which is the starting point of the program. `int` is the return value of the `main` function. After all the statements in the program have been executed, the last statement of the program will return an integer value to the operating system. The concepts will

Table 1.4 Escape sequences

Escape Sequence	Purpose
`\a`	Audible signal
`\b`	Backspace
`\t`	Tab
`\n`	New line
`\v`	Vertical tab
`\f`	New page\Clear screen
`\r`	Carriage return

be clear to us when we read this chapter in toto. So even if you do not understand certain things, do not worry.

`{ }` The two curly brackets are used to group all the related statements of the `main` function.

`printf("\n Welcome to the world of C ");` The `printf` function is defined in the `stdio.h` file and is used to print text on the screen. The message that has to be displayed on the screen is enclosed within double quotes and put inside brackets.

`\n` is an escape sequence and represents a newline character. It is used to print the message on a new line on the screen. Other escape sequences supported by C language are shown in Table 1.4.

`return 0;` This is a return command that is used to return value 0 to the operating system to give an indication that there were no errors during the execution of the program.

Note Every statement in the main function ends with a semi-colon (;).

`first.c.` If you are a Windows user, then open the command prompt by clicking Start→Run and typing "command" and clicking Ok. Using the command prompt, change to the directory in which you saved your file and then type:

```
C:\>tc first.c
```

In case you are working on UNIX/Linux operating system, then exit the text editor and type

```
$cc first.c -ofirst
```

The `-o` is for the output file name. If you leave out the `-o`, then the file name `a.out` is used.

This command is used to compile your C program. If there are any mistakes in the program, then the compiler will tell you what mistake(s) you have made and on which line the error has occurred. In case of errors, you need to re-open your `.c` file and correct the mistakes. However, if everything is right, then no error(s) will be reported and the compiler will create an `.exe` file for your program. This `.exe` file can be directly run by typing

`"first.exe"` for Windows and `"./first"` for UNIX/Linux operating system

When you run the `.exe` file, the output of the program will be displayed on screen. That is,

```
Welcome to the world of C
```

Note The printf and return statements have been indented or moved away from the left side. This is done to make the code more readable.

Using Comments

Comments are a way of explaining what a program does. C supports two types of comments.

- // is used to comment a single statement.
- /* is used to comment multiple statements. A /* is ended with */ and all statements that lie between these characters are commented.

Note that comment statements are not executed by the compiler. Rather, they are ignored by the compiler as they are simply added in programs to make the code understandable by programmers as well as other users. It is a good habit to always put a comment at the top of a program that tells you what the program does. This helps in defining the usage of the program the moment you open it.

Standard Header Files

Till now we have used `printf()` function, which is defined in the `stdio.h` header file. Even in other programs that we will be writing, we will use many functions that are not written by us. For example, to use the `strcmp()` function that compares two strings, we will pass string arguments and retrieve the result. We do not know the details of how these functions work. Such functions that are provided by all C compilers are included in standard header files. Examples of these standard header files include:

- `string.h` : for string handling functions
- `stdlib.h` : for some miscellaneous functions
- `stdio.h` : for standardized input and output functions
- `math.h` : for mathematical functions
- `alloc.h` : for dynamic memory allocation

All the header files are referenced at the start of the source code file that uses one or more functions from these files.

1.6 INPUT AND OUTPUT FUNCTIONS

The most fundamental operation in a C program is to accept *input* values from a standard input device and *output* the data produced by the program to a standard output device. As shown in Section 1.4, we can assign values to variables using the assignment operator '='. For example,

```
int a = 3;
```

What if we want to assign value to variable `a` that is inputted from the user at run-time? This is done by using the `scanf` function that reads data from the keyboard. Similarly, for outputting results of the program, `printf` function is used that sends results to a terminal. Like `printf` and `scanf`, there are different functions in C that can carry out the input–output operations. These functions are collectively known as Standard Input/Output Library. A program that uses standard input/output functions must contain the following statement at the beginning of the program:

```
#include <stdio.h>
```

scanf()

The `scanf()` function is used to read formatted data from the keyboard. The syntax of the `scanf()` function can be given as,

```
scanf ("control string", arg1, arg2, arg3...argn);
```

The control string specifies the type and format of the data that has to be obtained from the keyboard and stored in the memory locations pointed by the arguments, `arg1, arg2, ...,argn`. The prototype of the control string can be given as,

```
%[*][width][modifier]type
```

* is an optional argument that suppresses assignment of the input field. That is, it indicates that data should be read from the stream but ignored (not stored in the memory location).

width is an optional argument that specifies the maximum number of characters to be read. However, if the `scanf` function encounters a white space or an unconvertible character, input is terminated.

modifier is an optional argument (**h**, **l**, or **L**) , which modifies the type specifier. Modifier **h** is used for `short int` or `unsigned short int`, **l** is used for `long int`, `unsigned long int`, or `double` values. Finally, **L** is used for `long double` data values.

type specifies the type of data that has to be read. It also indicates how this data is expected to be read from the user. The type specifiers for `scanf` function are given in Table 1.5.

Table 1.5 Type specifiers

Type	Qualifying Input
%c	For single characters
%d, %i	For integer values
%e,%E,%f,%g,%G	For floating point numbers
%o	For octal numbers
%s	For a sequence of (string of) characters
%u	For unsigned integer values
%x,%X	For hexadecimal values

The `scanf` function ignores any blank spaces, tabs, and newlines entered by the user. The function simply returns the number of input fields successfully scanned and stored.

As we have not studied functions till now, understanding `scanf` function in depth will be a bit difficult here, but for now just understand that the `scanf` function is used to store values in memory locations associated with variables. For this, the function should have the address of the variables. The address of the variable is denoted by an & sign followed by the name of the variable. Look at the following code that shows how we can input value in a variable of `int` data type:

```
int num;
scanf(" %4d ", &num);
```

The `scanf` function reads first four digits into the address or the memory location pointed by `num`.

Note In case of reading strings, we do not use the & sign in the `scanf` function.

printf()

The `printf` function is used to display information required by the user and also prints the values of the variables. Its syntax can be given as:

```
printf ("control string", arg1,arg2,arg3,...,argn);
```

After the control string, the function can have as many arguments as specified in the control string. The control string contains format specifiers which are arranged in the order so that they correspond with the arguments in the variable list. It may also contain text to be printed such as instructions to the user, identifier names, or any other text to make the text readable.

Note that there must be enough arguments because if there are not enough arguments, then the result will be completely unpredictable. However, if by mistake you specify more number of arguments, the excess arguments will simply be ignored. The prototype of the control string can be given as below:

```
%[flags][width][.precision][modifier]type
```

Each control string must begin with a % sign.

flags is an optional argument, which specifies output justification like decimal point, numerical sign, trailing zeros or octadecimal or hexadecimal prefixes. Table 1.6 shows different types of flags with their descriptions.

Table 1.6 Flags in printf()

Flags	Description
-	Left-justify within the given field width
+	Displays the data with its numeric sign (either + or -)
#	Used to provide additional specifiers like o, x, X, 0, 0x, or 0X for octal and hexadecimal values respectively for values different than zero
0	The number is left-padded with zeroes (0) instead of spaces

width is an optional argument which specifies the minimum number of positions that the output characters will occupy. If the number of output characters is smaller than the specified width, then the output would be right justified with blank spaces to the left. However, if the number of characters is greater than the specified width, then all the characters would be printed.

precision is an optional argument which specifies the number of digits to print after the decimal point or the number of characters to print from a string.

modifier field is same as given for `scanf()` function.

type is used to define the type and the interpretation of the value of the corresponding argument. The type specifiers for `printf` function are given in Table 1.5.

The most simple `printf` statement is

```
printf ("Welcome to the world of C language");
```

The function when executed prompts the message enclosed in the quotation to be displayed on the screen.

For `float x = 8900.768`, the following examples show output under different format specifications:

`printf ("%f", x)`	8	9	0	0	.	7	6	8		
`printf("%10f", x);`			8	9	0	0	.	7	6	8
`printf("%9.2f", x);`			8	9	0	0	.	7	7	
`printf("%6f", x);`	8	9	0	0	.	7	6	8		

1.7 OPERATORS AND EXPRESSIONS

C language supports different types of operators, which can be used with variables and constants to form expressions. These operators can be categorized into the following major groups:

- Arithmetic operators
- Equality operators
- Unary operators
- Bitwise operators
- Comma operator
- Relational operators
- Logical operators
- Conditional operator
- Assignment operators
- Sizeof operator

We will now discuss all these operators.

Arithmetic Operators

Consider three variables declared as,

```
int a=9, b=3, result;
```

We will use these variables to explain arithmetic operators. Table 1.7 shows the arithmetic operators, their syntax, and usage in C language.

Table 1.7 Arithmetic operators

Operation	Operator	Syntax	Comment	Result
Multiply	*	a * b	result = a * b	27
Divide	/	a / b	result = a / b	3
Addition	+	a + b	result = a + b	12
Subtraction	–	a – b	result = a – b	6
Modulus	%	a % b	result = a % b	0

In Table 1.7, a and b (on which the operator is applied) are called **operands**. Arithmetic operators can be applied to any integer or floating point number. The addition, subtraction, multiplication, and division (+, -, *, and /) operators are the usual arithmetic operators, so you are already familiar with these operators.

However, the operator % might be new to you. The modulus operator (%) finds the remainder of an integer division. This operator can be applied only on integer operands and cannot be used on float or double operands.

While performing modulo division, the sign of the result is always the sign of the first operand (the dividend). Therefore,

```
 16    %    3 =  1
-16    %    3 = -1
 16    %   -3 =  1
-16    %   -3 = -1
```

When both operands of the division operator (/) are integers, the division is performed as an integer division. Integer division always results in an integer result. So, the result is always rounded-off by ignoring the remainder. Therefore,

```
9/4 = 2  and  -9/4 = -3
```

> **Note** It is not possible to divide any number by zero. This is an illegal operation that results in a run-time division-by-zero exception thereby terminating the program.

Except for modulus operator, all other arithmetic operators can accept a mix of integer and floating point numbers. If both operands are integers, the result will be an integer; if one or both operands are floating point numbers then the result would be a floating point number.

All the arithmetic operators bind from left to right. Multiplication, division, and modulus operators have higher precedence over addition and subtraction operators. Thus, if an arithmetic expression consists of a mix of operators, then multiplication, division, and modulus will be carried out first in a left to right order, before any addition and subtraction can be performed. For example,

```
     3 + 4 * 7
=    3 + 28
=    31
```

Relational Operators

Table 1.8 Relational operators

Operator	Meaning	Example
<	Less than	3 < 5 gives 1
>	Greater than	7 > 9 gives 0
<=	Less than or equal to	100 <= 100 gives 1
>=	Greater than equal to	50 >=100 gives 0

A relational operator, also known as a comparison operator, is an operator that compares two values or expressions. Relational operators return true or false value, depending on whether the conditional relationship between the two operands holds or not.

For example, to test if x is less than y, relational operator < is used as x < y. This expression will return true value if x is less than y; otherwise the value of the expression will be false. C provides four relational operators which are illustrated in Table 1.8. These operators are evaluated from left to right.

Equality Operators

C language also supports two equality operators to compare operands for strict equality or inequality. They are equal to (==) and not equal to (!=) operators. The equality operators have lower precedence than the relational operators.

The equal-to operator (==) returns true (1) if operands on both sides of the operator have the same value; otherwise, it returns false (0). On the contrary, the not-equal-to operator (!=) returns true (1) if the operands do not have the same value; else it returns false (0). Table 1.9 summarizes equality operators.

Table 1.9 Equality operators

Operator	Meaning
`==`	`Returns 1 if both operands are equal, 0 otherwise`
`!=`	`Returns 1 if operands do not have the same value, 0 otherwise`

Logical Operators

C language supports three logical operators. They are logical AND (&&), logical OR (||), and logical NOT (!). As in case of arithmetic expressions, logical expressions are evaluated from left to right.

Logical AND (&&)

Logical AND is a binary operator, which simultaneously evaluates two values or relational expressions. If both the operands are true, then the whole expression is true. If both or one of the operands is false, then the whole expression evaluates to false. The truth table of logical AND operator is given in Table 1.10.

Table 1.10 Truth table of logical AND

A	B	A && B
0	0	0
0	1	0
1	0	0
1	1	1

For example,

```
(a < b) && (b > c)
```

The whole expression is true only if both expressions are true, i.e., if `b` is greater than `a` and `c`.

Logical OR (||)

Logical OR returns a false value if both the operands are false. Otherwise it returns a true value. The truth table of logical OR operator is given in Table 1.11. For example,

Table 1.11 Truth table of logical OR

A	B	A || B
0	0	0
0	1	1
1	0	1
1	1	1

```
(a < b) || (b > c)
```

The whole expression is true if either `b` is greater than `a` or `b` is greater than `c` or `b` is greater than both `a` and `c`.

Logical NOT (!)

The logical NOT operator takes a single expression and produces a zero if the expression evaluates to a non-zero value and produces a 1 if the expression produces a zero. The truth table of logical NOT operator is given in Table 1.12. For example,

Table 1.12 Truth table of logical NOT

A	! A
0	1
1	0

```
int a = 10, b;
b = !a;
```

Now the value of `b = 0`. This is because value of `a = 10. !a = 0`. The value of `!a` is assigned to `b`, hence the result.

Unary Operators

Unary operators act on single operands. C language supports three unary operators. They are unary minus, increment, and decrement operators.

Unary Minus (–)

Unary minus operator negates the value of its operand. For example, if a number is positive then it becomes negative when preceded with a unary minus operator. Similarly, if the number is negative, it becomes positive after applying the unary minus operator. For example,

```
int a, b = 10;
a = -(b);
```

The result of this expression is `a = -10`, because variable `b` has a positive value. After applying unary minus operator (–) on the operand `b`, the value becomes –10, which indicates it has a negative value.

Increment Operator (++) and Decrement Operator (––)

The increment operator is a unary operator that increases the value of its operand by 1. Similarly, the decrement operator decreases the value of its operand by 1. For example, `--x` is equivalent to writing `x = x - 1`.

The increment/decrement operators have two variants: *prefix* and *postfix*. In a prefix expression (`++x` or `--x`), the operator is applied before the operand while in a postfix expression (`x++` or `x--`), the operator is applied after the operand.

An important point to note about unary increment and decrement operators is that `++x` is not same as `x++`. Similarly, `--x` is not the same as `x--`. Although, `x++` and `++x` both increment the value of `x` by 1, in the former case, the value of `x` is returned before it is incremented. Whereas in the latter case, the value of `x` is returned after it is incremented. For example,

```
int x = 10, y;
```

`y = x++;` is equivalent to writing

```
y = x;
x = x + 1;
```

Whereas `y = ++x;` is equivalent to writing

```
x = x + 1;
y = x;
```

The same principle applies to unary decrement operators. Note that unary operators have a higher precedence than the binary operators. And if in an expression we have more than one unary operator then they are evaluated from right to left.

Conditional Operator

The syntax of the conditional operator is

```
exp1 ? exp2 : exp3
```

`exp1` is evaluated first. If it is true, then `exp2` is evaluated and becomes the result of the expression, otherwise `exp3` is evaluated and becomes the result of the expression. For example,

```
large = (a > b) ? a : b
```

The conditional operator is used to find the larger of two given numbers. First `exp1`, that is `a > b`, is evaluated. If `a` is greater than `b`, then `large = a`, else `large = b`. Hence, `large` is equal to either `a` or `b`, but not both.

Conditional operators make the program code more compact, more readable, and safer to use as it is easier to both check and guarantee the arguments that are used for evaluation. Conditional operator is also known as ternary operator as it takes three operands.

Bitwise Operators

As the name suggests, bitwise operators perform operations at the bit level. These operators include: bitwise AND, bitwise OR, bitwise XOR, and shift operators.

Bitwise AND

Like boolean AND (&&), bitwise AND operator (&) performs operation on bits instead of bytes, chars, integers, etc. When we use the bitwise AND operator, the bit in the first operand is ANDed with the corresponding bit in the second operand. The truth table is the same as we had seen in logical AND operation. The bitwise AND operator compares each bit of its first operand with the corresponding bit of its second operand. If both bits are 1, the corresponding bit in the result is 1 and 0 otherwise. For example,

```
10101010 & 01010101 = 00000000
```

Bitwise OR

When we use the bitwise OR operator (|), the bit in the first operand is ORed with the corresponding bit in the second operand. The truth table is the same as we had seen in logical OR operation. The bitwise OR operator compares each bit of its first operand with the corresponding bit of its second operand. If one or both bits are 1, the corresponding bit in the result is 1 and 0 otherwise. For example,

```
10101010 | 01010101 = 11111111
```

Table 1.13 Truth table of bitwise XOR

A	B	A ^ B
0	0	0
0	1	1
1	0	1
1	1	0

Bitwise XOR

When we use the bitwise XOR operator, the bit in the first operand is XORed with the corresponding bit in the second operand. The truth table of bitwise XOR operator is shown in Table 1.13. The bitwise XOR operator compares each bit of its first operand with the corresponding bit of its second operand. If one of the bits is 1, the corresponding bit in the result is 1 and 0 otherwise. For example,

```
10101010 ^ 01010101 = 11111111
```

Bitwise NOT (~)

The bitwise NOT or complement is a unary operator that performs logical negation on each bit of the operand. By performing negation of each bit, it actually produces the one's complement of the given binary value. Bitwise NOT operator sets the bit to 1 if it was initially 0 and sets it to 0 if it was initially 1. For example,

```
~10101011 = 01010100
```

Shift Operators

C supports two bitwise shift operators. They are shift left (<<) and shift right (>>). The syntax for a shift operation can be given as

```
operand op num
```

where the bits in the operand are shifted left or right depending on the operator (left, if the operator is << and right, if the operator is >>) by number of places denoted by `num`. For example, if we have

```
x = 0001 1101
```

then `x << 1` produces `0011 1010`

When we apply a left shift, every bit in `x` is shifted to the left by one place. So, the MSB (most significant bit) of `x` is lost, the LSB (least significant bit) of `x` is set to 0. Therefore, if we have `x = 0001 1101`, then

```
x << 3 gives result = 1110 1000
```

On the contrary, when we apply a right shift, every bit in `x` is shifted to the right by one place. So, the LSB of `x` is lost, the MSB of `x` is set to 0. For example, if we have `x = 0001 1101`, then

```
x >> 1 gives result = 0000 1110
```

Similarly, if we have `x = 0001 1101`, then

```
x >> 4 gives result = 0000 0001
```

> **Note** The expression `x << y` is equivalent to multiplication of x by 2^y. And the expression `x >> y` is equivalent to division of x by 2^y if x is unsigned or has a non-negative value.

Assignment Operators

In C language, the assignment operator is responsible for assigning values to the variables. While the equal sign (=) is the fundamental assignment operator, C also supports other assignment operators that provide shorthand ways to represent common variable assignments.

When an equal sign is encountered in an expression, the compiler processes the statement on the right side of the sign and assigns the result to the variable on the left side. For example,

```
int x;
x = 10;
```

assigns the value 10 to variable `x`. The assignment operator has right-to-left associativity, so the expression

```
a = b = c = 10;
```

is evaluated as

```
(a = (b = (c = 10)));
```

First 10 is assigned to `c`, then the value of `c` is assigned to `b`. Finally, the value of `b` is assigned to `a`. Table 1.14 contains a list of other assignment operators that are supported by C.

Table 1.14 Assignment operators

Operator	Example
/=	float a=9.0; float b=3.0; a /= b;
\=	int a= 9; int b = 3; a \= b;
*=	int a= 9; int b = 3; a *= b;
+=	int a= 9; int b = 3; a += b;
-=	int a= 9; int b = 3; a -= b;
&=	int a = 10; int b = 20; a &= b;
^=	int a = 10; int b = 20; a ^= b;
<<=	int a= 9; int b = 3; a <<= b;
>>=	int a= 9; int b = 3; a >>= b;

Comma Operator

The comma operator, which is also called the sequential-evaluation operator, takes two operands. It works by evaluating the first expression and discarding its value, and then evaluates the second expression and returns the value as the result of the expression. Comma-separated expressions when chained together are evaluated in left-to-right sequence with the right-most value yielding the result of the expression. Among all the operators, the comma operator has the lowest precedence.

Therefore, when a comma operator is used, the entire expression evaluates to the value of the right expression. For example, the following statement first increments `a`, then increments `b`, and then assigns the value of `b` to `x`.

```
int a=2, b=3, x=0;
x = (++a, b+=a);
```

Now, the value of `x = 6`.

`sizeof` *Operator*

`sizeof` is a unary operator used to calculate the size of data types. This operator can be applied to all data types. When using this operator, the keyword `sizeof` is followed by a type name, variable, or expression. The operator returns the size of the data type, variable, or expression in bytes. That is, the `sizeof` operator is used to determine the amount of memory space that the data type/variable/expression will take.

When a type name is used, it is enclosed in parentheses, but in case of variable names and expressions, they can be specified with or without parentheses. A `sizeof` expression returns an unsigned value that specifies the size of the space in bytes required by the data type, variable, or expression. For example, `sizeof(char)` returns 1, that is the size of a character data type. If we have,

```
int a = 10;
unsigned int result;
result = sizeof(a);
```

then `result = 2`, that is, space required to store the variable *a* in memory. Since `a` is an integer, it requires 2 bytes of storage space.

Operator Precedence Chart

Table 1.15 lists the operators that C language supports in the order of their *precedence* (highest to lowest). The *associativity* indicates the order in which the operators of equal precedence in an expression are evaluated.

Table 1.15 Operators precedence chart

Operator	Associativity
() [] . ->	left-to-right
++(postfix) --(postfix)	right-to-left
++(prefix) --(prefix) +(unary) - (unary) ! ~ (type) *(indirection) &(address) sizeof	right-to-left
* / %	left-to-right
+ -	left-to-right
<< >>	left-to-right
< <= > >=	left-to-right
== !=	left-to-right
&	left-to-right
^	left-to-right
|	left-to-right
&&	left-to-right
||	left-to-right
?:	right-to-left
= += -= *= /= %= &= ^= |= <<= >>=	right-to-left
,(comma)	left-to-right

Examples of Expressions Using the Precedence Chart

If we have the following variable declarations:

```
int a = 0, b = 1, c = -1;
float x = 2.5, y = 0.0;
```

then,

```
(a)  a && b = 0
(b)  a < b && c < b = 1
(c)  b + c || ! a
     = ( b + c) || (!a)
     = 0 ||1
     = 1
(d)  x * 5 && 5 || ( b / c)
     = ((x * 5) && 5) || (b / c)
     = (12.5 && 5) || (1/-1)
     = 1
(e)  a <= 10 && x >= 1 && b
     = ((a <= 10) && (x >= 1)) && b
     = (1 && 1) && 1
     = 1
(f)  !x || !c || b + c
     = ((!x) || (!c)) || (b + c)
     = (0 || 0) || 0
     = 0
(g)  x * y < a + b || c
     = ((x * y) < (a + b)) || c
     = (0 < 1) || -1
     = 1
(h)  (x > y) + !a || c++
     = ((x > y) + (!a)) || (c++)
     = (1 + 1) || 0
     = 1
```

Programming Example

1. Write a program to calculate the area of a circle.

```
#include <stdio.h>
int main()
{
        float radius;
        double area;
        printf("\n Enter the radius of the circle : ");
        scanf("%f", &radius);
        area = 3.14 * radius * radius;
```

```
        printf(" \n Area = %.2lf", area);
        return 0;
}
```

Output

```
Enter the radius of the circle : 7
Area = 153.86
```

1.8 TYPE CONVERSION AND TYPECASTING

Type conversion or typecasting of variables refers to changing a variable of one data type into another. While type conversion is done implicitly, casting has to be done explicitly by the programmer. We will discuss both these concepts here.

Type Conversion

Type conversion is done when the expression has variables of different data types. So to evaluate the expression, the data type is promoted from lower to higher level where the hierarchy of data types can be given as: `double`, `float`, `long`, `int`, `short`, and `char`. For example, type conversion is automatically done when we assign an integer value to a floating point variable. Consider the following code:

```
float x;
int y = 3;
x = y;
```

Now, `x = 3.0`, as integer value is automatically converted into its equivalent floating point representation.

Typecasting

Typecasting is also known as *forced conversion*. It is done when the value of one data type has to be converted into the value of another data type. The code to perform typecasting can be given as:

```
float salary = 10000.00;
int sal;
sal = (int) salary;
```

When floating point numbers are converted to integers, the digits after the decimal are truncated. Therefore, data is lost when floating point representations are converted to integral representations.

As we can see in the code, typecasting can be done by placing the destination data type in parentheses followed by the variable name that has to be converted. Hence, we conclude that typecasting is done to make a variable of one data type to act like a variable of another type.

Programming Example

2. Write a program to convert an integer into the corresponding floating point number.

```
#include <stdio.h>
int main()
{
        float f_num;
        int i_num;
        printf("\n Enter any integer: ");
        scanf("%d", &i_num);
        f_num = (float)i_num;
        printf("\n The floating point variant of %d is = %f", i_num, f_num);
        return 0;
}
```

Output

```
Enter any integer: 56
The floating point variant of 56 is = 56.000000
```

1.9 CONTROL STATEMENTS

Till now we know that the code in the C program is executed sequentially from the first line of the program to its last line. That is, the second statement is executed after the first, the third statement is executed after the second, so on and so forth. Although this is true, in some cases we want only selected statements to be executed. Control flow statements enable programmers to conditionally execute a particular block of code. There are three types of control statements: decision control (branching), iterative (looping), and jump statements. While branching means deciding what actions have to be taken, looping, on the other hand, decides how many times the action has to be taken. Jump statements transfer control from one point to another point.

1.9.1 Decision Control Statements

C supports decision control statements that can alter the flow of a sequence of instructions. These statements help to jump from one part of the program to another depending on whether a particular condition is satisfied or not. These decision control statements include:

(a) `if` statement, (b) `if-else` statement,
(c) `if-else-if` statement, and (d) `switch-case` statement.

`if` *Statement*

`if` statement is the simplest decision control statement that is frequently used in decision making. The general form of a simple `if` statement is shown in Fig. 1.2.

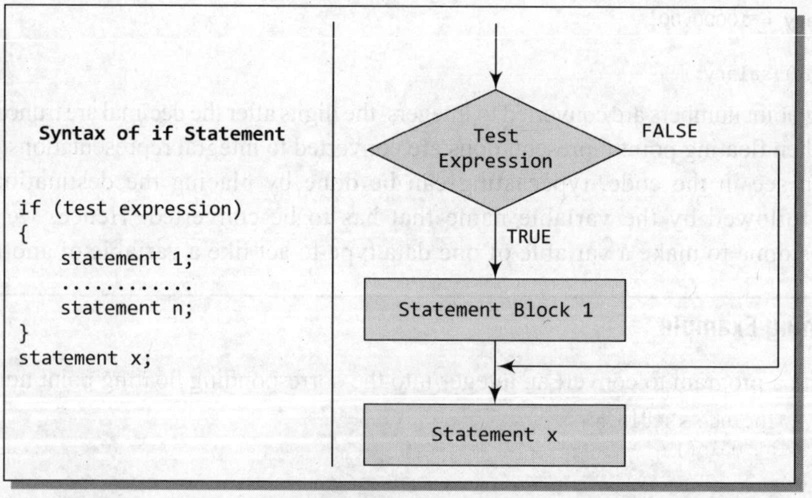

Figure 1.2 `if` statement construct

The `if` block may include 1 statement or *n* statements enclosed within curly brackets. First the test expression is evaluated. If the test expression is true, the statements of the `if` block are executed, otherwise these statements will be skipped and the execution will jump to statement `x`.

The statement in an `if` block is any valid C language statement, and the test expression is any valid C language expression that evaluates to either true or false. In addition to simple relational expressions, we can also use compound expressions formed using logical operators. Note that there is no semi-colon after the test expression. This is because the condition and statement should be put together as a single statement.

```
int main()
{
            int x=10;
            if (x>0) x++;
            printf("\n x = %d", x);
            return 0;
}
```

In the above code, we take a variable `x` and initialize it to 10. In the test expression, we check if the value of `x` is greater than 0. As 10 > 0, the test expression evaluates to true, and the value of `x` is incremented. After that, the value of `x` is printed on the screen. The output of this program is

```
x = 11
```

Observe that the `printf` statement will be executed even if the test expression is false.

> **Note** In case the statement block contains only one statement, putting curly brackets becomes optional. If there are more than one statement in the statement block, putting curly brackets becomes mandatory.

`if-else` *Statement*

We have studied that using `if` statement plays a vital role in conditional branching. Its usage is very simple. The test expression is evaluated, if the result is true, the statement(s) followed by the expression is executed, else if the expression is false, the statement is skipped by the compiler.

What if you want a separate set of statements to be executed if the expression returns a false value? In such cases, we can use an `if-else` statement rather than using a simple `if` statement. The general form of simple `if-else` statement is shown in Fig. 1.3.

Syntax of if-else Statement

```
if (test expression)
{
    statement block 1;
}
else
{
    statement block 2;
}
statement x;
```

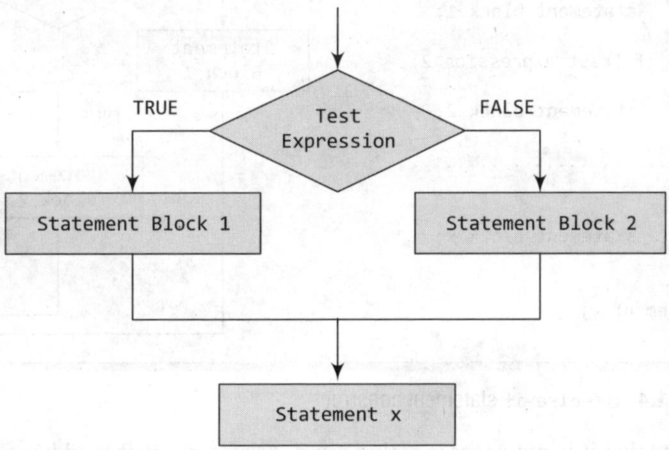

Figure 1.3 `if-else` statement construct

In the `if-else` construct, first the test expression is evaluated. If the expression is true, statement block 1 is executed and statement block 2 is skipped. Otherwise, if the expression is false, statement block 2 is executed and statement block 1 is ignored. In any case after the statement block 1 or 2 gets executed, the control will pass to statement `x`. Therefore, statement `x` is executed in every case.

Programming Example

3. Write a program to find whether a number is even or odd.

```
int main()
{
        int a;
        printf("\n Enter the value of a : ");
        scanf("%d", &a);
        if(a%2==0)
                printf("\n %d is even", a);
        else
                printf("\n %d is odd", a);
        return 0;
}
```

Output

```
Enter the value of a : 6
6 is even
```

`if-else-if` *Statement*

C language supports `if-else-if` statements to test additional conditions apart from the initial test expression. The `if-else-if` construct works in the same way as a normal `if` statement. Its construct is given in Fig. 1.4.

Syntax of if-else-if Statement

```
if (test expression 1)
{
        statement block 1;
}
else if (test expression 2)
{
        statement block 2;
}
...........................
else
{
        statement block x;
}
statement y;
```

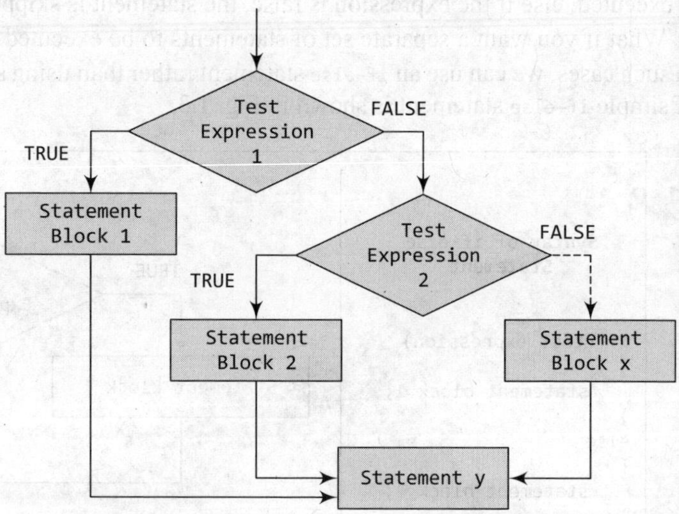

Figure 1.4 `if-else-if` statement construct

Note that it is not necessary that every `if` statement should have an `else` block as C supports simple `if` statements. After the first test expression or the first `if` branch, the programmer can have as many `else-if` branches as he wants depending on the expressions that have to be tested. For example, the following code tests whether a number entered by the user is negative, positive, or equal to zero.

```
int main()
{
        int num;
        printf("\n Enter any number : ");
```

```
    scanf("%d", &num);
    if(num==0)
            printf("\n The value is equal to zero");
    else if(num>0)
            printf("\n The number is positive");
    else
            printf("\n The number is negative");
    return 0;
}
```

Note that if the first test expression evaluates to a true value, i.e., `num=0`, then the rest of the statements in the code will be ignored and after executing the `printf` statement that displays 'The value is equal to zero', the control will jump to `return 0` statement.

`switch-case` *Statement*

A `switch-case` statement is a multi-way decision statement that is a simplified version of an `if-else-if` block. The general form of a `switch` statement is shown in Fig. 1.5.

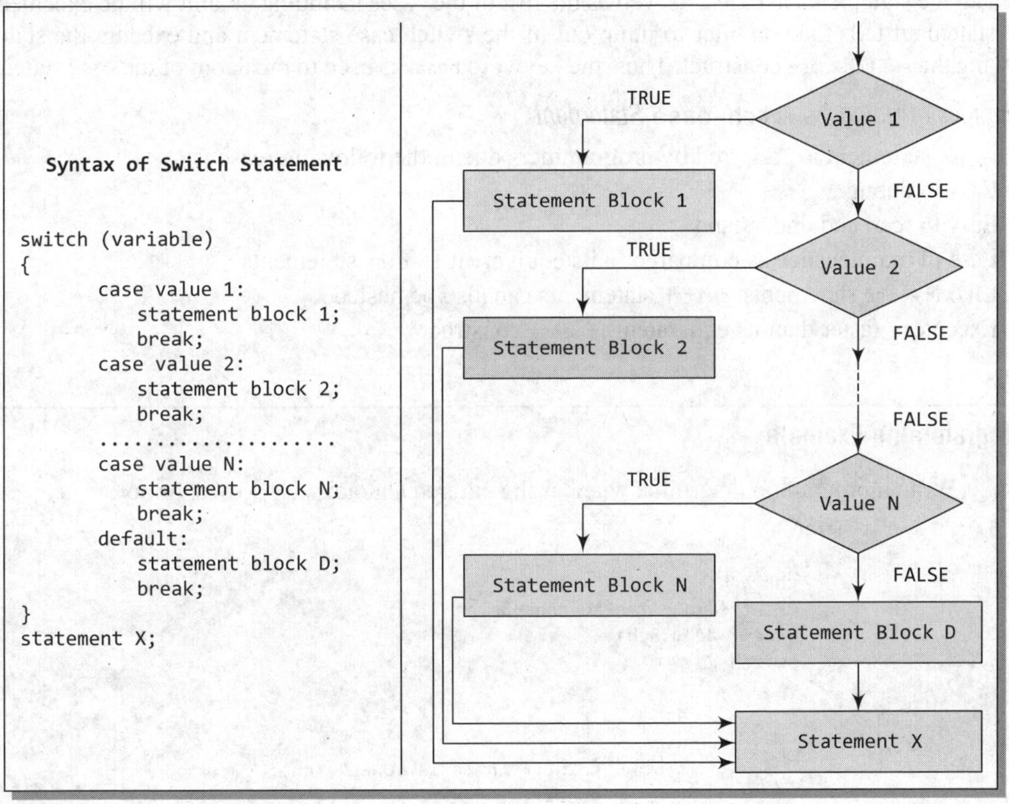

Figure 1.5 `switch-case` statement construct

The power of nested `if-else-if` statements lies in the fact that it can evaluate more than one expression in a single logical structure. `switch` statements are mostly used in two situations:

- When there is only one variable to evaluate in the expression
- When many conditions are being tested for

When there are many conditions to test, using the `if` and `else-if` constructs becomes complicated and confusing. Therefore, `switch case` statements are often used as an alternative to long `if` statements that compare a variable to several 'integral' values (integral values are those values that can be expressed as an integer, such as the value of a `char`). `Switch` statements are also used to handle the input given by the user.

We have already seen the syntax of the `switch` statement. The `switch case` statement compares the value of the variable given in the `switch` statement with the value of each case statement that follows. When the value of the `switch` and the `case` statement matches, the statement block of that particular case is executed.

Did you notice the keyword `default` in the syntax of the `switch case` statement? Default is the case that is executed when the value of the variable does not match with any of the values of the `case` statements. That is, default case is executed when no match is found between the values of `switch` and `case` statements and thus there are no statements to be executed. Although the default case is optional, it is always recommended to include it as it handles any unexpected case.

In the syntax of the `switch-case` statement, we have used another keyword `break`. The `break` statement must be used at the end of each case because if it is not used, then the case that matched and all the following cases will be executed. For example, if the value of `switch` statement matched with that of case 2, then all the statements in case 2 as well as the rest of the cases including default will be executed. The `break` statement tells the compiler to jump out of the switch case statement and execute the statement following the `switch-case` construct. Thus, the keyword `break` is used to break out of the case statements.

Advantages of Using a `switch-case` *Statement*

`Switch-case` statement is preferred by programmers due to the following reasons:

- Easy to debug
- Easy to read and understand
- Ease of maintenance as compared to its equivalent `if-else` statements
- Like `if-else` statements, `switch` statements can also be nested
- Executes faster than its equivalent `if-else` construct

Programming Example

4. Write a program to determine whether the entered character is a vowel or not.

```
int main()
{
        char ch;
        printf("\n Enter any character : ");
        scanf("%c", &ch);
        switch(ch)
        {
                case 'A':
                case 'a':
                        printf("\n %c is VOWEL", ch);
                        break;
                case 'E':
                case 'e':
                        printf("\n %c is VOWEL", ch);
                        break;
                case 'I':
                case 'i':
                        printf("\n %c is VOWEL", ch);
                        break;
                case 'O':
```

```
                case 'o':
                          printf("\n %c is VOWEL", ch);
                          break;
                case 'U':
                case 'u':
                          printf("\n %c is VOWEL", ch);
                          break;
                default: printf("\n %c is not a vowel", ch);
        }
        return 0;
}
```

Output

```
Enter any character : j
j is not a vowel
```

Note that there is no `break` statement after case `A`, so if the character `A` is entered then control will execute the statements given in case `a`.

1.9.2 Iterative Statements

Iterative statements are used to repeat the execution of a sequence of statements until the specified expression becomes false. C supports three types of iterative statements also known as looping statements. They are

- `while` loop
- `do-while` loop
- `for` loop

In this section, we will discuss all these statements.

`while` *Loop*

The `while` loop provides a mechanism to repeat one or more statements while a particular condition is true. Figure 1.6 shows the syntax and general form of a `while` loop.

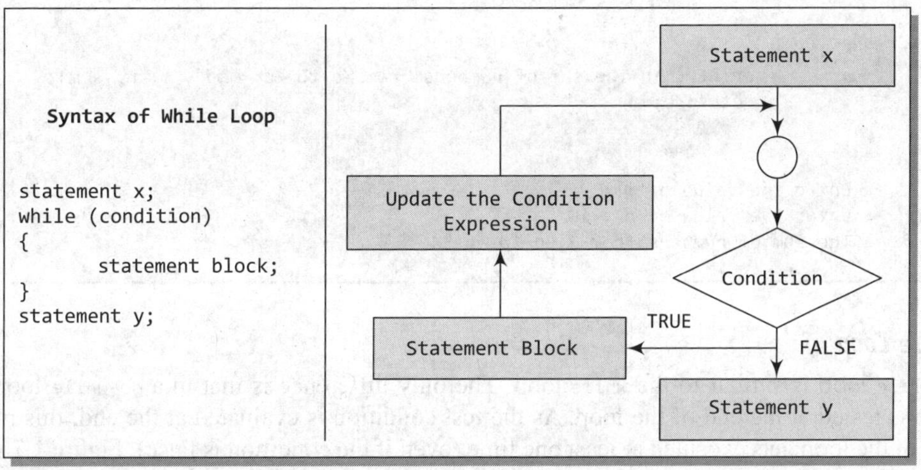

Figure 1.6 `while` loop construct

Note that in the `while` loop, the condition is tested before any of the statements in the statement block is executed. If the condition is true, only then the statements will be executed, otherwise if the condition is false, the control will jump to statement `y`, that is the immediate statement outside the `while` loop block.

In the flow diagram of Fig. 1.6, it is clear that we need to constantly update the condition of the `while` loop. It is this condition which determines when the loop will end. The `while` loop will execute as long as the condition is true. Note that if the condition is never updated and the condition never becomes false, then the computer will run into an infinite loop which is never desirable. For example, the following code prints the first 10 numbers using a `while` loop.

```
int main()
{
        int i = 1;
        while(i<=10)
        {
              printf("\n %d", i);
              i = i + 1;       // condition updated
        }
        return 0;
}
```

Note that initially `i = 1` and is less than 10, i.e., the condition is true, so in the `while` loop the value of `i` is printed and its value is incremented by 1. When `i=11`, the condition becomes false and the loop ends.

Programming Example

5. Write a program to calculate the sum of numbers from `m` to `n`.

```
int main()
{
      int n, m, i, sum =0;
      printf("\n Enter the value of m : ");
      scanf("%d", &m);
      i=m;
      printf("\n Enter the value of n : ");
      scanf("%d", &n);
      while(i<=n)
      {
            sum = sum + i;
            i = i + 1;
      }
      printf("\n The sum of numbers from %d to %d = %d", m, n, sum);
      return 0;
}
```

Output

```
Enter the value of m : 2
Enter the value of n : 10
The sum of numbers from 2 to 10  = 54
```

`do-while` *Loop*

The `do-while` loop is similar to the `while` loop. The only difference is that in a `do-while` loop, the test condition is tested at the end of the loop. As the test condition is evaluated at the end, this means that the body of the loop gets executed at least one time (even if the condition is false). Figure 1.7 shows the syntax and the general form of a `do-while` loop.

Note that the test condition is enclosed in parentheses and followed by a semi-colon. The statements in the statement block are enclosed within curly brackets. The curly brackets are optional if there is only one statement in the body of the `do-while` loop.

Syntax of do-While Loop

```
statement x;
do
{
        statement block;
}       while (condition);
statement y;
```

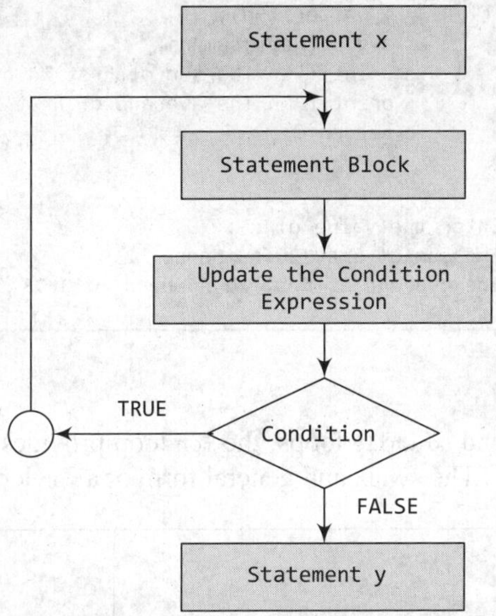

Figure 1.7 `Do-while` construct

The `do-while` loop continues to execute while the condition is true and when the condition becomes false, the control jumps to the statement following the `do-while` loop.

The major disadvantage of using a `do-while` loop is that it always executes at least once, so even if the user enters some invalid data, the loop will execute. However, `do-while` loops are widely used to print a list of options for menu-driven programs. For example, consider the following code.

```
int main()
{
        int i = 1;
        do
        {
                printf("\n %d", i);
                i = i + 1;
        } while(i<=10);
        return 0;
}
```

What do you think will be the output? Yes, the code will print numbers from 1 to 10.

Programming Example

6. Write a program to calculate the average of first *n* numbers.

```
int main()
{
        int n, i = 0, sum =0;
        float avg = 0.0;
        printf("\n Enter the value of n : ");
        scanf("%d", &n);
        do
        {
                sum = sum + i;
                i = i + 1;
```

```
        } while(i<=n);
        avg = (float)sum/n;
        printf("\n The sum of first %d numbers = %d",n, sum);
        printf("\n The average of first %d numbers = %.2f", n, avg);
        return 0;
}
```

Output

```
Enter the value of n : 20
The sum of first 20 numbers = 210
The average of first 20 numbers = 10.05
```

for *Loop*

Like the `while` and `do-while` loops, the `for` loop provides a mechanism to repeat a task till a particular condition is true. The synax and general form of a `for` loop is given in Fig. 1.8.

Syntax of for Loop

```
for (initialization; condition;
increment/decrement/update)
{
     statement block;
}
statement y;
```

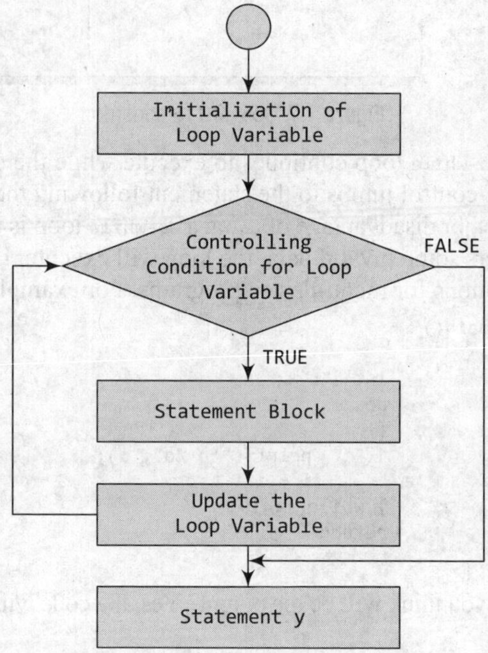

Figure 1.8 `for` loop construct

When a `for` loop is used, the loop variable is initialized only once. With every iteration, the value of the loop variable is updated and the condition is checked. If the condition is true, the statement block of the loop is executed, else the statements comprising the statement block of the `for` loop are skipped and the control jumps to the statement following the `for` loop body.

In the syntax of the `for` loop, initialization of the loop variable allows the programmer to give it a value. Second, the condition specifies that while the conditional expression is true, the loop should continue to repeat itself. Every iteration of the loop must make the condition to exit the loop approachable. So, with every iteration, the loop variable must be updated. Updating the loop variable may include incrementing the loop variable, decrementing the loop variable or setting it to some other value like, `i +=2`, where `i` is the loop variable.

Note that every section of the `for` loop is separated from the other with a semi-colon. It is possible that one of the sections may be empty, though the semi-colons still have to be there. However, if the condition is empty, it is evaluated as true and the loop will repeat until something else stops it.

The `for` loop is widely used to execute a single or a group of statements for a limited number of times. The following code shows how to print the first *n* numbers using a `for` loop.

```
int main()
{
        int i, n;
        printf("\n Enter the value of n :");
        scanf("%d", &n);
        for(i=1;i<=n;i++)
            printf("\n %d", i);
        return 0;
}
```

In the code, `i` is the loop variable. Initially, it is initialized with 1. Suppose the user enters 10 as the value of `n`. Then the condition is checked, since the condition is true as `i` is less than `n`, the statement in the `for` loop is executed and the value of `i` is printed. After every iteration, the value of `i` is incremented. When `i` exceeds the value of `n`, the control jumps to the `return 0` statement.

Programming Example

7. Write a program to determine whether a given number is a prime or a composite number.

```
#include <stdio.h>
int main()
{
        int flag = 0, i, num;
        printf("\n Enter any number : ");
        scanf("%d", &num);
        for(i=2; i<num/2;i++)
        {
                if(num%i == 0)
                {
                        flag =1;
                        break;
                }
        }
        if(flag == 1)
        printf("\n %d is a composite number", num);
        else
        printf("\n %d is a prime number", num);
        return 0;
}
```

Output

```
Enter any number : 37
37 is a prime number
```

1.9.3 Break and Continue Statements

`break` *Statement*

In C, the `break` statement is used to terminate the execution of the nearest enclosing loop in which it appears. We have already seen its use in the `switch` statement. The `break` statement is widely used with `for`, `while`, and `do-while` loops. When the compiler encounters a `break` statement, the control passes to the statement that follows the loop in which the `break` statement appears. Its syntax is quite simple, just type keyword `break` followed by a semi-colon.

```
break;
```

The example given below shows the manner in which `break` statement is used to terminate the loop in which it is embedded.

```
int main()
{
        int i = 0;
        while(i<=10)
        {
            if (i==5)
                 break;
            printf("\t %d", i);
            i = i + 1;
        }
        return 0;
}
```

Output

```
0 1 2 3 4
```

As soon as `i` becomes equal to 5, the `break` statement is executed and the control jumps to the statement following the `while` loop.

Hence, the `break` statement is used to exit a loop from any point within its body, bypassing its normal termination expression.

`continue` *Statement*

Like the `break` statement, the `continue` statement can only appear in the body of a loop. When the compiler encounters a `continue` statement, then the rest of the statements in the loop are skipped and the control is unconditionally transferred to the loop-continuation portion of the nearest enclosing loop. Its syntax is quite simple, just type keyword `continue` followed by a semi-colon.

```
continue;
```

Again like the `break` statement, the `continue` statement cannot be used without an enclosing `for`, `while`, or `do-while` loop. When the `continue` statement is encountered in the `while` loop and in the `do-while` loop, the control is transferred to the code that tests the controlling expression. However, if placed within a `for` loop, the `continue` statement causes a branch to the code that updates the loop variable. For example, consider the following code:

```
int main()
{
        int i;
        for(i=0; i<= 10; i++)
        {
            if (i==5)
                 continue;
            printf("\t %d", i);
        }
        return 0;
}
```

Output

```
0 1 2 3 4 6 7 8 9 10
```

Note that the code is meant to print numbers from 0 to 10. But as soon as `i` becomes equal to 5, the `continue` statement is encountered, so the `printf()` statement is skipped and the control passes to the expression that increments the value of `i`.

Hence, we conclude that the `continue` statement is somewhat the opposite of the `break` statement. It forces the next iteration of the loop to take place, skipping any code in between itself and the test condition of the loop. It is generally used to restart a statement sequence when an error occurs.

1.10 FUNCTIONS

C enables its programmers to break up a program into segments commonly known as *functions*, each of which can be written more or less independently of the others. Every function in the program is supposed to perform a well-defined task. Therefore, the program code of one function is completely insulated from the other functions.

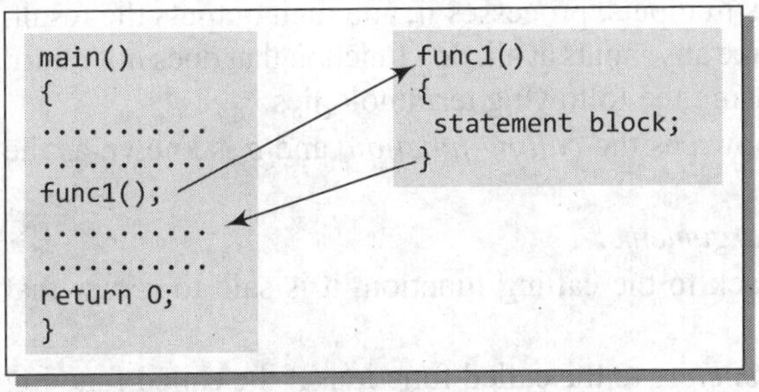

Figure 1.9 `main()` calls `func1()`

Every function interfaces to the outside world in terms of how information is transferred to it and how results generated by the function are transmitted back from it. This interface is basically specified by the function name. For example, look at Fig. 1.9 which explains how the `main()` function calls another function to perform a well-defined task.

In the figure, we can see that `main()` calls a function named `func1()`. Therefore, `main()` is known as the *calling function* and `func1()` is known as the *called function*. The moment the compiler encounters a function call, the control jumps to the statements that are a part of the called function. After the called function is executed, the control is returned to the calling program.

The `main()` function can call as many functions as it wants and as many times as it wants. For example, a function call placed within a `for` loop, `while` loop, or `do-while` loop may call the same function multiple times till the condition holds true.

Not only `main()`, any function can call any other function. For example, look at Fig. 1.10 which shows one function calling another, and the other function in turn calling some other function.

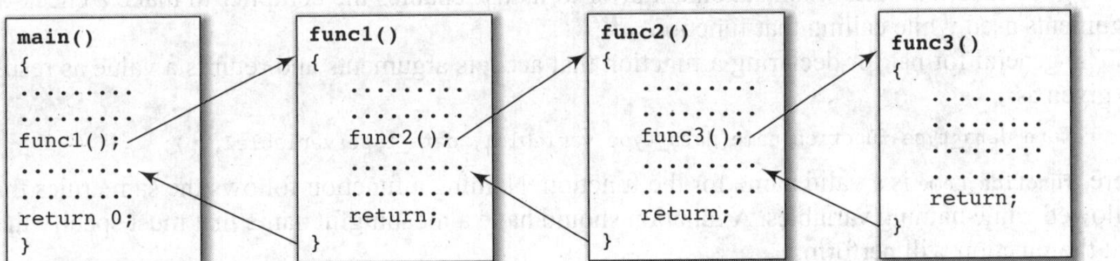

Figure 1.10 Function calling another function

1.10.1 Why are Functions Needed?

Let us analyse the reasons why segmenting a program into manageable chunks is an important aspect of programming.

- Dividing the program into separate well-defined functions facilitates each function to be written and tested separately. This simplifies the process of getting the total program to work.
- Understanding, coding, and testing multiple separate functions is easier than doing the same for one big function.

- If a big program has to be developed without using any function other than `main()`, then there will be countless lines in the `main()` function and maintaining that program will be a difficult task.
- All the libraries in C contain a set of functions that the programmers are free to use in their programs. These functions have been pre-written and pre-tested, so the programmers can use them without worrying about their code details. This speeds up program development, by allowing the programmer to concentrate only on the code that he has to write.
- Like C libraries, programmers can also write their own functions and use them from different points in the main program or any other program that needs its functionalities.
- When a big program is broken into comparatively smaller functions, then different programmers working on that project can divide the workload by writing different functions.

1.10.2 Using Functions

A function can be compared to a *black box* that takes in inputs, processes it, and then outputs the result. However, we may also have a function that does not take any inputs at all, or a function that does not return any value at all. While using functions, we will be using the following terminologies:

- A function *f* that uses another function g is known as the *calling function,* and g is known as the *called function.*
- The inputs that a function takes are known as *arguments.*
- When a called function returns some result back to the calling function, it is said to *return* that result.
- The calling function may or may not pass *parameters* to the called function. If the called function accepts arguments, the calling function will pass parameters, else not.
- *Function declaration* is a declaration statement that identifies a function's name, a list of arguments that it accepts, and the type of data it returns.
- *Function definition* consists of a function header that identifies the function, followed by the body of the function containing the executable code for that function.

Function Declaration

Before using a function, the compiler must know the number of parameters and the type of parameters that the function expects to receive and the data type of value that it will return to the calling program. Placing the function declaration statement prior to its use enables the compiler to make a check on the arguments used while calling that function.

The general format for declaring a function that accepts arguments and returns a value as result can be given as:

```
return_data_type function_name(data_type variable1, data_type variable2,..);
```

Here, **`function_name`** is a valid name for the function. Naming a function follows the same rules that are followed while naming variables. A function should have a meaningful name that must specify the task that the function will perform.

`return_data_type` specifies the data type of the value that will be returned to the calling function as a result of the processing performed by the called function.

`(data_type variable1, data_type variable2, ...)` is a list of variables of specified data types. These variables are passed from the calling function to the called function. They are also known as arguments or parameters that the called function accepts to perform its task.

> **Note** A function having void as its return type cannot return any value. Similarly, a function having void as its parameter list cannot accept any value.

Function Definition

When a function is defined, space is allocated for that function in the memory. A function definition comprises of two parts:

- Function header
- Function body

The syntax of a function definition can be given as:

```
return_data_type function_name(data_type variable1, data_type variable2,..)
{
            .............
            statements
            .............
            return(variable);
}
```

Note that the number of arguments and the order of arguments in the function header must be the same as that given in the function declaration statement.

While `return_data_type function_name(data_type variable1, data_type variable2,...)` is known as the function header, the rest of the portion comprising of program statements within the curly brackets { } is the function body which contains the code to perform the specific task.

Note that the function header is same as the function declaration. The only difference between the two is that a function header is not followed by a semi-colon.

Function Call

The function call statement invokes the function. When a function is invoked, the compiler jumps to the called function to execute the statements that are a part of that function. Once the called function is executed, the program control passes back to the calling function. A function call statement has the following syntax:

```
function_name(variable1, variable2, ...);
```

The following points are to be noted while calling a function:

- Function name and the number and the type of arguments in the function call must be same as that given in the function declaration and the function header of the function definition.
- Names (and not the types) of variables in function declaration, function call, and header of function definition may vary.
- Arguments may be passed in the form of expressions to the called function. In such a case, arguments are first evaluated and converted to the type of formal parameter and then the body of the function gets executed.
- If the return type of the function is not `void`, then the value returned by the called function may be assigned to some variable as given below.

```
variable_name = function_name(variable1, variable2, ...);
```

Programming Example

8. Write a program to find whether a number is even or odd using functions.

```
int evenodd(int);   //FUNCTION DECLARATION
int main()
{
        int num, flag;
        printf("\n Enter the number : ");
```

```
        scanf("%d", &num);
        flag = evenodd(num); //FUNCTION CALL
        if (flag == 1)
                printf("\n %d is EVEN", num);
        else
                printf("\n %d is ODD", num);
        return 0;
}
int evenodd(int a) // FUNCTION HEADER
{
                // FUNCTION BODY
        if(a%2 == 0)
                return 1;
        else
                return 0;
}
```

Output

```
Enter the number : 78
78 is EVEN
```

1.10.3 Passing Parameters to Functions

There are two ways in which arguments or parameters can be passed to the called function.

Call by value The values of the variables are passed by the calling function to the called function.

Call by reference The addresses of the variables are passed by the calling function to the called function.

Call by Value

In this method, the called function creates new variables to store the value of the arguments passed to it. Therefore, the called function uses a copy of the actual arguments to perform its intended task.

If the called function is supposed to modify the value of the parameters passed to it, then the change will be reflected only in the called function. In the calling function, no change will be made to the value of the variables. This is because all the changes are made to the copy of the variables and not to the actual variables. To understand this concept, consider the code given below. The function `add()` accepts an integer variable `num` and adds 10 to it. In the calling function, the value of `num = 2`. In `add()`, the value of `num` is modified to 12 but in the calling function, the change is not reflected.

```
void add(int n);
int main()
{
        int num = 2;
        printf("\n The value of num before calling the function = %d", num);
        add(num);
        printf("\n The value of num after calling the function = %d", num);
        return 0;
}
void add(int n)
{
        n = n + 10;
        printf("\n The value of num in the called function = %d", n);
}
```

Output

```
The value of num before calling the function = 2
The value of num in the called function = 12
The value of num after calling the function = 2
```

Following are the points to remember while passing arguments to a function using the call-by-value method:

- When arguments are passed by value, the called function creates new variables of the same data type as the arguments passed to it.
- The values of the arguments passed by the calling function are copied into the newly created variables.
- Values of the variables in the calling functions remain unaffected when the arguments are passed using the call-by-value technique.

Pros and cons

The biggest advantage of using the call-by-value technique is that arguments can be passed as variables, literals, or expressions, while its main drawback is that copying data consumes additional storage space. In addition, it can take a lot of time to copy, thereby resulting in performance penalty, especially if the function is called many times.

Call by Reference

When the calling function passes arguments to the called function using the call-by-value method, the only way to return the modified value of the argument to the caller is explicitly using the return statement. A better option is to pass arguments using the call-by-reference technique. In this method, we declare the function parameters as references rather than normal variables. When this is done, any changes made by the function to the arguments it received are also visible in the calling function.

To indicate that an argument is passed using call by reference, an asterisk (*) is placed after the type in the parameter list.

Hence, in the call-by-reference method, a function receives an implicit reference to the argument, rather than a copy of its value. Therefore, the function can modify the value of the variable and that change will be reflected in the calling function as well. The following code illustrates this concept.

```
void add(int *);
int main()
{
        int num = 2;
        printf("\n The value of num before calling the function = %d", num);
        add(&num);
        printf("\n The value of num after calling the function = %d", num);
        return 0;
}
void add(int *n)
{
        *n = *n + 10;
        printf("\n The value of num in the called function = %d", *n);
}
```

Output

```
The value of num before calling the function = 2
The value of num in the called function = 12
The value of num after calling the function = 12
```

Advantages

The advantages of using the call-by-reference technique of passing arguments include:

- Since arguments are not copied into the new variables, it provides greater time and space-efficiency.
- The function can change the value of the argument and the change is reflected in the calling function.
- A function can return only one value. In case we need to return multiple values, we can pass those arguments by reference, so that the modified values are visible in the calling function.

Disadvantages

However, the drawback of using this technique is that if inadvertent changes are caused to variables in called function then these changes would be reflected in calling function as original values would have been overwritten.

Consider the code given below which swaps the value of two integers. Note the value of integers in the calling function and called function.

```
//This function swaps the value of two variables
void swap_call_val(int, int);
void swap_call_ref(int *, int *);
int main()
{
    int a=1, b=2, c=3, d=4;
    printf("\n In main(), a = %d and b = %d", a, b);
    swap_call_val(a, b);
    printf("\n In main(), a = %d and b = %d", a, b);
    printf("\n\n In main(), c = %d and d = %d", c, d);
    swap_call_ref(&c, &d);
    printf("\n In main(), c = %d and d = %d", c, d);
    return 0;
}
void swap_call_val(int a, int b)
{
    int temp;
    temp = a;
    a = b;
    b = temp;
    printf("\n In function (Call By Value Method) - a = %d and b = %d", a, b);
}
void swap_call_ref(int *c, int *d)
{
    int temp;
    temp = *c;
    *c = *d;
    *d = temp;
    printf("\n In function (Call By Reference Method) - c = %d and d = %d", *c, *d);
}
```

Output

```
In main(), a = 1 and b = 2
In function (Call By Value Method) - a = 2 and b = 1
In main(), a = 1 and b = 2
In main(), c = 3 and d = 4
In function (Call By Reference Method) - c = 4 and d = 3
In main(), c = 4 and d = 3
```

1.11 POINTERS

Every variable in C has a name and a value associated with it. When a variable is declared, a specific block of memory within the computer is allocated to hold the value of that variable. The size of the allocated block depends on the data type.

Consider the following statement.

```
int x = 10;
```

When this statement executes, the compiler sets aside 2 bytes of memory to hold the value 10. It also sets up a symbol table in which it adds the symbol x and the relative address in the memory where those 2 bytes were set aside.

(Note the size of integer may vary from one system to another. On 32 bit systems, integer variable is allocated 4 bytes while on 16 bit systems it is allocated 2 bytes.)

Thus, every variable in C has a value and also a memory location (commonly known as *address*) associated with it. We will use terms `rvalue` and `lvalue` for the value and the address of the variable, respectively.

The `rvalue` appears on the right side of the assignment statement (10 in the above statement) and cannot be used on the left side of the assignment statement. Therefore, writing `10 = k;` is illegal. If we write,

```
int x, y;
x = 10;
y = x;
```

then, we have two integer variables `x` and `y`. The compiler reserves memory for the integer variable `x` and stores the `rvalue` 10 in it. When we say `y = x`, then `x` is interpreted as its `rvalue` since it is on the right hand side of the assignment operator `=`. Therefore, here `x` refers to the value stored at the memory location set aside for `x`, in this case 10. After this statement is executed, the `rvalue` of `y` is also 10.

You must be wondering why we are discussing addresses and `lvalues`. Actually pointers are nothing but memory addresses. A pointer is a variable that contains the memory location of another variable. Therefore, a pointer is a variable that represents the location of a data item, such as a variable or an array element. Pointers are frequently used in C, as they have a number of useful applications. These applications include:

- Pointers are used to pass information back and forth between functions.
- Pointers enable the programmers to return multiple data items from a function via function arguments.
- Pointers provide an alternate way to access the individual elements of an array.
- Pointers are used to pass arrays and strings as function arguments. We will discuss this in subsequent chapters.
- Pointers are used to create complex data structures, such as trees, linked lists, linked stacks, linked queues, and graphs.
- Pointers are used for the dynamic memory allocation of a variable (refer Appendix A on memory allocation in C programs).

1.11.1 Declaring Pointer Variables

The general syntax of declaring pointer variables can be given as below.

```
data_type *ptr_name;
```

Here, `data_type` is the data type of the value that the pointer will point to. For example,

```
int *pnum;
char *pch;
float *pfnum;
```

In each of the above statements, a pointer variable is declared to point to a variable of the specified data type. Although all these pointers (`pnum`, `pch`, and `pfnum`) point to different data types, they will occupy the same amount of space in the memory. But how much space they will occupy will depend on the platform where the code is going to run. Now let us declare an integer pointer variable and start using it in our program code.

```
int x= 10;
int *ptr;
ptr = &x;
```

In the above statement, `ptr` is the name of the pointer variable. The `*` informs the compiler that `ptr` is a pointer variable and the `int` specifies that it will store the address of an integer variable. An integer pointer variable, therefore, 'points to' an integer variable. In the last statement, `ptr` is assigned the address of `x`. The `&` operator retrieves the `lvalue` (address) of `x`, and copies that to the contents of the pointer `ptr`. Consider the memory cells given in Fig. 1.11.

			10						
1000	1001	1002	1003	1004	1005	1006	1007	1008	1009

Figure 1.11 Memory representation

Now, since `x` is an integer variable, it will be allocated 2 bytes. Assuming that the compiler assigns it memory locations 1003 and 1004, the address of `x` (written as `&x`) is equal to 1003, that is the starting address of `x` in the memory. When we write, `ptr = &x`, then `ptr = 1003`.

We can 'dereference' a pointer, *i.e.*, we can refer to the value of the variable to which it points by using the unary `*` operator as in `*ptr`. That is, `*ptr = 10`, since 10 is the value of `x`. Look at the following code which shows the use of a pointer variable:

```
int main()
{
        int num, *pnum;
        pnum = &num;
        printf("\n Enter the number : ");
        scanf("%d", &num);
        printf("\n The number that was entered is : %d", *pnum);
        return 0;
}
```

Output

```
Enter the number : 10
The number that was entered is : 10
```

What will be the value of `*(&num)`? It is equivalent to simply writing `num`.

1.11.2 Pointer Expressions and Pointer Arithmetic

Like other variables, pointer variables can also be used in expressions. For example, if `ptr1` and `ptr2` are pointers, then the following statements are valid:

```
int num1 = 2, num2 = 3, sum = 0, mul = 0, div = 1;
int *ptr1, *ptr2;
ptr1 = &num1;
ptr2 = &num2;
sum = *ptr1 + *ptr2;
mul = sum * (*ptr1);
*ptr2 += 1;
div = 9 + (*ptr1)/(*ptr2) - 30;
```

In C, the programmer may add integers to or subtract integers from pointers as well as subtract one pointer from the other. We can also use shorthand operators with the pointer variables as we use them with other variables.

C also allows comparing pointers by using relational operators in the expressions. For example, `p1>p2`, `p1==p2` and `p1!=p2` are all valid in C.

Postfix unary increment `(++)` and decrement `(--)` operators have greater precedence than the dereference operator `(*)`. Therefore, the expression `*ptr++` is equivalent to `*(ptr++)`, as `++` has greater operator precedence than `*`. Thus, the expression will increase the value of `ptr` so that it now points to the next memory location. This means that the statement `*ptr++` does not do the intended task. Therefore, to increment the value of the variable whose address is stored in `ptr`, you should write `(*ptr)++`.

1.11.3 Null Pointers

So far, we have studied that a pointer variable is a pointer to a variable of some data type. However, in some cases, we may prefer to have a *null pointer* which is a special pointer value and does not point to any value. This means that a `null` pointer does not point to any valid memory address.

To declare a null pointer, you may use the predefined constant `NULL` which is defined in several standard header files including `<stdio.h>`, `<stdlib.h>`, and `<string.h>`. After including any of these files in your program, you can write

```
int *ptr = NULL;
```

You can always check whether a given pointer variable stores the address of some variable or contains `NULL` by writing,

```
if (ptr == NULL)
{
        Statement block;
}
```

You may also initialize a pointer as a null pointer by using the constant 0

```
int *ptr,
ptr = 0;
```

This is a valid statement in C as `NULL` is a preprocessor macro, which typically has the value or replacement text 0. However, to avoid ambiguity, it is always better to use `NULL` to declare a null pointer. A function that returns pointer values can return a null pointer when it is unable to perform its task.

1.11.4 Generic Pointers

A generic pointer is a pointer variable that has *void* as its data type. The *void pointer*, or the generic pointer, is a special type of pointer that can point to variables of any data type. It is declared like a normal pointer variable but using the `void` keyword as the pointer's data type. For example,

```
void *ptr;
```

In C, since you cannot have a variable of type `void`, the void pointer will therefore not point to any data and, thus, cannot be dereferenced. You need to cast a void pointer to another kind of pointer before using it.

Generic pointers are often used when you want a pointer to point to data of different types at different times. For example, take a look at the following code.

```
int main()
{
        int x=10;
        char ch = 'A';
        void *gp;
        gp = &x;
        printf("\n Generic pointer points to the integer value = %d", *(int*)gp);
        gp = &ch;
        printf("\n Generic pointer now points to the character= %c", *(char*)gp);
        return 0;
}
```

Output

```
Generic pointer points to the integer value = 10
Generic pointer now points to the character = A
```

It is always recommended to avoid using void pointers unless absolutely necessary, as they effectively allow you to avoid type checking.

Programming Example

9. Write a program to add two integers using pointers and functions.

```
void sum (int*, int*, int*);
int main()
{
        int num1, num2, total;
        printf("\n Enter the first number : ");
        scanf("%d", &num1);
        printf("\n Enter the second number : ");
        scanf("%d", &num2);
        sum(&num1, &num2, &total);
        printf("\n Total = %d", total);
        return 0;
}
void sum (int *a, int *b, int *t)
{
        *t = *a + *b;
}
```

Output

```
Enter the first number : 23
Enter the second number : 34
Total = 57
```

1.11.5 Pointer to Pointers

In C, you can also use pointers that point to pointers. The pointers in turn point to data or even to other pointers. To declare pointers to pointers, just add an asterisk * for each level of reference.

For example, consider the following code:

```
int x=10;
int *px, **ppx;
px = &x;
ppx = &px;
```

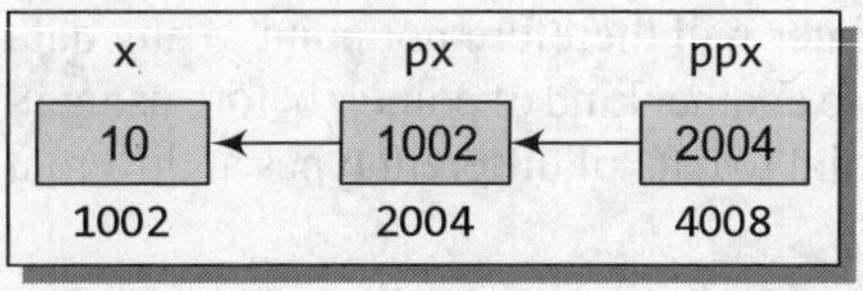

Figure 1.12 Pointer to pointer

Let us assume, the memory locations of these variables are as shown in Fig. 1.12.

Now if we write,

```
printf("\n %d", **ppx);
```

Then, it would print 10, the value of x.

1.11.6 Drawbacks of Pointers

Although pointers are very useful in C, they are not free from limitations. If used incorrectly, pointers can lead to bugs that are difficult to unearth. For example, if you use a pointer to read a memory location but that pointer is pointing to an incorrect location, then you may end up reading a wrong value. An erroneous input always leads to an erroneous output. Thus however efficient your program code may be, the output will always be disastrous. Same is the case when writing a value to a particular memory location.

Let us try to find some common errors when using pointers.

```
int x, *px;
x=10;
*px = 20;
```

Error: Un-initialized pointer. `px` is pointing to an unknown memory location. Hence it will overwrite that location's contents and store 20 in it.

```
int x, *px;
x=10;
px = x;
```

Error: It should be `px = &x;`

```
int x=10, y=20, *px, *py;
px = &x, py = &y;
if(px<py)
printf("\n x is less than y");
else
printf("\n y is less than x");
```

Error: It should be `if(*px< *py)`

Points to Remember

- C was developed in the early 1970s by Dennis Ritchie at Bell Laboratories.
- Every word in a C program is either an identifier or a keyword. Identifiers are the names given to program elements such as variables and functions. Keywords are reserved words which cannot be used as identifiers.
- C provides four basic data types: `char`, `int`, `float`, and `double`.
- A variable is defined as a meaningful name given to a data storage location in computer memory.
- Standard library function `scanf()` is used to input data in a specified format.`printf()`function is used to output data of different types in a specified format.
- C supports different types of operators which can be classified into following categories: arithmetic, relational, equality, logical, unary, conditional, bitwise, assignment, comma, and sizeof operators.
- Modulus operator (%) can only be applied on integer operands, and not on float or double operands.
- Equality operators have lower precedence than relational operators.
- Like arithmetic expressions, logical expressions are evaluated from left to right.
- Both x++ and ++x increment the value of x, but in the former case, the value of x is returned before it is incremented. Whereas in the latter case, the value of x is returned after it is incremented.
- Conditional operator is also known as ternary operator as it takes three operands.
- Bitwise NOT or complement produces one's complement of a given binary number.
- Among all the operators, comma operator has the lowest precedence.
- `sizeof` is a unary operator used to calculate the size of data types. This operator can be applied to all data types.
- While type conversion is done implicitly, typecasting has to be done explicitly by the programmer. Typecasting is done when the value of one data type has to be converted into the value of another data type.
- C supports three types of control statements: decision control statements, iterative statements, and jump statements.
- In a `switch` statement, if the value of the variable does not match with any of the values of case statements, then default case is executed.
- Iterative statements are used to repeat the execution of a list of statements until the specified expression becomes false.
- The `break` statement is used to terminate the execution of the nearest enclosing loop in which it appears.
- When the compiler encounters a `continue` statement, then the rest of the statements in the loop are skipped and the control is unconditionally transferred to the loop-continuation portion of the nearest enclosing loop.
- A C program contains one or more functions, where each function is defined as a group of statements that perform a specific task.

- Every C program contains a `main()` function which is the starting point of the program. It is the function that is called by the operating system when the user runs the program.
- Function declaration statement identifies a function's name and the list of arguments that it accepts and the type of data it returns.
- Function definition, on the other hand, consists of a function header that identifies the function, followed by the body of the function containing the executable code for that function. When a function is defined, space is allocated for that function in the memory.
- The moment the compiler encounters a function call, the control jumps to the statements that are a part of the called function. After the called function is executed, the control is returned back to the calling function.
- Placing the function declaration statement prior to its use enables the compiler to make a check on the arguments used while calling that function.
- A function having `void` as its return type cannot return any value. Similarly, a function having `void` as its parameter list cannot accept any value.
- Call by value method passes values of the variables to the called function. Therefore, the called function uses a copy of the actual arguments to perform its intended task. This method is used when the function does not need to modify the values of the original variables in the calling function.
- In call by reference method, addresses of the variables are passed by the calling function to the called function. Hence, in this method, a function receives an implicit reference to the argument, rather than a copy of its value. This allows the function to modify the value of the variable and that change is reflected in the calling function as well.
- A pointer is a variable that contains the memory address of another variable.
- The & operator retrieves the address of the variable.
- We can 'dereference' a pointer, i.e., refer to the value of the variable to which it points by using unary * operator.
- Null pointer is a special pointer variable that does not point to any variable. This means that a null pointer does not point to any valid memory address. To declare a null pointer we may use the predefined constant NULL.
- A generic pointer is pointer variable that has `void` as its data type. The generic pointer can point to variables of any data type.
- To declare pointer to pointers, we need to add an asterisk (*) for each level of reference.

Exercises

Review Questions

1. Discuss the structure of a C program.
2. Differentiate between declaration and definition.
3. How is memory reserved using a declaration statement?
4. What do you understand by identifiers and keywords?
5. Explain the terms variables and constants. How many types of variables are supported by C?
6. What does the data type of a variable signify?
7. Write a short note on basic data types that the C language supports.
8. Why do we include <stdio.h> in our programs?
9. What are header files? Explain their significance.
10. Write short notes on printf and scanf functions.
11. Write a short note on operators available in C language.
12. Draw the operator precedence chart.
13. Differentiate between typecasting and type conversion.
14. What are decision control statements? Explain in detail.
15. Write a short note on the iterative statements that C language supports.

16. When will you prefer to work with a switch statement?
17. Define function. Why are they needed?
18. Differentiate between function declaration and function definition.
19. Why is function declaration statement placed prior to function definition?
20. Explain the concept of making function calls.
21. Differentiate between call by value and call by reference using suitable examples.
22. Write a short note on pointers.
23. Explain the difference between a null pointer and a void pointer.
24. How are generic pointers different from other pointer variables?
25. Write a short note on pointers to pointers.

Programming Exercises

1. Write a program to read 10 integers. Display these numbers by printing three numbers in a line separated by commas.
2. Write a program to print the count of even numbers between 1–200. Also print their sum.
3. Write a program to count the number of vowels in a text.
4. Write a program to read the address of a user. Dis-play the result by breaking it in multiple lines.
5. Write a program to read two floating point numbers. Add these numbers and assign the result to an integer. Finally, display the value of all the three variables.
6. Write a program to read a floating point number. Display the rightmost digit of the integral part of the number.
7. Write a program to calculate simple interest and compound interest.
8. Write a program to calculate salary of an employee given his basic pay (to be entered by the user), HRA = 10% of the basic pay, TA = 5% of basic pay. Define HRA and TA as constants and use them to calculate the salary of the employee.
9. Write a program to prepare a grocery bill. Enter the name of the items purchased, quantity in which it is purchased, and its price per unit. Then display the bill in the following format:

```
************ B I L L ************
Item  Quantity  Price  Amount
_________________________________
_________________________________
Total Amount to be paid
_________________________________
```

10. Write a C program using printf statement to print BYE in the following format:

```
BBB      Y     Y      EEEE
B  B      Y   Y       E
BBB         Y         EEEE
B  B        Y
```

11. Write a program to read an integer. Display the value of that integer in decimal, octal, and hexadecimal notation.
12. Write a program that prints a floating point value in exponential format with the following specifications:
    (a) correct to two decimal places;
    (b) correct to four decimal places; and
    (c) correct to eight decimal places.
13. Write a program to find the smallest of three integers using functions.
14. Write a program to calculate area of a triangle using function.
15. Write a program to find whether a number is divisible by two or not using functions.
16. Write a program to print 'Programming in C is Fun' using pointers.
17. Write a program to read a character and print it. Also print its ASCII value. If the character is in lower case, print it in upper case and vice versa. Repeat the process until a '*' is entered.
18. Write a program to add three floating point numbers. The result should contain only two digits after the decimal.
19. Write a program to take input from the user and then check whether it is a number or a character. If it is a character, determine whether it is in upper case or lower case. Also print its ASCII value.
20. Write a program to display sum and average of numbers from `1` to `n`. Use `for` loop.
21. Write a program to print all odd numbers from `m` to `n`.
22. Write a program to print all prime numbers from `m` to `n`.

23. Write a program to read numbers until –1 is entered and display whether it is an Armstrong number or not.
24. Write a program to add two floating point numbers using pointers and functions.
25. Write a program to calculate area of a triangle using pointers.

Multiple-choice Questions

1. The operator which compares two values is
   (a) Assignment (b) Relational
   (c) Unary (d) Equality
2. Ternary operator operates on how many operands?
   (a) 1 (b) 2
   (c) 3 (d) 4
3. Which operator produces the one's complement of the given binary value?
   (a) Logical AND (b) Bitwise AND
   (c) Logical OR (d) Bitwise NOT
4. Which operator has the lowest precedence?
   (a) Sizeof (b) Unary
   (c) Assignment (d) Comma
5. Which of the following is the conversion character associated with short integer?
   (a) `%c` (b) `%h`
   (c) `%e` (d) `%f`
6. Which of the following is not a character constant?
   (a) 'A' (b) "A"
   (c) ' ' (d) '*'
7. Which of the following is a valid variable name?
   (a) Initial.Name (b) A+B
   (c) $amt (d) Floats
8. Which operator cannot be used with floating point numbers?
   (a) `+` (b) `–`
   (c) `%` (d) `*`
9. Identify the erroneous expression.
   (a) `X=y=2, 4;` (b) `res = ++a * 5;`
   (c) `res = /4;` (d) `res = a++ -b *2`
10. Function declaration statement identifies a function with its
    (a) Name
    (b) Arguments
    (c) Data type of return value
    (d) All of these
11. Which return type cannot return any value to the calling function?
    (a) int (b) float
    (c) void (d) double
12. Memory is allocated for a function when the function is
    (a) declared (b) defined
    (c) called (d) returned
13. `*(&num)` is equivalent to writing
    (a) `&num` (b) `*num`
    (c) `num` (d) None of these
14. Which operator retrieves the `lvalue` of a variable?
    (a) `&` (b) `*`
    (c) `->` (d) None of these
15. Which operator is used to dereference a pointer?
    (a) `&` (b) `*`
    (c) `->` (d) None of these

True or False

1. We can have only one function in a C program.
2. Keywords are case sensitive.
3. Variable 'first' is the same as 'First'.
4. Signed variables can increase the maximum positive range.
5. `Comment` statements are not executed by the compiler.
6. Equality operators have higher precedence than the relational operators.
7. Shifting once to the left multiplies the number by 2.
8. `Decision control` statements are used to repeat the execution of a list of statements.
9. `printf("%d", scanf("%d", &num));` is a valid C statement.
10. 1,234 is a valid integer constant.
11. A `printf` statement can generate only one line of output.
12. `stdio.h` is used to store the source code of the program.
13. The closing brace of `main()` is the logical end of the program.
14. The declaration section gives instructions to the computer.
15. Any valid printable ASCII character can be used for a variable name.
16. Underscore can be used anywhere in the variable name.
17. `void` is a data type in C.
18. All arithmetic operators have same precedence.
19. The modulus operator can be used only with integers.

20. The calling function always passes parameters to the called function.
21. The name of a function is global.
22. No function can be declared within the body of another function.
23. The `&` operator retrieves the `lvalue` of the variable.
24. Unary increment and decrement operators have greater precedence than the dereference operator.
25. On 32-bit systems, an integer variable is allocated 4 bytes.

Fill in the Blanks

1. C was developed by ______.
2. The execution of a C program begins at ______.
3. In the memory, characters are stored as ______.
4. `return 0` returns 0 to the ______.
5. ______ finds the remainder of an integer division.
6. `sizeof` is a ______ operator used to calculate the sizes of data types.
7. ______ is also known as forced conversion.
8. ______ is executed when the value of the variable does not match with any of the values of the case statement.
9. ______ function prints data on the monitor.
10. A C program ends with a ______.
11. ______ causes the cursor to move to the next line.
12. A variable can be made constant by declaring it with the qualifier ______ at the time of initialization.
13. ______ operator returns the number of bytes occupied by the operand.
14. The ______ specification is used to read/write a short integer.
15. The ______ specification is used to read/write a hexadecimal integer.
16. To print the data left-justified, ______ specification is used.
17. After the function is executed, the control passes back to the ______.
18. A function that uses another function is known as the ______.
19. The inputs that the function takes are known as ______.
20. Function definition consist of ______ and ______.
21. In ______ method, address of the variable is passed by the calling function to the called function.
22. Size of character pointer is ______.
23. ______ pointer does not point to any valid memory address.
24. The ______ appears on the right side of the assignment statement.
25. The ______ operator informs the compiler that the variable is a pointer variable.

CHAPTER 2

Introduction to Data Structures and Algorithms

LEARNING OBJECTIVE

In this chapter, we are going to discuss common data structures and algorithms which serve as building blocks for creating efficient programs. We will also discuss different approaches to designing algorithms and different notations for evaluating the performance of algorithms.

2.1 BASIC TERMINOLOGY

We have already learnt the basics of programming in C in the previous chapter and know how to write, debug, and run simple programs in C language. Our aim has been to design good programs, where a good program is defined as a program that

- runs correctly
- is easy to read and understand
- is easy to debug *and*
- is easy to modify.

A program should undoubtedly give correct results, but along with that it should also run efficiently. A program is said to be efficient when it executes in minimum time and with minimum memory space. In order to write efficient programs we need to apply certain data management concepts.

The concept of data management is a complex task that includes activities like data collection, organization of data into appropriate structures, and developing and maintaining routines for quality assurance.

Data structure is a crucial part of data management and in this book it will be our prime concern. A *data structure* is basically a group of data elements that are put together under one name, and which defines a particular way of storing and organizing data in a computer so that it can be used efficiently.

Data structures are used in almost every program or software system. Some common examples of data structures are arrays, linked lists, queues, stacks, binary trees, and hash tables. Data structures are widely applied in the following areas:

- Compiler design
- Statistical analysis package
- Numerical analysis
- Artificial intelligence
- Operating system
- DBMS
- Simulation
- Graphics

When you will study DBMS as a subject, you will realize that the major data structures used in the Network data model is graphs, Hierarchical data model is trees, and RDBMS is arrays.

Specific data structures are essential ingredients of many efficient algorithms as they enable the programmers to manage huge amounts of data easily and efficiently. Some formal design methods and programming languages emphasize data structures and the algorithms as the key organizing factor in software design. This is because representing information is fundamental to computer science. The primary goal of a program or software is not to perform calculations or operations but to store and retrieve information as fast as possible.

Be it any problem at hand, the application of an appropriate data structure provides the most efficient solution. A solution is said to be efficient if it solves the problem within the required resource constraints like the total space available to store the data and the time allowed to perform each subtask. And the best solution is the one that requires fewer resources than known alternatives. Moreover, the cost of a solution is the amount of resources it consumes. The cost of a solution is basically measured in terms of one key resource such as time, with the implied assumption that the solution meets the other resource constraints.

Today computer programmers do not write programs just to solve a problem but to write an efficient program. For this, they first analyse the problem to determine the performance goals that must be achieved and then think of the most appropriate data structure for that job. However, program designers with a poor understanding of data structure concepts ignore this analysis step and apply a data structure with which they can work comfortably. The applied data structure may not be appropriate for the problem at hand and therefore may result in poor performance (like slow speed of operations).

Conversely, if a program meets its performance goals with a data structure that is simple to use, then it makes no sense to apply another complex data structure just to exhibit the programmer's skill. When selecting a data structure to solve a problem, the following steps must be performed.

1. Analysis of the problem to determine the basic operations that must be supported. For example, basic operation may include inserting/deleting/searching a data item from the data structure.
2. Quantify the resource constraints for each operation.
3. Select the data structure that best meets these requirements.

This three-step approach to select an appropriate data structure for the problem at hand supports a data-centred view of the design process. In the approach, the first concern is the data and the operations that are to be performed on them. The second concern is the representation of the data, and the final concern is the implementation of that representation.

There are different types of data structures that the C language supports. While one type of data structure may permit adding of new data items only at the beginning, the other may allow it to be added at any position. While one data structure may allow accessing data items sequentially, the other may allow random access of data. So, selection of an appropriate data structure for the problem is a crucial decision and may have a major impact on the performance of the program.

2.1.1 Elementary Data Structure Organization

Data structures are building blocks of a program. A program built using improper data structures may not work as expected. So as a programmer it is mandatory to choose most appropriate data structures for a program.

The term *data* means a value or set of values. It specifies either the value of a variable or a constant (e.g., marks of students, name of an employee, address of a customer, value of *pi*, etc.).

While a data item that does not have subordinate data items is categorized as an elementary item, the one that is composed of one or more subordinate data items is called a group item. For example, a student's name may be divided into three sub-items—first name, middle name, and last name—but his roll number would normally be treated as a single item.

A *record* is a collection of data items. For example, the name, address, course, and marks obtained are individual data items. But all these data items can be grouped together to form a record.

A *file* is a collection of related records. For example, if there are 60 students in a class, then there are 60 records of the students. All these related records are stored in a file. Similarly, we can have a file of all the employees working in an organization, a file of all the customers of a company, a file of all the suppliers, so on and so forth.

Moreover, each record in a file may consist of multiple data items but the value of a certain data item uniquely identifies the record in the file. Such a data item K is called a *primary key*, and the values K_1, K_2 ... in such field are called keys or key values. For example, in a student's record that contains roll number, name, address, course, and marks obtained, the field roll number is a primary key. Rest of the fields (name, address, course, and marks) cannot serve as primary keys, since two or more students may have the same name, or may have the same address (as they might be staying at the same place), or may be enrolled in the same course, or have obtained same marks.

This organization and hierarchy of data is taken further to form more complex types of data structures, which is discussed in Section 2.2.

2.2 CLASSIFICATION OF DATA STRUCTURES

Data structures are generally categorized into two classes: *primitive* and *non-primitive* data structures.

Primitive and Non-primitive Data Structures

Primitive data structures are the fundamental data types which are supported by a programming language. Some basic data types are integer, real, character, and boolean. The terms 'data type', 'basic data type', and 'primitive data type' are often used interchangeably.

Non-primitive data structures are those data structures which are created using primitive data structures. Examples of such data structures include linked lists, stacks, trees, and graphs.
Non-primitive data structures can further be classified into two categories: *linear* and *non-linear* data structures.

Linear and Non-linear Structures

If the elements of a data structure are stored in a linear or sequential order, then it is a linear data structure. Examples include arrays, linked lists, stacks, and queues. Linear data structures can be represented in memory in two different ways. One way is to have to a linear relationship between elements by means of sequential memory locations. The other way is to have a linear relationship between elements by means of links.

However, if the elements of a data structure are not stored in a sequential order, then it is a non-linear data structure. The relationship of adjacency is not maintained between elements of a non-linear data structure. Examples include trees and graphs.

C supports a variety of data structures. We will now introduce all these data structures and they would be discussed in detail in subsequent chapters.

Arrays

An array is a collection of similar data elements. These data elements have the same data type. The elements of the array are stored in consecutive memory locations and are referenced by an *index* (also known as the *subscript*).
In C, arrays are declared using the following syntax:

```
type name[size];
```

For example,

```
int marks[10];
```

The above statement declares an array `marks` that contains 10 elements. In C, the array index starts from zero. This means that the array marks will contain 10 elements in all. The first element will be stored in `marks[0]`, second element in `marks[1]`, so on and so forth. Therefore, the last element, that is the 10th element, will be stored in `marks[9]`. In the memory, the array will be stored as shown in Fig. 2.1.

1st element	2nd element	3rd element	4th element	5th element	6th element	7th element	8th element	9th element	10th element
marks[0]	marks[1]	marks[2]	marks[3]	marks[4]	marks[5]	marks[6]	marks[7]	marks[8]	marks[9]

Figure 2.1 Memory representation of an array of 10 elements

Arrays are generally used when we want to store large amount of similar type of data. But they have the following limitations:

- Arrays are of fixed size.
- Data elements are stored in contiguous memory locations which may not be always available.
- Insertion and deletion of elements can be problematic because of shifting of elements from their positions.

However, these limitations can be solved by using linked lists. We will discuss more about arrays in Chapter 3.

Linked Lists

A linked list is a very flexible, dynamic data structure in which elements (called *nodes*) form a sequential list. In contrast to static arrays, a programmer need not worry about how many elements will be stored in the linked list. This feature enables the programmers to write robust programs which require less maintenance.

In a linked list, each node is allocated space as it is added to the list. Every node in the list points to the next node in the list. Therefore, in a linked list, every node contains the following two types of data:

- The value of the node or any other data that corresponds to that node
- A pointer or link to the next node in the list

The last node in the list contains a `NULL` pointer to indicate that it is the end or *tail* of the list. Since the memory for a node is dynamically allocated when it is added to the list, the total number of nodes that may be added to a list is limited only by the amount of memory available. Figure 2.2 shows a linked list of seven nodes.

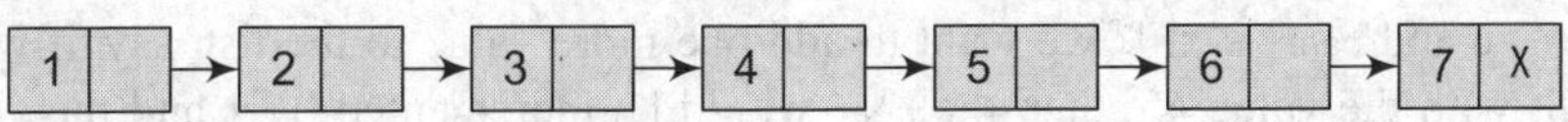

Figure 2.2 Simple linked list

Note *Advantage*: Easier to insert or delete data elements
Disadvantage: Slow search operation and requires more memory space

Stacks

A stack is a linear data structure in which insertion and deletion of elements are done at only one end, which is known as the `top` of the stack. Stack is called a last-in, first-out (LIFO) structure because the last element which is added to the stack is the first element which is deleted from the stack.

In the computer's memory, stacks can be implemented using arrays or linked lists. Figure 2.3 shows the array implementation of a stack. Every stack has a variable `top` associated with it. `top` is used to store the address of the topmost element of the stack. It is this position from where the element will be added or deleted. There is another variable `MAX`, which is used to store the maximum number of elements that the stack can store.

If `top = NULL`, then it indicates that the stack is empty and if `top = MAX-1`, then the stack is full.

A	AB	ABC	ABCD	ABCDE					
0	1	2	3	top = 4	5	6	7	8	9

Figure 2.3 Array representation of a stack

In Fig. 2.3, `top = 4`, so insertions and deletions will be done at this position. Here, the stack can store a maximum of 10 elements where the indices range from 0–9. In the above stack, five more elements can still be stored.

A stack supports three basic operations: `push`, `pop`, and `peep`. The `push` operation adds an element to the top of the stack. The `pop` operation removes the element from the top of the stack. And the `peep` operation returns the value of the topmost element of the stack (without deleting it).

However, before inserting an element in the stack, we must check for overflow conditions. An overflow occurs when we try to insert an element into a stack that is already full.

Similarly, before deleting an element from the stack, we must check for underflow conditions. An underflow condition occurs when we try to delete an element from a stack that is already empty.

Queues

A queue is a first-in, first-out (FIFO) data structure in which the element that is inserted first is the first one to be taken out. The elements in a queue are added at one end called the `rear` and removed from the other end called the `front`. Like stacks, queues can be implemented by using either arrays or linked lists.

Every queue has `front` and `rear` variables that point to the position from where deletions and insertions can be done, respectively. Consider the queue shown in Fig. 2.4.

Front					Rear				
12	9	7	18	14	36				
0	1	2	3	4	5	6	7	8	9

Figure 2.4 Array representation of a queue

Here, `front = 0` and `rear = 5`. If we want to add one more value to the list, say, if we want to add another element with the value 45, then the `rear` would be incremented by 1 and the value would be stored at the position pointed by the `rear`. The queue, after the addition, would be as shown in Fig. 2.5.

Here, `front = 0` and `rear = 6`. Every time a new element is to be added, we will repeat the same procedure.

Front						Rear			
12	9	7	18	14	36	45			
0	1	2	3	4	5	6	7	8	9

Figure 2.5 Queue after insertion of a new element

Now, if we want to delete an element from the queue, then the value of `front` will be incremented. Deletions are done only from this end of the queue. The queue after the deletion will be as shown in Fig. 2.6.

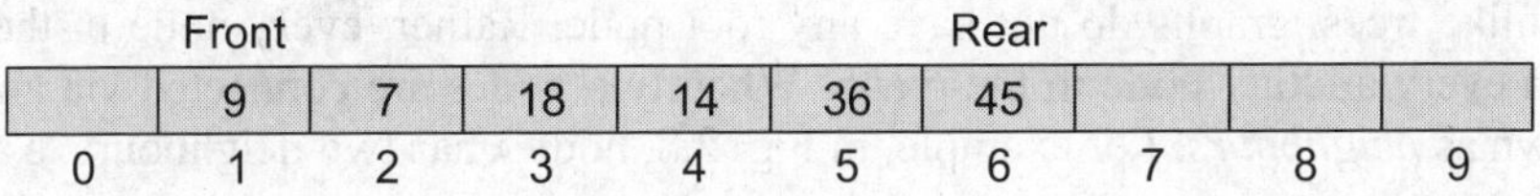

Figure 2.6 Queue after deletion of an element

However, before inserting an element in the queue, we must check for overflow conditions. An overflow occurs when we try to insert an element into a queue that is already full. A queue is full when `rear = MAX-1`, where `MAX` is the size of the queue, that is `MAX` specifies the maximum number of elements in the queue. Note that we have written `MAX-1` because the index starts from 0.

Similarly, before deleting an element from the queue, we must check for underflow conditions. An underflow condition occurs when we try to delete an element from a queue that is already empty. If `front = NULL` and `rear = NULL`, then there is no element in the queue.

Trees

A tree is a non-linear data structure which consists of a collection of nodes arranged in a hierarchical order. One of the nodes is designated as the root node, and the remaining nodes can be partitioned into disjoint sets such that each set is a sub-tree of the root.

The simplest form of a tree is a binary tree. A binary tree consists of a root node and left and right sub-trees, where both sub-trees are also binary trees. Each node contains a data element, a left pointer which points to the left sub-tree, and a right pointer which points to the right sub-tree. The root element is the topmost node which is pointed by a 'root' pointer. If `root = NULL` then the tree is empty.

Figure 2.7 shows a binary tree, where `R` is the root node and T_1 and T_2 are the left and right sub-trees of `R`. If T_1 is non-empty, then T_1 is said to be the left successor of `R`. Likewise, if T_2 is non-empty, then it is called the right successor of `R`.

In Fig. 2.7, node 2 is the left child and node 3 is the right child of the root node 1. Note that the left sub-tree of the root node consists of the nodes 2, 4, 5, 8, and 9. Similarly, the right sub-tree of the root node consists of the nodes 3, 6, 7, 10, 11, and 12.

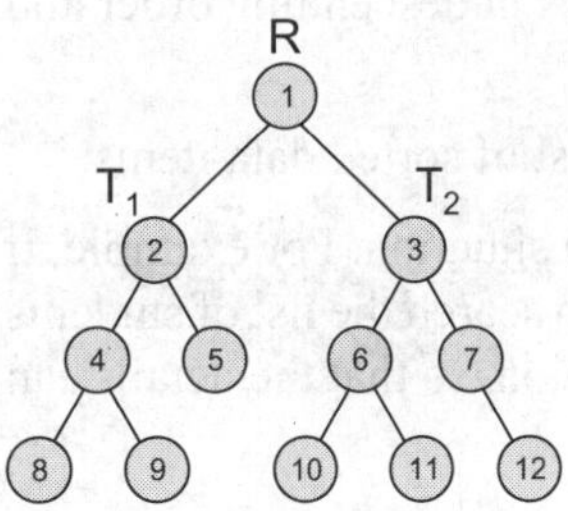

Figure 2.7 Binary tree

> **Note** *Advantage*: Provides quick search, insert, and delete operations
> *Disadvantage*: Complicated deletion algorithm

Graphs

A graph is a non-linear data structure which is a collection of *vertices* (also called *nodes*) and *edges* that connect these vertices. A graph is often viewed as a generalization of the tree structure, where instead of a purely parent-to-child relationship between tree nodes, any kind of complex relationships between the nodes can exist.

In a tree structure, nodes can have any number of children but only one parent, a graph on the other hand relaxes all such kinds of restrictions. Figure 2.8 shows a graph with five nodes.

A node in the graph may represent a city and the edges connecting the nodes can represent roads. A graph can also be used to represent a computer network where the nodes are workstations and the edges are the network connections. Graphs have so many applications in computer science and mathematics that several algorithms have been written to perform the standard graph operations, such as searching the graph and finding the shortest path between the nodes of a graph.

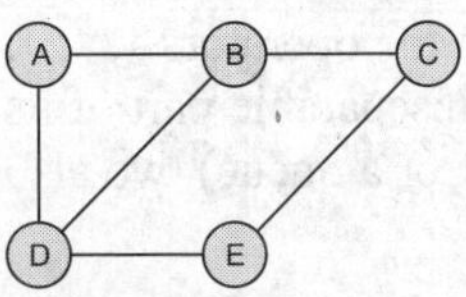

Figure 2.8 Graph

Note that unlike trees, graphs do not have any root node. Rather, every node in the graph can be connected with every another node in the graph. When two nodes are connected via an edge, the two nodes are known as *neighbours*. For example, in Fig. 2.8, node `A` has two neighbours: `B` and `D`.

Note *Advantage*: Best models real-world situations
Disadvantage: Some algorithms are slow and very complex

2.3 OPERATIONS ON DATA STRUCTURES

This section discusses the different operations that can be performed on the various data structures previously mentioned.

Traversing It means to access each data item exactly once so that it can be processed. For example, to print the names of all the students in a class.

Searching It is used to find the location of one or more data items that satisfy the given constraint. Such a data item may or may not be present in the given collection of data items. For example, to find the names of all the students who secured 100 marks in mathematics.

Inserting It is used to add new data items to the given list of data items. For example, to add the details of a new student who has recently joined the course.

Deleting It means to remove (delete) a particular data item from the given collection of data items. For example, to delete the name of a student who has left the course.

Sorting Data items can be arranged in some order like ascending order or descending order depending on the type of application. For example, arranging the names of students in a class in an alphabetical order, or calculating the top three winners by arranging the participants' scores in descending order and then extracting the top three.

Merging Lists of two sorted data items can be combined to form a single list of sorted data items.

Many a time, two or more operations are applied simultaneously in a given situation. For example, if we want to delete the details of a student whose name is X, then we first have to search the list of students to find whether the record of X exists or not and if it exists then at which location, so that the details can be deleted from that particular location.

2.4 ABSTRACT DATA TYPE

An *abstract data type* (ADT) is the way we look at a data structure, focusing on what it does and ignoring how it does its job. For example, stacks and queues are perfect examples of an ADT. We can implement both these ADTs using an array or a linked list. This demonstrates the 'abstract' nature of stacks and queues.

To further understand the meaning of an abstract data type, we will break the term into 'data type' and 'abstract', and then discuss their meanings.

Data type Data type of a variable is the set of values that the variable can take. We have already read the basic data types in C include `int`, `char`, `float`, and `double`.

When we talk about a primitive type (built-in data type), we actually consider two things: a data item with certain characteristics and the permissible operations on that data. For example, an `int` variable can contain any whole-number value from –32768 to 32767 and can be operated with the operators `+`, `-`, `*`, and `/`. In other words, the operations that can be performed on a data type are an inseparable part of its identity. Therefore, when we declare a variable of an abstract data type (e.g., stack or a queue), we also need to specify the operations that can be performed on it.

Abstract The word 'abstract' in the context of data structures means *considered apart from the detailed specifications or implementation*.

In C, an abstract data type can be a structure considered without regard to its implementation. It can be thought of as a 'description' of the data in the structure with a list of operations that can be performed on the data within that structure.

The end-user is not concerned about the details of how the methods carry out their tasks. They are only aware of the methods that are available to them and are only concerned about calling those methods and getting the results. They are not concerned about how they work.

For example, when we use a stack or a queue, the user is concerned only with the type of data and the operations that can be performed on it. Therefore, the fundamentals of how the data is stored should be invisible to the user. They should not be concerned with how the methods work or what structures are being used to store the data. They should just know that to work with stacks, they have `push()` and `pop()` functions available to them. Using these functions, they can manipulate the data (insertion or deletion) stored in the stack.

Advantage of using ADTs

In the real world, programs *evolve* as a result of new requirements or constraints, so a modification to a program commonly requires a change in one or more of its data structures. For example, if you want to add a new field to a student's record to keep track of more information about each student, then it will be better to replace an array with a linked structure to improve the program's efficiency. In such a scenario, rewriting every procedure that uses the changed structure is not desirable. Therefore, a better alternative is to *separate* the use of a data structure from the details of its implementation. This is the principle underlying the use of abstract data types.

2.5 ALGORITHMS

The typical definition of algorithm is 'a formally defined procedure for performing some calculation'. If a procedure is formally defined, then it can be implemented using a formal language, and such a language is known as a *programming language*. In general terms, an algorithm provides a blueprint to write a program to solve a particular problem. It is considered to be an effective procedure for solving a problem in finite number of steps. That is, a well-defined algorithm always provides an answer and is guaranteed to terminate.

Algorithms are mainly used to achieve *software reuse*. Once we have an idea or a blueprint of a solution, we can implement it in any high-level language like C, C++, or Java.

An algorithm is basically a set of instructions that solve a problem. It is not uncommon to have multiple algorithms to tackle the same problem, but the choice of a particular algorithm must depend on the time and space complexity of the algorithm.

2.6 DIFFERENT APPROACHES TO DESIGNING AN ALGORITHM

Algorithms are used to manipulate the data contained in data structures. When working with data structures, algorithms are used to perform operations on the stored data.

A complex algorithm is often divided into smaller units called modules. This process of dividing an algorithm into modules is called modularization. The key advantages of modularization are as follows:

- It makes the complex algorithm simpler to design and implement.
- Each module can be designed independently. While designing one module, the details of other modules can be ignored, thereby enhancing clarity in design which in turn simplifies implementation, debugging, testing, documenting, and maintenance of the overall algorithm.

There are two main approaches to design an algorithm—top-down approach and bottom-up approach, as shown in Fig. 2.9.

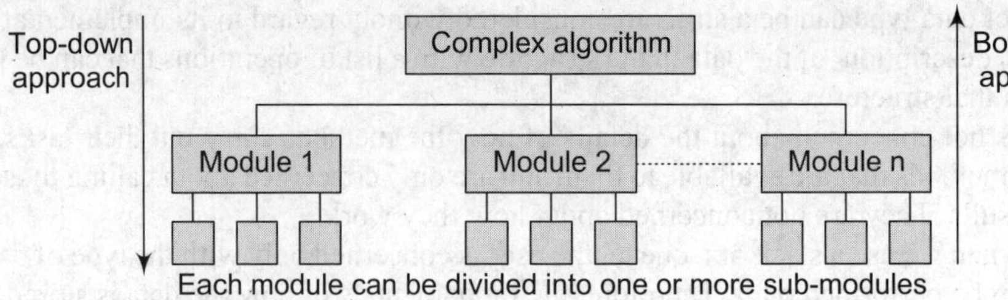

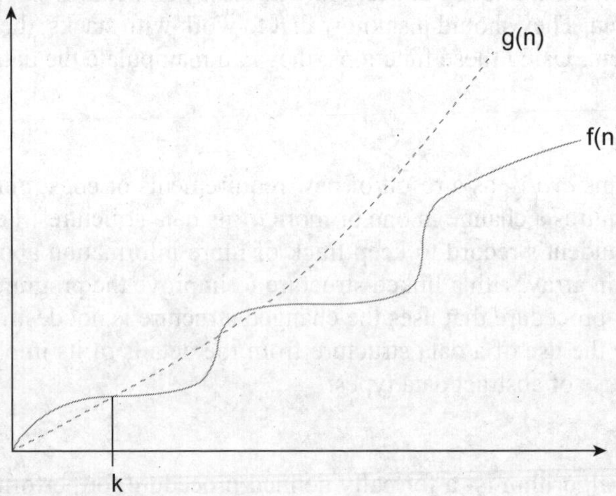

Figure 2.9 Different approaches of designing an algorithm. O(n) is the formal way to express the upper bound of an algorithm's running time. It measures the worst case time complexity or the longest amount of time an algorithm can possibly take to complete.

Top-down approach A top-down design approach starts by dividing the complex algorithm into one or more modules. These modules can further be decomposed into one or more sub-modules, and this process of decomposition is iterated until the desired level of module complexity is achieved. Top-down design method is a form of stepwise refinement where we begin with the topmost module and incrementally add modules that it calls.

Therefore, in a top-down approach, we start from an abstract design and then at each step, this design is refined into more concrete levels until a level is reached that requires no further refinement.

Bottom-up approach A bottom-up approach is just the reverse of top-down approach. In the bottom-up design, we start with designing the most basic or concrete modules and then proceed towards designing higher level modules. The higher level modules are implemented by using the operations performed by lower level modules. Thus, in this approach sub-modules are grouped together to form a higher level module. All the higher level modules are clubbed together to form even higher level modules. This process is repeated until the design of the complete algorithm is obtained.

Top-down vs bottom-up approach Whether the top-down strategy should be followed or a bottom-up is a question that can be answered depending on the application at hand.

While top-down approach follows a stepwise refinement by decomposing the algorithm into manageable modules, the bottom-up approach on the other hand defines a module and then groups together several modules to form a new higher level module.

Top-down approach is highly appreciated for ease in documenting the modules, generation of test cases, implementation of code, and debugging. However, it is also criticized because the sub-modules are

```
Step 1: Input first number as A
Step 2: Input second number as B
Step 3: SET SUM = A+B
Step 4: PRINT SUM
Step 5: END
```

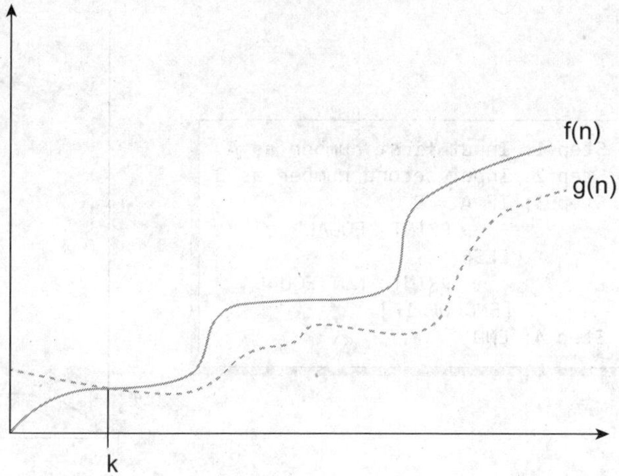

Figure 2.10 Algorithm to add two numbers. Ω(n) is the formal way to express the lower bound of an algorithm's running time. It measures the best case time complexity or the best amount of time an algorithm can possibly take to complete.

analysed in isolation without concentrating on their communication with other modules or on reusability of components and little attention is paid to data, thereby ignoring the concept of information hiding.

Although the bottom-up approach allows information hiding as it first identifies what has to be encapsulated within a module and then provides an abstract interface to define the module's boundaries as seen from the clients. But all this is difficult to be done in a strict bottom-up strategy. Some top-down activities need to be performed for this.

All in all, design of complex algorithms must not be constrained to proceed according to a fixed pattern but should be a blend of top-down and bottom-up approaches.

2.7 CONTROL STRUCTURES USED IN ALGORITHMS

An algorithm has a finite number of steps. Some steps may involve decision-making and repetition. Broadly speaking, an algorithm may employ one of the following control structures: (a) sequence, (b) decision, and (c) repetition.

Sequence

By sequence, we mean that each step of an algorithm is executed in a specified order. Let us write an algorithm to add two numbers. This algorithm performs the steps in a purely sequential order, as shown in Fig. 2.10.

Decision

Decision statements are used when the execution of a process depends on the outcome of some condition. For example, if `x = y`, then print `EQUAL`. So the general form of `IF` construct can be given as:

```
IF condition Then process
```

A condition in this context is any statement that may evaluate to either a true value or a false value. In the above example, a variable `x` can be either equal to `y` or not equal to `y`. However, it cannot be both true and false. If the condition is true, then the process is executed.

A decision statement can also be stated in the following manner:

```
IF condition
            Then process1
ELSE        process2
```

```
Step 1: Input first number as A
Step 2: Input second number as B
Step 3: IF A = B
            PRINT "EQUAL"
        ELSE
            PRINT "NOT EQUAL"
        [END OF IF]
Step 4: END
```

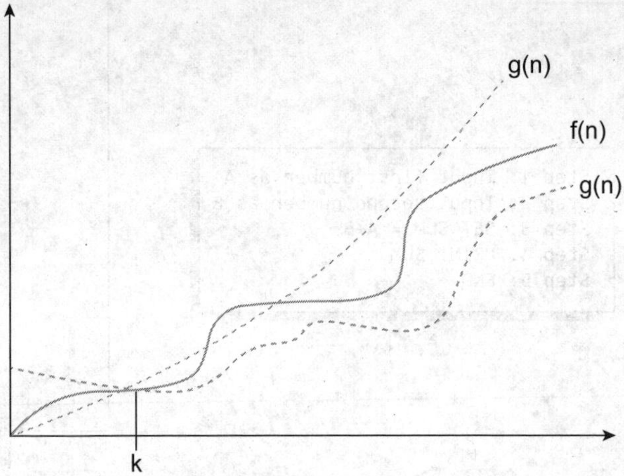

Figure 2.11 Algorithm to test for equality of of two numbers. θ(n) is the formal way to express both the lower bound and the upper bound of an algorithm's running time.

```
Step 1: [INITIALIZE] SET I = 1, N = 10
Step 2: Repeat Steps 3 and 4 while I<=N
Step 3: PRINT I
Step 4: SET I = I+1
        [END OF LOOP]
Step 5: END
```

Figure 2.12 Algorithm to print the first 10 natural

This form is popularly known as the `IF-ELSE` construct. Here, if the condition is true, then `process1` is executed, else `process2` is executed. Figure 2.11 shows an algorithm to check if two numbers are equal.

Repetition

Repetition, which involves executing one or more steps for a number of times, can be implemented using constructs such as `while`, `do-while`, and `for` loops. These loops execute one or more steps until some condition is true. Figure 2.12 shows an algorithm that prints the first 10 natural numbers.

Programming Examples

1. Write an algorithm for swapping two values.

```
Step 1: Input first number as A
Step 2: Input second number as B
Step 3: SET TEMP = A
Step 4: SET A = B
Step 5: SET B = TEMP
Step 6: PRINT A, B
Step 7: END
```

2. Write an algorithm to find the larger of two numbers.

```
Step 1: Input first number as A
Step 2: Input second number as B
Step 3: IF A>B
            PRINT A
        ELSE
            IF A<B
                PRINT B
        ELSE
```

```
                PRINT "The numbers are equal"
                [END OF IF]
        [END OF IF]
Step 4: END
```

3. Write an algorithm to find whether a number is even or odd.

```
Step 1: Input number as A
Step 2: IF A%2 =0
                PRINT "EVEN"
        ELSE
                PRINT "ODD"
        [END OF IF]
Step 3: END
```

4. Write an algorithm to print the grade obtained by a student using the following rules.

```
Step 1: Enter the Marks obtained as M
Step 2: IF M>75
                PRINT O
Step 3: IF M>=60 AND M<75
                PRINT A
Step 4: IF M>=50 AND M<60
                PRINT B
Step 5: IF M>=40 AND M<50
                PRINT C
        ELSE
                PRINT D
        [END OF IF]
Step 6: END
```

Marks	Grade
Above 75	O
60-75	A
50-59	B
40-49	C
Less then 40	D

5. Write an algorithm to find the sum of first N natural numbers.

```
Step 1: Input N
Step 2: SET I = 1, SUM = 0
Step 3: Repeat Step 4 while I <= N
Step 4:         SET SUM = SUM + I
                SET I = I + 1
        [END OF LOOP]
Step 5: PRINT SUM
Step 6: END
```

2.8 TIME AND SPACE COMPLEXITY

Analysing an algorithm means determining the amount of resources (such as time and memory) needed to execute it. Algorithms are generally designed to work with an arbitrary number of inputs, so the efficiency or complexity of an algorithm is stated in terms of time and space complexity.

The *time complexity* of an algorithm is basically the running time of a program as a function of the input size. Similarly, the *space complexity* of an algorithm is the amount of computer memory that is required during the program execution as a function of the input size.

In other words, the number of machine instructions which a program executes is called its time complexity. This number is primarily dependent on the size of the program's input and the algorithm used.

Generally, the space needed by a program depends on the following two parts:

- *Fixed part*: It varies from problem to problem. It includes the space needed for storing instructions, constants, variables, and structured variables (like arrays and structures).
- *Variable part*: It varies from program to program. It includes the space needed for recursion stack, and for structured variables that are allocated space dynamically during the runtime of a program.

However, running time requirements are more critical than memory requirements. Therefore, in this section, we will concentrate on the running time efficiency of algorithms.

2.8.1 Worst-case, Average-case, Best-case, and Amortized Time Complexity

Worst-case running time This denotes the behaviour of an algorithm with respect to the worst-possible case of the input instance. The worst-case running time of an algorithm is an upper bound on the running time for any input. Therefore, having the knowledge of worst-case running time gives us an assurance that the algorithm will never go beyond this time limit.

Average-case running time The average-case running time of an algorithm is an estimate of the running time for an 'average' input. It specifies the expected behaviour of the algorithm when the input is randomly drawn from a given distribution. Average-case running time assumes that all inputs of a given size are equally likely.

Best-case running time The term 'best-case performance' is used to analyse an algorithm under optimal conditions. For example, the best case for a simple linear search on an array occurs when the desired element is the first in the list. However, while developing and choosing an algorithm to solve a problem, we hardly base our decision on the best-case performance. It is always recommended to improve the average performance and the worst-case performance of an algorithm.

Amortized running time Amortized running time refers to the time required to perform a sequence of (related) operations averaged over all the operations performed. Amortized analysis guarantees the average performance of each operation in the worst case.

2.8.2 Time–Space Trade-off

The best algorithm to solve a particular problem at hand is no doubt the one that requires less memory space and takes less time to complete its execution. But practically, designing such an ideal algorithm is not a trivial task. There can be more than one algorithm to solve a particular problem. One may require less memory space, while the other may require less CPU time to execute. Thus, it is not uncommon to sacrifice one thing for the other. Hence, there exists a time–space trade-off among algorithms.

So, if space is a big constraint, then one might choose a program that takes less space at the cost of more CPU time. On the contrary, if time is a major constraint, then one might choose a program that takes minimum time to execute at the cost of more space.

2.8.3 Expressing Time and Space Complexity

The time and space complexity can be expressed using a function `f(n)` where `n` is the input size for a given instance of the problem being solved. Expressing the complexity is required when

- We want to predict the rate of growth of complexity as the input size of the problem increases.
- There are multiple algorithms that find a solution to a given problem and we need to find the algorithm that is most efficient.

The most widely used notation to express this function `f(n)` is the Big O notation. It provides the upper bound for the complexity.

2.8.4 Algorithm Efficiency

If a function is linear (without any loops or recursions), the efficiency of that algorithm or the running time of that algorithm can be given as the number of instructions it contains. However, if an algorithm contains loops, then the efficiency of that algorithm may vary depending on the number of loops and the running time of each loop in the algorithm.

Let us consider different cases in which loops determine the efficiency of an algorithm.

Linear Loops

To calculate the efficiency of an algorithm that has a single loop, we need to first determine the number of times the statements in the loop will be executed. This is because the number of iterations is directly proportional to the loop factor. Greater the loop factor, more is the number of iterations. For example, consider the loop given below:

```
for(i=0;i<100;i++)
    statement block;
```

Here, 100 is the loop factor. We have already said that efficiency is directly proportional to the number of iterations. Hence, the general formula in the case of linear loops may be given as

```
f(n) = n
```

However calculating efficiency is not as simple as is shown in the above example. Consider the loop given below:

```
for(i=0;i<100;i+=2)
     statement block;
```

Here, the number of iterations is half the number of the loop factor. So, here the efficiency can be given as

```
f(n) = n/2
```

Logarithmic Loops

We have seen that in linear loops, the loop updation statement either adds or subtracts the loop-controlling variable. However, in logarithmic loops, the loop-controlling variable is either multiplied or divided during each iteration of the loop. For example, look at the loops given below:

```
for(i=1;i<1000;i*=2)
    statement block;
```

```
for(i=1000;i>=1;i/=2)
    statement block;
```

Consider the first `for` loop in which the loop-controlling variable `i` is multiplied by 2. The loop will be executed only 10 times and not 1000 times because in each iteration the value of `i` doubles. Now, consider the second loop in which the loop-controlling variable `i` is divided by 2. In this case also, the loop will be executed 10 times. Thus, the number of iterations is a function of the number by which the loop-controlling variable is divided or multiplied. In the examples discussed, it is 2. That is, when `n = 1000`, the number of iterations can be given by `log 1000` which is approximately equal to 10.

Therefore, putting this analysis in general terms, we can conclude that the efficiency of loops in which iterations divide or multiply the loop-controlling variables can be given as

```
f(n) = log n
```

Nested Loops

Loops that contain loops are known as *nested loops*. In order to analyse nested loops, we need to determine the number of iterations each loop completes. The total is then obtained as the product of the number of iterations in the inner loop and the number of iterations in the outer loop.

In this case, we analyse the efficiency of the algorithm based on whether it is a linear logarithmic, quadratic, or dependent quadratic nested loop.

Linear logarithmic loop Consider the following code in which the loop-controlling variable of the inner loop is multiplied after each iteration. The number of iterations in the inner loop is `log 10`. This inner loop is controlled by an outer loop which iterates 10 times. Therefore, according to the formula, the number of iterations for this code can be given as `10 log 10`.

```
for(i=0;i<10;i++)
        for(j=1; j<10;j*=2)
                statement block;
```

In more general terms, the efficiency of such loops can be given as `f(n) = n log n`.

Quadratic loop In a quadratic loop, the number of iterations in the inner loop is equal to the number of iterations in the outer loop. Consider the following code in which the outer loop executes 10 times and for each iteration of the outer loop, the inner loop also executes 10 times. Therefore, the efficiency here is 100.

```
for(i=0;i<10;i++)
    for(j=0; j<10;j++)
        statement block;
```

The generalized formula for quadratic loop can be given as `f(n) = n²`.

Dependent quadratic loop In a dependent quadratic loop, the number of iterations in the inner loop is dependent on the outer loop. Consider the code given below:

```
for(i=0;i<10;i++)
    for(j=0; j<=i;j++)
        statement block;
```

In this code, the inner loop will execute just once in the first iteration, twice in the second iteration, thrice in the third iteration, so on and so forth. In this way, the number of iterations can be calculated as

```
1 + 2 + 3 + ... + 9 + 10 = 55
```

If we calculate the average of this loop (55/10 = 5.5), we will observe that it is equal to the number of iterations in the outer loop (10) plus 1 divided by 2. In general terms, the inner loop iterates `(n + 1)/2` times. Therefore, the efficiency of such a code can be given as

```
f(n) = n (n + 1)/2
```

2.9 BIG O NOTATION

In today's era of massive advancement in computer technology, we are hardly concerned about the efficiency of algorithms. Rather, we are more interested in knowing the generic order of the magnitude of the algorithm. If we have two different algorithms to solve the same problem where one algorithm executes in 10 iterations and the other in 20 iterations, the difference between the two algorithms is not much. However, if the first algorithm executes in 10 iterations and the other in 1000 iterations, then it is a matter of concern.

We have seen that the number of statements executed in the program for `n` elements of the data is a function of the number of elements, expressed as `f(n)`. Even if the expression derived for a function is complex, a dominant factor in the expression is sufficient to determine the order of the magnitude of the result and, hence, the efficiency of the algorithm. This factor is the `Big O`, and is expressed as `O(n)`.

The Big O notation, where O stands for 'order of', is concerned with what happens for very large values of `n`. For example, if a sorting algorithm performs n^2 operations to sort just `n` elements, then that algorithm would be described as an $O(n^2)$ algorithm.

When expressing complexity using the Big O notation, constant multipliers are ignored. So, an `O(4n)` algorithm is equivalent to `O(n)`, which is how it should be written.

If `f(n)` and `g(n)` are the functions defined on a positive integer number `n`, then

```
f(n) = O(g(n))
```

That is, `f of n is Big-O of g of n` if and only if positive constants `c` and `n` exist, such that $f(n) \leq cg(n)$. It means that for large amounts of data, `f(n)` will grow no more than a constant factor than `g(n)`. Hence, `g` provides an upper bound. Note that here `c` is a constant which depends on the following factors:

- the programming language used,

- the quality of the compiler or interpreter,
- the CPU speed,
- the size of the main memory and the access time to it,
- the knowledge of the programmer, and
- the algorithm itself, which may require simple but also time-consuming machine instructions.

We have seen that the Big O notation provides a strict upper bound for `f(n)`. This means that the function `f(n)` can do better but not worse than the specified value. Big O notation is simply written as `f(n) ∈ O(g(n))` or as `f(n) = O(g(n))`.

Here, `n` is the problem size and `O(g(n))` = `{h(n): ∃ positive constants c,` n_0 `such that 0 ≤ h(n) ≤ cg(n), ∀ n ≥` n_0`}`. Hence, we can say that `O(g(n))` comprises a set of all the functions `h(n)` that are less than or equal to `cg(n)` for all values of $n \geq n_0$.

If $f(n) \leq cg(n)$, $c > 0$, $\forall n \geq n_0$, then $f(n) = O(g(n))$ and `g(n)` is an asymptotically tight upper bound for `f(n)`.

Examples of functions in $O(n^3)$ include: $n^{2.9}$, n^3, $n^3 + n$, $540n^3 + 10$.
Examples of functions not in $O(n^3)$ include: $n^{3.2}$, n^2, $n^2 + n$, $540n + 10$, $2n$
To summarize,

- Best case O describes an upper bound for all combinations of input. It is possibly lower than the worst case. For example, when sorting an array the best case is when the array is already correctly sorted.
- Worst case O describes a lower bound for worst case input combinations. It is possibly greater than the best case. For example, when sorting an array the worst case is when the array is sorted in reverse order.
- If we simply write O, it means same as worst case O.

Now let us look at some examples of `g(n)` and `f(n)`. Table 2.1 shows the relationship between `g(n)` and `f(n)`. Note that the constant values will be ignored because the main purpose of the Big O notation is to analyse the algorithm in a general fashion, so the anomalies that appear for small input sizes are simply ignored.

Table 2.1 Examples of `f(n)` and `g(n)`

g(n)	f(n) = O(g(n))
10	O(1)
$2n^3 + 1$	$O(n^3)$
$3n^2 + 5$	$O(n^2)$
$2n^3 + 3n^2 + 5n - 10$	$O(n^3)$

Categories of Algorithms

According to the Big O notation, we have five different categories of algorithms:

- Constant time algorithm: running time complexity given as `O(1)`
- Linear time algorithm: running time complexity given as `O(n)`
- Logarithmic time algorithm: running time complexity given as `O(log n)`
- Polynomial time algorithm: running time complexity given as $O(n^k)$ where $k > 1$
- Exponential time algorithm: running time complexity given as $O(2^n)$

Table 2.2 shows the number of operations that would be performd for various values of `n`.

Table 2.2 Number of operations for different functions of `n`

n	O(1)	O(log n)	O(n)	O(n log n)	$O(n^2)$	$O(n^3)$
1	1	1	1	1	1	1
2	1	1	2	2	4	8
4	1	2	4	8	16	64
8	1	3	8	24	64	512
16	1	4	16	64	256	4096

Example 2.1 Show that $4n^2 = O(n^3)$.

Solution By definition, we have

$0 \le h(n) \le cg(n)$

Substituting $4n^2$ as $h(n)$ and n^3 as $g(n)$, we get

$0 \le 4n^2 \le cn^3$

Dividing by n^3

$0/n^3 \le 4n^2/n^3 \le cn^3/n^3$

$0 \le 4/n \le c$

Now to determine the value of c, we see that 4/n is maximum when n=1. Therefore, c=4.

To determine the value of n_0,

$0 \le 4/n_0 \le 4$

$0 \le 4/4 \le n_0$

$0 \le 1 \le n_0$

This means n_0=1. Therefore, $0 \le 4n^2 \le 4n^3 \; \forall \; n \ge n_0=1$.

Example 2.2 Show that $400n^3 + 20n^2 = O(n^3)$.

Solution By definition, we have

$0 \le h(n) \le cg(n)$

Substituting $400n^3 + 20n^2$ as $h(n)$ and n^3 as $g(n)$, we get

$0 \le 400n^3 + 20n^2 \le cn^3$

Dividing by n^3

$0/n^3 \le 400n^3/n^3 + 20n^2/n^3 \le cn^3/n^3$

$0 \le 400 + 20/n \le c$

Note that $20/n \rightarrow 0$ as $n \rightarrow \infty$, and 20/n is maximum when n = 1. Therefore,

$0 \le 400 + 20/1 \le c$

This means, c = 420

To determine the value of n_0,

$0 \le 400 + 20/n_0 \le 420$

$-400 \le 400 + 20/n_0 - 400 \le 420 - 400$

$-400 \le 20/n_0 \le 20$

$-20 \le 1/n_0 \le 1$

$-20\ n_0 \le 1 \le n_0$. This implies $n_0 = 1$.

Hence, $0 \le 400n^3 + 20n^2 \le 420n^3 \; \forall \; n \ge n_0=1$.

Example 2.3 Show that $n = O(n\log n)$.

Solution By definition, we have

$0 \le h(n) \le cg(n)$

Substituting n as h(n) and nlogn as g(n), we get

$0 \le n \le c\ n \log n$

Dividing by nlogn, we get

$0/n \log n \le n/n \log n \le c\ n \log n / n \log n$

$0 \le 1/\log n \le c$

We know that $1/\log n \rightarrow 0$ as $n \rightarrow \infty$

To determine the value of c, it is clearly evident that $1/\log n$ is greatest when n=2. Therefore,

$0 \le 1/\log 2 \le c = 1$. Hence c = 1.

To determine the value of n_0, we can write

$0 \le 1/\log n_0 \le 1$

$0 \le 1 \le \log n_0$

Now, $\log n_0 = 1$, when $n_0 = 2$.

Hence, $0 \le n \le cn \log n$ when $c= 1$ and $\forall\ n \ge n_0=2$.

Example 2.4 Show that $10n^3 + 20n \ne O(n^2)$.

Solution By definition, we have

$$0 \le h(n) \le cg(n)$$

Substituting $10n^3 + 20n$ as $h(n)$ and n^2 as $g(n)$, we get

$$0 \le 10n^3 + 20n \le cn^2$$

Dividing by n^2

$$0/n^2 \le 10n^3/n^2 + 20n/n^2 \le cn^2/n^2$$
$$0 \le 10n + 20/n \le c$$
$$0 \le (10n^2 + 20)/n \le c$$

Hence, $10n^3 + 20n \ne O^2(n^2)$

Limitations of Big O Notation

There are certain limitations with the Big O notation of expressing the complexity of algorithms. These limitations are as follows:

- Many algorithms are simply too hard to analyse mathematically.
- There may not be sufficient information to calculate the behaviour of the algorithm in the average case.
- Big O analysis only tells us how the algorithm grows with the size of the problem, not how efficient it is, as it does not consider the programming effort.
- It ignores important constants. For example, if one algorithm takes $O(n^2)$ time to execute and the other takes $O(100000n^2)$ time to execute, then as per Big O, both algorithm have equal time complexity. In real-time systems, this may be a serious consideration.

2.10 OMEGA NOTATION (Ω)

The Omega notation provides a tight lower bound for $f(n)$. This means that the function can never do better than the specified value but it may do worse.
Ω notation is simply written as, $f(n) \in \Omega(g(n))$, where n is the problem size and
$\Omega(g(n)) = \{h(n)\text{: } \exists$ positive constants $c > 0$, n_0 such that $0 \le cg(n) \le h(n),\ \forall\ n \ge n_0\}$.

Hence, we can say that $\Omega(g(n))$ comprises a set of all the functions $h(n)$ that are greater than or equal to $cg(n)$ for all values of $n \ge n_0$.

If $cg(n) \le f(n)$, $c > 0$, $\forall\ n \ge n_0$, then $f(n) \in \Omega(g(n))$ and $g(n)$ is an asymptotically tight lower bound for $f(n)$.

Examples of functions in $\Omega(n^2)$ include: n^2, $n^{2.9}$, $n^3 + n^2$, n^3
Examples of functions not in $\Omega(n^3)$ include: n, $n^{2.9}$, n^2
To summarize,

- Best case Ω describes a lower bound for all combinations of input. This implies that the function can never get any better than the specified value. For example, when sorting an array the best case is when the array is already correctly sorted.
- Worst case Ω describes a lower bound for worst case input combinations. It is possibly greater than best case. For example, when sorting an array the worst case is when the array is sorted in reverse order.
- If we simply write Ω, it means same as best case Ω.

Example 2.5 Show that $5n^2 + 10n = \Omega(n^2)$.

Solution By the definition, we can write

$$0 \le cg(n) \le h(n)$$
$$0 \le cn^2 \le 5n^2 + 10n$$

Dividing by n^2

$$0/n^2 \le cn^2/n^2 \le 5n^2/n^2 + 10n/n^2$$
$$0 \le c \le 5 + 10/n$$

Now, $\lim_{n\to\infty} 5 + 10/n = 5$.

Therefore, $0 \le c \le 5$.

Hence, $c = 5$

Now to determine the value of n_0

$$0 \le 5 \le 5 + 10/n_0$$
$$-5 \le 5 - 5 \le 5 + 10/n_0 - 5$$
$$-5 \le 0 \le 10/n_0$$

So $n_0 = 1$ as $\lim_{n\to\infty} 1/n = 0$

Hence, $5n^2 + 10n = \Omega(n^2)$ for $c=5$ and $\forall\ n \ge n_0=1$.

Example 2.6 Show that $7n \ne \Omega(n^2)$.

Solution By the definition, we can write

$$0 \le cg(n) \le h(n)$$
$$0 \le cn^2 \le 7n$$

Dividing by n^2, we get

$$0/n^2 \le cn^2/n^2 \le 7n/n^2$$
$$0 \le c \le 7/n$$

Thus, from the above statement, we see that the value of c depends on the value of n. There does not exist a value of n_0 that satisfies the condition as n increases. This could fairly be possible if $c = 0$ but it is not allowed as the definition by itself says that $\lim_{n\to\infty} 1/n = 0$.

2.11 THETA NOTATION (Θ)

Theta notation provides an asymptotically tight bound for $f(n)$. Θ notation is simply written as, $f(n) \in \Theta(g(n))$, where n is the problem size and

$\Theta(g(n)) = \{h(n)$: $\exists$ positive constants c_1, c_2, and n_0 such that $0 \le c_1g(n) \le h(n) \le c_2g(n)$, $\forall\ n \ge n_0\}$.

Hence, we can say that $\Theta(g(n))$ comprises a set of all the functions $h(n)$ that are between $c_1g(n)$ and $c_2g(n)$ for all values of $n \ge n_0$.

If $f(n)$ is between $c_1g(n)$ and $c_2g(n)$, $\forall\ n \ge n_0$, then $f(n) \in \Theta(g(n))$ and $g(n)$ is an asymptotically tight bound for $f(n)$ and $f(n)$ is amongst $h(n)$ in the set.

To summarize,

- The best case in Θ notation is not used.
- Worst case Θ describes asymptotic bounds for worst case combination of input values.
- If we simply write Θ, it means same as worst case Θ.

Example 2.7 Show that $n^2/2 - 2n = \Theta(n^2)$.

Solution By the definition, we can write

$$c_1g(n) \le h(n) \le c_2g(n)$$
$$c_1n^2 \le n^2/2 - 2n \le c_2n^2$$

Dividing by n^2, we get

$$c_1 n^2/n^2 \le n^2/2n^2 - 2n/n^2 \le c_2 n^2/n^2$$
$$c_1 \le 1/2 - 2/n \le c_2$$

This means $c_2 = 1/2$ because $\lim_{n\to\infty} 1/2 - 2/n = 1/2$ (Big O notation)

To determine c_1 using Ω notation, we can write

$$0 < c_1 \le 1/2 - 2/n$$

We see that $0 < c_1$ is minimum when $n = 5$. Therefore,

$$0 < c_1 \le 1/2 - 2/5$$

Hence, $c_1 = 1/10$

Now let us determine the value of n_0

$$1/10 \le 1/2 - 2/n_0 \le 1/2$$
$$2/n_0 \le 1/2 - 1/10 \le 1/2$$
$$2/n_0 \le 2/5 \le 1/2$$
$$n_0 \ge 5$$

You may verify this by substituting the values as shown below.

$$c_1 n^2 \le n^2/2 - 2n \le c_2 n^2$$
$$c_1 = 1/10,\ c_2 = 1/2 \text{ and } n_0 = 5$$
$$1/10(25) \le 25/2 - 20/2 \le 25/2$$
$$5/2 \le 5/2 \le 25/2$$

Thus, in general, we can write, $1/10n^2 \le n^2/2 - 2n \le 1/2n^2$ for $n \ge 5$.

2.12 OTHER USEFUL NOTATIONS

There are other notations like little o notation and little ω notation which have been discussed below.

Little o Notation

This notation provides a non-asymptotically tight upper bound for $f(n)$. To express a function using this notation, we write

$f(n) \in o(g(n))$ where

$o(g(n)) = \{h(n) : \exists$ positive constants c, n_0 such that for any $c > 0, n_0 > 0$, and $0 \le h(n) \le cg(n), \forall n \ge n_0\}$.

This is unlike the Big O notation where we say for some $c > 0$ (not any). For example, $5n^3 = O(n^3)$ is asymptotically tight upper bound but $5n^2 = o(n^3)$ is non-asymptotically tight bound for $f(n)$.

Examples of functions in $o(n^3)$ include: $n^{2.9}$, $n^3 / \log n$, $2n^2$

Examples of functions not in $o(n^3)$ include: $3n^3$, n^3, $n^3 / 1000$

Example 2.8 Show that $n^3 / 1000 \ne o(n^3)$.

Solution By definition, we have

$0 \le h(n) < cg(n)$, for any constant $c > 0$

$$0 \le n^3 / 1000 \le cn^3$$

This is in contradiction with selecting any $c < 1/1000$.

An imprecise analogy between the asymptotic comparison of functions $f(n)$ and $g(n)$ and the relation between their values can be given as:

$f(n) = O(g(n)) \approx f(n) \le g(n)$ $\quad$ $f(n) = o(g(n)) \approx f(n) < g(n)$ $\quad$ $f(n) = \Theta(g(n)) \approx f(n) = g(n)$

Little Omega Notation (ω)

This notation provides a non-asymptotically tight lower bound for $f(n)$. It can be simply written as, $f(n) \in \omega(g(n))$, where

$\omega(g(n)) = \{h(n) : \exists$ positive constants c, n_0 such that for any $c > 0, n_0 > 0$, and $0 \leq cg(n) < h(n), \forall n \geq n_0\}$.
This is unlike the Ω notation where we say for some $c > 0$ (not any). For example, $5n^3 = \Omega(n^3)$ is asymptotically tight upper bound but $5n^2 = \omega(n^3)$ is non-asymptotically tight bound for $f(n)$.
Example of functions in $\omega(g(n))$ include: $n^3 = \omega(n^2)$, $n^{3.001} = \omega(n^3)$, $n^2\log n = \omega(n^2)$
Example of a function not in $\omega(g(n))$ is $5n^2 \neq \omega(n^2)$ (just as $5 \neq 5$)

Example 2.9 Show that $50n^3/100 \neq \omega(n^3)$.

Solution By definition, we have

$0 \leq cg(n) < h(n)$, for any constant $c > 0$

$$0 \leq cn^3 < 50n^3/100$$

Dividing by n^3, we get

$$0 \leq c < 50/100$$

This is a contradictory value as for any value of c as it cannot be assured to be less than 50/100 or 1/2.

An imprecise analogy between the asymptotic comparison of functions $f(n)$ and $g(n)$ and the relation between their values can be given as:
$f(n) = \Omega(g(n)) \approx f(n) \geq g(n)$ $\qquad$ $f(n) = \omega(g(n)) \approx f(n) > g(n)$

2.13 NEED FOR DATA STRUCTURE

These days, we have a complex set of applications that needs to process huge amounts of data. For example, we have to frequently perform the following operations.

As applications are getting complex and data rich, there are three common problems that applications face now-a-days.

Data Search – Consider a scenario where a company has 1 million customers worldwide and they wish to give a heavy discount to those who had been loyal to them for last 10 years. The application needs to search such customers from 1 million entries.

Processor speed – Even if the processor speed is high, it will be very limited if the data grows to billion records.

Multiple requests – As thousands of users can search data simultaneously on a web server, even the fast server will fail to perform optimally.

The only way to rescue from the above problems is to organize the data in a data structure in such a way that all items may not be required to be searched, and the required data can be searched almost instantly.

Representing information is fundamental to computer science. The main aim of most computer programs is not to perform calculations, but to store and retrieve information efficiently at a fast pace. For this reason, the study of data structures is at the heart of computer science.

A solution is said to be efficient if it solves the problem within the required resource constraints.

Having a good information about different data structures help us to know the following details.

The tradeoffs, which highlights the costs and benefits associated with every data structure or algorithm. These tradeoffs can be understood by analyzing the amount of space and time required for typical operations.

Measure of the effectiveness of the data structure. This would help us to determine which data structure is most appropriate for a new problem. To solve a problem, we need a data structure that makes efficient use of the computer's resources.

2.14 SELECTING A DATA STRUCTURE

When selecting a data structure to solve a problem, follow these steps given below.

- Analyze the problem to determine the basic operations (like insertion, deletion, searching items in data structure) that must be supported.
- Quantify the resource constraints for each operation.
- Select the data structure that best meets these requirements.

There steps operationalize a data-centered view of the design process as the main concern here is for the data and the operations to be performed on them. The subsequent concerns are the representation for those data and the implementation of that representation.

Resource constraints on certain key operations drive the selection of a suitable data structure. For example, to determine an appropriate data structure, we must try to find answers to the following questions.

1. Is there a need to inset all data items at the beginning, or can insertions be done at any point in time? Note that static applications where all the data is inserted at the beginning and never change can be represented using a simpler data structure to get an efficient implementation. Dynamic applications require complicated solutions.
2. Is there a need to delete data items be deleted? If yes, then the we need a little complicated data structure that supports efficient deletion of data items. Else, a simpler one would suffice.
3. Are all data items processed in some well-defined order, or is search for specific data items allowed? Random access requires more complex data structures.

Case Study: A bank supports its customers to open accounts, close accounts, and add money or withdraw money from accounts. The most frequently used transactions are those that add/ remove money to/ from the account. And these transactions do not modify the database significantly. Adding or withdrawing money simply changes the value stored in an account record.

While selecting a suitable data structure to manage customer accounts, we can give less importance to deletion as these cases are less. We must opt for a data structure that is highly efficient for search and moderately efficient for insertion. In this case, **hash table** is a good choice as it performs extremely fast exact-match search. A record can be modified quickly provided that the modification does not affect its space requirements. Hash tables also support efficient insertion and deletion of records, but too many deletions may lead to performance degradation.

Case Study: The government is planning to store information about all the major cities including its size, population, etc. A data structure is required to facilitate range queries. For example, finding all cities that match a particular value or range of values for attributes such as location or population size.

In this case, hash table will not be a good choice as it cannot perform efficient range queries. So, we can choose **B+-tree** as it supports efficient insertion, deletion and range queries on large databases.

Let us now summarize which data structure should be used when.

Linked List	Circular Linked List
• Constant time for insertion and deletion. • Data grows dynamically. • Random access of elements is not required. • Insertion can be done in any position of the list. • Number of elements not known beforehand	• Develop the buffer memory. • Browser cache allows hitting the BACK button. • Implement the Most Recently Used (MRU) list. • Implement Undo functionality.

Doubly Linked List	**Stack**
• Easier to delete the node. • It can be iterated in reverse order without recursion implementation. • Faster insertion and deletion.	• To evaluate expression. • For syntax parsing. • Finding the correct path in a maze using backtracking. • Managing runtime memory. • Implement recursive function. • If the most recently inserted element needs to be accessed/deleted each time.
Queue	**Binary Search Tree**
• A queue is maintained to process in order. • Processed in First In First Out order. • Perform addition or deletion from both ends.	• To make efficient use of memory. • Store and work on sorted data • Search for a range of values. • Minimize reduce the running time. • During insertions, if the order of elements needs to be maintained. • Searching for a particular element when there is an order to the elements and if the maximum number of elements to be stored is unknown beforehand.
Heap	**Hash table**
• Implement Priority Queue. • Quick access to the largest (or smallest) item. • No quadratic worst-case scenarios exist. • To reduce runtime order of graph traversal. • If insertion needs to maintain the order of elements needs to be maintained.	• Constant time operation. • To support slow insertion but faster reads • To implement an associative array that map keys to values. • Searching is more efficient. • Route the data from one computer to another in a network router. • To implement internet search engine effectively. • Searching for a particular element when the order of elements needs to be maintained and if the maximum number of elements to be stored is known beforehand.
Graph	**Red-Black Tree**
• To implement network algorithms. • Finding the shortest path between the cities. • Solving the maze game.	• Implement Java TreeMap and C++ map • Computational Geometry Data structures. • Implement scheduler applications.
Array	**Matrix**
• Elements are randomly accessed using the index. • Size/ number of elements are already known so that memory can be easily defined. • Fast iteration through all the elements is needed in the sequence. • Amount of memory needs to be reduced. (Note that linked list takes more memory than arrays).	• Graph needs to be represented efficiently. • Data needs to be stored using rows and columns. • Matrix arithmetic needs to be performed. • Quadratic forms and linear algebra solution needs to be implemented.
Splay Tree	**AVL Tree**
• Need to access to the recent data easily. • Allow duplicate items. • Simple implementation that takes less memory. • When large amounts of data need to be processed and stored.	• When the height of should be either 0, -1 or 1. • Performs fast looking element.

Trie

- There is a fixed dictionary and fast look up is required.
- Less storage is required for a large dictionary.
- Sentences are matched during string matching.
- Predictable O(k) lookup time is required where k is the size of the key.
- Support for ordered traversal is required.
- Deletion has to be made a simple and straightforward process.

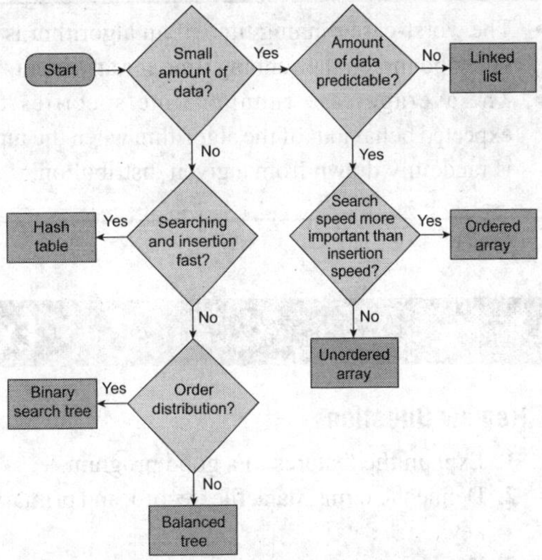

Points to Remember

- A data structure is a particular way of storing and organizing data either in computer's memory or on the disk storage so that it can be used efficiently.
- There are two types of data structures: primitive and non-primitive data structures. Primitive data structures are the fundamental data types which are supported by a programming language. Non-primitive data structures are those data structures which are created using primitive data structures.
- Non-primitive data structures can further be classified into two categories: linear and non-linear data structures.
- If the elements of a data structure are stored in a linear or sequential order, then it is a linear data structure. However, if the elements of a data structure are not stored in sequential order, then it is a non-linear data structure.
- An array is a collection of similar data elements which are stored in consecutive memory locations.
- A linked list is a linear data structure consisting of a group of elements (called nodes) which together represent a sequence.
- A stack is a last-in, first-out (LIFO) data structure in which insertion and deletion of elements are done at only one end, which is known as the top of the stack.
- A queue is a first-in, first-out (FIFO) data structure in which the element that is inserted first is the first to be taken out. The elements in a queue are added at one end called the rear and removed from the other end called the front.
- A tree is a non-linear data structure which consists of a collection of nodes arranged in a hierarchical tree structure.
- The simplest form of a tree is a binary tree. A binary tree consists of a root node and left and right sub-trees, where both sub-trees are also binary trees.
- A graph is often viewed as a generalization of the tree structure, where instead of a purely parent-to-child relationship between tree nodes, any kind of complex relationships can exist between the nodes.
- An abstract data type (ADT) is the way we look at a data structure, focusing on what it does and ignoring how it does its job.
- An algorithm is basically a set of instructions that solve a problem.
- The time complexity of an algorithm is basically the running time of the program as a function of the input size.
- The space complexity of an algorithm is the amount of computer memory required during the program execution as a function of the input size.

- The worst-case running time of an algorithm is an upper bound on the running time for any input.
- The average-case running time specifies the expected behaviour of the algorithm when the input is randomly drawn from a given distribution.
- Amortized analysis guarantees the average performance of each operation in the worst case.
- The efficiency of an algorithm is expressed in terms of the number of elements that has to be processed and the type of the loop that is being used.

Exercises

Review Questions

1. Explain the features of a good program.
2. Define the terms: data, file, record, and primary key.
3. Define data structures. Give some examples.
4. In how many ways can you categorize data structures? Explain each of them.
5. Discuss the applications of data structures.
6. Write a short note on different operations that can be performed on data structures.
7. Compare a linked list with an array.
8. Write a short note on abstract data type.
9. Explain the different types of data structures. Also discuss their merits and demerits.
10. Define an algorithm. Explain its features with the help of suitable examples.
11. Explain and compare the approaches for designing an algorithm.
12. What is modularization? Give its advantages.
13. Write a brief note on trees as a data structure.
14. What do you understand by a graph?
15. Explain the criteria that you will keep in mind while choosing an appropriate algorithm to solve a particular problem.
16. What do you understand by time–space trade-off?
17. What do you understand by the efficiency of an algorithm?
18. How will you express the time complexity of a given algorithm?
19. Discuss the significance and limitations of the Big O notation.
20. Discuss the best case, worst case, average case, and amortized time complexity of an algorithm.
21. Categorize algorithms based on their running time complexity.
22. Give examples of functions that are in Big O notation as well as functions that are not in Big O notation.
23. Explain the little o notation.
24. Give examples of functions that are in little o notation as well as functions that are not in little o notation.
25. Differentiate between Big O and little o notations.
26. Explain the Ω notation.
27. Give examples of functions that are in Ω notation as well as functions that are not in Ω notation.
28. Explain the Θ notation.
29. Give examples of functions that are in Θ notation as well as functions that are not in Θ notation.
30. Explain the ω notation.
31. Give examples of functions that are in ω notation as well as functions that are in ω notation.
32. Differentiate between Big omega and little omega notations.
33. Show that $n^2 + 50n = O(n^2)$.
34. Show that $n^2+n^2+n^2 = 3n^2 = O(n^3)$.
35. Prove that $n^3 \neq O(n^2)$.
36. Show that $\sqrt{n} = \Omega(\lg n)$.
37. Prove that $3n + 5 \neq \Omega(n^2)$.
38. Show that $\frac{1}{2}n^2 - 3n \in \Theta(n^2)$.

Multiple-choice Questions

1. Which data structure is defined as a collection of similar data elements?
   (a) Arrays (b) Linked lists
   (c) Trees (d) Graphs

2. The data structure used in hierarchical data model is
   (a) Array (b) Linked list
   (c) Tree (d) Graph
3. In a stack, insertion is done at
   (a) Top (b) Front
   (c) Rear (d) Mid
4. The position in a queue from which an element is deleted is called as
   (a) Top (b) Front
   (c) Rear (d) Mid
5. Which data structure has fixed size?
   (a) Arrays (b) Linked lists
   (c) Trees (d) Graphs
6. If `TOP = MAX-1`, then that the stack is
   (a) Empty (b) Full
   (c) Contains some data (d) None of these
7. Which among the following is a LIFO data structure?
   (a) Stacks (b) Linked lists
   (c) Queues (d) Graphs
8. Which data structure is used to represent complex relationships between the nodes?
   (a) Arrays (b) Linked lists
   (c) Trees (d) Graphs
9. Examples of linear data structures include
   (a) Arrays (b) Stacks
   (c) Queues (d) All of these
10. The running time complexity of a linear time algorithm is given as
    (a) $O(1)$ (b) $O(n)$
    (c) $O(n \log n)$ (d) $O(n^2)$
11. Which notation provides a strict upper bound for f(n)?
    (a) Omega notation (b) Big O notation
    (c) Small o notation (d) Theta Notation
12. Which notation comprises a set of all functions h(n) that are greater than or equal to cg(n) for all values of $n \geq n_0$?
    (a) Omega notation (b) Big O notation
    (c) Small o notation (d) Theta Notation
13. Function in $o(n^2)$ notation is
    (a) $10n^2$ (b) $n^{1.9}$
    (c) $n^2/100$ (d) n^2

True or False

1. Trees and graphs are the examples of linear data structures.
2. Queue is a FIFO data structure.
3. Trees can represent any kind of complex relationship between the nodes.
4. The average-case running time of an algorithm is an upper bound on the running time for any input.
5. Array is an abstract data type.
6. Array elements are stored in continuous memory locations.
7. The pop operation adds an element to the top of a stack.
8. Graphs have a purely parent-to-child relationship between their nodes.
9. The worst-case running time of an algorithm is a lower bound on the running time for any input.
10. In top-down approach, we start with designing the most basic or concrete modules and then proceed towards designing higher-level modules.
11. o(g(n)) comprises a set of all functions h(n) that are less than or equal to cg(n) for all values of $n \geq n_0$.
12. Simply Ω means same as best case Ω.
13. Small omega notation provides an asymptotically tight bound for f(n).
14. Theta notation provides a non-asymptotically tight lower bound for f(n).
15. $n^{3.001} \neq \omega(n^3)$.

Fill in the Blanks

1. ______ is an arrangement of data either in the computer's memory or on the disk storage.
2. ______ are used to manipulate the data contained in various data structures.
3. In ______, the elements of a data structure are stored sequentially.
4. ______ of a variable specifies the set of values that the variable can take.
5. A tree is empty if ______.
6. Abstract means ______.
7. The time complexity of an algorithm is the running time given as a function of ______.

8. ______ analysis guarantees the average performance of each operation in the worst case.
9. The elements of an array are referenced by an ______.
10. ______ is used to store the address of the topmost element of a stack.
11. The ______ operation returns the value of the topmost element of a stack.
12. An overflow occurs when ______.
13. ______ is a FIFO data structure.
14. The elements in a queue are added at ______ and removed from ______.
15. If the elements of a data structure are stored sequentially, then it is a ______.
16. ______ is basically a set of instructions that solve a problem.
17. The number of machine instructions that a program executes during its execution is called its ______.
18. ______ specifies the expected behaviour of an algorithm when an input is randomly drawn from a given distribution.
19. The running time complexity of a constant time algorithm is given as ______.
20. A complex algorithm is often divided into smaller units called ______.
21. ______ design approach starts by dividing the complex algorithm into one or more modules.
22. ______ case is when the array is sorted in reverse order.
23. ______ notation provides a tight lower bound for `f(n)`.
24. The small o notation provides a ______ tight upper bound for `f(n)`.
25. $540n^2 + 10$ ____ $\Omega(n^2)$.

CHAPTER 3

Arrays

LEARNING OBJECTIVE

In this chapter, we will discuss arrays. An array is a user-defined data type that stores related information together. All the information stored in an array belongs to the same data type. So, in this chapter, we will learn how arrays are defined, declared, initialized, and accessed. We will also discuss the different operations that can be performed on array elements and the different types of arrays such as two-dimensional arrays, multi-dimensional arrays, and sparse matrices.

3.1 INTRODUCTION

We will explain the concept of arrays using an analogy. Consider a situation in which we have 20 students in a class and we have been asked to write a program that reads and prints the marks of all the 20 students. In this program, we will need 20 integer variables with different names, as shown in Fig. 3.1.

Now to read the values of these 20 variables, we must have 20 read statements. Similarly, to print the value of these variables, we need 20 write statements. If it is just a matter of 20 variables, then it might be acceptable for the user to follow this approach. But would it be possible to follow this approach if we have to read and print the marks of students,

- in the entire course (say 100 students)
- in the entire college (say 500 students)
- in the entire university (say 10,000 students)

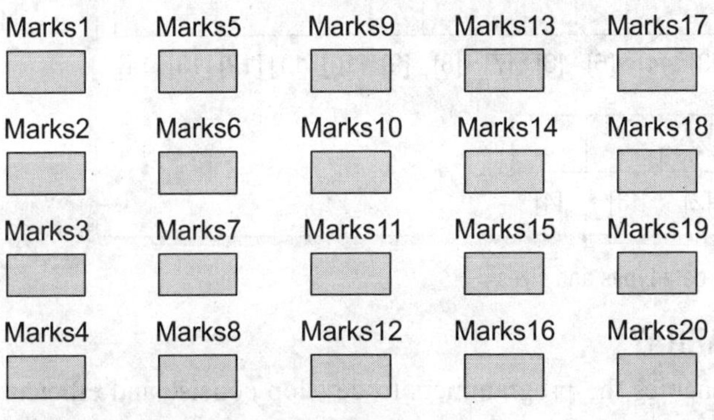

Figure 3.1 Twenty variables for 20 students

The answer is no, definitely not! To process a large amount of data, we need a data structure known as *array*.

An array is a collection of similar data elements. These data elements have the same data type. The elements of the array are stored in consecutive memory locations and are referenced by an `index` (also known as the *subscript*). The subscript is an ordinal number which is used to identify an element of the array.

3.2 DECLARATION OF ARRAYS

We have already seen that every variable must be declared before it is used. The same concept holds true for array variables. An array must be declared before being used. Declaring an array means specifying the following:

- *Data type*—the kind of values it can store, for example, `int`, `char`, `float`, `double`.
- *Name*—to identify the array.
- *Size*—the maximum number of values that the array can hold.

Arrays are declared using the following syntax:

```
type name[size];
```

The type can be either `int`, `float`, `double`, `char`, or any other valid data type. The number within brackets indicates the size of the array, i.e., the maximum number of elements that can be stored in the array. For example, if we write,

```
int marks[10];
```

then the statement declares `marks` to be an array containing 10 elements. In C, the array index starts from zero. The first element will be stored in `marks[0]`, second element in `marks[1]`, and so on. Therefore, the last element, that is the 10th element, will be stored in `marks[9]`. Note that `0, 1, 2, 3` written within square brackets are the subscripts. In the memory, the array will be stored as shown in Fig. 3.2.

1st element	2nd element	3rd element	4th element	5th element	6th element	7th element	8th element	9th element	10th element
marks[0]	marks[1]	marks[2]	marks[3]	marks[4]	marks[5]	marks[6]	marks[7]	marks[8]	marks[9]

Figure 3.2 Memory representation of an array of 10 elements

Figure 3.3 shows how different types of arrays are declared.

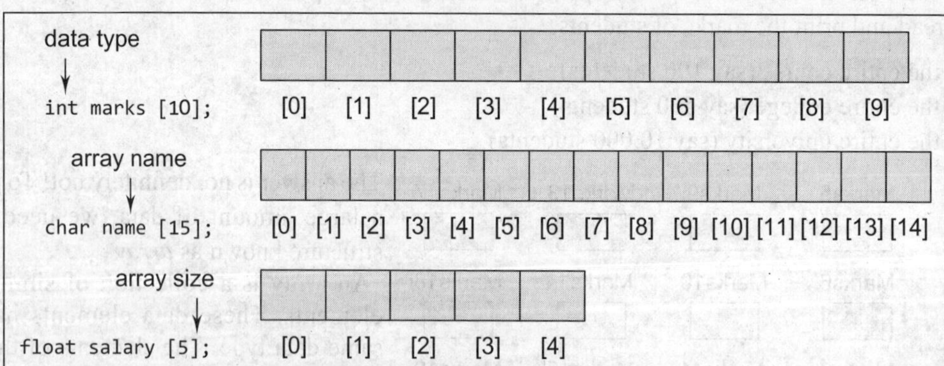

Figure 3.3 Declaring arrays of different data types and sizes

3.3 ACCESSING THE ELEMENTS OF AN ARRAY

Storing related data items in a single array enables the programmers to develop concise and efficient programs. But there is no single function that can operate on all the elements of an array. To access all the elements, we must use a loop. That is, we can access all the elements of an array by varying the value

```
// Set each element of the array to -1
int i, marks[10];
for(i=0;i<10;i++)
      marks[i] = -1;
```

Figure 3.4 Code to initialize each element of the array to –1

of the subscript into the array. But note that the subscript must be an integral value or an expression that evaluates to an integral value. As shown in Fig. 3.2, the first element of the array `marks[10]` can be accessed by writing `marks[0]`. Now to process all the elements of the array, we use a loop as shown in Fig. 3.4.

Figure 3.5 shows the result of the code shown in Fig. 3.4. The code accesses every individual element of the array and sets its value to –1. In the `for` loop, first the value of `marks[0]` is set to –1, then the value of the index `(i)` is incremented and the next value, that is, `marks[1]` is set to –1. The procedure continues until all the 10 elements of the array are set to –1.

– 1	– 1	– 1	– 1	– 1	– 1	– 1	– 1	– 1	– 1
[0]	[1]	[2]	[3]	[4]	[5]	[6]	[7]	[8]	[9]

Figure 3.5 Array `marks` after executing the code given in Fig. 3.4

Note There is no single statement that can read, access, or print all the elements of an array. To do this, we have to use a loop to execute the same statement with different index values.

3.3.1 Calculating the Address of Array Elements

You must be wondering how C gets to know where an individual element of an array is located in the memory. The answer is that the array name is a symbolic reference to the address of the first byte of the array. When we use the array name, we are actually referring to the first byte of the array.

The subscript or the index represents the offset from the beginning of the array to the element being referenced. That is, with just the array name and the index, C can calculate the address of any element in the array.

Since an array stores all its data elements in consecutive memory locations, storing just the base address, that is the address of the first element in the array, is sufficient. The address of other data elements can simply be calculated using the base address. The formula to perform this calculation is,

```
Address of data element, A[k] = BA(A) + w(k - lower_bound)
```

Here, `A` is the array, `k` is the index of the element of which we have to calculate the address, `BA` is the base address of the array `A`, and `w` is the size of one element in memory, for example, size of `int` is 2.

Example 3.1 Given an array `int marks[]={99,67,78,56,88,90,34,85}`, calculate the address of `marks[4]` if the `base address = 1000`.

Solution

99	67	78	56	**88**	90	34	85
marks[0]	marks[1]	marks[2]	marks[3]	**marks[4]**	marks[5]	marks[6]	marks[7]
1000	1002	1004	1006	**1008**	1010	1012	1014

We know that storing an integer value requires 2 bytes, therefore, its size is 2 bytes.

```
marks[4] = 1000 + 2(4 - 0)
         = 1000 + 2(4) = 1008
```

3.3.2 Calculating the Length of an Array

The length of an array is given by the number of elements stored in it. The general formula to calculate the length of an array is

```
Length = upper_bound - lower_bound + 1
```

where `upper_bound` is the index of the last element and `lower_bound` is the index of the first element in the array.

Example 3.2 Let `Age[5]` be an array of integers such that

```
Age[0] = 2, Age[1] = 5, Age[2] = 3, Age[3] = 1, Age[4] = 7
```

Show the memory representation of the array and calculate its length.

Solution

The memory representation of the array `Age[5]` is given as below.

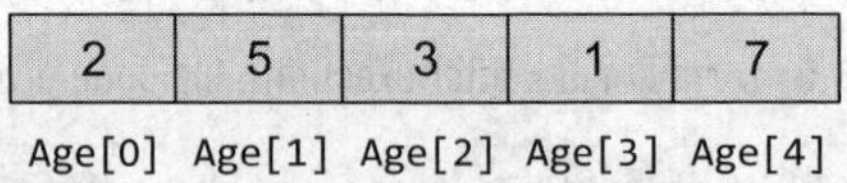


```
Length = upper_bound - lower_bound + 1
```

Here, `lower_bound = 0, upper_bound = 4`

Therefore, `length = 4 - 0 + 1 = 5`

3.4 STORING VALUES IN ARRAYS

When we declare an array, we are just allocating space for its elements; no values are stored in the array. There are three ways to store values in an array. First, to initialize the array elements during declaration; second, to input values for individual elements from the keyboard; third, to assign values to individual elements. This is shown in Fig. 3.6.

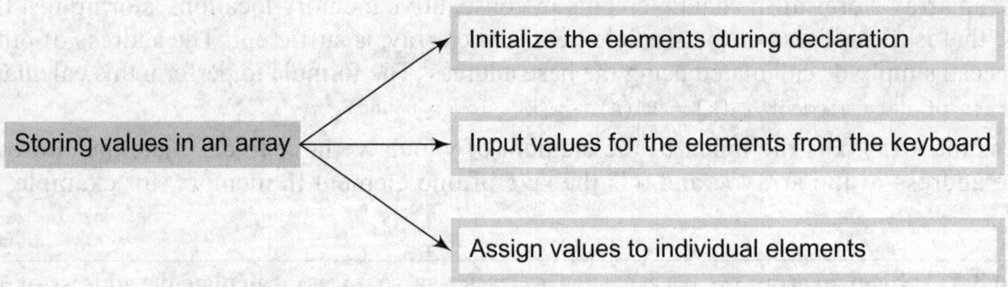

Figure 3.6 Storing values in an array

Initializing Arrays during Declaration

The elements of an array can be initialized at the time of declaration, just as any other variable. When an array is initialized, we need to provide a value for every element in the array. Arrays are initialized by writing,

```
type array_name[size]={list of values};
```

Note that the values are written within curly brackets and every value is separated by a comma. It is a compiler error to specify more values than there are elements in the array. When we write,

```
int marks[5]={90, 82, 78, 95, 88};
```

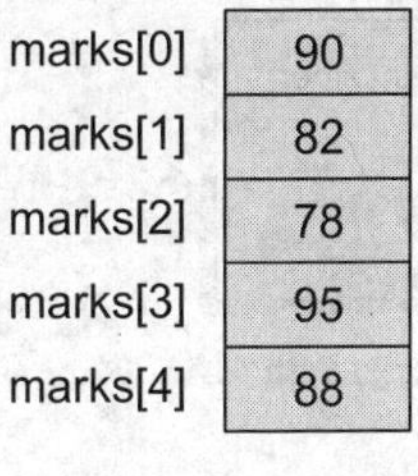

Figure 3.7 Initialization of array `marks[5]`

An array with the name `marks` is declared that has enough space to store five elements. The first element, that is, `marks[0]` is assigned value 90. Similarly, the second element of the array, that is `marks[1]`, is assigned 82, and so on. This is shown in Fig. 3.7.

While initializing the array at the time of declaration, the programmer may omit the size of the array. For example,

```
int marks[]= {98, 97, 90};
```

The above statement is absolutely legal. Here, the compiler will allocate enough space for all the initialized elements. Note that if the number of values provided is less than the number of elements in the array, the un-assigned elements are filled with zeros. Figure 3.8 shows the initialization of arrays.

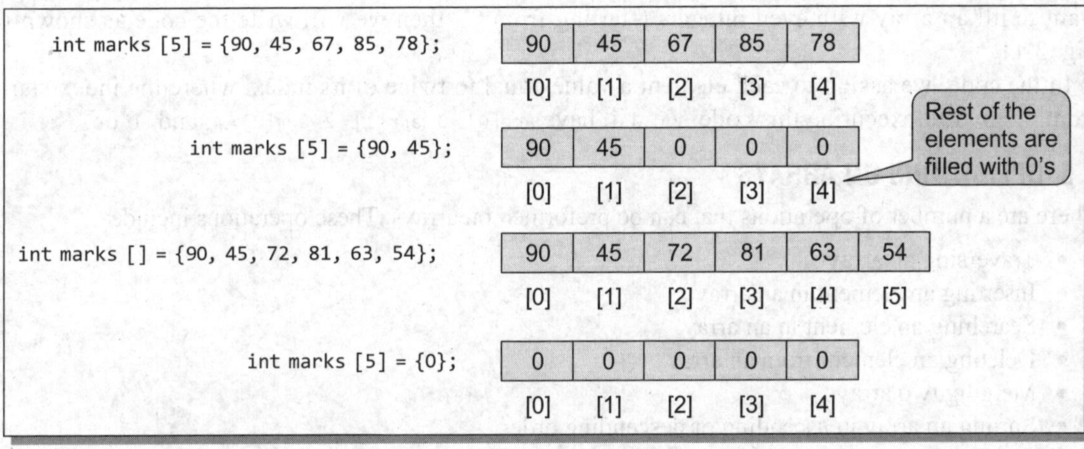

Figure 3.8 Initialization of array elements

Inputting Values from the Keyboard

```
int i, marks[10];
for(i=0;i<10;i++)
      scanf("%d", &marks[i]);
```

Figure 3.9 Code for inputting each element of the array

An array can be initialized by inputting values from the keyboard. In this method, a `while/do-while` or a `for` loop is executed to input the value for each element of the array. For example, look at the code shown in Fig. 3.9.

In the code, we start at the index `i` at 0 and input the value for the first element of the array. Since the array has 10 elements, we must input values for elements whose index varies from 0 to 9.

Assigning Values to Individual Elements

The third way is to assign values to individual elements of the array by using the assignment operator. Any value that evaluates to the data type as that of the array can be assigned to the individual array element. A simple assignment statement can be written as

```
marks[3] = 100;
```

Here, 100 is assigned to the fourth element of the array which is specified as `marks[3]`.

Note that we cannot assign one array to another array, even if the two arrays have the same type and size. To copy an array, you must copy the value of every element of the first array into the elements of the second array. Figure 3.10 illustrates the code to copy an array.

In Fig. 3.10, the loop accesses each element of the first array and simultaneously assigns its value to the corresponding element of the second array. The index value `i` is incremented to access the next

```
int i, arr1[10], arr2[10];
arr1[10] = {0,1,2,3,4,5,6,7,8,9};
for(i=0;i<10;i++)
        arr2[i] = arr1[i];
```

Figure 3.10 Code to copy an array at the individual element level

```
// Fill an array with even numbers
int i,arr[10];
for(i=0;i<10;i++)
        arr[i] = i*2;
```

Figure 3.11 Code for filling an array with even numbers

element in succession. Therefore, when this code is executed, `arr2[0] = arr1[0]`, `arr2[1] = arr1[1]`, `arr2[2] = arr1[2]`, and so on.

We can also use a loop to assign a pattern of values to the array elements. For example, if we want to fill an array with even integers (starting from 0), then we will write the code as shown in Fig. 3.11.

In the code, we assign to each element a value equal to twice of its index, where the index starts from 0. So after executing this code, we will have `arr[0]=0`, `arr[1]=2`, `arr[2]=4`, and so on.

3.5 OPERATIONS ON ARRAYS

There are a number of operations that can be preformed on arrays. These operations include:

- Traversing an array
- Inserting an element in an array
- Searching an element in an array
- Deleting an element from an array
- Merging two arrays
- Sorting an array in ascending or descending order

We will discuss all these operations in detail in this section, except searching and sorting, which will be discussed in Chapter 14.

3.5.1 Traversing an Array

Traversing an array means accessing each and every element of the array for a specific purpose.

Traversing the data elements of an array `A` can include printing every element, counting the total number of elements, or performing any process on these elements. Since, array is a linear data structure (because all its elements form a sequence), traversing its elements is very simple and straightforward. The algorithm for array traversal is given in Fig. 3.12.

```
Step 1: [INITIALIZATION] SET I = lower_bound
Step 2: Repeat Steps 3 to 4 while I <= upper_bound
Step 3:         Apply Process to A[I]
Step 4:         SET I = I + 1
        [END OF LOOP]
Step 5: EXIT
```

Figure 3.12 Algorithm for array traversal

In Step 1, we initialize the index to the lower bound of the array. In Step 2, a `while` loop is executed. Step 3 processes the individual array element as specified by the array name and index value. Step 4 increments the index value so that the next array element could be processed. The `while` loop in Step 2 is executed until all the elements in the array are processed, i.e., until `I` is less than or equal to the upper bound of the array.

Programming Examples

1. Write a program to read and display *n* numbers using an array.

```
#include <stdio.h>
int main()
{
        int i, n, arr[20];
        printf("\n Enter the number of elements in the array : ");
        scanf("%d", &n);
        for(i=0;i<n;i++)
        {
                printf("\n arr[%d] = ", i);
                scanf("%d",&arr[i]);
        }
        printf("\n The array elements are ");
        for(i=0;i<n;i++)
                printf("\t %d", arr[i]);
        return 0;
}
```

Output

```
Enter the number of elements in the array : 5
arr[0] = 1
arr[1] = 2
arr[2] = 3
arr[3] = 4
arr[4] = 5
The array elements are    1    2    3    4    5
```

2. Write a program to find the mean of *n* numbers using arrays.

```
#include <stdio.h>
int main()
{
        int i, n, arr[20], sum =0;
        float mean = 0.0;
        printf("\n Enter the number of elements in the array : ");
        scanf("%d", &n);
        for(i=0;i<n;i++)
        {
                printf("\n arr[%d] = ", i);
                scanf("%d",&arr[i]);
        }
        for(i=0;i<n;i++)
                sum += arr[i];
        mean = (float)sum/n;
        printf("\n The sum of the array elements = %d", sum);
        printf("\n The mean of the array elements = %.2f", mean);
        return 0;
}
```

Output

```
Enter the number of elements in the array : 5
arr[0] = 1
arr[1] = 2
arr[2] = 3
arr[3] = 4
arr[4] = 5
The sum of the array elements = 15
The mean of the array elements = 3.00
```

3. Write a program to print the position of the smallest number of *n* numbers using arrays.

```
#include <stdio.h>
int main()
{
	int i, n, arr[20], small, pos;
	printf("\n Enter the number of elements in the array : ");
	scanf("%d", &n);
	printf("\n Enter the elements : ");
	for(i=0;i<n;i++)
		scanf("%d",&arr[i]);
	small = arr[0];
	pos =0;
	for(i=1;i<n;i++)
	{
		if(arr[i]<small)
		{
			small = arr[i];
			pos = i;
		}
	}
	printf("\n The smallest element is : %d", small);
	printf("\n The position of the smallest element in the array is : %d", pos);
	return 0;
}
```

Output

```
Enter the number of elements in the array : 5
Enter the elements : 7 6 5 14 3
The smallest element is : 3
The position of the smallest element in the array is : 4
```

4. Write a program to find the second largest of *n* numbers using an array.

```
#include <stdio.h>
int main()
{
	int i, n, arr[20], large, second_large;
	printf("\n Enter the number of elements in the array : ");
	scanf("%d", &n);
	printf("\n Enter the elements");
	for(i=0;i<n;i++)
		scanf("%d",&arr[i]);
	large = arr[0];
	for(i=1;i<n;i++)
	{
		if(arr[i]>large)
			large = arr[i];
	}
	second_large = arr[1];
	for(i=0;i<n;i++)
	{
		if(arr[i] != large)
		{
			if(arr[i]>second_large)
				second_large = arr[i];
		}
	}
	printf("\n The numbers you entered are : ");
```

```
    for(i=0;i<n;i++)
        printf("\t %d", arr[i]);
    printf("\n The largest of these numbers is : %d",large);
    printf("\n The second largest of these numbers is : %d",second_large);
    return 0;
}
```

Output

```
Enter the number of elements in the array : 5
Enter the elements 1 2 3 4 5
The numbers you entered are :      1      2      3      4      5
The largest of these numbers is : 5
The second largest of these numbers is : 4
```

5. Write a program to enter *n* number of digits. Form a number using these digits.

```
#include <stdio.h>
#include <math.h>
int main()
{
    int number=0, digit[10], numofdigits,i;
    printf("\n Enter the number of digits : ");
    scanf("%d", &numofdigits);
    for(i=0;i<numofdigits;i++)
    {
        printf("\n Enter the digit at position %d", i+1);
        scanf("%d", &digit[i]);
    }
    i=0;
    while(i<numofdigits)
    {
        number = number + digit[i] * pow(10,i);
        i++;
    }
    printf("\n The number is : %d", number);
    return 0;
}
```

Output

```
Enter the number of digits : 4
Enter the digit at position 1: 2
Enter the digit at position 2 : 3
Enter the digit at position 3 : 0
Enter the digit at position 4 : 9
The number is : 9032
```

6. Write a program to find whether the array of integers contains a duplicate number.

```
#include <stdio.h>
int main()
{
    int array[10], i, n, j, flag =0;
    printf("\n Enter the size of the array : ");
    scanf("%d", &n);
    for(i=0;i<n;i++)
    {
        printf("\n array[%d] = ", i);
        scanf("%d", &array[i]);
    }
    for(i=0;i<n;i++)
```

```
        {
                for(j=i+1;j<n;j++)
                {
                        if(array[i] == array[j] && i!=j)
                        {
                        flag =1;
                        printf("\n Duplicate numbers found at locations %d and %d", i,
j);
                        }
                }
        }
        if(flag==0)
                printf("\n No Duplicates Found");
        return 0;
}
```

Output

```
Enter the size of the array : 5
array[0] = 1
array[1] = 2
array[2] = 3
array[3] = 2
array[4] = 5
Duplicate numbers found at locations 1 and 3
```

```
Step 1: Set upper_bound = upper_bound + 1
Step 2: Set A[upper_bound] = VAL
Step 3: EXIT
```

Figure 3.13 Algorithm to append a new element to an existing array

3.5.2 Inserting an Element in an Array

If an element has to be inserted at the end of an existing array, then the task of insertion is quite simple. We just have to add 1 to the `upper_bound` and assign the value. Here, we assume that the memory space allocated for the array is still available. For example, if an array is declared to contain 10 elements, but currently it has only 8 elements, then obviously there is space to accommodate two more elements. But if it already has 10 elements, then we will not be able to add another element to it.

Figure 3.13 shows an algorithm to insert a new element to the end of an array. In Step 1, we increment the value of the `upper_bound`. In Step 2, the new value is stored at the position pointed by the `upper_bound`. For example, let us assume an array has been declared as

```
int marks[60];
```

The array is declared to store the marks of all the students in a class. Now, suppose there are 54 students and a new student comes and is asked to take the same test. The marks of this new student would be stored in `marks[55]`. Assuming that the student secured 68 marks, we will assign the value as

```
marks[55] = 68;
```

However, if we have to insert an element in the middle of the array, then this is not a trivial task. On an average, we might have to move as much as half of the elements from their positions in order to accommodate space for the new element.

For example, consider an array whose elements are arranged in ascending order. Now, if a new element has to be added, it will have to be added probably somewhere in the middle of the array. To do this, we must first find the location where the new element will be inserted and then move all the elements (that have a value greater than that of the new element) one position to the right so that space can be created to store the new value.

Example 3.3 `Data[]` is an array that is declared as `int Data[20];` and contains the following values:

`Data[] = {12, 23, 34, 45, 56, 67, 78, 89, 90, 100};`

(a) Calculate the length of the array.
(b) Find the `upper_bound` and `lower_bound`.
(c) Show the memory representation of the array.
(d) If a new data element with the value 75 has to be inserted, find its position.
(e) Insert a new data element 75 and show the memory representation after the insertion.

Solution

(a) Length of the array = number of elements
Therefore, `length of the array = 10`

(b) By default, `lower_bound = 0` and `upper_bound = 9`

(c)

12	23	34	45	56	67	78	89	90	100
Data[0]	Data[1]	Data[2]	Data[3]	Data[4]	Data[5]	Data[6]	Data[7]	Data[8]	Data[9]

(d) Since the elements of the array are stored in ascending order, the new data element will be stored after 67, i.e., at the 6th location. So, all the array elements from the 6th position will be moved one position towards the right to accommodate the new value

(e)

12	23	34	45	56	67	75	78	89	90	100
Data[0]	Data[1]	Data[2]	Data[3]	Data[4]	Data[5]	Data[6]	Data[7]	Data[8]	Data[9]	Data[10]

Algorithm to Insert an Element in the Middle of an Array

The algorithm `INSERT` will be declared as `INSERT (A, N, POS, VAL)`. The arguments are

(a) `A`, the array in which the element has to be inserted
(b) `N`, the number of elements in the array
(c) `POS`, the position at which the element has to be inserted
(d) `VAL`, the value that has to be inserted

```
Step 1: [INITIALIZATION] SET I = N
Step 2: Repeat Steps 3 and 4 while I >= POS
Step 3:         SET A[I + 1] = A[I]
Step 4:         SET I = I - 1
        [END OF LOOP]
Step 5: SET N = N + 1
Step 6: SET A[POS] = VAL
Step 7: EXIT
```

Figure 3.14 Algorithm to insert an element in the middle of an array.

In the algorithm given in Fig. 3.14, in Step 1, we first initialize I with the total number of elements in the array. In Step 2, a `while` loop is executed which will move all the elements having an index greater than `POS` one position towards right to create space for the new element. In Step 5, we increment the total number of elements in the array by 1 and finally in Step 6, the new value is inserted at the desired position.

Now, let us visualize this algorithm by taking an example.

Initial `Data[]` is given as below.

45	23	34	12	56	20
Data[0]	Data[1]	Data[2]	Data[3]	Data[4]	Data[5]

Calling `INSERT(Data, 6, 3, 100)` will lead to the following processing in the array:

45	23	34	12	56	20	20
Data[0]	Data[1]	Data[2]	Data[3]	Data[4]	Data[5]	Data[6]

45	23	34	12	56	56	20
Data[0]	Data[1]	Data[2]	Data[3]	Data[4]	Data[5]	Data[6]

45	23	34	12	12	56	20
Data[0]	Data[1]	Data[2]	Data[3]	Data[4]	Data[5]	Data[6]

45	23	34	100	12	56	20
Data[0]	Data[1]	Data[2]	Data[3]	Data[4]	Data[5]	Data[6]

Programming Examples

7. Write a program to insert a number at a given location in an array.

```
#include <stdio.h>
int main()
{
        int i, n, num, pos, arr[10];
        printf("\n Enter the number of elements in the array : ");
        scanf("%d", &n);
        for(i=0;i<n;i++)
        {
                printf("\n arr[%d] = ", i);
                scanf("%d", &arr[i]);
        }
        printf("\n Enter the number to be inserted : ");
        scanf("%d", &num);
        printf("\n Enter the position at which the number has to be added :");
        scanf("%d", &pos);
        for(i=n-1;i>=pos;i--)
                arr[i+1] = arr[i];
        arr[pos] = num;
        n = n+1;
        printf("\n The array after insertion of %d is : ", num);
        for(i=0;i<n;i++)
            printf("\n arr[%d] = %d", i, arr[i]);
        return 0;
}
```

Output

```
Enter the number of elements in the array : 5
arr[0] = 1
arr[1] = 2
arr[2] = 3
arr[3] = 4
arr[4] = 5
Enter the number to be inserted : 0
Enter the position at which the number has to be added : 3
```

```
The array after insertion of 0 is :
arr[0] = 1
arr[1] = 2
arr[2] = 3
arr[3] = 0
arr[4] = 4
arr[5] = 5
```

8. Write a program to insert a number in an array that is already sorted in ascending order.

```
#include <stdio.h>
int main()
{
        int i, n, j, num, arr[10];
        printf("\n Enter the number of elements in the array : ");
        scanf("%d", &n);
        for(i=0;i<n;i++)
        {
                printf("\n arr[%d] = ", i);
                scanf("%d", &arr[i]);
        }
        printf("\n Enter the number to be inserted : ");
        scanf("%d", &num);
        for(i=0;i<n;i++)
        {
                if(arr[i] > num)
                {
                        for(j = n-1; j>=i; j--)
                                arr[j+1] = arr[j];
                        arr[i] = num;
                        break;
                }
        }
        n = n+1;
        printf("\n The array after insertion of %d is : ", num);
        for(i=0;i<n;i++)
                printf("\n arr[%d] = %d", i, arr[i]);
        return 0;
}
```

Output

```
Enter the number of elements in the array : 5
arr[0] = 1
arr[1] = 2
arr[2] = 4
arr[3] = 5
arr[4] = 6
Enter the number to be inserted : 3
The array after insertion of 3 is :
arr[0] = 1
arr[1] = 2
arr[2] = 3
arr[3] = 4
arr[4] = 5
arr[5] = 6
```

3.5.3 Deleting an Element from an Array

Deleting an element from an array means removing a data element from an already existing array. If the element has to be deleted from the end of the existing array, then the task of deletion is quite simple. We just have to subtract 1 from the `upper_bound`. Figure 3.15 shows an algorithm to delete an element from the end of an array.

For example, if we have an array that is declared as

```
int marks[60];
```

The array is declared to store the marks of all the students in the class. Now, suppose there are 54 students and the student with roll number 54 leaves the course. The score of this student was stored in `marks[54]`. We just have to decrement the `upper_bound`. Subtracting 1 from the `upper_bound` will indicate that there are 53 valid data in the array.

```
Step 1: SET upper_bound = upper_bound - 1
Step 2: EXIT
```

Figure 3.15 Algorithm to delete the last element of an array

However, if we have to delete an element from the middle of an array, then it is not a trivial task. On an average, we might have to move as much as half of the elements from their positions in order to occupy the space of the deleted element.

For example, consider an array whose elements are arranged in ascending order. Now, suppose an element has to be deleted, probably from somewhere in the middle of the array. To do this, we must first find the location from where the element has to be deleted and then move all the elements (having a value greater than that of the element) one position towards left so that the space vacated by the deleted element can be occupied by rest of the elements.

Example 3.4 `Data[]` is an array that is declared as `int Data[10];` and contains the following values:

```
Data[] = {12, 23, 34, 45, 56, 67, 78, 89, 90, 100};
```

(a) If a data element with value 56 has to be deleted, find its position.

(b) Delete the data element 56 and show the memory representation after the deletion.

Solution

(a) Since the elements of the array are stored in ascending order, we will compare the value that has to be deleted with the value of every element in the array. As soon as `VAL = Data[I]`, where `I` is the index or subscript of the array, we will get the position from which the element has to be deleted. For example, if we see this array, here `VAL = 56`. `Data[0] = 12` which is not equal to 56. We will continue to compare and finally get the value of `POS = 4`.

(b)

12	23	34	45	67	78	89	90	100
Data[0]	Data[1]	Data[2]	Data[3]	Data[4]	Data[5]	Data[6]	Data[7]	Data[8]

```
Step 1: [INITIALIZATION] SET I = POS
Step 2: Repeat Steps 3 and 4 while I <= N - 1
Step 3:         SET A[I] = A[I + 1]
Step 4:         SET I = I + 1
        [END OF LOOP]
Step 5: SET N = N - 1
Step 6: EXIT
```

Figure 3.16 Algorithm to delete an element from the middle of an array

Algorithm to Delete an Element from the Middle of an Array

The algorithm `DELETE` will be declared as `DELETE(A, N, POS)`. The arguments are:

(a) `A`, the array from which the element has to be deleted

(b) `N`, the number of elements in the array

45	23	34	12	56	20
Data[0]	Data[1]	Data[2]	Data[3]	Data[4]	Data[5]

45	23	12	12	56	20
Data[0]	Data[1]	Data[2]	Data[3]	Data[4]	Data[5]

45	23	12	56	56	20
Data[0]	Data[1]	Data[2]	Data[3]	Data[4]	Data[5]

45	23	12	56	20	20
Data[0]	Data[1]	Data[2]	Data[3]	Data[4]	Data[5]

45	23	12	56	20
Data[0]	Data[1]	Data[2]	Data[3]	Data[4]

Figure 3.17 Deleting elements from an array

(c) `POS`, the position from which the element has to be deleted

Figure 3.16 shows the algorithm in which we first initialize `I` with the position from which the element has to be deleted. In Step 2, a `while` loop is executed which will move all the elements having an index greater than `POS` one space towards left to occupy the space vacated by the deleted element. When we say that we are deleting an element, actually we are overwriting the element with the value of its successive element. In Step 5, we decrement the total number of elements in the array by 1.

Now, let us visualize this algorithm by taking an example given in Fig. 3.17. Calling `DELETE(Data, 6, 2)` will lead to the following processing in the array.

Programming Example

9. Write a program to delete a number from a given location in an array.

```
#include <stdio.h>
int main()
{
        int i, n, pos, arr[10];
        printf("\n Enter the number of elements in the array : ");
        scanf("%d", &n);
        for(i=0;i<n;i++)
        {
                printf("\n arr[%d] = ", i);
                scanf("%d", &arr[i]);
        }
        printf("\nEnter the position from which the number has to be deleted : ");
        scanf("%d", &pos);
        for(i=pos; i<n-1;i++)
                arr[i] = arr[i+1];
        n--;
        printf("\n The array after deletion is : ");
        for(i=0;i<n;i++)
                printf("\n arr[%d] = %d", i, arr[i]);
        return 0;
}
```

Output

```
Enter the number of elements in the array : 5
arr[0] = 1
arr[1] = 2
arr[2] = 3
arr[3] = 4
arr[4] = 5
Enter the position from which the number has to be deleted : 3
The array after deletion is :
arr[0] = 1
arr[1] = 2
arr[2] = 3
arr[3] = 5
```

10. Write a program to delete a number from an array that is already sorted in ascending order.

```
#include <stdio.h>
int main()
{
	int i, n, j, num, arr[10];
	printf("\n Enter the number of elements in the array : ");
	scanf("%d", &n);
	for(i=0;i<n;i++)
	{
		printf("\n arr[%d] = ", i);
		scanf("%d", &arr[i]);
	}
	printf("\n Enter the number to be deleted : ");
	scanf("%d", &num);
	for(i=0;i<n;i++)
	{
		if(arr[i] == num)
		{
			for(j=i; j<n-1;j++)
				arr[j] = arr[j+1];
		}
	}
	n = n-1;
	printf("\n The array after deletion is : ");
	for(i=0;i<n;i++)
		printf("\n arr[%d] = %d", i, arr[i]);
	return 0;
}
```

Output

```
Enter the number of elements in the array : 5
arr[0] = 1
arr[1] = 2
arr[2] = 3
arr[3] = 4
arr[4] = 5
Enter the number to be deleted : 3
The array after deletion is :
arr[0] = 1
arr[1] = 2
arr[2] = 4
arr[3] = 5
```

3.5.4 Merging Two Arrays

Merging two arrays in a third array means first copying the contents of the first array into the third array and then copying the contents of the second array into the third array. Hence, the merged array contains the contents of the first array followed by the contents of the second array.

If the arrays are unsorted, then merging the arrays is very simple, as one just needs to copy the contents of one array into another. But merging is not a trivial task when the two arrays are sorted and the merged array also needs to be sorted. Let us first discuss the merge operation on unsorted arrays. This operation is shown in Fig 3.18.

Array 1-	90	56	89	77	69							
Array 2-	45	88	76	99	12	58	81					
Array 3-	90	56	89	77	69	45	88	76	99	12	58	81

Figure 3.18 Merging of two unsorted arrays

Programming Example

11. Write a program to merge two unsorted arrays.

```
#include <stdio.h>
int main()
{
        int arr1[10], arr2[10], arr3[20];
        int i, n1, n2, m, index=0;
        printf("\n Enter the number of elements in array1 : ");
        scanf("%d", &n1);
        printf("\n\n Enter the elements of the first array");
        for(i=0;i<n1;i++)
        {
                printf("\n arr1[%d] = ", i);
                scanf("%d", &arr1[i]);
        }
        printf("\n Enter the number of elements in array2 : ");
        scanf("%d", &n2);
        printf("\n\n Enter the elements of the second array");
        for(i=0;i<n2;i++)
        {
                printf("\n arr2[%d] = ", i);
                scanf("%d", &arr2[i]);
        }
        m = n1+n2;
        for(i=0;i<n1;i++)
        {
            arr3[index] = arr1[i];
            index++;
        }
        for(i=0;i<n2;i++)
        {
                arr3[index] = arr2[i];
                index++;
        }
        printf("\n\n The merged array is");
        for(i=0;i<m;i++)
                printf("\n arr[%d] = %d", i, arr3[i]);
        return 0;
}
```

Output

```
Enter the number of elements in array1 : 3
Enter the elements of the first array
arr1[0] = 1
arr1[1] = 2
arr1[2] = 3
```

```
Enter the number of elements in array2 : 3
Enter the elements of the second array
arr2[0] = 4
arr2[1] = 5
arr2[2] = 6
The merged array is
arr[0] = 1
arr[1] = 2
arr[2] = 3
arr[3] = 4
arr[4] = 5
arr[5] = 6
```

If we have two sorted arrays and the resultant merged array also needs to be a sorted one, then the task of merging the arrays becomes a little difficult. The task of merging can be explained using Fig. 3.19.

Array 1-	20	30	40	50	60							
Array 2-	15	22	31	45	56	62	78					
Array 3-	15	20	22	30	31	40	45	50	56	60	62	78

Figure 3.19 Merging of two sorted arrays

Figure 3.19 shows how the merged array is formed using two sorted arrays. Here, we first compare the 1st element of `array1` with the 1st element of `array2`, and then put the smaller element in the merged array. Since 20 > 15, we put 15 as the first element in the merged array. We then compare the 2nd element of the second array with the 1st element of the first array. Since 20 < 22, now 20 is stored as the second element of the merged array. Next, the 2nd element of the first array is compared with the 2nd element of the second array. Since 30 > 22, we store 22 as the third element of the merged array. Now, we will compare the 2nd element of the first array with the 3rd element of the second array. Because 30 < 31, we store 30 as the 4th element of the merged array. This procedure will be repeated until elements of both the arrays are placed in the right location in the merged array.

Programming Example

12. Write a program to merge two sorted arrays.

```
#include <stdio.h>
int main()
{
        int arr1[10], arr2[10], arr3[20];
        int i, n1, n2, m, index=0;
        int index_first = 0, index_second = 0;
        printf("\n Enter the number of elements in array1 : ");
        scanf("%d", &n1);
        printf("\n\n Enter the elements of the first array");
        for(i=0;i<n1;i++)
        {
                printf("\n arr1[%d] = ", i);
                scanf("%d", &arr1[i]);
        }
```

```
        printf("\n Enter the number of elements in array2 : ");
        scanf("%d", &n2);
        printf("\n\n Enter the elements of the second array");
        for(i=0;i<n2;i++)
        {
                printf("\n arr2[%d] = ", i);
                scanf("%d", &arr2[i]);
        }
        m = n1+n2;
        while(index_first < n1 && index_second < n2)
        {
                if(arr1[index_first]<arr2[index_second])
                {
                        arr3[index] = arr1[index_first];
                        index_first++;
                }
                else
                {
                        arr3[index] = arr2[index_second];
                        index_second++;
                }
                index++;
        }
        // if elements of the first array are over and the second array has some
elements
        if(index_first == n1)
        {
                while(index_second<n2)
                {
                        arr3[index] = arr2[index_second];
                        index_second++;
                        index++;
                }
        }
        // if elements of the second array are over and the first array has some
elements
        else if(index_second == n2)
        {
                while(index_first<n1)
                {
                        arr3[index] = arr1[index_first];
                        index_first++;
                        index++;
                }
        }
        printf("\n\n The merged array is");
        for(i=0;i<m;i++)
                printf("\n arr[%d] = %d", i, arr3[i]);
        return 0;
}
```

Output

```
Enter the number of elements in array1 : 3
Enter the elements of the first array
arr1[0] = 1
arr1[1] = 3
arr1[2] = 5
```

```
Enter the number of elements in array2 : 3
Enter the elements of the second array
arr2[0] = 2
arr2[1] = 4
arr2[2] = 6
The merged array is
arr[0] = 1
arr[1] = 2
arr[2] = 3
arr[3] = 4
arr[4] = 5
arr[5] = 6
```

3.6 PASSING ARRAYS TO FUNCTIONS

Like variables of other data types, we can also pass an array to a function. In some situations, you may want to pass individual elements of the array; while in other situations, you may want to pass the entire array. In this section, we will discuss both the cases. Look at Fig. 3.20 which will help you understand the concept.

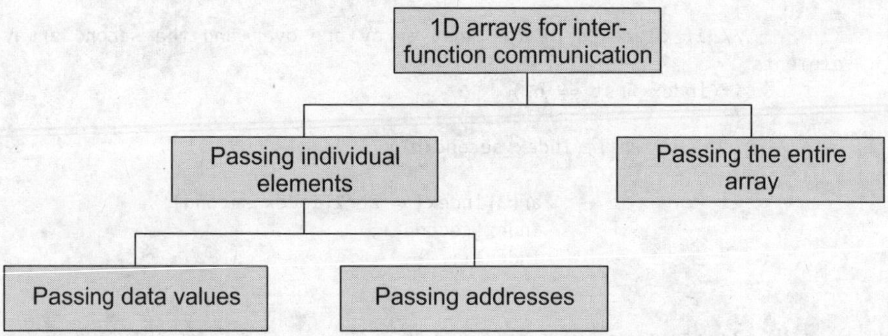

Figure 3.20 One dimensional arrays for inter-function communication

3.6.1 Passing Individual Elements

The individual elements of an array can be passed to a function by passing either their data values or addresses.

Passing Data Values

Individual elements can be passed in the same manner as we pass variables of any other data type. The condition is just that the data type of the array element must match with the type of the function parameter. Look at Fig. 3.21(a) which shows the code to pass an individual array element by passing the data value.

Calling function

```
main()
{
        int arr[5] ={1, 2, 3, 4, 5};
        func(arr[3]);
}
```

Called function

```
void func(int num)
{
        printf("%d", num);
}
```

Figure 3.21(a) Passing values of individual array elements to a function

In the above example, only one element of the array is passed to the called function. This is done by using the index expression. Here, `arr[3]` evaluates to a single integer value. The called function hardly bothers whether a normal integer variable is passed to it or an array value is passed.

Passing Addresses

Like ordinary variables, we can pass the address of an individual array element by preceding the indexed array element with the address operator. Therefore, to pass the address of the fourth element of the array to the called function, we will write `&arr[3]`.

However, in the called function, the value of the array element must be accessed using the indirection (`*`) operator. Look at the code shown in Fig. 3.21(b).

Calling function	Called function

`main()`
`{`
`    int arr[5] ={1, 2, 3, 4, 5};`
`    func(&arr[3]);`
`}`
	`void func(int *num)`
	`{`
	`    printf("%d", *num);`
	`}`

Figure 3.21(b) Passing addresses of individual array elements to a function

3.6.2 Passing the Entire Array

We have discussed that in C the array name refers to the first byte of the array in the memory. The address of the remaining elements in the array can be calculated using the array name and the index value of the element. Therefore, when we need to pass an entire array to a function, we can simply pass the name of the array. Figure 3.22 illustrates the code which passes the entire array to the called function.

Calling function	Called function

`main()`
`{`
`    int arr[5] ={1, 2, 3, 4, 5};`
`    func(arr);`
`}`
	`void func(int arr[5])`
	`{`
	`    int i;`
	`    for(i=0;i<5;i++)`
	`        printf("%d", arr[i]);`
	`}`

Figure 3.22 Passing entire array to a function

A function that accepts an array can declare the formal parameter in either of the two following ways.

`func(int arr[]);` or `func(int *arr);`

When we pass the name of an array to a function, the address of the zeroth element of the array is copied to the local pointer variable in the function. When a formal parameter is declared in a function header as an array, it is interpreted as a pointer to a variable and not as an array. With this pointer variable you can access all the elements of the array by using the expression: `array_name + index`. You can also pass the size of the array as another parameter to the function. So for a function that accepts an array as parameter, the declaration should be as follows.

`func(int arr[], int n);` or `func(int *arr, int n);`

It is not necessary to pass the whole array to a function. We can also pass a part of the array known as a sub-array. A pointer to a sub-array is also an array pointer. For example, if we want to send the array starting from the third element then we can pass the address of the third element and the size of the sub-array, i.e., if there are 10 elements in the array, and we want to pass the array starting from the third element, then only eight elements would be part of the sub-array. So the function call can be written as

```
func(&arr[2], 8);
```

Note that in case we want the called function to make no changes to the array, the array must be received as a constant array by the called function. This prevents any type of unintentional modifications of the array elements. To declare an array as a constant array, simply add the keyword `const` before the data type of the array.

Look at the following programs which illustrate the use of pointers to pass an array to a function.

Programming Examples

13. Write a program to read an array of *n* numbers and then find the smallest number.

```
#include <stdio.h>
void read_array(int arr[], int n);
int find_small(int arr[], int n);
int main()
{
        int num[10], n, smallest;
        printf("\n Enter the size of the array : ");
        scanf("%d", &n);
        read_array(num, n);
        smallest = find_small(num, n);
        printf("\n The smallest number in the array is = %d", smallest);
        return 0;
}
void read_array(int arr[10], int n)
{
        int i;
        for(i=0;i<n;i++)
        {
                printf("\n arr[%d] = ", i);
                scanf("%d", &arr[i]);
        }
}
int find_small(int arr[10], int n)
{
        int i = 0, small = arr[0];
        for(i=1;i<n;i++)
        {
                if(arr[i] < small)
                        small = arr[i];
        }
        return small;
}
```

Output

```
Enter the size of the array : 5
arr[0] = 1
arr[1] = 2
arr[2] = 3
arr[3] = 4
arr[4] = 5
The smallest number in the array is = 1
```

14. Write a program to interchange the largest and the smallest number in an array.

```
#include <stdio.h>
void read_array(int my_array[], int);
void display_array(int my_array[], int);
void interchange(int arr[], int);
int find_biggest_pos(int my_array[10], int n);
int find_smallest_pos(int my_array[10], int n);
int main()
{
          int arr[10], n;
          printf("\n Enter the size of the array : ");
          scanf("%d", &n);
          read_array(arr, n);
          interchange(arr, n);
          printf("\n The new array is: ");
          display_array(arr,n);
          return 0;
}
void read_array(int my_array[10], int n)
{
          int i;
          for(i=0;i<n;i++)
          {
                    printf("\n arr[%d] = ", i);
                    scanf("%d", &my_array[i]);
          }
}
void display_array(int my_array[10], int n)
{
          int i;
          for(i=0;i<n;i++)
                    printf("\n arr[%d] = %d", i, my_array[i]);
}
void interchange(int my_array[10], int n)
{
          int temp, big_pos, small_pos;
          big_pos = find_biggest_pos(my_array, n);
          small_pos = find_smallest_pos(my_array,n);
          temp = my_array[big_pos];
          my_array[big_pos] = my_array[small_pos];
          my_array[small_pos] = temp;
}
int find_biggest_pos(int my_array[10], int n)
{
          int i, large = my_array[0], pos=0;
          for(i=1;i<n;i++)
          {
                    if (my_array[i] > large)
                    {
                              large = my_array[i];
                              pos=i;
                    }
          }
          return pos;
}
int find_smallest_pos (int my_array[10], int n)
{
          int i, small = my_array[0], pos=0;
```

```
            for(i=1;i<n;i++)
            {
                    if (my_array[i] < small)
                    {
                            small = my_array[i];
                            pos=i;
                    }
            }
            return pos;
    }
```

Output

```
Enter the size of the array : 5
arr[0] = 5
arr[1] = 1
arr[2] = 6
arr[3] = 3
arr[4] = 2
The new array is :
arr[0] = 5
arr[1] = 6
arr[2] = 1
arr[3] = 3
arr[4] = 2
```

3.7 POINTERS AND ARRAYS

The concept of array is very much bound to the concept of pointer. Consider Fig. 3.23. For example, if we have an array declared as,

```
int arr[] = {1, 2, 3, 4, 5};
```

then in memory it would be stored as shown in Fig. 3.23.

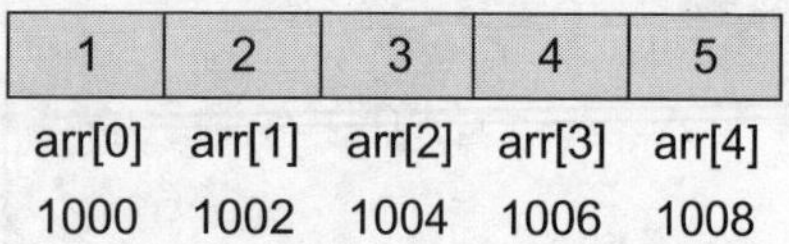

Figure 3.23 Memory representation of `arr[]`

Array notation is a form of pointer notation. The name of the array is the starting address of the array in memory. It is also known as the base address. In other words, base address is the address of the first element in the array or the address of `arr[0]`. Now let us use a pointer variable as given in the statement below.

```
int *ptr;
ptr = &arr[0];
```

Programming Tip

The name of an array is actually a pointer that points to the first element of the array.

Here, `ptr` is made to point to the first element of the array. Execute the code given below and observe the output which will make the concept clear to you.

```
main()
{
    int arr[]={1,2,3,4,5};
    printf("\n Address of array = %p %p %p", arr, &arr[0], &arr);
}
```

Similarly, writing `ptr = &arr[2]` makes `ptr` to point to the third element of the array that has index `2`. Figure 3.24 shows `ptr` pointing to the third element of the array.

If pointer variable `ptr` holds the address of the first element in the array, then the address of successive elements can be calculated by writing `ptr++`.

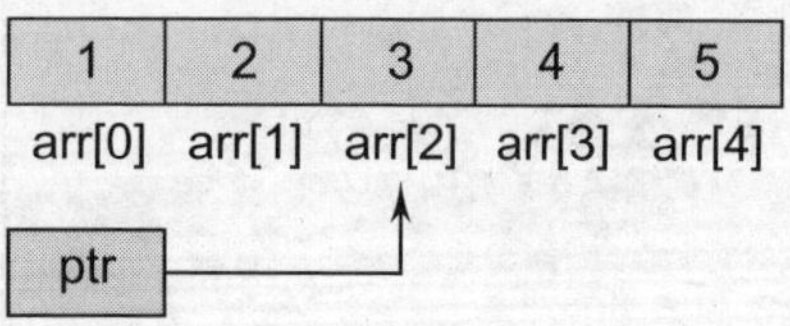

Figure 3.24 Pointer pointing to the third element of the array

> **Programming Tip**
>
> An error is generated if an attempt is made to change the address of the array.

```
int *ptr = &arr[0];
ptr++;
printf("\n The value of the second element of the array is %d",
*ptr);
```

The `printf()` function will print the value `2` because after being incremented `ptr` points to the next location. One point to note here is that if `x` is an integer variable, then `x++;` adds `1` to the value of x. But `ptr` is a pointer variable, so when we write `ptr+i`, then adding `i` gives a pointer that points `i` elements further along an array than the original pointer.

Since `++ptr` and `ptr++` are both equivalent to `ptr+1`, incrementing a pointer using the unary `++` operator, increments the address it stores by the amount given by `sizeof(type)` where `type` is the data type of the variable it points to (i.e., `2` for an integer). For example, consider Fig. 3.25.

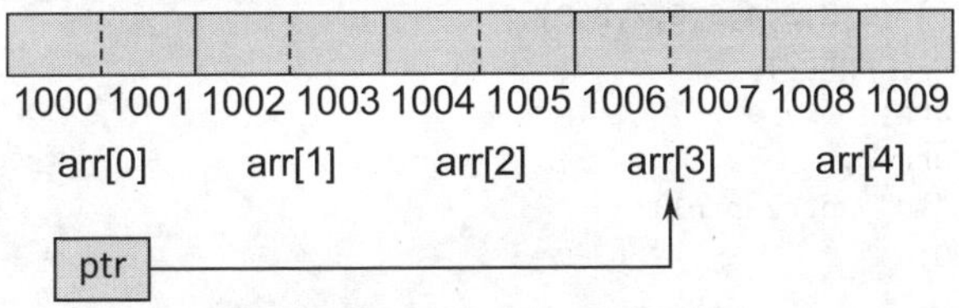

Figure 3.25 Pointer (ptr) pointing to the fourth element of the array

> **Programming Tip**
>
> When an array is passed to a function, we are actually passing a pointer to the function. Therefore, in the function declaration you must declare a pointer to receive the array name.

If `ptr` originally points to `arr[2]`, then `ptr++` will make it to point to the next element, i.e., `arr[3]`. This is shown in Fig. 3.25.

Had this been a character array, every byte in the memory would have been used to store an individual character. `ptr++` would then add only 1 byte to the address of `ptr`.

When using pointers, an expression like `arr[i]` is equivalent to writing `*(arr+i)`.

Many beginners get confused by thinking of array name as a pointer. For example, while we can write

```
ptr = arr;    // ptr = &arr[0]
```

we cannot write

```
arr = ptr;
```

This is because while `ptr` is a variable, `arr` is a constant. The location at which the first element of `arr` will be stored cannot be changed once `arr[]` has been declared. Therefore, an array name is often known to be a constant pointer.

To summarize, the name of an array is equivalent to the address of its first element, as a pointer is equivalent to the address of the element that it points to. Therefore, arrays and pointers use the same concept.

> **Note** arr[i], i[arr], *(arr+i), *(i+arr) gives the same value.

Look at the following code which modifies the contents of an array using a pointer to an array.

```
int main()
{
        int arr[]={1,2,3,4,5};
        int *ptr, i;
        ptr=&arr[2];
        *ptr = -1;
        *(ptr+1) = 0;
        *(ptr-1) = 1;
        printf("\n Array is: ");
```

```
        for(i=0;i<5;i++)
                printf(" %d", *(arr+i));
        return 0;
}
```

Output

```
Array is: 1 1 -1 0 5
```

In C we can add or subtract an integer from a pointer to get a new pointer, pointing somewhere other than the original position. C also permits addition and subtraction of two pointer variables. For example, look at the code given below.

```
int main()
{
        int arr[]={1,2,3,4,5,6,7,8,9};
        int *ptr1, *ptr2;
        ptr1 = arr;
        ptr2 = arr+2;
        printf("%d", ptr2-ptr1);
        return 0;
}
```

Output

```
2
```

In the code, ptr1 and ptr2 are pointers pointing to the elements of the same array. We may subtract two pointers as long as they point to the same array. Here, the output is 2 because there are two elements between ptr1 and ptr2 in the array arr. Both the pointers must point to the same array or one past the end of the array, otherwise this behaviour cannot be defined.

Moreover, C also allows pointer variables to be compared with each other. Obviously, if two pointers are equal, then they point to the same location in the array. However, if one pointer is less than the other, it means that the pointer points to some element nearer to the beginning of the array. Like with other variables, relational operators (>, <, >=, etc.) can also be applied to pointer variables.

Programming Example

15. Write a program to display an array of given numbers.

```
#include <stdio.h>
int main()
{
        int arr[]={1,2,3,4,5,6,7,8,9};
        int *ptr1, *ptr2;
        ptr1 = arr;
        ptr2 = &arr[8];
        while(ptr1<=ptr2)
        {
                printf("%d", *ptr1);
                ptr1++;
        }
        return 0;
}
```

Output

```
1 2 3 4 5 6 7 8 9
```

3.8 ARRAYS OF POINTERS

An array of pointers can be declared as

```
int *ptr[10];
```

The above statement declares an array of 10 pointers where each of the pointer points to an integer variable. For example, look at the code given below.

```
int *ptr[10];
int p = 1, q = 2, r = 3, s = 4, t = 5;
ptr[0] = &p;
ptr[1] = &q;
ptr[2] = &r;
ptr[3] = &s;
ptr[4] = &t;
```

Can you tell what will be the output of the following statement?

```
printf("\n %d", *ptr[3]);
```

The output will be `4` because `ptr[3]` stores the address of integer variable `s` and `*ptr[3]` will therefore print the value of s that is `4`. Now look at another code in which we store the address of three individual arrays in the array of pointers:

```
int main()
{
        int arr1[]={1,2,3,4,5};
        int arr2[]={0,2,4,6,8};
        int arr3[]={1,3,5,7,9};
        int *parr[3] = {arr1, arr2, arr3};
        int i;
        for(i = 0;i<3;i++)
                printf(«%d», *parr[i]);
        return 0;
}
```

Output

```
1 0 1
```

Surprised with this output? Try to understand the concept. In the `for` loop, `parr[0]` stores the base address of `arr1` (or, `&arr1[0]`). So writing `*parr[0]` will print the value stored at `&arr1[0]`. Same is the case with `*parr[1]` and `*parr[2]`.

3.9 TWO-DIMENSIONAL ARRAYS

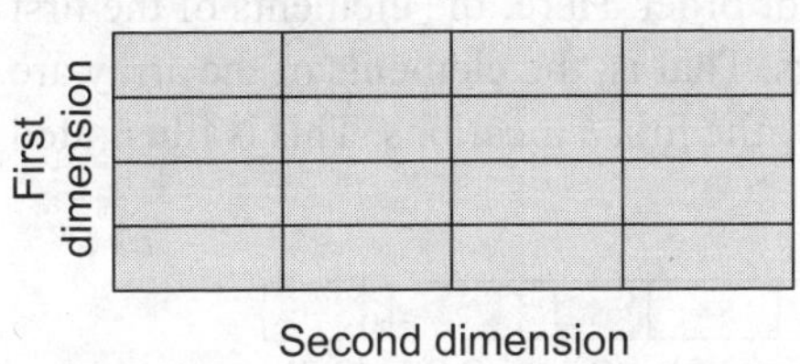

Figure 3.26 Two-dimensional array

Till now, we have only discussed one-dimensional arrays. One-dimensional arrays are organized linearly in only one direction. But at times, we need to store data in the form of grids or tables. Here, the concept of single-dimension arrays is extended to incorporate two-dimensional data structures. A two-dimensional array is specified using two subscripts where the first subscript denotes the row and the second denotes the column. The C compiler treats a two-dimensional array as an array of one-dimensional arrays. Figure 3.26 shows a two-dimensional array which can be viewed as an array of arrays.

3.9.1 Declaring Two-dimensional Arrays

Any array must be declared before being used. The declaration statement tells the compiler the name of the array, the data type of each element in the array, and the size of each dimension. A two-dimensional array is declared as:

```
data_type array_name[row_size][column_size];
```

Therefore, a two-dimensional `m×n` array is an array that contains `m × n` data elements and each element is accessed using two subscripts, `i` and `j`, where `i<=m` and `j<=n`.

For example, if we want to store the marks obtained by three students in five different subjects, we can declare a two-dimensional array as:

```
int marks[3][5];
```

In the above statement, a two-dimensional array called `marks` has been declared that has `m(3)` rows and `n(5)` columns. The first element of the array is denoted by `marks[0][0]`, the second element as `marks[0][1]`, and so on. Here, `marks[0][0]` stores the marks obtained by the first student in the first subject, `marks[1][0]` stores the marks obtained by the second student in the first subject.

The pictorial form of a two-dimensional array is shown in Fig. 3.27.

Rows / Columns	Col 0	Col 1	Col 2	Col 3	Col 4
Row 0	marks[0][0]	marks[0][1]	marks[0][2]	marks[0][3]	marks[0][4]
Row 1	marks[1][0]	marks[1][1]	marks[1][2]	marks[1][3]	marks[1][4]
Row 2	marks[2][0]	marks[2][1]	marks[2][2]	marks[2][3]	marks[2][4]

Figure 3.27 Two-dimensional array

Hence, we see that a 2D array is treated as a collection of 1D arrays. Each row of a 2D array corresponds to a 1D array consisting of `n` elements, where `n` is the number of columns. To understand this, we can also see the representation of a two-dimensional array as shown in Fig. 3.28.

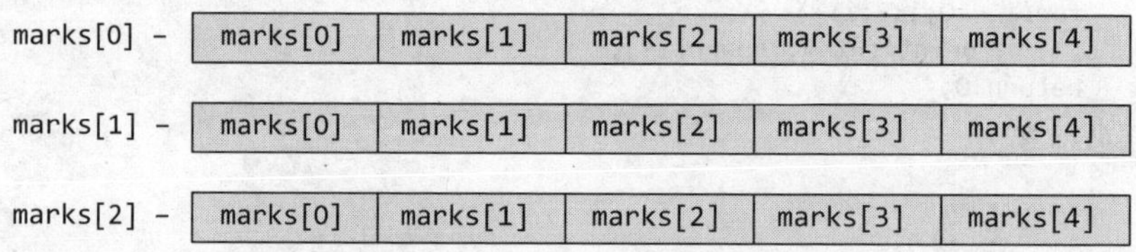

Figure 3.28 Representation of two-dimensional array `marks[3][5]`

Although we have shown a rectangular picture of a two-dimensional array, in the memory, these elements actually will be stored sequentially. There are two ways of storing a two-dimensional array in the memory. The first way is the *row major order* and the second is the *column major order*. Let us see how the elements of a 2D array are stored in a row major order. Here, the elements of the first row are stored before the elements of the second and third rows. That is, the elements of the array are stored row by row where `n` elements of the first row will occupy the first `n` locations. This is illustrated in Fig. 3.29.

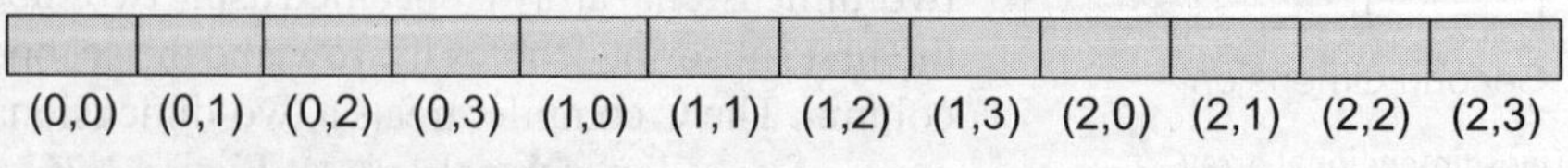

Figure 3.29 Elements of a 3 × 4 2D array in row major order

However, when we store the elements in a column major order, the elements of the first column are stored before the elements of the second and third column. That is, the elements of the array are stored column by column where `m` elements of the first column will occupy the first `m` locations. This is illustrated in Fig. 3.30.

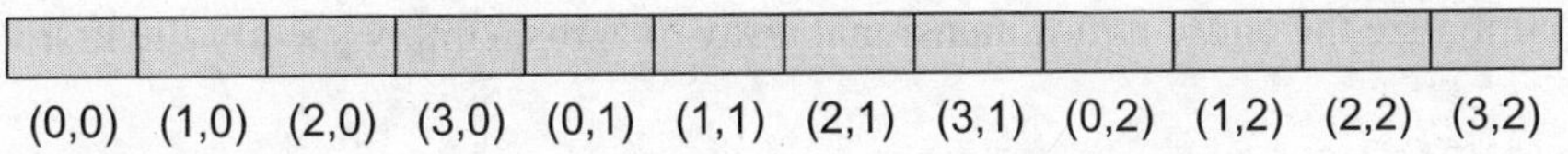

Figure 3.30 Elements of a 4 × 3 2D array in column major order

In one-dimensional arrays, we have seen that the computer does not keep track of the address of every element in the array. It stores only the address of the first element and calculates the address of other elements from the base address (address of the first element). Same is the case with a two-dimensional array. Here also, the computer stores the base address, and the address of the other elements is calculated using the following formula.

If the array elements are stored in column major order,

```
Address(A[I][J]) = Base_Address + w{M ( J - 1) + (I - 1)}
```

And if the array elements are stored in row major order,

```
Address(A[I][J]) = Base_Address + w{N ( I - 1) + (J - 1)}
```

where `w` is the number of bytes required to store one element, `N` is the number of columns, `M` is the number of rows, and `I` and `J` are the subscripts of the array element.

Example 3.5 Consider a 20 × 5 two-dimensional array `marks` which has its base address = 1000 and the size of an element = 2. Now compute the address of the element, `marks[18][4]` assuming that the elements are stored in row major order.

Solution

```
Address(A[I][J]) = Base_Address + w{N (I - 1) + (J - 1)}
Address(marks[18][4]) = 1000 + 2 {5(18 - 1) + (4 - 1)}
                      = 1000 + 2 {5(17) + 3}
                      = 1000 + 2 (88)
                      = 1000 + 176 = 1176
```

3.9.2 Initializing Two-dimensional Arrays

Like in the case of other variables, declaring a two-dimensional array only reserves space for the array in the memory. No values are stored in it. A two-dimensional array is initialized in the same way as a one-dimensional array is initialized. For example,

```
int marks[2][3]={90, 87, 78, 68, 62, 71};
```

Note that the initialization of a two-dimensional array is done row by row. The above statement can also be written as:

```
int marks[2][3]={{90,87,78},{68, 62, 71}};
```

The above two-dimensional array has two rows and three columns. First, the elements in the first row are initialized and then the elements of the second row are initialized.

Therefore,

```
marks[0][0] = 90    marks[0][1] = 87    marks[0][2] = 78
marks[1][0] = 68    marks[1][1] = 62    marks[1][2] = 71
```

In the above example, each row is defined as a one-dimensional array of three elements that are enclosed in braces. Note that the commas are used to separate the elements in the row as well as to separate the elements of two rows.

In case of one-dimensional arrays, we have discussed that if the array is completely initialized, we may omit the size of the array. The same concept can be applied to a two-dimensional array, except that only the size of the first dimension can be omitted. Therefore, the declaration statement given below is valid.

```
int marks[][3]={{90,87,78},{68, 62, 71}};
```

In order to initialize the entire two-dimensional array to zeros, simply specify the first value as zero. That is,

```
int marks[2][3] = {0};
```

The individual elements of a two-dimensional array can be initialized using the assignment operator as shown here.

```
marks[1][2] = 79;
```

or

```
marks[1][2] = marks[1][1] + 10;
```

3.9.3 Accessing the Elements of Two-dimensional Arrays

The elements of a 2D array are stored in contiguous memory locations. In case of one-dimensional arrays, we used a single `for` loop to vary the index `i` in every pass, so that all the elements could be scanned. Since the two-dimensional array contains two subscripts, we will use two `for` loops to scan the elements. The first `for` loop will scan each row in the 2D array and the second `for` loop will scan individual columns for every row in the array. Look at the programs which use two `for` loops to access the elements of a 2D array.

Programming Examples

16. Write a program to print the elements of a 2D array.

```
#include <stdio.h>
int main()
{
        int arr[2][2] = {12, 34, 56,32};
        int i, j;
        for(i=0;i<2;i++)
        {
              printf("\n");
              for(j=0;j<2;j++)
                     printf("%d\t", arr[i][j]);
        }
        return 0;
}
```

Output

```
12      34
56      32
```

17. Write a program to generate Pascal's triangle.

```
#include <stdio.h>
int main()
{
        int arr[7][7]={0};
        int row=2, col, i, j;
        arr[0][0] = arr[1][0] = arr[1][1] = 1;
        while(row <= 7)
        {
                arr[row][0] = 1;
                for(col = 1; col <= row; col++)
                arr[row][col] = arr[row-1][col-1] + arr[row-1][col];
                row++;
        }
        for(i=0; i<7; i++)
```

```
        {
                printf("\n");
                for(j=0; j<=i; j++)
                        printf("\t %d", arr[i][j]);
        }
        return 0;
}
```

Output

```
1
1       1
1       2       1
1       3       3       1
1       4       6       4       1
1       5       10      10      5       1
1       6       15      20      15      6       1
```

18. In a small company there are five salesmen. Each salesman is supposed to sell three products. Write a program using a 2D array to print (i) the total sales by each salesman and (ii) total sales of each item.

```
#include <stdio.h>
int main()
{
        int sales[5][3], i, j, total_sales=0;
        //INPUT DATA
        printf("\n ENTER THE DATA");
        printf("\n *****************");
        for(i=0; i<5; i++)
        {
                printf("\n Enter the sales of 3 items sold by salesman %d: ", i+1);
                for(j=0; j<3; j++)
                        scanf("%d", &sales[i][j]);
        }
        // PRINT TOTAL SALES BY EACH SALESMAN
        for(i=0; i<5; i++)
        {
                total_sales = 0;
                for(j=0; j<3; j++)
                        total_sales += sales[i][j];
                printf("\n Total Sales By Salesman %d = %d", i+1, total_sales);
        }
        // TOTAL SALES OF EACH ITEM
        for(i=0; i<3; i++)// for each item
        {
                total_sales=0;
                for(j=0; j<5; j++)// for each salesman
                        total_sales += sales[j][i];
                printf("\n Total sales of item %d = %d", i+1, total_sales);
        }
        return 0;
}
```

Output

```
ENTER THE DATA
*****************
Enter the sales of 3 items sold by salesman 1: 23 23 45
Enter the sales of 3 items sold by salesman 2: 34 45 63
Enter the sales of 3 items sold by salesman 3: 36 33 43
```

```
Enter the sales of 3 items sold by salesman 4: 33 52 35
Enter the sales of 3 items sold by salesman 5: 32 45 64
Total Sales By Salesman 1 = 91
Total Sales By Salesman 2 = 142
Total Sales By Salesman 3 = 112
Total Sales By Salesman 4 = 120
Total Sales By Salesman 5 = 141
Total sales of item 1 = 158
Total sales of item 2 = 198
Total sales of item 3 = 250
```

19. Write a program to read a 2D array `marks` which stores the marks of five students in three subjects. Write a program to display the highest marks in each subject.

```
#include <stdio.h>
int main()
{
        int marks[5][3], i, j, max_marks;
        for(i=0; i<5; i++)
        {
                printf("\n Enter the marks obtained by student %d",i+1);
                for(j=0; j<3; j++)
                {
                        printf("\n marks[%d][%d] = ", i, j);
                        scanf("%d", &marks[i][j]);
                }
        }
        for(j=0; j<3; j++)
        {
                max_marks = -999;
                for(i=0; i<5; i++)
                {
                        if(marks[i][j]>max_marks)
                        max_marks = marks[i][j];
                }
                printf("\n The highest marks obtained in the subject %d = %d", j+1, max_marks);
        }
        return 0;
}
```

Output

```
Enter the marks obtained by student 1
marks[0][0] = 89
marks[0][1] = 76
marks[0][2] = 100
Enter the marks obtained by student 2
marks[1][0] = 99
marks[1][1] = 90
marks[1][2] = 89
Enter the marks obtained by student 3
marks[2][0] = 67
marks[2][1] = 76
marks[2][2] = 56
Enter the marks obtained by student 4
marks[3][0] = 88
marks[3][1] = 77
marks[3][2] = 66
Enter the marks obtained by student 5
marks[4][0] = 67
```

```
marks[4][1] = 78
marks[4][2] = 89
The highest marks obtained in the subject 1 = 99
The highest marks obtained in the subject 2 = 90
The highest marks obtained in the subject 3 = 100
```

3.10 OPERATIONS ON TWO-DIMENSIONAL ARRAYS

Two-dimensional arrays can be used to implement the mathematical concept of matrices. In mathematics, a matrix is a grid of numbers, arranged in rows and columns. Thus, using two-dimensional arrays, we can perform the following operations on an $m \times n$ matrix:

Transpose Transpose of an $m \times n$ matrix A is given as a $n \times m$ matrix B, where $B_{i,j} = A_{j,i}$.

Sum Two matrices that are compatible with each other can be added together, storing the result in the third matrix. Two matrices are said to be compatible when they have the same number of rows and columns. The elements of two matrices can be added by writing:

$$C_{i,j} = A_{i,j} + B_{i,j}$$

Difference Two matrices that are compatible with each other can be subtracted, storing the result in the third matrix. Two matrices are said to be compatible when they have the same number of rows and columns. The elements of two matrices can be subtracted by writing:

$$C_{i,j} = A_{i,j} - B_{i,j}$$

Product Two matrices can be multiplied with each other if the number of columns in the first matrix is equal to the number of rows in the second matrix. Therefore, $m \times n$ matrix A can be multiplied with a $p \times q$ matrix B if $n=p$. The dimension of the product matrix is $m \times q$. The elements of two matrices can be multiplied by writing:

$$C_{i,j} = \Sigma A_{i,k} B_{k,j} \text{ for } k=1 \text{ to } n$$

Programming Examples

20. Write a program to read and display a 3×3 matrix.

```
#include <stdio.h>
int main()
{
        int i, j, mat[3][3];
        printf("\n Enter the elements of the matrix ");
        for(i=0;i<3;i++)
        {
                for(j=0;j<3;j++)
                {
                    scanf("%d",&mat[i][j]);
                }
        }
        printf("\n The elements of the matrix are ");
        for(i=0;i<3;i++)
        {
                printf("\n");
                for(j=0;j<3;j++)
                        printf("\t %d",mat[i][j]);
        }
```

```
        return 0;
    }
```

Output

```
Enter the elements of the matrix
1 2 3 4 5 6 7 8 9
The elements of the matrix are
1 2 3
4 5 6
7 8 9
```

21. Write a program to transpose a 3×3 matrix.

```
#include <stdio.h>
int main()
{
        int i, j, mat[3][3], transposed_mat[3][3];
        printf("\n Enter the elements of the matrix ");
        for(i=0;i<3;i++)
        {
                for(j=0;j<3;j++)
                {
                        scanf("%d", &mat[i][j]);
                }
        }
        printf("\n The elements of the matrix are ");
        for(i=0;i<3;i++)
        {
                printf("\n");
                for(j=0;j<3;j++)
                        printf("\t %d", mat[i][j]);
        }
        for(i=0;i<3;i++)
        {
                for(j=0;j<3;j++)
                        transposed_mat[i][j] = mat[j][i];
        }
        printf("\n The elements of the transposed matrix are ");
        for(i=0;i<3;i++)
        {
                printf("\n");
                for(j=0;j<3;j++)
                        printf("\t %d",transposed_mat[i][j]);
        }
        return 0;
}
```

Output

```
Enter the elements of the matrix
1 2 3 4 5 6 7 8 9
The elements of the matrix are
1 2 3
4 5 6
7 8 9
The elements of the transposed matrix are
1 4 7
2 5 8
3 6 9
```

22. Write a program to input two m × n matrices and then calculate the sum of their corresponding elements and store it in a third m × n matrix.

```
#include <stdio.h>
int main()
{
        int i, j;
        int rows1, cols1, rows2, cols2, rows_sum, cols_sum;
        int mat1[5][5], mat2[5][5], sum[5][5];
        printf("\n Enter the number of rows in the first matrix : ");
        scanf("%d",&rows1);
        printf("\n Enter the number of columns in the first matrix : ");
        scanf("%d",&cols1);
        printf("\n Enter the number of rows in the second matrix : ");
        scanf("%d",&rows2);
        printf("\n Enter the number of columns in the second matrix : ");
        scanf("%d",&cols2);
        if(rows1 != rows2 || cols1 != cols2)
        {
             printf("\n Number of rows and columns of both matrices must be equal");
             exit();
        }
        rows_sum = rows1;
        cols_sum = cols1;
        printf("\n Enter the elements of the first matrix ");
        for(i=0;i<rows1;i++)
        {
                for(j=0;j<cols1;j++)
                {
                        scanf("%d",&mat1[i][j]);
                }
        }
        printf("\n Enter the elements of the second matrix ");
        for(i=0;i<rows2;i++)
        {
                for(j=0;j<cols2;j++)
                {
                        scanf("%d",&mat2[i][j]);
                }
        }
        for(i=0;i<rows_sum;i++)
        {
                for(j=0;j<cols_sum;j++)
                        sum[i][j] = mat1[i][j] + mat2[i][j];
        }
        printf("\n The elements of the resultant matrix are ");
        for(i=0;i<rows_sum;i++)
        {
                printf("\n");
                for(j=0;j<cols_sum;j++)
                        printf("\t %d", sum[i][j]);
        }
        return 0;
}
```

Output

```
Enter the number of rows in the first matrix: 2
Enter the number of columns in the first matrix: 2
Enter the number of rows in the second matrix: 2
```

```
Enter the number of columns in the second matrix: 2
Enter the elements of the first matrix
1 2 3 4
Enter the elements of the second matrix
5 6 7 8
The elements of the resultant matrix are
6 8
10 12
```

23. Write a program to multiply two m × n matrices.

```
#include <stdio.h>
int main()
{
        int i, j, k;
        int rows1, cols1, rows2, cols2, res_rows, res_cols;
        int mat1[5][5], mat2[5][5], res[5][5];
        printf("\n Enter the number of rows in the first matrix : ");
        scanf("%d",&rows1);
        printf("\n Enter the number of columns in the first matrix : ");
        scanf("%d",&cols1);
        printf("\n Enter the number of rows in the second matrix : ");
        scanf("%d",&rows2);
        printf("\n Enter the number of columns in the second matrix : ");
        scanf("%d",&cols2);
        if(cols1 != rows2)
        {
                printf("\n The number of columns in the first matrix must be
                equal to the number of rows in the second matrix");
                exit();
        }
        res_rows = rows1;
        res_cols = cols2;
        printf("\n Enter the elements of the first matrix ");
        for(i=0;i<rows1;i++)
        {
                for(j=0;j<cols1;j++)
                {
                        scanf("%d",&mat1[i][j]);
                }
        }
        printf("\n Enter the elements of the second matrix ");
        for(i=0;i<rows2;i++)
        {
                for(j=0;j<cols2;j++)
                {
                        scanf("%d",&mat2[i][j]);
                }
        }
        for(i=0;i<res_rows;i++)
        {
                for(j=0;j<res_cols;j++)
                {
                        res[i][j]=0;
                        for(k=0; k<res_cols;k++)
                        res[i][j] += mat1[i][k] * mat2[k][j];
                }
        }
        printf("\n The elements of the product matrix are ");
```

```
        for(i=0;i<res_rows;i++)
        {
                printf("\n");
                for(j=0;j<res_cols;j++)
                        printf("\t %d",res[i][j]);
        }
        return 0;
}
```

Output

```
Enter the number of rows in the first matrix: 2
Enter the number of columns in the first matrix: 2
Enter the number of rows in the second matrix: 2
Enter the number of columns in the second matrix: 2
Enter the elements of the first matrix
1 2 3 4
Enter the elements of the second matrix
5 6 7 8
The elements of the product matrix are
19 22
43 50
```

3.11 PASSING TWO-DIMENSIONAL ARRAYS TO FUNCTIONS

There are three ways of passing a two-dimensional array to a function. First, we can pass individual elements of the array. This is exactly the same as passing an element of a one-dimensional array. Second, we can pass a single row of the two-dimensional array. This is equivalent to passing the entire one-dimensional array to a function that has already been discussed in a previous section. Third, we can pass the entire two-dimensional array to the function. Figure 3.31 shows the three ways of using two-dimensional arrays for inter-functon communication.

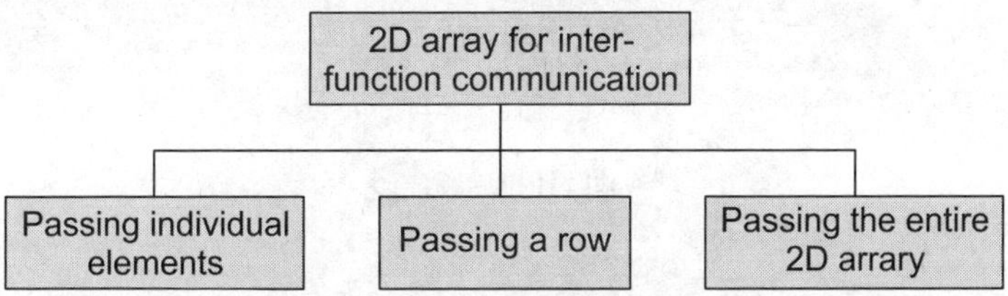

Figure 3.31 2D arrays for inter-function communication

Passing a Row

A row of a two-dimensional array can be passed by indexing the array name with the row number. Look at Fig. 3.32 which illustrates how a single row of a two-dimensional array can be passed to the called function.

Calling function	Called function

`main()`
`{`
`      int arr[2][3] = ({1, 2, 3}, {4, 5, 6});`
`      func(arr[1]);`
`}`
	`void func(int arr[])`
	`{`
	`      int i;`
	`      for(i=0;i<3;i++)`
	`        printf("%d", arr[i] * 10);`
	`}`

Figure 3.32 Passing a row of a 2D array to a function

Passing the Entire 2D Array

To pass a two-dimensional array to a function, we use the array name as the actual parameter (the way we did in case of a 1D array). However, the parameter in the called function must indicate that the array has two dimensions. Look at the following program which passes entire 2D array to a function.

Programming Example

24. Write a program to fill a square matrix with value zero on the diagonals, 1 on the upper right triangle, and –1 on the lower left triangle.

```
#include <stdio.h>
void read_matrix(int mat[5][5], int);
void display_matrix(int mat[5][5], int);
int main()
{
        int row;
        int mat1[5][5];
        printf("\n Enter the number of rows and columns of the matrix:");
        scanf("%d", &row);
        read_matrix(mat1, row);
        display_matrix(mat1, row);
        return 0;
}

void read_matrix(int mat[5][5], int r)
{
        int i, j;
        for(i=0; i<r; i++)
        {
              for(j=0; j<r; j++)
              {
                     if(i==j)
                         mat[i][j] = 0;
                     else if(i>j)
                         mat[i][j] = -1;
                     else
                         mat[i][j] = 1;
              }
        }
}
void display_matrix(int mat[5][5], int r)
{
        int i, j;
        for(i=0; i<r; i++)
        {
        printf("\n");
        for(j=0; j<r; j++)
                 printf("\t %d", mat[i][j]);
        }
}
```

Output

```
Enter the number of rows and columns of the matrix: 2
 0              1
-1              0
```

3.12 POINTERS AND TWO-DIMENSIONAL ARRAYS

Consider a two-dimensional array declared as

```
int mat[5][5];
```

To declare a pointer to a two-dimensional array, you may write

```
int **ptr
```

Here `int **ptr` is an array of pointers (to one-dimensional arrays), while `int mat[5][5]` is a 2D array. They are not the same type and are not interchangeable.

Individual elements of the array `mat` can be accessed using either:

```
mat[i][j] or
*(*(mat + i) + j) or
*(mat[i]+j);
```

To understand more fully the concept of pointers, let us replace `*(multi + row)` with `X` so the expression `*(*(mat + i) + j)` becomes `*(X + col)`

Using pointer arithmetic, we know that the address pointed to by (i.e., value of) `X + col + 1` must be greater than the address `X + col` by an amount equal to `sizeof(int)`.

Since `mat` is a two-dimensional array, we know that in the expression `multi + row` as used above, `multi + row + 1` must increase in value by an amount equal to that needed to *point to* the next row, which in this case would be an amount equal to `COLS * sizeof(int)`.

Thus, in case of a two-dimensional array, in order to evaluate expression (for a row major 2D array), we must know a total of 4 values:

1. The address of the first element of the array, which is given by the name of the array, i.e., `mat` in our case.
2. The size of the type of the elements of the array, i.e., size of integers in our case.
3. The specific index value for the row.
4. The specific index value for the column.

Note that

```
int (*ptr)[10];
```

declares `ptr` to be a pointer to an array of 10 integers. This is different from

```
int *ptr[10];
```

which would make `ptr` the name of an array of 10 pointers to type `int`. You must be thinking how pointer arithmetic works if you have an array of pointers. For example:

```
int * arr[10] ;
int ** ptr = arr ;
```

In this case, `arr` has type `int **`. Since all pointers have the same size, the address of `ptr + i` can be calculated as:

```
addr(ptr + i) = addr(ptr) + [sizeof(int *) * i]
= addr(ptr) + [2 * i]
```

Since `arr` has type `int **`,

```
arr[0] = &arr[0][0],
arr[1] = &arr[1][0], and in general,
arr[i] = &arr[i][0].
```

According to pointer arithmetic, `arr + i = & arr[i]`, yet this skips an entire row of 5 elements, i.e., it skips complete 10 bytes (5 elements each of 2 bytes size). Therefore, if `arr` is address **1000**, then `arr + 2` is address **1010**. To summarize, `&arr[0][0]`, `arr[0]`, `arr`, and `&arr[0]` point to the base address.

```
&arr[0][0] + 1 points to arr[0][1]
arr[0] + 1 points to arr[0][1]
arr + 1 points to arr[1][0]
&arr[0] + 1 points to arr[1][0]
```

To conclude, a two-dimensional array is not the same as an array of pointers to 1D arrays. Actually a two-dimensional array is declared as:

```
int (*ptr)[10] ;
```

Here `ptr` is a pointer to an array of 10 elements. The parentheses are not optional. In the absence of these parentheses, `ptr` becomes an array of 10 pointers, not a pointer to an array of 10 ints.

Look at the code given below which illustrates the use of a pointer to a two-dimensional array.

```
#include <stdio.h>
int main()
{
        int arr[2][2]={{1,2}, {3,4}};
        int i,j, (*parr)[2];
        parr = arr;
        for(i = 0; i < 2; i++)
        {
                for(j = 0; j < 2 ;j++)
                        printf(" %d", (*(parr+i))[j]);
        }
        return 0;
}
```

Output

```
1 2 3 4
```

The golden rule to access an element of a two-dimensional array can be given as

```
arr[i][j] = (*(arr+i))[j] = *((*arr+i))+j) = *(arr[i]+j)
```

Therefore,

```
arr[0][0] = *(arr)[0] = *((*arr)+0) = *(arr[0]+0)
arr[1][2] = (*(arr+1))[2] = *((*(arr+1))+2) = *(arr[1]+2)
```

If we declare an array of pointers using, `data_type *array_name[SIZE];` Here `SIZE` represents the number of rows and the space for columns that can be dynamically allocated.	If we declare a pointer to an array using, `data_type (*array_name)[SIZE];` Here `SIZE` represents the number of columns and the space for rows that may be dynamically allocated (refer Appendix A to see how memory is dynamically allocated).

Programming Example

25. Write a program to read and display a 3 × 3 matrix.

```
#include <stdio.h>
void display(int (*)[3]);
int main()
{
        int i, j, mat[3][3];
        printf("\n Enter the elements of the matrix");
        for(i=0;i<3;i++)
        {
                for(j = 0; j < 3; j++)
```

```
                {
                        scanf("%d", &mat[i][j]);
                }
        }
        display(mat);
        return 0;
}
void display(int (*mat)[3])
{
        int i, j;
        printf("\n The elements of the matrix are");
        for(i = 0; i < 3; i++)
        {
                printf("\n");
                for(j=0;j<3;j++)
                printf("\t %d",*(*(mat + i)+j));
        }
}
```

Output

```
Enter the elements of the matrix
1 2 3 4 5 6 7 8 9
The elements of the matrix are
1 2 3
4 5 6
7 8 9
```

Note A double pointer cannot be used as a 2D array. Therefore, it is wrong to declare: 'int **mat' and then use 'mat' as a 2D array. These are two very different data types used to access different locations in memory. So running such a code may abort the program with a 'memory access violation' error.

A 2D array is not equivalent to a double pointer. A 'pointer to pointer of T' cannot serve as a '2D array of T'. The 2D array is equivalent to a pointer to row of T, and this is very different from pointer to pointer of T.

When a double pointer that points to the first element of an array is used with the subscript notation ptr[0][0], it is fully dereferenced two times and the resulting object will have an address equal to the value of the first element of the array

3.13 MULTI-DIMENSIONAL ARRAYS

A multi-dimensional array in simple terms is an array of arrays. As we have one index in a one-dimensional array, two indices in a two-dimensional array, in the same way, we have n indices in an n-dimensional array or multi-dimensional array. Conversely, an n-dimensional array is specified using n indices. An n-dimensional $m_1 \times m_2 \times m_3 \times \cdots \times m_n$ array is a collection of $m_1 \times m_2 \times m_3 \times \cdots \times m_n$ elements. In a multi-dimensional array, a particular element is specified by using n subscripts as $A[I_1][I_2][I_3]\ldots[I_n]$, where

$$I_1 <= M_1,\ I_2 <= M_2,\ I_3 <= M_3,\ \ldots I_n <= M_n$$

A multi-dimensional array can contain as many indices as needed and as the requirement of memory increases with the number of indices used. However, in practice, we hardly use more than three indices in any program. Figure 3.33 shows a three-dimensional array. The array has three pages, four rows, and two columns.

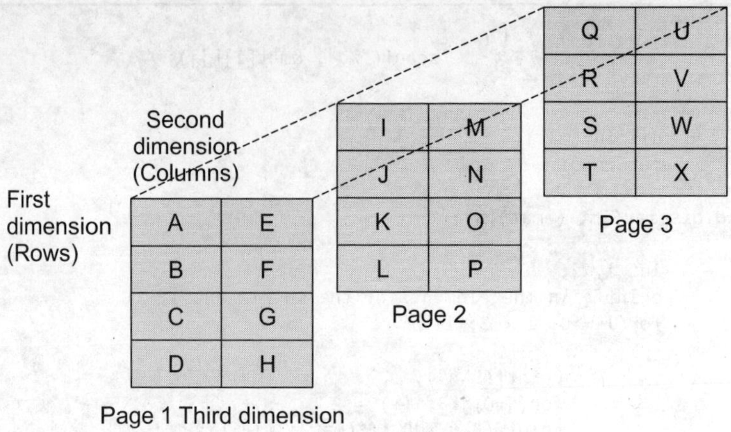

Figure 3.33 Three-dimensional array

> **Note** A multi-dimensional array is declared and initialized the same way we declare and initialize one- and two-dimensional arrays.

Example 3.6 Consider a three-dimensional array defined as `int A[2][2][3]`. Calculate the number of elements in the array. Also, show the memory representation of the array in the row major order and the column major order.

Solution

A three-dimensional array consists of pages. Each page, in turn, contains `m` rows and `n` columns.

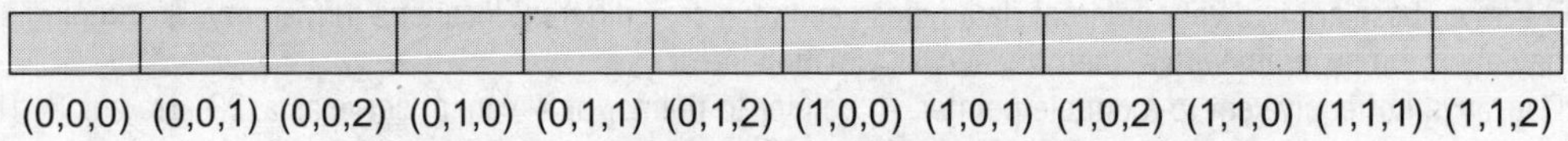

(a) Row major order

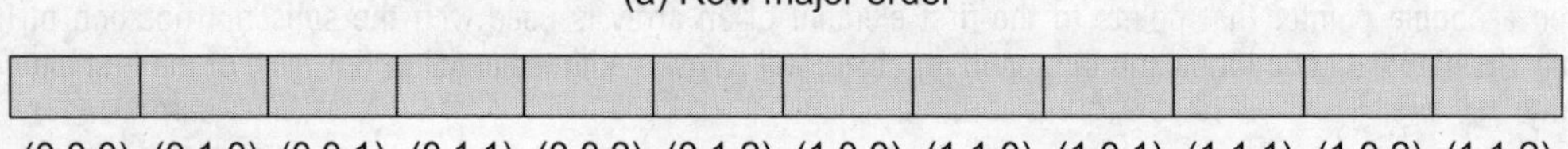

(b) Column major order

The three-dimensional array will contain $2 \times 2 \times 3 = 12$ elements.

Programming Example

26. Write a program to read and display a 2×2×2 array.

```
#include <stdio.h>
int main()
{
        int array[2][2][2], i, j, k;
        printf("\n Enter the elements of the matrix");
        for(i=0;i<2;i++)
        {
```

```
            for(j=0;j<2;j++)
            {
                    for(k=0;k<2;k++)
                    {
                            scanf("%d", &array[i][j][k]);
                    }
            }
        }
        printf("\n The matrix is : ");
        for(i=0;i<2;i++)
        {
            printf("\n");
            for(j=0;j<2;j++)
            {
                    printf("\n");
                    for(k=0;k<2;k++)
                            printf("\t array[%d][%d][%d]  =  %d", i, j, k,
array[i][j][k]);
            }
        }
        return 0;
}
```

Output

```
Enter the elements of the matrix
1 2 3 4 5 6 7 8
The matrix is
arr[0][0][0] = 1 arr[0][0][1] = 2
arr[0][1][0] = 3 arr[0][1][1] = 4
arr[1][0][0] = 5 arr[1][0][1] = 6
arr[1][1][0] = 7 arr[1][1][1] = 8
```

3.14 POINTERS AND THREE-DIMENSIONAL ARRAYS

In this section, we will see how pointers can be used to access a three-dimensional array. We have seen that pointer to a one-dimensional array can be declared as,

```
int arr[]={1,2,3,4,5};
int *parr;
parr = arr;
```

Similarly, pointer to a two-dimensional array can be declared as,

```
int arr[2][2]={{1,2},{3,4}};
int (*parr)[2];
parr = arr;
```

A pointer to a three-dimensional array can be declared as,

```
int arr[2][2][2]={1,2,3,4,5,6,7,8};
int (*parr)[2][2];
parr = arr;
```

We can access an element of a three-dimensional array by writing,

```
arr[i][j][k] = *(*(*(arr+i)+j)+k)
```

Programming Example

27. Write a program which illustrates the use of a pointer to a three-dimensional array.

```
#include <stdio.h>
int main()
{
          int i,j,k;
          int arr[2][2][2];
          int (*parr)[2][2]= arr;
          printf("\n Enter the elements of a 2 × 2 × 2 array: ");
          for(i = 0; i < 2; i++)
          {
                    for(j = 0; j < 2; j++)
                    {
                              for(k = 0; k < 2; k++)
                                        scanf("%d", &arr[i][j][k]);
                    }
          }
          printf("\n The elements of the 2 × 2 × 2 array are: ");
          for(i = 0; i < 2; i++)
          {
                    for(j = 0; j < 2; j++)
                    {
                              for(k = 0; k < 2; k++)
                                        printf("%d", *(*(*(parr+i)+j)+k));
                    }
          }
          return 0;
}
```

Output

```
Enter the elements of a 2 × 2 × 2 array: 1 2 3 4 5 6 7 8
The elements of the 2 × 2 × 2 array are: 1 2 3 4 5 6 7 8
```

Note In the printf statement, you could also have used `*(*(*(arr+i)+j+)+k)` instead of `*(*(*(parr+i)+j)+k))`.

3.15 SPARSE MATRICES

Sparse matrix is a matrix that has large number of elements with a zero value. In order to efficiently utilize the memory, specialized algorithms and data structures that take advantage of the sparse structure should be used. If we apply the operations using standard matrix structures and algorithms to sparse matrices, then the execution will slow down and the matrix will consume large amount of memory. Sparse data can be easily compressed, which in turn can significantly reduce memory usage.

There are two types of sparse matrices. In the first type of sparse matrix, all elements above the main diagonal have a zero value. This type of sparse matrix is also called a (*lower*) *triagonal matrix* because if you see it pictorially, all the elements with a non-zero value appear below the diagonal. In a lower triangular matrix, $A_{i,j}=0$ where $i<j$. An $n \times n$ lower-triangular matrix A has one non-zero element in the first row, two non-zero elements in the second row and likewise n non-zero elements in the *n*th row. Look at Fig. 3.34 which shows a lower-triangular matrix.

$$\begin{bmatrix} 1 & & & & \\ 5 & 3 & & & \\ 2 & 7 & -1 & & \\ 3 & 1 & 4 & 2 & \\ -9 & 2 & -8 & 1 & 7 \end{bmatrix}$$

Figure 3.34 Lower-triangular matrix

To store a lower-triangular matrix efficiently in the memory, we can use a one-dimensional array which stores only non-zero elements. The mapping between a two-dimensional matrix and a one-dimensional array can be done in any one of the following ways:

(a) Row-wise mapping—Here the contents of array `A[]` will be {1, 5, 3, 2, 7, –1, 3, 1, 4, 2, –9, 2, –8, 1, 7}

(b) Column-wise mapping—Here the contents of array `A[]` will be {1, 5, 2, 3, –9, 3, 7, 1, 2, –1, 4, –8, 2, 1, 7}

$$\begin{bmatrix} 1 & 2 & 3 & 4 & 5 \\ & 3 & 6 & 7 & 8 \\ & & -1 & 9 & 1 \\ & & & 9 & 2 \\ & & & & 7 \end{bmatrix}$$

Figure 3.35 Upper-triangular matrix

In an *upper-triangular matrix*, $A_{i,j}$=0 where `i>j`. An `n×n` upper-triangular matrix `A` has `n` non-zero elements in the first row, `n-1` non-zero elements in the second row and likewise one non-zero element in the *n*th row. Look at Fig. 3.35 which shows an upper-triangular matrix.

There is another variant of a sparse matrix, in which elements with a non-zero value can appear only on the diagonal or immediately above or below the diagonal. This type of matrix is also called a *tri-diagonal matrix*. Hence in a tridiagonal matrix, $A_{i,j}$=0, where `|i - j| > 1`. In a tridiagonal matrix, if elements are present on

(a) the main diagonal, it contains non-zero elements for `i=j`. In all, there will be `n` elements.

(b) below the main diagonal, it contains non-zero elements for `i=j+1`. In all, there will be `n-1` elements.

(c) above the main diagonal, it contains non-zero elements for `i=j-1`. In all, there will be `n-1` elements.

$$\begin{bmatrix} 4 & 1 & & & & \\ 5 & 1 & 2 & & & \\ & 9 & 3 & 1 & & \\ & & 4 & 2 & 2 & \\ & & & 5 & 1 & 9 \\ & & & & 8 & 7 \end{bmatrix}$$

Figure 3.36 Tri-diagonal matrix

Figure 3.36 shows a tri-diagonal matrix. To store a tri-diagonal matrix efficiently in the memory, we can use a one-dimensional array that stores only non-zero elements. The mapping between a two-dimensional matrix and a one-dimensional array can be done in any one of the following ways:

(a) Row-wise mapping—Here the contents of array `A[]` will be {4, 1, 5, 1, 2, 9, 3, 1, 4, 2, 2, 5, 1, 9, 8, 7}

(b) Column-wise mapping—Here the contents of array `A[]` will be {4, 5, 1, 1, 9, 2, 3, 4, 1, 2, 5, 2, 1, 8, 9, 7}

(c) Diagonal-wise mapping—Here the contents of array `A[]` will be {5, 9, 4, 5, 8, 4, 1, 3, 2, 1, 7, 1, 2, 1, 2, 9}

3.16 APPLICATIONS OF ARRAYS

Arrays are frequently used in C, as they have a number of useful applications. These applications are

- Arrays are widely used to implement mathematical vectors, matrices, and other kinds of rectangular tables.
- Many databases include one-dimensional arrays whose elements are records.
- Arrays are also used to implement other data structures such as strings, stacks, queues, heaps, and hash tables. We will read about these data structures in the subsequent chapters.
- Arrays can be used for sorting elements in ascending or descending order.

Points to Remember

- An array is a collection of elements of the same data type.
- The elements of an array are stored in consecutive memory locations and are referenced by an index (also known as the subscript).
- The index specifies an offset from the beginning of the array to the element being referenced.
- Declaring an array means specifying three parameters: data type, name, and its size.
- The length of an array is given by the number of elements stored in it.
- There is no single function that can operate on all the elements of an array. To access all the elements, we must use a loop.
- The name of an array is a symbolic reference to the address of the first byte of the array. Therefore, whenever we use the array name, we are actually referring to the first byte of that array.
- C considers a two-dimensional array as an array of one-dimensional arrays.
- A two-dimensional array is specified using two subscripts where the first subscript denotes the row and the second subscript denotes the column of the array.
- Using two-dimensional arrays, we can perform the different operations on matrices: transpose, addition, subtraction, multiplication.
- A multi-dimensional array is an array of arrays. Like we have one index in a one-dimensional array, two indices in a two-dimensional array, in the same way we have *n* indices in an *n*-dimensional or multi-dimensional array. Conversely, an *n*-dimensional array is specified using *n* indices.
- Multi-dimensional arrays can be stored in either row major order or column major order.
- Sparse matrix is a matrix that has large number of elements with a zero value.
- There are two types of sparse matrices. In the first type, all the elements above the main diagonal have a zero value. This type of sparse matrix is called a lower-triangular matrix. In the second type, all the elements below the main diagonal have a zero value. This type of sparse matrix is called an upper-triangular matrix.
- There is another variant of a sparse matrix, in which elements with a non-zero value can appear only on the diagonal or immediately above or below the diagonal. This type of sparse matrix is called a tridiagonal matrix.

Exercises

Review Questions

1. What are arrays and why are they needed?
2. How is an array represented in the memory?
3. How is a two-dimensional array represented in the memory?
4. What is the use of multi-dimensional arrays?
5. Explain sparse matrix.
6. How are pointers used to access two-dimensional arrays?
7. Why does storing of sparse matrices need extra consideration? How are sparse matrices stored efficiently in the computer's memory?
8. For an array declared as `int arr[50]`, calculate the address of `arr[35]`, if `Base(arr) = 1000` and `w = 2`.
9. Consider a two-dimensional array `Marks[10][5]` having its base address as 2000 and the number of bytes per element of the array is 2. Now, compute the address of the element, `Marks[8][5]`, assuming that the elements are stored in row major order.
10. How are arrays related to pointers?
11. Briefly explain the concept of array of pointers.
12. How can one-dimensional arrays be used for inter-function communication?
13. Consider a two-dimensional array `arr[10][10]` which has base address = 1000 and the number of bytes per element of the array = 2. Now, compute the address of the element `arr[8][5]` assuming that the elements are stored in column major order.

14. Consider the array given below:

`Name[0]`	Adam
`Name[1]`	Charles
`Name[2]`	Dicken
`Name[3]`	Esha
`Name[4]`	Georgia
`Name[5]`	Hillary
`Name[6]`	Mishael

(a) How many elements would be moved if the name Andrew has to be added in it?
(i) 7 (ii) 4
(iii) 5 (iv) 6

(b) How many elements would be moved if the name Esha has to be deleted from it?
(i) 3 (ii) 4
(iii) 5 (iv) 6

15. What happens when an array is initialized with
(a) fewer initializers as compared to its size?
(b) more initializers as compared to its size?

Programming Exercises

1. Consider an array `MARKS[20][5]` which stores the marks obtained by 20 students in 5 subjects. Now write a program to
(a) find the average marks obtained in each subject.
(b) find the average marks obtained by every student.
(c) find the number of students who have scored below 50 in their average.
(d) display the scores obtained by every student.

2. Write a program that reads an array of 100 integers. Display all the pairs of elements whose sum is 50.

3. Write a program to interchange the second element with the second last element.

4. Write a program that calculates the sum of squares of the elements.

5. Write a program to compute the sum and mean of the elements of a two-dimensional array.

6. Write a program to read and display a square (using functions).

7. Write a program that computes the sum of the elements that are stored on the main diagonal of a matrix using pointers.

8. Write a program to add two 3×3 matrix using pointers.

9. Write a program that computes the product of the elements that are stored on the diagonal above the main diagonal.

10. Write a program to count the total number of non-zero elements in a two-dimensional array.

11. Write a program to input the elements of a two-dimensional array. Then from this array, make two arrays—one that stores all odd elements of the two-dimensional array and the other that stores all even elements of the array.

12. Write a program to read two floating point number arrays. Merge the two arrays and display the resultant array in reverse order.

13. Write a program using pointers to interchange the second biggest and the second smallest number in the array.

14. Write a menu driven program to read and display a `p×q×r` matrix. Also, find the sum, transpose, and product of the two `p×q×r` matrices.

15. Write a program that reads a matrix and displays the sum of its diagonal elements.

16. Write a program that reads a matrix and displays the sum of the elements above the main diagonal. (*Hint: Calculate the sum of elements* A_{ij} *where* `i<j`)

17. Write a program that reads a matrix and displays the sum of the elements below the main diagonal.
(*Hint: Calculate the sum of elements* A_{ij} *where* `i>j`)

18. Write a program that reads a square matrix of size `n×n`. Write a function `int isUpperTriangular (int a[][], int n)` that returns 1 if the matrix is upper triangular.
(*Hint: Array* `A` *is upper triangular if* A_{ij} `= 0` *and* `i>j`)

19. Write a program that reads a square matrix of size `n×n`. Write a function `int isLowerTriangular (int a[][], int n)` that returns 1 if the matrix is lower triangular.
(*Hint: Array* `A` *is lower triangular if* A_{ij} `= 0` *and* `i<j`)

20. Write a program that reads a square matrix of size `n×n`. Write a function `int isSymmetric (int a[][], int n)` that returns 1 if the matrix is symmetric. (*Hint: Array* `A` *is symmetric if* $A_{ij} = A_{ji}$ *for all values of* `i` *and* `j`)

21. Write a program to calculate `XA + YB` where `A` and `B` are matrices and `X=2` and `Y=3`.
22. Write a program to illustrate the use of a pointer that points to a 2D array.
23. Write a program to enter a number and break it into `n` number of digits.
24. Write a program to delete all the duplicate entries from an array of `n` integers.
25. Write a program to read a floating point array. Update the array to insert a new number at the specified location.

Multiple-choice Questions

1. If an array is declared as `arr[] = {1,3,5,7,9};` then what is the value of `sizeof(arr[3])`?
   (a) 1 (b) 2
   (c) 3 (d) 8
2. If an array is declared as `arr[] = {1,3,5,7,9};` then what is the value of `arr[3]`?
   (a) 1 (b) 7
   (c) 9 (d) 5
3. If an array is declared as double `arr[50];` how many bytes will be allocated to it?
   (a) 50 (b) 100
   (c) 200 (d) 400
4. If an array is declared as `int arr[50]`, how many elements can it hold?
   (a) 49 (b) 50
   (c) 51 (d) 0
5. If an array is declared as `int arr[5][5]`, how many elements can it store?
   (a) 5 (b) 25
   (c) 10 (d) 0
6. Given an integer array `arr[]`; the `i`th element can be accessed by writing
   (a) `*(arr+i)` (b) `*(i+arr)`
   (c) `arr[i]` (d) All of these

True or False

1. An array is used to refer multiple memory locations having the same name.
2. An array name can be used as a pointer.
3. A loop is used to access all the elements of an array.
4. An array stores all its data elements in non-consecutive memory locations.
5. Lower bound is the index of the last element in an array.
6. Merged array contains contents of the first array followed by the contents of the second array.
7. It is possible to pass an entire array as a function argument.
8. `arr[i]` is equivalent to writing `*(arr+i)`.
9. Array name is equivalent to the address of its last element.
10. `mat[i][j]` is equivalent to `*(*(mat + i) + j)`.
11. An array contains elements of the same data type.
12. When an array is passed to a function, C passes the value for each element.
13. A two-dimensional array contains data of two different types.
14. The maximum number of dimensions that an array can have is 4.
15. By default, the first subscript of the array is zero.

Fill in the Blanks

1. Each array element is accessed using a ______.
2. The elements of an array are stored in ______ memory locations.
3. An *n*-dimensional array contains ______ subscripts.
4. Name of the array acts as a ______.
5. Declaring an array means specifying the ______, ______, and ______.
6. ______ is the address of the first element in the array.
7. Length of an array is given by the number of ______.
8. A multi-dimensional array, in simple terms, is an ______.
9. An expression that evaluates to an ______ value may be used as an index.
10. `arr[3] = 10;` initializes the ______ element of the array with value 10.

CHAPTER 4

Strings

LEARNING OBJECTIVE

In the last chapter, we discussed array of integers. Taking a step further, in this chapter, we will discuss array of characters commonly known as strings. We will see how strings are stored, declared, initialized, and accessed. We will learn about different operations that can be performed on strings as well as about array of strings.

4.1 INTRODUCTION

Nowadays, computers are widely used for word processing applications such as creating, inserting, updating, and modifying textual data. Besides this, we need to search for a particular pattern within a text, delete it, or replace it with another pattern. So, there is a lot that we as users do to manipulate the textual data.

In C, a string is a null-terminated character array. This means that after the last character, a `null` character (`'\0'`) is stored to signify the end of the character array. For example, if we write

```
char str[] = "HELLO";
```

then we are declaring an array that has five characters, namely, `H`, `E`, `L`, `L`, and `O`. Apart from these characters, a `null` character (`'\0'`) is stored at the end of the string. So, the internal representation of the string becomes `HELLO'\0'`. To store a string of length 5, we need 5 + 1 locations (1 extra for the `null` character). The name of the character array (or the string) is a pointer to the beginning of the string. Figure 4.1 shows the difference between character storage and string storage.

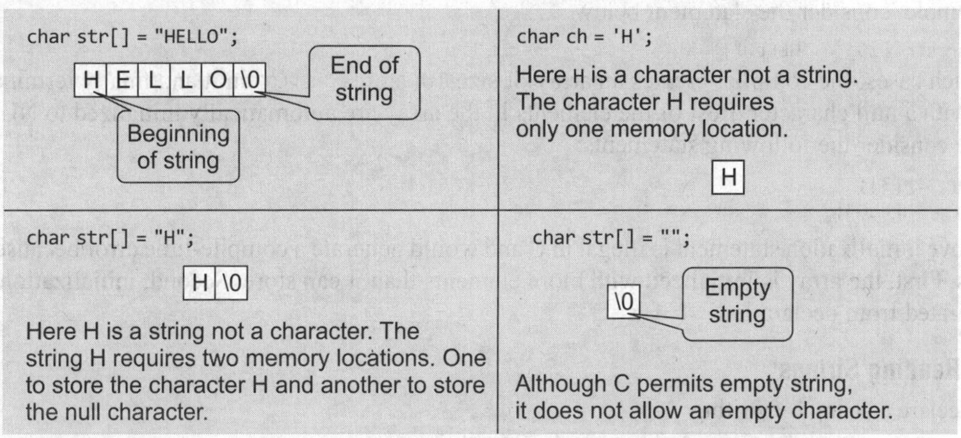

Figure 4.1 Difference between character storage and string storage

str[0]	1000	H
str[1]	1001	E
str[2]	1002	L
str[3]	1003	L
str[4]	1004	O
str[5]	1005	\0

Figure 4.2 Memory representation of a character array

If we had declared str as

```
char str[5] = "HELLO";
```

then the `null` character will not be appended automatically to the character array. This is because `str` can hold only 5 characters and the characters in `HELLO` have already filled the space allocated to it.

Like we use subscripts (also known as index) to access the elements of an array, we can also use subscripts to access the elements of a string. The subscript starts with a zero (0). All the characters of a string are stored in successive memory locations. Figure 4.2 shows how `str[]` is stored in the memory.

Thus, in simple terms, a string is a sequence of characters. In Fig. 4.2, 1000, 1001, 1002, etc., are the memory addresses of individual characters. For simplicity, the figure shows that `H` is stored at memory location 1000 but in reality, the ASCII code of a character is stored in the memory and not the character itself. So, at address 1000, 72 will be stored as the ASCII code for `H` is 72.

Programming Tip

When allocating memory space for a string, reserve space to hold the null character also.

The statement

```
char str[] = "HELLO";
```

declares a constant string, as we have assigned a value to it while declaring the string. However, the general form of declaring a string is

```
char str[size];
```

When we declare the string like this, we can store `size-1` characters in the array because the last character would be the null character. For example, `char mesg[100];` can store a maximum of 99 characters.

Till now, we have only seen one way of initializing strings. The other way to initialize a string is to initialize it as an array of characters. For example,

```
char str[] = {'H', 'E', 'L', 'L', 'O', '\0'};
```

In this example, we have explicitly added the null character. Also observe that we have not mentioned the size of the string. Here, the compiler will automatically calculate the size based on the number of characters. So, in this example six memory locations will be reserved to store the string variable, `str`.

We can also declare a string with size much larger than the number of elements that are initialized. For example, consider the statement below.

```
char str [10] = "HELLO";
```

In such cases, the compiler creates an array of size 10; stores `"HELLO"` in it and finally terminates the string with a null character. Rest of the elements in the array are automatically initialized to NULL.

Now consider the following statements:

```
char str[3];
str = "HELLO";
```

The above initialization statement is illegal in C and would generate a compile-time error because of two reasons. First, the array is initialized with more elements than it can store. Second, initialization cannot be separated from declaration.

4.1.1 Reading Strings

If we declare a string by writing

```
char str[100];
```

Then `str` can be read by the user in three ways:

1. using scanf function,
2. using gets() function, and
3. using getchar(),getch() function repeatedly.

Strings can be read using scanf() by writing

```
scanf("%s", str);
```

Although the syntax of using scanf() function is well known and easy to use, the main pitfall of using this function is that the function terminates as soon as it finds a blank space. For example, if the user enters Hello World, then the str will contain only Hello. This is because the moment a blank space is encountered, the string is terminated by the scanf() function. You may also specify a field width to indicate the maximum number of characters that can be read. Remember that extra characters are left unconsumed in the input buffer.

Programming Tip

Using & operand with a string variable in the scanf statement generates an error.

Unlike int, float, and char values, %s format does not require the ampersand before the variable str.

The next method of reading a string is by using the gets() function. The string can be read by writing

```
gets(str);
```

gets() is a simple function that overcomes the drawbacks of the scanf() function. The gets() function takes the starting address of the string which will hold the input. The string inputted using gets() is automatically terminated with a null character.

Strings can also be read by calling the getchar() function repeatedly to read a sequence of single characters (unless a terminating character is entered) and simultaneously storing it in a character array as shown below.

```
i=0;()
ch = getchar;// Get a character
while(ch != '*')
{
        str[i] = ch;// Store the read character in str
        i++;
        ch = getchar();// Get another character
}
str[i] = '\0';// Terminate str with null character
```

Note that in this method, you have to deliberately append the string with a null character. The other two functions automatically do this.

4.1.2 Writing Strings

Strings can be displayed on the screen using the following three ways:

1. using printf() function,
2. using puts() function, and
3. using putchar() function repeatedly.

Strings can be displayed using printf() by writing

```
printf("%s", str);
```

We use the format specifier %s to output a string. Observe carefully that there is no '&' character used with the string variable. We may also use width and precision specifications along with %s. The width specifies the minimum output field width. If the string is short, the extra space is either left padded or right padded. A negative width left pads short string rather than the default right justification. The precision specifies the maximum number of characters to be displayed, after which the string is truncated. For example,

```
printf ("%5.3s", str);
```

The above statement would print only the first three characters in a total field of five characters. Also these characters would be right justified in the allocated width. To make the string left justified, we must use a minus sign. For example,

```
printf ("%-5.3s", str);
```

Note When the field width is less than the length of the string, the entire string will be printed. If the number of characters to be printed is specified as zero, then nothing is printed on the screen.

The next method of writing a string is by using `puts()` function. A string can be displayed by writing

```
puts(str);
```

`puts()` is a simple function that overcomes the drawbacks of the `printf()` function.

Strings can also be written by calling the `putchar()` function repeatedly to print a sequence of single characters.

```
i=0;
while(str[i] != '\0')
{
        putchar(str[i]);// Print the character on the screen
        i++;
}
```

4.2 OPERATIONS ON STRINGS

In this section, we will learn about different operations that can be performed on strings.

Finding Length of a String

The number of characters in a string constitutes the length of the string. For example, `LENGTH("C PROGRAMMING IS FUN")` will return 20. Note that even blank spaces are counted as characters in the string.

```
Step 1: [INITIALIZE] SET I = 0
Step 2: Repeat Step 3 while STR[I] != NULL
Step 3:     SET I = I + 1
        [END OF LOOP]
Step 4: SET LENGTH = I
Step 5: END
```

Figure 4.3 Algorithm to calculate the length of a string

Figure 4.3 shows an algorithm that calculates the length of a string. In this algorithm, `I` is used as an index for traversing string `STR`. To traverse each and every character of `STR`, we increment the value of `I`. Once we encounter the `null` character, the control jumps out of the `while` loop and the length is initialized with the value of `I`.

Note The library function `strlen(s1)` which is defined in `string.h` returns the length of string `s1`.

Programming Example

1. Write a program to find the length of a string.

```
#include <stdio.h>
int main()
{
        char str[100], i = 0, length;
        printf("\n Enter the string : ");
        gets(str);
        while(str[i] != '\0')
```

```
                i++;
        length = i;
        printf("\n The length of the string is : %d", length);
        return 0;
    }
```

Output

```
    Enter the string : HELLO
    The length of the string is : 5
```

```
Step 1: [INITIALIZE] SET I=0
Step 2: Repeat Step 3 while STR[I] != NULL
Step 3:   IF STR[I] >= 'a' AND STR[I] <= 'z'
             SET UPPERSTR[I] = STR[I] -32
          ELSE
             SET UPPERSTR[I] = STR[I]
          [END OF IF]
          SET I = I + 1
       [END OF LOOP]
Step 4: SET UPPERSTR[I] = NULL
Step 5: EXIT
```

Figure 4.4 Algorithm to convert characters of a string into upper case

Converting Characters of a String into Upper/ Lower Case

We have already discussed that in the memory ASCII codes are stored instead of the real values. The ASCII code for `A-Z` varies from 65 to 91 and the ASCII code for `a-z` ranges from 97 to 123. So, if we have to convert a lower case character into uppercase, we just need to subtract 32 from the ASCII value of the character. And if we have to convert an upper case character into lower case, we need to add 32 to the ASCII value of the character. Figure 4.4 shows an algorithm that converts the lower case characters of a string into upper case.

Note The library functions `toupper()` and `tolower()` which are defined in `ctype.h` convert a character into upper and lower case, respectively.

In the algorithm, we initialize `I` to zero. Using `I` as the index of `STR`, we traverse each character of `STR` from Step 2 to 3. If the character is in lower case, then it is converted into upper case by subtracting 32 from its ASCII value. But if the character is already in upper case, then it is copied into the `UPPERSTR` string. Finally, when all the characters have been traversed, a `null` character is appended to `UPPERSTR` (as done in Step 4).

Programming Example

2. Write a program to convert the lower case characters of a string into upper case.

```
#include <stdio.h>
int main()
{
        char str[100], upper_str[100];
        int i=0;
        printf("\n Enter the string :");
        gets(str);
        while(str[i] != '\0')
        {
                if(str[i]>='a' && str[i]<='z')
                        upper_str[i] = str[i] - 32;
                else
                        upper_str[i] = str[i];
```

```
            i++;
        }
        upper_str[i] = '\0';
        printf("\n The string converted into upper case is : ");
        puts(upper_str);
        return 0;
    }
```

Output

```
    Enter the string : Hello
    The string converted into upper case is : HELLO
```

Appending a String to Another String

Appending one string to another string involves copying the contents of the source string at the end of the destination string. For example, if `S1` and `S2` are two strings, then appending `S1` to `S2` means we have to add the contents of `S1` to `S2`. So, `S1` is the source string and `S2` is the destination string. The appending operation would leave the source string `S1` unchanged and the destination string `S2 = S2 + S1`. Figure 4.5 shows an algorithm that appends two strings.

Note The library function `strcat(s1, s2)` which is defined in `string.h` concatenates string `s2` to `s1`.

```
Step 1: [INITIALIZE] SET I=0 and J=0
Step 2: Repeat Step 3 while DEST_STR[I] != NULL
Step 3:         SET I = I + 1
        [END OF LOOP]
Step 4: Repeat Steps 5 to 7 while SOURCE_STR[J] != NULL
Step 5:         DEST_STR[I] = SOURCE_STR[J]
Step 6:         SET I = I + 1
Step 7:         SET J = J + 1
        [END OF LOOP]
Step 8: SET DEST_STR[I] = NULL
Step 9: EXIT
```

Figure 4.5 Algorithm to append a string to another string

In this algorithm, we first traverse through the destination string to reach its end, that is, reach the position where a `null` character is encountered. The characters of the source string are then copied into the destination string starting from that position. Finally, a `null` character is added to terminate the destination string.

Programming Example

3. Write a program to append a string to another string.

```
    #include <stdio.h>
    int main()
    {
            char Dest_Str[100], Source_Str[50];
            int i=0, j=0;
            printf("\n Enter the source string : ");
            gets(Source_Str);
            printf("\n Enter the destination string : ");
```

```
        gets(Dest_Str);
        while(Dest_Str[i] != '\0')
                i++;
        while(Source_Str[j] != '\0')
        {
                Dest_Str[i] = Source_Str[j];
                i++;
                j++;
        }
        Dest_Str[i] = '\0';
        printf("\n After appending, the destination string is : ");
        puts(Dest_Str);
        return 0;
}
```

Output

```
Enter the source string : How are you?
Enter the destination string : Hello,
After appending, the destination string is : Hello, How are you?
```

Comparing Two Strings

If S1 and S2 are two strings, then comparing the two strings will give either of the following results:

(a) S1 and S2 are equal
(b) S1>S2, when in dictionary order, S1 will come after S2
(c) S1<S2, when in dictionary order, S1 precedes S2

To compare the two strings, each and every character is compared from both the strings. If all the characters are the same, then the two strings are said to be equal. Figure 4.6 shows an algorithm that compares two strings.

```
Step 1: [INITIALIZE] SET I=0, SAME =0
Step 2: SET LEN1 = Length(STR1), LEN2 = Length(STR2)
Step 3: IF LEN1 != LEN2
            Write "Strings Are Not Equal"
        ELSE
            Repeat while I<LEN1
                IF STR1[I] == STR2[I]
                    SET I = I + 1
                ELSE
                    Go to Step 4
                [END OF IF]
            [END OF LOOP]
            IF I = LEN1
                SET SAME =1
                Write "Strings are Equal"
            [END OF IF]
Step 4: IF SAME = 0,
            IF STR1[I] > STR2[I]
                Write "String1 is greater than String2"
            ELSE IF STR1[I] < STR2[I]
                Write "String2 is greater than String1"
            [END OF IF]
        [END OF IF]
Step 5: EXIT
```

Figure 4.6 Algorithm to compare two strings

Note The library function `strcmp(s1, s2)` which is defined in `string.h` compares string `s1` with `s2`.

In this algorithm, we first check whether the two strings are of the same length. If not, then there is no point in moving ahead, as it straight away means that the two strings are not the same. However, if the two strings are of the same length, then we compare character by character to check if all the characters are same. If yes, then the variable `SAME` is set to 1. Else, if `SAME = 0`, then we check which string precedes the other in the dictionary order and print the corresponding message.

Programming Example

4. Write a program to compare two strings.

```
#include <stdio.h>
#include <string.h>
int main()
{
        char str1[50], str2[50];
        int i=0, len1=0, len2=0, same=0;
        printf("\n Enter the first string : ");
        gets(str1);
        printf("\n Enter the second string : ");
        gets(str2);
        len1 = strlen(str1);
        len2 = strlen(str2);
        if(len1 == len2)
        {
                while(i<len1)
                {
                        if(str1[i] == str2[i])
                                i++;
                        else break;
                }
                if(i==len1)
                {
                        same=1;
                        printf("\n The two strings are equal");
                }
        }
        if(len1!=len2)
                printf("\n The two strings are not equal");
        if(same == 0)
        {
                if(str1[i]>str2[i])
                        printf("\n String 1 is greater than string 2");
                else if(str1[i]<str2[i])
                        printf("\n String 2 is greater than string 1");
        }
        return 0;
}
```

Output

```
Enter the first string : Hello
Enter the second string : Hello
The two strings are equal
```

Reversing a String

If `S1="HELLO"`, then reverse of `S1="OLLEH"`. To reverse a string, we just need to swap the first character with the last, second character with the second last character, and so on. Figure 4.7 shows an algorithm that reverses a string.

Note The library function `strrev(s1)` which is defined in `string.h` reverses all the characters in the string except the `null` character.

In Step 1, `I` is initialized to zero and `J` is initialized to the length of the string `-1`. In Step 2, a `while` loop is executed until all the characters of the string are accessed. In Step 4, we swap the `i`th character of `STR` with its `j`th character. As a result, the first character of `STR` will be replaced with its last character, the second character will be replaced with the second last character of `STR`, and so on. In Step 4, the value of `I` is incremented and `J` is decremented to traverse `STR` in the forward and backward directions, respectively.

```
Step 1: [INITIALIZE] SET I=0, J= Length(STR)-1
Step 2: Repeat Steps 3 and 4 while I < J
Step 3:      SWAP(STR(I), STR(J))
Step 4:      SET I = I + 1, J = J - 1
        [END OF LOOP]
Step 5: EXIT
```

Figure 4.7 Algorithm to reverse a string

Programming Example

5. Write a program to reverse a given string.

```
#include <stdio.h>
#include <string.h>
int main()
{
          char str[100], reverse_str[100], temp;
          int i=0, j=0;
          printf("\n Enter the string : ");
          gets(str);
          j=strlen(str)-1;
          while(i<j)
          {
                    temp = str[j];
                    str[j] = str[i];
                    str[i] = temp;
                    i++;
                    j--;
          }
          printf("\n The reversed string is : ");
          puts(str);
          return 0;
}
```

Output

```
Enter the string: Hi there
The reversed string is: ereht iH
```

Extracting a Substring from a String

To extract a substring from a given string, we need the following three parameters:

1. the main string,
2. the position of the first character of the substring in the given string, and

```
Step 1: [INITIALIZE] Set I=M, J=0
Step 2: Repeat Steps 3 to 6
          while STR[I] != NULL and N>0
Step 3:  SET SUBSTR[J] = STR[I]
Step 4:  SET I = I + 1
Step 5:  SET J = J + 1
Step 6:  SET N = N - 1
        [END OF LOOP]
Step 7: SET SUBSTR[J] = NULL
Step 8: EXIT
```

Figure 4.8 Algorithm to extract a substring from the middle of a string

3. the maximum number of characters/length of the substring.

For example, if we have a string

```
str[] = "Welcome to the world of programming";
```

Then,

```
SUBSTRING(str, 15, 5) = world
```

Figure 4.8 shows an algorithm that extracts a substring from the middle of a string.

In this algorithm, we initialize a loop counter `I` to `M`, that is, the position from which the characters have to be copied. Steps 3 to 6 are repeated until `N` characters have been copied. With every character copied, we decrement the value of `N`. The characters of the string are copied into another string called the `SUBSTR`. At the end, a null character is appended to `SUBSTR` to terminate the string.

Programming Example

6. Write a program to extract a substring from the middle of a given string.

```
#include <stdio.h>
int main()
{
        char str[100], substr[100];
        int i=0, j=0, n, m;
        printf("\n Enter the main string : ");
        gets(str);
        printf("\n Enter the position from which to start the substring: ");
        scanf("%d", &m);
        printf("\n Enter the length of the substring: ");
        scanf("%d", &n);
        i=m;
        while(str[i] != '\0' && n>0)
        {
                substr[j] = str[i];
                i++;
                j++;
                n--;
        }
        substr[j] = '\0';
        printf("\n The substring is : ");
        puts(substr);
        return 0;
}
```

Output

```
Enter the main string : Hi there
Enter the position from which to start the substring: 1
Enter the length of the substring: 4
 The substring is : i th
```

```
Step 1: [INITIALIZE] SET I=0, J=0 and K=0
Step 2: Repeat Steps 3 to 4 while TEXT[I] != NULL
Step 3: IF I = pos
          Repeat while Str[K] != NULL
              new_str[J] = Str[K]
              SET J=J+1
              SET K = K+1
          [END OF INNER LOOP]
        ELSE
          new_str[J] = TEXT[I]
          set J = J+1
        [END OF IF]
Step 4: set I = I+1
        [END OF OUTER LOOP]
Step 5: SET new_str[J] = NULL
Step 6: EXIT
```

Figure 4.9 Algorithm to insert a string in a given text at the specified position

Inserting a String in the Main String

The insertion operation inserts a string `S` in the main text `T` at the `k`th position. The general syntax of this operation is `INSERT(text, position, string)`. For example, `INSERT("XYZXYZ", 3, "AAA") = "XYZAAAXYZ"`

Figure 4.9 shows an algorithm to insert a string in a given text at the specified position.

This algorithm first initializes the indices into the string to zero. From Steps 3 to 5, the contents of `NEW_STR` are built. If `I` is exactly equal to the position at which the substring has to be inserted, then the inner loop copies the contents of the substring into `NEW_STR`. Otherwise, the contents of the text are copied into it.

Programming Example

7. Write a program to insert a string in the main text.

```
#include <stdio.h>
int main()
{
          char text[100], str[20], ins_text[100];
          int i=0, j=0, k=0,pos;
          printf("\n Enter the main text : ");
          gets(text);
          printf("\n Enter the string to be inserted : ");
          gets(str);
          printf("\n Enter the position at which the string has to be inserted:");
          scanf("%d", &pos);
          while(text[i] !='\0')
          {
                    if(i==pos)
                    {
                              while(str[k]!='\0')
                              {
                                        ins_text[j]=str[k];
                                        j++;
                                        k++;
                              }
                    }
                    else
                    {
                              ins_text[j]=text[i];
                              j++;
                    }
                    i++;
          }
          ins_text[j]='\0';
          printf("\n The new string is : ");
          puts(ins_text);
          return 0;
}
```

Output

```
Enter the main text : newsman
Enter the string to be inserted : paper
Enter the position at which the string has to be inserted: 4
The new string is: newspaperman
```

Pattern Matching

This operation returns the position in the string where the string pattern first occurs. For example,

```
INDEX("Welcome to the world of programming", "world") = 15
```

However, if the pattern does not exist in the string, the `INDEX` function returns 0. Figure 4.10 shows an algorithm to find the index of the first occurrence of a string within a given text.

```
Step 1: [INITIALIZE] SET I=0 and MAX = Length(TEXT)-Length(STR)+1
Step 2: Repeat Steps 3 to 6 while I < MAX
Step 3:   Repeat Step 4 for K = 0 To Length(STR)
Step 4:          IF STR[K] != TEXT[I + K], then Goto step 6
          [END OF INNER LOOP]
Step 5:   SET INDEX = I. Goto Step 8
Step 6:   SET I = I+1
        [END OF OUTER LOOP]
Step 7: SET INDEX = -1
Step 8: EXIT
```

Figure 4.10 Algorithm to find the index of the first occurrence of a string within a given text

In this algorithm, `MAX` is initialized to `length(TEXT) - Length(STR) + 1`. For example, if a text contains `'Welcome To Programming'` and the string contains `'World'`, in the main text, we will look for at the most 22 – 5 + 1 = 18 characters because after that there is no scope left for the string to be present in the text.

Steps 3 to 6 are repeated until each and every character of the text has been checked for the occurrence of the string within it. In the inner loop in Step 3, we check the `n` characters of string with the `n` characters of text to find if the characters are same. If it is not the case, then we move to Step 6, where `I` is incremented. If the string is found, then the index is initialized with `I`, else it is set to –1. For example, if

```
TEXT = WELCOME TO THE WORLD
STRING = COME
```

In the first pass of the inner loop, we will compare `COME` with `WELC` character by character. As `W` and `C` do not match, the control will move to Step 6 and then `ELCO` will be compared with `COME`. In the fourth pass, `COME` will be compared with `COME`.

We will be using the programming code of pattern matching operation in the operations that follow.

Deleting a Substring from the Main String

The deletion operation deletes a substring from a given text. We can write it as `DELETE(text, position, length)`. For example,

```
DELETE("ABCDXXXABCD", 4, 3) = "ABCDABCD"
```

Figure 4.11 shows an algorithm to delete a substring from a given text.

In this algorithm, we first initialize the indices to zero. Steps 3 to 6 are repeated until all the characters of the text are scanned. If `I` is exactly equal to `M` (the position from which deletion has to be done), then the index of the text is incremented and `N` is decremented. `N` is the number of characters that have to be deleted starting from position `M`. However, if `I` is not equal to `M`, then the characters of the text are simply copied into the `NEW_STR`.

Programming Example

8. Write a program to delete a substring from a text.

```
#include <stdio.h>
int main()
{
          char text[200], str[20], new_text[200];
          int i=0, j=0, found=0, k, n=0, copy_loop=0;
          printf("\n Enter the main text : ");
          gets(text);
          printf("\n Enter the string to be deleted : ");
          gets(str);
          while(text[i]!='\0')
          {
                    j=0, found=0, k=i;
                    while(text[k]==str[j] && str[j]!='\0')
                    {
                              k++;
                              j++;
                    }
                    if(str[j]=='\0')
                              copy_loop=k;
                    new_text[n] = text[copy_loop];
                    i++;
                    copy_loop++;
                    n++;
          }
          new_str[n]='\0';
          printf("\n The new string is : ");
          puts(new_str);
          return 0;
}
```

Output

```
Enter the main text : Hello, how are you?
Enter the string to be deleted : , how are you?
The new string is : Hello
```

Replacing a Pattern with Another Pattern in a String

```
Step 1: [INITIALIZE] SET I=0 and J=0
Step 2: Repeat Steps 3 to 6 while TEXT[I] != NULL
Step 3:  IF I=M
              Repeat while N>0
                    SET I = I+1
                    SET N = N - 1
              [END OF INNER LOOP]
         [END OF IF]
Step 4: SET NEW_STR[J] = TEXT[I]
Step 5: SET J = J + 1
Step 6: SET I = I + 1
        [END OF OUTER LOOP]
Step 7: SET NEW_STR[J] = NULL
Step 8: EXIT
```

Figure 4.11 Algorithm to delete a substring from a text

The replacement operation is used to replace the pattern P_1 by another pattern P_2. This is done by writing REPLACE(text, $pattern_1$, $pattern_2$). For example,

```
("AAABBBCCC", "BBB", "X") = AAAXCCC
("AAABBBCCC", "X", "YYY")= AAABBBCC
```

In the second example, there is no change as X does not appear in the text. Figure 4.12 shows an algorithm to replace a pattern P_1 with another pattern P_2 in the text.

The algorithm is very simple, where we first find the position POS, at which the pattern occurs in the text, then delete the existing pattern from that position and insert a new pattern there.

```
Step 1: [INITIALIZE] SET POS = INDEX(TEXT, P1)
Step 2: SET TEXT = DELETE(TEXT, POS, LENGTH(P1))
Step 3: INSERT(TEXT, POS, P2)
Step 4: EXIT
```

Figure 4.12 Algorithm to replace a pattern P_1 with another pattern P_2 in the text

Programming Example

9. Write a program to replace a pattern with another pattern in the text.

```
#include <stdio.h>
main()
{
        char str[200], pat[20], new_str[200], rep_pat[100];
        int i=0, j=0, k, n=0, copy_loop=0, rep_index=0;
        printf("\n Enter the string : ");
        gets(str);
        printf("\n Enter the pattern to be replaced: ");
        gets(pat);
        printf("\n Enter the replacing pattern: ");
        gets(rep_pat);
        while(str[i]!='\0')
        {
                j=0,k=i;
                while(str[k]==pat[j] && pat[j]!='\0')
                {
                        k++;
                        j++;
                }
                if(pat[j]=='\0')
                {
                        copy_loop=k;
                        while(rep_pat[rep_index] !='\0')
                        {
                        new_str[n] = rep_pat[rep_index];
                        rep_index++;
                        n++;
                        }
                }
                new_str[n] = str[copy_loop];
                i++;
                copy_loop++;
                n++;
        }
        new_str[n]='\0';
        printf("\n The new string is : ");
        puts(new_str);
        return 0;
}
```

Output

```
Enter the string : How ARE you?
```

```
Enter the pattern to be replaced : ARE
Enter the replacing pattern : are
The new string is : How are you?
```

4.3 ARRAYS OF STRINGS

Till now we have seen that a string is an array of characters. For example, if we say `char name[] = "Mohan"`, then the name is a string (character array) that has five characters.

Now, suppose that there are 20 students in a class and we need a string that stores the names of all the 20 students. How can this be done? Here, we need a string of strings or an array of strings. Such an array of strings would store 20 individual strings. An array of strings is declared as

```
char names[20][30];
```

Here, the first index will specify how many strings are needed and the second index will specify the length of every individual string. So here, we will allocate space for 20 names where each name can be a maximum 30 characters long.

Let us see the memory representation of an array of strings. If we have an array declared as

```
char name[5][10] = {"Ram", "Mohan", "Shyam", "Hari", "Gopal"};
```

Then in the memory, the array will be stored as shown in Fig. 4.13.

name[0]	R	A	M	'\0'						
name[1]	M	O	H	A	N	'\0'				
name[2]	S	H	Y	A	M	'\0'				
name[3]	H	A	R	I	'\0'					
name[4]	G	O	P	A	L	'\0'				

Figure 4.13 Memory representation of a 2D character array

```
Step 1: [INITIALIZE] SET I=0
Step 2: Repeat Step 3 while I< N
Step 3:      Apply Process to NAMES[I]
        [END OF LOOP]
Step 4: EXIT
```

Figure 4.14 Algorithm to process individual string from an array of strings

By declaring the array names, we allocate 50 bytes. But the actual memory occupied is 27 bytes. Thus, we see that about half of the memory allocated is wasted. Figure 4.14 shows an algorithm to process individual string from an array of strings.

In Step 1, we initialize the index variable `I` to zero. In Step 2, a `while` loop is executed until all the strings in the array are accessed. In Step 3, each individual string is processed.

Programming Examples

10. Write a program to sort the names of students.

```
#include <stdio.h>
#include <string.h>
int main()
{
        char names[5][10], temp[10];
        int i, n, j;
        printf("\n Enter the number of students : ");
        scanf("%d", &n);
        for(i=0;i<n;i++)
        {
                printf("\n Enter the name of student %d : ", i+1);
```

```
            gets(names[i]);
        }
        for(i=0;i<n;i++)
        {
            for(j=0;j<n-i-1;j++)
            {
                if(strcmp(names[j], names[j+1])>0)
                {
                    strcpy(temp, names[j]);
                    strcpy(names[j], names[j+1]);
                    strcpy(names[j+1], temp);
                }
            }
        }
        printf("\n Names of the students in alphabetical order are : ");
        for(i=0;i<n;i++)
            puts(names[i]);
        return 0;
    }
```

Output

```
Enter the number of students : 3
Enter the name of student 1 : Goransh
Enter the name of student 2 : Aditya
Enter the name of student 3 : Sarthak
Names of the students in alphabetical order are : Aditya Goransh Sarthak
```

11. Write a program to read multiple lines of text and then count the number of characters, words, and lines in the text.

```
#include <stdio.h>
int main()
{
        char str[1000];
        int i=0, word_count = 1, line_count =1, char_count = 1;
        printf("\n Enter a '*' to end");
        printf("\n **************");
        printf("\n Enter the text : ");
        scanf("%c", &str[i]);
        while(str[i] != '*')
        {
            i++;
            scanf("%c", &str[i]);
        }
        str[i] = '\0';
        i=0;
        while(str[i] != '\0')
        {
            if(str[i] == '\n' || i==79)
                line_count++;
            if(str[i] == ' ' &&str[i+1] != ' ')
                word_count++;
            char_count++;
            i++;
        }
        printf("\n The total count of words is : %d", word_count);
        printf("\n The total count of lines is : %d", line_count);
        printf("\n The total count of characters is : %d", char_count);
        return 0;
}
```

Output

```
Enter a '*' to end
**************
Enter the text : Hi there*
The total count of words is : 2
The total count of lines is : 1
The total count of characters is : 9
```

12. Write a program to find whether a string is a palindrome or not.

```
#include <stdio.h>
int main()
{
        char str[100];
        int i = 0, j, length = 0;
        printf("\n Enter the string : ");
        gets(str);
        while(str[i] != '\0')
        {
                length++ ;
                i++ ;
        }
        i=0;
        j = length - 1;
        while(i <= length/2)
        {
                if(str[i] == str[j])
                {
                        i++;
                        j--;
                }
                else
                        break;
        }
        if(i>=j)
                printf("\n PALINDROME");
        else
                printf("\n NOT A PALINDROME");
        return 0;
}
```

Output

```
Enter the string: madam
PALINDROME
```

4.4 POINTERS AND STRINGS

In C, strings are treated as arrays of characters that are terminated with a binary zero character (written as `'\0'`). Consider, for example,

```
char str[10];
str[0] = 'H';
str[1] = 'i';
str[2] = '!':
str[3] = '\0';
```

C provides two alternate ways of declaring and initializing a string. First, you may write

```
char str[10] = {'H', 'i', '!', '\0'};
```

But this also takes more typing than is convenient. So, C permits

```
char str[10] = "Hi!";
```

When the double quotes are used, a `null` character (`'\0'`) is automatically appended to the end of the string.

When a string is declared like this, the compiler sets aside a contiguous block of the memory, i.e., 10 bytes long, to hold characters and initializes its first four characters as `Hi!\0`.

Now, consider the following program that prints a text.

```
#include <stdio.h>
int main()
{
		char str[] = "Hello";
		char *pstr;
		pstr = str;
		printf("\n The string is : ");
		while(*pstr != '\0')
		{
			printf("%c", *pstr);
			pstr++;
		}
		return 0;
}
```

Output

```
The string is: Hello
```

In this program, we declare a character pointer `*pstr` to show the string on the screen. We then point the pointer `pstr` to `str`. Then, we print each character of the string using the `while` loop. Instead of using the `while` loop, we could straightaway use the function `puts()`, as shown below

```
puts(pstr);
```

The function prototype for `puts()` is as follows:

```
int puts(const char *s);
```

Here the `const` modifier is used to assure that the function dose not modify the contents pointed to by the source pointer. The address of the string is passed to the function as an argument.

The parameter passed to `puts()` is a pointer which is nothing but the address to which it points to or simply an address. Thus, writing `puts(str)` means passing the address of `str[0]`. Similarly when we write `puts(pstr);` we are passing the same address, because we have written `pstr = str;`.

Consider another program that reads a string and then scans each character to count the number of upper and lower case characters entered.

```
#include <stdio.h>
int main()
{
		char str[100], *pstr;
		int upper = 0, lower = 0;
		printf("\n Enter the string : ");
		gets(str);
		pstr = str;
		while(*pstr != '\0')
		{
			if(*pstr >= 'A' && *pstr <= 'Z')
				upper++;
			else if(*pstr >= 'a' && *pstr <= 'z')
				lower++;
			pstr++;
		}
		printf("\n Total number of upper case characters = %d", upper);
```

```
        printf("\n Total number of lower case characters = %d", lower);
        return 0;
}
```

Output

```
Enter the string : How are you
Total number of upper case characters = 1
Total number of lower case characters = 8
```

Programming Examples

13. Write a program to copy a string into another string.

```
#include <stdio.h>
int main()
{
        char str[100], copy_str[100];
        char *pstr, *pcopy_str;
        pstr = str;
        pcopy_str = copy_str;
        printf("\n Enter the string : ");
        gets(str);
        while(*pstr != '\0')
        {
                *pcopy_str = *pstr;
                pstr++, pcopy_str++;
        }
        *pcopy_str = '\0';
        printf("\n The copied text is : ");
        while(*pcopy_str != '\0')
        {
                printf("%c", *pcopy_str);
                pcopy_str++;
        }
        return 0;
}
```

Output

```
Enter the string : C Programming
The copied text is : C Programming
```

14. Write a program to concatenate two strings.

```
#include <stdio.h>
int main()
{
        char str1[100], str2[100], copy_str[200];
        char *pstr1, *pstr2, *pcopy_str;
        pstr1 = str1;
        pstr2 = str2;
        pcopy_str = copy_str;
        printf("\n Enter the first string : ");
        gets(str1);
        printf("\n Enter the second string : ");
        gets(str2);
        while(*pstr1 != '\0')
        {
                *pcopy_str = *pstr1;
```

```
                pcopy_str++, pstr1++;
        }
        while(*pstr2 != '\0')
        {
                *pcopy_str = *pstr2;
                pcopy_str++, pstr2++;
        }
        *pcopy_str = '\0';
        printf("\n The concatenated text is : ");
        while(*pcopy_str != '\0')
        {
                printf("%c", *pcopy_str);
                pcopy_str++;
        }
        return 0;
}
```

Output

```
Enter the first string : Data Structures Using C by
Enter the second string : Reema Thareja
 The concatenated text is : Data Structures Using C by Reema Thareja
```

Points to Remember

- A string is a null-terminated character array.
- Individual characters of strings can be accessed using a subscript that starts from zero.
- All the characters of a string are stored in successive memory locations.
- Strings can be read by a user using three ways: using `scanf()` function, using `gets()` function, or using `getchar()` function repeatedly.
- The `scanf()` function terminates as soon as it finds a blank space.
- The `gets()` function takes the starting address of the string which will hold the input. The string inputted using `gets()` is automatically terminated with a `null` character.
- Strings can also be read by calling `getchar()` repeatedly to read a sequence of single characters.
- Strings can be displayed on the screen using three ways: using `printf` function, using `puts()` function, or using `putchar()`function repeatedly.
- ∑ C standard library supports a number of pre-defined functions for manipulating strings or changing the contents of strings. Many of these functions are defined in the header file string.h.
- Alternatively we can also develop functions which perform the same task as the pre-defined string handling functions. The most basic function is the `length` function which returns the number of characters in a string.
- Name of a string acts as a pointer to the string. In the declaration `char str[5] = "hello";` `str` is a pointer which holds the address of the first character, i.e., `'h'`.
- An array of strings can be declared as `char strings [20][30];` where the first subscript denotes the number of strings and the second subscript denotes the length of every individual string.

Exercises

Review Questions

1. What are strings? Discuss some of the operations that can be performed on strings.
2. Explain how strings are represented in the main memory.
3. How are strings read from the standard input device? Explain the different functions used to perform the string input operation.
4. Explain how strings can be displayed on the screen.
5. Explain the syntax of `printf()` and `scanf()`.
6. List all the substrings that can be formed from the string 'ABCD'.
7. What do you understand by pattern matching? Give an algorithm for it.
8. Write a short note on array of strings.
9. Explain with an example how an array of strings is stored in the main memory.
10. Explain how pointers and strings are related to each other with the help of a suitable program.
11. If the substring function is given as `SUBSTRING (string, position, length)`, then find `S(5,9)` if `S = "Welcome to World of C Programming"`
12. If the index function is given as `INDEX(text, pattern)`, then find `index(T, P)` where `T = "Welcome to World of C Programming"` and `P = "of"`
13. Differentiate between `gets()` and `scanf()`.
14. Give the drawbacks of getchar() and scanf().
15. Which function can be used to overcome the shortcomings of `getchar()` and `scanf()`?
16. How can `putchar()` be used to print a string?
17. Differentiate between a character and a string.
18. Differentiate between a character array and a string.

Programming Exercises

1. Write a program in which a string is passed as an argument to a function.
2. Write a program in C to concatenate first `n` characters of a string with another string.
3. Write a program in C that compares first `n` characters of one string with first `n` characters of another string.
4. Write a program in C that removes leading and trailing spaces from a string.
5. Write a program in C that replaces a given character with another character in a string.
6. Write a program to count the number of digits, upper case characters, lower case characters, and special characters in a given string.
7. Write a program to count the total number of occurrences of a given character in the string.
8. Write a program to accept a text. Count and display the number of times the word 'the' appears in the text.
9. Write a program to count the total number of occurrences of a word in the text.
10. Write a program to find the last instance of occurrence of a sub-string within a string.
11. Write a program to input an array of strings. Then, reverse the string in the format shown below. `"HAPPY BIRTHDAY TO YOU"` should be displayed as `"YOU TO BIRTHDAY HAPPY"`
12. Write a program to append a given string in the following format. `"GOOD MORNING MORNING GOOD"`
13. Write a program to input a text of at least two paragraphs. Interchange the first and second paragraphs and then re-display the text on the screen.
14. Write a program to input a text of at least two paragraphs. Construct an array `PAR` such that `PAR[I]` contains the location of the ith paragraph in text.
15. Write a program to convert the given string `"GOOD MORNING"` to `"good morning"`.
16. Write a program to concatenate two given strings `"Good Morning"` and `"World"`. Display the resultant string.
17. Write a program to check whether the two given strings `"Good Morning"` and `"GOOD MORNING"` are same.
18. Write a program to convert the given string `"hello world"` to `"dlrow olleh"`.
19. Write a program to extract the string `"od Mo"` from the given string `"Good Morning"`.
20. Write a program to insert `"University"` in the given string `"Oxford Press"` so that the string should read as `"Oxford University Press"`.

21. Write a program to read a text, delete all the semi-colons it has, and finally replace all '.' with a ','.
22. Write a program to copy the last n characters of a character array in another character array. Also, convert the lower case letters into upper case letters while copying.
23. Write a program to rewrite the string "Good Morning" to "Good Evening".
24. Write a program to read and display names of employees in a department.
25. Write a program to read a line until a newline is entered.
26. Write a program to read a short story. Rewrite the story by printing the line number before the starting of each line.
27. Write a program to enter a text that contains multiple lines. Display the n lines of text starting from the mth line.
28. Write a program to check whether a pattern exists in a text. If it does, delete the pattern and display it.
29. Write a program to insert a new name in the string array STUD[][], assuming that names are sorted alphabetically.
30. Write a program to delete a name in the string array STUD[][], assuming that names are sorted alphabetically.

Multiple-choice Questions

1. Insert("XXXYYYZZZ", 1, "PPP") =
   (a) PPPXXXYYYZZZ
   (b) XPPPXXYYYZZZ
   (c) XXXYYYZZZPPP
2. Delete("XXXYYYZZZ", 4,3) =
   (a) XXYZ (b) XXXYYZZ
   (c) XXXYZZ
3. If str[] = "Welcome to the world of programming", then SUBSTRING(str, 15, 5) =
   (a) world (b) programming
   (c) welcome (d) none of these
4. strcat() is defined in which header file?
   (a) ctype.h (b) stdio.h
   (c) string.h (d) math.h
5. A string can be read using which function(s)?
   (a) gets() (b) scanf()
   (c) getchar() (d) all of these
6. Replace("XXXYYYZZZ", "XY", "AB") =
   (a) XXABYYZZZ (b) XABYYYZZZ
   (c) ABXXXYYYZZZ
7. The index of U in Oxford University Press is?
   (a) 5 (b) 6
   (c) 7 (d) 8
8. s1 = "HI", s2 = "HELLO", s3 = "BYE". How can we concatenate the three strings?
   (a) strcat(s1,s2,s3)
   (b) strcat(s1(strcat(s2,s3)))
   (c) strcpy(s1, strcat(s2,s3))
9. strlen("Oxford University Press") is ?
   (a) 22 (b) 23
   (c) 24 (d) 25
10. Which function adds a string to the end of another string?
    (a) stradd() (b) strcat()
    (c) strtok() (d) strcpy()

True or False

1. String Hello World can be read using scanf().
2. A string when read using scanf() needs an ampersand character.
3. The gets() function takes the starting address of a string which will hold the input.
4. tolower() is defined in ctype.h header file.
5. If S_1 and S_2 are two strings, then the concatenation operation produces a string which contains the characters of S_2 followed by the characters of S_1.
6. Appending one string to another string involves copying the contents of the source string at the end of the destination string.
7. S1<S2, when in dictionary order, S1 precedes S2.
8. If S1 = "GOOD MORNING", then Substr_Right (S1, 5) = MORNING.
9. Replace ("AAABBBCCC", "X", "YYY")= AAABBBCC.
10. Initializing a string as char str[] = "HELLO"; is incorrect as a null character has not been explicitly added.
11. The scanf() function automatically appends a null character at the end of the string read from the keyboard.
12. String variables can be present either on the left or on the right side of the assignment operator.
13. When a string is initialized during its declaration, the string must be explicitly terminated with a null character.

14. `strcmp("and", "ant");` will return a positive value.

15. Assignment operator can be used to copy the contents of one string into another.

Fill in the blanks

1. Strings are ______.
2. Every string is terminated with a ______.
3. If a string is given as `"AB CD"`, the length of this string is ______.
4. The subscript of a string starts with ______.
5. Characters of a string are stored in ______ memory locations.
6. `char mesg[100];` can store a maximum of ______ characters.
7. ______ function terminates as soon as it finds a blank space.
8. The ASCII code for `A-Z` varies from ______.
9. `toupper()` is used to ______.
10. `S1>S2` means ______.
11. The function to reverse a string is ______.
12. If `S1 = "GOOD MORNING"`, then `Substr_Left (S1, 7) =` ______.
13. `INDEX("Welcome to the world of programming", "world") =` ______.
14. ______ returns the position in the string where the string pattern first occurs.
15. strcmp(str1, str2) returns 1 if ______.
16. ______ function computes the length of a string.
17. Besides printf(), ______ function can be used to print a line of text on the screen.

CHAPTER 5

Structures and Unions

LEARNING OBJECTIVE

Today's modern applications need complex data structures to support them. A structure is a collection of related data items of different data types. It extends the concept of arrays by storing related information of heterogeneous data types together under a single name. It is useful for applications that need a lot more features than those provided by the primitive data types. A union is also a collection of variables of different data types, except that in case of unions, you can only store information in one field at any one time. In this chapter, we will learn how structures and unions are declared, defined, and accessed using the C language.

5.1 INTRODUCTION

A structure is in many ways similar to a record. It stores related information about an entity. Structure is basically a user-defined data type that can store related information (even of different data types) together. The major difference between a structure and an array is that an array can store only information of same data type.

A structure is therefore a collection of variables under a single name. The variables within a structure are of different data types and each has a name that is used to select it from the structure.

5.1.1 Structure Declaration

A structure is declared using the keyword `struct` followed by the structure name. All the variables of the structure are declared within the structure. A structure type is generally declared by using the following syntax:

```
struct struct-name
{
            data_type var-name;
                  data_type var-name;
            ...............
};
```

For example, if we have to define a structure for a student, then the related information for a student probably would be: `roll_number`, `name`, `course`, and `fees`. This structure can be declared as:

```
struct student
{
            int r_no;
            char name[20];
            char course[20];
            float fees;
};
```

Programming Tip

Do not forget to place a semicolon after the declaration of structures and unions.

Now the structure has become a user-defined data type. Each variable name declared within a structure is called a member of the structure. The structure declaration, however, does not allocate any memory or consume storage space. It just gives a template that conveys to the C compiler how the structure would be laid out in the memory and also gives the details of member names. Like any other data type, memory is allocated for the structure when we declare a variable of the structure. For example, we can define a variable of `student` by writing:

```
struct student stud1;
```

Here, `struct student` is a data type and `stud1` is a variable. Look at another way of declaring variables. In the following syntax, the variables are declared at the time of structure declaration.

```
struct student
{
    int r_no;
    char name[20];
    char course[20];
    float fees;
} stud1, stud2;
```

In this declaration we declare two variables `stud1` and `stud2` of the structure `student`. So if you want to declare more than one variable of the structure, then separate the variables using a comma. When we declare variables of the structure, separate memory is allocated for each variable. This is shown in Fig. 5.1.

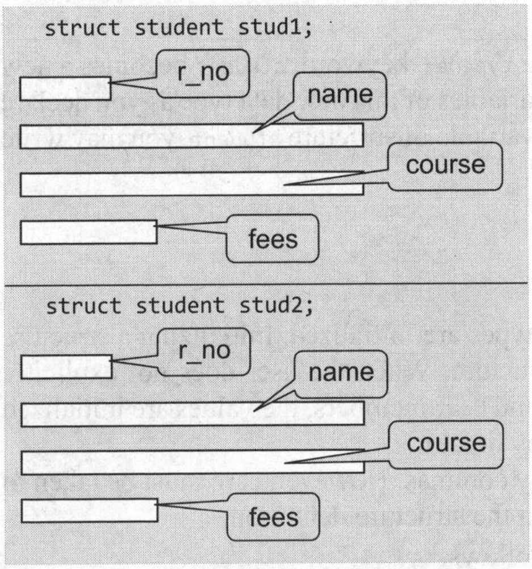

Figure 5.1 Memory allocation for a structure variable

Note Structure type and variable declaration of a structure can be either local or global depending on their placement in the code.

Last but not the least, structure member names and names of the structure follow the same rules as laid down for the names of ordinary variables. However, care should be taken to ensure that the name of structure and the name of a structure member should not be the same. Moreover, structure name and its variable name should also be different.

5.1.2 `Typedef` Declarations

The `typedef` (derived from type definition) keyword enables the programmer to create a new data type name by using an existing data type. By using `typedef`, no new data is created, rather an alternate name is given to a known data type. The general syntax of using the `typedef` keyword is given as:

```
typedef existing_data_type new_data_type;
```

Programming Tip

C does not allow declaration of variables at the time of creating a typedef definition. So variables must be declared in an independent statement.

Note that `typedef` statement does not occupy any memory; it simply defines a new type. For example, if we write

```
typedef int INTEGER;
```

then `INTEGER` is the new name of data type `int`. To declare variables using the new data type name, precede the variable name with the data type name (new). Therefore, to define an integer variable, we may now write

```
INTEGER num=5;
```

When we precede a `struct` name with the `typedef` keyword, then the `struct` becomes a new type. It is used to make the construct shorter with more meaningful names for types already defined by C or for types that you have declared. For example, consider the following declaration:

```
typedef struct student
{
        int r_no;
        char name[20];
        char course[20];
        float fees;
};
```

Now that you have preceded the structure's name with the `typedef` keyword, `student` becomes a new data type. Therefore, now you can straightaway declare the variables of this new data type as you declare the variables of type `int`, `float`, `char`, `double`, etc. To declare a variable of structure `student`, you may write

```
student stud1;
```

Note that we have not written `struct student stud1`.

5.1.3 Initialization of Structures

A structure can be initialized in the same way as other data types are initialized. Initializing a structure means assigning some constants to the members of the structure. When the user does not explicitly initialize the structure, then C automatically does it. For `int` and `float` members, the values are initialized to zero, and `char` and string members are initialized to `'\0'` by default.

The initializers are enclosed in braces and are separated by commas. However, care must be taken to ensure that the initializers match their corresponding types in the structure definition.

The general syntax to initialize a structure variable is as follows:

```
struct struct_name
{
        data_type member_name1;
        data_type member_name2;
        data_type member_name3;
        .......................
}struct_var = {constant1, constant2, constant3,...};
```

or

```
struct struct_name
{
        data_type member_name1;
        data_type member_name2;
        data_type member_name3;
        .......................
};
struct struct_name struct_var = {constant1, constant2, constant 3,...};
```

For example, we can initialize a student structure by writing,

Programming Tip

It is an error to assign a structure of one type to a structure of another type.

```
struct student
{
  int r_no;
  char name[20];
  char course[20];
        float fees;
     }stud1 = {01, "Rahul", "BCA", 45000};
```

Or, by writing,

```
struct student stud1 = {01, "Rahul", "BCA", 45000};
```

Figure 5.2 illustrates how the values will be assigned to individual fields of the structure.

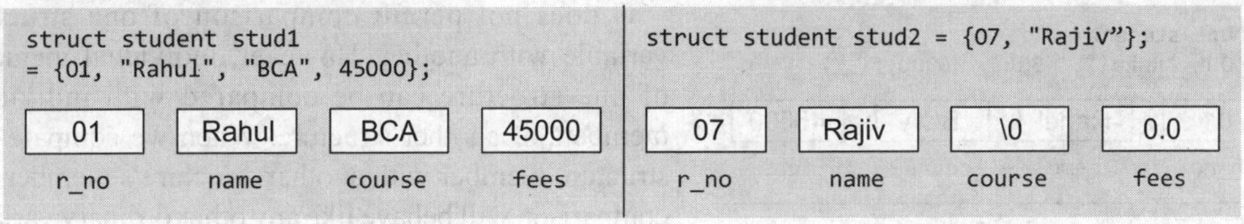

Figure 5.2 Assigning values to structure elements

When all the members of a structure are not initialized, it is called partial initialization. In case of partial initialization, first few members of the structure are initialized and those that are uninitialized are assigned default values.

5.1.4 Accessing the Members of a Structure

Each member of a structure can be used just like a normal variable, but its name will be a bit longer. A structure member variable is generally accessed using a '.' (dot) operator. The syntax of accessing a structure or a member of a structure can be given as:

```
struct_var.member_name
```

The dot operator is used to select a particular member of the structure. For example, to assign values to the individual data members of the structure variable `stud1`, we may write

```
stud1.r_no = 01;
stud1.name = "Rahul";
stud1.course = "BCA";
stud1.fees = 45000;
```

To input values for data members of the structure variable `stud1`, we may write

```
scanf("%d", &stud1.r_no);
scanf("%s", stud1.name);
```

Similarly, to print the values of structure variable `stud1`, we may write

```
printf("%s", stud1.course);
printf("%f", stud1.fees);
```

Memory is allocated only when we declare the variables of the structure. In other words, the memory is allocated only when we instantiate the structure. In the absence of any variable, structure definition is just a template that will be used to reserve memory when a variable of type `struct` is declared.

Once the variables of a structure are defined, we can perform a few operations on them. For example, we can use the assignment operator `(=)` to assign the values of one variable to another.

Note Of all the operators –>, . , ( ), and [] have the highest priority. This is evident from the following statement `stud1.fees++` will be interpreted as `(stud1.fees)++`.

5.1.5 Copying and Comparing Structures

We can assign a structure to another structure of the same type. For example, if we have two structure variables `stud1` and `stud2` of type `struct student` given as

```
struct student stud1 = {01, "Rahul", "BCA", 45000};
struct student stud2;
```

Then to assign one structure variable to another, we will write

```
stud2 = stud1;
```

This statement initializes the members of `stud2` with the values of members of `stud1`. Therefore, now the values of `stud1` and `stud2` can be given as shown in Fig. 5.3.

Programming Tip

An error will be generated if you try to compare two structure variables.

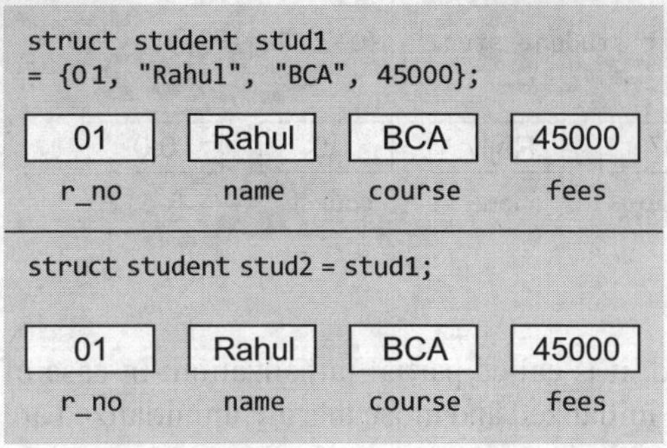

Figure 5.3 Values of structure variables

C does not permit comparison of one structure variable with another. However, individual members of one structure can be compared with individual members of another structure. When we compare one structure member with another structure's member, the comparison will behave like any other ordinary variable comparison. For example, to compare the fees of two students, we will write

```
    if(stud1.fees > stud2.fees) //to check if fees of
stud1 is greater than stud2
```

Programming Examples

1. Write a program using structures to read and display the information about a student.

```
#include <stdio.h>
int main()
{
        struct student
        {
                int roll_no;
                char name[80];
                float fees;
                char DOB[80];
        };
        struct student stud1;
        printf("\n Enter the roll number : ");
        scanf("%d", &stud1.roll_no);
        printf("\n Enter the name : ");
        scanf("%s", stud1.name);
        printf("\n Enter the fees : ");
        scanf("%f", &stud1.fees);
        printf("\n Enter the DOB : ");
        scanf("%s", stud1.DOB);
        printf("\n ********STUDENT'S DETAILS *******");
        printf("\n ROLL No. = %d", stud1.roll_no);
        printf("\n NAME = %s", stud1.name);
        printf("\n FEES = %f", stud1.fees);
        printf("\n DOB = %s", stud1.DOB);
        return 0;
}
```

Output

```
Enter the roll number : 01
Enter the name : Rahul
Enter the fees : 45000
Enter the DOB : 25-09-1991
*******STUDENT'S DETAILS *******
ROLL No. = 01
NAME = Rahul
FEES = 45000.00
DOB = 25-09-1991
```

2. Write a program to read, display, add, and subtract two complex numbers.

```
#include <stdio.h>
int main()
```

```
{
         typedef struct complex
         {
                  int real;
                  int imag;
         }COMPLEX;
         COMPLEX c1, c2, sum_c, sub_c;
         int option;
         do
         {
                  printf("\n ******** MAIN MENU *********");
                  printf("\n 1. Read the complex numbers");
                  printf("\n 2. Display the complex numbers");
                  printf("\n 3. Add the complex numbers");
                  printf("\n 4. Subtract the complex numbers");
                  printf("\n 5. EXIT");
                  printf("\n Enter your option : ");
                  scanf("%d", &option);
                  switch(option)
                  {
                           case 1:
                                    printf("\n Enter the real and imaginary parts of
the                                         first complex number : ");
                                    scanf("%d %d", &c1.real, &c1.imag);
                                    printf("\n Enter the real and imaginary parts of
the                                          second complex number : ");
                                    scanf("%d %d", &c2.real, &c2.imag);
                                    break;
                           case 2:
                                    printf("\n The first complex number is : %d+%di",
                                        c1.real,c1.imag);
                                    printf("\n The second complex number is : %d+%di",
                                        c2.real,c2.imag);
                                    break;
                           case 3:
                                    sum_c.real = c1.real + c2.real;
                                    sum_c.imag = c1.imag + c2.imag;
                                    printf("\n The sum of two complex numbers is :
                                        %d+%di",sum_c.real, sum_c.imag);
                                    break;
                           case 4:
                                    sub_c.real = c1.real - c2.real;
                                    sub_c.imag = c1.imag - c2.imag;
                                    printf("\n The difference between two complex
numbers                                      is :%d+%di", sub_c.real, sub_c.imag);
                                    break;
                  }
          }while(option != 5);
          return 0;
}
```

Output

```
******** MAIN MENU *********
1. Read the complex numbers
2. Display the complex numbers
3. Add the complex numbers
4. Subtract the complex numbers
5. EXIT
```

Because of constraint of space, we will show the MENU only once in all the menu-driven programs.

```
Enter your option : 1
Enter the real and imaginary parts of the first complex number : 2 3
Enter the real and imaginary parts of the second complex number : 4 5
Enter your option : 2
The first complex numbers is : 2+3i
The second complex numbers is : 4+5i
Enter your option : 3
The sum of two complex numbers is : 6+8i
Enter your option : 5
```

5.2 NESTED STRUCTURES

A structure can be placed within another structure, i.e., a structure may contain another structure as its member. A structure that contains another structure as its member is called a *nested structure*.

Let us now see how we declare nested structures. Although it is possible to declare a nested structure with one declaration, it is not recommended. The easier and clearer way is to declare the structures separately and then group them in the higher level structure. When you do this, take care to check that nesting must be done from inside out (from lowest level to the most inclusive level), i.e., declare the innermost structure, then the next level structure, working towards the outer (most inclusive) structure.

```
typedef struct
{
        char first_name[20];
        char mid_name[20];
        char last_name[20];
}NAME;
typedef struct
{
        int dd;
        int mm;
        int yy;
}DATE;
typedef struct
{
        int r_no;
        NAME name;
        char course[20];
        DATE DOB;
        float fees;
} student;
```

In this example, we see that the structure `student` contains two other structures, `NAME` and `DATE`. Both these structures have their own fields. The structure `NAME` has three fields: `first_name`, `mid_name`, and `last_name`. The structure `DATE` also has three fields: `dd`, `mm`, and `yy`, which specify the day, month, and year of the date. Now, to assign values to the structure fields, we will write

```
student stud1;
stud1.r_no = 01;
stud1.name.first_name = "Janak";
stud1.name.mid_name = "Raj";
stud1.name.last_name = "Thareja";
stud1.course = "BCA";
stud1.DOB.dd = 15;
stud1.DOB.mm = 09;
stud1.DOB.yy = 1990;
stud1.fees = 45000;
```

In case of nested structures, we use the dot operator in conjunction with the structure variables to access the members of the innermost as well as the outermost structures. The use of nested structures is illustrated in the next program.

Programming Example

3. Write a program to read and display the information of a student using a nested structure.

```
#include <stdio.h>
int main()
{
        struct DOB
        {
                int day;
                int month;
                int year;
        };
        struct student
        {
                int roll_no;
                char name[100];
                float fees;
                struct DOB date;
        };
        struct student stud1;
        printf("\n Enter the roll number : ");
        scanf("%d", &stud1.roll_no);
        printf("\n Enter the name : ");
        scanf("%s", stud1.name);
        printf("\n Enter the fees : ");
        scanf("%f", &stud1.fees);
        printf("\n Enter the DOB : ");
        scanf("%d %d %d", &stud1.date.day, &stud1.date.month, &stud1.date.year);
        printf("\n ********STUDENT'S DETAILS *******");
        printf("\n ROLL No. = %d", stud1.roll_no);
        printf("\n NAME = %s", stud1.name);
        printf("\n FEES = %f", stud1.fees);
        printf("\n DOB = %d - %d - %d", stud1.date.day, stud1.date.month, stud1.date.
year);
        return 0;
}
```

Output

```
Enter the roll number : 01
Enter the name : Rahul
Enter the fees : 45000
Enter the DOB : 25 09 1991
********STUDENT'S DETAILS *******
ROLL No. = 01
NAME = Rahul
FEES = 45000.00
DOB = 25 - 09 - 1991
```

5.3 ARRAYS OF STRUCTURES

In the above examples, we have seen how to declare a structure and assign values to its data members. Now, we will discuss how an array of structures is declared. For this purpose, let us first analyse where we would need an array of structures.

In a class, we do not have just one student. But there may be at least 30 students. So, the same definition of the structure can be used for all the 30 students. This would be possible when we make an array of structures. An array of structures is declared in the same way as we declare an array of a built-in data type.

Another example where an array of structures is desirable is in case of an organization. An organization has a number of employees. So, defining a separate structure for every employee is not a viable solution. So, here we can have a common structure definition for all the employees. This can again be done by declaring an array of structure employee.

The general syntax for declaring an array of structures can be given as,

```
struct struct_name
{
        data_type member_name1;
        data_type member_name2;
        data_type member_name3;
        .......................
};
struct struct_name struct_var[index];
```

Consider the given structure definition.

```
struct student
{
        int r_no;
        char name[20];
        char course[20];
        float fees;
};
```

A student array can be declared by writing,

```
struct student stud[30];
```

Now, to assign values to the `ith` student of the class, we will write

```
stud[i].r_no = 09;
stud[i].name = "RASHI";
stud[i].course = "MCA";
stud[i].fees = 60000;
```

In order to initialize the array of structure variables at the time of declaration, we can write as follows:

```
struct student stud[3] = {{01, "Aman", "BCA", 45000},{02, "Aryan", "BCA", 60000}, {03,
"John", "BCA", 45000}};
```

Programming Example

4. Write a program to read and display the information of all the students in a class. Then edit the details of the ith student and redisplay the entire information.

```
#include <stdio.h>
#include <string.h>
int main()
{
        struct student
        {
                int roll_no;
                char name[80];
```

```
            int fees;
            char DOB[80];
        };
        struct student stud[50];
        int n, i, num, new_rolno;
        int new_fees;
        char new_DOB[80], new_name[80];
        printf("\n Enter the number of students : ");
        scanf("%d", &n);
        for(i=0;i<n;i++)
        {
            printf("\n Enter the roll number : ");
            scanf("%d", &stud[i].roll_no);
            printf("\n Enter the name : ");
            fgets(stud[i].name, sizeof(stud[i].name), stdin);
            printf("\n Enter the fees : ");
            scanf("%d",&stud[i].fees); getchar();
            printf("\n Enter the DOB : ");
            fgets(stud[i].DOB, sizeof(stud[i].DOB), stdin);
        }
        for(i=0;i<n;i++)
        {
            printf("\n ********DETAILS OF STUDENT %d*******", i+1);
            printf("\n ROLL No. = %d", stud[i].roll_no);
            printf("\n NAME = %s", stud[i].name);
            printf("\n FEES = %d", stud[i].fees);
            printf("\n DOB = %s", stud[i].DOB);
        }
        printf("\n Enter the student number whose record has to be edited : ");
        scanf("%d", &num);
        num= num-1;
        printf("\n Enter the new roll number : ");
        scanf("%d", &new_rolno);
        printf("\n Enter the new name : ");
        fgets(new_name, sizeof(new_name), stdin);
        printf("\n Enter the new fees : ");
        scanf("%d", &new_fees);
        printf("\n Enter the new DOB : ");
        fgets(new_DOB, sizeof(new_DOB), stdin);
        stud[num].roll_no = new_rolno;
        strcpy(stud[num].name, new_name);
        stud[num].fees = new_fees;
        strcpy (stud[num].DOB, new_DOB);
        for(i=0;i<n;i++)
        {
            printf("\n ********DETAILS OF STUDENT %d*******", i+1);
            printf("\n ROLL No. = %d", stud[i].roll_no);
            printf("\n NAME = %s", stud[i].name);
            printf("\n FEES = %d", stud[i].fees);
            printf("\n DOB = %s", stud[i].DOB);
        }
        return 0;
}
```

Output

```
Enter the number of students : 2
Enter the roll number : 1
Enter the name : kirti
```

```
Enter the fees : 5678
Enter the DOB : 9 9 91
Enter the roll number : 2
Enter the name : kangana
Enter the fees : 5678
Enter the DOB : 27 8 91
********DETAILS OF STUDENT 1*******
ROLL No. = 1
NAME = kirti
FEES = 5678
DOB = 9 9 91
********DETAILS OF STUDENT 2*******
ROLL No. = 2
NAME = kangana
FEES = 5678
DOB = 27 8 91
Enter the student number whose record has to be edited : 2
Enter the new roll number : 2
Enter the new name : kangana khullar
Enter the new fees : 7000
Enter the new DOB : 27 8 92
********DETAILS OF STUDENT 1*******
ROLL No. = 1
NAME = kirti
FEES = 5678
DOB = 9 9 91
********DETAILS OF STUDENT 2*******
ROLL No. = 2
NAME = kangana khullar
FEES = 7000
DOB = 27 8 92
```

5.4 STRUCTURES AND FUNCTIONS

For structures to be fully useful, we must have a mechanism to pass them to functions and return them. A function may access the members of a structure in three ways as shown in Fig. 5.4.

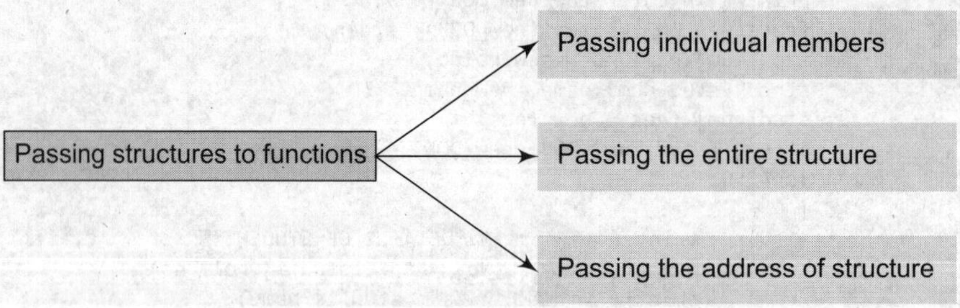

Figure 5.4 Different ways of passing structures to functions

5.4.1 Passing Individual Members

To pass any individual member of a structure to a function, we must use the direct selection operator to refer to the individual members. The called program does not know if a variable is an ordinary variable or a structured member. Look at the code given below which illustrates this concept.

```
#include <stdio.h>
typedef struct
```

```
{
        int x;
        int y;
}POINT;
void display(int, int);
int main()
{
        POINT p1 = {2, 3};
        display(p1.x, p1.y);
        return 0;
}
void display(int a, int b)
{
        printf(" The coordinates of the point are: %d %d", a, b);
}
```

Output

```
The coordinates of the point are: 2 3
```

5.4.2 Passing the Entire Structure

Just like any other variable, we can pass an entire structure as a function argument. When a structure is passed as an argument, it is passed using the call by value method, i.e., a copy of each member of the structure is made.

The general syntax for passing a structure to a function and returning a structure can be given as,

```
struct struct_name func_name(struct struct_name struct_var);
```

The above syntax can vary as per the requirement. For example, in some situations, we may want a function to receive a structure but return a void or the value of some other data type. The code given below passes a structure to a function using the call by value method.

```
#include <stdio.h>
typedef struct
{
        int x;
        int y;
}POINT;
void display(POINT);
int main()
{
        POINT p1 = {2, 3};
        display(p1);
        return 0;
}
void display(POINT p)
{
        printf("The coordinates of the point are: %d %d", p.x, p.y);
}
```

Programming Example

5. Write a program to read, display, add, and subtract two distances. Distance must be defined using kms and meters.

```
#include <stdio.h>
typedef struct distance
{
```

```
        int kms;
        int meters;
}DISTANCE;
DISTANCE add_distance (DISTANCE, DISTANCE);
DISTANCE subtract_distance (DISTANCE, DISTANCE);
DISTANCE d1, d2, d3, d4;
int main()
{
        int option;
        do
        {
                printf("\n ******** MAIN MENU *********");
                printf("\n 1. Read the distances ");
                printf("\n 2. Display the distances");
                printf("\n 3. Add the distances");
                printf("\n 4. Subtract the distances");
                printf("\n 5. EXIT");
                printf("\n Enter your option : ");
                scanf("%d", &option);
                switch(option)
                {
                        case 1:
                            printf("\n Enter the first distance in kms and meters:
");
                            scanf("%d %d", &d1.kms, &d1.meters);
                            printf("\n Enter the second distance in kms and meters:
");
                            scanf("%d %d", &d2.kms, &d2.meters);
                            break;
                        case 2:
                            printf("\n The first distance is : %d kms %d meters",
    d1.kms, d1.meters);
                            printf("\n The second distance is : %d kms %d meters",
d2.kms, d2.meters);
                            break;
                        case 3:
                            d3 = add_distance(d1, d2);
                            printf("\n The sum of two distances is : %d kms %d
meters", d3.kms, d3.meters);
                            break;
                        case 4:
                            d4 = subtract_distance(d1, d2);
                            printf("\n The difference between two distances is :
%d kms %d meters", d4.kms, d4.meters);
                            break;
                }
        }while(option != 5);
        return 0;
}
DISTANCE add_distance(DISTANCE d1, DISTANCE d2)
{
        DISTANCE sum;
        sum.meters = d1.meters + d2.meters;
        sum.kms = d1.kms + d2.kms;
        while (sum.meters >= 1000)
```

```
        {
                sum.meters = sum.meters % 1000;
                sum.kms += 1;
        }
        return sum;
}
DISTANCE subtract_distance(DISTANCE d1, DISTANCE d2)
{
        DISTANCE sub;
        if(d1.kms > d2.kms)
        {
                sub.meters = d1.meters - d2.meters;
                sub.kms = d1.kms - d2.kms;
        }
        else
        {
                sub.meters = d2.meters - d1.meters;
                sub.kms = d2.kms - d1.kms;
        }
        if(sub.meters < 0)
        {
                sub.kms = sum.kms - 1;
                sub.meters = sum.meters + 1000;
        }
        return sub;
}
```

Output

```
******** MAIN MENU *********
1. Read the distances
2. Display the distances
3. Add the distances
4. Subtract the distances
5. EXIT
Enter your option : 1
Enter the first distance in kms and meters: 5 300
Enter the second distance in kms and meters: 3 400
Enter your option : 3
The sum of two distances is: 8 kms 700 meters
Enter your option : 5
```

Let us summarize some points that must be considered while passing a structure to the called function.

- If the called function is returning a copy of the entire structure then it must be declared as `struct` followed by the structure name.
- The structure variable used as parameter in the function declaration must be the same as that of the actual argument in the called function (and that should be the name of the `struct` type).
- When a function returns a structure, then in the calling function the returned structure must be assigned to a structure variable of the same type.

5.4.3 Passing Structures through Pointers

Passing large structures to functions using the call by value method is very inefficient. Therefore, it is preferred to pass structures through pointers. It is possible to create a pointer to almost any type in C, including the user-defined types. It is extremely common to create pointers to structures. Like in other cases, a pointer to a structure is never itself a structure, but merely a variable that holds the address of a structure. The syntax to declare a pointer to a structure can be given as,

```
struct struct_name
{
            data_type member_name1;
            data_type member_name2;
            data_type member_name3;
            .......................
}*ptr;
```

or,

```
struct struct_name *ptr;
```

For our `student` structure, we can declare a pointer variable by writing

```
struct student *ptr_stud, stud;
```

The next thing to do is to assign the address of `stud` to the pointer using the address operator (`&`), as we would do in case of any other pointer. So to assign the address, we will write

```
ptr_stud = &stud;
```

To access the members of a structure, we can write

```
/* get the structure, then select a member */
(*ptr_stud).roll_no;
```

Since parentheses have a higher precedence than `*`, writing this statement would work well. But this statement is not easy to work with, especially for a beginner. So, C introduces a new operator to do the same task. This operator is known as 'pointing-to' operator (->). It can be used as:

```
/* the roll_no in the structure ptr_stud points to */
ptr_stud -> roll_no = 01;
```

This statement is far easier than its alternative.

Programming Tip

The selection operator (->) is a single token, so do not place any white space between them.

Programming Examples

6. Write a program to initialize the members of a structure by using a pointer to the structure.

```
#include <stdio.h>
struct student
{
        int r_no;
        char name[20];
        char course[20];
        int fees;
};
int main()
{
        struct student stud1, *ptr_stud1;
        ptr_stud1 = &stud1;
        printf("\n Enter the details of the student :");
        printf("\n Enter the Roll Number =");
        scanf("%d", &ptr_stud1 -> r_no); getchar();
        printf("\n Enter the Name = ");
        fgets(ptr_stud1 -> name, sizeof(ptr_stud1 -> name), stdin);
        printf("\n Enter the Course = ");
        fgets(ptr_stud1 -> course, sizeof(ptr_stud1 -> course), stdin);
        printf("\n Enter the Fees = ");
```

```
        scanf("%d", &ptr_stud1->fees);
        printf("\n DETAILS OF THE STUDENT");
        printf("\n ROLL NUMBER = %d", ptr_stud1 -> r_no);
        printf("\n NAME = %s", ptr_stud1 -> name);
        printf("\n COURSE = %s", ptr_stud1 -> course);
        printf("\n FEES = %d", ptr_stud1 -> fees);
        return 0;
}
```

Output

```
Enter the details of the student:
Enter the Roll Number = 02
Enter the Name = Aditya
Enter the Course = MCA
Enter the Fees = 60000
DETAILS OF THE STUDENT
ROLL NUMBER = 02
NAME = Aditya
COURSE = MCA
FEES = 60000
```

7. Write a program, using an array of pointers to a structure, to read and display the data of students.

```
#include <stdio.h>
#include <stdlib.h>
struct student
{
        int r_no;
        char name[20];
        char course[20];
        int fees;
};
struct student *ptr_stud[10];
int main()
{
        int i, n;
        printf("\n Enter the number of students : ");
        scanf("%d", &n);
        for(i=0;i<n;i++)
        {
        ptr_stud[i] = (struct student *)malloc(sizeof(struct student));
        printf("\n Enter the data for student %d ", i+1);
        printf("\n ROLL NO.: ");
        scanf("%d", &ptr_stud[i]->r_no);
        printf("\n NAME: ");
        fgets(ptr_stud[i]->name, sizeof(ptr_stud[i] -> name), stdin);
        printf("\n COURSE: ");
        fgets(ptr_stud[i]->course, sizeof(ptr_stud[i] -> course),
        printf("\n FEES: ");
        scanf("%d", &ptr_stud[i]->fees);
        }
printf("\n DETAILS OF STUDENTS");
for(i=0;i<n;i++)
        {
        printf("\n ROLL NO. = %d", ptr_stud[i]->r_no);
        printf("\n NAME = %s", ptr_stud[i]->name);
        printf("\n COURSE = %s", ptr_stud[i]->course);
        printf("\n FEES = %d", ptr_stud[i]->fees);
        }
for(i=0;i<n;i++)
        free(ptr_stud[i]);
return 0;
}
```

Output

```
Enter the number of students : 1
Enter the data for student 1
ROLL NO.: 01
NAME: Rahul
COURSE: BCA
FEES: 45000
DETAILS OF STUDENTS
ROLL NO. = 01
NAME = Rahul
COURSE = BCA
FEES = 45000
```

8. Write a program that passes a pointer to a structure to a function.

```
#include <stdio.h>
#include <stdlib.h>
struct student
{
        int r_no;
        char name[20];
        char course[20];
        int fees;
};
void display (struct student *);
int main()
{
        struct student *ptr;
        ptr = (struct student *)malloc(sizeof(struct student));
        printf("\n Enter the data for the student ");
        printf("\n ROLL NO.: ");
        scanf("%d", &ptr->r_no); getchar();
        printf("\n NAME: ");
        fgets(ptr->name, sizeof(ptr -> name), stdin);
        printf("\n COURSE: ");
        fgets(ptr->course, sizeof(ptr -> course), stdin); //
        printf("\n FEES: ");
        scanf("%d", &ptr->fees);
        display(ptr); free(ptr);
        return 0;
}
void display(struct student *ptr)
{
        printf("\n DETAILS OF STUDENT");
        printf("\n ROLL NO. = %d", ptr->r_no);
        printf("\n NAME = %s", ptr->name);
        printf("\n COURSE = %s ", ptr->course);
        printf("\n FEES = %d", ptr->fees);
}
```

Output

```
Enter the data for the student
ROLL NO.: 01
NAME: Rahul
COURSE: BCA
FEES: 45000
DETAILS OF STUDENT
ROLL NO. = 01
NAME = Rahul
COURSE = BCA
FEES = 45000
```

5.5 SELF-REFERENTIAL STRUCTURES

Self-referential structures are those structures that contain a reference to the data of its same type. That is, a self-referential structure, in addition to other data, contains a pointer to a data that is of the same type as that of the structure. For example, consider the structure node given below.

```
struct node
    {
            int val;
            struct node *next;
    };
```

Here, the structure node will contain two types of data: an integer `val` and a pointer `next`. You must be wondering why we need such a structure. Actually, self-referential structure is the foundation of other data structures. We will be using them throughout this book and their purpose will be clearer to you when we discuss linked lists, trees, and graphs.

5.6 UNIONS

Similar to structures, a union is a collection of variables of different data types. The only difference between a structure and a union is that in case of unions, you can only store information in one field at any one time. To better understand a union, think of it as a chunk of memory that is used to store variables of different types. When a new value is assigned to a field, the existing data is replaced with the new data.

Thus, unions are used to save memory. They are useful for applications that involve multiple members, where values need not be assigned to all the members at any one time.

Programming Tip

It is an error to use a structure/ union variable as a member of its own struct type structure or union type union, respectively.

5.6.1 Declaring a Union

The syntax for declaring a union is the same as that of declaring a structure. The only difference is that instead of using the keyword `struct`, the keyword `union` would be used. The syntax for union declaration can be given as

```
union union-name
    {
      data_type var-name;
      data_type var-name;
      ..................
    };
```

Again the `typedef` keyword can be used to simplify the declaration of union variables. The most important thing to remember about a union is that the size of a union is the size of its largest field. This is because sufficient number of bytes must be reserved to store the largest sized field.

Programming Tip

Variable of a structure or a union can be declared at the time of structure/union definition by placing the variable name after the closing brace and before the semicolon.

5.6.2 Accessing a Member of a Union

A member of a union can be accessed using the same syntax as that of a structure. To access the fields of a union, use the dot operator (.), i.e., the union variable name followed by the dot operator followed by the member name.

5.6.3 Initializing Unions

The difference between a structure and a union is that in case of a union, the fields share the same memory space, so new data replaces any existing data. Look at the following code and observe the difference between a structure and union when their fields are to be initialized.

```
#include <stdio.h>
typedef struct POINT1
{
        int x, y;
};
typedef union POINT2
{
        int x;
        int y;
};
int main()
{
        struct POINT1 P1 = {2,3};
        // POINT2 P2 ={4,5}; Illegal in case of unions
        union POINT2 P2;
        P2.x = 4;
        P2.y = 5;
        printf("\n The coordinates of P1 are %d and %d", P1.x, P1.y);
        printf("\n The coordinates of P2 are %d and %d", P2.x, P2.y);
        return 0;
}
```

Output

```
The coordinates of P1 are 2 and 3
The coordinates of P2 are 5 and 5
```

In this code, `POINT1` is a structure name and `POINT2` is a union name. However, both the declarations are almost same (except the keywords—`struct` and `union`). In `main()`, we can see the difference between structures and unions while initializing values. The fields of a union cannot be initialized all at once.

Programming Tip

The size of a union is equal to the size of its largest member.

Look at the output carefully. For the structure variable the output is as expected but for the union variable the answer does not seem to be correct. To understand the concept of union, execute the following code. The code given below just re-arranges the `printf` statements. You will be surprised to see the result.

```
#include <stdio.h>
typedef struct POINT1
{
        int x, y;
};
typedef union POINT2
{
        int x;
        int y;
};
int main()
{
        struct POINT1 P1 = {2,3};
        union POINT2 P2;
        printf("\n The coordinates of P1 are %d and %d", P1.x, P1.y);
        P2. x = 4;
        printf("\n The x coordinate of P2 is %d", P2.x);
        P2.y = 5;
```

```
        printf("\n The y coordinate of P2 is %d", P2.y);
        return 0;
}
```

Output

```
The coordinates of P1 are 2 and 3
The x coordinate of P2 is 4
The y coordinate of P2 is 5
```

Here although the output is correct, the data is still overwritten in memory.

5.7 ARRAYS OF UNION VARIABLES

Like structures we can also have an array of union variables. However, because of the problem of new data overwriting existing data in the other fields, the program may not display the accurate results.

```
#include <stdio.h>
union POINT
{
        int x, y;
};
int main()
{
        int i;
        union POINT points[3];
        points[0].x = 2;
        points[0].y = 3;
        points[1].x = 4;
        points[1].y = 5;
        points[2].x = 6;
        points[2].y = 7;
        for(i=0;i<3;i++)
                printf("\n Coordinates of Point[%d] are %d and %d", i, points[i].x,
                points[i].y);
        return 0;
}
```

Output

```
Coordinates of Point[0] are 3 and 3
Coordinates of Point[1] are 5 and 5
Coordinates of Point[2] are 7 and 7
```

5.8 UNIONS INSIDE STRUCTURES

Generally, unions can be very useful when declared inside a structure. Consider an example in which you want a field of a structure to contain a string or an integer, depending on what the user specifies. The following code illustrates such a scenario:

```
#include <stdio.h>
struct student
{
        union
        {
                char name[20];
                int roll_no;
        };
        int marks;
};
int main()
```

```
{
        struct student stud;
        char choice;
        printf("\n You can enter the name or roll number of the student");
        printf("\n Do you want to enter the name? (Y or N): ");
        scanf(" %c", &choice);
        if(choice=='y' || choice=='Y')
        {
                printf("\n Enter the name: ");
                scanf(" %[^\n]", stud.name
        }
        else
        {
                printf("\n Enter the roll number: ");
                scanf("%d", &stud.roll_no); getchar();
        }
        printf("\n Enter the marks: ");
        scanf("%d", &stud.marks);
        if(choice=='y' || choice=='Y')
                printf("\n Name: %s ", stud.name);
        else
                printf("\n Roll Number: %d ", stud.roll_no);
        printf("\n Marks: %d", stud.marks);
        return 0;
}
```

Now in this code, we have a union embedded within a structure. We know the fields of a union will share memory, so in the main program we ask the user which data he/she would like to store and depending on his/her choice the appropriate field is used.

Points to Remember

- Structure is a user-defined data type that can store related information (even of different data types) together.
- A structure is declared using the keyword `struct`, followed by the structure name.
- The structure definition does not allocate any memory or consume storage space. It just gives a template that conveys to the C compiler how the structure is laid out in the memory and gives details of the member names. Like any data type, memory is allocated for the structure when we declare a variable of the structure.
- When a `struct` name is preceded with the keyword `typedef`, then the `struct` becomes a new type.
- When the user does not explicitly initialize the structure, then C automatically does it. For `int` and `float` members, the values are initialized to zero and `char` and string members are initialized to `'\0'` by default.
- A structure member variable is generally accessed using a `'.'` (dot) operator.
- A structure can be placed within another structure. That is, a structure may contain another structure as its member. Such a structure is called a nested structure.
- Self-referential structures are those structures that contain a reference to data of its same type. That is, a self-referential structure, in addition to other data, contains a pointer to a data that is of the same type as that of the structure.
- A union is a collection of variables of different data types in which memory is shared among these variables. The size of a union is equal to the size of its largest member.
- The only difference between a structure and a union is that in case of unions information can only be stored in one member at a time.

Exercises

Review Questions

1. What is the advantage of using structures?
2. Structure declaration reserves memory for the structure. Comment on this statement with valid justifications.
3. Differentiate between a structure and an array.
4. Write a short note on structures and inter-process communication.
5. Explain the utility of the keyword `typedef` in structures.
6. Explain with an example how structures are initialized.
7. Is it possible to create an array of structures? Explain with the help of an example.
8. What do you understand by a union?
9. Differentiate between a structure and a union.
10. How is a structure name different from a structure variable?
11. Explain how members of a union are accessed.
12. Write a short note on nested structures.
13. In which applications unions can be useful?

Programming Exercises

1. Declare a structure that represents the following hierarchical information.
   (a) Student
   (b) Roll Number
   (c) Name
      (i) First name
      (ii) Middle Name
      (iii) Last Name
   (d) Sex
   (e) Date of Birth
      (i) Day
      (ii) Month
      (iii) Year
   (f) Marks
      (i) English
      (ii) Mathematics
      (iii) Computer Science
2. Define a structure to store the name, an array `marks[]` which stores the marks of three different subjects, and a character grade. Write a program to display the details of the student whose name is entered by the user. Use the structure definition of the first question to make an array of students. Display the name of the students who have secured less than 40% of the aggregate.
3. Modify Question 2 to print each student's average marks and the class average (that includes average of all the student's marks).
4. Make an array of students as illustrated in Question 1 and write a program to display the details of the student with the given Date of Birth.
5. Write a program to find smallest of three numbers using structures.
6. Write a program to calculate the distance between the given points (6,3) and (2,2).
7. Write a program to read and display the information about all the employees in a department. Edit the details of the ith employee and redisplay the information.
8. Write a program to add and subtract height 6'2" and 5'4".
9. Write a program to add and subtract 10hrs 20mins 50sec and 5hrs 30min 40sec.
10. Write a program using structure to check if the current year is leap year or not.
11. Write a program using pointer to structure to initialize the members of an employee structure. Use functions to print the employee's information.
12. Write a program to create a structure with the information given below. Then, read and print the data.
    Employee[10]
    (a) Emp_Id
    (b) Name
       (i) First Name
       (ii) Middle Name
       (iii) Last Name
    (c) Address
       (i) Area
       (ii) City
       (iii) State
    (d) Age
    (e) Salary
    (f) Designation

13. Define a structure date containing three integers—day, month, and year. Write a program using functions to read data, to validate the date entered by the user and then print the date on the screen. For example, if you enter 29,2,2010 then that is an invalid date as 2010 is not a leap year. Similarly 31,6,2007 is invalid as June does not have 31 days.
14. Using the structure definition of the above program, write a function to increment the date. Make sure that the incremented date is a valid date.
15. Modify the above program to add a specific number of days to the given date.
16. Write a program to define a structure vector. Then write functions to read data, print data, add two vectors and scale the members of a vector by a factor of 10.
17. Write a program to define a structure for a hotel that has members— name, address, grade, number of rooms, and room charges. Write a function to print the names of hotels in a particular grade. Also write a function to print names of hotels that have room charges less than the specified value.
18. Write a program to define a union and a structure both having exactly the same members. Using the `sizeof` operator, print the size of structure variable as well as union variable and comment on the result.
19. Declare a structure time that has three fields—hr, min, sec. Create two variables start_time and end_time. Input their values from the user. Then while start_time does not reach the end_time, display GOOD DAY on the screen.
20. Declare a structure fraction that has two fields—numerator and denominator. Create two variables and compare them using function. Return 0 if the two fractions are equal, –1 if the first fraction is less than the second and 1 otherwise. You may convert a fraction into a floating point number for your convenience.
21. Declare a structure POINT. Input the coordinates of a point variable and determine the quadrant in which it lies. The following table can be used to determine the quadrant

Quadrant	X	Y
1	Positive	Positive
2	Negative	Positive
3	Negative	Negative
4	Positive	Negative

22. Write a program to calculate the area of one of the geometric figures—circle, rectangle or a triangle. Write a function to calculate the area. The function must receive one parameter which is a structure that contains the type of figure and the size of the components needed to calculate the area must be a part of a union. Note that a circle requires just one component, rectangle requires two components and a triangle requires the size of three components to calculate the area.

Multiple-choice Questions

1. A data structure that can store related information together is called
   (a) Array (b) String
   (c) Structure (d) All of these
2. A data structure that can store related information of different data types together is called
   (a) Array (b) String
   (c) Structure (d) All of these
3. Memory for a structure is allocated at the time of
   (a) Structure definition
   (b) Structure variable declaration
   (c) Structure declaration
   (d) Function declaration
4. A structure member variable is generally accessed using
   (a) Address operator (b) Dot operator
   (c) Comma operator (d) Ternary operator
5. A structure that can be placed within another structure is known as
   (a) Self-referential structure
   (b) Nested structure
   (c) Parallel structure
   (d) Pointer to structure
6. A union member variable is generally accessed using the
   (a) Address operator (b) Dot operator
   (c) Comma operator (d) Ternary operator
7. `typedef` can be used with which of these data types?
   (a) struct (b) union
   (c) enum (d) all of these

True or False

1. Structures contain related information of the same data type.
2. Structure declaration reserves memory for the structure.

3. When the user does not explicitly initialize the structure, then C automatically does it.
4. The dereference operator is used to select a particular member of the structure.
5. A nested structure contains another structure as its member.
6. A struct type is a primitive data type.
7. C permits copying of one structure variable to another.
8. Unions and structures are initialized in the same way.
9. A structure cannot have a union as its member.
10. C permits nested unions.
11. A field in a structure can itself be a structure.
12. No two members of a union should have the same name.
13. A union can have another union as its member.
14. New variables can be created using the typedef keyword.

Fill in the Blanks

1. Structure is a ______ data type.
2. ______ is just a template that will be used to reserve memory when a variable of type `struct` is declared.
3. A structure is declared using the keyword `struct` followed by a ______.
4. When we precede a `struct` name with ______, then the `struct` becomes a new type.
5. For `int` and `float` structure members, the values are initialized to ______.
6. `char` and `string` structure members are initialized to ______ by default.
7. A structure member variable is generally accessed using a ______.
8. A structure placed within another structure is called a ______.
9. ______ structures contain a reference to data of its same type.
10. Memory is allocated for a structure when ______ is done.
11. ______ is a collection of data under one name in which memory is shared among the members.
12. The selection operator is used to ______.
13. ______ permits sharing of memory among different types of data.

CHAPTER 6

Linked Lists

LEARNING OBJECTIVE

A linked list is a collection of data elements called nodes in which the linear representation is given by links from one node to the next node. In this chapter, we are going to discuss different types of linked lists and the operations that can be performed on these lists.

6.1 INTRODUCTION

We have studied that an array is a linear collection of data elements in which the elements are stored in consecutive memory locations. While declaring arrays, we have to specify the size of the array, which will restrict the number of elements that the array can store. For example, if we declare an array as `int marks[10]`, then the array can store a maximum of 10 data elements but not more than that. But what if we are not sure of the number of elements in advance? Moreover, to make efficient use of memory, the elements must be stored randomly at any location rather than in consecutive locations. So, there must be a data structure that removes the restrictions on the maximum number of elements and the storage condition to write efficient programs.

Linked list is a data structure that is free from the aforementioned restrictions. A linked list does not store its elements in consecutive memory locations and the user can add any number of elements to it. However, unlike an array, a linked list does not allow random access of data. Elements in a linked list can be accessed only in a sequential manner. But like an array, insertions and deletions can be done at any point in the list in a constant time.

6.1.1 Basic Terminologies

A linked list, in simple terms, is a linear collection of data elements. These data elements are called *nodes*. Linked list is a data structure which in turn can be used to implement other data structures. Thus, it acts as a building block to implement data structures such as stacks, queues, and their variations. A linked list can be perceived as a train or a sequence of nodes in which each node contains one or more data fields and a pointer to the next node.

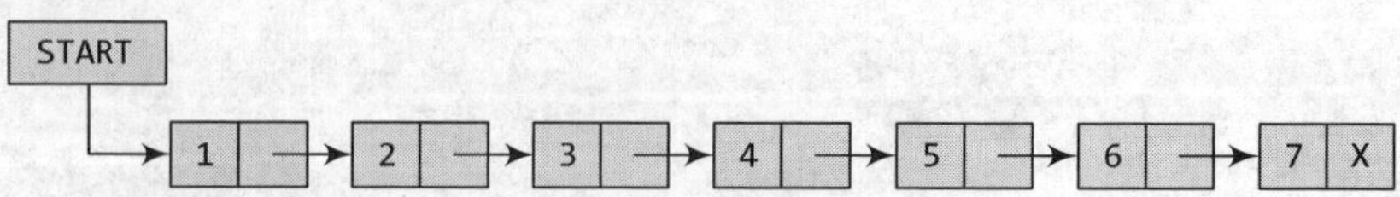

Figure 6.1 Simple linked list

In Fig. 6.1, we can see a linked list in which every node contains two parts, an integer and a pointer to the next node. The left part of the node which contains data may include a simple data type, an array, or a structure. The right part of the node contains a pointer to the next node (or address of the next node in sequence). The last node will have no next node connected to it, so it will store a special value called `NULL`. In Fig. 6.1, the `NULL` pointer is represented by `X`. While programming, we usually define `NULL` as –1. Hence, a `NULL` pointer denotes the end of the list. Since in a linked list, every node contains a pointer to another node which is of the same type, it is also called a *self-referential data type.*

Linked lists contain a pointer variable `START` that stores the address of the first node in the list. We can traverse the entire list using `START` which contains the address of the first node; the next part of the first node in turn stores the address of its succeeding node. Using this technique, the individual nodes of the list will form a chain of nodes. If `START = NULL`, then the linked list is empty and contains no nodes.

In C, we can implement a linked list using the following code:

```
struct node
{
        int data;
        struct node *next;
};
```

Note Linked lists provide an efficient way of storing related data and perform basic operations such as insertion, deletion, and updation of information at the cost of extra space required for storing address of the next node.

START: 1

	Data	Next
1	H	4
2		
3		
4	E	7
5		
6		
7	L	8
8	L	10
9		
10	O	-1

Figure 6.2 `START` pointing to the first element of the linked list in the memory

Let us see how a linked list is maintained in the memory. In order to form a linked list, we need a structure called *node* which has two fields, `DATA` and `NEXT`. `DATA` will store the information part and `NEXT` will store the address of the next node in sequence. Consider Fig. 6.2.

In the figure, we can see that the variable `START` is used to store the address of the first node. Here, in this example, `START = 1`, so the first data is stored at address 1, which is `H`. The corresponding `NEXT` stores the address of the next node, which is 4. So, we will look at address 4 to fetch the next data item. The second data element obtained from address 4 is `E`. Again, we see the corresponding `NEXT` to go to the next node. From the entry in the `NEXT`, we get the next address, that is 7, and fetch `L` as the data. We repeat this procedure until we reach a position where the `NEXT` entry contains –1 or `NULL`, as this would denote the end of the linked list. When we traverse `DATA` and `NEXT` in this manner, we finally see that the linked list in the above example stores characters that when put together form the word `HELLO`.

Note that Fig. 6.2 shows a chunk of memory locations which range from 1 to 10. The shaded portion contains data for other applications. Remember that the nodes of a linked list need not be in consecutive memory locations. In our example, the nodes for the linked list are stored at addresses 1, 4, 7, 8, and 10.

Let us take another example to see how two linked lists are maintained together in the computer's memory. For example, the students of Class XI of Science group are asked to choose between Biology and Computer Science. Now, we will maintain two linked lists, one for each subject. That is, the first linked list will contain the roll numbers of all the students who have opted for Biology and the second list will contain the roll numbers of students who have chosen Computer Science.

Now, look at Fig. 6.3, two different linked lists are simultaneously maintained in the memory. There is no ambiguity in traversing through the list because each list maintains a separate `START` pointer, which gives the address of the first node of their respective linked lists. The rest of the nodes are reached by looking at the value stored in the `NEXT`.

START 1 (Biology): 1

START 2 (Computer Science): 2

	Roll No	Next
1	S01	3
2	S02	5
3	S03	8
4		
5	S04	7
6		
7	S05	10
8	S06	11
9		
10	S07	12
11	S08	13
12	S09	-1
13	S10	15
14		
15	S11	-1

Figure 6.3 Two linked lists which are simultaneously maintained in the memory

By looking at the figure, we can conclude that roll numbers of the students who have opted for Biology are S01, S03, S06, S08, S10, and S11. Similarly, roll numbers of the students who chose Computer Science are S02, S04, S05, S07, and S09.

We have already said that the DATA part of a node may contain just a single data item, an array, or a structure. Let us take an example to see how a structure is maintained in a linked list that is stored in the memory.

Consider a scenario in which the roll number, name, aggregate, and grade of students are stored using linked lists. Now, we will see how the NEXT pointer is used to store the data alphabetically. This is shown in Fig. 6.4.

6.1.2 Linked Lists versus Arrays

Both arrays and linked lists are a linear collection of data elements. But unlike an array, a linked list does not store its nodes in consecutive memory locations. Another point of difference between an array and a linked list is that a linked list does not allow random access of data. Nodes in a linked list can be accessed only in a sequential manner. But like an array, insertions and deletions can be done at any point in the list in a constant time.

START: 18

	Roll No	Name	Aggregate	Grade	Next
1	S01	Ram	78	Distinction	6
2	S02	Shyam	64	First division	14
3					
4	S03	Mohit	89	Outstanding	17
5					
6	S04	Rohit	77	Distinction	2
7	S05	Varun	86	Outstanding	10
8	S06	Karan	65	First division	12
9					
10	S07	Veena	54	Second division	-1
11	S08	Meera	67	First division	4
12	S09	Krish	45	Third division	13
13	S10	Kusum	91	Outstanding	11
14	S11	Silky	72	First division	7
15					
16					
17	S12	Monica	75	Distinction	1
18	S13	Ashish	63	First division	19
19	S14	Gaurav	61	First division	8

Figure 6.4 Students' linked list

Another advantage of a linked list over an array is that we can add any number of elements in the list. This is not possible in case of an array. For example, if we declare an array as `int marks[20]`, then the array can store a maximum of 20 data elements only. There is no such restriction in case of a linked list.

Thus, linked lists provide an efficient way of storing related data and performing basic operations such as insertion, deletion, and updation of information at the cost of extra space required for storing the address of next nodes.

6.1.3 Memory Allocation and De-allocation for a Linked List

We have seen how a linked list is represented in the memory. If we want to add a node to an already existing linked list in the memory, we first find free space in the memory and then use it to store the information. For example, consider the linked list shown in Fig. 6.5. The linked list contains the roll number of students, marks obtained by them in Biology, and finally a NEXT field which stores the address of the next node in sequence. Now, if a new student joins the class and is asked to appear for the same test that the other students had taken, then the new student's marks should also be recorded in the linked list. For this purpose, we find a free space and store the information there. In Fig. 6.5 the grey shaded portion shows free space, and thus we have 4 memory locations available. We can use any one of them to store our data. This is illustrated in Figs 6.5(a) and (b).

Now, the question is which part of the memory is available and which part is occupied? When we delete a node from a linked list, then who changes the status of the memory occupied by it from occupied to available? The answer is the operating system. Discussing the mechanism of how the operating system does all this is out of the scope of this book. So, in simple language, we can say that the computer does it on its own without any intervention from the user or the programmer. As a programmer, you just have to take care of the code to perform insertions and deletions in the list.

However, let us briefly discuss the basic concept behind it. The computer maintains a list of all free memory cells. This list of available space is called the *free pool.*

START = 1 (Biology)

	Roll No	Marks	Next
1	S01	78	2
2	S02	84	3
3	S03	45	5
4			
5	S04	98	7
6			
7	S05	55	8
8	S06	34	10
9			
10	S07	90	11
11	S08	87	12
12	S09	86	13
13	S10	67	15
14			
15	S11	56	-1

(a)

START = 1 (Biology)

	Roll No	Marks	Next
1	S01	78	2
2	S02	84	3
3	S03	45	5
4	S12	75	-1
5	S04	98	7
6			
7	S05	55	8
8	S06	34	10
9			
10	S07	90	11
11	S08	87	12
12	S09	86	13
13	S10	67	15
14			
15	S11	56	4

(b)

Figure 6.5 (a) Students' linked list and (b) linked list after the insertion of new student's record

We have seen that every linked list has a pointer variable START which stores the address of the first node of the list. Likewise, for the free pool (which is a linked list of all free memory cells), we have a

START: 1 (Biology)

AVAIL: 4

	Roll No	Marks	Next
1	S01	78	2
2	S02	84	3
3	S03	45	5
4			6
5	S04	98	7
6			9
7	S05	55	8
8	S06	34	10
9			14
10	S07	90	11
11	S08	87	12
12	S09	86	13
13	S10	67	15
14			–1
15	S11	56	–1

Figure 6.6 Linked list with AVAIL and START pointers

pointer variable AVAIL which stores the address of the first free space. Let us revisit the memory representation of the linked list storing all the students' marks in Biology.

Now, when a new student's record has to be added, the memory address pointed by AVAIL will be taken and used to store the desired information. After the insertion, the next available free space's address will be stored in AVAIL. For example, in Fig. 6.6, when the first free memory space is utilized for inserting the new node, AVAIL will be set to contain address 6.

This was all about inserting a new node in an already existing linked list. Now, we will discuss deleting a node or the entire linked list. When we delete a particular node from an existing linked list or delete the entire linked list, the space occupied by it must be given back to the free pool so that the memory can be reused by some other program that needs memory space.

The operating system does this task of adding the freed memory to the free pool. The operating system will perform this operation whenever it finds the CPU idle or whenever the programs are falling short of memory space. The operating system scans through all the memory cells and marks those cells that are being used by some program. Then it collects all the cells which are not being used and adds their address to the free pool, so that these cells can be reused by other programs. This process is called *garbage collection*.

There are different types of linked lists which we will discuss in the next section.

6.2 SINGLY LINKED LISTS

A singly linked list is the simplest type of linked list in which every node contains some data and a pointer to the next node of the same data type. By saying that the node contains a pointer to the next node, we mean that the node stores the address of the next node in sequence. A singly linked list allows traversal of data only in one way. Figure 6.7 shows a singly linked list.

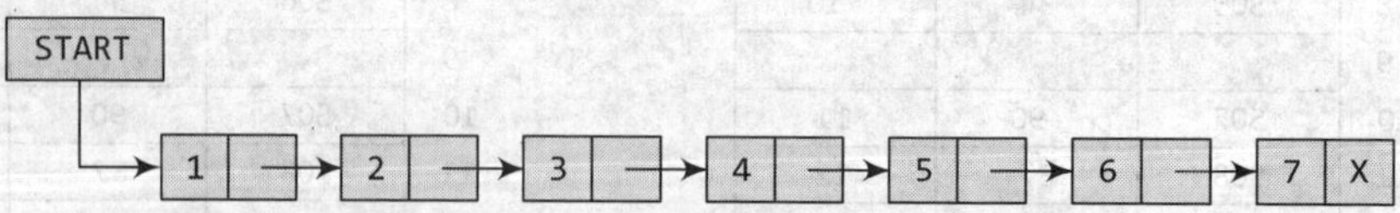

Figure 6.7 Singly linked list

6.2.1 Traversing a Linked List

Traversing a linked list means accessing the nodes of the list in order to perform some processing on them. Remember a linked list always contains a pointer variable START which stores the address of the first node of the list. End of the list is marked by storing NULL or –1 in the NEXT field of the last node. For traversing the linked list, we also make use of another pointer variable PTR which points to the node that is currently being accessed. The algorithm to traverse a linked list is shown in Fig. 6.8.

```
Step 1: [INITIALIZE] SET PTR = START
Step 2: Repeat Steps 3 and 4 while PTR != NULL
Step 3:         Apply Process to PTR->DATA
Step 4:         SET PTR = PTR->NEXT
        [END OF LOOP]
Step 5: EXIT
```

Figure 6.8 Algorithm for traversing a linked list

In this algorithm, we first initialize PTR with the address of START. So now, PTR points to the first node of the linked list. Then in Step 2, a while loop is executed which is repeated till PTR processes the last node, that is until it encounters NULL. In Step 3, we apply the process (e.g., print) to the current node, that is, the node pointed by PTR. In Step 4, we move to the next node by making the PTR variable point to the node whose address is stored in the NEXT field.

```
Step 1: [INITIALIZE] SET COUNT = 0
Step 2: [INITIALIZE] SET PTR = START
Step 3: Repeat Steps 4 and 5 while PTR != NULL
Step 4:         SET COUNT = COUNT + 1
Step 5:         SET PTR = PTR->NEXT
        [END OF LOOP]
Step 6: Write COUNT
Step 7: EXIT
```

Figure 6.9 Algorithm to print the number of nodes in a linked list

Let us now write an algorithm to count the number of nodes in a linked list. To do this, we will traverse each and every node of the list and while traversing every individual node, we will increment the counter by 1. Once we reach NULL, that is, when all the nodes of the linked list have been traversed, the final value of the counter will be displayed. Figure 6.9 shows the algorithm to print the number of nodes in a linked list.

6.2.2 Searching for a Value in a Linked List

Searching a linked list means to find a particular element in the linked list. As already discussed, a linked list consists of nodes which are divided into two parts, the information part and the next part. So searching means finding whether a given value is present in the information part of the node or not. If it is present, the algorithm returns the address of the node that contains the value.

```
Step 1: [INITIALIZE] SET PTR = START
Step 2: Repeat Step 3 while PTR != NULL
Step 3:     IF VAL = PTR->DATA
                SET POS = PTR
                Go To Step 5
            ELSE
                SET PTR = PTR->NEXT
            [END OF IF]
        [END OF LOOP]
Step 4: SET POS = NULL
Step 5: EXIT
```

Figure 6.10 Algorithm to search a linked list

Figure 6.10 shows the algorithm to search a linked list.

In Step 1, we initialize the pointer variable PTR with START that contains the address of the first node. In Step 2, a while loop is executed which will compare every node's DATA with VAL for which the search is being made. If the search is successful, that is, VAL has been found, then the address of that node is stored in POS and the control jumps to the last statement of the algorithm. However, if the search is unsuccessful, POS is set to NULL which indicates that VAL is not present in the linked list.

Consider the linked list shown in Fig. 6.11. If we have VAL = 4, then the flow of the algorithm can be explained as shown in the figure.

6.2.3 Inserting a New Node in a Linked List

In this section, we will see how a new node is added into an already existing linked list. We will take four cases and then see how insertion is done in each case.

Case 1: The new node is inserted at the beginning.
Case 2: The new node is inserted at the end.
Case 3: The new node is inserted after a given node.
Case 4: The new node is inserted before a given node.

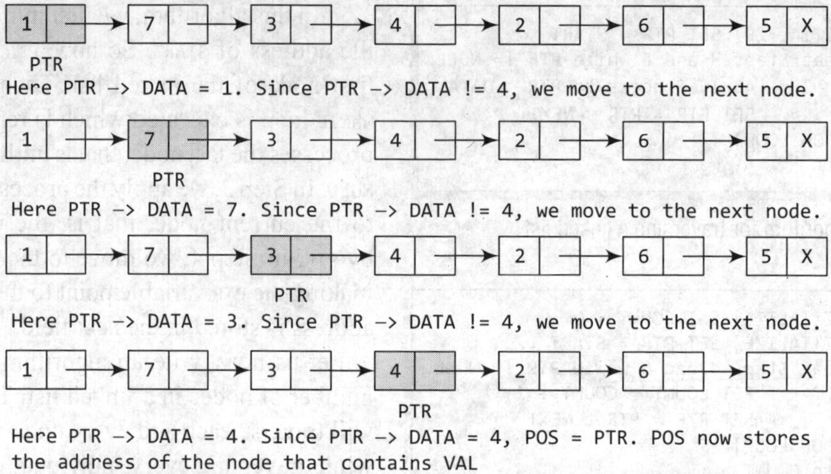

Figure 6.11 Searching a linked list

Before we describe the algorithms to perform insertions in all these four cases, let us first discuss an important term called `OVERFLOW`. Overflow is a condition that occurs when `AVAIL = NULL` or no free memory cell is present in the system. When this condition occurs, the program must give an appropriate message.

Inserting a Node at the Beginning of a Linked List

Consider the linked list shown in Fig. 6.12. Suppose we want to add a new node with data 9 and add it as the first node of the list. Then the following changes will be done in the linked list.

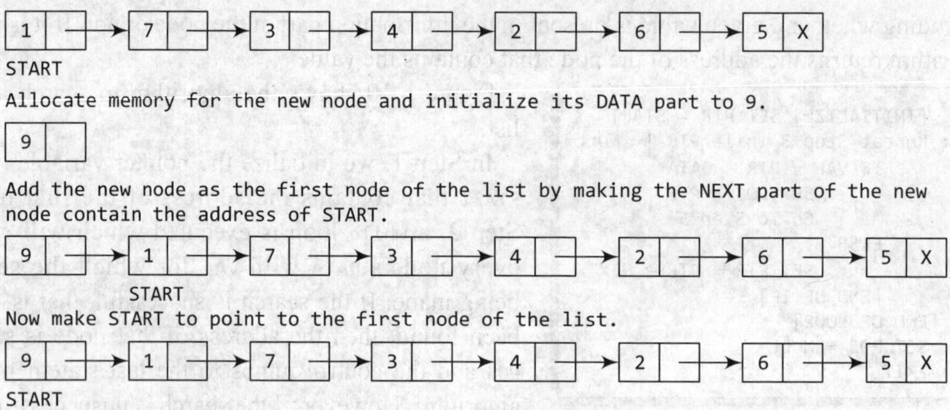

Figure 6.12 Inserting an element at the beginning of a linked list

Figure 6.13 shows the algorithm to insert a new node at the beginning of a linked list. In Step 1, we first check whether memory is available for the new node. If the free memory has exhausted, then an `OVERFLOW` message is printed. Otherwise, if a free memory cell is available, then we allocate space for the new node. Set its `DATA` part with the given `VAL` and the `NEXT` part is initialized with the address of the first node of the list, which is stored in `START`. Now, since the new node is added as the first node of the list, it will now be known as the `START` node, that is, the `START` pointer variable will now hold the address of the `NEW_NODE`. Note the following two steps:

```
Step 2: SET NEW_NODE = AVAIL
Step 3: SET AVAIL = AVAIL -> NEXT
```

```
Step 1: IF AVAIL = NULL
            Write OVERFLOW
            Go to Step 7
        [END OF IF]
Step 2: SET NEW_NODE = AVAIL
Step 3: SET AVAIL = AVAIL -> NEXT
Step 4: SET NEW_NODE -> DATA = VAL
Step 5: SET NEW_NODE -> NEXT = START
Step 6: SET START = NEW_NODE
Step 7: EXIT
```

Figure 6.13 Algorithm to insert a new node at the beginning

These steps allocate memory for the new node. In C, there are functions like `malloc()`, `alloc`, and `calloc()` which automatically do the memory allocation on behalf of the user.

Inserting a Node at the End of a Linked List

Consider the linked list shown in Fig. 6.14. Suppose we want to add a new node with data 9 as the last node of the list. Then the following changes will be done in the linked list.

Figure 6.15 shows the algorithm to insert a new node at the end of a linked list. In Step 6, we take a pointer variable PTR and initialize it with START. That is, PTR now points to the first node of the linked list. In the `while` loop, we traverse through the linked list to reach the last node. Once we reach the last node, in Step 9, we change the NEXT pointer of the last node to store the address of the new node. Remember that the NEXT field of the new node contains NULL, which signifies the end of the linked list.

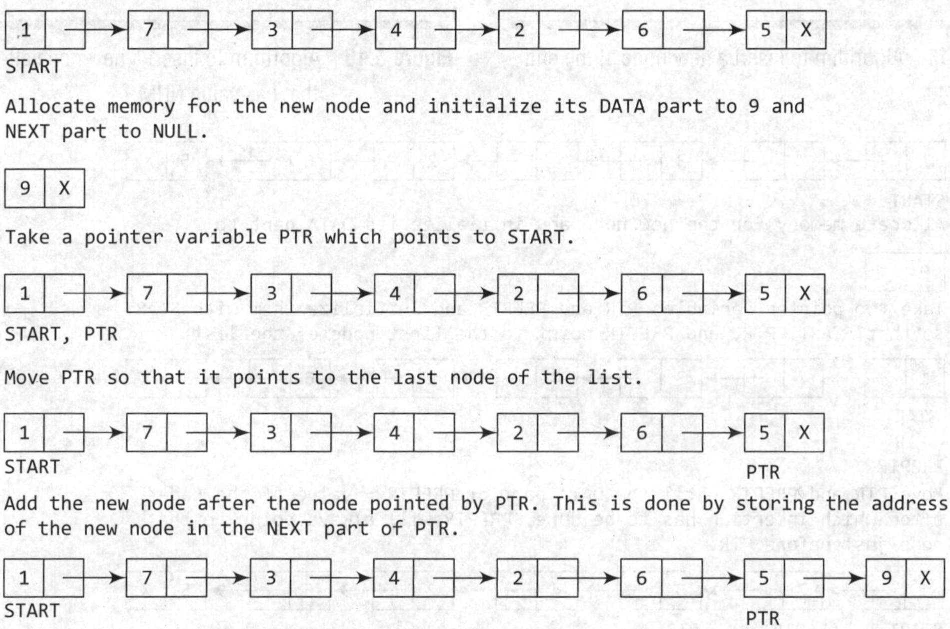

Figure 6.14 Inserting an element at the end of a linked list

Inserting a Node After a Given Node in a Linked List

Consider the linked list shown in Fig. 6.17. Suppose we want to add a new node with value 9 after the node containing data 3. Before discussing the changes that will be done in the linked list, let us first look at the algorithm shown in Fig. 6.16.

In Step 5, we take a pointer variable PTR and initialize it with START. That is, PTR now points to the first node of the linked list. Then we take another pointer variable PREPTR which will be used to store the address of the node preceding PTR. Initially, PREPTR is initialized to PTR. So now, PTR, PREPTR, and START are all pointing to the first node of the linked list.

In the `while` loop, we traverse through the linked list to reach the node that has its value equal to NUM. We need to reach this node because the new node will be inserted after this node. Once we reach this node, in Steps 10 and 11, we change the NEXT pointers in such a way that new node is inserted after the desired node.

```
Step 1: IF AVAIL = NULL
            Write OVERFLOW
            Go to Step 10
        [END OF IF]
Step 2: SET NEW_NODE = AVAIL
Step 3: SET AVAIL = AVAIL->NEXT
Step 4: SET NEW_NODE->DATA = VAL
Step 5: SET NEW_NODE->NEXT = NULL
Step 6: SET PTR = START
Step 7: Repeat Step 8 while PTR->NEXT != NULL
Step 8:     SET PTR = PTR->NEXT
        [END OF LOOP]
Step 9: SET PTR->NEXT = NEW_NODE
Step 10: EXIT
```

Figure 6.15 Algorithm to insert a new node at the end

```
Step 1: IF AVAIL = NULL
            Write OVERFLOW
            Go to Step 12
        [END OF IF]
Step 2: SET NEW_NODE = AVAIL
Step 3: SET AVAIL = AVAIL->NEXT
Step 4: SET NEW_NODE->DATA = VAL
Step 5: SET PTR = START
Step 6: SET PREPTR = PTR
Step 7: Repeat Steps 8 and 9 while PREPTR->DATA
        != NUM
Step 8:     SET PREPTR = PTR
Step 9:     SET PTR = PTR->NEXT
        [END OF LOOP]
Step 10: PREPTR->NEXT = NEW_NODE
Step 11: SET NEW_NODE->NEXT = PTR
Step 12: EXIT
```

Figure 6.16 Algorithm to insert a new node after a node that has value NUM

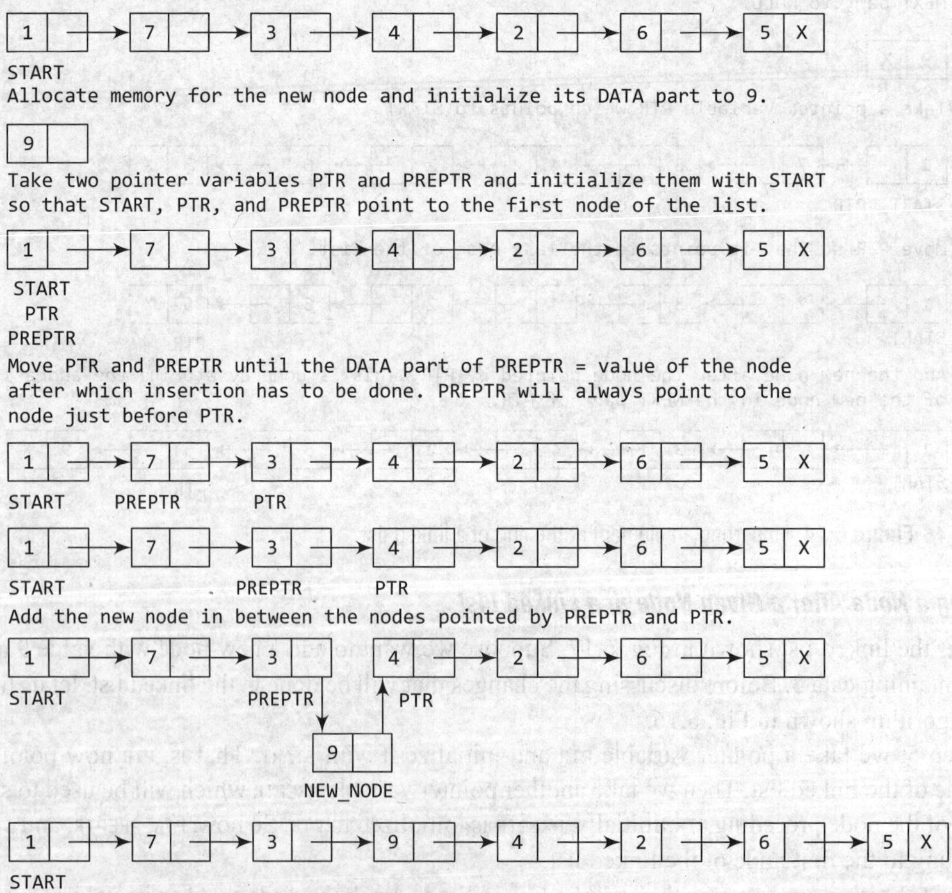

Figure 6.17 Inserting an element after a given node in a linked list

```
Step 1: IF AVAIL = NULL
            Write OVERFLOW
            Go to Step 12
        [END OF IF]
Step 2: SET NEW_NODE = AVAIL
Step 3: SET AVAIL = AVAIL->NEXT
Step 4: SET NEW_NODE->DATA = VAL
Step 5: SET PTR = START
Step 6: SET PREPTR = PTR
Step 7: Repeat Steps 8 and 9 while PTR->DATA != NUM
Step 8:         SET PREPTR = PTR
Step 9:         SET PTR = PTR->NEXT
         [END OF LOOP]
Step 10: PREPTR->NEXT = NEW_NODE
Step 11: SET NEW_NODE->NEXT = PTR
Step 12: EXIT
```

Figure 6.18 Algorithm to insert a new node before a node that has value NUM

Inserting a Node Before a Given Node in a Linked List

Consider the linked list shown in Fig. 6.19. Suppose we want to add a new node with value 9 before the node containing 3. Before discussing the changes that will be done in the linked list, let us first look at the algorithm shown in Fig. 6.18.

In Step 5, we take a pointer variable PTR and initialize it with START. That is, PTR now points to the first node of the linked list. Then, we take another pointer variable PREPTR and initialize it with PTR. So now, PTR, PREPTR, and START are all pointing to the first node of the linked list.

In the while loop, we traverse through the linked list to reach the node that has its value equal to NUM. We need to reach this node because the new node will be inserted before this node. Once we reach this node, in Steps 10 and 11, we change the NEXT pointers in such a way that the new node is inserted before the desired node.

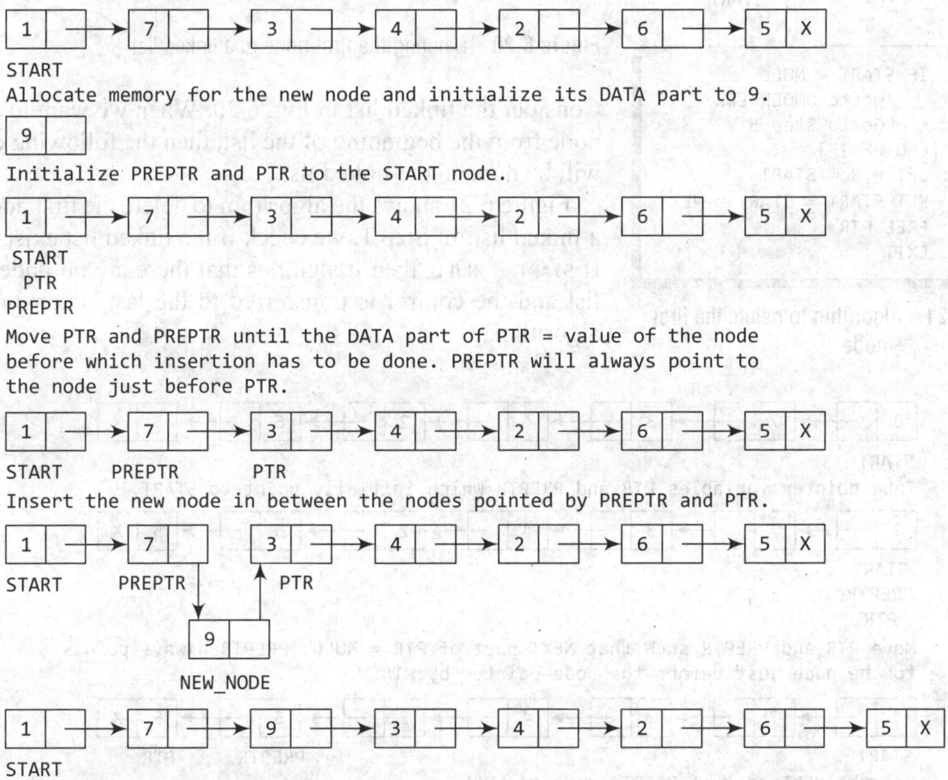

Figure 6.19 Inserting an element before a given node in a linked list

6.2.4 Deleting a Node from a Linked List

In this section, we will discuss how a node is deleted from an already existing linked list. We will consider three cases and then see how deletion is done in each case.

Case 1: The first node is deleted.
Case 2: The last node is deleted.
Case 3: The node after a given node is deleted.

Before we describe the algorithms in all these three cases, let us first discuss an important term called UNDERFLOW. Underflow is a condition that occurs when we try to delete a node from a linked list that is empty. This happens when START = NULL or when there are no more nodes to delete. Note that when we delete a node from a linked list, we actually have to free the memory occupied by that node. The memory is returned to the free pool so that it can be used to store other programs and data. Whatever be the case of deletion, we always change the AVAIL pointer so that it points to the address that has been recently vacated.

Deleting the First Node from a Linked List

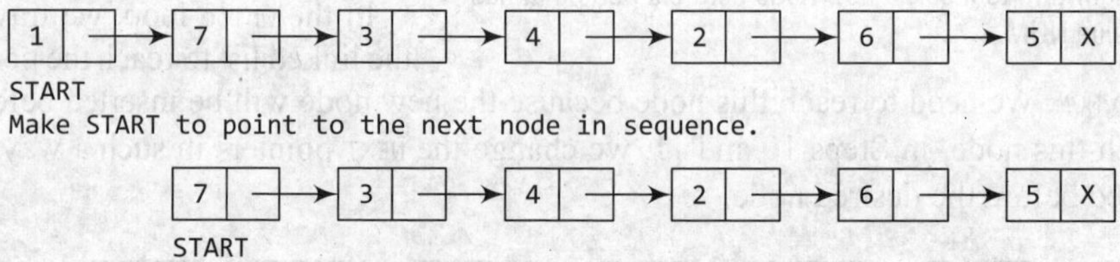

Figure 6.20 Deleting the first node of a linked list

```
Step 1: IF START = NULL
            Write UNDERFLOW
            Go to Step 5
        [END OF IF]
Step 2: SET PTR = START
Step 3: SET START = START -> NEXT
Step 4: FREE PTR
Step 5: EXIT
```

Figure 6.21 Algorithm to delete the first node

Consider the linked list in Fig. 6.20. When we want to delete a node from the beginning of the list, then the following changes will be done in the linked list.

Figure 6.21 shows the algorithm to delete the first node from a linked list. In Step 1, we check if the linked list exists or not. If START = NULL, then it signifies that there are no nodes in the list and the control is transferred to the last statement of the algorithm.

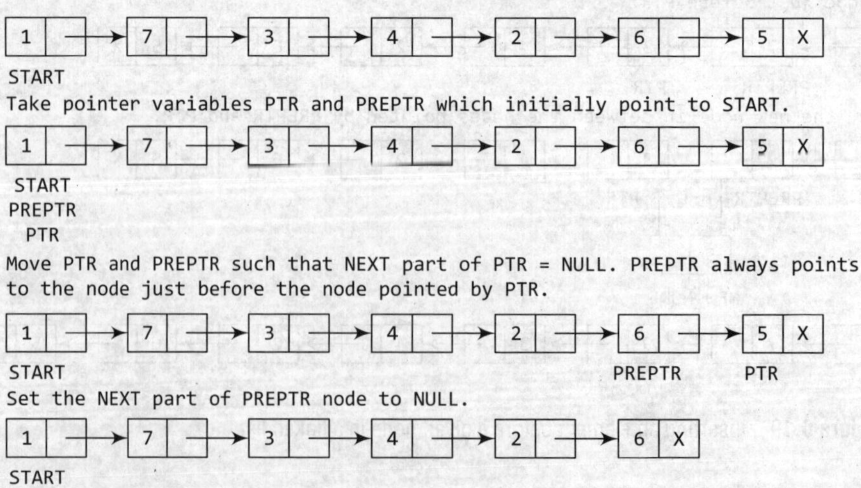

Figure 6.22 Deleting the last node of a linked list

```
Step 1: IF START = NULL
            Write UNDERFLOW
            Go to Step 8
        [END OF IF]
Step 2: SET PTR = START
Step 3: Repeat Steps 4 and 5 while PTR -> NEXT != NULL
Step 4:     SET PREPTR = PTR
Step 5:     SET PTR = PTR -> NEXT
        [END OF LOOP]
Step 6: SET PREPTR -> NEXT = NULL
Step 7: FREE PTR
Step 8: EXIT
```

Figure 6.23 Algorithm to delete the last node

However, if there are nodes in the linked list, then we use a pointer variable PTR that is set to point to the first node of the list. For this, we initialize PTR with START that stores the address of the first node of the list. In Step 3, START is made to point to the next node in sequence and finally the memory occupied by the node pointed by PTR (initially the first node of the list) is freed and returned to the free pool.

Deleting the Last Node from a Linked List

Consider the linked list shown in Fig. 6.22. Suppose we want to delete the last node from the linked list, then the following changes will be done in the linked list.

Figure 6.23 shows the algorithm to delete the last node from a linked list. In Step 2, we take a pointer variable PTR and initialize it with START. That is, PTR now points to the first node of the linked list. In the while loop, we take another pointer variable PREPTR such that it always points to one node before the PTR. Once we reach the last node and the second last node, we set the NEXT pointer of the second last node to NULL, so that it now becomes the (new) last node of the linked list. The memory of the previous last node is freed and returned back to the free pool.

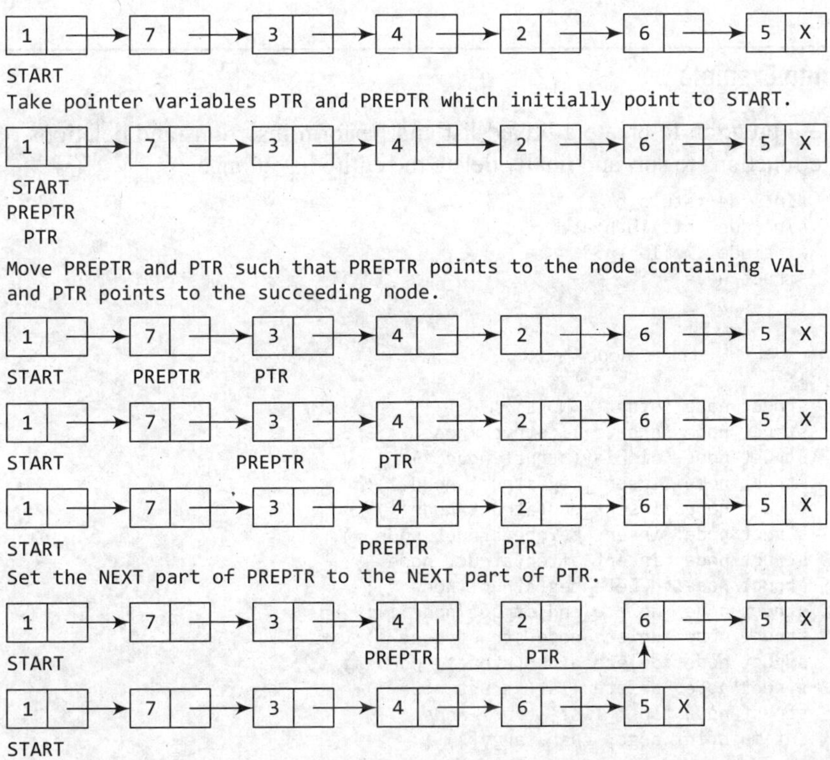

Figure 6.24 Deleting the node after a given node in a linked list

Deleting the Node After a Given Node in a Linked List

Consider the linked list shown in Fig. 6.24. Suppose we want to delete the node that succeeds the node which contains data value 4. Then the following changes will be done in the linked list.

Figure 6.25 shows the algorithm to delete the node after a given node from a linked list. In Step 2, we take a pointer variable PTR and initialize it with START. That is, PTR now points to the first node of the linked list. In the while loop, we take another pointer variable PREPTR such that it always points to one node before the PTR. Once we reach the node containing VAL and the node succeeding it, we set the next pointer of the node containing VAL to the address contained in next field of the node succeeding it. The memory of the node succeeding the given node is freed and returned back to the free pool.

```
Step 1: IF START = NULL
            Write UNDERFLOW
            Go to Step 10
        [END OF IF]
Step 2: SET PTR = START
Step 3: SET PREPTR = PTR
Step 4: Repeat Steps 5 and 6 while PREPTR->DATA != NUM
Step 5:     SET PREPTR = PTR
Step 6:     SET PTR = PTR->NEXT
        [END OF LOOP]
Step 7: SET TEMP = PTR
Step 8: SET PREPTR->NEXT = PTR->NEXT
Step 9: FREE TEMP
Step 10: EXIT
```

Figure 6.25 Algorithm to delete the node after a given node

Programming Example

1. Write a program to create a linked list and perform insertions and deletions of all cases. Write functions to sort and finally delete the entire list at once.

```
#include <stdio.h>
#include <stdlib.h>
#include <malloc.h>
struct node
{
        int data;
        struct node *next;
};
struct node *start = NULL;
struct node *create_ll(struct node *);
struct node *display(struct node *);
struct node *insert_beg(struct node *);
struct node *insert_end(struct node *);
struct node *insert_before(struct node *);
struct node *insert_after(struct node *);
struct node *delete_beg(struct node *);
struct node *delete_end(struct node *);
struct node *delete_node(struct node *);
struct node *delete_after(struct node *);
struct node *delete_list(struct node *);
struct node *sort_list(struct node *);
int main(int argc, char *argv[]) {
        int option;
```

```
        do
        {
                printf("\n\n *****MAIN MENU *****");
                printf("\n 1:  Create a list");
                printf("\n 2:  Display the list");
                printf("\n 3:  Add a node at the beginning");
                printf("\n 4:  Add a node at the end");
                printf("\n 5:  Add a node before a given node");
                printf("\n 6:  Add a node after a given node");
                printf("\n 7:  Delete a node from the beginning");
                printf("\n 8:  Delete a node from the end");
                printf("\n 9:  Delete a given node");
                printf("\n 10: Delete a node after a given node");
                printf("\n 11: Delete the entire list");
                printf("\n 12: Sort the list");
                printf("\n 13: EXIT");
                printf("\n\n Enter your option : ");
                scanf("%d", &option);
                switch(option)
                {
                case 1: start = create_ll(start);
                        printf("\n LINKED LIST CREATED");
                        break;
                case 2: start = display(start);
                        break;
                case 3: start = insert_beg(start);
                        break;
                case 4: start = insert_end(start);
                        break;
                case 5: start = insert_before(start);
                        break;
                case 6: start = insert_after(start);
                        break;
                case 7: start = delete_beg(start);
                        break;
                case 8: start = delete_end(start);
                        break;
                case 9: start = delete_node(start);
                        break;
                case 10: start = delete_after(start);
                        break;
                case 11: start = delete_list(start);
                        printf("\n LINKED LIST DELETED");
                        break;
                case 12: start = sort_list(start);
                        break;
                }
        }while(option !=13);
        return 0;
}
struct node *create_ll(struct node *start)
{
        struct node *new_node, *ptr;
        int num;
        printf("\n Enter -1 to end");
        printf("\n Enter the data : ");
        scanf("%d", &num);
        while(num!=-1)
        {
                new_node = (struct node*)malloc(sizeof(struct node));
                new_node -> data=num;
```

```
                if(start==NULL)
                {
                        new_node -> next = NULL;
                        start = new_node;
                }
                else
                {
                        ptr=start;
                        while(ptr->next!=NULL)
                        ptr=ptr->next;
                        ptr->next = new_node;
                        new_node->next=NULL;
                }
                printf("\n Enter the data : ");
                scanf("%d", &num);
        }
        return start;
}
struct node *display(struct node *start)
{
        struct node *ptr;
        ptr = start;
        if(ptr==NULL)
        {
                printf("LIST IS EMPTY!");
                return 0;
        }
        while(ptr != NULL)
        {
                printf("\t %d", ptr -> data);
                ptr = ptr -> next;
        }
        return start;
}
struct node *insert_beg(struct node *start)
{
        struct node *new_node;
        int num;
        printf("\n Enter the data : ");
        scanf("%d", &num);
        new_node = (struct node *)malloc(sizeof(struct node));
        new_node -> data = num;
        new_node -> next = start;
        start = new_node;
        return start;
}
struct node *insert_end(struct node *start)
{
        struct node *ptr, *new_node;
        int num;
        printf("\n Enter the data : ");
        scanf("%d", &num);
        new_node = (struct node *)malloc(sizeof(struct node));
        new_node -> data = num;
        new_node -> next = NULL;
        ptr = start;
        while(ptr -> next != NULL)
        ptr = ptr -> next;
        ptr -> next = new_node;
        return start;
}
```

```
struct node *insert_before(struct node *start)
{
        struct node *new_node, *ptr, *preptr;
        int num, val;
        printf("\n Enter the data : ");
        scanf("%d", &num);
        printf("\n Enter the value before which the data has to be inserted : ");
        scanf("%d", &val);
        new_node = (struct node *)malloc(sizeof(struct node));
        new_node -> data = num;
        ptr = start;
        while(ptr -> data != val)
        {
                preptr = ptr;
                ptr = ptr -> next;
        }
        preptr -> next = new_node;
        new_node -> next = ptr;
        return start;
}
struct node *insert_after(struct node *start)
{
        struct node *new_node, *ptr, *preptr;
        int num, val;
        printf("\n Enter the data : ");
        scanf("%d", &num);
        printf("\n Enter the value after which the data has to be inserted : ");
        scanf("%d", &val);
        new_node = (struct node *)malloc(sizeof(struct node));
        new_node -> data = num;
        ptr = start;
        preptr = ptr;
        while(preptr -> data != val)
        {
                preptr = ptr;
                ptr = ptr -> next;
        }
        preptr -> next=new_node;
        new_node -> next = ptr;
        return start;
}
struct node *delete_beg(struct node *start)
{
        struct node *ptr;
        ptr = start;
        start = start -> next;
        free(ptr);
        return start;
}
struct node *delete_end(struct node *start)
{
        struct node *ptr, *preptr;
        ptr = start;
        while(ptr -> next != NULL)
        {
                preptr = ptr;
                ptr = ptr -> next;
        }
        preptr -> next = NULL;
        free(ptr);
        return start;
}
```

```
struct node *delete_node(struct node *start)
{
        struct node *ptr, *preptr;
        int val;
        printf("\n Enter the value of the node which has to be deleted : ");
        scanf("%d", &val);
        ptr = start;
        if(ptr -> data == val)
        {
                start = delete_beg(start);
                return start;
        }
        else
        {
                while(ptr -> data != val)
                {
                        preptr = ptr;
                        ptr = ptr -> next;
                }
                preptr -> next = ptr -> next;
                free(ptr);
                return start;
        }
}
struct node *delete_after(struct node *start)
{
        struct node *ptr, *preptr;
        int val;
        printf("\n Enter the value after which the node has to deleted : ");
        scanf("%d", &val);
        ptr = start;
        preptr = ptr;
        while(preptr -> data != val)
        {
                preptr = ptr;
                ptr = ptr -> next;
        }
        preptr -> next=ptr -> next;
        free(ptr);
        return start;
}
struct node *delete_list(struct node *start)
{
        struct node *ptr; // Lines 252-254 were modified from original code to fix
unresposiveness in output window
        if(start!=NULL){
                ptr=start;
                while(ptr != NULL)
                {
                        printf("\n %d is to be deleted next", ptr -> data);
                        start = delete_beg(ptr);
                        ptr = start;
                }
        }

        return start;
}
struct node *sort_list(struct node *start)
{
        struct node *ptr1, *ptr2;
        int temp;
        ptr1 = start;
```

```
            while(ptr1 -> next != NULL)
            {
                ptr2 = ptr1 -> next;
                while(ptr2 != NULL)
                {
                    if(ptr1 -> data > ptr2 -> data)
                    {
                        temp = ptr1 -> data;
                        ptr1 -> data = ptr2 -> data;
                        ptr2 -> data = temp;
                    }
                    ptr2 = ptr2 -> next;
                }
                ptr1 = ptr1 -> next;
            }
            return start;
        }
```

Output

```
*****MAIN MENU *****
1: Create a list
2: Display the list
3: Add a node at the beginning
4: Add the node at the end
5: Add the node before a given node
6: Add the node after a given node
7: Delete a node from the beginning
8: Delete a node from the end
9: Delete a given node
10: Delete a node after a given node
11: Delete the entire list
12: Sort the list
13: Exit
Enter your option : 3
Enter your option : 73
```

6.3 CIRCULAR LINKED LISTS

In a circular linked list, the last node contains a pointer to the first node of the list. We can have a circular singly linked list as well as a circular doubly linked list. While traversing a circular linked list, we can begin at any node and traverse the list in any direction, forward or backward, until we reach the same node where we started. Thus, a circular linked list has no beginning and no ending. Figure 6.26 shows a circular linked list.

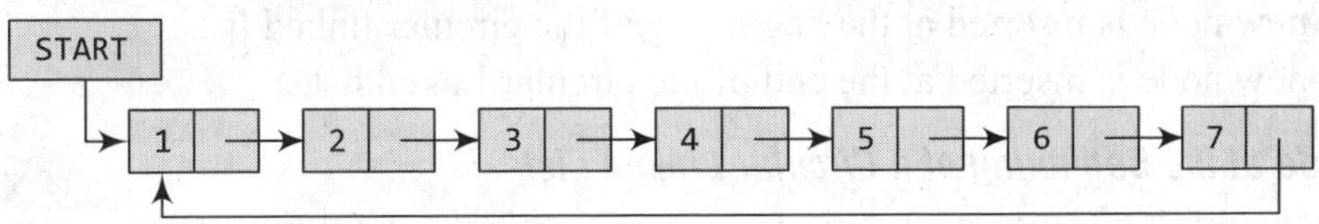

Figure 6.26 Circular linked list

The only downside of a circular linked list is the complexity of iteration. Note that there are no NULL values in the NEXT part of any of the nodes of list.

Circular linked lists are widely used in operating systems for task maintenance. We will now discuss an example where a circular linked list is used. When we are surfing the Internet, we can use the Back button and the Forward button to move to the previous pages that we have already visited. How is this done? The answer is simple. A circular linked list is used to maintain the sequence of the Web pages visited. Traversing this circular linked list either in forward or backward direction helps to revisit the pages again using Back and Forward buttons. Actually, this is done using either the circular stack or the circular queue. We will read about circular queues in Chapter 8. Consider Fig. 6.27.

START = 1

	DATA	NEXT
1	H	4
2		
3		
4	E	7
5		
6		
7	L	8
8	L	10
9		
10	O	1

Figure 6.27 Memory representation of a circular linked list

We can traverse the list until we find the `NEXT` entry that contains the address of the first node of the list. This denotes the end of the linked list, that is, the node that contains the address of the first node is actually the last node of the list. When we traverse the `DATA` and `NEXT` in this manner, we will finally see that the linked list in Fig. 6.27 stores characters that when put together form the word `HELLO`.

Now, look at Fig. 6.28. Two different linked lists are simultaneously maintained in the memory. There is no ambiguity in traversing through the list because each list maintains a separate `START` pointer which gives the address of the first node of the respective linked list. The remaining nodes are reached by looking at the value stored in `NEXT`.

By looking at the figure, we can conclude that the roll numbers of the students who have opted for Biology are `S01`, `S03`, `S06`, `S08`, `S10`, and `S11`. Similarly, the roll numbers of the students who chose Computer Science are `S02`, `S04`, `S05`, `S07`, and `S09`.

START (Biology) = 1

START (Computer Science) = 2

	Roll No	NEXT
1	S01	3
2	S02	5
3	S03	8
4		
5	S04	7
6		
7	S05	10
8	S06	11
9		
10	S07	12
11	S08	13
12	S09	1
13	S10	15
14		
15	S11	2

Figure 6.28 Memory representation of two circular linked lists stored in the memory

6.3.1 Inserting a New Node in a Circular Linked List

In this section, we will see how a new node is added into an already existing linked list. We will take two cases and then see how insertion is done in each case.

Case 1: The new node is inserted at the beginning of the circular linked list.

Case 2: The new node is inserted at the end of the circular linked list.

Inserting a Node at the Beginning of a Circular Linked List

Consider the linked list shown in Fig. 6.29. Suppose we want to add a new node with data 9 as the first node of the list. Then the following changes will be done in the linked list.

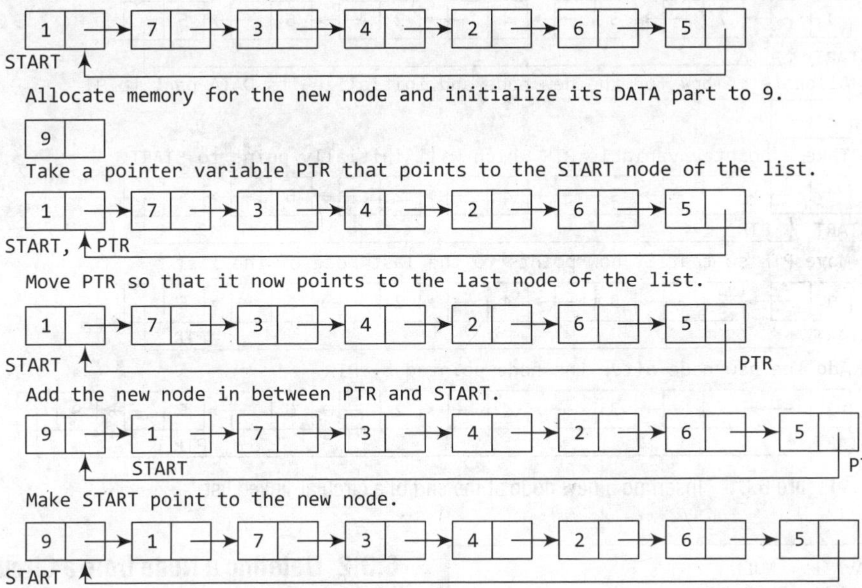

Figure 6.29 Inserting a new node at the beginning of a circular linked list

```
Step 1: IF AVAIL = NULL
            Write OVERFLOW
            Go to Step 11
        [END OF IF]
Step 2: SET NEW_NODE = AVAIL
Step 3: SET AVAIL = AVAIL -> NEXT
Step 4: SET NEW_NODE -> DATA = VAL
Step 5: SET PTR = START
Step 6: Repeat Step 7 while PTR -> NEXT != START
Step 7:     PTR = PTR -> NEXT
        [END OF LOOP]
Step 8: SET NEW_NODE -> NEXT = START
Step 9: SET PTR -> NEXT = NEW_NODE
Step 10: SET START = NEW_NODE
Step 11: EXIT
```

Figure 6.30 Algorithm to insert a new node at the beginning

Figure 6.30 shows the algorithm to insert a new node at the beginning of a linked list. In Step 1, we first check whether memory is available for the new node. If the free memory has exhausted, then an OVERFLOW message is printed. Otherwise, if free memory cell is available, then we allocate space for the new node. Set its DATA part with the given VAL and the NEXT part is initialized with the address of the first node of the list, which is stored in START. Now, since the new node is added as the first node of the list, it will now be known as the START node, that is, the START pointer variable will now hold the address of the NEW_NODE.

While inserting a node in a circular linked list, we have to use a `while` loop to traverse to the last node of the list. Because the last node contains a pointer to START, its NEXT field is updated so that after insertion it points to the new node which will be now known as START.

Inserting a Node at the End of a Circular Linked List

Consider the linked list shown in Fig. 6.31. Suppose we want to add a new node with data 9 as the last node of the list. Then the following changes will be done in the linked list.

Figure 6.32 shows the algorithm to insert a new node at the end of a circular linked list. In Step 6, we take a pointer variable PTR and initialize it with START. That is, PTR now points to the first node of the linked list. In the `while` loop, we traverse through the linked list to reach the last node. Once we reach the last node, in Step 9, we change the NEXT pointer of the last node to store the address of the new node. Remember that the NEXT field of the new node contains the address of the first node which is denoted by START.

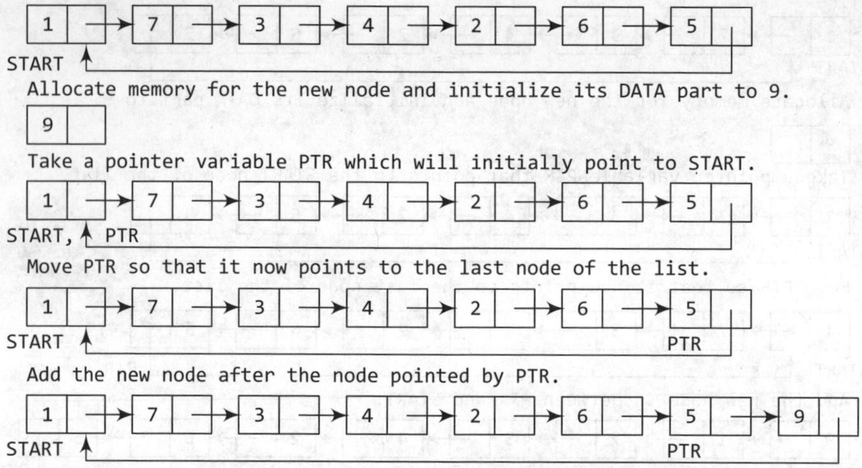

Figure 6.31 Inserting a new node at the end of a circular linked list

```
Step 1: IF AVAIL = NULL
            Write OVERFLOW
            Go to Step 10
        [END OF IF]
Step 2: SET NEW_NODE = AVAIL
Step 3: SET AVAIL = AVAIL -> NEXT
Step 4: SET NEW_NODE -> DATA = VAL
Step 5: SET NEW_NODE -> NEXT = START
Step 6: SET PTR = START
Step 7: Repeat Step 8 while PTR -> NEXT != START
Step 8:     SET PTR = PTR -> NEXT
        [END OF LOOP]
Step 9: SET PTR -> NEXT = NEW_NODE
Step 10: EXIT
```

Figure 6.32 Algorithm to insert a new node at the end

6.3.2 Deleting a Node from a Circular Linked List

In this section, we will discuss how a node is deleted from an already existing circular linked list. We will take two cases and then see how deletion is done in each case. Rest of the cases of deletion are same as that given for singly linked lists.

Case 1: The first node is deleted.

Case 2: The last node is deleted.

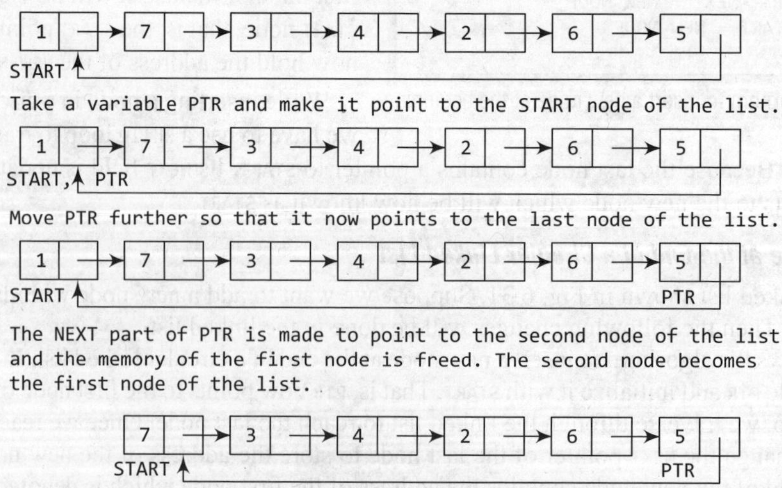

Figure 6.33 Deleting the first node from a circular linked list

```
Step 1: IF START = NULL
             Write UNDERFLOW
             Go to Step 8
        [END OF IF]
Step 2: SET PTR = START
Step 3: Repeat Step 4 while PTR->NEXT != START
Step 4:      SET PTR = PTR->NEXT
        [END OF LOOP]
Step 5: SET PTR->NEXT = START->NEXT
Step 6: FREE START
Step 7: SET START = PTR->NEXT
Step 8: EXIT
```

Figure 6.34 Algorithm to delete the first node

Deleting the First Node from a Circular Linked List

Consider the circular linked list shown in Fig. 6.33. When we want to delete a node from the beginning of the list, then the following changes will be done in the linked list.

Figure 6.34 shows the algorithm to delete the first node from a circular linked list. In Step 1 of the algorithm, we check if the linked list exists or not. If `START = NULL`, then it signifies that there are no nodes in the list and the control is transferred to the last statement of the algorithm.

However, if there are nodes in the linked list, then we use a pointer variable `PTR` which will be used to traverse the list to ultimately reach the last node. In Step 5, we change the next pointer of the last node to point to the second node of the circular linked list. In Step 6, the memory occupied by the first node is freed. Finally, in Step 7, the second node now becomes the first node of the list and its address is stored in the pointer variable `START`.

Deleting the Last Node from a Circular Linked List

Consider the circular linked list shown in Fig. 6.35. Suppose we want to delete the last node from the linked list, then the following changes will be done in the linked list.

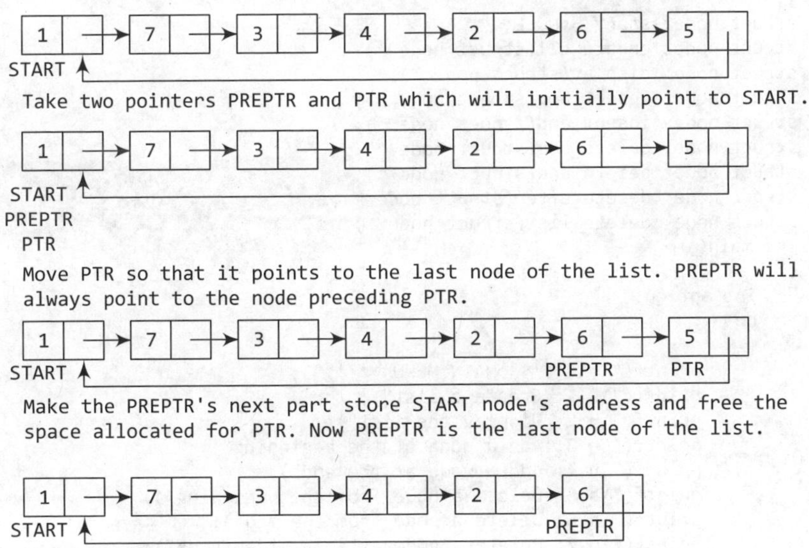

Figure 6.35 Deleting the last node from a circular linked list

Figure 6.36 shows the algorithm to delete the last node from a circular linked list. In Step 2, we take a pointer variable `PTR` and initialize it with `START`. That is, `PTR` now points to the first node of the linked list. In the `while` loop, we take another pointer variable `PREPTR` such that `PREPTR` always points to one node before `PTR`. Once we reach the last node and the second last node, we set the next pointer of the second last node to `START`, so that it now becomes the (new) last node of the linked list. The memory of the previous last node is freed and returned to the free pool.

```
Step 1: IF START = NULL
                Write UNDERFLOW
                Go to Step 8
            [END OF IF]
Step 2: SET PTR = START
Step 3: Repeat Steps 4 and 5 while PTR->NEXT != START
Step 4:         SET PREPTR = PTR
Step 5:         SET PTR = PTR->NEXT
            [END OF LOOP]
Step 6: SET PREPTR->NEXT = START
Step 7: FREE PTR
Step 8: EXIT
```

Figure 6.36 Algorithm to delete the last node

Programming Example

2. Write a program to create a circular linked list. Perform insertion and deletion at the beginning and end of the list.

```
#include <stdio.h>
#include <malloc.h>
struct node
{
    int data;
    struct node *next;
};
struct node *start = NULL;
struct node *create_cll(struct node *);
struct node *display(struct node *);
struct node *insert_beg(struct node *);
struct node *insert_end(struct node *);
struct node *delete_beg(struct node *);
struct node *delete_end(struct node *);
struct node *delete_after(struct node *);
struct node *delete_list(struct node *);
int main()
{
    int option;
    do
    {
        printf("\n\n *****MAIN MENU *****");
        printf("\n 1: Create a list");
        printf("\n 2: Display the list");
        printf("\n 3: Add a node at the beginning");
        printf("\n 4: Add a node at the end");
        printf("\n 5: Delete a node from the beginning");
        printf("\n 6: Delete a node from the end");
        printf("\n 7: Delete a node after a given node");
        printf("\n 8: Delete the entire list");
        printf("\n 9: EXIT");
        printf("\n\n Enter your option : ");
        scanf("%d", &option);
        switch(option)
        {
                case 1: start = create_cll(start);
                        printf("\n CIRCULAR LINKED LIST CREATED");
                        break;
```

```
                case 2: start = display(start);
                        break;
                case 3: start = insert_beg(start);
                        break;
                case 4: start = insert_end(start);
                        break;
                case 5: start = delete_beg(start);
                        break;
                case 6: start = delete_end(start);
                        break;
                case 7: start = delete_after(start);
                        break;
                case 8: start = delete_list(start);
                        printf("\n CIRCULAR LINKED LIST DELETED");
                        break;
            }
        }while(option !=9);
        return 0;
    }
    struct node *create_cll(struct node *start)
    {
            struct node *new_node, *ptr;
            int num;
            printf("\n Enter -1 to end");
            printf("\n Enter the data : ");
            scanf("%d", &num);
            while(num!=-1)
            {
                    new_node = (struct node*)malloc(sizeof(struct node));
                    new_node -> data = num;
                    if(start == NULL)
                    {
                            new_node -> next = new_node;
                            start = new_node;
                    }
                    else
                    {       ptr = start;
                            while(ptr -> next != start)
                                    ptr = ptr -> next;
                            ptr -> next = new_node;
                            new_node -> next = start;
                    }
                    printf("\n Enter the data : ");
                    scanf("%d", &num);
            }
            return start;
    }
    struct node *display(struct node *start)
    {
            struct node *ptr;
            ptr=start;
            if(ptr==NULL)
            {
                    printf("LIST IS EMPTY!");
                    return 0;
            }
            while(ptr -> next != start)
            {
                    printf("\t %d", ptr -> data);
                    ptr = ptr -> next;
            }
            printf("\t %d", ptr -> data);
```

```
        return start;
}
struct node *insert_beg(struct node *start)
{
        struct node *new_node, *ptr;
        int num;
        printf("\n Enter the data : ");
        scanf("%d", &num);
        new_node = (struct node *)malloc(sizeof(struct node));
        new_node -> data = num;
        ptr = start;
        while(ptr -> next != start)
                ptr = ptr -> next;
        ptr -> next = new_node;
        new_node -> next = start;
        start = new_node;
        return start;
}
struct node *insert_end(struct node *start)
{
        struct node *ptr, *new_node;
        int num;
        printf("\n Enter the data : ");
        scanf("%d", &num);
        new_node = (struct node *)malloc(sizeof(struct node));
        new_node -> data = num;
        ptr = start;
        while(ptr -> next != start)
                ptr = ptr -> next;
        ptr -> next = new_node;
        new_node -> next = start;
        return start;
}
struct node *delete_beg(struct node *start)
{
        struct node *ptr;
        ptr = start;
        while(ptr -> next != start)
                ptr = ptr -> next;
        ptr -> next = start -> next;
        free(start);
        start = ptr -> next;
        return start;
}
struct node *delete_end(struct node *start)
{
        struct node *ptr, *preptr;
        ptr = start;
        while(ptr -> next != start)
        {
                preptr = ptr;
                ptr = ptr -> next;
        }
        preptr -> next = ptr -> next;
        free(ptr);
        return start;
}
struct node *delete_after(struct node *start)
{
        struct node *ptr, *preptr;
        int val;
        printf("\n Enter the value after which the node has to deleted : ");
```

```
        scanf("%d", &val);
        ptr = start;
        preptr = ptr;
        while(preptr -> data != val)
        {
                preptr = ptr;
                ptr = ptr -> next;
        }
        preptr -> next = ptr -> next;
        if(ptr == start)
                start = preptr -> next;
        free(ptr);
        return start;
}
struct node *delete_list(struct node *start)
{
        struct node *ptr;
        ptr = start;
        while(ptr -> next != start)
                start = delete_end(start);
        free(start);
        return start;
}
```

Output

```
*****MAIN MENU *****
1: Create a list
2: Display the list
3: Add a node at the beginning
________________________
8: Delete the entire list
9: EXIT
Enter your option : 1
Enter -1 to end
Enter the data: 1
Enter the data: 2
Enter the data: 4
Enter the data: -1
CIRCULAR LINKED LIST CREATED
Enter your option : 3
Enter your option : 5
Enter your option : 2
5   1   2   4
Enter your option : 9
```

6.4 DOUBLY LINKED LISTS

A doubly linked list or a two-way linked list is a more complex type of linked list which contains a pointer to the next as well as the previous node in the sequence. Therefore, it consists of three parts—data, a pointer to the next node, and a pointer to the previous node as shown in Fig. 6.37.

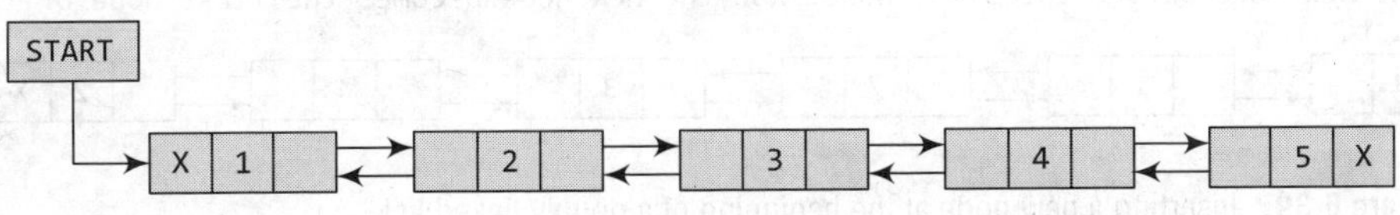

Figure 6.37 Doubly linked list

In C, the structure of a doubly linked list can be given as,

```
struct node
{
        struct node *prev;
        int data;
        struct node *next;
};
```

The PREV field of the first node and the NEXT field of the last node will contain NULL. The PREV field is used to store the address of the preceding node, which enables us to traverse the list in the backward direction.

Thus, we see that a doubly linked list calls for more space per node and more expensive basic operations. However, a doubly linked list provides the ease to manipulate the elements of the list as it maintains pointers to nodes in both the directions (forward and backward). The main advantage of using a doubly linked list is that it makes searching twice as efficient. Let us view how a doubly linked list is maintained in the memory. Consider Fig. 6.38.

START = 1

	DATA	PREV	NEXT
1	H	-1	3
2			
3	E	1	6
4			
5			
6	L	3	7
7	L	6	9
8			
9	O	7	-1

Figure 6.38 Memory representation of a doubly linked list

In the figure, we see that a variable START is used to store the address of the first node. In this example, START = 1, so the first data is stored at address 1, which is H. Since this is the first node, it has no previous node and hence stores NULL or –1 in the PREV field. We will traverse the list until we reach a position where the NEXT entry contains –1 or NULL. This denotes the end of the linked list. When we traverse the DATA and NEXT in this manner, we will finally see that the linked list in the above example stores characters that when put together form the word HELLO.

6.4.1 Inserting a New Node in a Doubly Linked List

In this section, we will discuss how a new node is added into an already existing doubly linked list. We will take four cases and then see how insertion is done in each case.

Case 1: The new node is inserted at the beginning.
Case 2: The new node is inserted at the end.
Case 3: The new node is inserted after a given node.
Case 4: The new node is inserted before a given node.

Inserting a Node at the Beginning of a Doubly Linked List

Consider the doubly linked list shown in Fig. 6.39. Suppose we want to add a new node with data 9 as the first node of the list. Then the following changes will be done in the linked list.

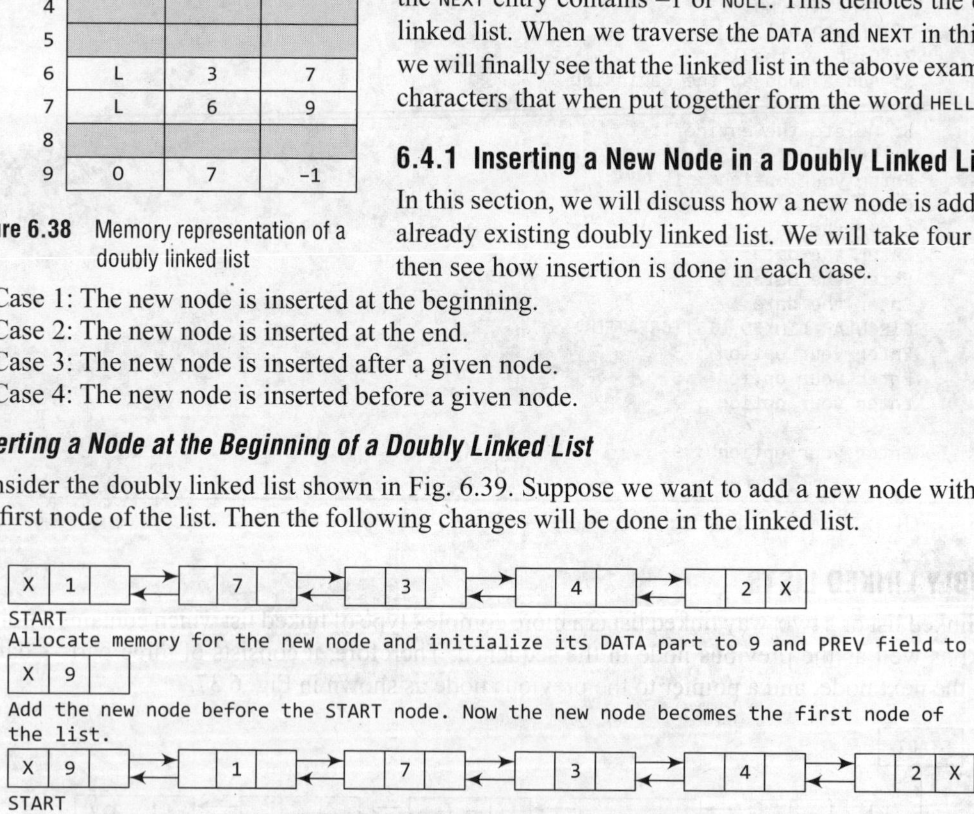

Figure 6.39 Inserting a new node at the beginning of a doubly linked list

Figure 6.40 shows the algorithm to insert a new node at the beginning of a doubly linked list. In Step 1, we first check whether memory is available for the new node. If the free memory has exhausted, then

```
Step 1: IF AVAIL = NULL
            Write OVERFLOW
            Go to Step 9
        [END OF IF]
Step 2: SET NEW_NODE = AVAIL
Step 3: SET AVAIL = AVAIL -> NEXT
Step 4: SET NEW_NODE -> DATA = VAL
Step 5: SET NEW_NODE -> PREV = NULL
Step 6: SET NEW_NODE -> NEXT = START
Step 7: SET START -> PREV = NEW_NODE
Step 8: SET START = NEW_NODE
Step 9: EXIT
```

Figure 6.40 Algorithm to insert a new node at the beginning

an OVERFLOW message is printed. Otherwise, if free memory cell is available, then we allocate space for the new node. Set its DATA part with the given VAL and the NEXT part is initialized with the address of the first node of the list, which is stored in START. Now, since the new node is added as the first node of the list, it will now be known as the START node, that is, the START pointer variable will now hold the address of NEW_NODE.

Inserting a Node at the End end of a Doubly Linked List

Consider the doubly linked list shown in Fig. 6.41. Suppose we want to add a new node with data 9 as the last node of the list. Then the following changes will be done in the linked list.

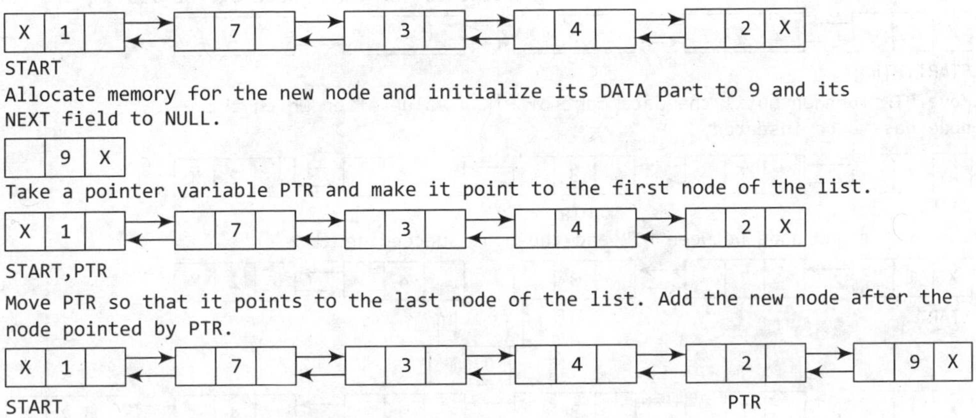

Figure 6.41 Inserting a new node at the end of a doubly linked list

Figure 6.42 shows the algorithm to insert a new node at the end of a doubly linked list. In Step 6, we take a pointer variable PTR and initialize it with START. In the while loop, we traverse through the linked list to reach the last node. Once we reach the last node, in Step 9, we change the NEXT pointer of the last

```
Step 1: IF AVAIL = NULL
            Write OVERFLOW
            Go to Step 11
        [END OF IF]
Step 2: SET NEW_NODE = AVAIL
Step 3: SET AVAIL = AVAIL -> NEXT
Step 4: SET NEW_NODE -> DATA = VAL
Step 5: SET NEW_NODE -> NEXT = NULL
Step 6: SET PTR = START
Step 7: Repeat Step 8 while PTR -> NEXT != NULL
Step 8:         SET PTR = PTR -> NEXT
        [END OF LOOP]
Step 9: SET PTR -> NEXT = NEW_NODE
Step 10: SET NEW_NODE -> PREV = PTR
Step 11: EXIT
```

Figure 6.42 Algorithm to insert a new node at the end

```
Step 1: IF AVAIL = NULL
            Write OVERFLOW
            Go to Step 12
        [END OF IF]
Step 2: SET NEW_NODE = AVAIL
Step 3: SET AVAIL = AVAIL -> NEXT
Step 4: SET NEW_NODE -> DATA = VAL
Step 5: SET PTR = START
Step 6: Repeat Step 7 while PTR -> DATA != NUM
Step 7:         SET PTR = PTR -> NEXT
        [END OF LOOP]
Step 8: SET NEW_NODE -> NEXT = PTR -> NEXT
Step 9: SET NEW_NODE -> PREV = PTR
Step 10: SET PTR -> NEXT = NEW_NODE
Step 11: SET PTR -> NEXT -> PREV = NEW_NODE
Step 12: EXIT
```

Figure 6.43 Algorithm to insert a new node after a given node

node to store the address of the new node. Remember that the NEXT field of the new node contains NULL which signifies the end of the linked list. The PREV field of the NEW_NODE will be set so that it points to the node pointed by PTR (now the second last node of the list).

Inserting a Node After a Given Node in a Doubly Linked List

Consider the doubly linked list shown in Fig. 6.44. Suppose we want to add a new node with value 9 after the node containing 3. Before discussing the changes that will be done in the linked list, let us first look at the algorithm shown in Fig. 6.43.

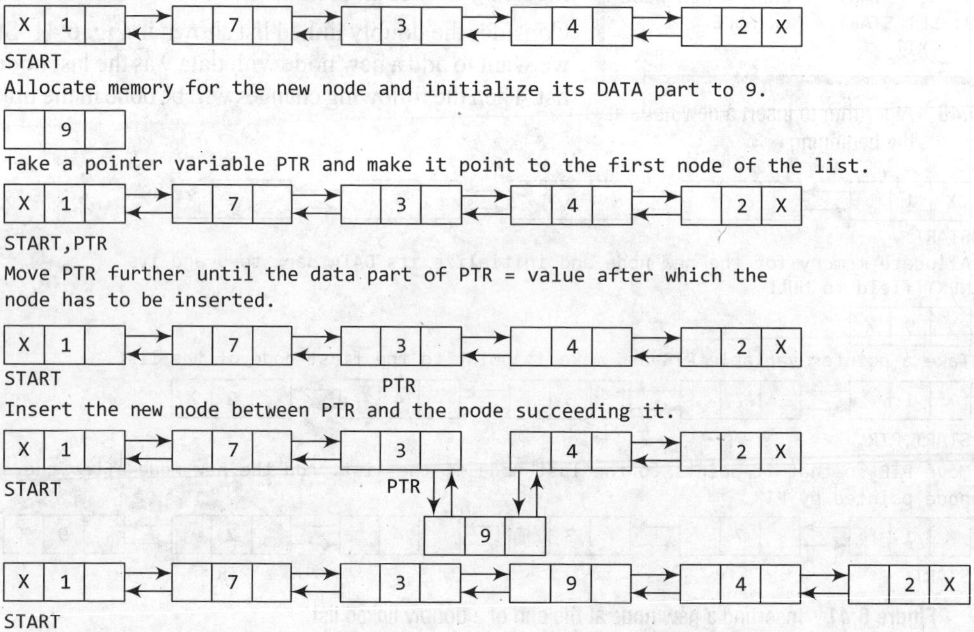

Figure 6.44 Inserting a new node after a given node in a doubly linked list

```
Step 1: IF AVAIL = NULL
            Write OVERFLOW
            Go to Step 12
        [END OF IF]
Step 2: SET NEW_NODE = AVAIL
Step 3: SET AVAIL = AVAIL -> NEXT
Step 4: SET NEW_NODE -> DATA = VAL
Step 5: SET PTR = START
Step 6: Repeat Step 7 while PTR -> DATA != NUM
Step 7:     SET PTR = PTR -> NEXT
        [END OF LOOP]
Step 8: SET NEW_NODE -> NEXT = PTR
Step 9: SET NEW_NODE -> PREV = PTR -> PREV
Step 10: SET PTR -> PREV = NEW_NODE
Step 11: SET PTR -> PREV -> NEXT = NEW_NODE
Step 12: EXIT
```

Figure 6.45 Algorithm to insert a new node before a given node

Figure 6.43 shows the algorithm to insert a new node after a given node in a doubly linked list. In Step 5, we take a pointer PTR and initialize it with START. That is, PTR now points to the first node of the linked list. In the while loop, we traverse through the linked list to reach the node that has its value equal to NUM. We need to reach this node because the new node will be inserted after this node. Once we reach this node, we change the NEXT and PREV fields in such a way that the new node is inserted after the desired node.

Inserting a Node Before a Given Node in a Doubly Linked List

Consider the doubly linked list shown in Fig. 6.46. Suppose we want to add a new node with value 9 before the node containing 3. Before discussing the changes that will be done in the linked list, let us first look at the algorithm shown in Fig. 6.45.

In Step 1, we first check whether memory is available for the new node. In Step 5, we take a pointer variable PTR and initialize it with START. That is, PTR now points to the first node of the linked list. In the while loop, we traverse through the linked list to reach the node that has its value equal to NUM. We need to reach this node because the new node will be inserted before this node. Once we reach this node, we change the NEXT and PREV fields in such a way that the new node is inserted before the desired node.

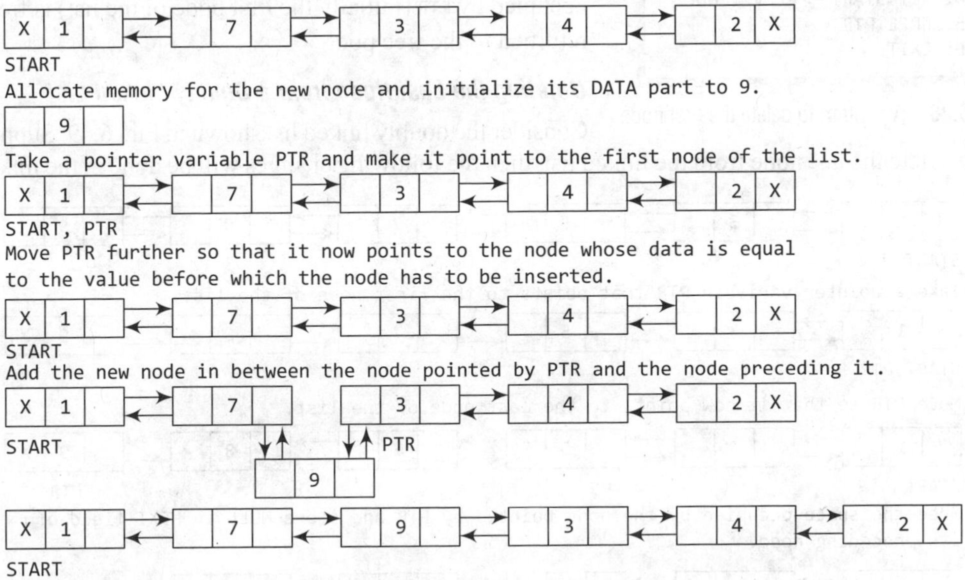

Figure 6.46 Inserting a new node before a given node in a doubly linked list

6.4.2 Deleting a Node from a Doubly Linked List

In this section, we will see how a node is deleted from an already existing doubly linked list. We will take four cases and then see how deletion is done in each case.

Case 1: The first node is deleted.
Case 2: The last node is deleted.
Case 3: The node after a given node is deleted.
Case 4: The node before a given node is deleted.

Deleting the First Node from a Doubly Linked List

Consider the doubly linked list shown in Fig. 6.47. When we want to delete a node from the beginning of the list, then the following changes will be done in the linked list.

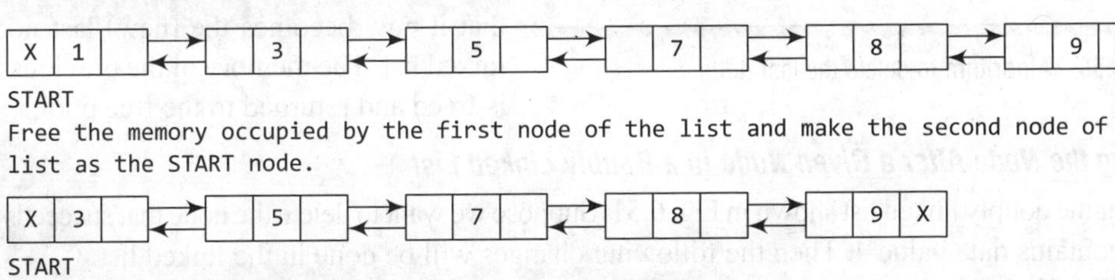

Figure 6.47 Deleting the first node from a doubly linked list

Figure 6.48 shows the algorithm to delete the first node of a doubly linked list. In Step 1 of the algorithm, we check if the linked list exists or not. If START = NULL, then it signifies that there are no nodes in the list and the control is transferred to the last statement of the algorithm.

```
Step 1: IF START = NULL
            Write UNDERFLOW
            Go to Step 6
        [END OF IF]
Step 2: SET PTR = START
Step 3: SET START = START -> NEXT
Step 4: SET START -> PREV = NULL
Step 5: FREE PTR
Step 6: EXIT
```

Figure 6.48 Algorithm to delete the first node

However, if there are nodes in the linked list, then we use a temporary pointer variable PTR that is set to point to the first node of the list. For this, we initialize PTR with START that stores the address of the first node of the list. In Step 3, START is made to point to the next node in sequence and finally the memory occupied by PTR (initially the first node of the list) is freed and returned to the free pool.

Deleting the Last Node from a Doubly Linked List

Consider the doubly linked list shown in Fig. 6.49. Suppose we want to delete the last node from the linked list, then the following changes will be done in the linked list.

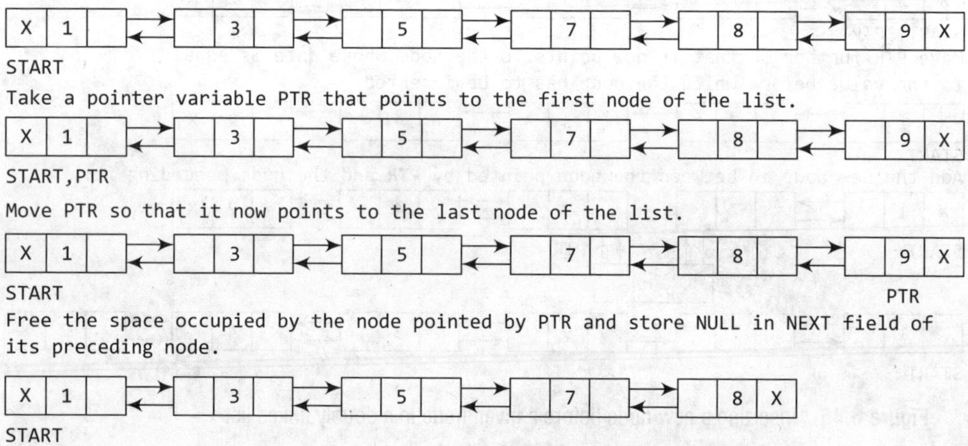

Figure 6.49 Deleting the last node from a doubly linked list

```
Step 1: IF START = NULL
            Write UNDERFLOW
            Go to Step 7
        [END OF IF]
Step 2: SET PTR = START
Step 3: Repeat Step 4 while PTR -> NEXT != NULL
Step 4:     SET PTR = PTR -> NEXT
        [END OF LOOP]
Step 5: SET PTR -> PREV -> NEXT = NULL
Step 6: FREE PTR
Step 7: EXIT
```

Figure 6.50 Algorithm to delete the last node

Figure 6.50 shows the algorithm to delete the last node of a doubly linked list. In Step 2, we take a pointer variable PTR and initialize it with START. That is, PTR now points to the first node of the linked list. The while loop traverses through the list to reach the last node. Once we reach the last node, we can also access the second last node by taking its address from the PREV field of the last node. To delete the last node, we simply have to set the next field of second last node to NULL, so that it now becomes the (new) last node of the linked list. The memory of the previous last node is freed and returned to the free pool.

Deleting the Node After a Given Node in a Doubly Linked List

Consider the doubly linked list shown in Fig. 6.51. Suppose we want to delete the node that succeeds the node which contains data value 4. Then the following changes will be done in the linked list.

Figure 6.52 shows the algorithm to delete a node after a given node of a doubly linked list. In Step 2, we take a pointer variable PTR and initialize it with START. That is, PTR now points to the first node of the doubly linked list. The while loop traverses through the linked list to reach the given node. Once we reach the node containing VAL, the node succeeding it can be easily accessed by using the address stored in its NEXT field. The NEXT field of the given node is set to contain the contents in the NEXT field of the succeeding

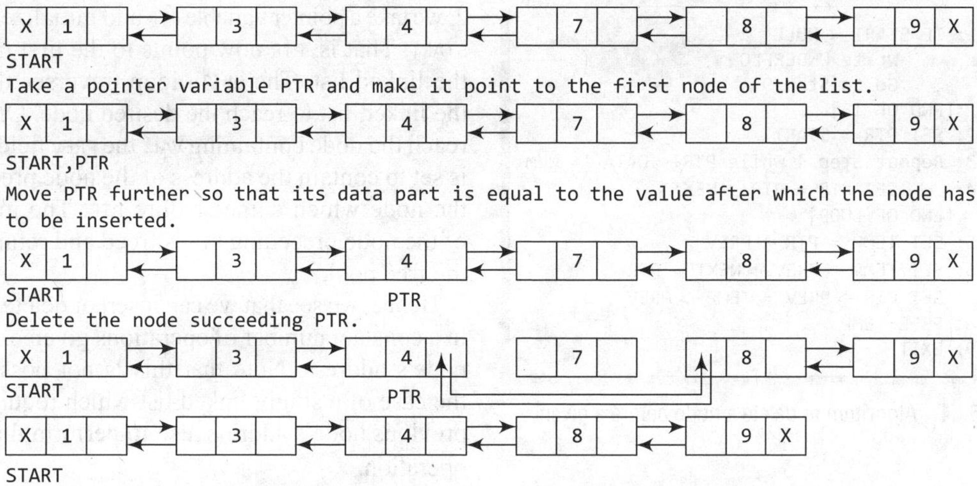

Figure 6.51 Deleting the node after a given node in a doubly linked list

```
Step 1: IF START = NULL
            Write UNDERFLOW
            Go to Step 9
        [END OF IF]
Step 2: SET PTR = START
Step 3: Repeat Step 4 while PTR -> DATA != NUM
Step 4:         SET PTR = PTR -> NEXT
        [END OF LOOP]
Step 5: SET TEMP = PTR -> NEXT
Step 6: SET PTR -> NEXT = TEMP -> NEXT
Step 7: SET TEMP -> NEXT -> PREV = PTR
Step 8: FREE TEMP
Step 9: EXIT
```

Figure 6.52 Algorithm to delete a node after a given node

node. Finally, the memory of the node succeeding the given node is freed and returned to the free pool.

Deleting the Node Before a Given Node in a Doubly Linked List

Consider the doubly linked list shown in Fig. 6.53. Suppose we want to delete the node preceding the node with value 4. Before discussing the changes that will be done in the linked list, let us first look at the algorithm.

Figure 6.54 shows the algorithm to delete a node before a given node of a doubly linked list. In Step

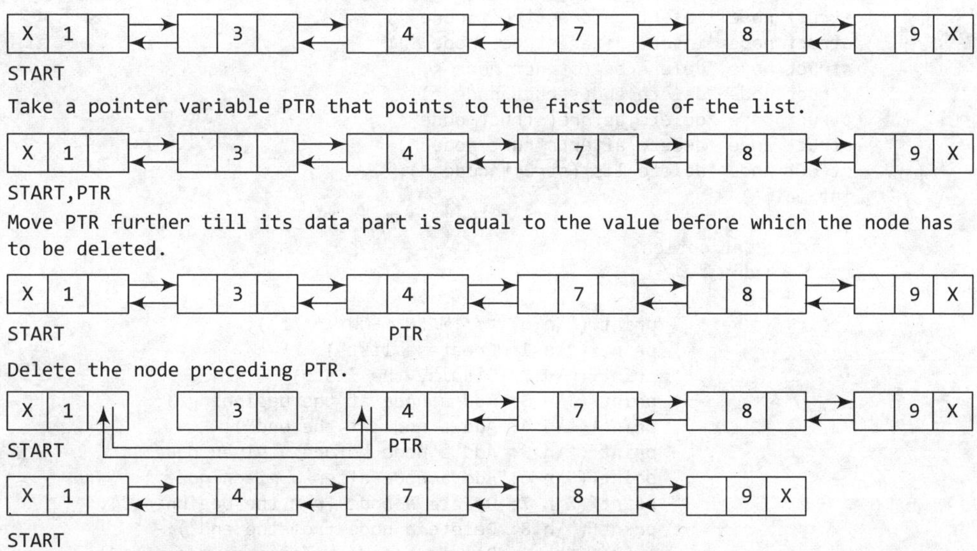

Figure 6.53 Deleting a node before a given node in a doubly linked list

```
Step 1: IF START = NULL
            Write UNDERFLOW
            Go to Step 9
        [END OF IF]
Step 2: SET PTR = START
Step 3: Repeat Step 4 while PTR -> DATA != NUM
Step 4:     SET PTR = PTR -> NEXT
        [END OF LOOP]
Step 5: SET TEMP = PTR -> PREV
Step 6: SET TEMP -> PREV -> NEXT = PTR
Step 7: SET PTR -> PREV = TEMP -> PREV
Step 8: FREE TEMP
Step 9: EXIT
```

Figure 6.54 Algorithm to delete a node before a given node

2, we take a pointer variable PTR and initialize it with START. That is, PTR now points to the first node of the linked list. The while loop traverses through the linked list to reach the desired node. Once we reach the node containing VAL, the PREV field of PTR is set to contain the address of the node preceding the node which comes before PTR. The memory of the node preceding PTR is freed and returned to the free pool.

Hence, we see that we can insert or delete a node in a constant number of operations given only that node's address. Note that this is not possible in the case of a singly linked list which requires the previous node's address also to perform the same operation.

Programming Example

3. Write a program to create a doubly linked list and perform insertions and deletions in all cases.

```
#include <stdio.h>
#include <malloc.h>
struct node
{
        struct node *next;
        int data;
        struct node *prev;
};
struct node *start = NULL;
struct node *create_ll(struct node *);
struct node *display(struct node *);
struct node *insert_beg(struct node *);
struct node *insert_end(struct node *);
struct node *insert_before(struct node *);
struct node *insert_after(struct node *);
struct node *delete_beg(struct node *);
struct node *delete_end(struct node *);
struct node *delete_before(struct node *);
struct node *delete_after(struct node *);
struct node *delete_list(struct node *);
int main()
{
        int option;
        do
        {
                printf("\n\n *****MAIN MENU *****");
                printf("\n 1: Create a list");
                printf("\n 2: Display the list");
                printf("\n 3: Add a node at the beginning");
                printf("\n 4: Add a node at the end");
                printf("\n 5: Add a node before a given node");
                printf("\n 6: Add a node after a given node");
                printf("\n 7: Delete a node from the beginning");
                printf("\n 8: Delete a node from the end");
                printf("\n 9: Delete a node before a given node");
```

```
                printf("\n 10: Delete a node after a given node");
                printf("\n 11: Delete the entire list");
                printf("\n 12: EXIT");
                printf("\n\n Enter your option : ");
                scanf("%d", &option);
                switch(option)
                {
                        case 1:  start = create_ll(start);
                                 printf("\n DOUBLY LINKED LIST CREATED");
                                 break;
                        case 2:  start = display(start);
                                 break;
                        case 3:  start = insert_beg(start);
                                 break;
                        case 4:  start = insert_end(start);
                                 break;
                        case 5:  start = insert_before(start);
                                 break;
                        case 6:  start = insert_after(start);
                                 break;
                        case 7:  start = delete_beg(start);
                                 break;
                        case 8:  start = delete_end(start);
                                 break;
                        case 9:  start = delete_before(start);
                                 break;
                        case 10: start = delete_after(start);
                                 break;
                        case 11: start = delete_list(start);
                                 printf("\n DOUBLY LINKED LIST DELETED");
                                 break;
                }
        }while(option != 12);
        return 0;
}
struct node *create_ll(struct node *start)
{
        struct node *new_node, *ptr;
        int num;
        printf("\n Enter -1 to end");
        printf("\n Enter the data : ");
        scanf("%d", &num);
        while(num != -1)
        {
                if(start == NULL)
                {
                        new_node = (struct node*)malloc(sizeof(struct node));
                        new_node -> prev = NULL;
                        new_node -> data = num;
                        new_node -> next = NULL;
                        start = new_node;
                }
                else
                {
                        ptr=start;
                        new_node = (struct node*)malloc(sizeof(struct node));
                        new_node->data=num;
                        while(ptr->next!=NULL)
                                ptr = ptr->next;
                        ptr->next = new_node;
```

```
                    new_node->prev=ptr;
                    new_node->next=NULL;
                }
                printf("\n Enter the data : ");
                scanf("%d", &num);
        }
        return start;
}
struct node *display(struct node *start)
{
        struct node *ptr;
        ptr=start;
        if(ptr==NULL)
        {
                printf("LIST IS EMPTY!");
                return 0;
        }
        while(ptr!=NULL)
        {
                printf("\t %d", ptr -> data);
                ptr = ptr -> next;
        }
        return start;
}
struct node *insert_beg(struct node *start)
{
        struct node *new_node;
        int num;
        printf("\n Enter the data : ");
        scanf("%d", &num);
        new_node = (struct node *)malloc(sizeof(struct node));
        new_node -> data = num;
        start -> prev = new_node;
        new_node -> next = start;
        new_node -> prev = NULL;
        start = new_node;
        return start;
}
struct node *insert_end(struct node *start)
{
        struct node *ptr, *new_node;
        int num;
        printf("\n Enter the data : ");
        scanf("%d", &num);
        new_node = (struct node *)malloc(sizeof(struct node));
        new_node -> data = num;
        ptr=start;
        while(ptr -> next != NULL)
                ptr = ptr -> next;
        ptr -> next = new_node;
        new_node -> prev = ptr;
        new_node -> next = NULL;
        return start;
}
struct node *insert_before(struct node *start)
{
        struct node *new_node, *ptr;
        int num, val;
        printf("\n Enter the data : ");
        scanf("%d", &num);
        printf("\n Enter the value before which the data has to be inserted:");
        scanf("%d", &val);
```

```
        new_node = (struct node *)malloc(sizeof(struct node));
        new_node -> data = num;
        ptr = start;
        while(ptr -> data != val)
                ptr = ptr -> next;
        new_node -> next = ptr;
        new_node -> prev = ptr-> prev;
        ptr -> prev -> next = new_node;
        ptr -> prev = new_node;
        return start;
}
struct node *insert_after(struct node *start)
{
        struct node *new_node, *ptr;
        int num, val;
        printf("\n Enter the data : ");
        scanf("%d", &num);
        printf("\n Enter the value after which the data has to be inserted:");
        scanf("%d", &val);
        new_node = (struct node *)malloc(sizeof(struct node));
        new_node -> data = num;
        ptr = start;
        while(ptr -> data != val)
                ptr = ptr -> next;
        new_node -> prev = ptr;
        new_node -> next = ptr -> next;
        ptr -> next -> prev = new_node;
        ptr -> next = new_node;
        return start;
}
struct node *delete_beg(struct node *start)
{
        struct node *ptr;
        ptr = start;
        start = start -> next;
        start -> prev = NULL;
        free(ptr);
        return start;
}
struct node *delete_end(struct node *start)
{
        struct node *ptr;
        ptr = start;
        while(ptr -> next != NULL)
                ptr = ptr -> next;
        ptr -> prev -> next = NULL;
        free(ptr);
        return start;
}
struct node *delete_after(struct node *start)
{
        struct node *ptr, *temp;
        int val;
        printf("\n Enter the value after which the node has to deleted : ");
        scanf("%d", &val);
        ptr = start;
        while(ptr -> data != val)
                ptr = ptr -> next;
        temp = ptr -> next;
        ptr -> next = temp -> next;
        temp -> next -> prev = ptr;
        free(temp);
```

```
        return start;
}
struct node *delete_before(struct node *start)
{
        struct node *ptr, *temp;
        int val;
        printf("\n Enter the value before which the node has to deleted:");
        scanf("%d", &val);
        ptr = start;
        while(ptr -> data != val)
                ptr = ptr -> next;
        temp = ptr -> prev;
        if(temp == start)
                start = delete_beg(start);
        else
        {
                ptr -> prev = temp -> prev;
                temp -> prev -> next = ptr;
        }
        free(temp);
        return start;
}
struct node *delete_list(struct node *start)
{
        while(start != NULL)
                start = delete_beg(start);
        return start;
}
```

Output

```
*****MAIN MENU *****
1: Create a list
2: Display the list
---------------------------
11: Delete the entire list
12: EXIT
Enter your option : 1
Enter -1 to end
Enter the data: 1
Enter the data: 3
Enter the data: 4
Enter the data: -1
DOUBLY LINKED LIST CREATED
Enter your option : 12
```

6.5 CIRCULAR DOUBLY LINKED LISTS

A circular doubly linked list or a circular two-way linked list is a more complex type of linked list which contains a pointer to the next as well as the previous node in the sequence. The difference between a doubly linked and a circular doubly linked list is same as that exists between a singly linked list and a circular linked list. The circular doubly linked list does not contain NULL in the previous field of the first node and the next field of the last node. Rather, the next field of the last node stores the address of the first node of the list, i.e., START. Similarly, the previous field of the first field stores the address of the last node. A circular doubly linked list is shown in Fig. 6.55.

Since a circular doubly linked list contains three parts in its structure, it calls for more space per node and more expensive basic operations. However, a circular doubly linked list provides the ease to manipulate the elements of the list as it maintains pointers to nodes in both the directions (forward and backward). The main advantage of using a circular doubly linked list is that it makes search operation twice as efficient.

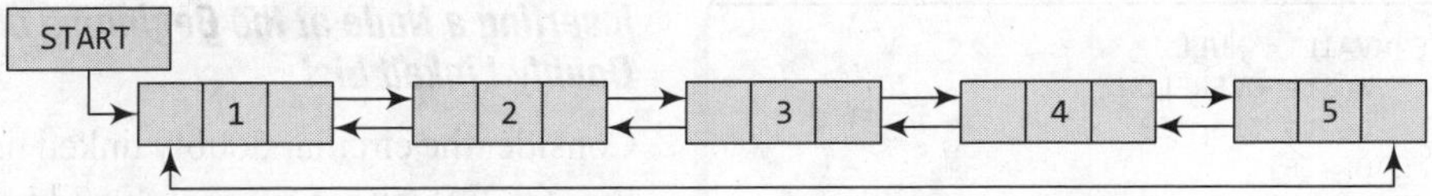

Figure 6.55 Circular doubly linked list

START: 1

	DATA	PREV	Next
1	H	9	3
2			
3	E	1	6
4			
5			
6	L	3	7
7	L	6	9
8			
9	O	7	1

Figure 6.56 Memory representation of a circular doubly linked list

Let us view how a circular doubly linked list is maintained in the memory. Consider Fig. 6.56. In the figure, we see that a variable `START` is used to store the address of the first node. Here in this example, `START = 1`, so the first data is stored at address 1, which is `H`. Since this is the first node, it stores the address of the last node of the list in its previous field. The corresponding `NEXT` stores the address of the next node, which is 3. So, we will look at address 3 to fetch the next data item. The previous field will contain the address of the first node. The second data element obtained from address 3 is `E`. We repeat this procedure until we reach a position where the `NEXT` entry stores the address of the first element of the list. This denotes the end of the linked list, that is, the node that contains the address of the first node is actually the last node of the list.

6.5.1 Inserting a New Node in a Circular Doubly Linked List

In this section, we will see how a new node is added into an already existing circular doubly linked list. We will take two cases and then see how insertion is done in each case. Rest of the cases are similar to that given for doubly linked lists.

Case 1: The new node is inserted at the beginning.

Case 2: The new node is inserted at the end.

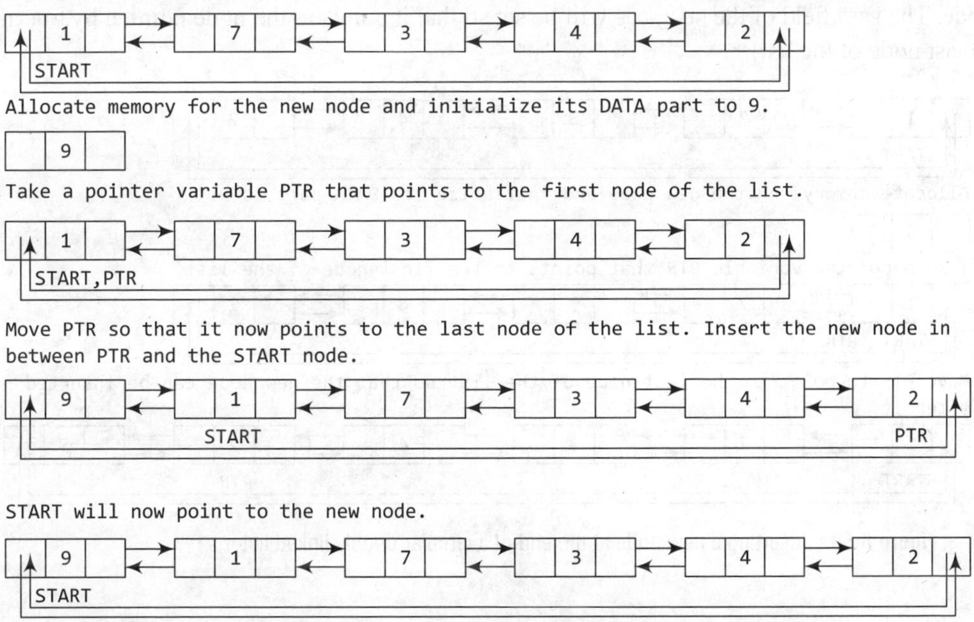

Figure 6.57 Inserting a new node at the beginning of a circular doubly linked list

```
Step 1: IF AVAIL = NULL
            Write OVERFLOW
            Go to Step 13
        [END OF IF]
Step 2: SET NEW_NODE = AVAIL
Step 3: SET AVAIL = AVAIL -> NEXT
Step 4: SET NEW_NODE -> DATA = VAL
Step 5: SET PTR = START
Step 6: Repeat Step 7 while PTR -> NEXT != START
Step 7:     SET PTR = PTR -> NEXT
        [END OF LOOP]
Step 8: SET PTR -> NEXT = NEW_NODE
Step 9: SET NEW_NODE -> PREV = PTR
Step 10: SET NEW_NODE -> NEXT = START
Step 11: SET START -> PREV = NEW_NODE
Step 12: SET START = NEW_NODE
Step 13: EXIT
```

Figure 6.58 Algorithm to insert a new node at the beginning

Inserting a Node at the Beginning of a Circular Doubly Linked List

Consider the circular doubly linked list shown in Fig. 6.57. Suppose we want to add a new node with data 9 as the first node of the list. Then, the following changes will be done in the linked list.

Figure 6.58 shows the algorithm to insert a new node at the beginning of a circular doubly linked list. In Step 1, we first check whether memory is available for the new node. If the free memory has exhausted, then an OVERFLOW message is printed. Otherwise, we allocate space for the new node. Set its data part with the given VAL and its next part is initialized with the address of the first node of the list, which is stored in START. Now since the new node is added as the first node of the list, it will now be known as the START node, that is, the START pointer variable will now hold the address of NEW_NODE. Since it is a circular doubly linked list, the PREV field of the NEW_NODE is set to contain the address of the last node.

Inserting a Node at the End of a Circular Doubly Linked List

Consider the circular doubly linked list shown in Fig. 6.59. Suppose we want to add a new node with data 9 as the last node of the list. Then the following changes will be done in the linked list.

Figure 6.60 shows the algorithm to insert a new node at the end of a circular doubly linked list. In Step 6, we take a pointer variable PTR and initialize it with START. That is, PTR now points to the first node of the linked list. In the while loop, we traverse through the linked list to reach the last node. Once we reach the last node, in Step 9, we change the NEXT pointer of the last node to store the address of the new node. The PREV field of the NEW_NODE will be set so that it points to the node pointed by PTR (now the second last node of the list).

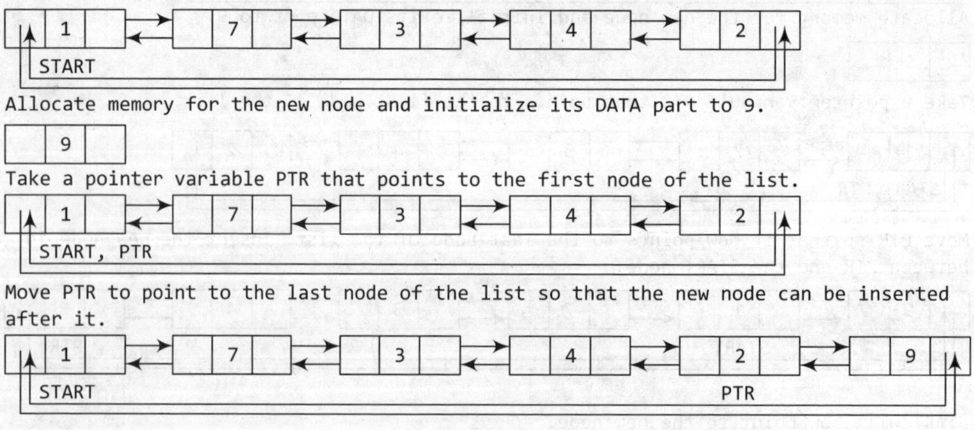

Figure 6.59 Inserting a new node at the end of a circular doubly linked list

```
Step 1: IF AVAIL = NULL
            Write OVERFLOW
            Go to Step 12
        [END OF IF]
Step 2: SET NEW_NODE = AVAIL
Step 3: SET AVAIL = AVAIL -> NEXT
Step 4: SET NEW_NODE -> DATA = VAL
Step 5: SET NEW_NODE -> NEXT = START
Step 6: SET PTR = START
Step 7: Repeat Step 8 while PTR -> NEXT != START
Step 8:         SET PTR = PTR -> NEXT
        [END OF LOOP]
Step 9: SET PTR -> NEXT = NEW_NODE
Step 10: SET NEW_NODE -> PREV = PTR
Step 11: SET START -> PREV = NEW_NODE
Step 12: EXIT
```

Figure 6.60 Algorithm to insert a new node at the end

6.5.2 Deleting a Node from a Circular Doubly Linked List

In this section, we will see how a node is deleted from an already existing circular doubly linked list. We will take two cases and then see how deletion is done in each case. Rest of the cases are same as that given for doubly linked lists.

Case 1: The first node is deleted.

Case 2: The last node is deleted.

Deleting the First Node from a Circular Doubly Linked List

Consider the circular doubly linked list shown in Fig. 6.61. When we want to delete a node from the beginning of the list, then the following changes will be done in the linked list.

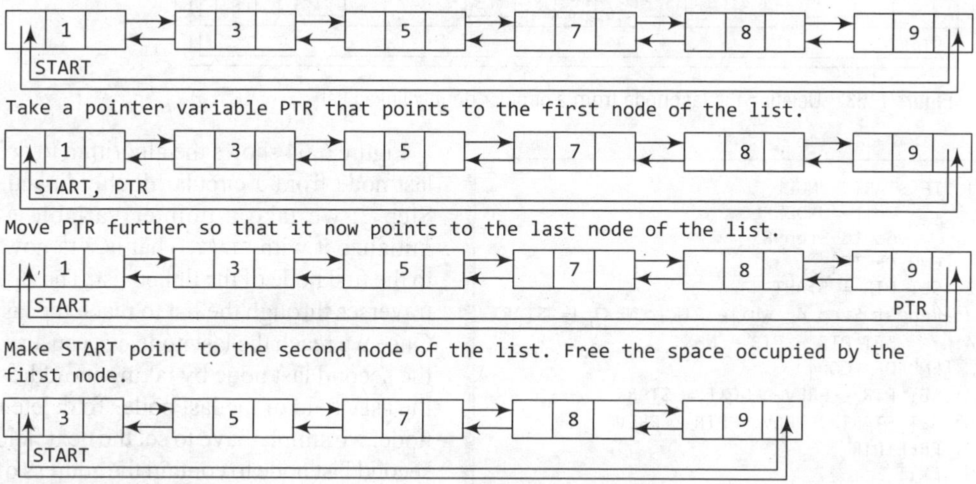

Figure 6.61 Deleting the first node from a circular doubly linked list

```
Step 1: IF START = NULL
            Write UNDERFLOW
            Go to Step 8
        [END OF IF]
Step 2: SET PTR = START
Step 3: Repeat Step 4 while PTR -> NEXT != START
Step 4:         SET PTR = PTR -> NEXT
        [END OF LOOP]
Step 5: SET PTR -> NEXT = START -> NEXT
Step 6: SET START -> NEXT -> PREV = PTR
Step 7: FREE START
Step 8: SET START = PTR -> NEXT
```

Figure 6.62 Algorithm to delete the first node

Figure 6.62 shows the algorithm to delete the first node from a circular doubly linked list. In Step 1 of the algorithm, we check if the linked list exists or not. If `START = NULL`, then it signifies that there are no nodes in the list and the control is transferred to the last statement of the algorithm.

However, if there are nodes in the linked list, then we use a pointer variable `PTR` that is set to point to the first node of the list. For this, we initialize `PTR` with `START` that stores the address of the first node of the list. The `while` loop traverses through the list to reach the last node. Once we reach the last node, the `NEXT` pointer of `PTR` is set to contain the address of the node that succeeds START. Finally, START is made to point to the next node in the sequence and the memory occupied by the first node of the list is freed and returned to the free pool.

Deleting the Last Node from a Circular Doubly Linked List

Consider the circular doubly linked list shown in Fig. 6.63. Suppose we want to delete the last node from the linked list, then the following changes will be done in the linked list.

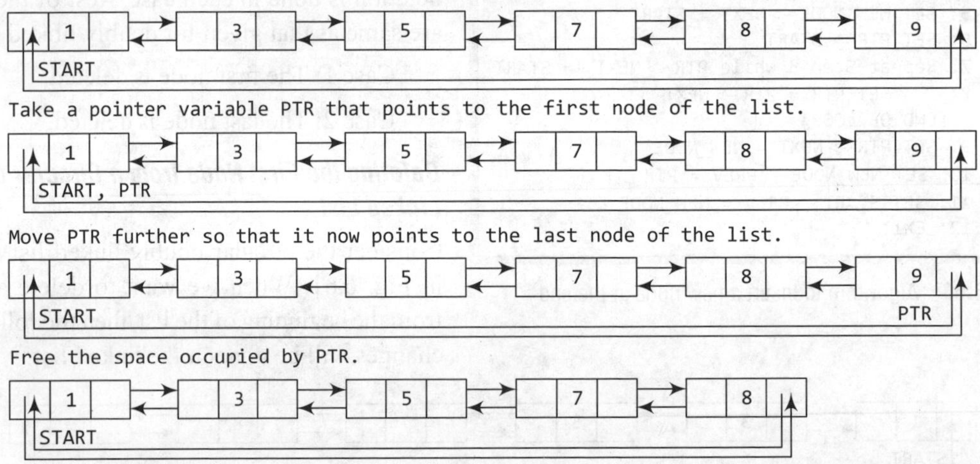

Figure 6.63 Deleting the last node from a circular doubly linked list

```
Step 1: IF START = NULL
            Write UNDERFLOW
            Go to Step 8
        [END OF IF]
Step 2: SET PTR = START
Step 3: Repeat Step 4  while PTR->NEXT != START
Step 4:     SET PTR = PTR->NEXT
        [END OF LOOP]
Step 5: SET PTR->PREV->NEXT = START
Step 6: SET START->PREV = PTR->PREV
Step 7: FREE PTR
Step 8: EXIT
```

Figure 6.64 Algorithm to delete the last node

Figure 6.64 shows the algorithm to delete the last node from a circular doubly linked list. In Step 2, we take a pointer variable PTR and initialize it with START. That is, PTR now points to the first node of the linked list. The while loop traverses through the list to reach the last node. Once we reach the last node, we can also access the second last node by taking its address from the PREV field of the last node. To delete the last node, we simply have to set the next field of the second last node to contain the address of START, so that it now becomes the (new) last node of the linked list. The memory of the previous last node is freed and returned to the free pool.

Programming Example

4. Write a program to create a circular doubly linked list and perform insertions and deletions at the beginning and end of the list.

```
#include <stdio.h>
#include <malloc.h>
#include <stdlib.h>
struct node
{
          struct node *next;
          int data;
          struct node *prev;
};
```

```
struct node *start = NULL;
struct node *create_ll(struct node *);
struct node *display(struct node *);
struct node *insert_beg(struct node *);
struct node *insert_end(struct node *);
struct node *delete_beg(struct node *);
struct node *delete_end(struct node *);
struct node *delete_node(struct node *);
struct node *delete_list(struct node *);
int main()
{
        int option;
        do
        {
                printf("\n\n *****MAIN MENU *****");
                printf("\n 1: Create a list");
                printf("\n 2: Display the list");
                printf("\n 3: Add a node at the beginning");
                printf("\n 4: Add a node at the end");
                printf("\n 5: Delete a node from the beginning");
                printf("\n 6: Delete a node from the end");
                printf("\n 7: Delete a given node");
                printf("\n 8: Delete the entire list");
                printf("\n 9: EXIT");
                printf("\n\n Enter your option : ");
                scanf("%d", &option);
                switch(option)
                {
                        case 1: start = create_ll(start);
                                printf("\n CIRCULAR DOUBLY LINKED LIST CREATED");
                                break;
                        case 2: start = display(start);
                                break;
                        case 3: start = insert_beg(start);
                                break;
                        case 4: start = insert_end(start);
                                break;
                        case 5: start = delete_beg(start);
                                break;
                        case 6: start = delete_end(start);
                                break;
                        case 7: start = delete_node(start);
                                break;
                        case 8: start = delete_list(start);
                                printf("\n CIRCULAR DOUBLY LINKED LIST DELETED");
                                break;
                }
        }while(option != 9);
        return 0;
}
struct node *create_ll(struct node *start)
{
        struct node *new_node, *ptr;
        int num;
        printf("\n Enter -1 to end");
        printf("\n Enter the data : ");
        scanf("%d", &num);
        while(num != -1)
```

```
        {
                if(start == NULL)
                {
                        new_node = (struct node*)malloc(sizeof(struct node));
                        new_node -> prev = NULL;
                        new_node -> data = num;
                        new_node -> next = start;
                        start = new_node;
                }
                else
                {
                        new_node = (struct node*)malloc(sizeof(struct node));
                        new_node -> data = num;
                        ptr = start;
                        while(ptr -> next != start)
                                ptr = ptr -> next;
                        new_node -> prev = ptr;
                        ptr -> next = new_node;
                        new_node -> next = start;
                        start -> prev = new_node;
                }
                printf("\n Enter the data : ");
                scanf("%d", &num);
        }
        return start;
}
struct node *display(struct node *start)
{
        struct node *ptr;
        ptr = start;
        if(ptr==NULL)
        {
                printf("LIST IS EMPTY!");
                return 0;
        }
        while(ptr -> next != start)
        {
                printf("\t %d", ptr -> data);
                ptr = ptr -> next;
        }
        printf("\t %d", ptr -> data);
        return start;
}
struct node *insert_beg(struct node *start)
{
        struct node *new_node, *ptr;
        int num;
        printf("\n Enter the data : ");
        scanf("%d", &num);
        new_node = (struct node *)malloc(sizeof(struct node));
        new_node-> data = num;
        ptr = start;
        while(ptr -> next != start)
                ptr = ptr -> next;
        new_node -> prev = ptr;
        ptr -> next = new_node;
        new_node -> next = start;
        start -> prev = new_node;
        start = new_node;
        return start;
}
```

```
struct node *insert_end(struct node *start)
{
        struct node *ptr, *new_node;
        int num;
        printf("\n Enter the data : ");
        scanf("%d", &num);
        new_node = (struct node *)malloc(sizeof(struct node));
        new_node -> data = num;
        ptr = start;
        while(ptr -> next != start)
                ptr = ptr -> next;
        ptr -> next = new_node;
        new_node -> prev = ptr;
        new_node -> next = start;
        start-> prev = new_node;
        return start;
}
struct node *delete_beg(struct node *start)
{
        struct node *ptr, *temp;
        ptr = start;
        while(ptr -> next != start)
                ptr = ptr -> next;
        ptr -> next = start -> next;
        temp = start;
        start=start->next;
        start->prev=ptr;
        free(temp);
        return start;
}
struct node *delete_end(struct node *start)
{
        struct node *ptr;
        ptr=start;
        while(ptr -> next != start)
                ptr = ptr -> next;
        ptr -> prev -> next = start;
        start -> prev = ptr -> prev;
        free(ptr);
        return start;
}
struct node *delete_node(struct node *start)
{
        struct node *ptr;
        int val;
        printf("\n Enter the value of the node which has to be deleted : ");
        scanf("%d", &val);
        ptr = start;
        if(ptr -> data == val)
        {
                start = delete_beg(start);
                return start;
        }
        else
        {
                while(ptr -> data != val)
                        ptr = ptr -> next;
                ptr -> prev -> next = ptr -> next;
                ptr -> next -> prev = ptr -> prev;
                free(ptr);
                return start;
        }
```

```
}
struct node *delete_list(struct node *start)
{
          struct node *ptr;
          ptr = start;
          while(ptr -> next != start)
                    start = delete_end(start);
          free(start);
          return start;
}
```

Output

```
*****MAIN MENU *****
1: Create a list
2: Display the list
------------------------
8: Delete the entire list
9: EXIT
Enter your option : 1
Enter -1 to end
Enter the data: 2
Enter the data: 3
Enter the data: 4
Enter the data: -1
CIRCULAR DOUBLY LINKED LIST CREATED
Enter your option : 8
CIRCULAR DOUBLY LINKED LIST DELETED
Enter your options : 9
```

6.6 HEADER LINKED LISTS

A header linked list is a special type of linked list which contains a header node at the beginning of the list. So, in a header linked list, START will not point to the first node of the list but START will contain the address of the header node. The following are the two variants of a header linked list:

- *Grounded header linked list* which stores NULL in the next field of the last node.
- *Circular header linked list* which stores the address of the header node in the next field of the last node. Here, the header node will denote the end of the list.

Look at Fig. 6.65 which shows both the types of header linked lists.

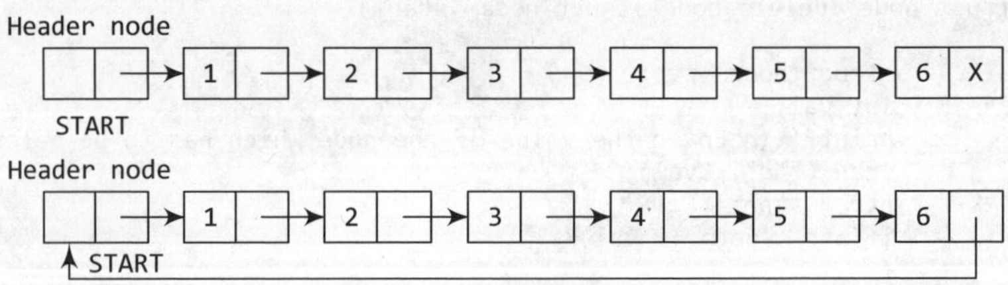

Figure 6.65 Header linked list

As in other linked lists, if START = NULL, then this denotes an empty header linked list. Let us see how a grounded header linked list is stored in the memory. In a grounded header linked list, a node has two fields, DATA and NEXT. The DATA field will store the information part and the NEXT field will store the address of the node in sequence. Consider Fig. 6.66.

Note that START stores the address of the header node. The shaded row denotes a header node. The NEXT field of the header node stores the address of the first node of the list. This node stores H. The corresponding NEXT field stores the address of the next node, which is 3. So, we will look at address 3 to fetch the next data item.

START: 5 (→ 5)

	DATA	NEXT
1	H	3
2		
3	E	6
4		
5	1234	1
6	L	7
7	L	9
8		
9	O	-1

Figure 6.66 Memory representation of a header linked list

START: 5 (→ 5)

	DATA	NEXT
1	H	3
2		
3	E	6
4		
5	1234	1
6	L	7
7	L	9
8		
9	O	5

Figure 6.67 Memory representation of a circular header linked list

```
Step 1: SET PTR = START -> NEXT
Step 2: Repeat Steps 3 and 4 while PTR != START
Step 3:           Apply PROCESS to PTR -> DATA
Step 4:           SET PTR = PTR -> NEXT
        [END OF LOOP]
Step 5: EXIT
```

Figure 6.68 Algorithm to traverse a circular header linked list

Hence, we see that the first node can be accessed by writing FIRST_NODE = START –> NEXT and not by writing START = FIRST_NODE. This is because START points to the header node and the header node points to the first node of the header linked list.

Let us now see how a circular header linked list is stored in the memory. Look at Fig. 6.67. Note that the last node in this case stores the address of the header node (instead of –1).

Hence, we see that the first node can be accessed by writing FIRST_NODE = START –> NEXT and not writing START = FIRST_NODE. This is because START points to the header node and the header node points to the first node of the header linked list.

Let us quickly look at Figs 6.68, 6.69, and 6.70 that show the algorithms to traverse a circular header linked list, insert a new node in it, and delete an existing node from it.

After discussing linked lists in such detail, these algorithms are self-explanatory. There is actually just one small difference between these algorithms and the algorithms that we have discussed earlier. Like we have a header list and a circular header list, we also have a two-way (doubly) header list and a circular two-way (doubly) header list. The algorithms to perform all the basic operations will be exactly the same except that the first node will be accessed by writing START –> NEXT instead of START.

```
Step 1: IF AVAIL = NULL
            Write OVERFLOW
            Go to Step 10
       [END OF IF]
Step 2: SET NEW_NODE = AVAIL
Step 3: SET AVAIL = AVAIL -> NEXT
Step 4: SET PTR = START -> NEXT
Step 5: SET NEW_NODE -> DATA = VAL
Step 6: Repeat Step 7 while PTR -> DATA != NUM
Step 7:     SET PTR = PTR -> NEXT
       [END OF LOOP]
Step 8: NEW_NODE -> NEXT = PTR -> NEXT
Step 9: SET PTR -> NEXT = NEW_NODE
Step 10: EXIT
```

Figure 6.69 Algorithm to insert a new node in a circular header linked list

```
Step 1: SET PTR = START->NEXT
Step 2: Repeat Steps 3 and 4 while
          PTR -> DATA != VAL
Step 3:     SET PREPTR = PTR
Step 4:     SET PTR = PTR -> NEXT
          [END OF LOOP]
Step 5: SET PREPTR -> NEXT = PTR -> NEXT
Step 6: FREE PTR
Step 7: EXIT
```

Figure 6.70 Algorithm to delete a node from a circular header linked list

Programming Example

5. Write a program to implement a header linked list.

```
#include <stdio.h>
#include <malloc.h>
#include <stdlib.h>
struct node
{
        int data;
        struct node *next;
};
struct node *start = NULL;
struct node *create_hll(struct node *);
struct node *display(struct node *);
int main()
{
        int option;
        do
        {
                printf("\n\n *****MAIN MENU *****");
                printf("\n 1: Create a list");
                printf("\n 2: Display the list");
                printf("\n 3: EXIT");
                printf("\n Enter your option : ");
                scanf("%d", &option);
                switch(option)
                {
                        case 1: start = create_hll(start);
                               printf("\n HEADER LINKED LIST CREATED");
                               break;
                        case 2: start = display(start);
                               break;
                }
        }while(option !=3);
        return 0;
}
struct node *create_hll(struct node *start)
{
        struct node *new_node, *ptr;
        int num;
        printf("\n Enter -1 to end");
        printf("\n Enter the data : ");
        scanf("%d", &num);
        while(num!=-1)
        {
                new_node = (struct node*)malloc(sizeof(struct node));
                new_node->data=num;
                new_node->next=NULL;
                if(start==NULL)
                {
                        start = (struct node*)malloc(sizeof(struct node));
                        start->next=new_node;
                }
                else
                {
                        ptr=start;
                        while(ptr->next!=NULL)
                                ptr=ptr->next;
                        ptr->next=new_node;
                }
```

```
                printf("\n Enter the data : ");
                scanf("%d", &num);
        }
        return start;
}
struct node *display(struct node *start)
{
        struct node *ptr;
        ptr=start;
        while(ptr!=NULL)
        {
                printf("\t %d", ptr->data);
                ptr = ptr->next;
        }
        return start;
}
```

Output

```
*****MAIN MENU *****
1: Create a list
2: Display the list
3: EXIT
Enter your option : 1
Enter -1 to end
Enter the data: 1
Enter the data: 2
Enter the data: 4
Enter the data: -1
HEADER LINKED LIST CREATED
Enter your option : 3
```

6.7 MULTI-LINKED LISTS

In a multi-linked list, each node can have `n` number of pointers to other nodes. A doubly linked list is a special case of multi-linked lists. However, unlike doubly linked lists, nodes in a multi-linked list may or may not have inverses for each pointer. We can differentiate a doubly linked list from a multi-linked list in two ways:

(a) A doubly linked list has exactly two pointers. One pointer points to the previous node and the other points to the next node. But a node in the multi-linked list can have any number of pointers.

(b) In a doubly linked list, pointers are exact inverses of each other, i.e., for every pointer which points to a previous node there is a pointer which points to the next node. This is not true for a multi-linked list.

Multi-linked lists are generally used to organize multiple orders of one set of elements. For example, if we have a linked list that stores name and marks obtained by students in a class, then we can organize the nodes of the list in two ways:

(i) Organize the nodes alphabetically (according to the name)

(ii) Organize the nodes according to decreasing order of marks so that the information of student who got highest marks comes before other students.

Figure 6.71 shows a multi-linked list in which students' nodes are organized by both the aforementioned ways.

A new node can be inserted in a multi-linked list in the same way as it is done for a doubly linked list.

Note In multi-linked lists, we can have inverses of each pointer as in a doubly linked list. But for that we must have four pointers in a single node.

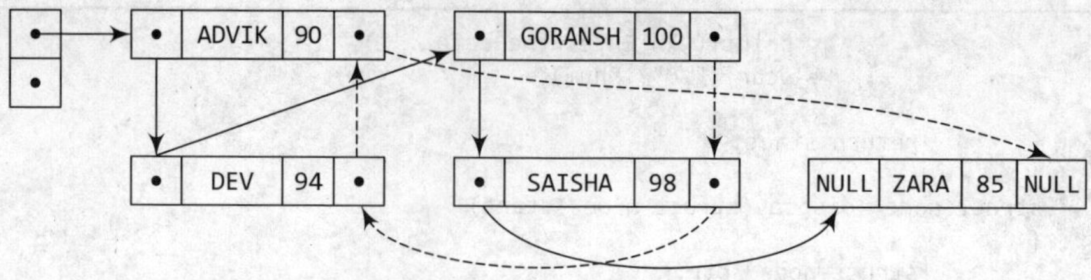

Figure 6.71 Multi-linked list that stores names alphabetically as well as according to decreasing order of marks

y \ x	0	1	2
0	0	25	0
1	0	0	0
2	17	0	5
3	19	0	0

Figure 6.72 Sparse matrix

Multi-linked lists are also used to store sparse matrices. In Chapter 3 we have read about sparse matrices. Such matrices have very few non-zero values stored and most of the entries are zero. Sparse matrices are very common in engineering applications. If we use a normal array to store such matrices, we will end up wasting a lot of space. Therefore, a better solution is to represent these matrices using multi-linked lists.

The sparse matrix shown in Fig. 6.72 can be represented using a linked list for every row and column. Since a value is in exactly one row and one column, it will appear in both lists exactly once. A node in the multi-linked will have four parts. First stores the data, second stores a pointer to the next node in the row, third stores a pointer to the next node in the column, and the fourth stores the coordinates or the row and column number in which the data appears in the matrix. However, as in case of doubly linked lists, we can also have a corresponding inverse pointer for every pointer in the multi-linked list representation of a sparse matrix.

Note When a non-zero value in the sparse matrix is set to zero, the corresponding node in the multi-linked list must be deleted.

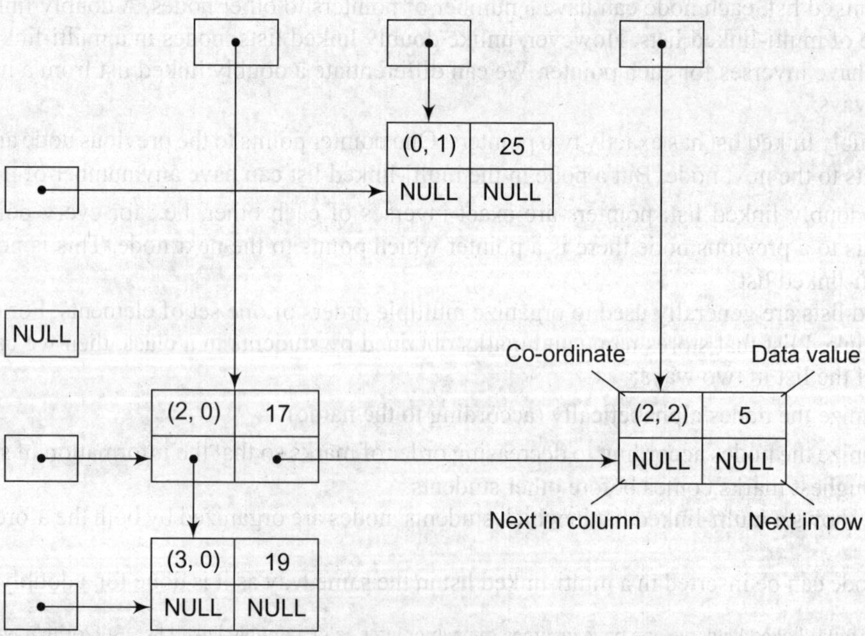

Figure 6.73 Multi-linked representation of sparse matrix shown in Fig. 6.72

6.8 APPLICATIONS OF LINKED LISTS

Linked lists can be used to represent polynomials and the different operations that can be performed on them. In this section, we will see how polynomials are represented in the memory using linked lists.

6.8.1 Polynomial Representation

Let us see how a polynomial is represented in the memory using a linked list. Consider a polynomial $6x^3 + 9x^2 + 7x + 1$. Every individual term in a polynomial consists of two parts, a coefficient and a power. Here, 6, 9, 7, and 1 are the coefficients of the terms that have 3, 2, 1, and 0 as their powers respectively.

Every term of a polynomial can be represented as a node of the linked list. Figure 6.74 shows the linked representation of the terms of the above polynomial.

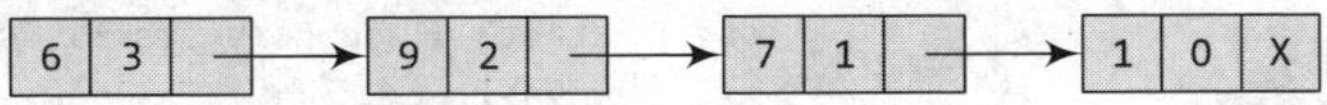

Figure 6.74 Linked representation of a polynomial

Now that we know how polynomials are represented using nodes of a linked list, let us write a program to perform operations on polynomials.

Programming Example

6. Write a program to store a polynomial using linked list. Also, perform addition and subtraction on two polynomials.

```
#include <stdio.h>
#include <malloc.h>
#include <stdlib.h>
struct node
{
        int num;
        int coeff;
        struct node *next;
};
struct node *start1 = NULL;
struct node *start2 = NULL;
struct node *start3 = NULL;
struct node *start4 = NULL;
struct node *last3 = NULL;
struct node *create_poly(struct node *);
struct node *display_poly(struct node *);
struct node *add_poly(struct node *, struct node *, struct node *);
struct node *sub_poly(struct node *, struct node *, struct node *);
struct node *add_node(struct node *, int, int);
int main()
{
        int option;
        do
        {
                printf("\n******* MAIN MENU *******");
                printf("\n 1. Enter the first polynomial");
                printf("\n 2. Display the first polynomial");
                printf("\n 3. Enter the second polynomial");
                printf("\n 4. Display the second polynomial");
                printf("\n 5. Add the polynomials");
                printf("\n 6. Display the result");
                printf("\n 7. Subtract the polynomials");
                printf("\n 8. Display the result");
```

```
                printf("\n 9. EXIT");
                printf("\n\n Enter your option : ");
                scanf("%d", &option);
                switch(option)
                {
                        case 1: start1 = create_poly(start1);
                                break;
                        case 2: start1 = display_poly(start1);
                                break;
                        case 3: start2 = create_poly(start2);
                                break;
                        case 4: start2 = display_poly(start2);
                                break;
                        case 5: start3 = add_poly(start1, start2, start3);
                                break;
                        case 6: start3 = display_poly(start3);
                                break;
                        case 7: start4 = sub_poly(start1, start2, start4);
                                break;
                        case 8: start4 = display_poly(start4);
                                break;
                }
        }while(option!=9);
        return 0;
}
struct node *create_poly(struct node *start)
{
        struct node *new_node, *ptr;
        int n, c;
        printf("\n Enter the number : ");
        scanf("%d", &n);
        printf("\t Enter its coefficient : ");
        scanf("%d", &c);
        while(n != -1)
        {
                if(start==NULL)
                {
                        new_node = (struct node *)malloc(sizeof(struct node));
                        new_node -> num = n;
                        new_node -> coeff = c;
                        new_node -> next = NULL;
                        start = new_node;
                }
                else
                {
                        ptr = start;
                        while(ptr -> next != NULL)
                                ptr = ptr -> next;
                        new_node = (struct node *)malloc(sizeof(struct node));
                        new_node -> num = n;
                        new_node -> coeff = c;
                        new_node -> next = NULL;
                        ptr -> next = new_node;
                }
                printf("\n Enter the number : ");
                scanf("%d", &n);
                if(n == -1)
                        break;
                printf("\t Enter its coefficient : ");
```

```
			scanf("%d", &c);
		}
		return start;
	}
	struct node *display_poly(struct node *start)
	{
		struct node *ptr;
		ptr = start;
		while(ptr != NULL)
		{
			printf("\n%d x %d\t", ptr -> num, ptr -> coeff);
			ptr = ptr -> next;
		}
		return start;
	}
	struct node *add_poly(struct node *start1, struct node *start2, struct node *start3)
	{
		struct node *ptr1, *ptr2;
		int sum_num, c;
		ptr1 = start1, ptr2 = start2;
		while(ptr1 != NULL && ptr2 != NULL)
		{
			if(ptr1 -> coeff == ptr2 -> coeff)
			{
				sum_num = ptr1 -> num + ptr2 -> num;
				start3 = add_node(start3, sum_num, ptr1 -> coeff);
				ptr1 = ptr1 -> next;
				ptr2 = ptr2 -> next;
			}
			else if(ptr1 -> coeff > ptr2 -> coeff)
			{
				start3 = add_node(start3, ptr1 -> num, ptr1 -> coeff);
				ptr1 = ptr1 -> next;
			}
			else if(ptr1 -> coeff < ptr2 -> coeff)
			{
				start3 = add_node(start3, ptr2 -> num, ptr2 -> coeff);
				ptr2 = ptr2 -> next;
			}
		}
		if(ptr1 == NULL)
		{
			while(ptr2 != NULL)
			{
				start3 = add_node(start3, ptr2 -> num, ptr2 -> coeff);
				ptr2 = ptr2 -> next;
			}
		}
		if(ptr2 == NULL)
		{
			while(ptr1 != NULL)
			{
				start3 = add_node(start3, ptr1 -> num, ptr1 -> coeff);
				ptr1 = ptr1 -> next;
			}
		}
		return start3;
	}
	struct node *sub_poly(struct node *start1, struct node *start2, struct node *start4)
```

```
{
        struct node *ptr1, *ptr2;
        int sub_num, c;
        ptr1 = start1, ptr2 = start2;
        do
        {
                if(ptr1 -> coeff == ptr2 -> coeff)
                {
                        sub_num = ptr1 -> num - ptr2 -> num;
                        start4 = add_node(start4, sub_num, ptr1 -> coeff);
                        ptr1 = ptr1 -> next;
                        ptr2 = ptr2 -> next;
                }
                else if(ptr1 -> coeff > ptr2 -> coeff)
                {
                        start4 = add_node(start4, ptr1 -> num, ptr1 -> coeff);
                        ptr1 = ptr1 -> next;
                }
                else if(ptr1 -> coeff < ptr2 -> coeff)
                {
                        start4 = add_node(start4, ptr2 -> num, ptr2 -> coeff);
                        ptr2 = ptr2 -> next;
                }
        }while(ptr1 != NULL || ptr2 != NULL);
        if(ptr1 == NULL)
        {
                while(ptr2 != NULL)
                {
                        start4 = add_node(start4, ptr2 -> num, ptr2 -> coeff);
                        ptr2 = ptr2 -> next;
                }
        }
        if(ptr2 == NULL)
        {
                while(ptr1 != NULL)
                {
                        start4 = add_node(start4, ptr1 -> num, ptr1 -> coeff);
                        ptr1 = ptr1 -> next;
                }
        }
        return start4;
}
struct node *add_node(struct node *start, int n, int c)
{
        struct node *ptr, *new_node;
        if(start == NULL)
        {
                new_node = (struct node *)malloc(sizeof(struct node));
                new_node -> num = n;
                new_node -> coeff = c;
                new_node -> next = NULL;
                start = new_node;
        }
        else
        {
                ptr = start;
                while(ptr -> next != NULL)
                        ptr = ptr -> next;
                new_node = (struct node *)malloc(sizeof(struct node));
```

```
                new_node -> num = n;
                new_node -> coeff = c;
                new_node -> next = NULL;
                ptr -> next = new_node;
        }
        return start;
}
```

Output

```
******* MAIN MENU *******
1. Enter the first polynomial
2. Display the first polynomial
-------------------------------
9. EXIT
Enter your option : 1
Enter the number : 6        Enter its coefficient : 2
Enter the number : 5        Enter its coefficient : 1
Enter the number : -1
Enter your option : 2
6 x 2    5 x 1
Enter your option : 9
```

Points to Remember

- A linked list is a linear collection of data elements called as nodes in which linear representation is given by links from one node to another.
- Linked list is a data structure which can be used to implement other data structures such as stacks, queues, and their variations.
- Before we insert a new node in linked lists, we need to check for `OVERFLOW` condition, which occurs when no free memory cell is present in the system.
- Before we delete a node from a linked list, we must first check for `UNDERFLOW` condition which occurs when we try to delete a node from a linked list that is empty.
- When we delete a node from a linked list, we have to actually free the memory occupied by that node. The memory is returned back to the free pool so that it can be used to store other programs and data.
- In a circular linked list, the last node contains a pointer to the first node of the list. While traversing a circular linked list, we can begin at any node and traverse the list in any direction forward or backward until we reach the same node where we had started.
- A doubly linked list or a two-way linked list is a linked list which contains a pointer to the next as well as the previous node in the sequence. Therefore, it consists of three parts—data, a pointer to the next node, and a pointer to the previous node.
- The `PREV` field of the first node and the `NEXT` field of the last node contain `NULL`. This enables to traverse the list in the backward direction as well.
- Thus, a doubly linked list calls for more space per node and more expensive basic operations. However, a doubly linked list provides the ease to manipulate the elements of the list as it maintains pointers to nodes in both the directions (forward and backward). The main advantage of using a doubly linked list is that it makes search operation twice as efficient.
- A circular doubly linked list or a circular two-way linked list is a more complex type of linked list which contains a pointer to the next as well as previous node in the sequence. The difference between a doubly linked and a circular doubly linked list is that the circular doubly linked list does not contain `NULL` in the previous field of the first node and the next field of the last node. Rather, the next field of the last node stores the address of the first node of the list. Similarly, the previous field of the first field stores the address of the last node.
- A header linked list is a special type of linked list which contains a header node at the beginning of the list. So, in a header linked list `START` will not point to the first node of the list but `START` will contain the address of the header node.
- Multi-linked lists are generally used to organize multiple orders of one set of elements. In a multi-linked list, each node can have n number of pointers to other nodes.

Exercises

Review Questions

1. Make a comparison between a linked list and a linear array. Which one will you prefer to use and when?
2. Why is a doubly linked list more useful than a singly linked list?
3. Give the advantages and uses of a circular linked list.
4. Specify the use of a header node in a header linked list.
5. Give the linked representation of the following polynomial:

$$7x^3y^2 - 8x^2y + 3xy + 11x - 4$$

6. Explain the difference between a circular linked list and a singly linked list.
7. Form a linked list to store students' details.
8. Use the linked list of the above question to insert the record of a new student in the list.
9. Delete the record of a student with a specified roll number from the list maintained in Question 7.
10. Given a linked list that contains English alphabet. The characters may be in upper case or in lower case. Create two linked lists—one which stores upper case characters and the other that stores lower case characters.
11. Create a linked list which stores names of the employees. Then sort these names and re-display the contents of the linked list.

Programming Exercises

1. Write a program that removes all nodes that have duplicate information.
2. Write a program to print the total number of occurrences of a given item in the linked list.
3. Write a program to multiply every element of the linked list with 10.
4. Write a program to print the number of non-zero elements in the list.
5. Write a program that prints whether the given linked list is sorted (in ascending order) or not.
6. Write a program that copies a circular linked list.
7. Write a program to merge two linked lists.
8. Write a program to sort the values stored in a doubly circular linked list.
9. Write a program to merge two sorted linked lists. The resultant list must also be sorted.
10. Write a program to delete the first, last, and middle node of a header linked list.
11. Write a program to create a linked list from an already given list. The new linked list must contain every alternate element of the existing linked list.
12. Write a program to concatenate two doubly linked lists.
13. Write a program to delete the first element of a doubly linked list. Add this node as the last node of the list.
14. Write a program to
    (a) Delete the first occurrence of a given character in a linked list
    (b) Delete the last occurrence of a given character
    (c) Delete all the occurrences of a given character
15. Write a program to reverse a linked list using recursion.
16. Write a program to input an n digit number. Now, break this number into its individual digits and then store every single digit in a separate node thereby forming a linked list. For example, if you enter 12345, then there will 5 nodes in the list containing nodes with values 1, 2, 3, 4, 5.
17. Write a program to add the values of the nodes of a linked list and then calculate the mean.
18. Write a program that prints minimum and maximum values in a linked list that stores integer values.
19. Write a program to interchange the value of the first element with the last element, second element with second last element, so on and so forth of a doubly linked list.
20. Write a program to make the first element of singly linked list as the last element of the list.
21. Write a program to count the number of occurrences of a given value in a linked list.
22. Write a program that adds 10 to the values stored in the nodes of a doubly linked list.
23. Write a program to form a linked list of floating point numbers. Display the sum and mean of these numbers.
24. Write a program to delete the kth node from a linked list.

25. Write a program to perform deletions in all the cases of a circular header linked list.
26. Write a program to multiply a polynomial with a given number.
27. Write a program to count the number of non-zero values in a circular linked list.
28. Write a program to create a linked list which stores the details of employees in a department. Read and print the information stored in the list.
29. Use the linked list of Question 28 so that it displays the record of a given employee only.
30. Use the linked list of Question 28 and insert information about a new employee.
31. Use the linked list of Question 28 and delete information about an existing employee.
32. Write a program to move a middle node of a doubly link list to the top of the list.
33. Write a program to create a singly linked list and reverse the list by interchanging the links and not the data.
34. Write a program that prints the nth element from the end of a linked list in a single pass.
35. Write a program that creates a singly linked list. Use a function isSorted that returns 1 if the list is sorted and 0 otherwise.
36. Write a program to interchange the kth and the `(k+1)`th node of a circular doubly linked list.
37. Write a program to create a header linked list.
38. Write a program to delete a node from a circular header linked list.
39. Write a program to delete all nodes from a header linked list that has negative values in its data part.

Multiple-choice Questions

1. A linked list is a
   (a) Random access structure
   (b) Sequential access structure
   (c) Both
   (d) None of these
2. An array is a
   (a) Random access structure
   (b) Sequential access structure
   (c) Both
   (d) None of these
3. Linked list is used to implement data structures like
   (a) Stacks (b) Queues
   (c) Trees (d) All of these
4. Which type of linked list contains a pointer to the next as well as the previous node in the sequence?
   (a) Singly linked list (b) Circular linked list
   (c) Doubly linked list (d) All of these
5. Which type of linked list does not store NULL in next field?
   (a) Singly linked list (b) Circular linked list
   (c) Doubly linked list (d) All of these
6. Which type of linked list stores the address of the header node in the next field of the last node?
   (a) Singly linked list
   (b) Circular linked list
   (c) Doubly linked list
   (d) Circular header linked list
7. Which type of linked list can have four pointers per node?
   (a) Circular doubly linked list
   (b) Multi-linked list
   (c) Header linked list
   (d) Doubly linked list

True or False

1. A linked list is a linear collection of data elements.
2. A linked list can grow and shrink during run time.
3. A node in a linked list can point to only one node at a time.
4. A node in a singly linked list can reference the previous node.
5. A linked list can store only integer values.
6. Linked list is a random access structure.
7. Deleting a node from a doubly linked list is easier than deleting it from a singly linked list.
8. Every node in a linked list contains an integer part and a pointer.
9. `START` stores the address of the first node in the list.
10. Underflow is a condition that occurs when we try to delete a node from a linked list that is empty.

Fill in the Blanks

1. ______ is used to store the address of the first free memory location.
2. The complexity to insert a node at the beginning of the linked list is ______.
3. The complexity to delete a node from the end of the linked list is ______.

4. Inserting a node at the beginning of the doubly linked list needs to modify ______ pointers.
5. Inserting a node in the middle of the singly linked list needs to modify ______ pointers.
6. Inserting a node at the end of the circular linked list needs to modify ______ pointers.
7. Inserting a node at the beginning of the circular doubly linked list needs to modify ______ pointers.
8. Deleting a node from the beginning of the singly linked list needs to modify ______ pointers
9. Deleting a node from the middle of the doubly linked list needs to modify ______ pointers.
10. Deleting a node from the end of a circular linked list needs to modify ______ pointers.
11. Each element in a linked list is known as a ______.
12. First node in the linked list is called the ______.
13. Data elements in a linked list are known as ______.
14. Overflow occurs when ______.
15. In a circular linked list, the last node contains a pointer to the ______ node of the list.

Coding Challenges

1. Write a program to find the kth smallest element in a linked list.
2. Write a program to find the intersection point of two singly linked lists.
3. Write a program to find the smallest missing positive number in a linked list containing both positive and negative numbers.
4. Write a program to swap every two nodes in a linked list (e.g., given 1->2->3->4, the program should return 2->1->4->3).
5. Write a program to find the median of a sorted circular linked list.

CHAPTER 7

Stacks

LEARNING OBJECTIVE

A stack is an important data structure which is extensively used in computer applications. In this chapter we will study about the important features of stacks to understand how and why they organize the data so uniquely. The chapter will also illustrate the implementation of stacks by using both arrays as well as linked lists. Finally, the chapter will discuss in detail some of the very useful areas where stacks are primarily used.

7.1 INTRODUCTION

Stack is an important data structure which stores its elements in an ordered manner. We will explain the concept of stacks using an analogy. You must have seen a pile of plates where one plate is placed on top of another as shown in Fig. 7.1. Now, when you want to remove a plate, you remove the topmost plate first. Hence, you can add and remove an element (i.e., a plate) only at/from one position which is the topmost position.

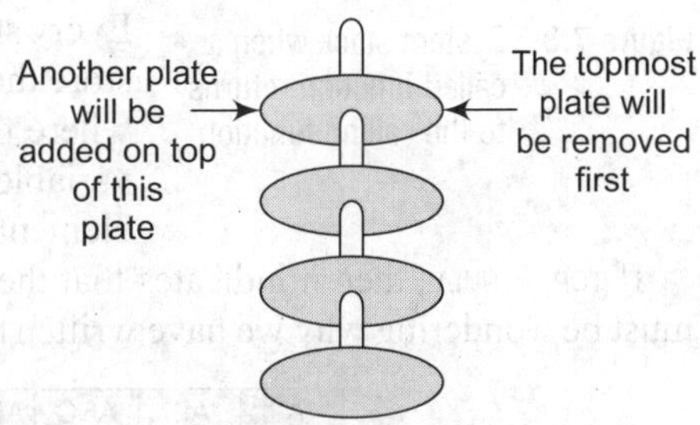

Figure 7.1 Stack of plates

A stack is a linear data structure which uses the same principle, i.e., the elements in a stack are added and removed only from one end, which is called the TOP. Hence, a stack is called a LIFO (Last-In-First-Out) data structure, as the element that was inserted last is the first one to be taken out.

Now the question is where do we need stacks in computer science? The answer is in function calls. Consider an example, where we are executing function A. In the course of its execution, function A calls another function B. Function B in turn calls another function C, which calls function D.

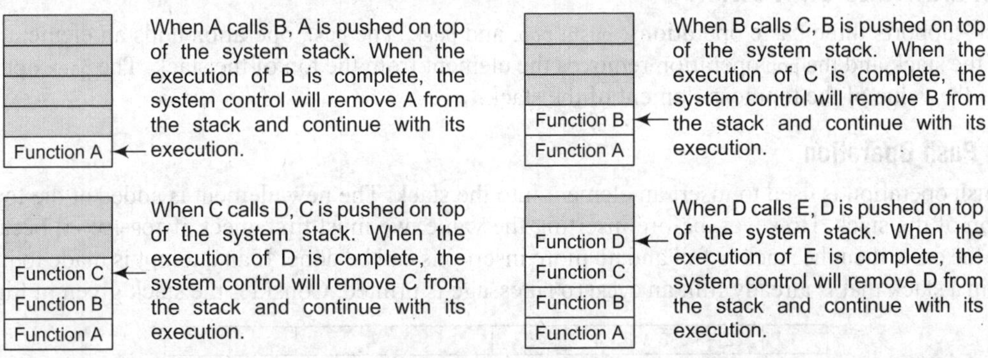

Figure 7.2 System stack in the case of function calls

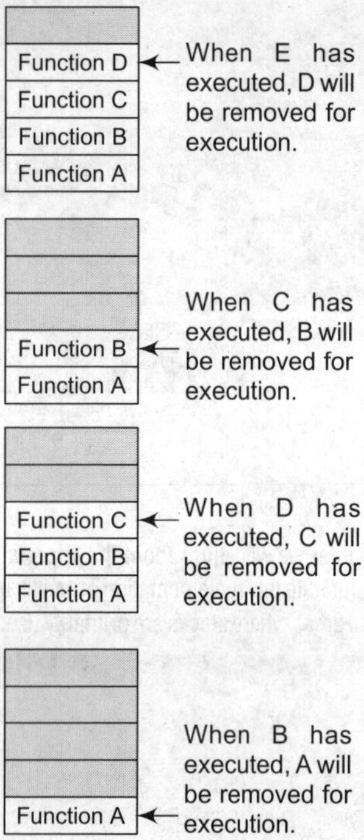

Figure 7.3 System stack when a called function returns to the calling function

In order to keep track of the returning point of each active function, a special stack called system stack or call stack is used. Whenever a function calls another function, the calling function is pushed onto the top of the stack. This is because after the called function gets executed, the control is passed back to the calling function. Look at Fig. 7.2 which shows this concept.

Now when function `E` is executed, function `D` will be removed from the top of the stack and executed. Once function `D` gets completely executed, function `C` will be removed from the stack for execution. The whole procedure will be repeated until all the functions get executed. Let us look at the stack after each function is executed. This is shown in Fig. 7.3.

The system stack ensures a proper execution order of functions. Therefore, stacks are frequently used in situations where the order of processing is very important, especially when the processing needs to be postponed until other conditions are fulfilled.

Stacks can be implemented using either arrays or linked lists. In the following sections, we will discuss both array and linked list implementation of stacks.

7.2 ARRAY REPRESENTATION OF STACKS

In the computer's memory, stacks can be represented as a linear array. Every stack has a variable called `TOP` associated with it, which is used to store the address of the topmost element of the stack. It is this position where the element will be added to or deleted from. There is another variable called `MAX`, which is used to store the maximum number of elements that the stack can hold.

If `TOP = NULL`, then it indicates that the stack is empty and if `TOP = MAX-1`, then the stack is full. (You must be wondering why we have written `MAX-1`. It is because array indices start from 0.) Look at Fig. 7.4.

A	AB	ABC	ABCD	ABCDE					
0	1	2	3	TOP = 4	5	6	7	8	9

Figure 7.4 Stack

The stack in Fig. 7.4 shows that `TOP = 4`, so insertions and deletions will be done at this position. In the above stack, five more elements can still be stored.

7.3 OPERATIONS ON A STACK

A stack supports three basic operations: `push`, `pop`, and `peek`. The `push` operation adds an element to the top of the stack and the `pop` operation removes the element from the top of the stack. The `peek` operation returns the value of the topmost element of the stack.

7.3.1 Push Operation

The push operation is used to insert an element into the stack. The new element is added at the topmost position of the stack. However, before inserting the value, we must first check if `TOP=MAX-1`, because if that is the case, then the stack is full and no more insertions can be done. If an attempt is made to insert a value in a stack that is already full, an `OVERFLOW` message is printed. Consider the stack given in Fig. 7.5.

1	2	3	4	5					
0	1	2	3	TOP = 4	5	6	7	8	9

Figure 7.5 Stack

To insert an element with value 6, we first check if `TOP=MAX-1`. If the condition is false, then we increment the value of `TOP` and store the new element at the position given by `stack[TOP]`. Thus, the updated stack becomes as shown in Fig. 7.6.

1	2	3	4	5	6				
0	1	2	3	4	**TOP = 5**	6	7	8	9

Figure 7.6 Stack after insertion

```
Step 1: IF TOP = MAX-1
            PRINT "OVERFLOW"
            Goto Step 4
        [END OF IF]
Step 2: SET TOP = TOP + 1
Step 3: SET STACK[TOP] = VALUE
Step 4: END
```

Figure 7.7 Algorithm to insert an element in a stack

Figure 7.7 shows the algorithm to insert an element in a stack. In Step 1, we first check for the `OVERFLOW` condition. In Step 2, `TOP` is incremented so that it points to the next location in the array. In Step 3, the value is stored in the stack at the location pointed by `TOP`.

7.3.2 Pop Operation

The `pop` operation is used to delete the topmost element from the stack. However, before deleting the value, we must first check if `TOP=NULL` because if that is the case, then it means the stack is empty and no more deletions can be done. If an attempt is made to delete a value from a stack that is already empty, an `UNDERFLOW` message is printed. Consider the stack given in Fig. 7.8.

1	2	3	4	5					
0	1	2	3	**TOP = 4**	5	6	7	8	9

Figure 7.8 Stack

To delete the topmost element, we first check if `TOP=NULL`. If the condition is false, then we decrement the value pointed by `TOP`. Thus, the updated stack becomes as shown in Fig. 7.9.

1	2	3	4						
0	1	2	**TOP = 3**	4	5	6	7	8	9

Figure 7.9 Stack after deletion

Figure 7.10 shows the algorithm to delete an element from a stack. In Step 1, we first check for the `UNDERFLOW` condition. In Step 2, the value of the location in the stack pointed by `TOP` is stored in `VAL`. In Step 3, `TOP` is decremented.

```
Step 1: IF TOP = NULL
            PRINT "UNDERFLOW"
            Goto Step 4
        [END OF IF]
Step 2: SET VAL = STACK[TOP]
Step 3: SET TOP = TOP - 1
Step 4: END
```

Figure 7.10 Algorithm to delete an element from a stack

7.3.3 Peek Operation

`Peek` is an operation that returns the value of the topmost element of the stack without deleting it from the stack. The algorithm for `Peek` operation is given in Fig. 7.11.

However, the `Peek` operation first checks if the stack is empty, i.e., if `TOP = NULL`, then an appropriate message is printed, else the value is returned. Consider the stack given in Fig. 7.12.

```
Step 1: IF TOP = NULL
            PRINT "STACK IS EMPTY"
            Goto Step 3
Step 2: RETURN STACK[TOP]
Step 3: END
```

Figure 7.11 Algorithm for `Peek` operation

1	2	3	4	5					
0	1	2	3	**TOP = 4**	5	6	7	8	9

Figure 7.12 Stack

Here, the `Peek` operation will return 5, as it is the value of the topmost element of the stack.

Programming Example

1. Write a program to perform Push, Pop, and Peek operations on a stack.

```
#include <stdio.h>
#include <stdlib.h>
#define MAX 3

int st[MAX], top=-1;
void push(int st[], int val);
int pop(int st[]);
int peek(int st[]);
void display(int st[]);

int main(int argc, char *argv[]) {
        int val, option;
        do
        {
                printf("\n *****MAIN MENU*****");
                printf("\n 1. PUSH");
                printf("\n 2. POP");
                printf("\n 3. PEEK");
                printf("\n 4. DISPLAY");
                printf("\n 5. EXIT");
                printf("\n Enter your option: ");
                scanf("%d", &option);
                switch(option)
                {
                case 1:
                        printf("\n Enter the number to be pushed on stack: ");
                        scanf("%d", &val);
                        push(st, val);
                        break;
                case 2:
                        val = pop(st);
                        if(val != -1)
                        printf("\n The value deleted from stack is: %d", val);
                        break;
                case 3:
                        val = peek(st);
                        if(val != -1)
                        printf("\n The value stored at top of stack is: %d", val);
                        break;
                case 4:
                        display(st);
                        break;
                }
        }while(option != 5);
        return 0;
}
void push(int st[], int val)
{
        if(top == MAX-1)
        {
                printf("\n STACK OVERFLOW");
        }
        else
        {
                top++;
```

```
                st[top] = val;
        }
}
int pop(int st[])
{
        int val;
        if(top == -1)
        {
                printf("\n STACK UNDERFLOW");
                return -1;
        }
        else
        {
                val = st[top];
                top--;
                return val;
        }
}
void display(int st[])
{
        int i;
        if(top == -1)
        printf("\n STACK IS EMPTY");
        else
        {
                for(i=top;i>=0;i--)
                printf("\n %d",st[i]);
                printf("\n");
        }
}
int peek(int st[])
{
        if(top == -1)
        {
                printf("\n STACK IS EMPTY");
                return -1;
        }
        else
        return (st[top]);
}
```

Output

```
*****MAIN MENU*****
1. PUSH
2. POP
3. PEEK
4. DISPLAY
5. EXIT
Enter your option : 1
Enter the number to be pushed on stack : 500
```

7.4 LINKED REPRESENTATION OF STACKS

We have seen how a stack is created using an array. This technique of creating a stack is easy, but the drawback is that the array must be declared to have some fixed size. In case the stack is a very small one or its maximum size is known in advance, then the array implementation of the stack gives an efficient implementation. But if the array size cannot be determined in advance, then the other alternative, i.e., linked representation, is used.

The storage requirement of linked representation of the stack with `n` elements is `O(n)`, and the typical time requirement for the operations is `O(1)`.

In a linked stack, every node has two parts—one that stores data and another that stores the address of the next node. The `START` pointer of the linked list is used as `TOP`. All insertions and deletions are done at the node pointed by `TOP`. If `TOP = NULL`, then it indicates that the stack is empty.

The linked representation of a stack is shown in Fig. 7.13.

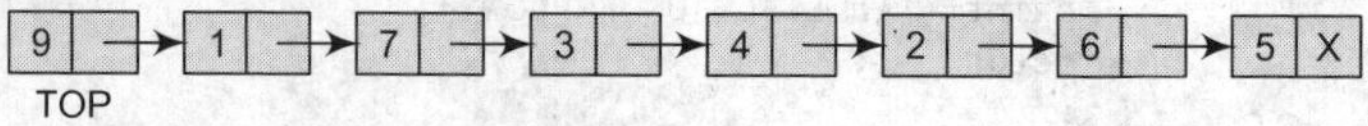

Figure 7.13 Linked stack

7.5 OPERATIONS ON A LINKED STACK

A linked stack supports all the three stack operations, that is, `push`, `pop`, and `peek`.

7.5.1 Push Operation

The `push` operation is used to insert an element into the stack. The new element is added at the topmost position of the stack. Consider the linked stack shown in Fig. 7.14.

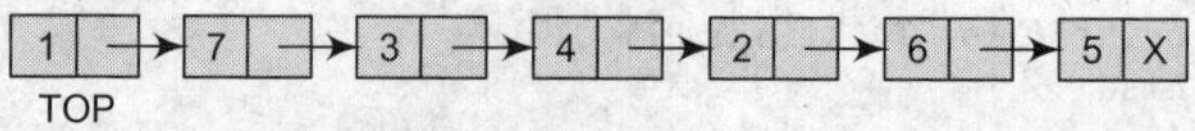

Figure 7.14 Linked stack

To insert an element with value 9, we first check if `TOP=NULL`. If this is the case, then we allocate memory for a new node, store the value in its `DATA` part and `NULL` in its `NEXT` part. The new node will then be called `TOP`. However, if `TOP!=NULL`, then we insert the new node at the beginning of the linked stack and name this new node as `TOP`. Thus, the updated stack becomes as shown in Fig. 7.15.

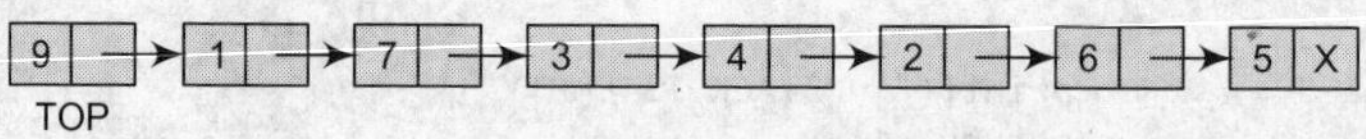

Figure 7.15 Linked stack after inserting a new node

```
Step 1: Allocate memory for the new
        node and name it as NEW_NODE
Step 2: SET NEW_NODE -> DATA = VAL
Step 3: IF TOP = NULL
              SET NEW_NODE -> NEXT = NULL
              SET TOP = NEW_NODE
        ELSE
              SET NEW_NODE -> NEXT = TOP
              SET TOP = NEW_NODE
        [END OF IF]
Step 4: END
```

Figure 7.16 Algorithm to insert an element in a linked stack

Figure 7.16 shows the algorithm to push an element into a linked stack. In Step 1, memory is allocated for the new node. In Step 2, the `DATA` part of the new node is initialized with the value to be stored in the node. In Step 3, we check if the new node is the first node of the linked list. This is done by checking if `TOP = NULL`. In case the `IF` statement evaluates to true, then `NULL` is stored in the `NEXT` part of the node and the new node is called `TOP`. However, if the new node is not the first node in the list, then it is added before the first node of the list (that is, the `TOP` node) and termed as `TOP`.

7.5.2 Pop Operation

The `pop` operation is used to delete the topmost element from a stack. However, before deleting the value, we must first check if `TOP=NULL`, because if this is the case, then it means that thestack is empty and no more deletions can be done. If an attempt is made to delete a value from a stack that is already empty, an `UNDERFLOW` message is printed. Consider the stack shown in Fig. 7.17.

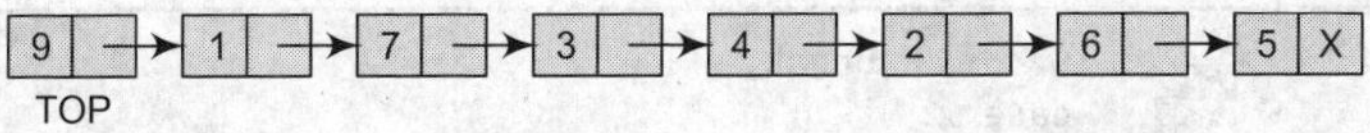

Figure 7.17 Linked stack

In case `TOP!=NULL`, then we will delete the node pointed by `TOP`, and make `TOP` point to the second element of the linked stack. Thus, the updated stack becomes as shown in Fig. 7.18.

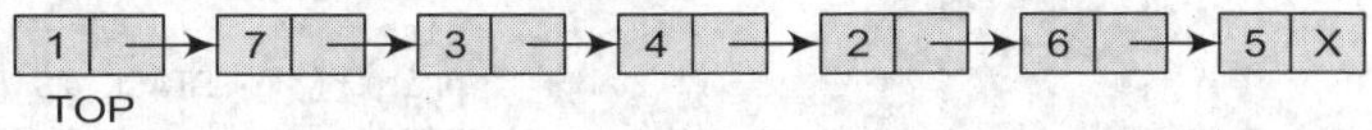

Figure 7.18 Linked stack after deletion of the topmost element

```
Step 1: IF TOP = NULL
            PRINT "UNDERFLOW"
            Goto Step 5
        [END OF IF]
Step 2: SET PTR = TOP
Step 3: SET TOP = TOP -> NEXT
Step 4: FREE PTR
Step 5: END
```

Figure 7.19 Algorithm to delete an element from a linked stack

Figure 7.19 shows the algorithm to delete an element from a stack. In Step 1, we first check for the `UNDERFLOW` condition. In Step 2, we use a pointer `PTR` that points to `TOP`. In Step 3, `TOP` is made to point to the next node in sequence. In Step 4, the memory occupied by `PTR` is given back to the free pool.

Programming Example

2. Write a program to implement a linked stack.

```
##include <stdio.h>
#include <stdlib.h>
#include <malloc.h>
struct stack
{
        int data;
        struct stack *next;
};
struct stack *top = NULL;
struct stack *push(struct stack *, int);
struct stack *display(struct stack *);
struct stack *pop(struct stack *);
int peek(struct stack *);

int main(int argc, char *argv[]) {
        int val, option;
        do
        {
                printf("\n *****MAIN MENU*****");
                printf("\n 1. PUSH");
                printf("\n 2. POP");
                printf("\n 3. PEEK");
                printf("\n 4. DISPLAY");
                printf("\n 5. EXIT");
                printf("\n Enter your option: ");
                scanf("%d", &option);
                switch(option)
                {
                case 1:
                        printf("\n Enter the number to be pushed on stack: ");
                        scanf("%d", &val);
                        top = push(top, val);
```

```
                        break;
                case 2:
                        top = pop(top);
                        break;
                case 3:
                        val = peek(top);
                        if (val != -1)
                        printf("\n The value at the top of stack is: %d", val);
                        else
                        printf("\n STACK IS EMPTY");
                        break;
                case 4:
                        top = display(top);
                        break;
                }
        }while(option != 5);
        return 0;
}
struct stack *push(struct stack *top, int val)
{
        struct stack *ptr;
        ptr = (struct stack*)malloc(sizeof(struct stack));
        ptr -> data = val;
        if(top == NULL)
        {
                ptr -> next = NULL;
                top = ptr;
        }
        else
        {
                ptr -> next = top;
                top = ptr;
        }
        return top;
}
struct stack *display(struct stack *top)
{
        struct stack *ptr;
        ptr = top;
        if(top == NULL)
        printf("\n STACK IS EMPTY");
        else
        {
                while(ptr != NULL)
                {
                        printf("\n %d", ptr -> data);
                        ptr = ptr -> next;
                }
        }
        return top;
}
struct stack *pop(struct stack *top)
{
        struct stack *ptr;
        ptr = top;
        if(top == NULL)
        printf("\n STACK UNDERFLOW");
        else
```

```
		{
			top = top -> next;
			printf("\n The value being deleted is: %d", ptr -> data);
			free(ptr);
		}
		return top;
	}
	int peek(struct stack *top)
	{
		if(top==NULL)
		return -1;
		else
		return top ->data;
	}
```

Output

```
	*****MAIN MENU*****
	1. PUSH
	2. POP
	3. Peek
	4. DISPLAY
	5. EXIT
	Enter your option : 1
	Enter the number to be pushed on stack : 100
```

7.6 MULTIPLE STACKS

While implementing a stack using an array, we had seen that the size of the array must be known in advance. If the stack is allocated less space, then frequent OVERFLOW conditions will be encountered. To deal with this problem, the code will have to be modified to reallocate more space for the array.

In case we allocate a large amount of space for the stack, it may result in sheer wastage of memory. Thus, there lies a trade-off between the frequency of overflows and the space allocated.

So, a better solution to deal with this problem is to have multiple stacks or to have more than one stack in the same array of sufficient size. Figure 7.20 illustrates this concept.

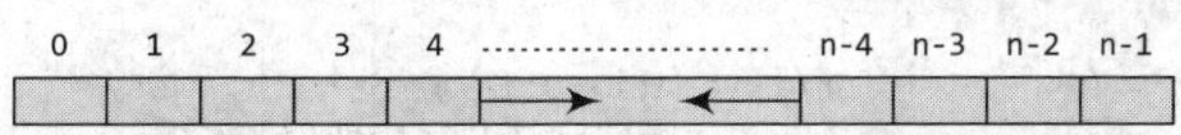

Figure 7.20 Multiple stacks

In Fig. 7.20, an array `STACK[n]` is used to represent two stacks, `Stack A` and `Stack B`. The value of `n` is such that the combined size of both the stacks will never exceed `n`. While operating on these stacks, it is important to note one thing—`Stack A` will grow from left to right, whereas `Stack B` will grow from right to left at the same time.

Extending this concept to multiple stacks, a `stack` can also be used to represent `n` number of stacks in the same array. That is, if we have a `STACK[n]`, then each `stack I` will be allocated an equal amount of space bounded by indices `b[i]` and `e[i]`. This is shown in Fig. 7.21.

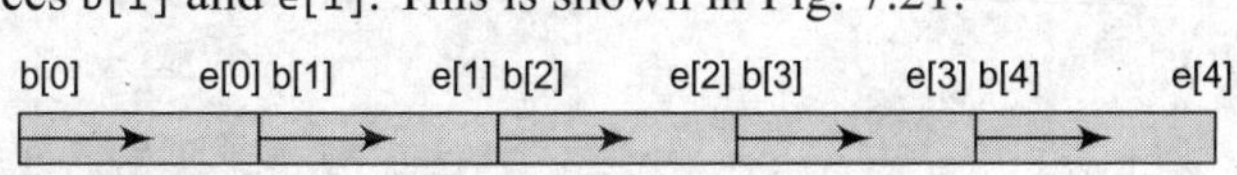

Figure 7.21 Multiple stacks

Programing Example

3. Write a program to implement multiple stacks.

```
#include <stdio.h>
#define MAX 10
int stack[MAX],topA=-1,topB=MAX;
void pushA(int val)
{
        if(topA==topB-1)
                printf("\n OVERFLOW");
        else
        {
                topA+= 1;
                stack[topA] = val;
        }
}
int popA()
{
        int val;
        if(topA==-1)
        {
                printf("\n UNDERFLOW");
                val = -999;
        }
        else
        {
                val = stack[topA];
                topA--;
        }
        return val;
}
void display_stackA()
{
        int i;
        if(topA==-1)
                printf("\n Stack A is Empty");
        else
        {
                for(i=topA;i>=0;i--)
                    printf("\t %d",stack[i]);
        }
}
void pushB(int val)
{
        if(topB-1==topA)
                printf("\n OVERFLOW");
        else
        {
                topB -= 1;
                stack[topB] = val;
        }
}
int popB()
{
        int val;
        if(topB==MAX)
        {
                printf("\n UNDERFLOW");
                val = -999;
```

```
            }
            else
            {
                    val = stack[topB];
                    topB++;
            }
    }
    void display_stackB()
    {
            int i;
            if(topB==MAX)
                    printf("\n Stack B is Empty");
            else
            {
                    for(i=topB;i<MAX;i++)
                        printf("\t %d",stack[i]);
            }
    }
    void main()
    {
            int option, val;
            do
            {
                    printf("\n *****MENU*****");
                    printf("\n 1. PUSH IN STACK A");
                    printf("\n 2. PUSH IN STACK B");
                    printf("\n 3. POP FROM STACK A");
                    printf("\n 4. POP FROM STACK B");
                    printf("\n 5. DISPLAY STACK A");
                    printf("\n 6. DISPLAY STACK B");
                    printf("\n 7. EXIT");
                    printf("\n Enter your choice");
                    scanf("%d",&option);
                    switch(option)
                    {
                    case 1: printf("\n Enter the value to push on Stack A : ");
                        scanf("%d",&val);
                        pushA(val);
                        break;
                    case 2: printf("\n Enter the value to push on Stack B : ");
                        scanf("%d",&val);
                        pushB(val);
                        break;
                    case 3: val=popA();
                        if(val!=-999)
                           printf("\n The value popped from Stack A = %d",val);
                        break;
                    case 4: val=popB();
                        if(val!=-999)
                           printf("\n The value popped from Stack B = %d",val);
                        break;
                    case 5: printf("\n The contents of Stack A are : \n");
                        display_stackA();
                        break;
                    case 6: printf("\n The contents of Stack B are : \n");
                        display_stackB();
                        break;
                    }
            }while(option!=7);
```

```
}
```

Output

```
*****MAIN MENU*****
1. PUSH IN STACK A
2. PUSH IN STACK B
3. POP FROM STACK A
4. POP FROM STACK B
5. DISPLAY STACK A
6. DISPLAY STACK B
7. EXIT
Enter your choice : 1
Enter the value to push on Stack A : 10
Enter the value to push on Stack A : 15
Enter your choice : 5
The content of Stack A are:
15      10
Enter your choice : 4
UNDERFLOW
Enter your choice : 7
```

7.7 APPLICATIONS OF STACKS

In this section we will discuss typical problems where stacks can be easily applied for a simple and efficient solution. The topics that will be discussed in this section include the following:

- Reversing a list
- Parentheses checker
- Conversion of an infix expression into a postfix expression
- Evaluation of a postfix expression
- Conversion of an infix expression into a prefix expression
- Evaluation of a prefix expression
- Recursion
- Tower of Hanoi

7.7.1 Reversing a List

A list of numbers can be reversed by reading each number from an array starting from the first index and pushing it on a stack. Once all the numbers have been read, the numbers can be popped one at a time and then stored in the array starting from the first index.

Programming Example

4. Write a program to reverse a list of given numbers.

```
#include <stdio.h>
int stk[10];
int top=-1;
int pop();
void push(int);
int main()
{
        int val, n, i,
        arr[10];
        printf("\n Enter the number of elements in the array : ");
```

```
            scanf("%d", &n);
            printf("\n Enter the elements of the array : ");
            for(i=0;i<n;i++)
                    scanf("%d", &arr[i]);
            for(i=0;i<n;i++)
                    push(arr[i]);
            for(i=0;i<n;i++)
            {
                    val = pop();
                    arr[i] = val;
            }
            printf("\n The reversed array is : ");
            for(i=0;i<n;i++)
                    printf("\n %d", arr[i]);
            getchar();
            return 0;
    }
    void push(int val)
    {
            stk[++top] = val;
    }
    int pop()
    {
            return(stk[top--]);
    }
```

Output

```
    Enter the number of elements in the array : 5
    Enter the elements of the array : 1 2 3 4 5
    The reversed array is : 5 4 3 2 1
```

7.7.2 Implementing Parentheses Checker

Stacks can be used to check the validity of parentheses in any algebraic expression. For example, an algebraic expression is valid if for every open bracket there is a corresponding closing bracket. For example, the expression (A+B} is invalid but an expression {A + (B – C)} is valid. Look at the program below which traverses an algebraic expression to check for its validity.

Programming Example

5. Write a program to check nesting of parentheses using a stack.

```
    #include <stdio.h>
    #include <string.h>
    #define MAX 10
    int top = -1;
    int stk[MAX];
    void push(char);
    char pop();
    void main()
    {
            char exp[MAX],temp;
            int i, flag=1;
            printf("Enter an expression : ");
            fgets(exp,MAX,stdin);
```

```
            for(i=0;i<strlen(exp);i++)
            {
                    if(exp[i]=='(' || exp[i]=='{' || exp[i]=='[')
                            push(exp[i]);
                    if(exp[i]==')' || exp[i]=='}' || exp[i]==']')
                            if(top == -1)
                                    flag=0;
                            else
                            {
                                    temp=pop();
                                    if(exp[i]==')' && (temp=='{' || temp=='['))
                                            flag=0;
                                    if(exp[i]=='}' && (temp=='(' || temp=='['))
                                            flag=0;
                                    if(exp[i]==']' && (temp=='(' || temp=='{'))
                                            flag=0;
                            }
            }
            if(top>=0)
                    flag=0;
            if(flag==1)
                    printf("\n Valid expression");
            else
                    printf("\n Invalid expression");
    }
    void push(char c)
    {
            if(top == (MAX-1))
                    printf("Stack Overflow\n");
            else
            {
                    top=top+1;
                    stk[top] = c;
            }
    }
    char pop()
    {
            if(top == -1)
                    printf("\n Stack Underflow");
            else
                    return(stk[top--]);
    }
```

Output

```
    Enter an expression : (A + (B - C))
    Valid Expression
```

7.7.3 Evaluation of Arithmetic Expressions

Polish Notations

Infix, postfix, and prefix notations are three different but equivalent notations of writing algebraic expressions. But before learning about prefix and postfix notations, let us first see what an infix notation is. We all are familiar with the infix notation of writing algebraic expressions. While writing an arithmetic expression using infix notation, the operator is placed in between the operands. For example, A+B; here, plus operator is placed between the two operandsA and B. Although it is easy for us to write expressions using infix notation, computers find it difficult to parse as the computer needs a lot of information to evaluate the expression. Information is needed about operator precedence and associativity rules, and brackets which override these rules. So, computers work more efficiently with expressions written using prefix and postfix notations.

Postfix notation was developed by Jan Łukasiewicz who was a Polish logician, mathematician, and philosopher. His aim was to develop a parenthesis-free prefix notation (also known as Polish notation) and a postfix notation, which is better known as Reverse Polish Notation or RPN.

In postfix notation, as the name suggests, the operator is placed after the operands. For example, if an expression is written as A+B in infix notation, the same expression can be written as AB+ in postfix notation. The order of evaluation of a postfix expression is always from left to right. Even brackets cannot alter the order of evaluation.

The expression (A + B) * C can be written as:

[AB+]*C

AB+C* in the postfix notation

Example 7.1 Convert the following infix expressions into postfix expressions.

Solution

```
(a) (A–B) * (C+D)
    [AB–] * [CD+]
    AB–CD+*
(b) (A + B) / (C + D) - (D * E)
    [AB+] / [CD+] - [DE*]
    [AB+CD+/] - [DE*]
    AB+CD+/DE*-
```

A postfix operation does not even follow the rules of operator precedence. The operator which occurs first in the expression is operated first on the operands. For example, given a postfix notation AB+C*. While evaluation, addition will be performed prior to multiplication.

Thus we see that in a postfix notation, operators are applied to the operands that are immediately left to them. In the example, AB+C*, + is applied on A and B, then * is applied on the result of addition and C.

Although a prefix notation is also evaluated from left to right, the only difference between a postfix notation and a prefix notation is that in a prefix notation, the operator is placed before the operands. For example, if A+B is an expression in infix notation, then the corresponding expression in prefix notation is given by +AB.

While evaluating a prefix expression, the operators are applied to the operands that are present immediately on the right of the operator. Like postfix, prefix expressions also do not follow the rules of operator precedence and associativity, and even brackets cannot alter the order of evaluation.

Conversion of an Infix Expression into a Postfix Expression

Example 7.2 Convert the following infix expressions into prefix expressions.

Solution

```
(a) (A + B) * C
    (+AB)*C
    *+ABC
(b) (A–B) * (C+D)
    [–AB] * [+CD]
    *–AB+CD
(c) (A + B) / ( C + D) - ( D * E)
    [+AB] / [+CD] - [*DE]
    [/+AB+CD] - [*DE]
    -/+AB+CD*DE
```

Let I be an algebraic expression written in infix notation. I may contain parentheses, operands, and operators. For simplicity of the algorithm we will use only +, –, *, /, % operators. The precedence of these operators can be given as follows:

Higher priority *, /, %

Lower priority +, -

No doubt, the order of evaluation of these operators can be changed by making use of parentheses. For example, if we have an expression A + B * C, then first B * C will be done and the result will be added to A. But the same expression if written as, (A + B) * C, will evaluate A + B first and then the result will be multiplied with C.

The algorithm given below transforms an infix expression into postfix expression, as shown in Fig. 7.22. The algorithm accepts an infix expression that may contain operators, operands, and parentheses. For simplicity, we assume that the infix operation contains only modulus (%), multiplication (*), division (/), addition (+), and subtraction (–) operators and that operators with same precedence are performed from left-to-right.

The algorithm uses a stack to temporarily hold operators. The postfix expression is obtained from left-to-right using the operands from the infix expression and the operators which are removed from the stack. The first step in this algorithm is to push a left parenthesis on the stack and to add a corresponding right parenthesis at the end of the infix expression. The algorithm is repeated until the stack is empty.

```
Step 1: Add ")" to the end of the infix expression
Step 2: Push "(" on to the stack
Step 3: Repeat until each character in the infix notation is scanned
        IF a "(" is encountered, push it on the stack
        IF an operand (whether a digit or a character) is encountered, add it to the
        postfix expression.
        IF a ")" is encountered, then
          a. Repeatedly pop from stack and add it to the postfix expression until a
             "(" is encountered.
          b. Discard the "(". That is, remove the "(" from stack and do not
             add it to the postfix expression
        IF an operator O is encountered, then
          a. Repeatedly pop from stack and add each operator (popped from the stack) to the
             postfix expression which has the same precedence or a higher precedence than O
          b. Push the operator O to the stack
        [END OF IF]
Step 4: Repeatedly pop from the stack and add it to the postfix expression until the stack is empty
Step 5: EXIT
```

Figure 7.22 Algorithm to convert an infix notation to postfix notation

Example 7.3 Convert the following infix expression into postfix expression using the algorithm given in Fig. 7.22.

(a) A – (B / C + (D % E * F) / G)* H

(b) A – (B / C + (D % E * F) / G)* H)

Solution

Infix Character Scanned	Stack	Postfix Expression
	(	
A	(	A
–	(–	A
(	(– (	A
B	(– (	A B
/	(– (/	A B
C	(– (/	A B C
+	(– (+	A B C /
(	(– (+ (	A B C /
D	(– (+ (	A B C / D
%	(– (+ (%	A B C / D
E	(– (+ (%	A B C / D E
*	(– (+ (% *	A B C / D E
F	(– (+ (% *	A B C / D E F
)	(– (+	A B C / D E F * %
/	(– (+ /	A B C / D E F * %
G	(– (+ /	A B C / D E F * % G
)	(–	A B C / D E F * % G / +
*	(– *	A B C / D E F * % G / +
H	(– *	A B C / D E F * % G / + H
)		A B C / D E F * % G / + H * –

Programming Example

6. Write a program to convert an infix expression into its equivalent postfix notation.

```
#include <stdio.h>
#include <ctype.h>
#include <string.h>
#define MAX 100
char st[MAX];
int top=-1;
void push(char st[], char);
char pop(char st[]);
```

```
void InfixtoPostfix(char source[], char target[]);
int getPriority(char);
int main()
{
        char infix[100], postfix[100];
        printf("\n Enter any infix expression : ");
        fgets(infix,MAX,stdin);
        strcpy(postfix, "");
        InfixtoPostfix(infix, postfix);
        printf("\n The corresponding postfix expression is : ");
        puts(postfix);
        return 0;
}
void InfixtoPostfix(char source[], char target[])
{
        int i=0, j=0;
        char temp;
        strcpy(target, "");
        while(source[i]!='\0')
        {
                if(source[i]=='(')
                {
                        push(st, source[i]);
                        i++;
                }
                else if(source[i] == ')')
                {
                        while((top!=-1) && (st[top]!='('))
                        {
                                target[j] = pop(st);
                                j++;
                        }
                        if(top==-1)
                        {
                                printf("\n INCORRECT EXPRESSION");
                                exit(1);
                        }
                        temp = pop(st);//remove left parenthesis
                        i++;
                }
                else if(isdigit(source[i]) || isalpha(source[i]))
                {
                        target[j] = source[i];
                        j++;
                        i++;
                }
                else if (source[i] == '+' || source[i] == '-' || source[i] == '*'
|| source[i] == '/' || source[i] == '%')
                {
                        while( (top!=-1) && (st[top]!= '(') && (getPriority(st[top])
> getPriority(source[i])))
                        {
                                target[j] = pop(st);
                                j++;
                        }
                        push(st, source[i]);
                        i++;
                }
                else
```

```
                        {
                                printf("\n INCORRECT ELEMENT IN EXPRESSION");
                                exit(1);
                        }
                }
                while((top!=-1) && (st[top]!='('))
                {
                        target[j] = pop(st);
                        j++;
                }
                target[j]='\0';
        }
        int getPriority(char op)
        {
                if(op=='/' || op == '*' || op=='%')
                        return 1;
                else if(op=='+' || op=='-')
                        return 0;
        }
        void push(char st[], char val)
        {
                if(top==MAX-1)
                        printf("\n STACK OVERFLOW");
                else
                {
                        top++;
                        st[top]=val;
                }
        }
        char pop(char st[])
        {
                char val=' ';
                if(top==-1)
                        printf("\n STACK UNDERFLOW");
                else
                {
                        val=st[top];
                        top--;
                }
                return val;
        }
```

Output

```
Enter any infix expression : A+B-C*D
The corresponding postfix expression is : AB+CD*-
```

Evaluation of a Postfix Expression

The ease of evaluation acts as the driving force for computers to translate an infix notation into a postfix notation. That is, given an algebraic expression written in infix notation, the computer first converts the expression into the equivalent postfix notation and then evaluates the postfix expression.

Both these tasks—converting the infix notation into postfix notation and evaluating the postfix expression—make extensive use of stacks as the primary tool.

Using stacks, any postfix expression can be evaluated very easily. Every character of the postfix expression is scanned from left to right. If the character encountered is an operand, it is pushed on to the stack. However, if an operator is encountered, then the top two values are popped from the stack and the operator is applied on these values. The result is then pushed on to the stack. Let us look at Fig. 7.23 which shows the algorithm to evaluate a postfix expression.

```
Step 1: Add a ")" at the end of the
        postfix expression
Step 2: Scan every character of the
        postfix expression and repeat
        Steps 3 and 4 until ")"is encountered
Step 3: IF an operand is encountered,
        push it on the stack
        IF an operator O is encountered, then
        a. Pop the top two elements from the
           stack as A and B as A and B
        b. Evaluate B O A, where A is the
           topmost element and B
           is the element below A.
        c. Push the result of evaluation
           on the stack
        [END OF IF]
Step 4: SET RESULT equal to the topmost element
        of the stack
Step 5: EXIT
```

Figure 7.23 Algorithm to evaluate a postfix expression

Table 7.1 Evaluation of a postfix expression

Character Scanned	Stack
9	9
3	9, 3
4	9, 3, 4
*	9, 12
8	9, 12, 8
+	9, 20
4	9, 20, 4
/	9, 5
-	4

Let us now take an example that makes use of this algorithm. Consider the infix expression given as `9 - ((3 * 4) + 8) / 4`. Evaluate the expression.

The infix expression `9 - ((3 * 4) + 8) / 4` can be written as `9 3 4 * 8 + 4 / -` using postfix notation. Look at Table 7.1, which shows the procedure.

Programming Example

7. Write a program to evaluate a postfix expression.

```
#include <stdio.h>
#include <stdlib.h>
#include <ctype.h>
#include <string.h>
#define MAX 100
float st[MAX];
int top=-1;
void push(float st[], float val);
float pop(float st[]);
float evaluatePostfixExp(char exp[]);
int main()
{
        float val;
        char exp[100];
        printf("\n Enter any postfix expression : ");
        fgets(exp, sizeof(exp), stdin);
        val = evaluatePostfixExp(exp);
        printf("\n Value of the postfix expression = %.2f", val);
        return 0;
}
float evaluatePostfixExp(char exp[])
{
        int i=0;
        float op1, op2, value;
        while(exp[i] != '\0')
        {
```

```
                if(isdigit(exp[i]))
                        push(st, (float)(exp[i]-'0'));
                else
                {
                        op2 = pop(st);
                        op1 = pop(st);
                        switch(exp[i])
                        {
                                case '+':
                                        value = op1 + op2;
                                        break;
                                case '-':
                                        value = op1 - op2;
                                        break;
                                case '/':
                                        value = op1 / op2;
                                        break;
                                case '*':
                                        value = op1 * op2;
                                        break;
                                case '%':
                                        value = (int)op1 % (int)op2;
                                        break;
                        }
                        push(st, value);
                }
                i++;
        }
        return(pop(st));
}
void push(float st[], float val)
{
        if(top==MAX-1)
                printf("\n STACK OVERFLOW");
        else
        {
                top++;
                st[top]=val;
        }
}
float pop(float st[])
{
        float val=-1;
        if(top==-1)
                printf("\n STACK UNDERFLOW");
        else
        {
                val=st[top];
                top--;
        }
        return val;
}
```

Output

```
Enter any postfix expression : 9 3 4 * 8 + 4 / -
Value of the postfix expression = 4.00
```

Conversion of an Infix Expression into a Prefix Expression

There are two algorithms to convert an infix expression into its equivalent prefix expression. The first algorithm is given in Fig. 7.24, while the second algorithm is shown in Fig. 7.25.

```
Step 1: Scan each character in the infix
        expression. For this, repeat Steps
        2-8 until the end of infix expression
Step 2: Push the operator into the operator stack,
        operand into the operand stack, and
        ignore all the left parentheses until
        a right parenthesis is encountered
Step 3: Pop operand 2 from operand stack
Step 4: Pop operand 1 from operand stack
Step 5: Pop operator from operator stack
Step 6: Concatenate operator and operand 1
Step 7: Concatenate result with operand 2
Step 8: Push result into the operand stack
Step 9: END
```

Figure 7.24 Algorithm to convert an infix expression into prefix expression

```
Step 1: Reverse the infix string. Note that
        while reversing the string you must
        interchange left and right parentheses.
Step 2: Obtain the postfix expression of the
        infix expression obtained in Step 1.
Step 3: Reverse the postfix expression to get
        the prefix expression
```

Figure 7.25 Algorithm to convert an infix expression into prefix expression

The corresponding prefix expression is obtained in the operand stack.

For example, given an infix expression `(A – B / C) * (A / K – L)`

Step 1: Reverse the infix string. Note that while reversing the string you must interchange left and right parentheses.

`(L – K / A) * (C / B – A)`

Step 2: Obtain the corresponding postfix expression of the infix expression obtained as a result of Step 1.

The expression is: `(L – K / A) * (C / B – A)`

Therefore, `[L – (K A /)] * [(C B /) – A]`

`= [LKA/–] * [CB/A–]`

`= L K A / – C B / A – *`

Step 3: Reverse the postfix expression to get the prefix expression

Therefore, the prefix expression is `* – A / B C – /A K L`

Programming Example

8. Write a program to convert an infix expression to a prefix expression.

```
#include <stdio.h>
#include <string.h>
#include <stdlib.h>
#include <ctype.h>
#define MAX 100
char st[MAX];
int top=-1;
void reverse(char str[]);
void push(char st[], char);
char pop(char st[]);
void InfixtoPostfix(char source[], char target[]);
int getPriority(char);
char infix[100], postfix[100], temp[100];
int main()
{
        printf("\\n Enter any infix expression : ");
        fgets(infix,MAX,stdin);
        infix[strcspn(infix, "\n")] = '\0';
        reverse(infix);
        strcpy(postfix, "");
        InfixtoPostfix(temp, postfix);
        printf("\n The corresponding postfix expression is : ");
        puts(postfix);
        strcpy(temp,"");
```

```
        reverse(postfix);
        printf("\n The prefix expression is : \n");
        puts(temp);
        getchar();
        return 0;
}
void reverse(char str[])
{
        int len, i=0, j=0;
        len=strlen(str);
        j=len-1;
        while(j>= 0)
        {
                if (str[j] == '(')
                        temp[i] = ')';
                else    if ( str[j] == ')')
                        temp[i] = '(';
                else
                        temp[i] = str[j];
                i++,    j--;
        }
        temp[i] = '\0';
}
void InfixtoPostfix(char source[], char target[])
{
        int i=0, j=0;
        char temp;
        strcpy(target, "");
        while(source[i]!= '\0')
        {
                if(source[i]=='(')
                {
                        push(st, source[i]);
                        i++;
                }
                else if(source[i] == ')')
                {
                        while((top!=-1) && (st[top]!='('))
                        {
                                target[j] = pop(st);
                                j++;
                        }
                        if(top==-1)
                        {
                                printf("\n INCORRECT EXPRESSION");
                                exit(1);
                        }
                        temp = pop(st); //remove left parentheses
                        i++;
                }
                else if(isdigit(source[i]) || isalpha(source[i]))
                {
                        target[j] = source[i];
                        j++;
                        i++;
                }
                else if( source[i] == '+' || source[i] == '-' || source[i] == '*'
                || source[i] == '/' || source[i] == '%')
                {
                        while( (top!=-1) && (st[top]!= '(') && (getPriority(st[top])
                        > getPriority(source[i])))
```

```
                        {
                                target[j] = pop(st);
                                j++;
                        }
                        push(st, source[i]);
                        i++;
                }
                else
                {
                        printf("\n INCORRECT ELEMENT IN EXPRESSION");
                        exit(1);
                }
        }
        while((top!=-1) && (st[top]!='('))
        {
                target[j] = pop(st);
                j++;
        }
        target[j]='\0';
}
int getPriority( char op)
{
        if(op=='/' || op == '*' || op=='%')
                return 1;
        else if(op=='+' || op=='-')
                return 0;
}
void push(char st[], char val)
{
        if(top==MAX-1)
                printf("\n STACK OVERFLOW");
        else
        {
                top++;
                st[top] = val;
        }
 }
char pop(char st[])
{
        char val=' ';
        if(top==-1)
                printf("\n STACK UNDERFLOW");
        else
        {
                val=st[top];
                top--;
        }
        return val;
}
```

Output

```
Enter any infix expression : A+B-C*D
The corresponding postfix expression is : AB+CD*-
The prefix expression is : -+AB*CD
```

Evaluation of a Prefix Expression

There are a number of techniques for evaluating a prefix expression. The simplest way of evaluation of a prefix expression is given in Fig. 7.26.

```
Step 1: Accept the prefix expression
Step 2: Repeat until all the characters
        in the prefix expression have
        been scanned
        (a) Scan the prefix expression
            from right, one character at a
            time.
        (b) If the scanned character is an
            operand, push it on the
            operand stack.
        (c) If the scanned character is an
            operator, then
              (i) Pop two values from the
                  operand stack
             (ii) Apply the operator on
                  the popped operands
            (iii) Push the result on the
                  operand stack
Step 3: END
```

Figure 7.26 Algorithm for evaluation of a prefix expression

For example, consider the prefix expression `+ - 9 2 7 * 8 / 4 12`. Let us now apply the algorithm to evaluate this expression.

Character scanned	Operand stack
12	12
4	12, 4
/	3
8	3, 8
*	24
7	24, 7
2	24, 7, 2
-	24, 5
+	29

Programming Example

9. Write a program to evaluate a prefix expression.

```
#include <stdio.h>
#include <string.h>
int stk[10];
int top=-1;
int pop();
void push(int);
int main()
{
    char prefix[10];
    int len, val, i, opr1, opr2, res;
    printf("\n Enter the prefix expression :
");
    fgets(prefix,10,stdin);
    len = strlen(prefix);
          for(i=len-1;i>=0;i--)
       {
    switch(get_type(prefix[i]))
             {
                 case 0:
                       val = prefix[i] - '0';
                       push(val);
                       break;
                 case 1:
                       opr1 = pop();
                       opr2 = pop();
                       switch(prefix[i])
                       {
                             case '+':
                                   res = opr1 + opr2;
                                   break;
                             case '-':
                                   res = opr1 - opr2;
                                   break;
                             case '*':
                                   res = opr1 * opr2;
                                   break;
                             case '/':
                                   res = opr1 / opr2;
                                   break;
                       }
                       push(res);
             }
      }
      printf("\n RESULT = %d", stk[0]);
      getchar();
      return 0;
}
void push(int val)
{
      stk[++top] = val;
}
```

```
int pop()
{
        return(stk[top--]);
}
int get_type(int c)
{
        if(c == '+' || c == '-' || c == '*' || c == '/')
                return 1;
        else return 0;
}
```

Output

```
Enter the prefix expression : +-927
RESULT = 14
```

7.7.4 Recursion

In this section we are going to discuss recursion which is an implicit application of the STACK ADT.

A *recursive function* is defined as a function that calls itself to solve a smaller version of its task until a final call is made which does not require a call to itself. Since a recursive function repeatedly calls itself, it makes use of the system stack to temporarily store the return address and local variables of the calling function. Every recursive solution has two major cases. They are

- *Base case,* in which the problem is simple enough to be solved directly without making any further calls to the same function.
- *Recursive case,* in which first the problem at hand is divided into simpler sub-parts. Second the function calls itself but with sub-parts of the problem obtained in the first step. Third, the result is obtained by combining the solutions of simpler sub-parts.

Therefore, recursion is defining large and complex problems in terms of smaller and more easily solvable problems. In recursive functions, a complex problem is defined in terms of simpler problems and the simplest problem is given explicitly.

To understand recursive functions, let us take an example of calculating factorial of a number. To calculate `n!`, we multiply the number with factorial of the number that is 1 less than that number. In other words, `n! = n × (n-1)!`

Let us say we need to find the value of `5!`

```
5! = 5 × 4 × 3 × 2 × 1
   = 120
```

This can be written as

```
5! = 5 × 4!, where 4!= 4 × 3!
```

Therefore,

```
5! = 5 × 4 × 3!
```

Similarly, we can also write,

```
5! = 5 × 4 × 3 × 2!
```

Expanding further

```
5! = 5 × 4 × 3 × 2 × 1!
```

We know, `1! = 1`

The series of problems and solutions can be given as shown in Fig. 7.27.

PROBLEM	SOLUTION
5!	5 × 4 × 3 × 2 × 1!
= 5 × 4!	= 5 × 4 × 3 × 2 × 1
= 5 × 4 × 3!	= 5 × 4 × 3 × 2
= 5 × 4 × 3 × 2!	= 5 × 4 × 6
= 5 × 4 × 3 × 2 × 1!	= 5 × 24
	= 120

Figure 7.27 Recursive factorial function

Now if you look at the problem carefully, you can see that we can write a recursive function to calculate the factorial of a number. Every recursive function must have a base case and a recursive case. For the factorial function,

> **Programming Tip**
>
> Every recursive function must have at least one base case. Otherwise, the recursive function will generate an infinite sequence of calls, thereby resulting in an error condition known as an infinite stack.

- **Base case** is when `n = 1`, because if `n = 1`, the result will be `1` as `1! = 1`.
- **Recursive case** of the factorial function will call itself but with a smaller value of `n`, this case can be given as

  `factorial(n) = n × factorial (n-1)`

Look at the following program which calculates the factorial of a number recursively.

Programming Example

10. Write a program to calculate the factorial of a given number.

```
#include <stdio.h>
int Fact(int);   // FUNCTION DECLARATION
int main()
{
          int num, val;
          printf("\n Enter the number: ");
          scanf("%d", &num);
          val = Fact(num);
          printf("\n Factorial of %d = %d", num, val);
          return 0;
}
int Fact(int n)
{
          if(n==1)
                    return 1;
          else
               return (n * Fact(n-1));
}
```

Output

```
Enter the number : 5
Factorial of 5 = 120
```

From the above example, let us analyse the steps of a recursive program.

Step 1: Specify the base case which will stop the function from making a call to itself.

Step 2: Check to see whether the current value being processed matches with the value of the base case. If yes, process and return the value.

Step 3: Divide the problem into smaller or simpler sub-problems.

Step 4: Call the function from each sub-problem.

Step 5: Combine the results of the sub-problems.

Step 6: Return the result of the entire problem.

Greatest Common Divisor

The greatest common divisor of two numbers (integers) is the largest integer that divides both the numbers. We can find the GCD of two numbers recursively by using the *Euclid's algorithm* that states

$$\text{GCD (a, b)} = \begin{cases} \text{b, if b divides a} \\ \text{GCD (b, a mod b), otherwise} \end{cases}$$

GCD can be implemented as a recursive function because if `b` does not divide `a`, then we call the same function (GCD) with another set of parameters that are smaller than the original ones.

Here we assume that `a > b`. However if `a < b`, then interchange `a` and `b` in the formula given above.

Working

Assume `a = 62` and `b = 8`

```
GCD(62, 8)
   rem = 62 % 8 = 6
   GCD(8, 6)
         rem = 8 % 6 = 2
         GCD(6, 2)
                  rem = 6 % 2 = 0
         Return 2
   Return 2
Return 2
```

Programming Example

11. Write a program to calculate the GCD of two numbers using recursive functions.

```
#include <stdio.h>
int GCD(int, int);
int main()
{
         int num1, num2, res;
         printf("\n Enter the two numbers: ");
         scanf("%d %d", &num1, &num2);
         res = GCD(num1, num2);
         printf("\n GCD of %d and %d = %d", num1, num2, res);
         return 0;
}

int GCD(int x, int y)
{
         int rem;
         rem = x%y;
         if(rem==0)
                  return y;
         else
                  return (GCD(y, rem));
}
```

Output

```
Enter the two numbers : 8 12
GCD of 8 and 12 = 4
```

Finding Exponents

We can also find exponent of a number using recursion. To find x^y, the base case would be when `y=0`, as we know that any number raised to the power `0` is `1`. Therefore, the general formula to find x^y can be given as

$$\text{EXP}(x, y) = \begin{cases} 1, & \text{if } y == 0 \\ x \times \text{EXP}(x^{y-1}), & \text{otherwise} \end{cases}$$

Working

```
exp_rec(2, 4) = 2 × exp_rec(2, 3)
               exp_rec(2, 3) = 2 × exp_rec(2, 2)
                     exp_rec(2, 2) 2 × exp_rec(2, 1)
                              exp_rec(2, 1) = 2 × exp_rec(2, 0)
                                      exp_rec(2, 0) = 1
                              exp_rec(2, 1) = 2 × 1 = 2
                     exp_rec(2, 2) = 2 × 2 = 4
```

```
        exp_rec(2, 3) = 2 × 4 = 8
exp_rec(2, 4) = 2 × 8 = 16
```

Programming Example

12. Write a program to calculate `exp(x,y)` using recursive functions.

```
#include <stdio.h>
int exp_rec(int, int);
int main()
{
        int num1, num2, res;
        printf("\n Enter the two numbers: ");
        scanf("%d %d", &num1, &num2);
        res = exp_rec(num1, num2);
        printf ("\n RESULT = %d", res);
        return 0;
}
int exp_rec(int x, int y)
{
        if(y==0)
                return 1;
        else
                return (x * exp_rec(x, y-1));
}
```

Output

```
Enter the two numbers : 3 4
RESULT = 81
```

The Fibonacci Series

The Fibonacci series can be given as

0 1 1 2 3 5 8 13 21 34 55 ......

That is, the third term of the series is the sum of the first and second terms. Similarly, fourth term is the sum of second and third terms, and so on. Now we will design a recursive solution to find the `nth` term of the Fibonacci series. The general formula to do so can be given as

As per the formula, `FIB(0) =0` and `FIB(1) = 1`. So we have two base cases. This is necessary because every problem is divided into two smaller problems.

$$\text{FIB}(n) = \begin{cases} 0, & \text{if } n = 0 \\ 1, & \text{if } n = 1 \\ \text{FIB}(n-1) + \text{FIB}(n-2), & \text{otherwise} \end{cases}$$

Programming Example

13. Write a program to print the Fibonacci series using recursion.

```
#include <stdio.h>
int Fibonacci(int);
int main()
{
        int n, i = 0, res;
        printf("Enter the number of terms\n");
        scanf("%d",&n);
        printf("Fibonacci series\n");
        for(i = 0; i < n; i++ )
        {
                res = Fibonacci(i);
```

```
                printf("%d\t",res);
            }
            return 0;
        }
        int Fibonacci(int n)
        {
            if ( n == 0 )
                return 0;
            else if ( n == 1 )
                return 1;
            else
                return ( Fibonacci(n-1) + Fibonacci(n-2) );
        }
```

Output

```
Enter the number of terms
Fibonacci series
   0    1    1    2    3
```

Types of Recursion

Recursion is a technique that breaks a problem into one or more sub-problems that are similar to the original problem. Any recursive function can be characterized based on:

- whether the function calls itself directly or indirectly (*direct or indirect recursion*),
- whether any operation is pending at each recursive call (*tail-recursive* or not), and
- the structure of the calling pattern (*linear or tree-recursive*).

In this section, we will read about all these types of recursions.

```
int Func (int n)
{
    if (n == 0)
        return n;
    else
        return (Func (n-1));
}
```

Figure 7.28 Direct recursion

Direct Recursion

A function is said to be *directly* recursiveif it explicitly calls itself. For example, consider the code shown in Fig. 7.28. Here, the function `Func()` calls itself for all positive values of `n`, so it is said to be a directly recursive function.

```
int Func1 (int n)
{
    if (n == 0)
        return n;
    else
        return Func2(n);
}
int Func2(int x)
{
    return Func1(x-1);
}
```

Figure 7.29 Indirect recursion

Indirect Recursion

A function is said to be *indirectly* recursive if it contains a call to another function which ultimately calls it. Look at the functions given below. These two functions are indirectly recursive as they both call each other (Fig. 7.29).

Tail Recursion

A recursive function is said to be *tail recursive* if no operations are pending to be performed when the recursive function returns to its caller. When the called function returns, the returned value is immediately returned from the calling function. Tail recursive functions are highly desirable because they are much more efficient to use as the amount of information that has to be stored on the system stack is independent of the number of recursive calls.

```
int Fact(int n)
{
    if (n == 1)
        return 1;
    else
        return (n * Fact(n-1));
}
```

Figure 7.30 Non-tail recursion

In Fig. 7.30, the factorial function that we have written is a non-tail-recursive function, because there is a pending operation of multiplication to be performed on return from each recursive call.

```
int Fact(n)
{
    return Fact1(n, 1);
}
int Fact1(int n, int res)
{
    if (n == 1)
        return res;
    else
      return Fact1(n-1, n*res);
}
```

Figure 7.31 Tail recursion

Whenever there is a pending operation to be performed, the function becomes non-tail recursive. In such a non-tail recursive function, information about each pending operation must be stored, so the amount of information directly depends on the number of calls.

However, the same factorial function can be written in a tail-recursive manner as shown Fig. 7.31.

In the code, `Fact1` function preserves the syntax of `Fact(n)`. Here the recursion occurs in the `Fact1` function and not in `Fact` function. Carefully observe that `Fact1` has no pending operation to be performed on return from recursive calls. The value computed by the recursive call is simply returned without any modification. So in this case, the amount of information to be stored on the system stack is constant (only the values of `n` and `res` need to be stored) and is independent of the number of recursive calls.

Converting Recursive Functions to Tail Recursive

A non-tail recursive function can be converted into a tail-recursive function by using an *auxiliary parameter* as we did in case of the Factorial function. The auxiliary parameter is used to form the result. When we use such a parameter, the pending operation is incorporated into the auxiliary parameter so that the recursive call no longer has a pending operation. We generally use an auxiliary function while using the auxiliary parameter. This is done to keep the syntax clean and to hide the fact that auxiliary parameters are needed.

Linear and Tree Recursion

Recursive functions can also be characterized depending on the way in which the recursion grows in a linear fashion or forming a tree structure (Fig. 7.32).

```
int Fibonacci(int num)
{
  if(num == 0)
    return 0;
  else if (num == 1)
    return 1;
    else
    return (Fibonacci(num - 1) + Fibonacci(num - 2));
}
```

Observe the series of function calls. When the function returns, the pending operations in turn calls the function

Fibonacci(7) = Fibonacci(6) + Fibonacci(5)
Fibonacci(6) = Fibonacci(5) + Fibonacci(4)
Fibonacci(5) = Fibonacci(4) + Fibonacci(3)
Fibonacci(4) = Fibonacci(3) + Fibonacci(2)
Fibonacci(3) = Fibonacci(2) + Fibonacci(1)
Fibonacci(2) = Fibonacci(1) + Fibonacci(0)

Now we have, Fibonacci(2) = 1 + 0 = 1

Fibonacci(3) = 1 + 1 = 2
Fibonacci(4) = 2 + 1 = 3
Fibonacci(5) = 3 + 2 = 5
Fibonacci(6) = 3 + 5 = 8
Fibonacci(7) = 5 + 8 = 13

Figure 7.32 Tree recursion

In simple words, a recursive function is said to be *linearly* recursive when the pending operation (if any) does not make another recursive call to the function. For example, observe the last line of recursive factorial function. The factorial function is linearly recursive as the pending operation involves only multiplication to be performed and does not involve another recursive call to `Fact`.

On the contrary, a recursive function is said to be *tree* recursive (or *non-linearly* recursive) if the pending operation makes another recursive call to the function. For example, the `Fibonacci` function in which the pending operations recursively call the `Fibonacci` function.

Tower of Hanoi

The tower of Hanoi is one of the main applications of recursion. It says, 'if you can solve `n-1` cases, then you can easily solve the `nth` case'.

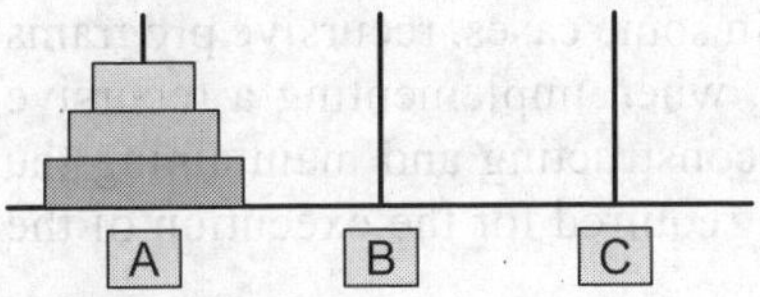

Figure 7.33 Tower of Hanoi

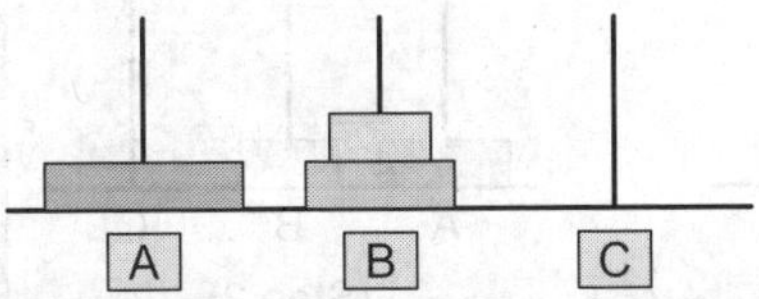

Figure 7.34 Move rings from A to B

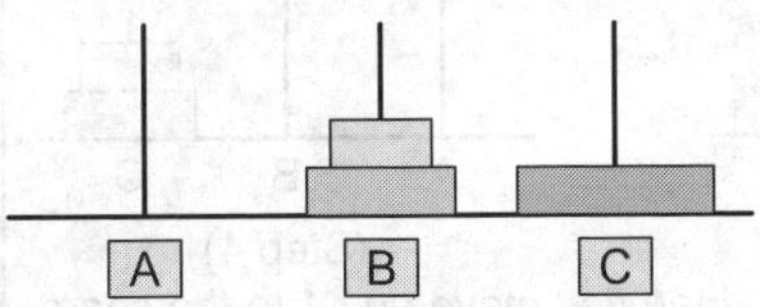

Figure 7.35 Move ring from A to C

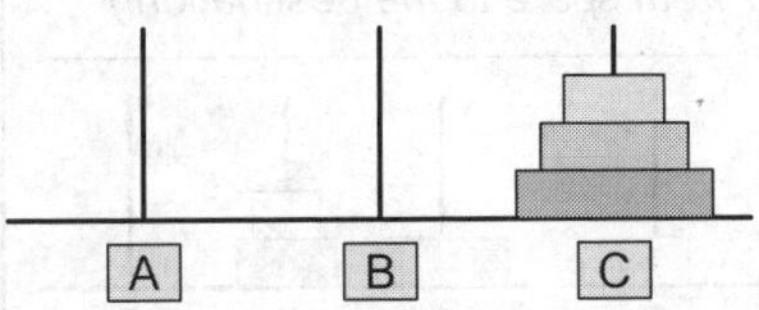

Figure 7.36 Move ring from B to C

Look at Fig. 7.33 which shows three rings mounted on pole A. The problem is to move all these rings from pole A to pole C while maintaining the same order. The main issue is that the smaller disk must always come above the larger disk.

We will be doing this using a spare pole. In our case, A is the source pole, C is the destination pole, and B is the spare pole. To transfer all the three rings from A to C, we will first shift the upper two rings `(n-1 rings)` from the source pole to the spare pole. We move the first two rings from pole A to B as shown in Fig. 7.34.

Now that `n-1` rings have been removed from pole A, the `nth` ring can be easily moved from the source pole (A) to the destination pole (C). Figure 7.35 shows this step.

The final step is to move the `n-1` rings from the spare pole (B) to the destination pole (C). This is shown in Fig. 7.36.

To summarize, the solution to our problem of moving n rings from A to C using B as spare can be given as:

Base case: `if n=1`

- Move the ring from A to C using B as spare

Recursive case:

- Move `n – 1` rings from A to B using C as spare
- Move the one ring left on A to C using B as spare
- Move `n – 1` rings from B to C using A as spare

The following code implements the solution of the Tower of Hanoi problem.

```
#include <stdio.h>
int main()
{
	int n;
	printf("\n Enter the number of rings: ");
	scanf("%d", &n);
	move(n,'A', 'C', 'B');
	return 0;
}
void move(int n, char source, char dest, char spare)
{
	if (n==1)
		printf("\n Move from %c to %c",source,dest);
	else
	{
		move(n-1,source,spare,dest);
		move(1,source,dest,spare);
		move(n-1,spare,dest,source);
	}
}
```

Let us look at the Tower of Hanoi problem in detail using the program given above. Figure 7.37 on the next page explains the working of the program using one, then two, and finally three rings.

Recursion versus Iteration

Recursion is more of a top-down approach to problem solving in which the original problem is divided into smaller sub-problems. On the contrary, iteration follows a bottom-up approach that begins with what is known and then constructing the solution step by step.

Recursion is an excellent way of solving complex problems especially when the problem can be defined in recursive terms. For such problems, a recursive code can be written and modified in a much simpler and clearer manner.

However, recursive solutions are not always the best solutions. In some cases, recursive programs may require substantial amount of run-time overhead. Therefore, when implementing a recursive solution, there is a trade-off involved between the time spent in constructing and maintaining the program and the cost incurred in running-time and memory space required for the execution of the program.

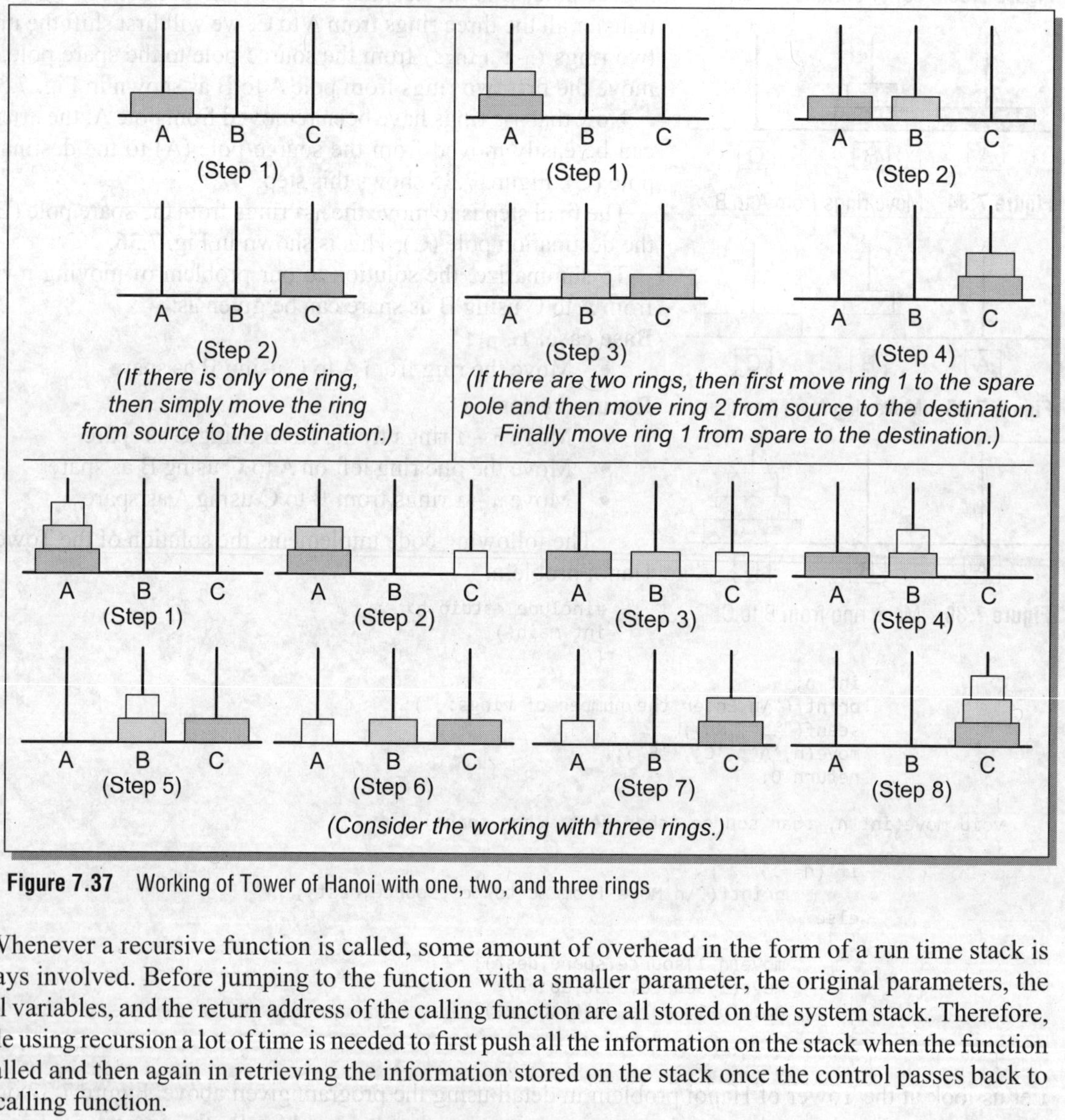

Figure 7.37 Working of Tower of Hanoi with one, two, and three rings

Whenever a recursive function is called, some amount of overhead in the form of a run time stack is always involved. Before jumping to the function with a smaller parameter, the original parameters, the local variables, and the return address of the calling function are all stored on the system stack. Therefore, while using recursion a lot of time is needed to first push all the information on the stack when the function is called and then again in retrieving the information stored on the stack once the control passes back to the calling function.

To conclude, one must use recursion only to find solution to a problem for which no obvious iterative solution is known. To summarize the concept of recursion, let us briefly discuss the pros and cons of recursion.

The advantages of using a recursive program include the following:

- Recursive solutions often tend to be shorter and simpler than non-recursive ones.
- Code is clearer and easier to use.
- Recursion works similar to the original formula to solve a problem.

- Recursion follows a divide and conquer technique to solve problems.
- In some (limited) instances, recursion may be more efficient.

The drawbacks/disadvantages of using a recursive program include the following:

- For some programmers and readers, recursion is a difficult concept.
- Recursion is implemented using system stack. If the stack space on the system is limited, recursion to a deeper level will be difficult to implement.
- Aborting a recursive program in midstream can be a very slow process.
- Using a recursive function takes more memory and time to execute as compared to its non-recursive counterpart.
- It is difficult to find bugs, particularly while using global variables.

The advantages of recursion pay off for the extra overhead involved in terms of time and space required.

Points to Remember

- A stack is a linear data structure in which elements are added and removed only from one end, which is called the top. Hence, a stack is called a LIFO (Last-In, First-Out) data structure as the element that is inserted last is the first one to be taken out.
- In the computer's memory, stacks can be implemented using either linked lists or single arrays.
- The storage requirement of linked representation of stack with `n` elements is `O(n)` and the typical time requirement for operations is `O(1)`.
- Infix, prefix, and postfix notations are three different but equivalent notations of writing algebraic expressions.
- In postfix notation, operators are placed after the operands, whereas in prefix notation, operators are placed before the operands.
- Postfix notations are evaluated using stacks. Every character of the postfix expression is scanned from left to right. If the character is an operand, it is pushed onto the stack. Else, if it is an operator, then the top two values are popped from the stack and the operator is applied on these values. The result is then pushed onto the stack.
- Multiple stacks means to have more than one stack in the same array of sufficient size.
- A recursive function is defined as a function that calls itself to solve a smaller version of its task until a final call is made which does not require a call to itself. They are implmented using system stack.

Exercises

Review Questions

1. What do you understand by stack overflow and underflow?
2. Differentiate between an array and a stack.
3. How does a stack implemented using a linked list differ from a stack implemented using an array?
4. Differentiate between `peek()` and `pop()` functions.
5. Why are parentheses not required in postfix/prefix expressions?
6. Explain how stacks are used in a non-recursive program?
7. What do you understand by a multiple stack? How is it useful?
8. Explain the terms infix expression, prefix expression, and postfix expression. Convert the following infix expressions to their postfix equivalents:
   (a) A – B + C (b) A * B + C / D
   (c) (A – B) + C * D / E – C
   (d) (A * B) + (C / D) – (D + E)
   (e) ((A – B) + D / ((E + F) * G))
   (f) (A – 2 * (B + C) / D * E) + F
   (g) 14 / 7 * 3 – 4 + 9 / 2

9. Convert the following infix expressions to their postfix equivalents:
   (a) A – B + C
   (b) A * B + C / D
   (c) (A – B) + C * D / E – C
   (d) (A * B) + (C / D) – (D + E)
   (e) ((A – B) + D / ((E + F) * G))
   (f) (A – 2 * (B + C) / D * E) + F
   (g) 14 / 7 * 3 – 4 + 9 / 2
10. Find the infix equivalents of the following postfix equivalents:
   (a) A B + C * D –   (b) ABC * + D –
11. Give the infix expression of the following prefix expressions.
   (a) * – + A B C D   (b) + – a * B C D
12. Convert the expression given below into its corresponding postfix expression and then evaluate it. Also write a program to evaluate a postfix expression.
   10 + ((7 – 5) + 10)/2
13. Write a function that accepts two stacks. Copy the contents of first stack in the second stack. Note that the order of elements must be preserved.
   (*Hint: use a temporary stack*)
14. Draw the stack structure in each case when the following operations are performed on an empty stack.
   (a) Add A, B, C, D, E, F
   (b) Delete two letters
   (c) Add G   (d) Add H
   (e) Delete four letters   (f) Add I
15. Differentiate between an iterative function and a recursive function. Which one will you prefer to use and in what circumstances?
16. Explain the Tower of Hanoi problem.

Programming Exercises

1. Write a program to implement a stack using a linked list.
2. Write a program to convert the expression "a+b" into "ab+".
3. Write a program to convert the expression "a+b" into "+ab".
4. Write a program to implement a stack that stores names of students in the class.
5. Write a program to input two stacks and compare their contents.
6. Write a program to compute `F(x, y)`, where
   `F(x, y)` = `F(x-y, y)` + 1 if y≤x
   And `F(x, y)` = 0 if x<y
7. Write a program to compute `F(n, r)` where `F(n, r)` can be recursively defined as:
   `F(n, r)` = `F(n-1, r)` + `F(n-1, r-1)`
8. Write a program to compute `Lambda(n)` for all positive values of `n` where `Lambda(n)` can be recursively defined as:
   `Lambda(n)` = `Lambda(n/2)` + `1 if n>1`
   and `Lambda(n)` = 0 if `n =1`
9. Write a program to compute `F(M, N)` where `F(M, N)` can be recursively defined as:
   `F(M,N)` = 1 if `M=0` or `M≥N≥1`
   and `F(M,N) = F(M-1,N) + F(M-1, N-1)`, otherwise
10. Write a program to reverse a string using recursion.

Multiple-choice Questions

1. Stack is a
   (a) LIFO   (b) FIFO   (c) FILO   (d) LILO
2. Which function places an element on the stack?
   (a) `Pop()`   (b) `Push()`
   (c) `Peek()`   (d) `isEmpty()`
3. Disks piled up one above the other represent a
   (a) Stack   (b) Queue
   (c) Linked List   (d) Array
4. Reverse Polish notation is the other name of
   (a) Infix expression   (b) Prefix expression
   (c) Postfix expression   (d) Algebraic expression

True or False

1. `Pop()` is used to add an element on the top of the stack.
2. Postfix operation does not follow the rules of operator precedence.
3. Recursion follows a divide-and-conquer technique to solve problems.
4. Using a recursive function takes more memory and time to execute.

5. Recursion is more of a bottom-up approach to problem solving.
6. *An indirect* recursive function if it contains a call to another function which ultimately calls it.
7. The peek operation displays the topmost value and deletes it from the stack.
8. In a stack, the element that was inserted last is the first one to be taken out.
9. Underflow occurs when TOP = MAX-1.
10. The storage requirement of linked representation of the stack with n elements is O(n).
11. A push operation on linked stack can be performed in O(n) time.
12. Overflow can never occur in case of multiple stacks.

Fill in the Blanks

1. ______ is used to convert an infix expression into a postfix expression.
2. ______ is used in a non-recursive implementation of a recursive algorithm.
3. The storage requirement of a linked stack with n elements is ______.
4. Underflow takes when ______.
5. The order of evaluation of a postfix expression is from ______.
6. Whenever there is a pending operation to be performed, the function becomes ______ recursive.
7. A function is said to be ______ recursive if it explicitly calls itself.

CHAPTER 8

Queues

LEARNING OBJECTIVE

A queue is an important data structure which is extensively used in computer applications. In this chapter we will study the operations that can be performed on a queue. The chapter will also discuss the implementation of a queue by using both arrays as well as linked lists. The chapter will illustrate different types of queues like multiple queues, double ended queues, circular queues, and priority queues. The chapter also lists some real-world applications of queues.

8.1 INTRODUCTION

Let us explain the concept of queues using the analogies given below.

- People moving on an escalator. The people who got on the escalator first will be the first one to step out of it.
- People waiting for a bus. The first person standing in the line will be the first one to get into the bus.
- People standing outside the ticketing window of a cinema hall. The first person in the line will get the ticket first and thus will be the first one to move out of it.
- Luggage kept on conveyor belts. The bag which was placed first will be the first to come out at the other end.
- Cars lined at a toll bridge. The first car to reach the bridge will be the first to leave.

In all these examples, we see that the element at the first position is served first. Same is the case with queue data structure. A queue is a `FIFO` (First-In, First-Out) data structure in which the element that is inserted first is the first one to be taken out. The elements in a queue are added at one end called the `REAR` and removed from the other end called the `FRONT`.

Queues can be implemented by using either arrays or linked lists. In this section, we will see how queues are implemented using each of these data structures.

8.2 ARRAY REPRESENTATION OF QUEUES

Queues can be easily represented using linear arrays. As stated earlier, every queue has `FRONT` and `REAR` variables that point to the position from where deletions and insertions can be done, respectively. The array representation of a queue is shown in Fig. 8.1.

Operations on Queues

In Fig. 8.1, `FRONT = 0` and `REAR = 5`. Suppose we want to add another element with value 45, then `REAR` would be incremented by 1 and the value would be stored at the position pointed by `REAR`. The queue after

12	9	7	18	14	36				
0	1	2	3	4	5	6	7	8	9

Figure 8.1 Queue

12	9	7	18	14	36	45			
0	1	2	3	4	5	6	7	8	9

Figure 8.2 Queue after insertion of a new element

	9	7	18	14	36	45			
0	1	2	3	4	5	6	7	8	9

Figure 8.3 Queue after deletion of an element

```
Step 1: IF REAR = MAX-1
            Write OVERFLOW
            Goto step 4
        [END OF IF]
Step 2: IF FRONT = -1 and REAR = -1
            SET FRONT = REAR = 0
        ELSE
            SET REAR = REAR + 1
        [END OF IF]
Step 3: SET QUEUE[REAR] = NUM
Step 4: EXIT
```

Figure 8.4 Algorithm to insert an element in a queue

```
Step 1: IF FRONT = -1 OR FRONT > REAR
            Write UNDERFLOW
        ELSE
            SET VAL = QUEUE[FRONT]
            SET FRONT = FRONT + 1
        [END OF IF]
Step 2: EXIT
```

Figure 8.5 Algorithm to delete an element from a queue

addition would be as shown in Fig. 8.2. Here, `FRONT = 0` and `REAR = 6`. Every time a new element has to be added, we repeat the same procedure.

If we want to delete an element from the queue, then the value of `FRONT` will be incremented. Deletions are done from only this end of the queue. The queue after deletion will be as shown in Fig. 8.3.

Here, `FRONT = 1` and `REAR = 6`.

However, before inserting an element in a queue, we must check for `overflow` conditions. An `overflow` will occur when we try to insert an element into a queue that is already full. When `REAR = MAX - 1`, where `MAX` is the size of the queue, we have an `overflow` condition. Note that we have written `MAX - 1` because the index starts from 0.

Similarly, before deleting an element from a queue, we must check for `underflow` conditions. An `underflow` condition occurs when we try to delete an element from a queue that is already empty. If `FRONT = -1` and `REAR = -1`, it means there is no element in the queue. Let us now look at Figs 8.4 and 8.5 which show the algorithms to insert and delete an element from a queue.

Figure 8.4 shows the algorithm to insert an element in a queue. In Step 1, we first check for the `overflow` condition. In Step 2, we check if the queue is empty. In case the queue is empty, then both `FRONT` and `REAR` are set to zero, so that the new value can be stored at the 0th location. Otherwise, if the queue already has some values, then `REAR` is incremented so that it points to the next location in the array. In Step 3, the value is stored in the queue at the location pointed by `REAR`.

Figure 8.5 shows the algorithm to delete an element from a queue. In Step 1, we check for `underflow` condition. An underflow occurs if `FRONT = -1` or `FRONT > REAR`. However, if queue has some values, then `FRONT` is incremented so that it now points to the next value in the queue.

Programming Example

1. Write a program to implement a linear queue.

```
##include <stdio.h>
#define MAX 10
int queue[MAX];
int front = -1, rear = -1;
void insert(void);
int delete_element(void);
int peek(void);
void display(void);
int main()
```

```
{
        int option, val;
        do
        {
                printf("\n\n ***** MAIN MENU *****");
                printf("\n 1. Insert an element");
                printf("\n 2. Delete an element");
                printf("\n 3. Peek");
                printf("\n 4. Display the queue");
                printf("\n 5. EXIT");
                printf("\n Enter your option : ");
                scanf("%d", &option);
                switch(option)
                {
                case 1:
                    insert();
                    break;
                case 2:
                    val = delete_element();
                    if (val != -1)
                    printf("\n The number deleted is : %d", val);
                    break;
                case 3:
                    val = peek();
                    if (val != -1)
                    printf("\n The first value in queue is : %d", val);
                    break;
                case 4:
                    display();
                    break;
                }
        }while(option != 5);
        return 0;
}
void insert()
{
        int num;
        printf("\n Enter the number to be inserted in the queue : ");
        scanf("%d", &num);
        if(rear == MAX-1)
        printf("\n OVERFLOW");
        else if(front == -1 && rear == -1)
        front = rear = 0;
        else
        rear++;
        queue[rear] = num;
}
int delete_element()
{
        int val;
        if(front == -1 || front>rear)
        {
                printf("\n UNDERFLOW");
                return -1;
        }
        else
        {
                val = queue[front];
```

```
            front++;
            if(front > rear)
            front = rear = -1;
            return val;
        }
    }
    int peek()
    {
        if(front==-1 || front>rear)
        {
            printf("\n QUEUE IS EMPTY");
            return -1;
        }
        else
        {
            return queue[front];
        }
    }
    void display()
    {
        int i;
        printf("\n");
        if(front == -1 || front > rear)
        printf("\n QUEUE IS EMPTY");
        else
        {
            for(i = front;i <= rear;i++)
            printf("\t %d", queue[i]);
        }
    }
```

Output

```
    ***** MAIN MENU *****"
    1. Insert an element
    2. Delete an element
    3. Peek
    4. Display the queue
    5. EXIT
    Enter your option : 1
    Enter the number to be inserted in the queue : 50
```

Note The process of inserting an element in the queue is called enqueue, and the process of deleting an element from the queue is called dequeue.

8.3 LINKED REPRESENTATION OF QUEUES

We have seen how a queue is created using an array. Although this technique of creating a queue is easy, its drawback is that the array must be declared to have some fixed size. If we allocate space for 50 elements in the queue and it hardly uses 20–25 locations, then half of the space will be wasted. And in case we allocate less memory locations for a queue that might end up growing large and large, then a lot of re-allocations will have to be done, thereby creating a lot of overhead and consuming a lot of time.

In case the queue is a very small one or its maximum size is known in advance, then the array implementation of the queue gives an efficient implementation. But if the array size cannot be determined in advance, the other alternative, i.e., the linked representation is used.

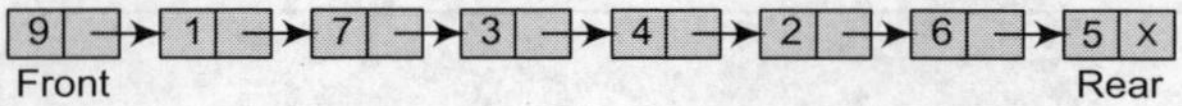

Figure 8.6 Linked queue

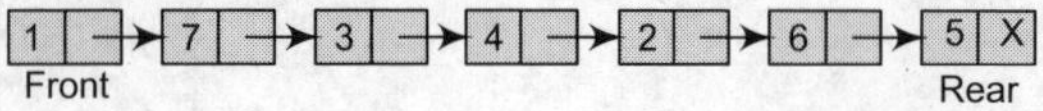

Figure 8.7 Linked queue

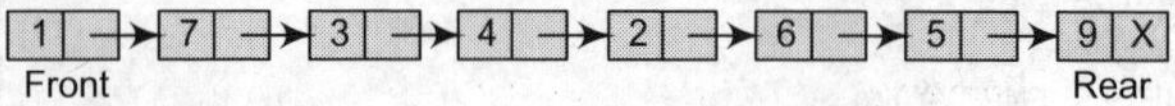

Figure 8.8 Linked queue after inserting a new node

```
Step 1: Allocate memory for the new node and name
        it as PTR
Step 2: SET PTR -> DATA = VAL
Step 3: IF FRONT = NULL
            SET FRONT = REAR = PTR
            SET FRONT -> NEXT = REAR -> NEXT = NULL
        ELSE
            SET REAR -> NEXT = PTR
            SET REAR = PTR
            SET REAR -> NEXT = NULL
        [END OF IF]
Step 4: END
```

Figure 8.9 Algorithm to insert an element in a linked queue

The storage requirement of linked representation of a queue with `n` elements is `O(n)` and the typical time requirement for operations is `O(1)`.

In a linked queue, every element has two parts, one that stores the data and another that stores the address of the next element. The `START` pointer of the linked list is used as `FRONT`. Here, we will also use another pointer called `REAR`, which will store the address of the last element in the queue. All insertions will be done at the rear end and all the deletions will be done at the front end. If `FRONT = REAR = NULL`, then it indicates that the queue is empty.

The linked representation of a queue is shown in Fig. 8.6.

Operations on Linked Queues

A queue has two basic operations: `insert` and `delete`. The `insert` operation adds an element to the end of the queue, and the `delete` operation removes an element from the front or the start of the queue. Apart from this, there is another operation `peek` which returns the value of the first element of the queue.

`Insert` *Operation*

The `insert` operation is used to insert an element into a queue. The new element is added as the last element of the queue. Consider the linked queue shown in Fig. 8.7.

To insert an element with value 9, we first check if `FRONT=NULL`. If the condition holds, then the queue is empty. So, we allocate memory for a new node, store the value in its `DATA` part and `NULL` in its `NEXT` part. The new node will then be called both `FRONT` and `REAR`. However, if `FRONT != NULL`, then we will insert the new node at the rear end of the linked queue and name this new node as `REAR`. Thus, the updated queue becomes as shown in Fig. 8.8.

Figure 8.9 shows the algorithm to insert an element in a linked queue. In Step 1, the memory is allocated for the new node. In Step 2, the `DATA` part of the new node is initialized with the value to be stored in the node. In Step 3, we check if the new node is the first node of the linked queue. This is done by checking if `FRONT = NULL`. If this is the case, then the new node is tagged as `FRONT` as well as `REAR`. Also `NULL` is stored in the `NEXT` part of the node (which is also the `FRONT` and the `REAR` node). However, if the new node is not the first node in the list, then it is added at the `REAR` end of the linked queue (or the last node of the queue).

`Delete` *Operation*

The `delete` operation is used to delete the element that is first inserted in a queue, i.e., the element whose address is stored in `FRONT`. However, before deleting the value, we must first check if `FRONT=NULL` because if this is the case, then the queue is empty and no more deletions can be done. If an attempt is made to delete a value from a queue that is already empty, an `underflow` message is printed. Consider the queue shown in Fig. 8.10.

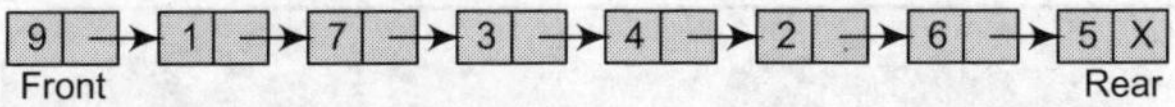

Figure 8.10 Linked queue

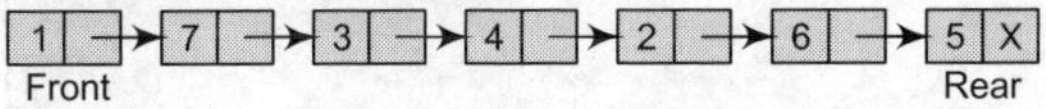

Figure 8.11 Linked queue after deletion of an element

```
Step 1: IF FRONT = NULL
            Write "Underflow"
            Go to Step 5
        [END OF IF]
Step 2: SET PTR = FRONT
Step 3: SET FRONT = FRONT -> NEXT
Step 4: FREE PTR
Step 5: END
```

Figure 8.12 Algorithm to delete an element from a linked queue

To delete an element, we first check if `FRONT=NULL`. If the condition is false, then we delete the first node pointed by `FRONT`. The `FRONT` will now point to the second element of the linked queue. Thus, the updated queue becomes as shown in Fig. 8.11.

Figure 8.12 shows the algorithm to delete an element from a linked queue. In Step 1, we first check for the `underflow` condition. If the condition is true, then an appropriate message is displayed, otherwise in Step 2, we use a pointer `PTR` that points to `FRONT`. In Step 3, `FRONT` is made to point to the next node in sequence. In Step 4, the memory occupied by `PTR` is given back to the free pool.

Programming Example

2. Write a program to implement a linked queue.

```
#include <stdio.h>
#include <malloc.h>
struct node
{
    int data;
    struct node *next;
};
struct queue
{
    struct node *front;
    struct node *rear;
};
struct queue *q;
void create_queue(struct queue *);
struct queue *insert(struct queue *,int);
struct queue *delete_element(struct queue *);
struct queue *display(struct queue *);
int peek(struct queue *);
int main()
{
    int val, option;
    q = (struct queue *)malloc(sizeof(struct queue));
    create_queue(q);
    do
    {
        printf("\n *****MAIN MENU*****");
        printf("\n 1. INSERT");
        printf("\n 2. DELETE");
        printf("\n 3. PEEK");
        printf("\n 4. DISPLAY");
        printf("\n 5. EXIT");
        printf("\n Enter your option : ");
        scanf("%d", &option);
        switch(option)
```

```
            {
                case 1:
                    printf("\n Enter the number to insert in the queue:");
                    scanf("%d", &val);
                    q = insert(q,val);
                    break;
                case 2:
                    q = delete_element(q);
                    break;
                case 3:
                    val = peek(q);
                    if(val != -1)
                        printf("\n The value at front of queue is : %d", val);
                    break;
                case 4:
                    q = display(q);
                    break;
            }
        }while(option != 5);
        return 0;
    }
    void create_queue(struct queue *q)
    {
        q -> rear = NULL;
        q -> front = NULL;
    }
    struct queue *insert(struct queue *q,int val)
    {
        struct node *ptr;
        ptr = (struct node*)malloc(sizeof(struct node));
        ptr -> data = val;
        if(q -> front == NULL)
        {
            q -> front = ptr;
            q -> rear = ptr;
            q -> front -> next = q -> rear -> next = NULL;
        }
        else
        {
            q -> rear -> next = ptr;
            q -> rear = ptr;
            q -> rear -> next = NULL;
        }
        return q;
    }
    struct queue *display(struct queue *q)
    {
        struct node *ptr;
        ptr = q -> front;
        if(ptr == NULL)
            printf("\n QUEUE IS EMPTY");
        else
        {
            printf("\n");
            while(ptr!=q -> rear)
            {
                printf("%d\t", ptr -> data);
                ptr = ptr -> next;
            }
            printf("%d\t", ptr -> data);
```

```
        }
        return q;
    }
    struct queue *delete_element(struct queue *q)
    {
        struct node *ptr;
        ptr = q -> front;
        if(q -> front == NULL)
            printf("\n UNDERFLOW");
        else
        {
            q -> front = q -> front -> next;
            printf("\n The value being deleted is : %d", ptr -> data);
            free(ptr);
        }
        return q;
    }
    int peek(struct queue *q)
    {
        if(q->front==NULL)
        {
            printf("\n QUEUE IS EMPTY");
            return -1;
        }
        else
            return q->front->data;
    }
```

Output

```
    *****MAIN MENU*****
    1. INSERT
    2. DELETE
    3. PEEK
    4. DISPLAY
    5. EXIT
    Enter your option : 3
    QUEUE IS EMPTY
    Enter your option : 5
```

8.4 TYPES OF QUEUES

A queue data structure can be classified into the following types:

1.Circular Queue 2. Deque 3. Priority Queue 4. Multiple Queue

We will discuss each of these queues in detail in the following sections.

8.4.1 Circular Queues

In linear queues, we have discussed so far that insertions can be done only at one end called the REAR and deletions are always done from the other end called the FRONT. Look at the queue shown in Fig. 8.13.

54	9	7	18	14	36	45	21	99	72
0	1	2	3	4	5	6	7	8	9

Figure 8.13 Linear queue

Here, FRONT = 0 and REAR = 9.

Now, if you want to insert another value, it will not be possible because the queue is completely full. There is no empty space where the value can be inserted. Consider a scenario in which two successive deletions are made. The queue will then be given as shown in Fig. 8.14.

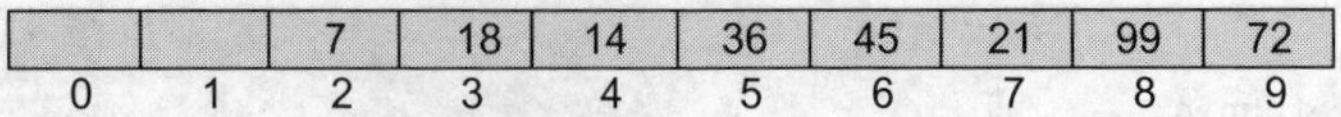

Figure 8.14 Queue after two successive deletions

Here, `FRONT = 2` and `REAR = 9`.

Suppose we want to insert a new element in the queue shown in Fig. 8.14. Even though there is space available, the `overflow` condition still exists because the condition `REAR = MAX - 1` still holds true. This is a major drawback of a linear queue.

To resolve this problem, we have two solutions. First, shift the elements to the left so that the vacant space can be occupied and utilized efficiently. But this can be very time-consuming, especially when the queue is quite large.

The second option is to use a circular queue. In the circular queue, the first index comes right after the last index. Conceptually, you can think of a circular queue as shown in Fig. 8.15.

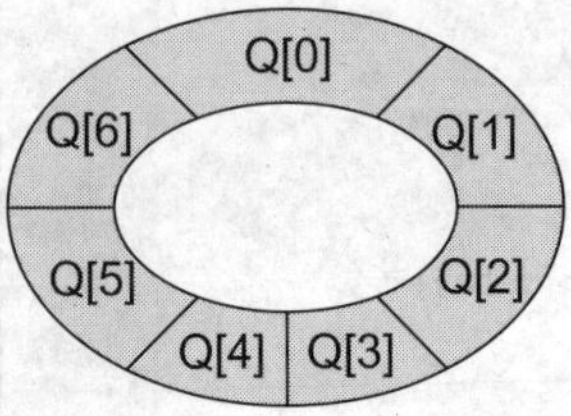

Figure 8.15 Circular queue

The circular queue will be full only when `FRONT = 0` and `REAR = Max - 1`. A circular queue is implemented in the same manner as a linear queue is implemented. The only difference will be in the code that performs insertion and deletion operations. For insertion, we now have to check for the following three conditions:

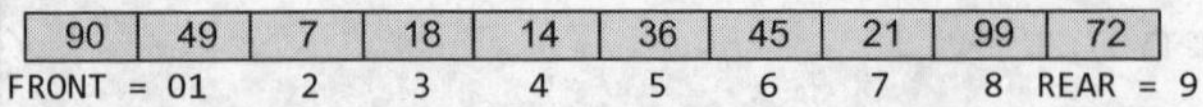

Figure 8.16 Full queue

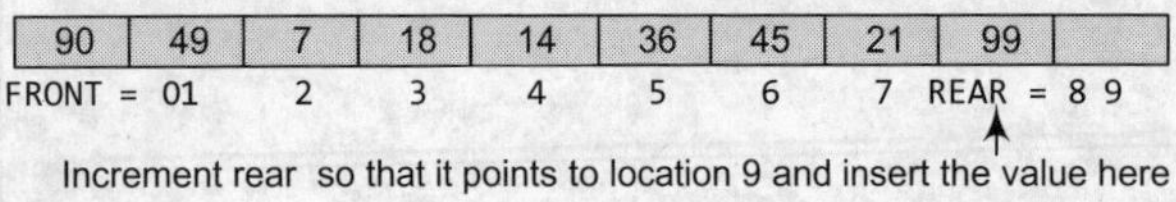

Figure 8.17 Queue with vacant locations

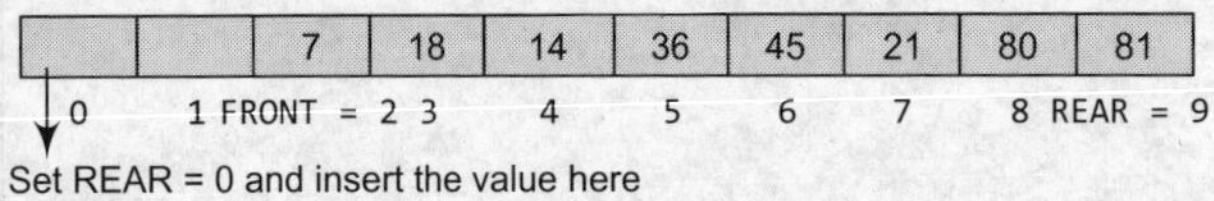

Figure 8.18 Inserting an element in a circular queue

- If `FRONT = 0` and `REAR = MAX - 1`, then the circular queue is full. Look at the queue given in Fig. 8.16 which illustrates this point.
- If `REAR != MAX - 1`, then `REAR` will be incremented and the value will be inserted as illustrated in Fig. 8.17.
- If `FRONT != 0` and `REAR = MAX - 1`, then it means that the queue is not full. So, set `REAR = 0` and insert the new element there, as shown in Fig. 8.18.

```
Step 1: IF FRONT = 0 and Rear = MAX - 1
            Write "OVERFLOW"
            Goto step 4
        [End OF IF]
Step 2: IF FRONT = -1 and REAR = -1
            SET FRONT = REAR = 0
        ELSE IF REAR = MAX - 1 and FRONT != 0
            SET REAR = 0
        ELSE
            SET REAR = REAR + 1
        [END OF IF]
Step 3: SET QUEUE[REAR] = VAL
Step 4: EXIT
```

Figure 8.19 Algorithm to insert an element in a circular queue

Let us look at Fig. 8.19 which shows the algorithm to insert an element in a circular queue. In Step 1, we check for the `overflow` condition. In Step 2, we make two checks. First to see if the queue is empty, and second to see if the `REAR` end has already reached the maximum capacity while there are certain free locations before the `FRONT` end. In Step 3, the value is stored in the queue at the location pointed by `REAR`.

After seeing how a new element is added in a circular queue, let us now discuss how deletions are performed in this case. To delete an element, again we check for three conditions.

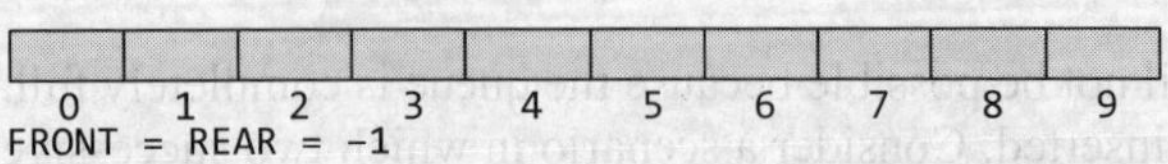

Figure 8.20 Empty queue

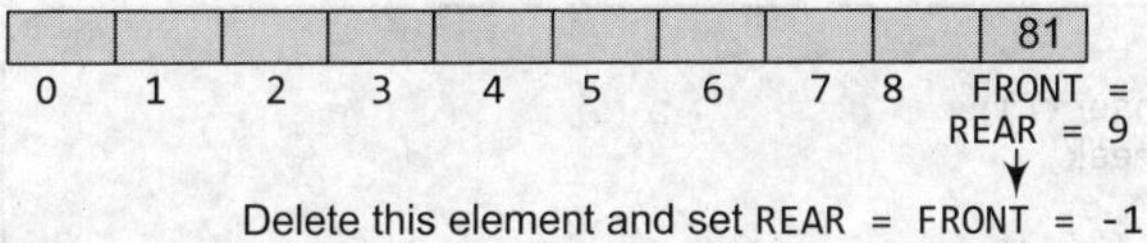

Figure 8.21 Queue with a single element

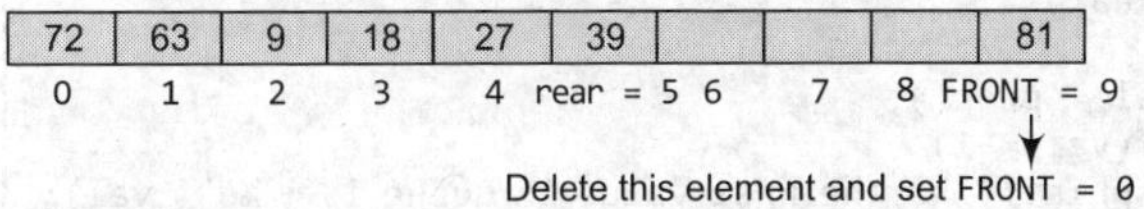

Figure 8.22 Queue where FRONT = MAX-1 before deletion

```
Step 1: IF FRONT = -1
             Write "UNDERFLOW"
             Goto Step 4
        [END of IF]
Step 2: SET VAL = QUEUE[FRONT]
Step 3: IF FRONT = REAR
             SET FRONT = REAR = -1
        ELSE
             IF FRONT = MAX -1
                   SET FRONT = 0
             ELSE
                   SET FRONT = FRONT + 1
             [END of IF]
        [END OF IF]
Step 4: EXIT
```

Figure 8.23 Algorithm to delete an element from a circular queue

- Look at Fig. 8.20. If FRONT = -1, then there are no elements in the queue. So, an underflow condition will be reported.
- If the queue is not empty and FRONT = REAR, then after deleting the element at the front the queue becomes empty and so FRONT and REAR are set to -1. This is illustrated in Fig. 8.21.
- If the queue is not empty and FRONT = MAX-1, then after deleting the element at the front, FRONT is set to 0. This is shown in Fig. 8.22.

Let us look at Fig. 8.23 which shows the algorithm to delete an element from a circular queue. In Step 1, we check for the underflow condition. In Step 2, the value of the queue at the location pointed by FRONT is stored in VAL. In Step 3, we make two checks. First to see if the queue has become empty after deletion and second to see if FRONT has reached the maximum capacity of the queue. The value of FRONT is then updated based on the outcome of these checks.

Programming Example

3. Write a program to implement a circular queue.

```
#include <stdio.h>
#define MAX 10
int queue[MAX];
int front=-1, rear=-1;
void insert(void);
int delete_element(void);
int peek(void);
void display(void);
int main()
{
        int option, val;
        do
        {
                printf("\n ***** MAIN MENU *****");
                printf("\n 1. Insert an element");
                printf("\n 2. Delete an element");
                printf("\n 3. Peek");
                printf("\n 4. Display the queue");
                printf("\n 5. EXIT");
                printf("\n Enter your option : ");
                scanf("%d", &option);
                switch(option)
                {
```

```
                case 1:
                        insert();
                        break;
                case 2:
                        val = delete_element();
                        if(val!=-1)
                          printf("\n The number deleted is : %d", val);
                        break;
                case 3:
                        val = peek();
                        if(val!=-1)
                          printf("\n The first value in queue is : %d", val);
                        break;
                case 4:
                        display();
                        break;
                }
        }while(option!=5);
        return 0;
}
void insert()
{
        int num;
        printf("\n Enter the number to be inserted in the queue : ");
        scanf("%d", &num);
        if(front==0 && rear==MAX-1)
                printf("\n OVERFLOW");
        else if(front==-1 && rear==-1)
        {
                front=rear=0;
                queue[rear]=num;
        }
        else if(rear==MAX-1 && front!=0)
        {
                rear=0;
                queue[rear]=num;
        }
        else
        {
                rear++;
                queue[rear]=num;
        }
}
int delete_element()
{
        int val;
        if(front==-1 && rear==-1)
         {
                printf("\n UNDERFLOW");
                return -1;
         }
        val = queue[front];
        if(front==rear)
                front=rear=-1;
        else
        {
                if(front==MAX-1)
                        front=0;
                else
                        front++;
        }
        return val;
}
```

```
int peek()
{
	if(front==-1 && rear==-1)
	{
		printf("\n QUEUE IS EMPTY");
		return -1;
	}
	else
	{
		return queue[front];
	}
}
void display()
{
	int i;
	printf("\n");
	if (front ==-1 && rear == -1)
		printf ("\n QUEUE IS EMPTY");
	else
	{
		if(front<rear)
		{
			for(i=front;i<=rear;i++)
				printf("\t %d", queue[i]);
		}
		else
		{
			for(i=front;i<MAX;i++)
				printf("\t %d", queue[i]);
			for(i=0;i<=rear;i++)
				printf("\t %d", queue[i]);
		}
	}
}
```

Output

```
***** MAIN MENU *****
1. Insert an element
2. Delete an element
3. Peek
4. Display the queue
5. EXIT
Enter your option : 1
Enter the number to be inserted in the queue : 25
Enter your option : 2
The number deleted is : 25
Enter your option : 3
QUEUE IS EMPTY
Enter your option : 5
```

8.4.2 Deques

A deque (pronounced as 'deck' or 'dequeue') is a list in which the elements can be inserted or deleted at either end. It is also known as a *head-tail linked list* because elements can be added to or removed from either the front (head) or the back (tail) end.

However, no element can be added and deleted from the middle. In the computer's memory, a deque is implemented using either a circular array or a circular doubly linked list. In a deque, two pointers are maintained, `LEFT` and `RIGHT`, which point to either end of the deque. The elements in a deque extend from the `LEFT` end to the `RIGHT` end and since it is circular, `Dequeue[N-1]` is followed by `Dequeue[0]`. Consider the deques shown in Fig. 8.24.

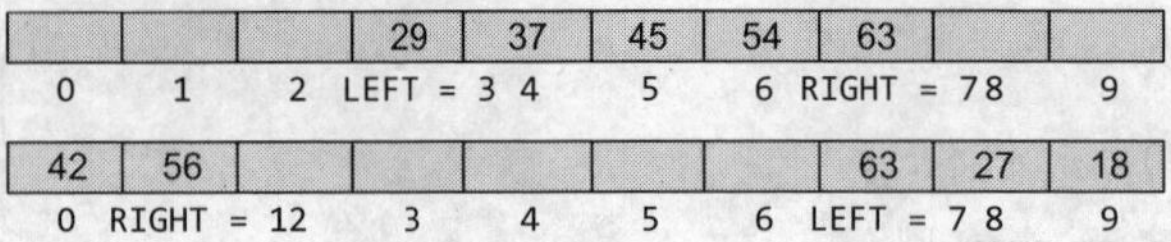

Figure 8.24 Double-ended queues

There are two variants of a double-ended queue. They include

- *Input restricted deque* In this dequeue, insertions can be done only at one of the ends, while deletions can be done from both ends.
- *Output restricted deque* In this dequeue, deletions can be done only at one of the ends, while insertions can be done on both ends.

Programming Example

4. Write a program to implement input and output restricted deques.

```
#include <stdio.h>
#define MAX 10
int deque[MAX];
int left = -1, right = -1;
void input_deque(void);
void output_deque(void);
void insert_left(void);
void insert_right(void);
void delete_left(void);
void delete_right(void);
void display(void);
int main()
{
        int option;
        printf("\n *****MAIN MENU*****");
        printf("\n 1.Input restricted deque");
        printf("\n 2.Output restricted deque");
        printf("Enter your option : ");
        scanf("%d",&option);
        switch(option)
        {
                case 1:
                        input_deque();
                        break;
                case 2:
                        output_deque();
                        break;
        }
        return 0;
}
void input_deque()
{
        int option;
        do
        {
                printf("\n INPUT RESTRICTED DEQUE");
                printf("\n 1.Insert at right");
                printf("\n 2.Delete from left");
                printf("\n 3.Delete from right");
                printf("\n 4.Display");
                printf("\n 5.Quit");
                printf("\n Enter your option : ");
                scanf("%d",&option);
                switch(option)
                {
                        case 1:
                                insert_right();
```

```
                        break;
                case 2:
                        delete_left();
                        break;
                case 3:
                        delete_right();
                        break;
                case 4:
                        display();
                        break;
                }
        }while(option!=5);
}
void output_deque()
{
        int option;
        do
        {
        printf("OUTPUT RESTRICTED DEQUE");
        printf("\n 1.Insert at right");
        printf("\n 2.Insert at left");
        printf("\n 3.Delete from left");
        printf("\n 4.Display");
        printf("\n 5.Quit");
        printf("\n Enter your option : ");
        scanf("%d",&option);
        switch(option)
                {
                case 1:
                        insert_right();
                        break;
                case 2:
                        insert_left();
                        break;
                case 3:
                        delete_left();
                        break;
                case 4:
                        display();
                        break;
                }
        }while(option!=5);
}
void insert_right()
{
        int val;
        printf("\n Enter the value to be added:");
        scanf("%d", &val);
        if((left == 0 && right == MAX-1) || (left == right+1))
        {
                printf("\n OVERFLOW");
                return;
        }
        if (left == -1) /* if queue is initially empty */
        {
                left = 0;
                right = 0;
        }
        else
        {
                if(right == MAX-1) /*right is at last position of queue */
                        right = 0;
                else
                        right = right+1;
```

```
        }
        deque[right] = val ;
}
void insert_left()
{
        int val;
        printf("\n Enter the value to be added:");
        scanf("%d", &val);
        if((left == 0 && right == MAX-1) || (left == right+1))
        {
                printf("\n OVERFLOW");
                return;
        }
        if (left == -1)/*If queue is initially empty*/
        {
                left = 0;
                right = 0;
        }
        else
        {
                if(left == 0)
                        left=MAX-1;
                else
                        left=left-1;
        }
        deque[left] = val;
}
void delete_left()
{
        if (left == -1)
        {
                printf("\n UNDERFLOW");
                return ;
        }
        printf("\n The deleted element is : %d", deque[left]);
        if(left == right) /*Queue has only one element */
        {
                left = -1;
                right = -1;
        }
        else
        {
                if(left == MAX-1)
                        left = 0;
                else
                        left = left+1;
        }
}
void delete_right()
{
        if (left == -1)
        {
                printf("\n UNDERFLOW");
                return ;
        }
        printf("\n The element deleted is : %d", deque[right]);
        if(left == right) /*queue has only one element*/
        {
                left = -1;
                right = -1;
        }
        else
        {
                if(right == 0)
```

```
                        right=MAX-1;
                else
                        right=right-1;
        }
}
void display()
{
        int front = left, rear = right;
        if(front == -1)
        {
                printf("\n QUEUE IS EMPTY");
                return;
        }
        printf("\n The elements of the queue are : ");
        if(front <= rear )
        {
                while(front <= rear)
                {
                        printf("%d",deque[front]);
                        front++;
                }
        }
        else
        {
                while(front <= MAX-1)
                {
                        printf("%d", deque[front]);
                        front++;
                }
                front = 0;
                while(front <= rear)
                {
                        printf("%d",deque[front]);
                        front++;
                }
        }
        printf("\n");
}
```

Output

```
***** MAIN MENU *****
1.Input restricted deque
2.Output restricted deque
Enter your option : 1
INPUT RESTRICTED DEQUEUE
1.Insert at right
2.Delete from left
3.Delete from right
4.Display
5.Quit
Enter your option : 1
Enter the value to be added : 5
Enter the value to be added : 10
Enter your option : 2
The deleted element is : 5
Enter your option : 5
```

8.4.3 Priority Queues

A priority queue is a data structure in which each element is assigned a priority. The priority of the element will be used to determine the order in which the elements will be processed. The general rules of processing the elements of a priority queue are

- An element with higher priority is processed before an element with a lower priority.
- Two elements with the same priority are processed on a first-come-first-served (FCFS) basis.

A priority queue can be thought of as a modified queue in which when an element has to be removed from the queue, the one with the highest-priority is retrieved first. The priority of the element can be set based on various factors. Priority queues are widely used in operating systems to execute the highest priority process first. The priority of the process may be set based on the CPU time it requires to get executed completely. For example, if there are three processes, where the first process needs 5 ns to complete, the second process needs 4 ns, and the third process needs 7 ns, then the second process will have the highest priority and will thus be the first to be executed. However, CPU time is not the only factor that determines the priority, rather it is just one among several factors. Another factor is the importance of one process over another. In case we have to run two processes at the same time, where one process is concerned with online order booking and the second with printing of stock details, then obviously the online booking is more important and must be executed first.

Implementation of a Priority Queue

There are two ways to implement a priority queue. We can either use a sorted list to store the elements so that when an element has to be taken out, the queue will not have to be searched for the element with the highest priority or we can use an unsorted list so that insertions are always done at the end of the list. Every time when an element has to be removed from the list, the element with the highest priority will be searched and removed. While a sorted list takes `O(n)` time to insert an element in the list, it takes only `O(1)` time to delete an element. On the contrary, an unsorted list will take `O(1)` time to insert an element and `O(n)` time to delete an element from the list.

Practically, both these techniques are inefficient and usually a blend of these two approaches is adopted that takes roughly `O(log n)` time or less.

Linked Representation of a Priority Queue

In the computer memory, a priority queue can be represented using arrays or linked lists. When a priority queue is implemented using a linked list, then every node of the list will have three parts: (a) the information or data part, (b) the priority number of the element, and (c) the address of the next element. If we are using a sorted linked list, then the element with the higher priority will precede the element with the lower priority.

Consider the priority queue shown in Fig. 8.25.

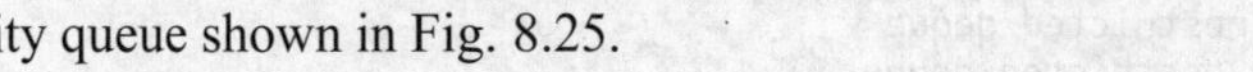

Figure 8.25 Priority queue

Lower priority number means higher priority. For example, if there are two elements `A` and `B`, where `A` has a priority number 1 and `B` has a priority number 5, then `A` will be processed before `B` as it has higher priority than `B`.

The priority queue in Fig. 8.25 is a sorted priority queue having six elements. From the queue, we cannot make out whether `A` was inserted before `E` or whether `E` joined the queue before `A` because the list is not sorted based on FCFS. Here, the element with a higher priority comes before the element with a lower priority. However, we can definitely say that `C` was inserted in the queue before `D` because when two elements have the same priority the elements are arranged and processed on FCFS principle.

Insertion When a new element has to be inserted in a priority queue, we have to traverse the entire list until we find a node that has a priority lower than that of the new element. The new node is inserted before the node with the lower priority. However, if there exists an element that has the same priority as the new element, the new element is inserted after that element. For example, consider the priority queue shown in Fig. 8.26.

Figure 8.26 Priority queue

If we have to insert a new element with `data = F` and `priority number = 4`, then the element will be inserted before `D` that has priority number 5, which is lower priority than that of the new element. So, the priority queue now becomes as shown in Fig. 8.27.

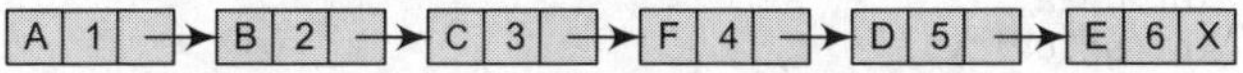

Figure 8.27 Priority queue after insertion of a new node

However, if we have a new element with `data = F` and `priority number = 2`, then the element will be inserted after `B`, as both these elements have the same priority but the insertions are done on FCFS basis as shown in Fig. 8.28.

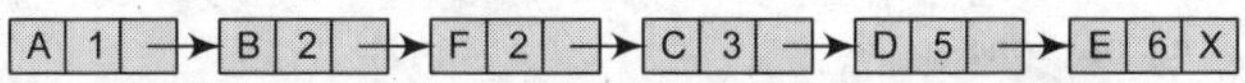

Figure 8.28 Priority queue after insertion of a new node

Deletion Deletion is a very simple process in this case. The first node of the list will be deleted and the data of that node will be processed first.

Array Representation of a Priority Queue

When arrays are used to implement a priority queue, then a separate queue for each priority number is maintained. Each of these queues will be implemented using circular arrays or circular queues. Every individual queue will have its own `FRONT` and `REAR` pointers.

We use a two-dimensional array for this purpose where each queue will be allocated the same amount of space. Look at the two-dimensional representation of a priority queue given below. Given the `FRONT` and `REAR` values of each queue, the two-dimensional matrix can be formed as shown in Fig. 8.29.

`FRONT[K]` and `REAR[K]` contain the front and rear values of row `K`, where `K` is the priority number. Note that here we are assuming that the row and column indices start from 1, not 0. Obviously, while programming, we will not take such assumptions.

FRONT	REAR
3	3
1	3
4	5
4	1

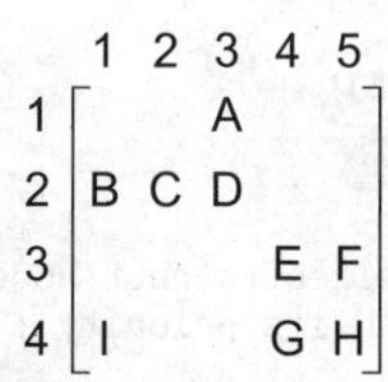

Figure 8.29 Priority queue matrix

Insertion To insert a new element with priority `K` in the priority queue, add the element at the rear end of row `K`, where `K` is the row number as well as the priority number of that element. For example, if we have to insert an element `R` with priority number 3, then the priority queue will be given as shown in Fig. 8.30.

FRONT	REAR
3	3
1	3
4	1
4	1

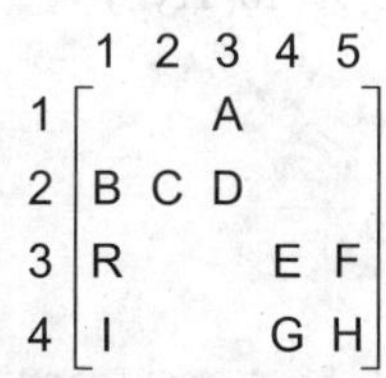

Figure 8.30 Priority queue matrix after insertion of a new element

Deletion To delete an element, we find the first non-empty queue and then process the front element of the first non-empty queue. In our priority queue, the first non-empty queue is the one with priority number 1 and the front element is `A`, so `A` will be deleted and processed first. In technical terms, find the element with the smallest `K`, such that `FRONT[K] != NULL`.

Programming Example

5. Write a program to implement a priority queue.

```
#include <stdio.h>
#include <malloc.h>
struct node
{
        int data;
        int priority;
        struct node *next;
};
struct node *start=NULL;
struct node *insert(struct node *);
struct node *delete(struct node *);
void display(struct node *);
int main()
{
        int option;
        do
        {
                printf("\n *****MAIN MENU*****");
                printf("\n 1. INSERT");
                printf("\n 2. DELETE");
                printf("\n 3. DISPLAY");
                printf("\n 4. EXIT");
                printf("\n Enter your option : ");
                scanf( "%d", &option);
                switch(option)
                {
                        case 1:
                              start=insert(start);
                              break;
                        case 2:
                              start = delete(start);
                              break;
                        case 3:
                              display(start);
                              break;
                }
        }while(option!=4);
}
struct node *insert(struct node *start)
{
        int val, pri;
        struct node *ptr, *p;
        ptr = (struct node *)malloc(sizeof(struct node));
        printf("\n Enter the value and its priority : " );
        scanf( "%d %d", &val, &pri);
        ptr->data = val;
        ptr->priority = pri;
        if(start==NULL || pri < start->priority )
        {
                ptr->next = start;
                start = ptr;
        }
        else
        {
                p = start;
                while(p->next != NULL && p->next->priority <= pri)
                        p = p->next;
                ptr->next = p->next;
                p->next = ptr;
        }
```

```
        return start;
    }
    struct node *delete(struct node *start)
    {
        struct node *ptr;
        if(start == NULL)
        {
            printf("\n UNDERFLOW" );
            return;
        }
        else
        {
            ptr = start;
            printf("\n Deleted item is: %d", ptr->data);
            start = start->next;
            free(ptr);
        }
        return start;
    }
    void display(struct node *start)
    {
        struct node *ptr;
        ptr = start;
        if(start == NULL)
            printf("\nQUEUE IS EMPTY" );
        else
        {
            printf("\n PRIORITY QUEUE IS : " );
            while(ptr != NULL)
            {
                printf( "\t%d[priority=%d]", ptr->data, ptr->priority );
                ptr=ptr->next;
            }
        }
    }
```

Output

```
*****MAIN MENU*****
1. INSERT
2. DELETE
3. DISPLAY
4. EXIT
Enter your option : 1
Enter the value and its priority : 5 2
Enter the value and its priority : 10 1
Enter your option : 3
PRIORITY QUEUE IS :
10[priority = 1] 5[priority = 2]
Enter your option : 4
```

8.4.4 Multiple Queues

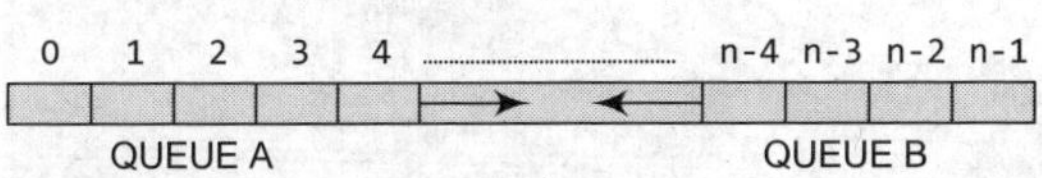

Figure 8.31 Multiple queues

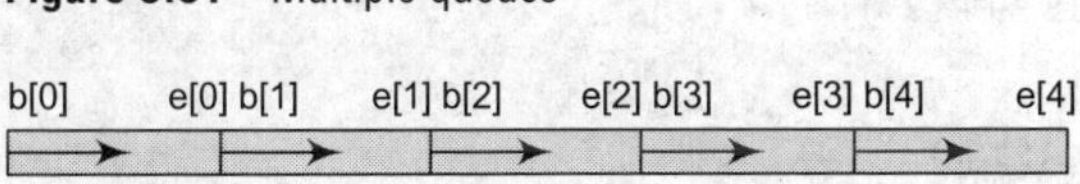

Figure 8.32 Multiple queues

When we implement a queue using an array, the size of the array must be known in advance. If the queue is allocated less space, then frequent overflow conditions will be encountered. To deal with this problem, the code will have to be modified to reallocate more space for the array.

In case we allocate a large amount of space for the queue, it will result in sheer wastage of the memory. Thus, there lies a tradeoff between the frequency of overflows and the space allocated.

So a better solution to deal with this problem is to have multiple queues or to have more than one queue in the same array of sufficient size. Figure 8.31 illustrates this concept.

In the figure, an array `QUEUE[n]` is used to represent two queues, `QUEUE A` and `QUEUE B`. The value of `n` is such that the combined size of both the queues will never exceed `n`. While operating on these queues, it is important to note one thing—`QUEUE A` will grow from left to right, whereas `QUEUE B` will grow from right to left at the same time.

Extending the concept to multiple queues, a queue can also be used to represent n number of queues in the same array. That is, if we have a QUEUE[n], then each queue I will be allocated an equal amount of space bounded by indices b[i] and e[i]. This is shown in Fig. 8.32.

Programming Example

6. Write a program to implement multiple queues.

```
#include <stdio.h>
#define MAX 10
int QUEUE[MAX], rearA=-1,frontA=-1, rearB=MAX, frontB = MAX;
void insertA(int val)
{
        if(rearA==rearB -1)
                printf("\n OVERFLOW");
        else
        {
                if(rearA ==-1 && frontA == -1)
                {       rearA = frontA = 0;
                        QUEUE[rearA] = val;
                }
                else
                        QUEUE[++rearA] = val;
        }
}
int deleteA()
{
        int val;
        if(frontA==-1)
        {
                printf("\n UNDERFLOW");
                return -1;
        }
        else
        {
                val = QUEUE[frontA];
                frontA++;
                if (frontA>rearA)
                        frontA=rearA=-1;
                return val;
        }
}

void display_queueA()
{
        int i;
        if(frontA==-1)
                printf("\n QUEUE A IS EMPTY");
        else
        {
                for(i=frontA;i<=rearA;i++)
                        printf("\t %d",QUEUE[i]);
        }
}
```

```
void insertB(int val)
{
        if(rearA==rearB-1)
                printf("\n OVERFLOW");
        else
        {
                if(rearB == MAX && frontB == MAX)
                {       rearB = frontB = MAX-1;
                        QUEUE[rearB] = val;
                }
                else
                        QUEUE[--rearB] = val;
        }
}

int deleteB()
{
        int val;
        if(frontB==MAX)
        {
                printf("\n UNDERFLOW");
                return -1;
        }

        else
        {
                val = QUEUE[frontB];
                frontB--;
                if (frontB<rearB)
                        frontB=rearB=MAX;
                return val;
        }
}

void display_queueB()
{
        int i;
        if(frontB==MAX)
                printf("\n QUEUE B IS EMPTY");
        else
        {
                for(i=frontB;i>=rearB;i--)
                        printf("\t %d",QUEUE[i]);
        }
}

int main()
{
        int option, val;
        do
        {
                printf("\n *******MENU******");
                printf("\n 1. INSERT IN QUEUE A");
                printf("\n 2. INSERT IN QUEUE B");
                printf("\n 3. DELETE FROM QUEUE A");
                printf("\n 4. DELETE FROM QUEUE B");
                printf("\n 5. DISPLAY QUEUE A");
                printf("\n 6. DISPLAY QUEUE B");
                printf("\n 7. EXIT");
                printf("\n Enter your option : ");
                scanf("%d",&option);
                switch(option)
                {
                case 1:  printf("\n Enter the value to be inserted in Queue A : ");
                        scanf("%d",&val);
                        insertA(val);
```

```
                        break;
                case 2: printf("\n Enter the value to be inserted in Queue B : ");
                        scanf("%d",&val);
                        insertB(val);
                        break;
                case 3: val=deleteA();
                        if(val!=-1)
                        printf("\n The value deleted from Queue A = %d",val);
                        break;
                case 4 : val=deleteB();
                        if(val!=-1)
                        printf("\n The value deleted from Queue B = %d",val);
                        break;
                case 5: printf("\n The contents of Queue A are : \n");
                        display_queueA();
                        break;
                case 6: printf("\n The contents of Queue B are : \n");
                        display_queueB();
                        break;
                }
        }while(option!=7);
}
```

Output

```
*******MENU******"
1. INSERT IN QUEUE A
2. INSERT IN QUEUE B
3. DELETE FROM QUEUE A
4. DELETE FROM QUEUE B
5. DISPLAY QUEUE A
6. DISPLAY QUEUE B
7. EXIT
Enter your option : 2
Enter the value to be inserted in Queue B : 10
Enter the value to be inserted in Queue B : 5
Enter your option: 6
The contents of Queue B are : 10 5
Enter your option : 7
```

8.5 APPLICATIONS OF QUEUES

- Queues are widely used as waiting lists for a single shared resource like printer, disk, CPU.
- Queues are used to transfer data asynchronously (data not necessarily received at same rate as sent) between two processes (IO buffers), e.g., pipes, file IO, sockets.
- Queues are used as buffers on MP3 players and portable CD players, iPod playlist.
- Queues are used in Playlist for jukebox to add songs to the end, play from the front of the list.
- Queues are used in operating system for handling interrupts. When programming a real-time system that can be interrupted, for example, by a mouse click, it is necessary to process the interrupts immediately, before proceeding with the current job. If the interrupts have to be handled in the order of arrival, then a FIFO queue is the appropriate data structure.

Josephus Problem

Let us see how queues can be used for finding a solution to the Josephus problem.

In Josephus problem, `n` people stand in a circle waiting to be executed. The counting starts at some point in the circle and proceeds in a specific direction around the circle. In each step, a certain number of people are skipped and the next person is executed (or eliminated). The elimination of people makes the circle smaller and smaller. At the last step, only one person remains who is declared the 'winner'.

Therefore, if there are `n` number of people and a number `k` which indicates that `k-1` people are skipped and `k-th` person in the circle is eliminated, then the problem is to choose a position in the initial circle so that the given person becomes the winner.

For example, if there are 5 (`n`) people and every second (`k`) person is eliminated, then first the person at position 2 is eliminated followed by the person at position 4 followed by person at position 1 and finally the person at position 5 is eliminated. Therefore, the person at position 3 becomes the winner.

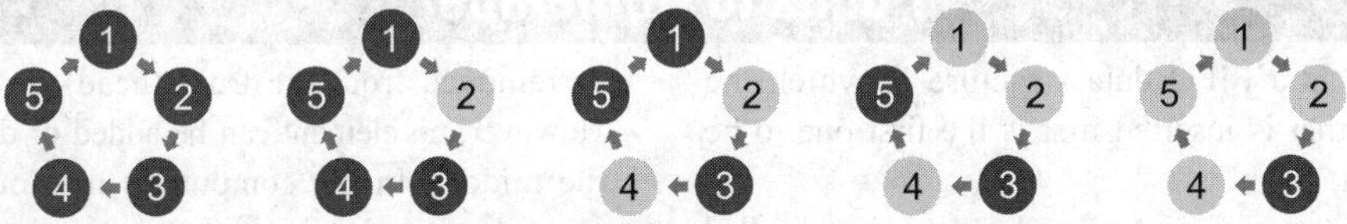

Try the same process with `n` = 7 and `k` =3. You will find that person at position 4 is the winner. The elimination goes in the sequence of 3, 6, 2, 7, 5 and 1.

Programming Example

7. Write a program which finds the solution of Josephus problem using a circular linked list.

```
#include <stdio.h>
#include <malloc.h>
struct node
{
          int player_id;
          struct node *next;
};
struct node *start, *ptr, *new_node;

int main()
{
          int n, k, i, count;
          printf("\n Enter the number of players : ");
          scanf("%d", &n);
          printf("\n Enter the value of k (every kth player gets eliminated): ");
          scanf("%d", &k);
          // Create circular linked list containing all the players
          start = malloc(sizeof(struct node));
          start->player_id = 1;
          ptr = start;
          for (i = 2; i <= n; i++)
          {
                    new_node = malloc(sizeof(struct node));
                    ptr->next = new_node;
                    new_node->player_id = i;
                    new_node->next=start;
                    ptr=new_node;
          }
          for (count = n; count > 1; count--)
          {
                    for (i = 0; i < k - 1; ++i)
                              ptr = ptr->next;
                    ptr->next = ptr->next->next; // Remove the eliminated player from
the circular linked list
          }
          printf("\n The Winner is Player %d", ptr->player_id);
          getchar();
          return 0;
}
```

Output

```
Enter the number of players : 5
Enter the value of k (every kth player gets eliminated): 2
The Winner is Player 3
```

Points to Remember

- A queue is a FIFO data structure in which the element that is inserted first is the first one to be taken out.
- The elements in a queue are added at one end called the `REAR` and removed from the other end called the `FRONT`.
- In the computer's memory, queues can be implemented using both arrays and linked lists.
- The storage requirement of linked representation of queue with n elements is `O(n)` and the typical time requirement for operations is `O(1)`.
- In a circular queue, the first index comes after the last index.
- Multiple queues means to have more than one queue in the same array of sufficient size.
- A deque is a list in which elements can be inserted or deleted at either end. It is also known as a head-tail linked list because elements can be added to or removed from the front (head) or back (tail). However, no element can be added or deleted from the middle. In the computer's memory, a deque is implemented using either a circular array or a circular doubly linked list.
- In an input restricted deque, insertions can be done only at one end, while deletions can be done from both the ends. In an output restricted deque, deletions can be done only at one end, while insertions can be done at both the ends.
- A priority queue is a data structure in which each element is assigned a priority. The priority of the element will be used to determine the order in which the elements will be processed.
- When a priority queue is implemented using a linked list, then every node of the list will have three parts: (a) the information or data part, (b) the priority number of the element, and (c) the address of the next element.

Exercises

Review Questions

1. What is a priority queue? Give its applications.
2. Explain the concept of a circular queue? How is it better than a linear queue?
3. Why do we use multiple queues?
4. Draw the queue structure in each case when the following operations are performed on an empty queue.
   (a) Add A, B, C, D, E, F
   (b) Delete two letters
   (c) Add G (d) Add H
   (e) Delete four letters (f) Add I
5. Consider the queue given below which has `FRONT = 1` and `REAR = 5`.

	A	B	C	D	E				

   Now perform the following operations on the queue:
   (a) Add F (b) Delete two letters
   (c) Add G (d) Add H
   (e) Delete four letters (f) Add I
6. Consider the dequeue given below which has `LEFT = 1` and `RIGHT = 5`.

	A	B	C	D	E				

   Now perform the following operations on the queue:
   (a) Add F on the left
   (b) Add G on the right
   (c) Add H on the right
   (d) Delete two letters from left
   (e) Add I on the right
   (f) Add J on the left
   (g) Delete two letters from right

Programming Exercises

1. Write a program to calculate the number of items in a queue.
2. Write a program to create a linear queue of 10 values.
3. Write a program to create a queue using arrays which permits insertion at both the ends.
4. Write a program to implement a dequeue with the help of a linked list.
5. Write a program to create a queue which permits insertion at any vacant location at the rear end.
6. Write a program to create a queue using arrays which permits deletion from both the ends.
7. Write a program to create a queue using arrays which permits insertion and deletion at both the ends.
8. Write a program to implement a priority queue.
9. Write a program to create a queue from a stack.
10. Write a program to create a stack from a queue.
11. Write a program to reverse the elements of a queue.
12. Write a program to input two queues and compare their contents.

Multiple-choice Questions

1. A line in a grocery store represents a
   (a) Stack (b) Queue
   (c) Linked List (d) Array
2. In a queue, insertion is done at
   (a) Rear (b) Front
   (c) Back (d) Top
3. The function that deletes values from a queue is called
   (a) enqueue (b) dequeue
   (c) pop (d) peek
4. Typical time requirement for operations on queues is
   (a) O(1) (b) O(n)
   (c) O(log n) (d) $O(n^2)$
5. The circular queue will be full only when
   (a) FRONT = MAX –1 and REAR = Max –1
   (b) FRONT = 0 and REAR = Max –1
   (c) FRONT = MAX –1 and REAR = 0
   (d) FRONT = 0 and REAR = 0

True or False

1. A queue stores elements in a manner such that the first element is at the beginning of the list and the last element is at the end of the list.
2. Elements in a priority queue are processed sequentially.
3. In a linked queue, a maximum of 100 elements can be added.
4. Conceptually a linked queue is same as that of a linear queue.
5. The size of a linked queue cannot change during run time.
6. In a priority queue, two elements with the same priority are processed on a FCFS basis.
7. Output-restricted deque allows deletions to be done only at one end of the dequeue, while insertions can be done at both the ends.
8. If `FRONT=MAX - 1` and `REAR= 0`, then the circular queue is full.

Fill in the Blanks

1. New nodes are added at ______ of the queue.
2. ______ allows insertion of elements at either ends but not in the middle.
3. The typical time requirement for operations in a linked queue is ______.
4. In ______, insertions can be done only at one end, while deletions can be done from both the ends.
5. Dequeue is implemented using ______.
6. ______ are appropriate data structures to process batch computer programs submitted to the computer centre.
7. ______ are appropriate data structures to process a list of employees having a contract for a seniority system for hiring and firing.

Coding Challenges

1. Write a program to find the largest element in a queue without removing it.
2. Implement a circular queue using an array that dynamically resizes itself when it becomes full.
3. Write a program to find the average waiting time of a set of processes in a queue. Each process has a burst time and arrival time, and the program should calculate the average time the processes wait in the queue before being executed.

CHAPTER 9

Trees

LEARNING OBJECTIVE

So far, we have discussed linear data structures such as arrays, strings, stacks, and queues. In this chapter, we will learn about a non-linear data structure called tree. A tree is a structure which is mainly used to store data that is hierarchical in nature. In this chapter, we will first discuss general trees and then binary trees. These binary trees are used to form binary search trees and heaps. They are widely used to manipulate arithmetic expressions, construct symbol tables, and for syntax analysis.

9.1 INTRODUCTION

A tree is recursively defined as a set of one or more nodes where one node is designated as the root of the tree and all the remaining nodes can be partitioned into non-empty sets each of which is a sub-tree of the root. Figure 9.1 shows a tree where node A is the root node; nodes B, C, and D are children of the root node and form sub-trees of the tree rooted at node A.

9.1.1 Basic Terminology

Root node The root node R is the topmost node in the tree. If R = NULL, then it means the tree is empty.

Sub-trees If the root node R is not NULL, then the trees T_1, T_2, and T_3 are called the sub-trees of R.

Leaf node A node that has no children is called the leaf node or the terminal node.

Path A sequence of consecutive edges is called a *path.* For example, in Fig. 9.1, the path from the root node A to node I is given as: A, D, and I.

Ancestor node An ancestor of a node is any predecessor node on the path from root to that node. The root node does not have any ancestors. In the tree given in Fig. 9.1, nodes A, C, and G are the ancestors of node K.

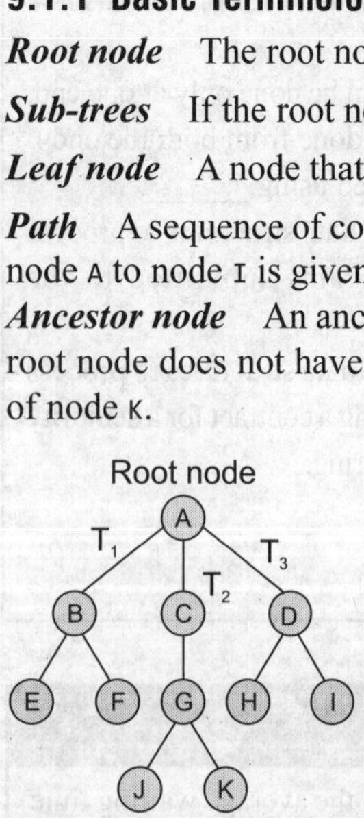

Figure 9.1 Tree

Descendant node A descendant node is any successor node on any path from the node to a leaf node. Leaf nodes do not have any descendants. In the tree given in Fig. 9.1, nodes C, G, J, and K are the descendants of node A.

Level number Every node in the tree is assigned a *level number* in such a way that the root node is at level 0, children of the root node are at level number 1. Thus, every node is at one level higher than its parent. So, all child nodes have a level number given by parent's `level number + 1`.

Degree Degree of a node is equal to the number of children that a node has. The degree of a leaf node is zero.

In-degree In-degree of a node is the number of edges arriving at that node.

Out-degree Out-degree of a node is the number of edges leaving that node.

9.2 TYPES OF TREES

Trees are of following 6 types:

1. General trees
2. Forests
3. Binary trees
4. Binary search trees
5. Expression trees
6. Tournament trees

9.2.1 General Trees

General trees are data structures that store elements hierarchically. The top node of a tree is the root node and each node, except the root, has a parent. A node in a general tree (except the leaf nodes) may have zero or more sub-trees. General trees which have 3 sub-trees per node are called ternary trees. However, the number of sub-trees for any node may be variable. For example, a node can have 1 sub-tree, whereas some other node can have 3 sub-trees.

Although general trees can be represented as ADTs, there is always a problem when another sub-tree is added to a node that already has the maximum number of sub-trees attached to it. Even the algorithms for searching, traversing, adding, and deleting nodes become much more complex as there are not just two possibilities for any node but multiple possibilities.

To overcome the complexities of a general tree, it may be represented as a graph data structure (to be discussed later), thereby losing many of the advantages of the tree processes. Therefore, a better option is to convert general trees into binary trees.

A general tree when converted to a binary tree may not end up being well formed or full, but the advantages of such a conversion enable the programmer to use the algorithms for processes that are used for binary trees with minor modifications.

9.2.2 Forests

A forest is a disjoint union of trees. A set of disjoint trees (or forests) is obtained by deleting the root and the edges connecting the root node to nodes at level 1.

We have already seen that every node of a tree is the root of some sub-tree. Therefore, all the sub-trees immediately below a node form a forest.

A forest can also be defined as an ordered set of zero or more general trees. While a general tree must have a root, a forest on the other hand may be empty because by definition it is a set, and sets can be empty.

We can convert a forest into a tree by adding a single node as the root node of the tree. For example, Fig. 9.2(a) shows a forest and Fig. 9.2(b) shows the corresponding tree.

Similarly, we can convert a general tree into a forest by deleting the root node of the tree.

9.2.3 Binary Trees

A binary tree is a data structure that is defined as a collection of elements called nodes. In a binary tree, the topmost element is called the root node, and each node has 0, 1, or at the most 2 children. A node that has zero children is called a leaf node or a terminal node. Every node contains a data element, a left pointer which points to the left child, and a right pointer which points to the right child. The root element is pointed by a `'root'` pointer. If `root = NULL`, then it means the tree is empty.

Figure 9.3 shows a binary tree. In the figure, R is the root node and the two trees T_1 and T_2 are called the left and right sub-trees of R. T_1 is said to be the left successor of R. Likewise, T_2 is called the right successor of R.

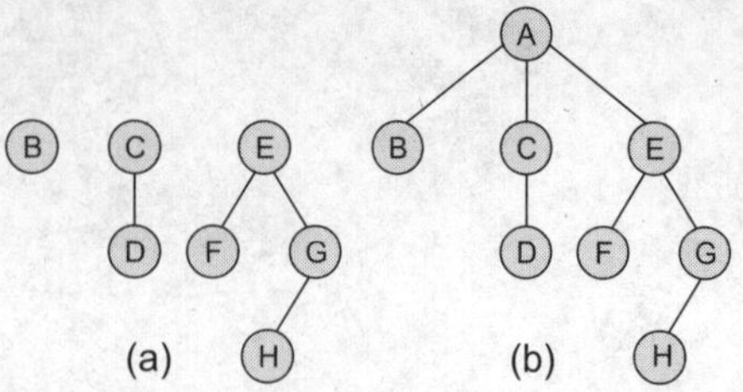

Figure 9.2 Forest and its corresponding tree

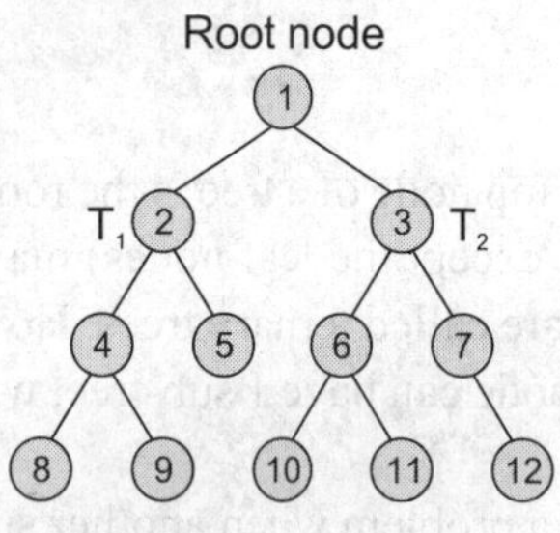

Figure 9.3 Binary tree

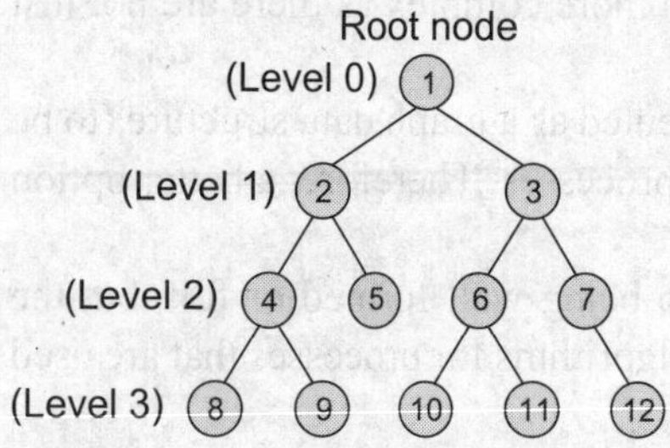

Figure 9.4 Levels in binary tree

Note that the left sub-tree of the root node consists of the nodes: 2, 4, 5, 8, and 9. Similarly, the right sub-tree of the root node consists of nodes: 3, 6, 7, 10, 11, and 12.

In the tree, root node 1 has two successors: 2 and 3. Node 2 has two successor nodes: 4 and 5. Node 4 has two successors: 8 and 9. Node 5 has no successor. Node 3 has two successor nodes: 6 and 7. Node 6 has two successors: 10 and 11. Finally, node 7 has only one successor: 12.

A binary tree is recursive by definition as every node in the tree contains a left sub-tree and a right sub-tree. Even the terminal nodes contain an empty left sub-tree and an empty right sub-tree. Look at Fig. 9.3, nodes 5, 8, 9, 10, 11, and 12 have no successors and thus said to have empty sub-trees.

Terminology

Parent If `N` is any node in `T` that has *left successor* S_1 and *right successor* S_2, then `N` is called the *parent* of S_1 and S_2. Correspondingly, S_1 and S_2 are called the left child and the right child of `N`. Every node other than the root node has a parent.

Level number Every node in the binary tree is assigned a *level number* (refer Fig. 9.4). The root node is defined to be at level 0. The left and the right child of the root node have a level number 1. Similarly, every node is at one level higher than its parents. So all child nodes are defined to have level number as `parent's level number + 1`.

Degree of a node It is equal to the number of children that a node has. The degree of a leaf node is zero. For example, in the tree, degree of node 4 is 2, degree of node 5 is zero and degree of node 7 is 1.

Sibling All nodes that are at the same level and share the same parent are called *siblings* (brothers). For example, nodes 2 and 3; nodes 4 and 5; nodes 6 and 7; nodes 8 and 9; and nodes 10 and 11 are siblings.

Leaf node A node that has no children is called a leaf node or a terminal node. The leaf nodes in the tree are: 8, 9, 5, 10, 11, and 12.

Similar binary trees Two binary trees `T` and `T′` are said to be similar if both these trees have the same structure. Figure 9.5 shows two *similar binary trees*.

Copies Two binary trees `T` and `T′` are said to be *copies* if they have similar structure and if they have same content at the corresponding nodes. Figure 9.6 shows that `T′` is a copy of `T`.

Edge It is the line connecting a node `N` to any of its successors. A binary tree of `n` nodes has exactly `n - 1` edges because every node except the root node is connected to its parent via an edge.

Path A sequence of consecutive edges. For example, in Fig. 9.4, the path from the root node to the node 8 is given as: 1, 2, 4, and 8.

Depth The *depth* of a node `N` is given as the length of the path from the root `R` to the node `N`. The depth of the root node is zero.

Height of a tree It is the total number of nodes on the path from the root node to the deepest node in the tree. A tree with only a root node has a height of 1.

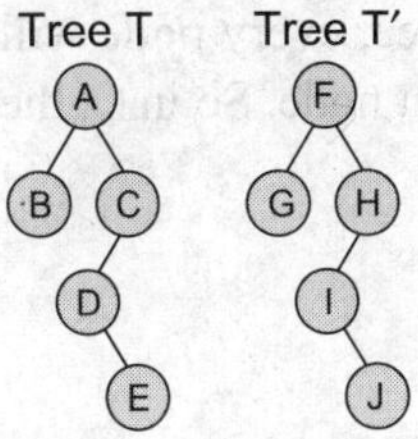

Figure 9.5 Similar binary trees

A binary tree of height h has at least h nodes and at most $2^h - 1$ nodes. This is because every level will have at least one node and can have at most 2 nodes. So, if every level has two nodes then a tree with height h will have at the most $2^h - 1$ nodes as at level 0, there is only one element called the root. The height of a binary tree with n nodes is at least $\log_2(n+1)$ and at most n.

In-degree/out-degree of a node It is the number of edges arriving at a node. The root node is the only node that has an in-degree equal to zero. Similarly, *out-degree* of a node is the number of edges leaving that node.

Binary trees are commonly used to implement binary search trees, expression trees, tournament trees, and binary heaps.

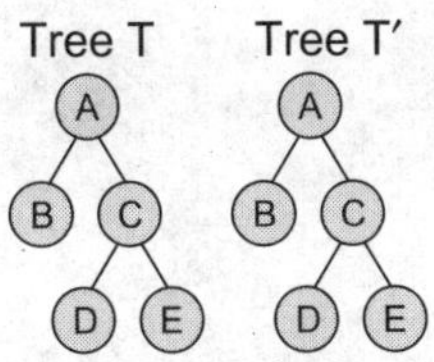

Figure 9.6 T′ is a copy of T

Complete Binary Trees

A *complete binary tree* is a binary tree that satisfies two properties. First, in a complete binary tree, every level, except possibly the last, is completely filled. Second, all nodes appear as far left as possible.

In a complete binary tree T_n, there are exactly n nodes and level r of T can have at most 2^r nodes. Figure 9.7 shows a complete binary tree.

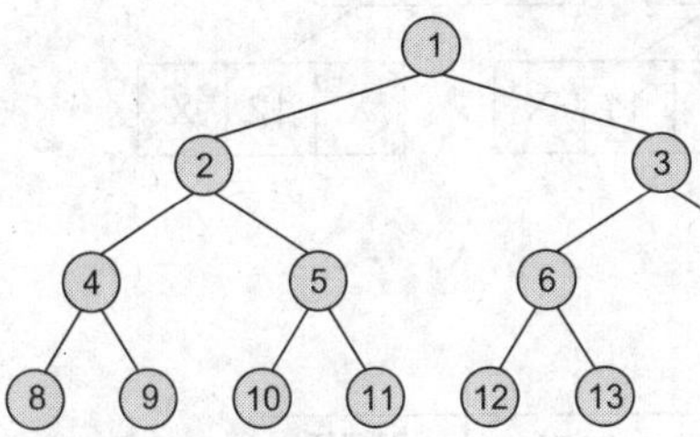

Figure 9.7 Complete binary tree

Note that in Fig. 9.7, level 0 has $2^0 = 1$ node, level 1 has $2^1 = 2$ nodes, level 2 has $2^2 = 4$ nodes, level 3 has 6 nodes which is less than the maximum of $2^3 = 8$ nodes.

In Fig. 9.7, tree T_{13} has exactly 13 nodes. They have been purposely labelled from 1 to 13, so that it is easy for the reader to find the parent node, the right child node, and the left child node of the given node. The formula can be given as—if K is a parent node, then its left child can be calculated as $2 \times K$ and its right child can be calculated as $2 \times K + 1$. For example, the children of the node 4 are 8 (2×4) and 9 $(2 \times 4 + 1)$. Similarly, the parent of the node K can be calculated as $| K/2 |$. Given the node 4, its parent can be calculated as $| 4/2 | = 2$. The height of a tree T_n having exactly n nodes is given as:

$$H_n = | \log_2 (n + 1) |$$

This means, if a tree T has 10,00,000 nodes, then its height is 21.

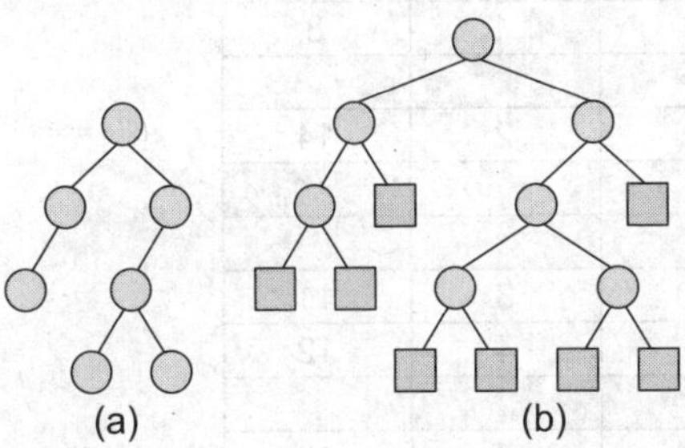

Figure 9.8 (a) Binary tree and (b) extended binary tree

Extended Binary Trees

A binary tree T is said to be an extended binary tree (or a 2-tree) if each node in the tree has either no child or exactly two children. Figure 9.8 shows how an ordinary binary tree is converted into an extended binary tree.

In an extended binary tree, nodes having two children are called *internal nodes* and nodes having no children are called *external nodes*. In Fig. 9.8, the internal nodes are represented using circles and the external nodes are represented using squares.

To convert a binary tree into an extended tree, every empty sub-tree is replaced by a new node. The original nodes in the tree are the internal nodes, and the new nodes added are called the external nodes.

Representation of Binary Trees in the Memory

In the computer's memory, a binary tree can be maintained either by using a linked representation or by using a sequential representation.

Linked representation of binary trees In the linked representation of a binary tree, every node will have three parts: the data element, a pointer to the left node, and a pointer to the right node. So in C, the binary tree is built with a node type given below.

```
struct node {
        struct node *left;
        int data;
        struct node *right;
};
```

Every binary tree has a pointer ROOT, which points to the root element (topmost element) of the tree. If ROOT = NULL, then the tree is empty. Consider the binary tree given in Fig. 9.3. The schematic diagram of the linked representation of the binary tree is shown in Fig. 9.9.

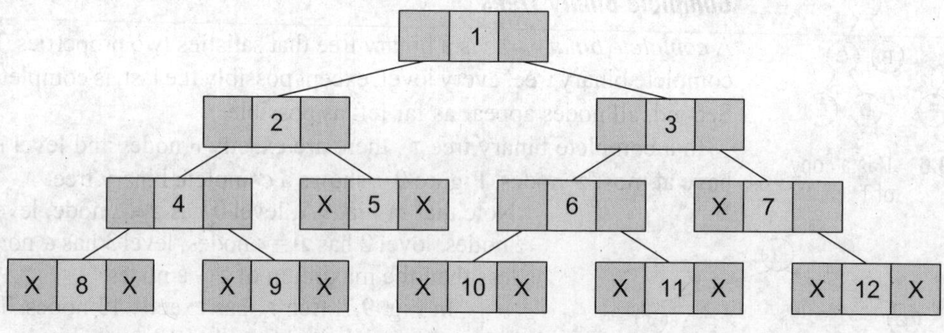

Figure 9.9 Linked representation of a binary tree

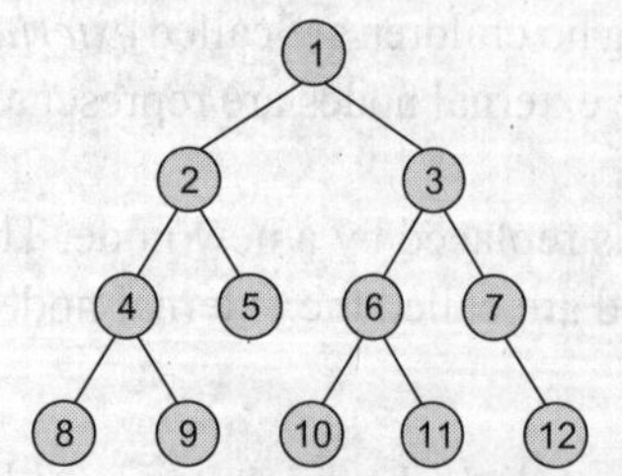

Figure 9.10 Binary tree T

ROOT = 3, AVAIL = 15

	LEFT	DATA	RIGHT
1	–1	8	–1
2	–1	10	–1
3	5	1	8
4			
5	9	2	14
6			
7			
8	20	3	11
9	1	4	12
10			
11	–1	7	18
12	–1	9	–1
13			
14	–1	5	–1
15			
16	–1	11	–1
17			
18	–1	12	–1
19			
20	2	6	16

Figure 9.11 Linked representation of binary tree T

In Fig. 9.9, the left position is used to point to the left child of the node or to store the address of the left child of the node. The middle position is used to store the data. Finally, the right position is used to point to the right child of the node or to store the address of the right child of the node. Empty sub-trees are represented using X (meaning NULL).

Look at the tree given in Fig. 9.10. Note how this tree is represented in the main memory using a linked list (Fig. 9.11).

Example 9.1 Given the memory representation of a tree that stores the names of family members, construct the corresponding tree from the given data.

Solution

ROOT 3

AVAIL 7

	LEFT	NAMES	RIGHT
1	12	Pallav	–1
2			
3	9	Amar	13
4			
5			
6	19	Deepak	17
7			
8			
9	1	Janak	–1
10			
11	–1	Kuvam	–1
12	–1	Rudraksh	–1
13	6	Raj	20
14			
15	–1	Kunsh	–1
16			
17	–1	Tanush	–1
18			
19	–1	Ridhiman	–1
20	11	Sanjay	15

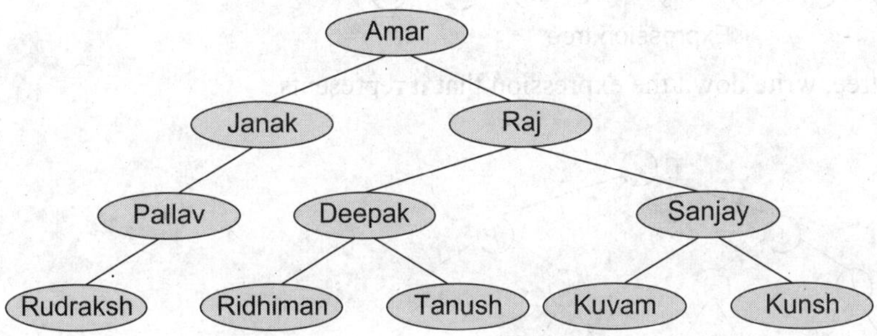

Sequential representation of binary trees Sequential representation of trees is done using single or one-dimensional arrays. Though it is the simplest technique for memory representation, it is inefficient as it requires a lot of memory space. A sequential binary tree follows the following rules:

- A one-dimensional array, called TREE, is used to store the elements of tree.
- The root of the tree will be stored in the first location. That is, TREE[1] will store the data of the root element.
- The children of a node stored in location K will be stored in locations (2 × K) and (2 × K+1).
- The maximum size of the array TREE is given as (2^h–1), where h is the height of the tree.
- An empty tree or sub-tree is specified using NULL. If TREE[1] = NULL, then the tree is empty.

Figure 9.12 shows a binary tree and its corresponding sequential representation. The tree has 11 nodes and its height is 4.

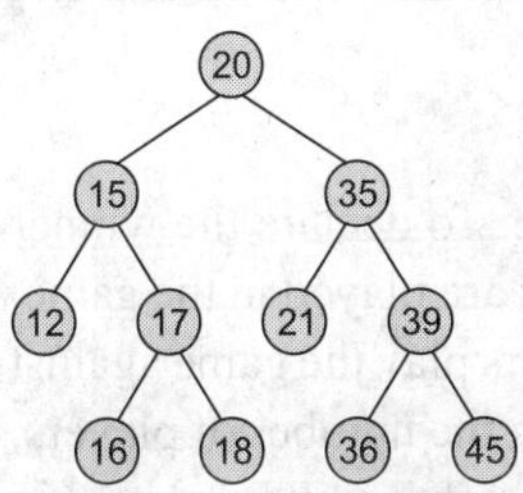

1	20
2	15
3	35
4	12
5	17
6	21
7	39
8	
9	
10	16
11	18
12	
13	
14	36
15	45

Figure 9.12 Binary tree and its sequential representation

9.2.4 Binary Search Trees

A binary search tree, also known as an ordered binary tree, is a variant of binary tree in which the nodes are arranged in an order. We will discuss the concept of binary search trees and different operations performed on them in the next chapter.

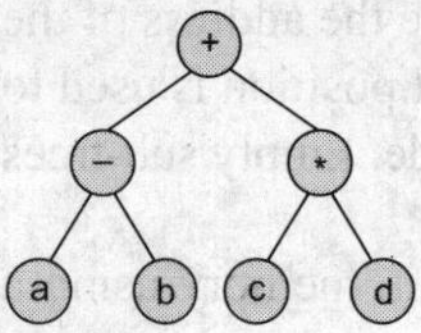

Figure 9.13 Expression tree

9.2.5 Expression Trees

Binary trees are widely used to store algebraic expressions. For example, consider the algebraic expression given as:

```
Exp = (a – b) + (c * d)
```

This expression can be represented using a binary tree as shown in Fig. 9.13.

Example 9.2 Given an expression, `Exp = ((a + b) – (c * d)) % ((e ^f) / (g – h))`, construct the corresponding binary tree.

Solution

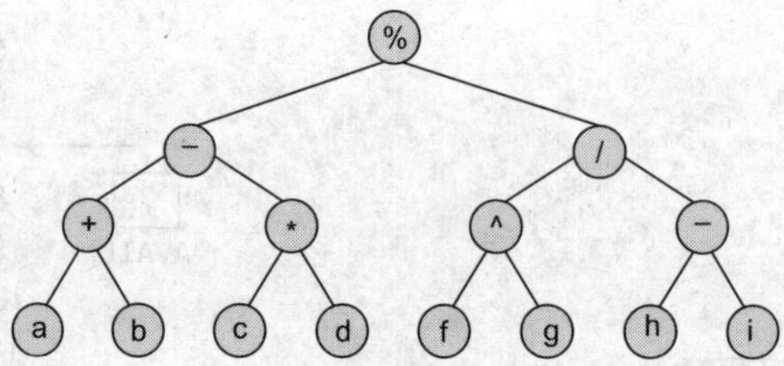

Expression tree

Example 9.3 Given the binary tree, write down the expression that it represents.

Solution

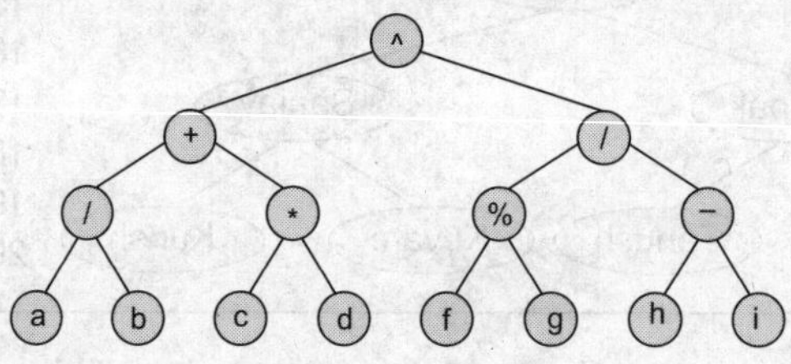

Expression for the above binary tree is
`[{(a/b) + (c*d)} ^ {(f % g)/(h – i)}]`

Example 9.4 Given the expression, `Exp = a + b / c * d – e`, construct the corresponding binary tree.

Solution Use the operator precedence chart to find the sequence in which operations will be performed. The given expression can be written as

```
Exp = ((a + ((b/c) * d)) – e)
```

9.2.6 Tournament Trees

We all know that in a tournament, say of chess, `n` number of players participate. To declare the winner among all these players, a couple of matches are played and usually three rounds are played in the game.

In every match of round 1, a number of matches are played in which two players play the game against each other. The number of matches that will be played in round 1 will depend on the number of players. For example, if there are 8 players participating in a chess tournament, then 4 matches will be played in round 1. Every match of round 1 will be played between two players.

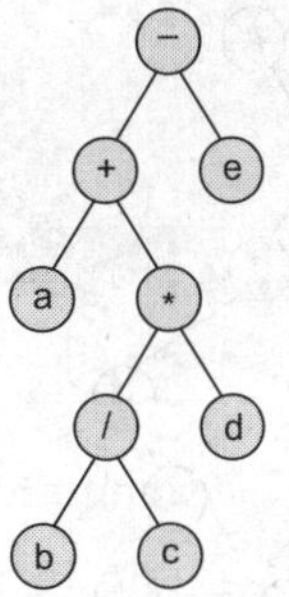

Expression tree

Then in round 2, the winners of round 1 will play against each other. Similarly, in round 3, the winners of round 2 will play against each other and the person who wins round 3 is declared the winner. Tournament trees are used to represent this concept.

In a tournament tree (also called a *selection tree*), each external node represents a player and each internal node represents the winner of the match played between the players represented by its children nodes. These tournament trees are also called *winner trees* because they are being used to record the winner at each level. We can also have a *loser tree* that records the loser at each level.

Consider the tournament tree given in Fig. 9.14. There are 8 players in total whose names are represented using a, b, c, d, e, f, g, and h. In round 1, a and b; c and d; e and f; and finally g and h play against each other. In round 2, the winners of round 1, that is, a, d, e, and g play against each other. In round 3, the winners of round 2, a and e play against each other. Whosoever wins is declared the winner. In the tree, the root node a specifies the winner.

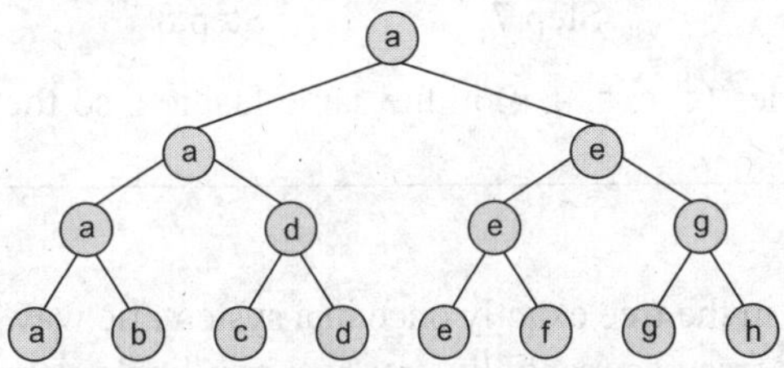

Figure 9.14 Tournament tree

9.3 CREATING A BINARY TREE FROM A GENERAL TREE

The rules for converting a general tree to a binary tree are given below. Note that a general tree is converted into a binary tree and not a binary search tree.

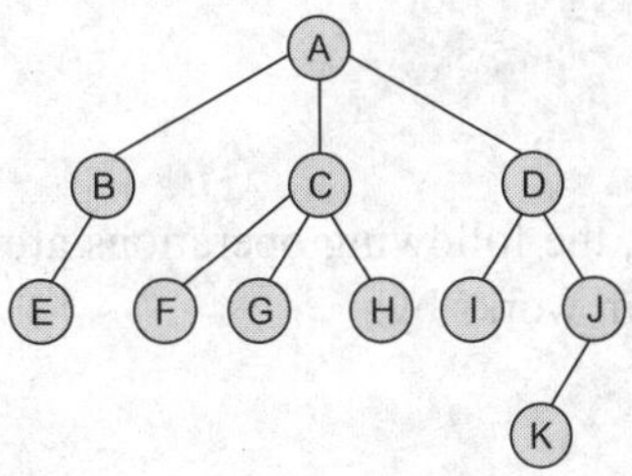

Rule 1: Root of the binary tree = Root of the general tree

Rule 2: Left child of a node in the binary tree = Leftmost child of the node in the general tree

Rule 3: Right child of a node in the binary tree = Right sibling of the node in the general tree

---

Example 9.5 Convert the given general tree into a binary tree.

Now let us build the binary tree.

Step 1: Node A is the root of the general tree, so it will also be the root of the binary tree.

Step 2: Left child of node A is the leftmost child of node A in the general tree and right child of node A is the right sibling of the node A in the general tree. Since node A has no right sibling in the general tree, it has no right child in the binary tree.

Step 3: Now process node B. Left child of B is E and its right child is C (right sibling in general tree).

Step 4: Now process node C. Left child of C is F (leftmost child) and its right child is D (right sibling in general tree).

Step 5: Now process node D. Left child of D is I (leftmost child). There will be no right child of D because it has no right sibling in the general tree.

Step 6: Now process node I. There will be no left child of I in the binary tree because I has no left child in the general tree. However, I has a right sibling J, so it will be added as the right child of I.

Step 7: Now process node J. Left child of J is K (leftmost child). There will be no right child of J because it has no right sibling in the general tree.

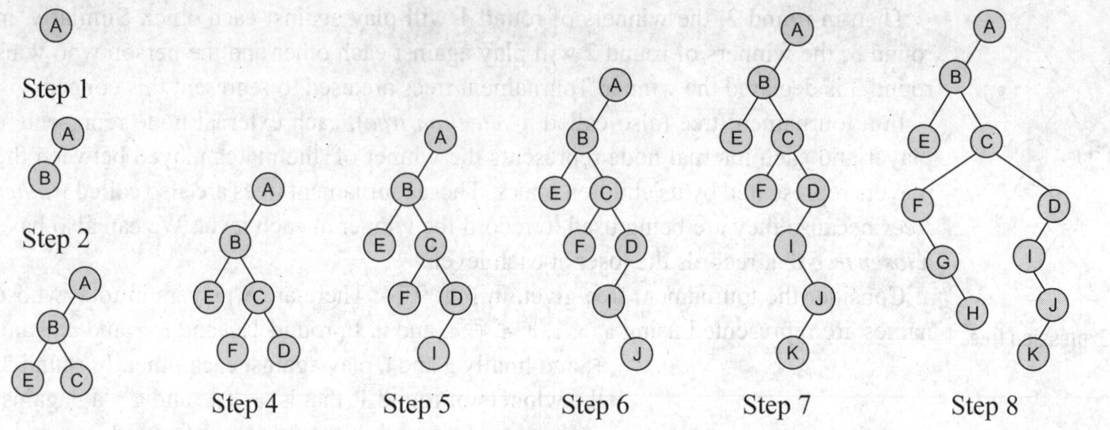

Step 8: Now process all the unprocessed nodes (E, F, G, H, K) in the same fashion, so the resultant binary tree can be given as follows.

9.4 TRAVERSING A BINARY TREE

Traversing a binary tree is the process of visiting each node in the tree exactly once in a systematic way. Unlike linear data structures in which the elements are traversed sequentially, tree is a non-linear data structure in which the elements can be traversed in many different ways. There are different algorithms for tree traversals. These algorithms differ in the order in which the nodes are visited. In this section, we will discuss these algorithms.

9.4.1 Pre-order Traversal

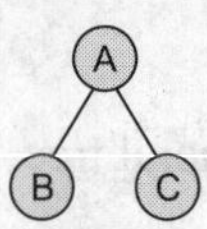

Figure 9.15 Binary tree

To traverse a non-empty binary tree in pre-order, the following operations are performed recursively at each node. The algorithm works by:

1. Visiting the root node,
2. Traversing the left sub-tree, and finally
3. Traversing the right sub-tree.

```
Step 1: Repeat Steps 2 to 4 while TREE != NULL
Step 2:             Write TREE -> DATA
Step 3:             PREORDER(TREE -> LEFT)
Step 4:             PREORDER(TREE -> RIGHT)
        [END OF LOOP]
Step 5: END
```

Figure 9.16 Algorithm for pre-order traversal

Consider the tree given in Fig. 9.15. The pre-order traversal of the tree is given as A, B, C. Root node first, the left sub-tree next, and then the right sub-tree. Pre-order traversal is also called as *depth-first traversal*. In this algorithm, the left sub-tree is always traversed before the right sub-tree. The word 'pre' in the pre-order specifies that the root node is accessed prior to any other nodes in the left and right sub-trees. Pre-order algorithm is also known as the NLR traversal algorithm (Node-Left-Right). The algorithm for pre-order traversal is shown in Fig. 9.16.

Pre-order traversal algorithms are used to extract a prefix notation from an expression tree. For example, consider the expressions given below. When we traverse the elements of a tree using the pre-order traversal algorithm, the expression that we get is a prefix expression.

```
+ - a b * c d (from Fig. 9.13)
% - + a b * c d / ^ e f - g h (from Fig of Example 9.2)
^ + / a b * c d / % f g - h i (from Fig of Example 9.3)
```

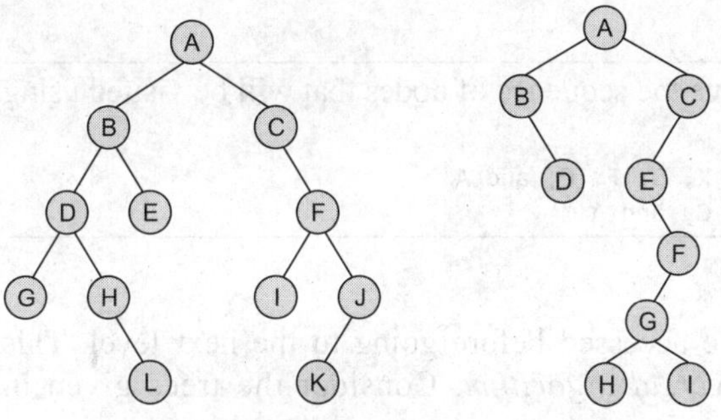

(a) (b)

Example 9.6 In Figs (a) and (b), find the sequence of nodes that will be visited using pre-order traversal algorithm.

Solution

```
TRAVERSAL ORDER: A, B, D, G, H, L, E, C, F, I, J,
    and K
TRAVERSAL ORDER: A, B, D, C, D, E, F, G, H, and I
```

9.4.2 In-order Traversal

To traverse a non-empty binary tree in in-order, the following operations are performed recursively at each node. The algorithm works by:

1. Traversing the left sub-tree,
2. Visiting the root node, and finally
3. Traversing the right sub-tree.

Consider the tree given in Fig. 9.15. The in-order traversal of the tree is given as B, A, and C. Left sub-tree first, the root node next, and then the right sub-tree. In-order traversal is also called as *symmetric traversal*. In this algorithm, the left sub-tree is always traversed before the root node and the right sub-tree. The word 'in' in the in-order specifies that the root node is accessed in between the left and the right sub-trees. In-order algorithm is also known as the LNR traversal algorithm (Left-Node-Right). The algorithm for in-order traversal is shown in Fig. 9.17.

In-order traversal algorithm is usually used to display the elements of a binary search tree. Here, all the elements with a value lower than a given value are accessed before the elements with a higher value. We will discuss binary search trees in detail in the next chapter.

Example 9.7 For the trees given in Example 9.6, find the sequence of nodes that will be visited using in-order traversal algorithm.

```
TRAVERSAL ORDER: G, D, H, L, B, E, A, C, I, F, K, and J
TRAVERSAL ORDER: B, D, A, E, H, G, I, F, and C
```

9.4.3 Post-order Traversal

```
Step 1: Repeat Steps 2 to 4 while TREE != NULL
Step 2:             INORDER(TREE -> LEFT)
Step 3:             Write TREE -> DATA
Step 4:             INORDER(TREE -> RIGHT)
        [END OF LOOP]
Step 5: END
```

Figure 9.17 Algorithm for in-order traversal

```
Step 1: Repeat Steps 2 to 4 while TREE != NULL
Step 2:             POSTORDER(TREE -> LEFT)
Step 3:             POSTORDER(TREE -> RIGHT)
Step 4:             Write TREE -> DATA
        [END OF LOOP]
Step 5: END
```

Figure 9.18 Algorithm for post-order traversal

To traverse a non-empty binary tree in post-order, the following operations are performed recursively at each node. The algorithm works by:

1. Traversing the left sub-tree,
2. Traversing the right sub-tree, and finally
3. Visiting the root node.

Consider the tree given in Fig. 9.18. The post-order traversal of the tree is given as B, C, and A. Left sub-tree first, the right sub-tree next, and finally the root node. In this algorithm, the left sub-tree is always traversed before the right sub-tree and the root node. The word 'post' in the post-order specifies that the root node is accessed after the left and the right sub-trees. Post-order algorithm is also known as the LRN traversal algorithm (Left-Right-Node). The algorithm for post-order traversal is shown in Fig. 9.18. Post-order traversals are used to extract postfix notation from an expression tree.

Example 9.8 For the trees given in Example 9.6, give the sequence of nodes that will be visited using post-order traversal algorithm.

```
TRAVERSAL ORDER: G, L, H, D, E, B, I, K, J, F, C, and A
TRAVERSAL ORDER: D, B, H, I, G, F, E, C, and A
```

9.4.4 Level-order Traversal

In level-order traversal, all the nodes at a level are accessed before going to the next level. This algorithm is also called as the *breadth-first traversal algorithm*. Consider the trees given in Fig. 9.19 and note the level order of these trees.

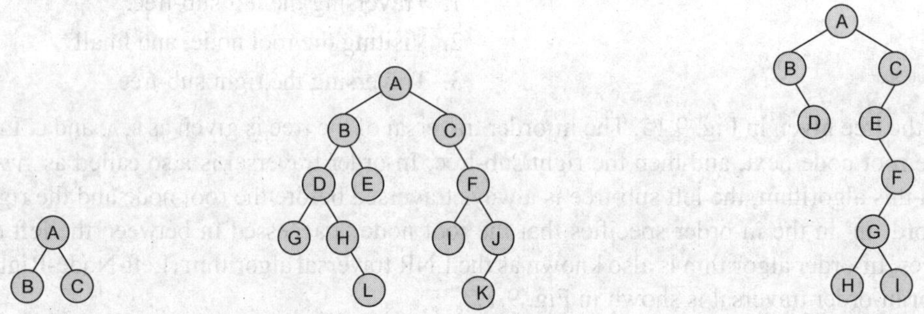

(a) TRAVERSAL ORDER: A, B, and C

(b) TRAVERSAL ORDER: A, B, C, D, E, F, G, H, I, J, L, and K

(c) TRAVERSAL ORDER: A, B, C, D, E, F, G, H, and I

Figure 9.19 Binary trees

9.4.5 Constructing a Binary Tree from Traversal Results

We can construct a binary tree if we are given at least two traversal results. The first traversal must be the in-order traversal and the second can be either pre-order or post-order traversal. The in-order traversal result will be used to determine the left and the right child nodes, and the pre-order/post-order can be used to determine the root node. For example, consider the traversal results given below:

```
In-order Traversal: D B E A F C G                    Pre-order Traversal: A B D E C F G
```

Here, we have the in-order traversal sequence and pre-order traversal sequence. Follow the steps given below to construct the tree:

Step 1 Use the pre-order sequence to determine the root node of the tree. The first element would be the root node.

Step 2 Elements on the left side of the root node in the in-order traversal sequence form the left sub-tree of the root node. Similarly, elements on the right side of the root node in the in-order traversal sequence form the right sub-tree of the root node.

Step 3 Recursively select each element from pre-order traversal sequence and create its left and right sub-trees from the in-order traversal sequence.

Look at Fig. 9.20 which constructs the tree from its traversal results. Now consider the in-order traversal and post-order traversal sequences of a given binary

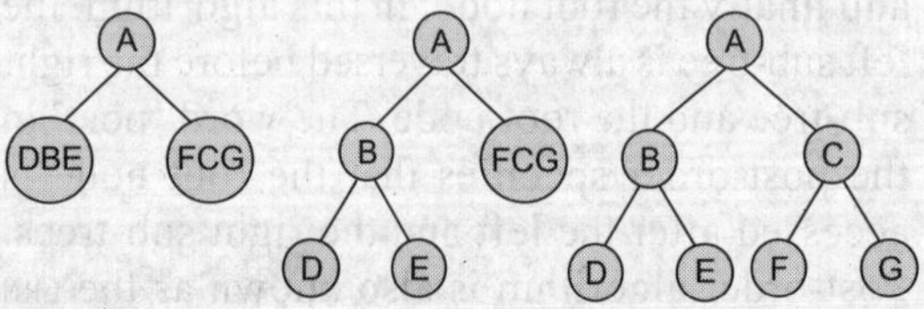

Figure 9.20

tree. Before constructing the binary tree, remember that in post-order traversal the root node is the last node. Rest of the steps will be the same as mentioned above Fig. 9.21.

In–order Traversal: D B H E I A F J C G   Post order Traversal: D H I E B J F G C A

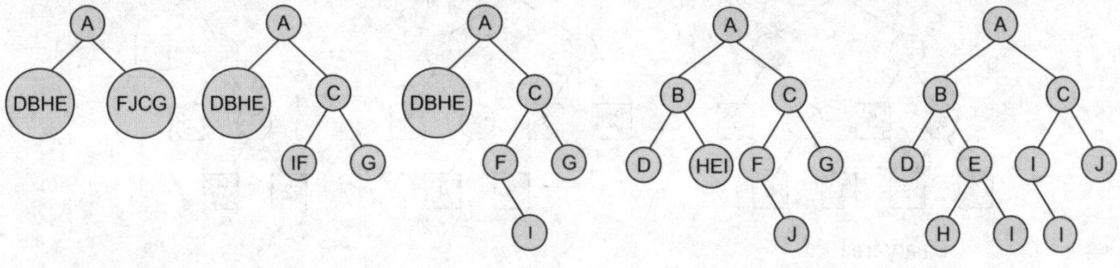

Figure 9.21 Steps to show binary tree

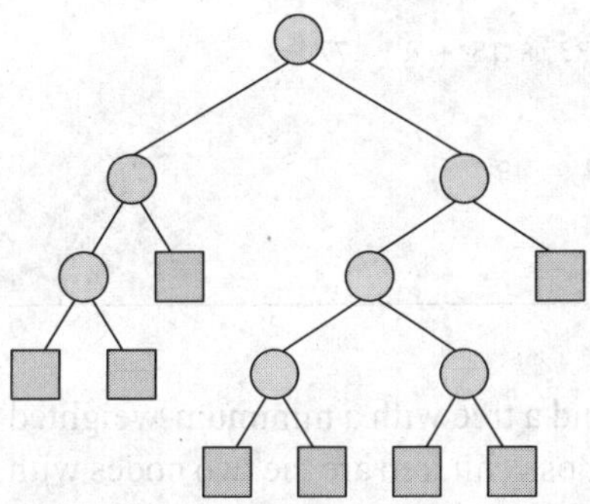

Figure 9.22 Binary tree

9.5 HUFFMAN'S TREE

Huffman coding is an entropy encoding algorithm developed by David A. Huffman that is widely used as a lossless data compression technique. The Huffman coding algorithm uses a variable-length code table to encode a source character where the variable-length code table is derived on the basis of the estimated probability of occurrence of the source character.

The key idea behind Huffman algorithm is that it encodes the most common characters using shorter strings of bits than those used for less common source characters.

The algorithm works by creating a binary tree of nodes that are stored in an array. A node can be either a leaf node or an internal node. Initially, all the nodes in the tree are at the leaf level and store the source character and its frequency of occurrence (also known as weight).

While the internal node is used to store the weight and contains links to its child nodes, the external node contains the actual character. Conventionally, a `'0'` represents following the left child and a `'1'` represents following the right child. A finished tree that has `n` leaf nodes will have `n - 1` internal nodes.

The running time of the algorithm depends on the length of the paths in the tree. So, before going into further details of Huffman coding, let us first learn how to calculate the length of the paths in the tree. The *external path length* of a binary tree is defined as the sum of all path lengths summed over each path from the root to an external node. The internal path length is also defined in the same manner. The *internal path length* of a binary tree is defined as the sum of all path lengths summed over each path from the root to an internal node. Look at the binary tree given in Fig. 9.22.

The internal path length, $L_I = 0 + 1 + 2 + 1 + 2 + 3 + 3 = 12$

The external path length, $L_E = 2 + 3 + 3 + 2 + 4 + 4 + 4 + 4 = 26$

Note that, $L_I + 2 * n = 12 + 2 * 7 = 12 + 14 = 26 = L_E$

Thus, $L_I + 2n = L_E$, where n is the number of internal nodes. Now if the tree has n external nodes and each external node is assigned a weight, then the weighted path length P is defined as the sum of the weighted path lengths.

Therefore, $P = W_1L_1 + W_2L_2 + ... + W_nL_n$

where W_i and L_i are the weight and path length of an external node N_i.

Example 9.9 Consider the trees T_1, T_2, and T_3 given below, calculate their weighted external path lengths.

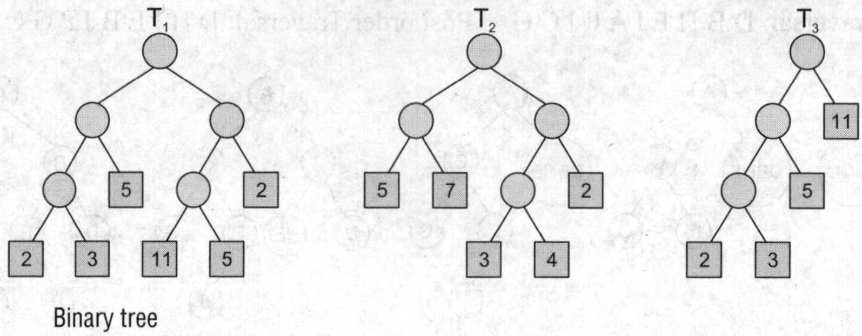

Solution

Weighted external path length of T_1 can be given as,

$$P_1 = 2\cdot3 + 3\cdot3 + 5\cdot2 + 11\cdot3 + 5\cdot3 + 2\cdot2 = 6 + 9 + 10 + 33 + 15 + 4 = 77$$

Weighted external path length of T_2 can be given as,

$$P_2 = 5\cdot2 + 7\cdot2 + 3\cdot3 + 4\cdot3 + 2\cdot2 = 10 + 14 + 9 + 12 + 4 = 49$$

Weighted external path length of T_3 can be given as,

$$P_3 = 2\cdot3 + 3\cdot3 + 5\cdot2 + 11\cdot1 = 6 + 9 + 10 + 11 = 36$$

Technique

Given n nodes and their weights, the Huffman algorithm is used to find a tree with a minimum-weighted path length. The process essentially begins by creating a new node whose children are the two nodes with the smallest weight, such that the new node's weight is equal to the sum of the children's weight. That is, the two nodes are merged into one node. This process is repeated until the tree has only one node. Such a tree with only one node is known as the Huffman tree.

The Huffman algorithm can be implemented using a priority queue in which all the nodes are placed in such a way that the node with the lowest weight is given the highest priority. The algorithm is shown in Fig. 9.23.

```
Step 1: Create a leaf node for each character. Add the character and its weight or frequency
        of occurrence to the priority queue.
Step 2: Repeat Steps 3 to 5 while the total number of nodes in the queue is greater than 1.
Step 3: Remove two nodes that have the lowest weight (or highest priority).
Step 4: Create a new internal node by merging these two nodes as children and with weight
        equal to the sum of the two nodes' weights.
Step 5: Add the newly created node to the queue.
```

Figure 9.23 Huffman algorithm

Example 9.10 Create a Huffman tree with the following nodes arranged in a priority queue.

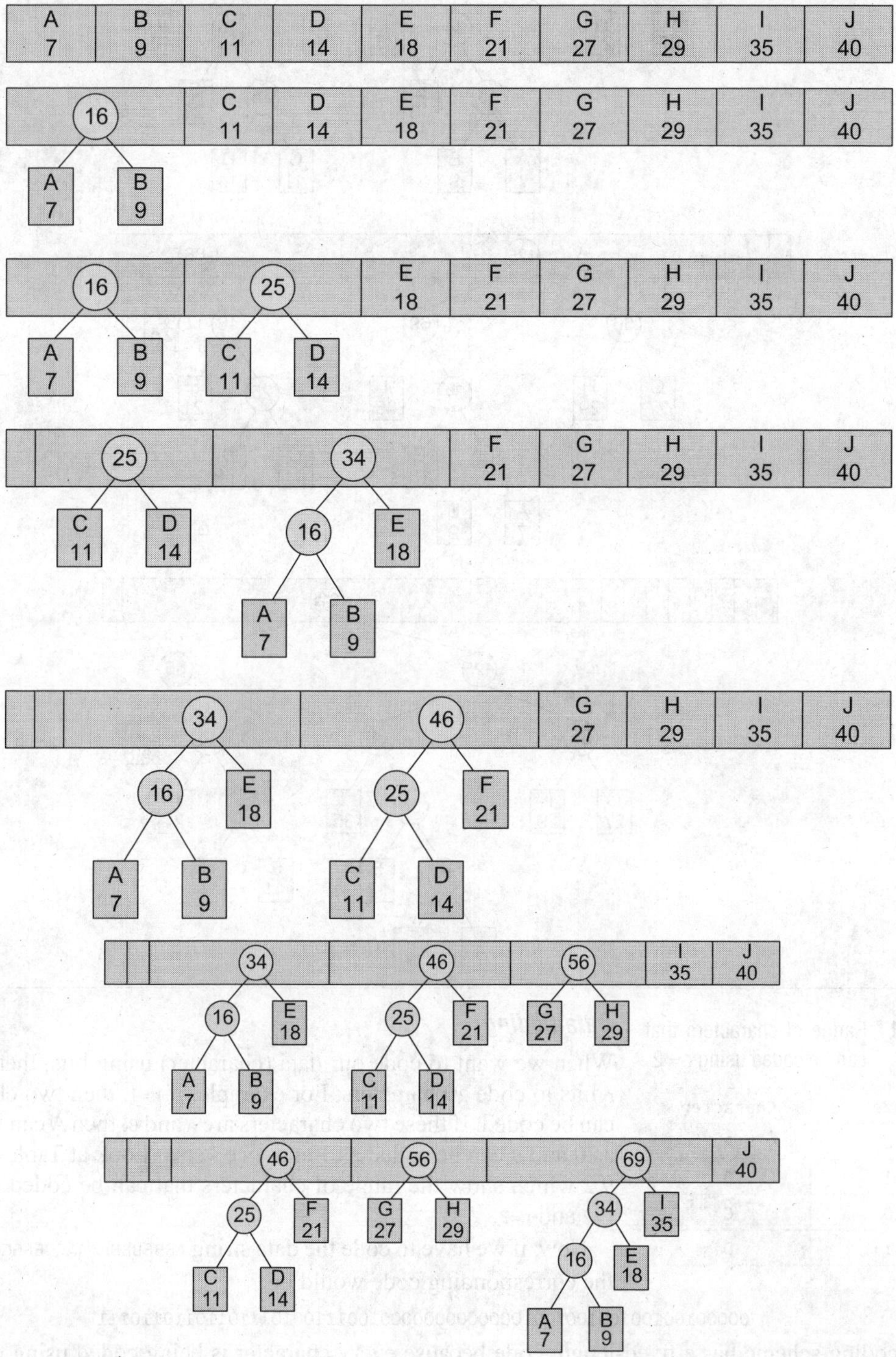

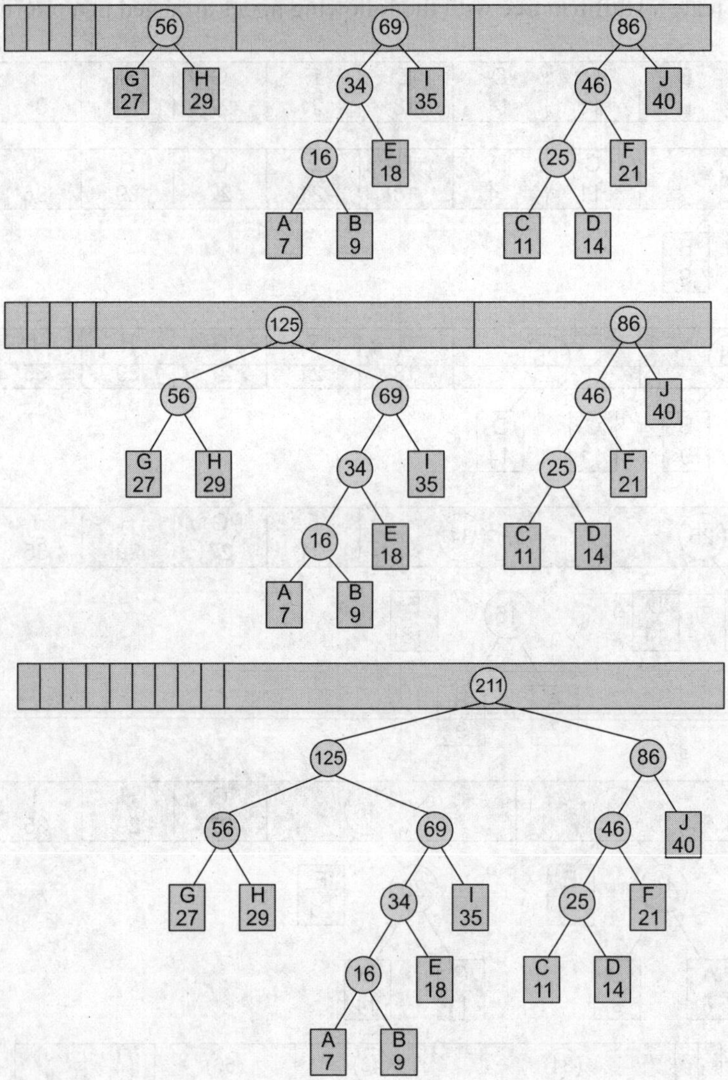

Table 9.1 Range of characters that can be coded using r = 2

Code	Character
00	A
01	B
10	C
11	D

Data Coding

When we want to code our data (character) using bits, then we use r bits to code 2^r characters. For example, if r=1, then two characters can be coded. If these two characters are A and B, then A can be coded as 0 and B can be coded as 1 and vice versa. Look at Tables 9.1 and 9.2 which show the range of characters that can be coded by using r=2 and r=3.

Now, if we have to code the data string ABBBBBBAAAACDEFGGGGH, then the corresponding code would be:

0000010010010010010010000000000000010011100101110110110110111

This coding scheme has a fixed-length code because every character is being coded using the same number of bits. Although this technique of coding is simple, coding the data can be made more efficient by using a variable-length code.

Table 9.2 Range of characters that can be coded using r = 3

Code	Character
000	A
001	B
010	C
011	D
100	E
101	F
110	G
111	H

You might have observed that when we write a text in English, all the characters are not used frequently. For example, characters like a, e, i, and r are used more frequently than w, x, y, z and so on. So, the basic idea is to assign a shorter code to the frequently occurring characters and a longer to less frequently occurring characters. Variable-length coding is preferred over fixed-length coding because it requires lesser number of bits to encode the same data.

For variable-length encoding, we first build a Huffman tree. First, arrange all the characters in a priority queue in which the character with the lowest frequency of occurrence has the highest priority. Then, create a Huffman tree as explained in the previous section. Figure 9.24 shows a Huffman tree that is used for encoding the data set.

In the Huffman tree, circles contain the cumulative weights of their child nodes. Every left branch is coded with 0 and every right branch is coded with 1. So, the characters A, E, R, W, X, Y, and Z are coded as shown in Table 9.3.

Table 9.3 Characters with their codes

Character	Code
A	00
E	01
R	11
W	1010
X	1000
Y	1001
Z	1011

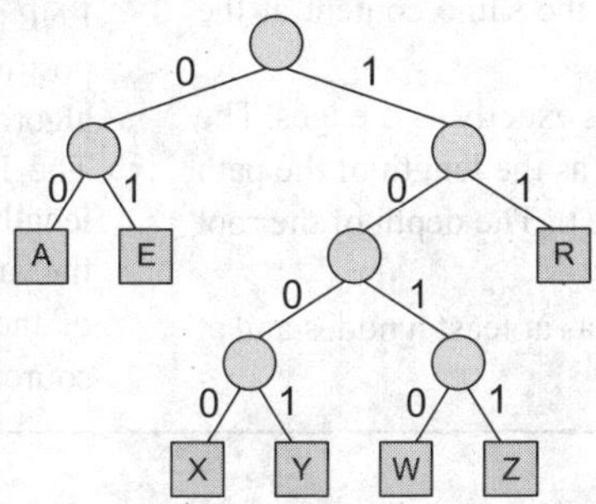

Figure 9.24 Huffman tree

Thus, we see that frequent characters have a shorter code and infrequent characters have a longer code.

9.6 APPLICATIONS OF TREES

- Trees are used to store simple as well as complex data. Here simple means an integer value, character value and complex data means a structure or a record.
- Trees are often used for implementing other types of data structures like hash tables, sets, and maps.
- A self-balancing tree, Red-black tree is used in kernel scheduling, to preempt massively multi-processor computer operating system use. (We will study red-black trees in next chapter.)
- Another variation of tree, B-trees are prominently used to store tree structures on disc. They are used to index a large number of records. (We will study B-Trees in Chapter 11.)
- B-trees are also used for secondary indexes in databases, where the index facilitates a select operation to answer some range criteria.
- Trees are an important data structure used for compiler construction.
- Trees are also used in database design.
- Trees are used in file system directories.
- Trees are also widely used for information storage and retrieval in symbol tables.

Points to Remember

- A tree is a data structure which is mainly used to store hierarchical data. A tree is recursively defined as collection of one or more nodes where one node is designated as the root of the tree and the remaining nodes can be partitioned into non-empty sets each of which is a sub-tree of the root.
- In a binary tree, every node has zero, one, or at the most two successors. A node that has no successors is called a leaf node or a terminal node. Every node other than the root node has a parent.
- The degree of a node is equal to the number of children that a node has. The degree of a leaf node is zero. All nodes that are at the same level and share the same parent are called siblings.
- Two binary trees having a similar structure are said to be copies if they have the same content at the corresponding nodes.
- A binary tree of `n` nodes has exactly `n - 1` edges. The depth of a node `N` is given as the length of the path from the root `R` to the node `N`. The depth of the root node is zero.
- A binary tree of height `h` has at least h nodes and at most 2^h - `1` nodes.
- The height of a binary tree with `n` nodes is at least $\log_2(n+1)$ and at most `n`. In-degree of a node is the number of edges arriving at that node. The root node is the only node that has an in-degree equal to zero. Similarly, out-degree of a node is the number of edges leaving that node.
- In a complete binary tree, every level (except possibly the last) is completely filled and nodes appear as far left as possibly.
- A binary tree `T` is said to be an extended binary tree (or a 2-tree) if each node in the tree has either no children or exactly two children.
- Pre-order traversal is also called as depth-first traversal. It is also known as the NLR traversal algorithm (Node-Left-Right) and is used to extract a prefix notation from an expression tree. In-order algorithm is known as the LNR traversal algorithm (Left-Node-Right). Similarly, post-order algorithm is known as the LRN traversal algorithm (Left-Right-Node).
- The Huffman coding algorithm uses a variable-length code table to encode a source character where the variable-length code table is derived on the basis of the estimated probability of occurrence of the source character.

Exercises

Review Questions

1. Explain the concept of a tree. Discuss its applications.
2. What are the two ways of representing binary trees in the memory? Which one do you prefer and why?
3. List all possible non-similar binary trees having four nodes.
4. Draw the binary expression tree that represents the following postfix expression:

   A B + C * D –

5. Write short notes on:
   (a) Complete binary trees
   (b) Extended binary trees
   (c) Tournament trees
   (d) Expression trees
   (e) Huffman trees
   (f) General trees
   (g) Forests
6. Consider the tree given below. Now, do the following:
   (a) Name the leaf nodes
   (b) Name the non-leaf nodes
   (c) Name the ancestors of E
   (d) Name the descendants of A
   (e) Name the siblings of C
   (f) Find the height of the tree
   (g) Find the height of sub-tree rooted at E
   (h) Find the level of node E
   (i) Find the in-order, pre-order, post-order, and level-order traversal

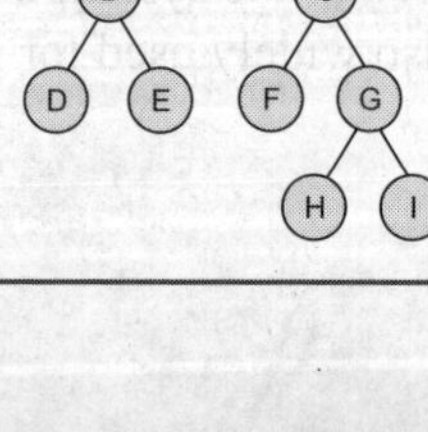

7. For the expression tree given below, do the following:

(a) Extract the infix expression it represents

(b) Find the corresponding prefix and postfix expressions

(c) Evaluate the infix expression, given a = 30, b = 10, c = 2, d = 30, e = 10

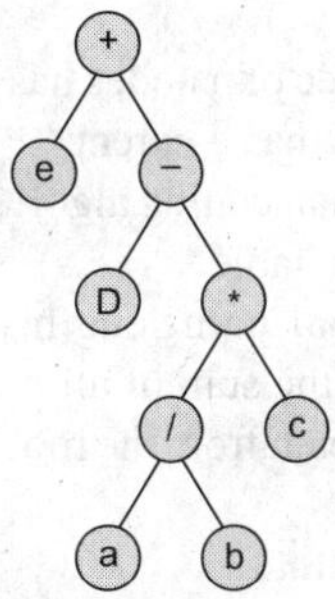

8. Convert the prefix expression `-/ab*+bcd` into infix expression and then draw the corresponding expression tree.

9. Consider the trees given below and state whether they are complete binary tree or full binary tree.

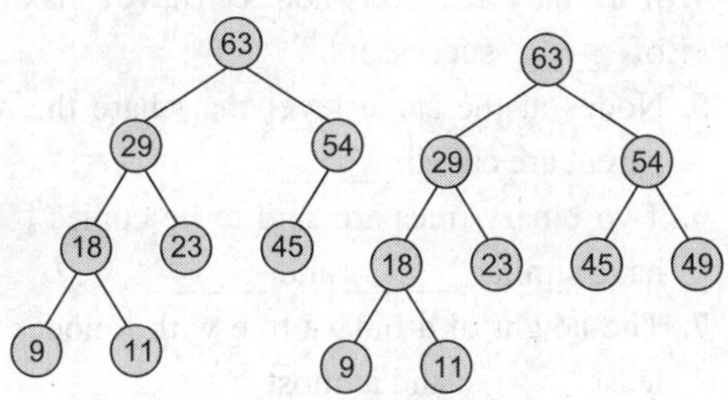

10. What is the maximum number of levels that a binary search tree with 100 nodes can have?

11. What is the maximum height of a tree with 32 nodes?

12. What is the maximum number of nodes that can be found in a binary tree at levels 3, 4, and 12?

13. Draw all possible non-similar binary trees having three nodes.

14. Draw the binary tree having the following memory representation:

ROOT 3 → 3

AVAIL 15 → 15

	LEFT	DATA	RIGHT
1	–1	8	–1
2	–1	10	–1
3	5	1	8
4			
5	9	2	14
6			
7			
8	20	3	11
9	1	4	12
10			
11	–1	7	18
12	–1	9	–1
13			
14	–1	5	–1
15			
16	–1	11	–1
17			
18	–1	12	–1
19			
20	2	6	16

15. Draw the memory representation of the binary tree given below.

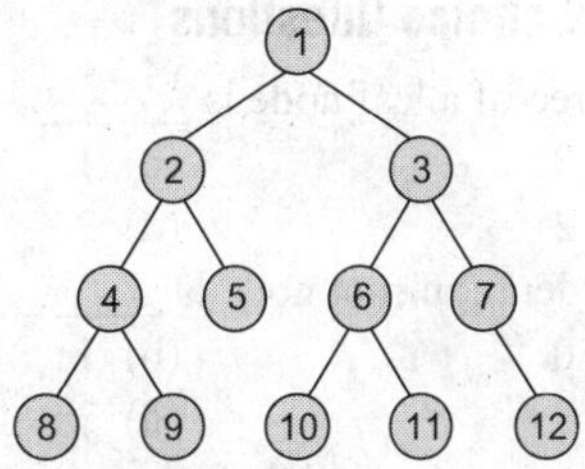

16. Consider the trees T_1, T_2, and T_3 given below and calculate their weighted path lengths.

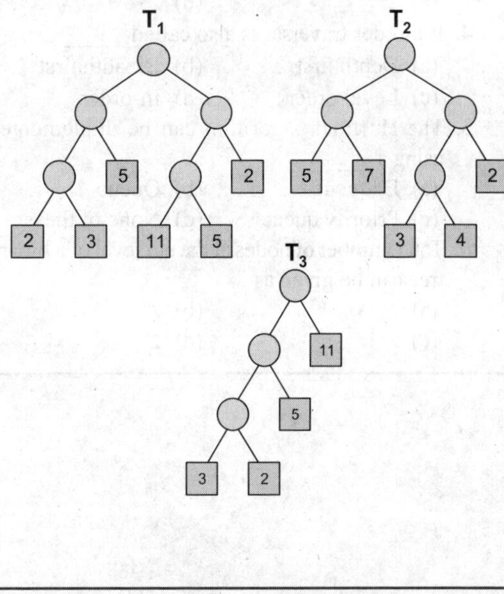

17. Consider the trees T_1, T_2, and T_3 given below and find the Huffman coding for the characters.

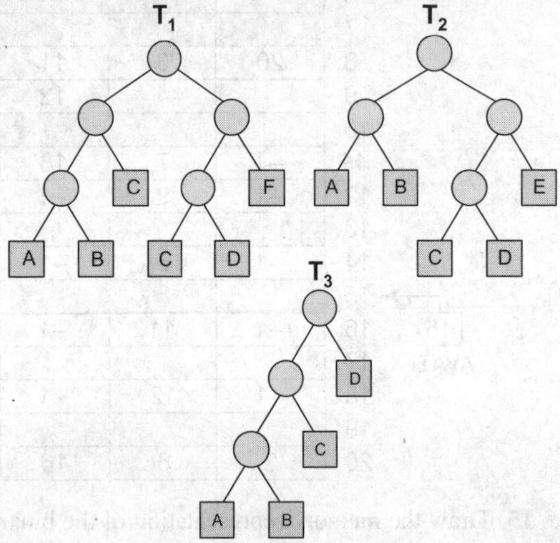

Multiple-choice Questions

1. Degree of a leaf node is ______.
   (a) 0 (b) 1
   (c) 2 (d) 3
2. The depth of root node is ______.
   (a) 0 (b) 1
   (c) 2 (d) 3
3. A binary tree of height h has at least h nodes and at most ______ nodes.
   (a) 2h (b) 2^h
   (c) 2^{h+1} (d) $2^h - 1$
4. Pre-order traversal is also called ______.
   (a) Depth first (b) Breadth first
   (c) Level order (d) In-order
5. The Huffman algorithm can be implemented using a ______.
   (a) Dequeue (b) Queue
   (c) Priority queue (d) None of these
6. Total number of nodes at the nth level of a binary tree can be given as
   (a) 2^n (b) 2^n
   (c) 2^{n+1} (d) 2^{n-1}

True or False

1. Nodes that branch into child nodes are called parent nodes.
2. The size of a tree is equal to the total number of nodes.
3. A leaf node does not branch out further.
4. A node that has no successors is called the root node.
5. A binary tree of n nodes has exactly n - 1 edges.
6. Every node has a parent.
7. The Huffman coding algorithm uses a variable-length code table.
8. The internal path length of a binary tree is defined as the sum of all path lengths summed over each path from the root to an external node.

Fill in the Blanks

1. Parent node is also known as the ______ node.
2. Size of a tree is basically the number of ______ in the tree.
3. The maximum number of nodes at the kth level of a binary tree is ______.
4. In a binary tree, every node can have a maximum of ______ successors.
5. Nodes at the same level that share the same parent are called ______.
6. Two binary trees are said to be copies if they have similar ______ and ______.
7. The height of a binary tree with n nodes is at least ______ and at most ______.
8. A binary tree T is said to be an extended binary tree if ______.
9. ______ traversal algorithm is used to extract a prefix notation from an expression tree.
10. In a Huffman tree, the code of a character depends on ______.

CHAPTER 10

Efficient Binary Trees

LEARNING OBJECTIVE

In this chapter, we will discuss efficient binary trees such as binary search trees, AVL trees, threaded binary trees, red-black trees, and splay trees. This chapter is an extension of binary trees.

10.1 BINARY SEARCH TREES

We have already discussed binary trees in the previous chapter. A binary search tree, also known as an ordered binary tree, is a variant of binary trees in which the nodes are arranged in an order. In a binary search tree, all the nodes in the left sub-tree have a value less than that of the root node. Correspondingly, all the nodes in the right sub-tree have a value either equal to or greater than the root node. The same rule is applicable to every sub-tree in the tree. (Note that a binary search tree may or may not contain duplicate values, depending on its implementation.)

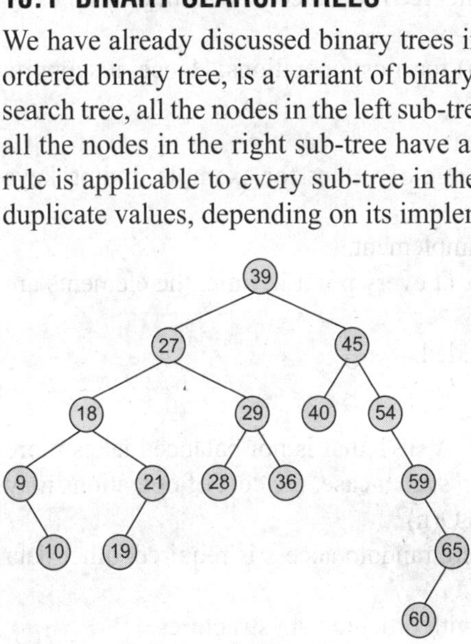

Figure 10.1 Binary search tree

Look at Fig. 10.1. The root node is 39. The left sub-tree of the root node consists of nodes 9, 10, 18, 19, 21, 27, 28, 29, and 36. All these nodes have smaller values than the root node. The right sub-tree of the root node consists of nodes 40, 45, 54, 59, 60, and 65. Recursively, each of the sub-trees also obeys the binary search tree constraint. For example, in the left sub-tree of the root node, 27 is the root and all elements in its left sub-tree (9, 10, 18, 19, 21) are smaller than 27, while all nodes in its right sub-tree (28, 29, and 36) are greater than the root node's value.

Since the nodes in a binary search tree are ordered, the time needed to search an element in the tree is greatly reduced. Whenever we search for an element, we do not need to traverse the entire tree. At every node, we get a hint regarding which sub-tree to search in. For example, in the given tree, if we have to search for 29, then we know that we have to scan only the left sub-tree. If the value is present in the tree, it will only be in the left sub-tree, as 29 is smaller than 39 (the root node's value). The left sub-tree has a root node with the value 27. Since 29 is greater than 27, we will move to the right sub-tree, where we will find the element. Thus, the average running time of a search operation is $O(\log_2 n)$, as at every step, we eliminate half of the sub-tree from the search process. Due to its efficiency in searching elements, binary search trees are widely used in dictionary problems where the code always inserts and searches the elements that are indexed by some key value.

Binary search trees also speed up the insertion and deletion operations. The tree has a speed advantage when the data in the structure changes rapidly.

Binary search trees are considered to be efficient data structures especially when compared with sorted linear arrays and linked lists. In a sorted array, searching can be done in $O(\log_2 n)$ time, but insertions and deletions are quite expensive. In contrast, inserting and deleting elements in a linked list is easier, but searching for an element is done in O(n) time.

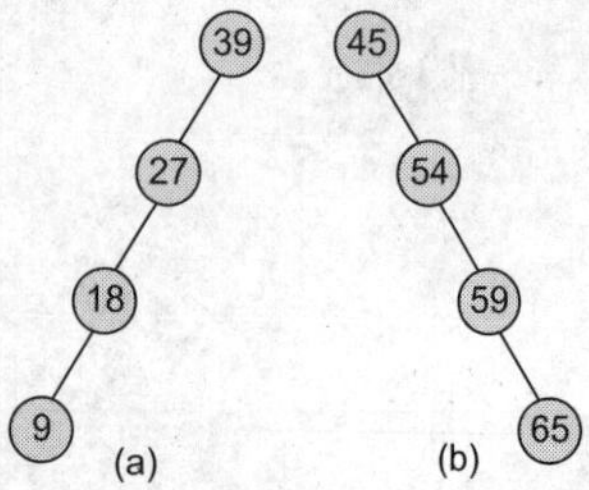

Figure 10.2 (a) Left skewed, and (b) right skewed binary search trees

However, in the worst case, a binary search tree will take O(n) time to search for an element. The worst case would occur when the tree is a linear chain of nodes as given in Fig. 10.2.

To summarize, a binary search tree is a binary tree with the following properties:

- The left sub-tree of a node N contains values that are less than N's value.
- The right sub-tree of a node N contains values that are greater than N's value.
- Both the left and the right binary trees also satisfy these properties and, thus, are binary search trees.

Advantages of Binary Search Tree:

- BST supports fast insertion and deletion operations (when the tree is balanced). The time complexity of these operations is O(log n).
- BST performs searching with a time complexity of O(log n) for most operations. Hence, it supports fast searching also.
- BST is efficient to implement.
- BST supports operations that can be easily applied to a range of values for example finding keys between N and M (N <= M).
- As compared to other data structures, BST code is easy to implement.
- BST automatically sorts elements while inserting them. So, at every point in time, the elements are always stored.
- BST is a flexible data structure as new data can be easily added.

Disadvantages of Binary Search Tree:

- The main limitation of a BST is that it should be balanced. A BST that is not balanced takes more time to perform the operations like insertion and deletion. In such a case, the cost of operations may not be logarithmic and the time complexity may degrade to O(n).
- BST does not support random data access. So, in cases where random access is required, other data structures like arrays or hash tables perform better.
- A BST does not support some operations that are possible with ordered data structures.

Example 10.1 State whether the binary trees in Fig. 10.3 are binary search trees or not.

Solution

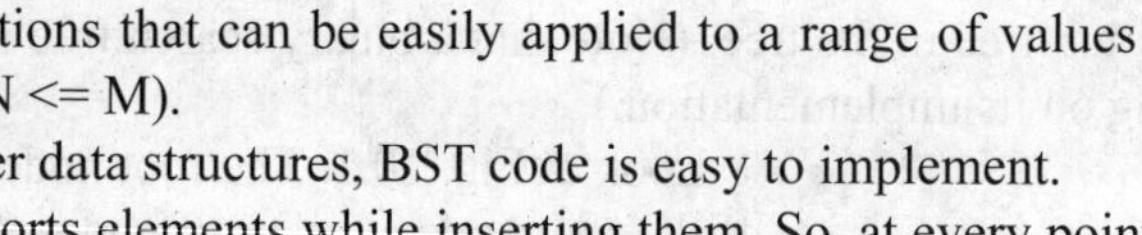

Figure 10.3 Binary trees

Example 10.2 Create a binary search tree using the following data elements:
45, 39, 56, 12, 34, 78, 32, 10, 89, 54, 67, 81

Solution

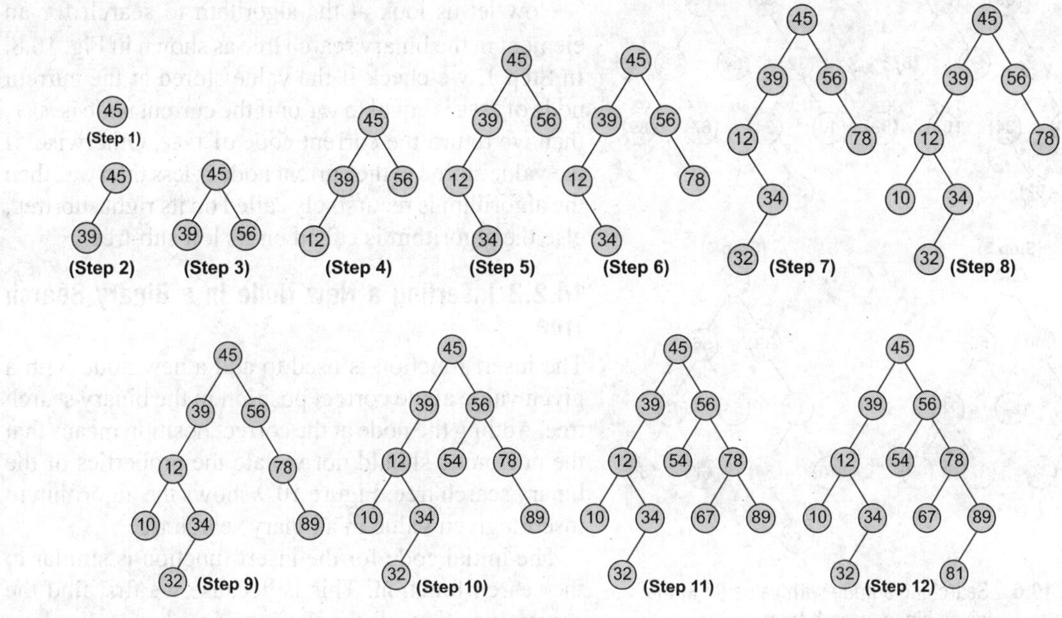

Figure 10.4 Binary search tree

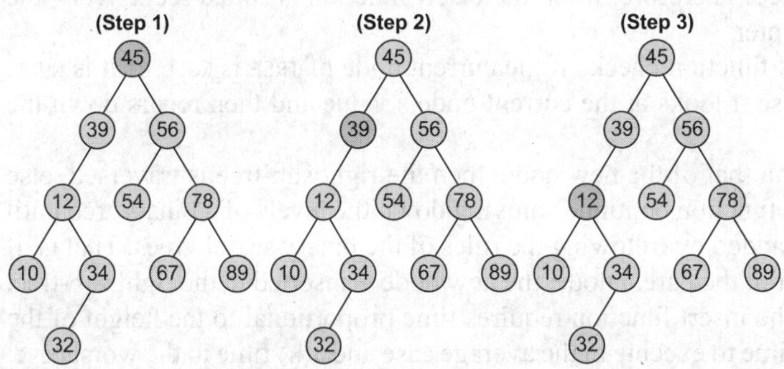

Figure 10.5 Searching a node with value 12 in the given binary search tree

10.2 OPERATIONS ON BINARY SEARCH TREES

In this section, we will discuss the different operations that are performed on a binary search tree. All these operations require comparisons to be made between the nodes.

10.2.1 Searching for a Node in a Binary Search Tree

The search function is used to find whether a given value is present in the tree or not. The searching process begins at the root node. The function first checks if the binary search tree is empty. If it is empty, then the value we are searching for is not present in the tree. So, the search algorithm terminates by displaying an appropriate message. However, if there are nodes in the tree, then the search function checks to see if the key value of the current node is equal to the value to be searched. If not, it checks if the value to be searched for is less than the value of the current node, in which case it should be recursively called on the left child node. In case the value is greater than the value of the current node, it should be recursively called on the right child node.

Look at Fig. 10.5. The figure shows how a binary tree is searched to find a specific element. First, see how the tree will be traversed to find the node with value 12. The procedure to find the node with value 67 is illustrated in Fig. 10.6.

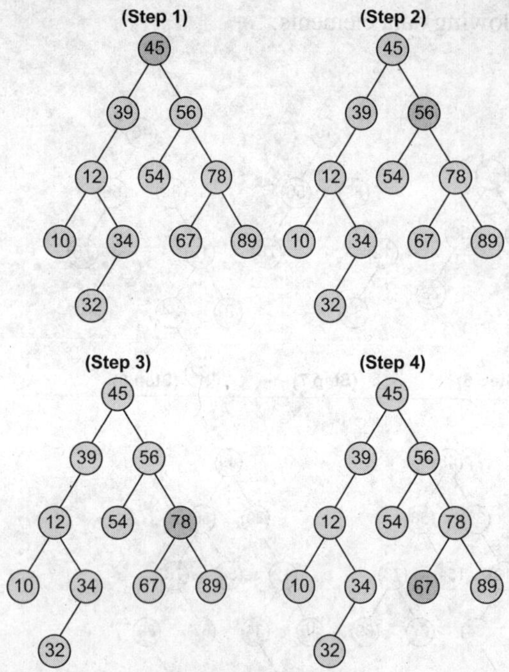

Figure 10.6 Searching a node with value 67 in the given binary search tree

The procedure to find the node with value 40 is shown in Fig. 10.7. The search would terminate after reaching node 39 as it does not have any right child.

Now let us look at the algorithm to search for an element in the binary search tree as shown in Fig. 10.8. In Step 1, we check if the value stored at the current node of `TREE` is equal to `VAL` or if the current node is `NULL`, then we return the current node of `TREE`. Otherwise, if the value stored at the current node is less than `VAL`, then the algorithm is recursively called on its right sub-tree, else the algorithm is called on its left sub-tree.

10.2.2 Inserting a New Node in a Binary Search Tree

The insert function is used to add a new node with a given value at the correct position in the binary search tree. Adding the node at the correct position means that the new node should not violate the properties of the binary search tree. Figure 10.9 shows the algorithm to insert a given value in a binary search tree.

The initial code for the insert function is similar to the search function. This is because we first find the correct position where the insertion has to be done and then add the node at that position. The insertion function changes the structure of the tree. Therefore, when the insert function is called recursively, the function should return the new tree pointer.

In Step 1 of the algorithm, the insert function checks if the current node of `TREE` is `NULL`. If it is `NULL`, the algorithm simply adds the node, else it looks at the current node's value and then recurs down the left or right sub-tree.

If the current node's value is less than that of the new node, then the right sub-tree is traversed, else the left sub-tree is traversed. The insert function continues moving down the levels of a binary tree until it reaches a leaf node. The new node is added by following the rules of the binary search trees. That is, if the new node's value is greater than that of the parent node, the new node is inserted in the right sub-tree, else it is inserted in the left sub-tree. The insert function requires time proportional to the height of the tree in the worst case. It takes `O(log n)` time to execute in the average case and `O(n)` time in the worst case.

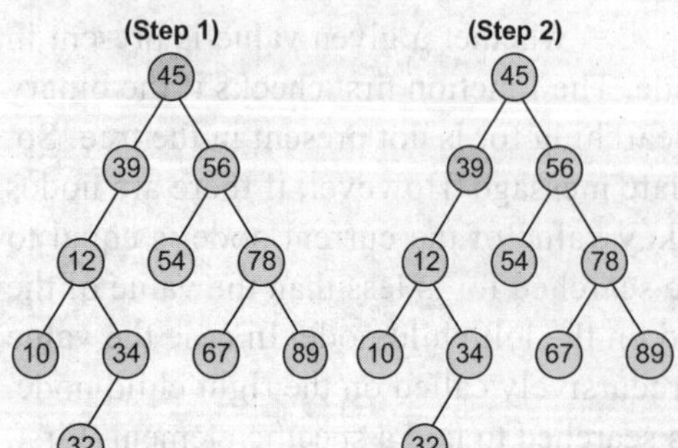

Figure 10.7 Searching a node with the value 40 in the given binary search tree

```
searchElement (TREE, VAL)

Step 1: IF TREE -> DATA = VAL OR TREE = NULL
           Return TREE
        ELSE
         IF VAL < TREE -> DATA
          Return searchElement(TREE -> LEFT, VAL)
         ELSE
          Return searchElement(TREE -> RIGHT, VAL)
         [END OF IF]
        [END OF IF]
Step 2: END
```

Figure 10.8 Algorithm to search for a given value in a binary search tree

```
Insert (TREE, VAL)

Step 1: IF TREE = NULL
             Allocate memory for TREE
             SET TREE -> DATA = VAL
             SET TREE -> LEFT = TREE -> RIGHT = NULL
        ELSE
             IF VAL < TREE -> DATA
                    Insert(TREE -> LEFT, VAL)
             ELSE
                    Insert(TREE -> RIGHT, VAL)
             [END OF IF]
        [END OF IF]
Step 2: END
```

Figure 10.9 Algorithm to insert a given value in a binary search tree

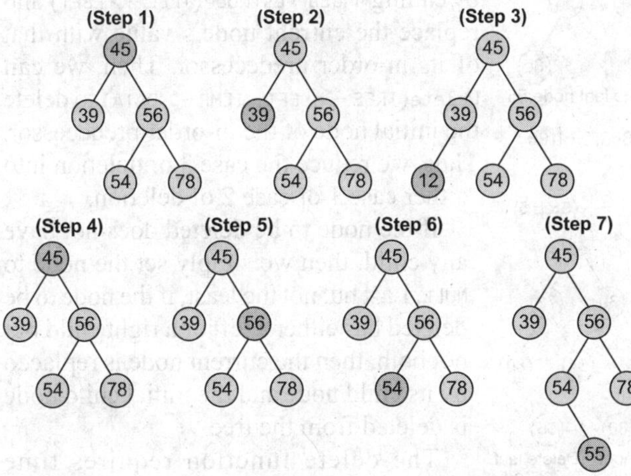

Figure 10.10 Inserting nodes with values 12 and 55 in the given binary search tree

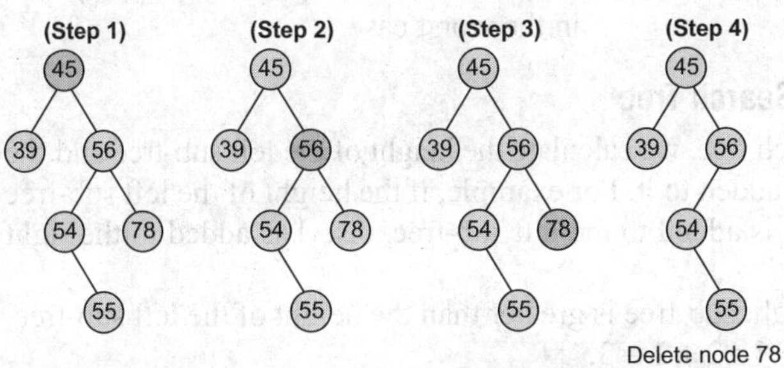

Figure 10.11 Deleting node 78 from the given binary search tree

Look at Fig. 10.10 which shows insertion of values in a given tree. We will take up the case of inserting 12 and 55.

10.2.3 Deleting a Node from a Binary Search Tree

The delete function deletes a node from the binary search tree. However, utmost care should be taken that the properties of the binary search tree are not violated and nodes are not lost in the process. We will take up three cases in this section and discuss how a node is deleted from a binary search tree.

Case 1: Deleting a Node that has No Children

Look at the binary search tree given in Fig. 10.11. If we have to delete node 78, we can simply remove this node without any issue. This is the simplest case of deletion.

Case 2: Deleting a Node with One Child

To handle this case, the node's child is set as the child of the node's parent. In other words, replace the node with its child. Now, if the node is the left child of its parent, the node's child becomes the left child of the node's parent. Correspondingly, if the node is the right child of its parent, the node's child becomes the right child of the node's parent. Look at the binary search tree shown in Fig. 10.12 and see how deletion of node 54 is handled.

Case 3: Deleting a Node with Two Children

To handle this case, replace the node's value with its *in-order predecessor* (largest value in the left sub-tree) or *in-order successor* (smallest value in the right sub-tree). The in-order predecessor or the successor can then be deleted using any of the above cases. Look at the binary search tree given in Fig. 10.13 and see how deletion of node with value 56 is handled.

This deletion could also be handled by replacing node 56 with its in-order successor, as shown in Fig. 10.14.

Now, let us look at Fig. 10.15 which shows the algorithm to delete a node from a binary search tree.

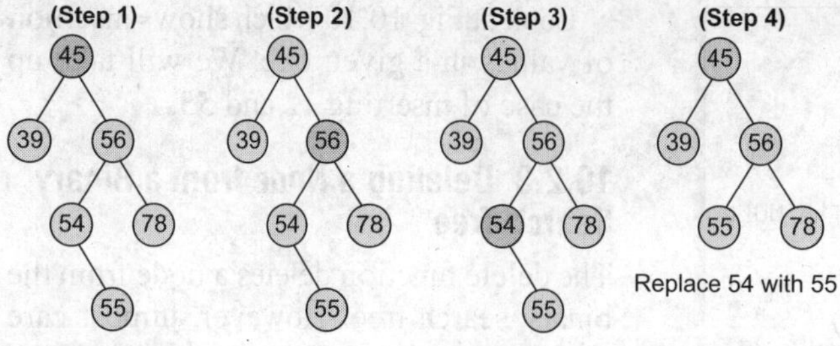

Figure 10.12 Deleting node 54 from the given binary search tree

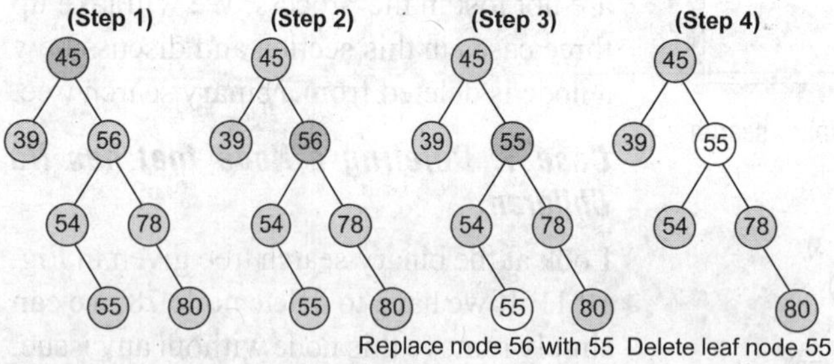

Figure 10.13 Deleting node 56 from the given binary search tree

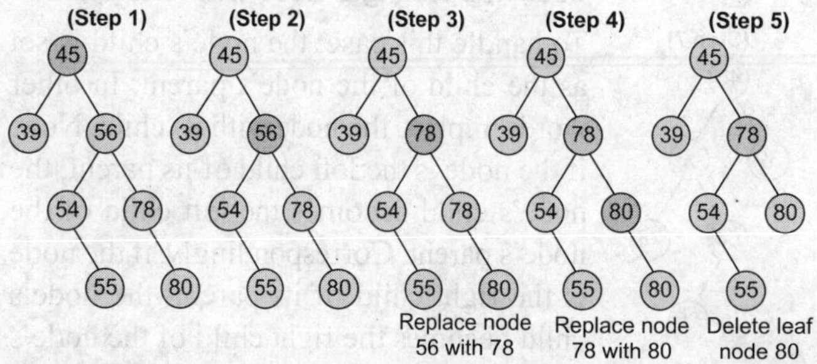

Figure 10.14 Deleting node 56 from the given binary search tree

In Step 1 of the algorithm, we first check if `TREE=NULL`, because if it is true, then the node to be deleted is not present in the tree. However, if that is not the case, then we check if the value to be deleted is less than the current node's data. In case the value is less, we call the algorithm recursively on the node's left sub-tree, otherwise the algorithm is called recursively on the node's right sub-tree.

Note that if we have found the node whose value is equal to `VAL`, then we check which case of deletion it is. If the node to be deleted has both left and right children, then we find the in-order predecessor of the node by calling `findLargestNode(TREE –> LEFT)` and replace the current node's value with that of its in-order predecessor. Then, we call `Delete(TREE –> LEFT, TEMP –> DATA)` to delete the initial node of the in-order predecessor. Thus, we reduce the case 3 of deletion into either case 1 or case 2 of deletion.

If the node to be deleted does not have any child, then we simply set the node to `NULL`. Last but not the least, if the node to be deleted has either a left or a right child but not both, then the current node is replaced by its child node and the initial child node is deleted from the tree.

The delete function requires time proportional to the height of the tree in the worst case. It takes `O(log n)` time to execute in the average case and Ω`(n)` time in the worst case.

10.2.4 Determining the Height of a Binary Search Tree

In order to determine the height of a binary search tree, we calculate the height of the left sub-tree and the right sub-tree. Whichever height is greater, 1 is added to it. For example, if the height of the left sub-tree is greater than that of the right sub-tree, then 1 is added to the left sub-tree, else 1 is added to the right sub-tree.

Look at Fig. 10.16. Since the height of the right sub-tree is greater than the height of the left sub-tree, the height of the tree = height (right sub-tree) + 1= 2 + 1= 3.

Figure 10.17 shows a recursive algorithm that determines the height of a binary search tree.

In Step 1 of the algorithm, we first check if the current node of the `TREE = NULL`. If the condition is true, then 0 is returned to the calling code. Otherwise, for every node, we recursively call the algorithm to calculate the height of its left sub-tree as well as its right sub-tree. The height of the tree at that node is given by adding 1 to the height of the left sub-tree or the height of right sub-tree, whichever is greater.

```
Delete (TREE, VAL)

Step 1: IF TREE = NULL
            Write "VAL not found in the tree"
        ELSE IF VAL < TREE -> DATA
            Delete(TREE->LEFT, VAL)
        ELSE IF VAL > TREE -> DATA
            Delete(TREE -> RIGHT, VAL)
        ELSE IF TREE -> LEFT AND TREE -> RIGHT
            SET TEMP = findLargestNode(TREE -> LEFT)
            SET TREE -> DATA = TEMP -> DATA
            Delete(TREE -> LEFT, TEMP -> DATA)
        ELSE
            SET TEMP = TREE
           IF TREE -> LEFT = NULL AND TREE -> RIGHT = NULL
                SET TREE = NULL
            ELSE IF TREE -> LEFT != NULL
                SET TREE = TREE -> LEFT
            ELSE
                SET TREE = TREE -> RIGHT
            [END OF IF]
            FREE TEMP
        [END OF IF]
Step 2: END
```

Figure 10.15 Algorithm to delete a node from a binary search tree

10.2.5 Determining the Number of Nodes

Determining the number of nodes in a binary search tree is similar to determining its height. To calculate the total number of elements/nodes in the tree, we count the number of nodes in the left sub-tree and the right sub-tree.

```
Number of nodes = totalNodes(left sub-tree) + totalNodes(right sub-tree) + 1
```

Consider the tree given in Fig. 10.18. The total number of nodes in the tree can be calculated as:

```
Total nodes of left sub-tree = 1
Total nodes of left sub-tree = 5
Total nodes of tree = (1 + 5) + 1
                    = 7
```

Figure 10.19 shows a recursive algorithm to calculate the number of nodes in a binary search tree. For every node, we recursively call the algorithm on its left sub-tree as well as the right sub-tree. The total number of nodes at a given node is then returned by adding 1 to the number of nodes in its left as well as right sub-tree. However if the tree is empty, that is `TREE = NULL`, then the number of nodes will be zero.

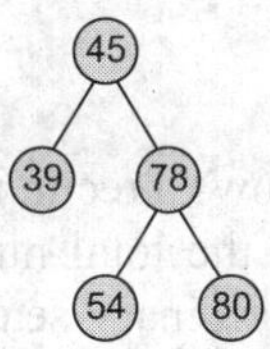

Figure 10.16 Binary search tree with height = 3

Determining the Number of Internal Nodes

To calculate the total number of internal nodes or non-leaf nodes, we count the number of internal nodes in the left sub-tree and the right sub-tree and add 1 to it (1 is added for the root node).

```
Number of internal nodes =    totalInternalNodes(left sub-tree) +
                              totalInternalNodes(right sub-tree) + 1
```

Consider the tree given in Fig. 10.18. The total number of internal nodes in the tree can be calculated as:

```
Total internal nodes of left sub-tree = 0
Total internal nodes of right sub-tree = 3
Total internal nodes of tree = (0 + 3) + 1
                             = 4
```

Figure 10.20 shows a recursive algorithm to calculate the total number of internal nodes in a binary search tree. For every node, we recursively

```
Height (TREE)

Step 1: IF TREE = NULL
            Return 0
        ELSE
          SET LeftHeight = Height(TREE -> LEFT)
          SET RightHeight = Height(TREE -> RIGHT)
           IF LeftHeight > RightHeight
                Return LeftHeight + 1
           ELSE
                Return RightHeight + 1
           [END OF IF]
        [END OF IF]
Step 2: END
```

Figure 10.17 Algorithm to determine the height of a binary search tree

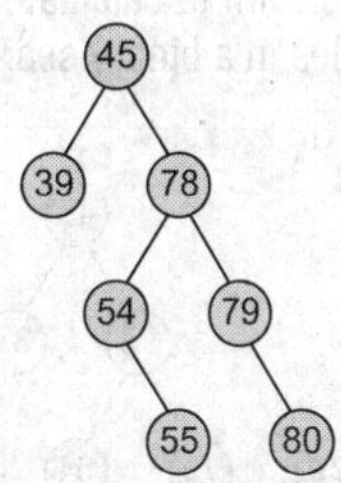

Figure 10.18 Binary search tree

```
totalNodes(TREE)

Step 1: IF TREE = NULL
            Return 0
        ELSE
            Return totalNodes(TREE -> LEFT)
                + totalNodes(TREE -> RIGHT) + 1
        [END OF IF]
Step 2: END
```

Figure 10.19 Algorithm to calculate the number of nodes in a binary search tree

```
totalInternalNodes(TREE)

Step 1: IF TREE = NULL
            Return 0
        [END OF IF]
        IF TREE -> LEFT = NULL AND TREE -> RIGHT = NULL
            Return 0
        ELSE
            Return totalInternalNodes(TREE -> LEFT) +
                totalInternalNodes(TREE -> RIGHT) + 1
        [END OF IF]
Step 2: END
```

Figure 10.20 Algorithm to calculate the total number of internal nodes in a binary search tree

call the algorithm on its left sub-tree as well as the right sub-tree. The total number of internal nodes at a given node is then returned by adding internal nodes in its left as well as right sub-tree. However, if the tree is empty, that is `TREE = NULL`, then the number of internal nodes will be zero. Also if there is only one node in the tree, then the number of internal nodes will be zero.

Determining the Number of External Nodes

To calculate the total number of external nodes or leaf nodes, we add the number of external nodes in the left sub-tree and the right sub-tree. However if the tree is empty, that is `TREE = NULL`, then the number of external nodes will be zero. But if there is only one node in the tree, then the number of external nodes will be one.

```
Number of external nodes =
totalExternalNodes(left sub-tree) +
    totalExternalNodes (right sub-tree)
```

Consider the tree given in Fig. 10.18. The total number of external nodes in the given tree can be calculated as:

```
Total external nodes of left sub-tree = 1
Total external nodes of left sub-tree = 2
Total external nodes of tree = 1 + 2
                             = 3
```

```
totalExternalNodes(TREE)

Step 1: IF TREE = NULL
            Return 0
        ELSE IF TREE -> LEFT = NULL AND TREE -> RIGHT = NULL
            Return 1
        ELSE
            Return totalExternalNodes(TREE -> LEFT) +
            totalExternalNodes(TREE -> RIGHT)
        [END OF IF]
Step 2: END
```

Figure 10.21 Algorithm to calculate the total number of external nodes in a binary search tree

Figure 10.21 shows a recursive algorithm to calculate the total number of external nodes in a binary search tree. For every node, we recursively call the algorithm on its left sub-tree as well as the right sub-tree. The total number of external nodes at a given node is then returned by adding the external nodes in its left as well as right sub-tree. However if the tree is empty, that is `TREE = NULL`, then the number of external nodes will be zero. Also if there is only one node in the tree, then there will be only one external node (that is the root node).

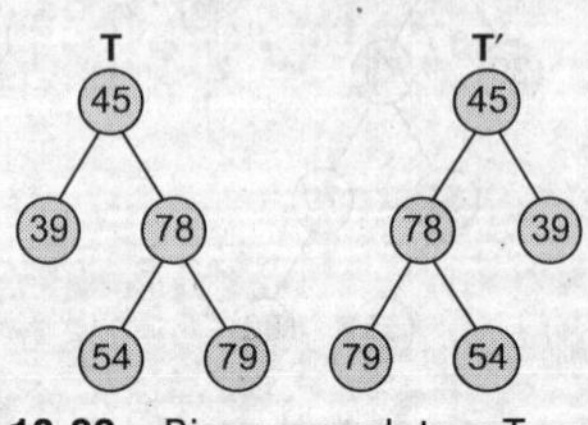

Figure 10.22 Binary search tree T and its

10.2.6 Finding the Mirror Image of a Binary Search Tree

Mirror image of a binary search tree is obtained by interchanging the left sub-tree with the right sub-tree at every node of the tree. For example, given a tree `T`, the mirror image of `T` can be obtained as `T′`. Consider the tree T given in Fig. 10.22.

```
MirrorImage(TREE)

Step 1: IF TREE != NULL
            MirrorImage(TREE -> LEFT)
            MirrorImage(TREE -> RIGHT)
            SET TEMP = TREE -> LEFT
            SET TREE -> LEFT = TREE -> RIGHT
            SET TREE -> RIGHT = TEMP
        [END OF IF]
Step 2: END
```

Figure 10.23 Algorithm to obtain the mirror image mirror image T′ of a binary search tree

Figure 10.23 shows a recursive algorithm to obtain the mirror image of a binary search tree. In the algorithm, if `TREE != NULL`, that is if the current node in the tree has one or more nodes, then the algorithm is recursively called at every node in the tree to swap the nodes in its left and right sub-trees.

10.2.7 Deleting a Binary Search Tree

To delete/remove an entire binary search tree from the memory, we first delete the elements/nodes in the left sub-tree and then delete the nodes in the right sub-tree. The algorithm shown in Fig. 10.24 gives a recursive procedure to remove the binary search tree.

```
deleteTree(TREE)

Step 1: IF TREE != NULL
            deleteTree (TREE -> LEFT)
            deleteTree (TREE -> RIGHT)
            Free (TREE)
        [END OF IF]
Step 2: END
```

Figure 10.24 Alogrithm to delete a binary search tree

10.2.8 Finding the Smallest Node in a Binary Search Tree

The very basic property of the binary search tree states that the smaller value will occur in the left sub-tree. If the left sub-tree is `NULL`, then the value of the root node will be smallest as compared to the nodes in the right sub-tree. So, to find the node with the smallest value, we find the value of the leftmost node of the left sub-tree. The recursive algorithm to find the smallest node in a binary search tree is shown in Fig. 10.25.

```
findSmallestElement(TREE)

Step 1: IF TREE = NULL OR TREE -> LEFT = NULL
            Returen TREE
        ELSE
            Return findSmallestElement(TREE -> LEFT)
        [END OF IF]
Step 2: END
```

Figure 10.25 Algorithm to find the smallest node in a binary search tree

10.2.9 Finding the Largest Node in a Binary Search Tree

To find the node with the largest value, we find the value of the rightmost node of the right sub-tree. However, if the right sub-tree is empty, then the root node will be the largest value in the tree. The recursive algorithm to find the largest node in a binary search tree is shown in Fig. 10.26.

```
findLargestElement(TREE)

Step 1: IF TREE = NULL OR TREE -> RIGHT = NULL
            Return TREE
        ELSE
           Return findLargestElement(TREE -> RIGHT)
        [END OF IF]
Step 2: END
```

Figure 10.26 Algorithm to find the largest node in a binary search tree

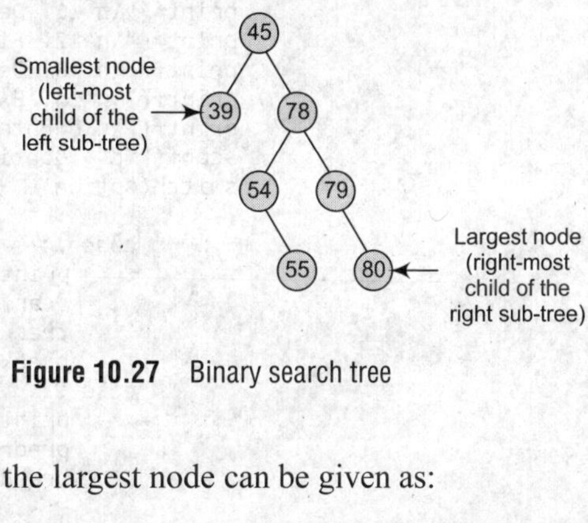

Figure 10.27 Binary search tree

Consider the tree given in Fig. 10.27. The smallest and the largest node can be given as:

Programming Example

1. Write a program to create a binary search tree and perform all the operations discussed in the preceding sections.

```
#include <stdio.h>
#include <malloc.h>
struct node
{
      int data;
      struct node *left;
      struct node *right;
};
struct node *tree;
void create_tree(struct node *);
struct node *insertElement(struct node *, int);
void preorderTraversal(struct node *);
void inorderTraversal(struct node *);
void postorderTraversal(struct node *);
struct node *findSmallestElement(struct node *);
struct node *findLargestElement(struct node *);
struct node *deleteElement(struct node *, int);
struct node *mirrorImage(struct node *);
int totalNodes(struct node *);
int totalExternalNodes(struct node *);
int totalInternalNodes(struct node *);
int Height(struct node *);
struct node *deleteTree(struct node *);
int main()
{
      int option, val;
      struct node *ptr;
      create_tree(tree);
      do
      {
            printf("\n ******MAIN MENU******* \n");
            printf("\n 1. Insert Element");
            printf("\n 2. Preorder Traversal");
            printf("\n 3. Inorder Traversal");
            printf("\n 4. Postorder Traversal");
            printf("\n 5. Find the smallest element");
            printf("\n 6. Find the largest element");
            printf("\n 7. Delete an element");
            printf("\n 8. Count the total number of nodes");
            printf("\n 9. Count the total number of external nodes");
            printf("\n 10. Count the total number of internal nodes");
            printf("\n 11. Determine the height of the tree");
            printf("\n 12. Find the mirror image of the tree");
            printf("\n 13. Delete the tree");
            printf("\n 14. Exit");
            printf("\n\n Enter your option : ");
            scanf("%d", &option);
            switch(option)
            {
                  case 1:
                        printf("\n Enter the value of the new node : ");
                        scanf("%d", &val);
                        tree = insertElement(tree, val);
                        break;
                  case 2:
                        printf("\n The elements of the tree are : \n");
                        preorderTraversal(tree);
                        break;
```

```
                case 3:
                    printf("\n The elements of the tree are : \n");
                    inorderTraversal(tree);
                    break;
                case 4:
                    printf("\n The elements of the tree are : \n");
                    postorderTraversal(tree);
                    break;
                case 5:
                    ptr = findSmallestElement(tree);
                    printf("\n Smallest element is :%d",ptr->data);
                    break;
                case 6:
                    ptr = findLargestElement(tree);
                    printf("\n Largest element is : %d", ptr->data);
                    break;
                case 7:
                    printf("\n Enter the element to be deleted : ");
                    scanf("%d", &val);
                    tree = deleteElement(tree, val);
                    break;
                case 8:
                    printf("\n Total no. of nodes = %d", totalNodes(tree));
                    break;
                case 9:
                    printf("\n Total no. of external nodes = %d",
                            totalExternalNodes(tree));
                    break;
                case 10:
                    printf("\n Total no. of internal nodes = %d",
                            totalInternalNodes(tree));
                    break;
                case 11:
                    printf("\n The height of the tree = %d",Height(tree));
                    break;
                case 12:
                    tree = mirrorImage(tree);
                    break;
                case 13:
                    tree = deleteTree(tree);
                    break;
            }
        }while(option!=14);
        getchar();
        return 0;
}
void create_tree(struct node *tree)
{
        tree = NULL;
}
struct node *insertElement(struct node *tree, int val)
{
        struct node *ptr, *nodeptr, *parentptr;
        ptr = (struct node*)malloc(sizeof(struct node));
        ptr->data = val;
        ptr->left = NULL;
        ptr->right = NULL;
        if(tree==NULL)
        {
                tree=ptr;
                tree->left=NULL;
                tree->right=NULL;
        }
        else
```

```
		{
			parentptr=NULL;
			nodeptr=tree;
			while(nodeptr!=NULL)
			{
				parentptr=nodeptr;
				if(val<nodeptr->data)
					nodeptr=nodeptr->left;
				else
					nodeptr = nodeptr->right;
			}
			if(val<parentptr->data)
				parentptr->left = ptr;
			else
				parentptr->right = ptr;
		}
		return tree;
	}
	void preorderTraversal(struct node *tree)
	{
		if(tree != NULL)
		{
			printf("%d\t", tree->data);
			preorderTraversal(tree->left);
			preorderTraversal(tree->right);
		}
	}
	void inorderTraversal(struct node *tree)
	{
		if(tree != NULL)
		{
			inorderTraversal(tree->left);
			printf("%d\t", tree->data);
			inorderTraversal(tree->right);
		}
	}
	void postorderTraversal(struct node *tree)
	{
		if(tree != NULL)
		{
			postorderTraversal(tree->left);
			postorderTraversal(tree->right);
			printf("%d\t", tree->data);
		}
	}
	struct node *findSmallestElement(struct node *tree)
	{
		if( (tree == NULL) || (tree->left == NULL))
			return tree;
		else
			return findSmallestElement(tree ->left);
	}
	struct node *findLargestElement(struct node *tree)
	{
		if( (tree == NULL) || (tree->right == NULL))
			return tree;
		else
			return findLargestElement(tree->right);
	}
	struct node *deleteElement(struct node *tree, int val)
	{
		struct node *cur, *parent, *suc, *psuc, *ptr;
		if(tree->left==NULL)
```

```
        {
                printf("\n The tree is empty ");
                return(tree);
        }
        parent = tree;
        cur = tree->left;
        while(cur!=NULL && val!= cur->data)
        {
                parent = cur;
                cur = (val<cur->data)? cur->left:cur->right;
        }
        if(cur == NULL)
        {
                printf("\n The value to be deleted is not present in the tree");
                return(tree);
        }
        if(cur->left == NULL)
                ptr = cur->right;
        else if(cur->right == NULL)
                ptr = cur->left;
        else
        {
                // Find the in-order successor and its parent
                psuc = cur;
                cur = cur->left;
                while(suc->left!=NULL)
                {
                        psuc = suc;
                        suc = suc->left;
                }
                if(cur==psuc)
                {
                        // Situation 1
                        suc->left = cur->right;
                }
                else
                {
                        // Situation 2
                        suc->left = cur->left;
                        psuc->left = suc->right;
                        suc->right = cur->right;
                }
                ptr = suc;
        }
        // Attach ptr to the parent node
        if(parent->left == cur)
                parent->left=ptr;
        else
                parent->right=ptr;
        free(cur);
        return tree;
}
int totalNodes(struct node *tree)
{
        if(tree==NULL)
                return 0;
        else
                return(totalNodes(tree->left) + totalNodes(tree->right) + 1);
}
int totalExternalNodes(struct node *tree)
```

```
{
        if(tree==NULL)
                return 0;
        else if((tree->left==NULL) && (tree->right==NULL))
                return 1;
        else
                return (totalExternalNodes(tree->left) +
                totalExternalNodes(tree->right));
}
int totalInternalNodes(struct node *tree)
{
        if( (tree==NULL) || ((tree->left==NULL) && (tree->right==NULL)))
                return 0;
        else
                return (totalInternalNodes(tree->left)
                + totalInternalNodes(tree->right) + 1);
}
int Height(struct node *tree)
{
        int leftheight, rightheight;
        if(tree==NULL)
                return 0;
        else
        {
                leftheight = Height(tree->left);
                rightheight = Height(tree->right);
                if(leftheight > rightheight)
                        return (leftheight + 1);
                else
                        return (rightheight + 1);
        }
}
struct node *mirrorImage(struct node *tree)
{
        struct node *ptr;
        if(tree!=NULL)
        {
                mirrorImage(tree->left);
                mirrorImage(tree->right);
                ptr=tree->left;
                ptr->left = ptr->right;
                tree->right = ptr;
        }
}
struct node *deleteTree(struct node *tree)
{
        if(tree!=NULL)
        {
                deleteTree(tree->left);
                deleteTree(tree->right);
                free(tree);
        }
}
```

Output

```
*******MAIN   MENU*******
1. Insert Element
2. Preorder Traversal
3. Inorder Traversal
4. Postorder Traversal
5. Find the smallest element
```

```
6. Find the largest element
7. Delete an element
8. Count the total number of nodes
9. Count the total number of external nodes
10. Count the total number of internal nodes
11. Determine the height of the tree
12. Find the mirror image of the tree
13. Delete the tree
14. Exit
Enter your option : 1
Enter the value of the new node : 1
Enter the value of the new node : 2
Enter the value of the new node : 4
Enter your option : 3
2    1    4
Enter your option : 14
```

10.3 THREADED BINARY TREES

A threaded binary tree is the same as that of a binary tree but with a difference in storing the NULL pointers. Consider the linked representation of a binary tree as given in Fig. 10.28.

In the linked representation, a number of nodes contain a NULL pointer, either in their left or right fields or in both. This space that is wasted in storing a NULL pointer can be efficiently used to store some other useful piece of information. For example, the NULL entries can be replaced to store a pointer to the in-order predecessor or the in-order successor of the node. These special pointers are called *threads* and binary trees containing threads are called *threaded trees*. In the linked representation of a threaded binary tree, threads will be denoted using arrows.

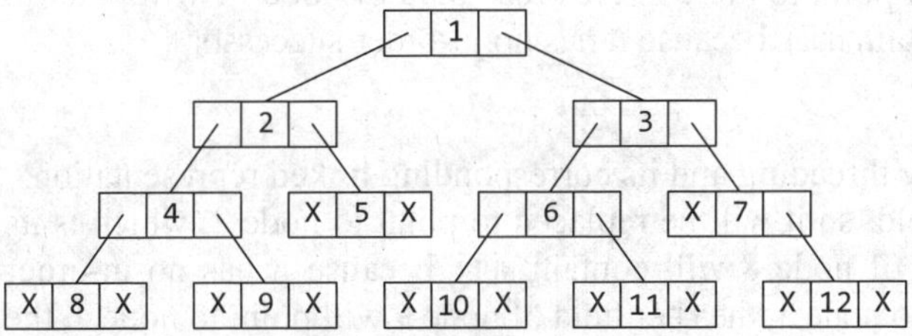

Figure 10.28 Linked representation of a binary tree

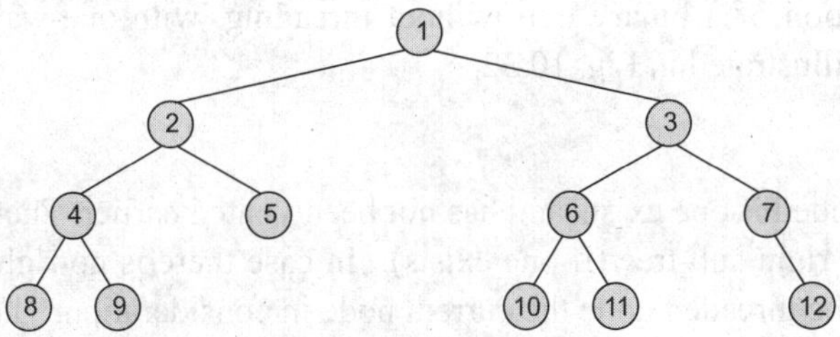

Figure 10.29 (a) Binary tree without threading

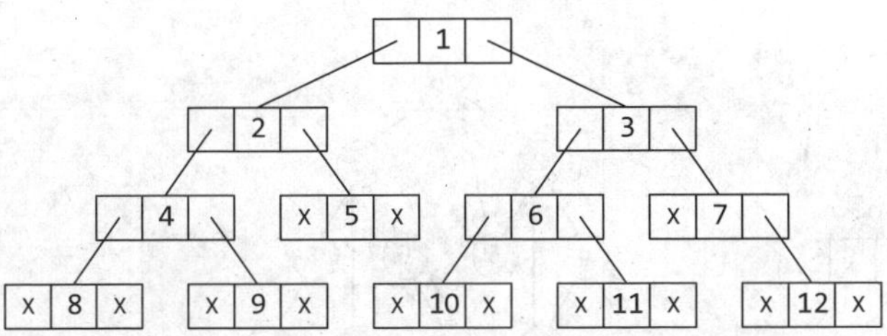

Figure 10.29 (b) Linked representation of the binary tree (without threading)

There are many ways of threading a binary tree and each type may vary according to the way the tree is traversed. In this book, we will discuss in-order traversal of the tree. Apart from this, a threaded binary tree may correspond to one-way threading or a two-way threading.

In one-way threading, a thread will appear either in the right field or the left field of the node. A one-way threaded tree is also called a single-threaded tree. If the thread appears in the left field, then the left field will be made to point to the in-order predecessor of the node. Such a one-way threaded tree is called a left-threaded binary tree. On the contrary, if the thread appears in the right field, then it will point to the in-order successor of the node. Such a one-way threaded tree is called a right-threaded binary tree.

In a two-way threaded tree, also called a double-threaded tree, threads will appear

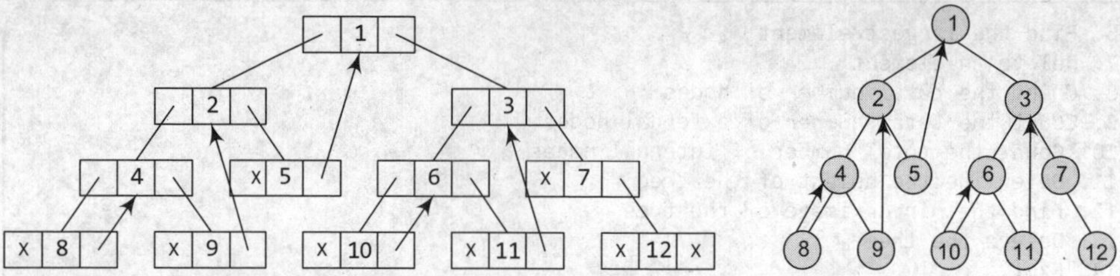

Figure 10.30 (a) Linked representation of the binary tree with one-way threading, (b) Binary tree with one-way threading

in both the left and the right field of the node. While the left field will point to the in-order predecessor of the node, the right field will point to its successor. A two-way threaded binary tree is also called a fully threaded binary tree. One-way threading and two-way threading of binary trees are explained below. Figure 10.29 shows a binary tree without threading and its corresponding linked representation.
The in-order traversal of the tree is given as 8, 4, 9, 2, 5, 1, 10, 6, 11, 3, 7, 12

One-way Threading

Figure 10.30 shows a binary tree with one-way threading and its corresponding linked representation.

Node 5 contains a NULL pointer in its RIGHT field, so it will be replaced to point to node 1, which is its in-order successor. Similarly, the RIGHT field of node 8 will point to node 4, the RIGHT field of node 9 will point to node 2, the RIGHT field of node 10 will point to node 6, the RIGHT field of node 11 will point to node 3, and the RIGHT field of node 12 will contain NULL because it has no in-order successor.

Two-way Threading

Figure 10.31 shows a binary tree with two-way threading and its corresponding linked representation.

Node 5 contains a NULL pointer in its LEFT field, so it will be replaced to point to node 2, which is its in-order predecessor. Similarly, the LEFT field of node 8 will contain NULL because it has no in-order predecessor, the LEFT field of node 7 will point to node 3, the LEFT field of node 9 will point to node 4, the LEFT field of node 10 will point to node 1, the LEFT field of node 11 will contain 6, and the LEFT field of node 12 will point to node 7.

Now, let us look at the memory representation of a binary tree without threading, with one-way threading, and with two-way threading. This is illustrated in Fig. 10.32.

10.3.1 Traversing a Threaded Binary Tree

For every node, visit the left sub-tree first, provided if one exists and has not been visited earlier. Then the node (root) itself is followed by visiting its right sub-tree (if one exists). In case there is no right sub-tree, check for the threaded link and make the threaded node the current node in consideration. The algorithm for in-order traversal of a threaded binary tree is given in Fig. 10.33.

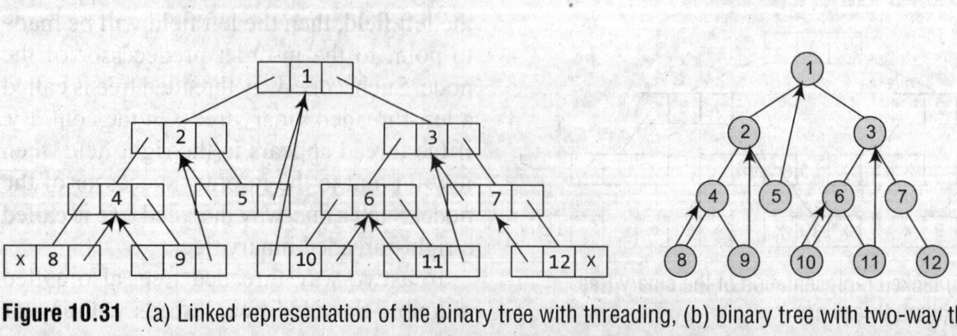

Figure 10.31 (a) Linked representation of the binary tree with threading, (b) binary tree with two-way threading

ROOT = 3, AVAIL = 15

	LEFT	DATA	RIGHT
1	-1	8	-1
2	-1	10	-1
3	5	1	8
4			
5	9	2	14
6			
7			
8	20	3	11
9	1	4	12
10			
11	-1	7	18
12	-1	9	-1
13			
14	-1	5	-1
15			
16	-1	11	-1
17			
18	-1	12	-1
19			
20	2	6	16

(a)

ROOT = 3, AVAIL = 15

	LEFT	DATA	RIGHT
1	-1	8	9
2	-1	10	20
3	5	1	8
4			
5	9	2	14
6			
7			
8	20	3	11
9	1	4	12
10			
11	-1	7	18
12	-1	9	5
13			
14	-1	5	3
15			
16	-1	11	8
17			
18	-1	12	-1
19			
20	2	6	16

(b)

ROOT = 3, AVAIL = 15

	LEFT	DATA	RIGHT
1	-1	8	9
2	3	10	20
3	5	1	8
4			
5	9	2	14
6			
7			
8	20	3	11
9	1	4	12
10			
11	8	7	18
12	9	9	5
13			
14	5	5	3
15			
16	20	11	8
17			
18	11	12	-1
19			
20	2	6	16

(c)

Figure 10.32 Memory representation of binary trees: (a) without threading, (b) with one-way, and (c) two-way threading

Step 1: Check if the current node has a left child that has not been visited. If a left child exists that has not been visited, go to Step 2, else go to Step 3.

Step 2: Add the left child in the list of visited nodes. Make it as the current node and then go to Step 6.

Step 3: If the current node has a right child, go to Step 4 else go to Step 5.

Step 4: Make that right child as current node and go to Step 6.

Step 5: Print the node and if there is a threaded node make it the current node.

Step 6: If all the nodes have visited then END else go to Step 1.

Figure 10.33 Algorithm for in-order traversal of a threaded binary tree

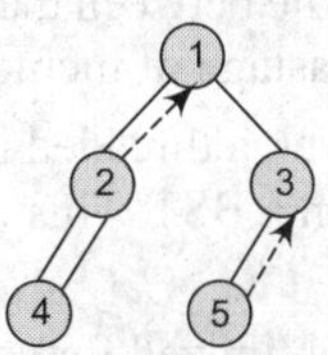

Figure 10.34 Threaded binary tree

Let's consider the threaded binary tree given in Fig. 10.34 and traverse it using the algorithm.

1. Node 1 has a left child i.e., 2 which has not been visited. So, add 2 in the list of visited nodes, make it as the current node.
2. Node 2 has a left child i.e., 4 which has not been visited. So, add 4 in the list of visited nodes, make it as the current node.
3. Node 4 does not have any left or right child, so print 4 and check for its threaded link. It has a threaded link to node 2, so make node 2 the current node.
4. Node 2 has a left child which has already been visited. However, it does not have a right child. Now, print 2 and follow its threaded link to node 1. Make node 1 the current node.

5. Node 1 has a left child that has been already visited. So print 1. Node 1 has a right child 3 which has not yet been visited, so make it the current node.
6. Node 3 has a left child (node 5) which has not been visited, so make it the current node.
7. Node 5 does not have any left or right child. So print 5. However, it does have a threaded link which points to node 3. Make node 3 the current node.
8. Node 3 has a left child which has already been visited. So print 3.
9. Now there are no nodes left, so we end here. The sequence of nodes printed is—4 2 1 5 3.

Advantages of Threaded Binary Tree

No need for stacks or recursion: Unlike binary trees, threaded binary trees do not use stack or recursion techniques for traversing the elements.

Optimal memory usage: It reduces memory wastage. For example, in binary trees, whenever a node's left or right pointer is NULL, memory is wasted. In case of a threaded binary tree, this node is used to store its inorder predecessor or successor.

Find Parent and Child Nodes: The tree enables finding parent node easily without explicitly using a parent pointer. Since threads point to successor and predecessor nodes, it is easier to obtain predecessor and successor node of any node quickly.

Finding these nodes in a non-threaded tree is much more time-consuming and tedious as it uses the stack to provide upward-pointing information in the tree.

Time complexity: In-order traversal in a threaded binary tree is faster than a binary tree. The time complexity of getting the next node is O(1) which is O(Height) in case of a binary tree.

Backward traversal: We can easily and quickly backward traverse a double-threaded binary tree.

Linear Traversal: The tree enables linear traversal of elements.

Faster traversal: Threaded Binary Tree provides much faster traversal than that of the Non-Threaded Binary Tree.

Ease of traversal: We can access any node from a given node. While links point downward, threads point upward, whereas the links are downward. This allows traversals in either direction as nodes are linked circularly. This is impossible in Non-Threaded Binary Tree which allows movement only in a downward direction beginning from the root.

Disadvantages of Threaded Binary Tree

Complicated insertion and deletion: Storing the inorder predecessor or successor of the node (having a NULL in its left or right pointer) makes the process of insertion and deletion more time-consuming and a highly complex process.

Extra memory usage: Extra memory is required to distinguish between a thread from an ordinary link. (Note that this problem can be handled by using more efficient methods to differentiate between the two). A skewed tree can result in a large number of additional pointers and thus more wastage of memory.

Complex structure: Implementing threads for every node is complicated. Moreover, a threaded binary tree requires more complex algorithms and data structures for implementation than a BST. This makes the code harder to read and debug.

Limited flexibility: Threaded binary trees are specialized data structures that are optimized for specific types of traversals. For those traversals, they are implemented to perform efficiently. But they may not be useful in other scenarios that involve lot of insertions and deletions.

Difficulty in parallelizing: It is difficult to parallelize operations on a threaded binary tree. This impacts its performance. The reason for this limitation is the that a threaded binary tree may have certain data dependencies which makes it very challenging to process nodes independently.

Applications of threaded binary tree

Expression evaluation: Threaded binary trees can be used to evaluate arithmetic expressions in a fast and efficient way by avoiding recursion through a stack. The tree can be constructed from the input expression, and then traversed in-order or pre-order to perform the evaluation.

Database indexing: Threaded binary trees can be used in databases to index data based on a specific field. For example, name of the course. The indexed values can be used as keys to facilitate data traversal (in-order traversal) in a sorted order.

Symbol table management: Threaded binary trees are used in a compiler or interpreter to store and manage symbol tables for variables and functions. The tree can be constructed with the symbols as keys. This tree can then be traversed in-order or pre-order to perform operations on the symbol table.

Disk-based data structures: Disk-based data structures like B-trees use threaded binary tree to improve performance. Threading allows traversal in a way that minimizes disk seeks and improves locality of reference.

Navigation of hierarchical data: Hierarchical data structures like file systems or web site directories uses threaded binary trees to support in-order or pre-order traversal to efficiently access the data in a specific order.

Thus, we see the basic difference between a binary tree and a threaded binary tree is that in binary trees a node stores a `NULL` pointer if it has no child and so there is no way to traverse back.

Programming Example

2. Write a program to implement simple right in-threaded binary trees.

```
#include <stdio.h>
struct tree
{
        int val;
        struct tree *right;
        struct tree *left;
        int thread;
};
struct tree *root = NULL;
struct tree* insert_node(struct tree *root, struct tree *ptr, struct tree *rt)
{
        if(root == NULL)
        {
                root = ptr;
                if(rt != NULL)
                {
                        root->right = rt;
                        root->thread = 1;
                }
        }
        else if(ptr->val < root->val)
                root->left = insert_node(root->left, ptr, root);
        else
                if(root->thread == 1)
                {
                        root->right = insert_node(NULL, ptr, rt);
                        root->thread=0;
                }
                else
                        root->right = insert_node(root->right, ptr, rt);
        return root;
}
```

```
struct tree* create_threaded_tree()
{
        struct tree *ptr;
        int num;
        printf("\n Enter the elements, press -1 to terminate ");
        scanf("%d", &num);
        while(num != -1)
        {
        ptr = (struct tree*)malloc(sizeof(struct tree));
                ptr->val = num;
                ptr->left = ptr->right = NULL;
                ptr->thread = 0;
                root = insert_node(root, ptr, NULL);
                printf(" \n Enter the next element ");
                fflush(stdin);
                scanf("%d", &num);
        }
        return root;
}
void inorder(struct tree *root)
{
        struct tree *ptr = root, *prev;
        do
        {
                while(ptr != NULL)
                {
                        prev = ptr;
                        ptr = ptr->left;
                }
                if(prev != NULL)
                {
                        printf(" %d", prev->val);
                        ptr = prev->right;
                        while(prev != NULL && prev->thread)
                        {
                                printf(" %d", ptr->val);
                                prev = ptr;
                                ptr = ptr->right;
                        }
                }
        }while(ptr != NULL);
}
void main()
{
    //  struct tree *root=NULL;
        create_threaded_tree();
        printf(" \n The in-order traversal of the tree can be given as : ");
        inorder(root);
        getchar();
}
```

Output

```
Enter the elements, press -1 to terminate 5
Enter the next element 8
Enter the next element 2
Enter the next element 3
Enter the next element 7
Enter the next element -1
The in-order traversal of the tree can be given as:
2        3        5        7        8
```

10.4 AVL TREES

AVL tree is a self-balancing binary search tree invented by G.M. Adelson-Velsky and E.M. Landis in 1962. The tree is named AVL in honour of its inventors. In an AVL tree, the heights of the two sub-trees of a node may differ by at most one. Due to this property, the AVL tree is also known as a height-balanced tree. The key advantage of using an AVL tree is that it takes `O(log n)` time to perform search, insert, and delete operations in an average case as well as the worst case because the height of the tree is limited to `O(log n)`.

The structure of an AVL tree is the same as that of a binary search tree but with a little difference. In its structure, it stores an additional variable called the `BalanceFactor`. Thus, every node has a balance factor associated with it. The balance factor of a node is calculated by subtracting the height of its right sub-tree from the height of its left sub-tree. A binary search tree in which every node has a balance factor of –1, 0, or 1 is said to be height balanced. A node with any other balance factor is considered to be unbalanced and requires rebalancing of the tree.

Balance factor = Height (left sub-tree) – Height (right sub-tree)

- If the balance factor of a node is 1, then it means that the left sub-tree of the tree is one level higher than that of the right sub-tree. Such a tree is therefore called as a *left-heavy tree*.
- If the balance factor of a node is 0, then it means that the height of the left sub-tree (longest path in the left sub-tree) is equal to the height of the right sub-tree.
- If the balance factor of a node is –1, then it means that the left sub-tree of the tree is one level lower than that of the right sub-tree. Such a tree is therefore called as a *right-heavy tree*.

Look at Fig. 10.35. Note that the nodes 18, 39, 54, and 72 have no children, so their balance factor = 0. Node 27 has one left child and zero right child. So, the height of left sub-tree = 1, whereas the height of right sub-tree = 0. Thus, its balance factor = 1. Look at node 36, it has a left sub-tree with height = 2, whereas the height of right sub-tree = 1. Thus, its balance factor = 2 – 1 = 1. Similarly, the balance factor of node 45 = 3 – 2 =1; and node 63 has a balance factor of 0 (1 – 1).

Now, look at Figs 10.35 (a) and (b) which show a right-heavy AVL tree and a balanced AVL tree.

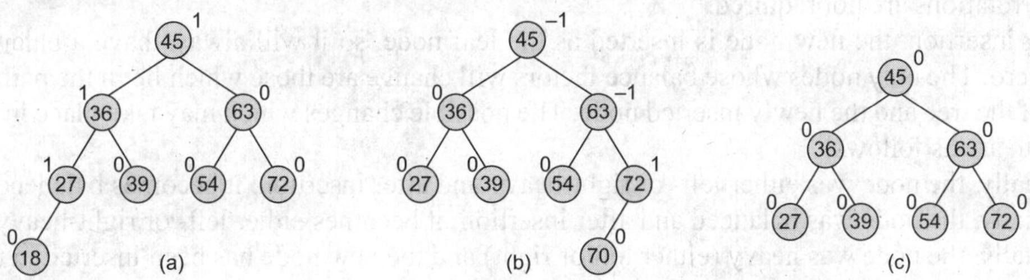

Figure 10.35 (a) Left-heavy AVL tree, (b) right-heavy tree, (c) balanced tree

The trees given in Fig. 10.35 are typical candidates of AVL trees because the balancing factor of every node is either 1, 0, or –1. However, insertions and deletions from an AVL tree may disturb the balance factor of the nodes and, thus, rebalancing of the tree may have to be done. The tree is rebalanced by performing rotation at the critical node. There are four types of rotations: LL rotation, RR rotation, LR rotation, and RL rotation. The type of rotation that has to be done will vary depending on the particular situation. In the following section, we will discuss insertion, deletion, searching, and rotations in AVL trees.

Advantages of AVL Trees

- The AVL tree's height never exceeds log N, where N is the total number of nodes in the tree. This ensures that the tree is always balanced.
- It provides better search time complexity than BST.
- AVL trees are self-balancing.

Disadvantages of AVL Trees

- AVL trees are difficult to implement.
- For some operations, AVL trees have significant constant factors.

- Red-black trees are more preferred than AVL trees in majority of STL implementations of the ordered associative containers (like sets, multisets, maps, and multimaps). This is because red-black trees, unlike AVL trees, need only one restructure for an insertion or deletion operation.

Applications of AVL Trees

- AVL trees are used to store most of the in-memory sets and dictionaries.
- AVL trees are used to implement database applications, where insertions and deletions are less common but frequent data lookups are required.
- AVL tree is a preferred choice in all applications that require better searching.
- AVL trees are used in games with plotlines as well.

10.4.1 Operations on AVL Trees

Searching for a Node in an AVL Tree

Searching in an AVL tree is performed exactly the same way as it is performed in a binary search tree. Due to the height-balancing of the tree, the search operation takes `O(log n)` time to complete. Since the operation does not modify the structure of the tree, no special provisions are required.

Inserting a New Node in an AVL Tree

Insertion in an AVL tree is also done in the same way as it is done in a binary search tree. In the AVL tree, the new node is always inserted as the leaf node. But the step of insertion is usually followed by an additional step of rotation. Rotation is done to restore the balance of the tree. However, if insertion of the new node does not disturb the balance factor, that is, if the balance factor of every node is still –1, 0, or 1, then rotations are not required.

During insertion, the new node is inserted as the leaf node, so it will always have a balance factor equal to zero. The only nodes whose balance factors will change are those which lie in the path between the root of the tree and the newly inserted node. The possible changes which may take place in any node on the path are as follows:

- Initially, the node was either left- or right-heavy and after insertion, it becomes balanced.
- Initially, the node was balanced and after insertion, it becomes either left- or right-heavy.
- Initially, the node was heavy (either left or right) and the new node has been inserted in the heavy sub-tree, thereby creating an unbalanced sub-tree. Such a node is said to be a *critical node*.

Consider the AVL tree given in Fig. 10.36.

If we insert a new node with the value 30, then the new tree will still be balanced and no rotations will be required in this case. Look at the tree given in Fig. 10.37 which shows the tree after inserting node 30.

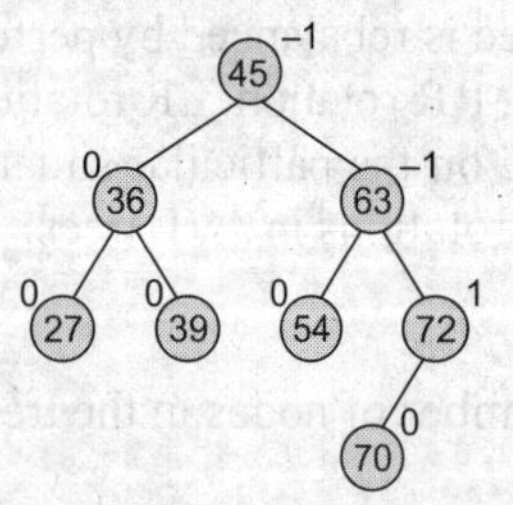

Figure 10.36 AVL tree

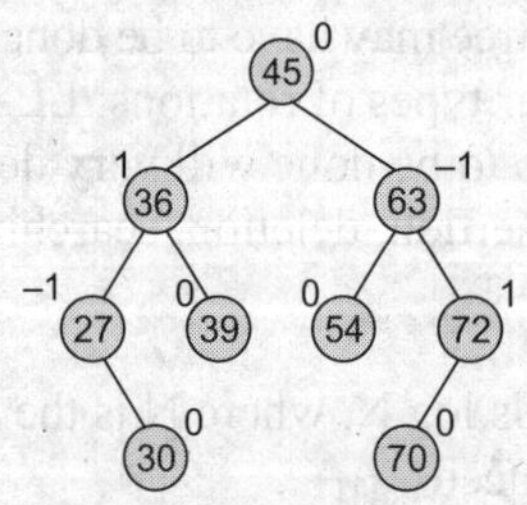

Figure 10.37 AVL tree after inserting a node with the value 30

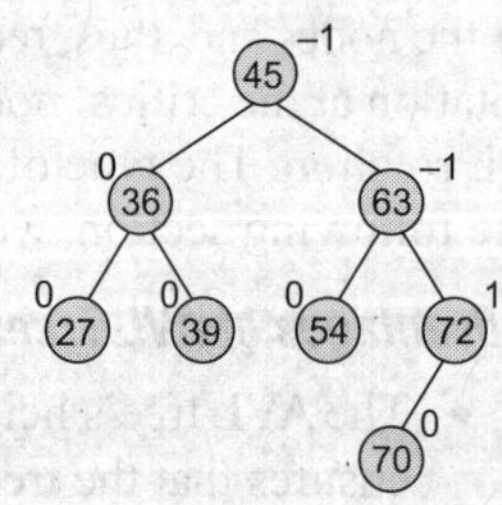

Figure 10.38 AVL tree

Let us take another example to see how insertion can disturb the balance factors of the nodes and how rotations are done to restore the AVL property of a tree. Look at the tree given in Fig. 10.38.

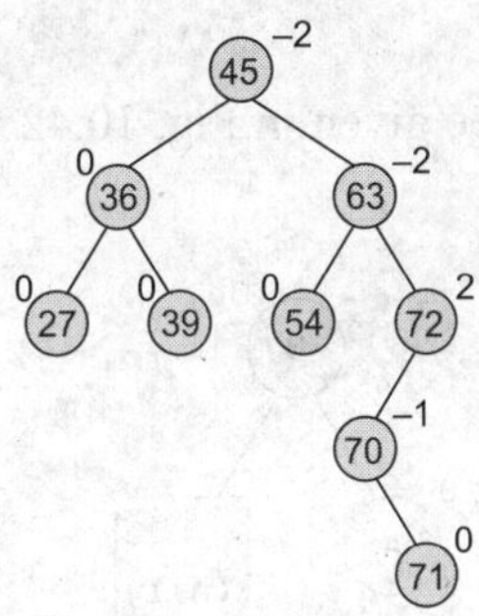

Figure 10.39 AVL tree after inserting a node with the value 71

After inserting a new node with the value 71, the new tree will be as shown in Fig. 10.39. Note that there are three nodes in the tree that have their balance factors 2, –2, and –2, thereby disturbing the *AVLness* of the tree. So, here comes the need to perform rotation. To perform rotation, our first task is to find the critical node. Critical node is the nearest ancestor node on the path from the inserted node to the root whose balance factor is neither –1, 0, nor 1. In the tree given above, the critical node is 72. The second task in rebalancing the tree is to determine which type of rotation has to be done. There are four types of rebalancing rotations and application of these rotations depends on the position of the inserted node with reference to the critical node. The four categories of rotations are:

- *LL rotation* The new node is inserted in the left sub-tree of the left sub-tree of the critical node.
- *RR rotation* The new node is inserted in the right sub-tree of the right sub-tree of thecritical node.
- *LR rotation* The new node is inserted in the right sub-tree of the left sub-tree of thecritical node.
- *RL rotation* The new node is inserted in the left sub-tree of the right sub-tree of thecritical node.

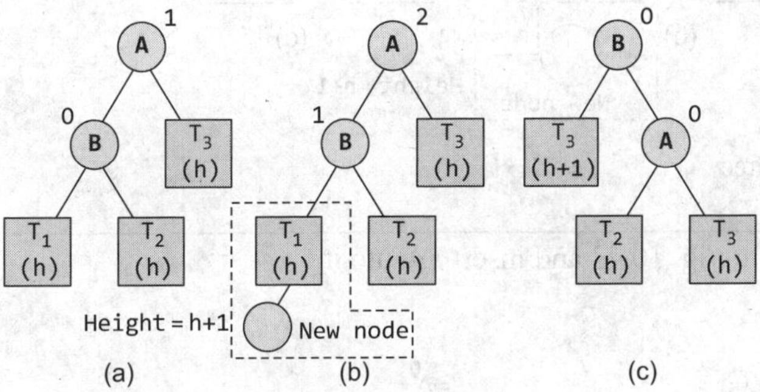

Figure 10.40 LL rotation in an AVL tree

LL Rotation

Let us study each of these rotations in detail. First, we will see where and how LL rotation is applied. Consider the tree given in Fig. 10.40 which shows an AVL tree.

Tree (a) is an AVL tree. In tree (b), a new node is inserted in the left sub-tree of the left sub-tree of the critical node A (node A is the critical node because it is the closest ancestor whose balance factor is not –1, 0, or 1), so we apply LL rotation as shown in tree (c).

Note The new node has now become a part of tree T_1.

While rotation, node B becomes the root, with T_1 and A as its left and right child. T_2 and T_3 become the left and right sub-trees of A.

Example 10.3 Consider the AVL tree given in Fig. 10.41 and insert 18 into it.

Solution

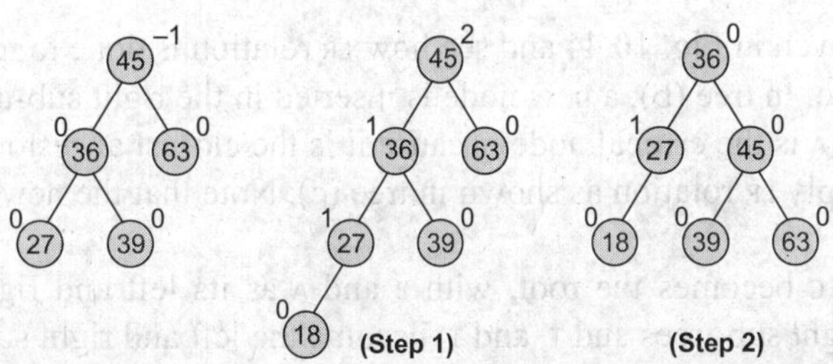

Figure 10.41 AVL tree

RR Rotation

Let us now discuss where and how RR rotation is applied. Consider the tree given in Fig. 10.42 which shows an AVL tree.

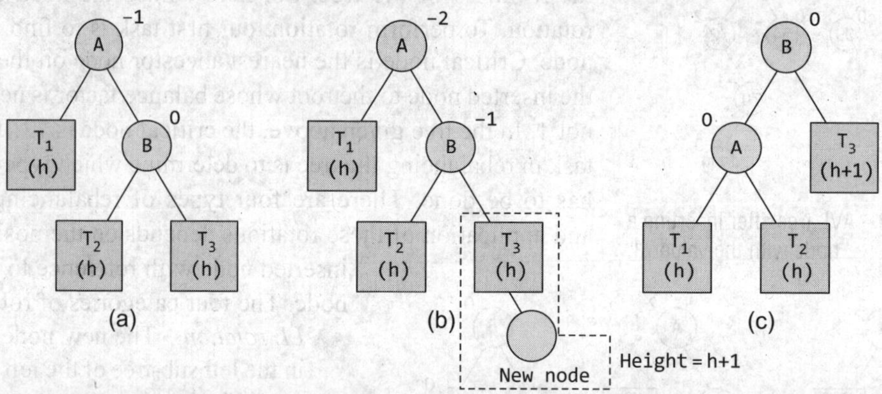

Figure 10.42 RR rotation in an AVL tree

Example 10.4 Consider the AVL tree given in Fig. 10.43 and insert 89 into it.

Solution

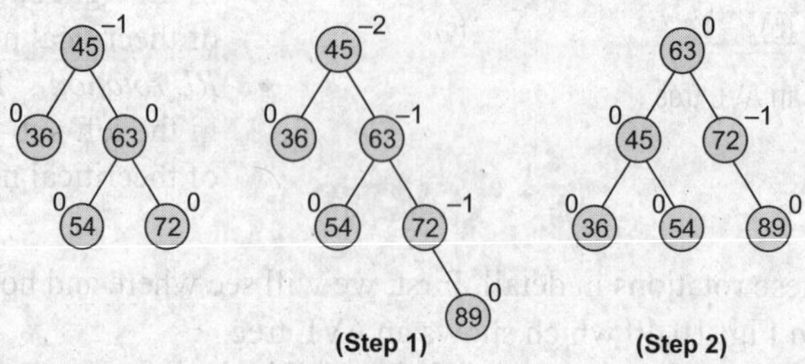

Figure 10.43 AVL tree

Tree (a) is an AVL tree. In tree (b), a new node is inserted in the right sub-tree of the right sub-tree of the critical node A (node A is the critical node because it is the closest ancestor whose balance factor is not –1, 0, or 1), so we apply RR rotation as shown in tree (c). Note that the new node has now become a part of tree T_3.

While rotation, node B becomes the root, with A and T_3 as its left and right child. T_1 and T_2 become the left and right sub-trees of A.

LR and RL Rotations

Consider the AVL tree given in Fig. 10.44 and see how LR rotation is done to rebalance the tree.

Tree (a) is an AVL tree. In tree (b), a new node is inserted in the right sub-tree of the left sub-tree of the critical node A (node A is the critical node because it is the closest ancestor whose balance factor is not –1, 0 or 1), so we apply LR rotation as shown in tree (c). Note that the new node has now become a part of tree T_2.

While rotation, node C becomes the root, with B and A as its left and right children. Node B has T_1 and T_2 as its left and right sub-trees and T_3 and T_4 become the left and right sub-trees of node A.

Now, consider the AVL tree given in Fig. 10.46 and see how RL rotation is done to rebalance the tree.

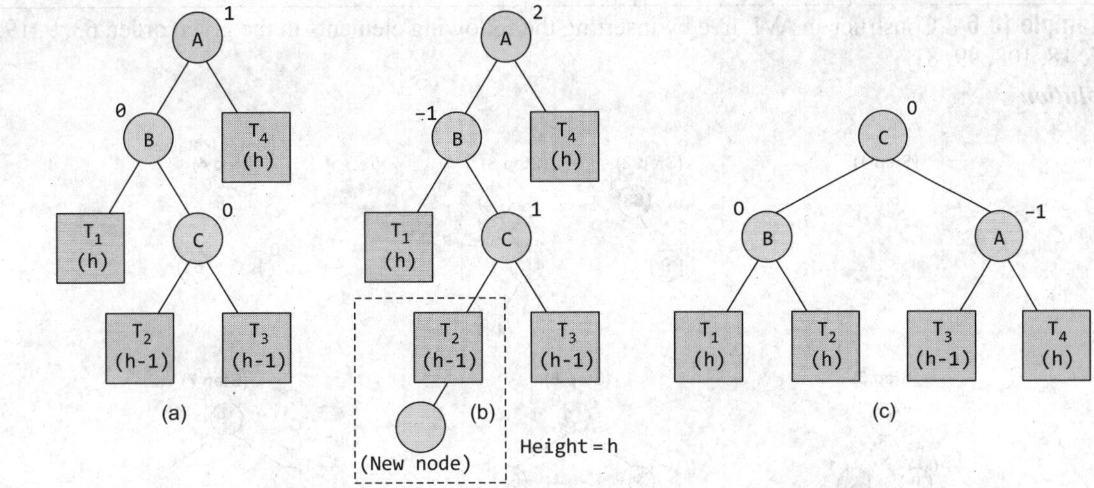

Figure 10.44 LR rotation in an AVL tree

Example 10.5 Consider the AVL tree given in Fig. 10.45 and insert 37 into it.

Solution

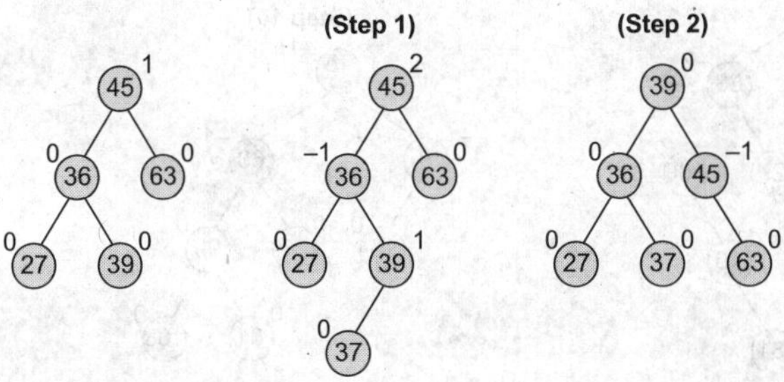

Figure 10.45 AVL tree

Tree (a) is an AVL tree. In tree (b), a new node is inserted in the left sub-tree of the right sub-tree of the critical node A (node A is the critical node because it is the closest ancestor whose balance factor is not –1, 0, or 1), so we apply RL rotation as shown in tree (c). Note that the new node has now become a part of tree T_2.

While rotation, node C becomes the root, with A and B as its left and right children. Node A has T_1 and T_2 as its left and right sub-trees and T_3 and T_4 become the left and right sub-trees of node B.

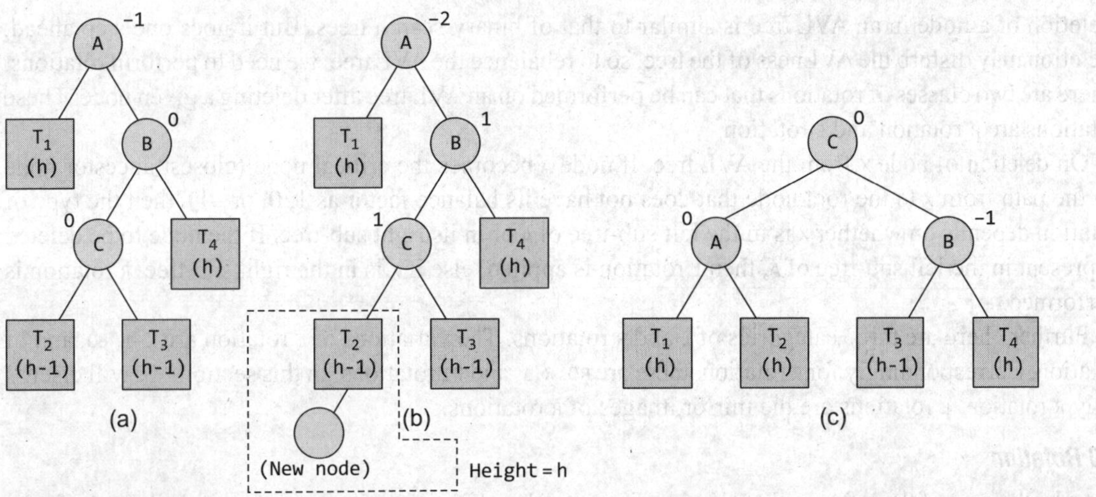

Figure 10.46 RL rotation in an AVL tree

Example 10.6 Construct an AVL tree by inserting the following elements in the given order. 63, 9, 19, 27, 18, 108, 99, 81.

Solution

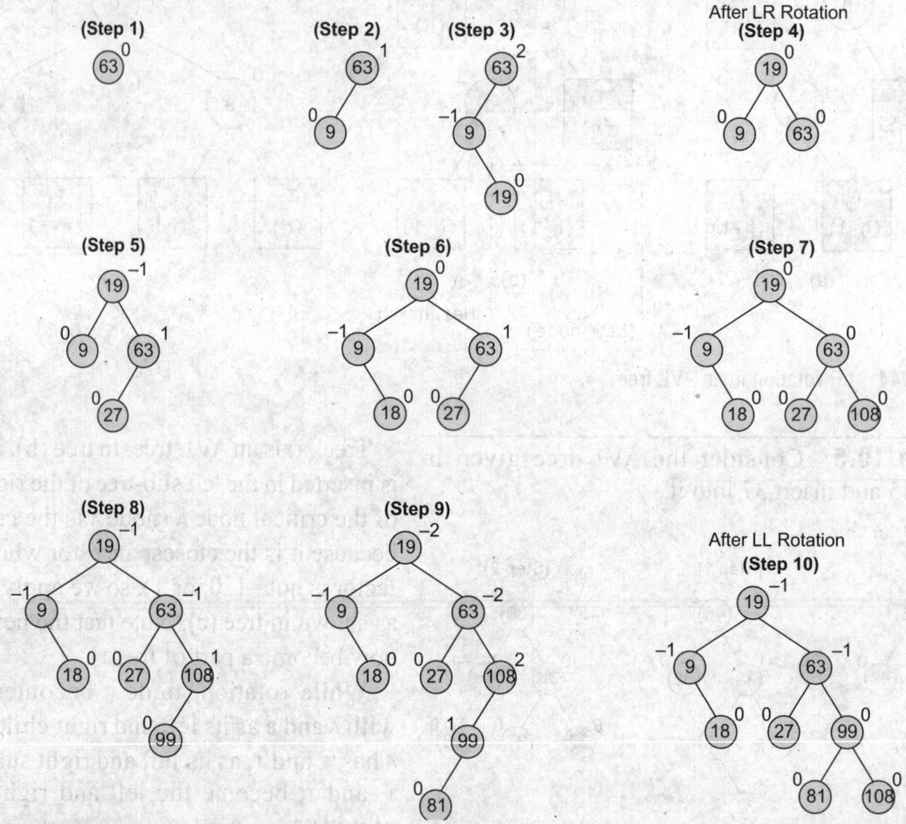

Figure 10.47 AVL tree

Deleting a Node from an AVL Tree

Deletion of a node in an AVL tree is similar to that of binary search trees. But it goes one step ahead. Deletion may disturb the AVLness of the tree, so to rebalance the AVL tree, we need to perform rotations. There are two classes of rotations that can be performed on an AVL tree after deleting a given node. These rotations are `R` rotation and `L` rotation.

On deletion of node `X` from the AVL tree, if node `A` becomes the critical node (closest ancestor node on the path from `X` to the root node that does not have its balance factor as 1, 0, or –1), then the type of rotation depends on whether `X` is in the left sub-tree of `A` or in its right sub-tree. If the node to be deleted is present in the left sub-tree of `A`, then `L` rotation is applied, else if `X` is in the right sub-tree, `R` rotation is performed.

Further, there are three categories of `L` and `R` rotations. The variations of `L` rotation are `L-1`, `L0`, and `L1` rotation. Correspondingly for `R` rotation, there are `R0`, `R-1`, and `R1` rotations. In this section, we will discuss only `R` rotation. `L` rotations are the mirror images of `R` rotations.

R0 Rotation

Let `B` be the root of the left or right sub-tree of `A` (critical node). `R0` rotation is applied if the balance factor of `B` is 0. This is illustrated in Fig. 10.48.

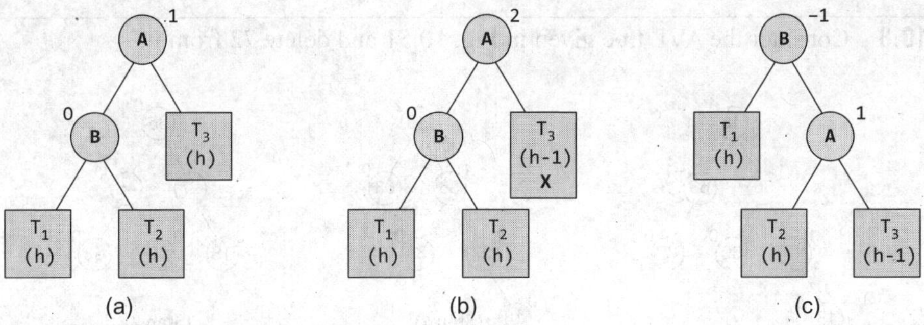

Figure 10.48 R0 rotation in an AVL tree

Tree (a) is an AVL tree. In tree (b), the node X is to be deleted from the right sub-tree of the critical node A (node A is the critical node because it is the closest ancestor whose balance factor is not –1, 0, or 1). Since the balance factor of node B is 0, we apply R0 rotation as shown in tree (c).

During the process of rotation, node B becomes the root, with T_1 and A as its left and right child. T_2 and T_3 become the left and right sub-trees of A.

R1 Rotation

Let B be the root of the left or right sub-tree of A (critical node). R1 rotation is applied if the balance factor of B is 1. Observe that R0 and R1 rotations are similar to LL rotations; the only difference is that R0 and R1 rotations yield different balance factors. This is illustrated in Fig. 10.50.

Tree (a) is an AVL tree. In tree (b), the node X is to be deleted from the right sub-tree of the critical node A (node A is the critical node because it is the closest ancestor whose balance factor is not –1, 0, or 1). Since the balance factor of node B is 1, we apply R1 rotation as shown in tree (c).

During the process of rotation, node B becomes the root, with T_1 and A as its left and right children. T_2 and T_3 become the left and right sub-trees of A.

Example 10.7 Consider the AVL tree given in Fig. 10.49 and delete 72 from it.

Solution

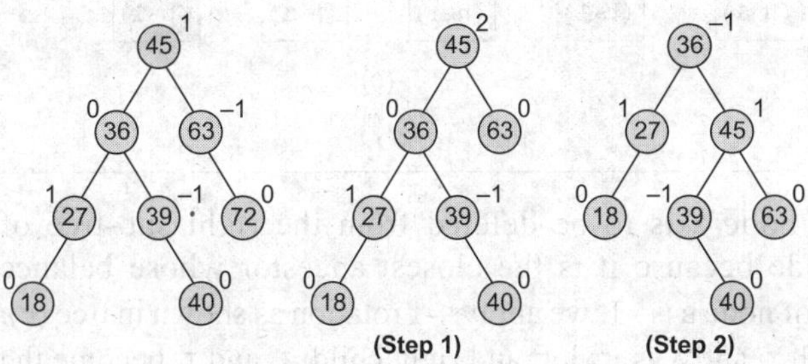

Figure 10.49 AVL tree

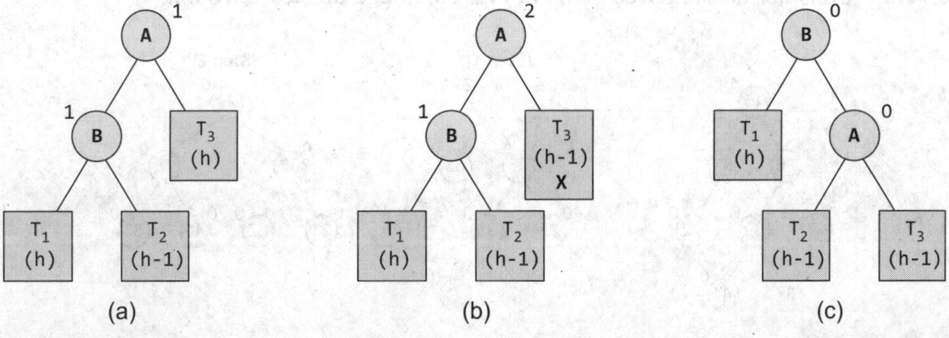

Figure 10.50 R1 rotation in an AVL tree

Example 10.8 Consider the AVL tree given in Fig. 10.51 and delete 72 from it.
Solution

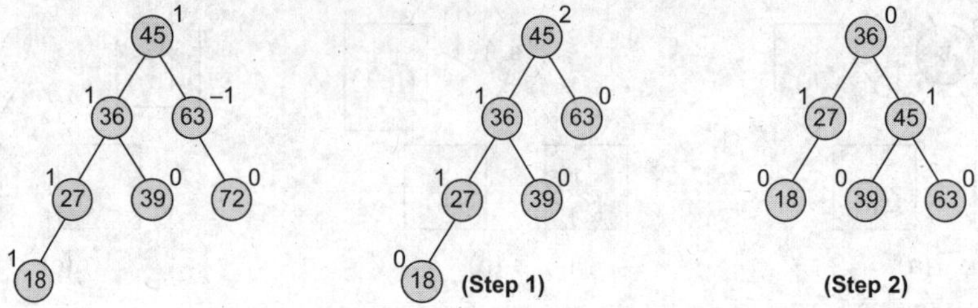

Figure 10.51 AVL tree

R–1 Rotation

Let B be the root of the left or right sub-tree of A (critical node). R-1 rotation is applied if the balance factor of B is –1. Observe that R-1 rotation is similar to LR rotation. This is illustrated in Fig. 10.52.

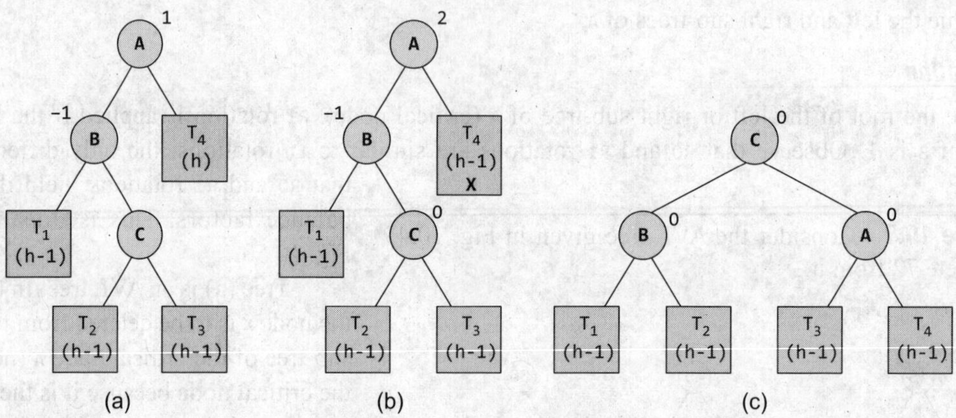

Figure 10.52 R1 Rotation in an AVL tree

Tree (a) is an AVL tree. In tree (b), the node X is to be deleted from the right sub-tree of the critical node A (node A is the critical node because it is the closest ancestor whose balance factor is not –1, 0 or 1). Since the balance factor of node B is –1, we apply R-1 rotation as shown in tree (c).

While rotation, node C becomes the root, with T_1 and A as its left and right child. T_2 and T_3 become the left and right sub-trees of A.

Example 10.9 Consider the AVL tree given in Fig. 10.53 and delete 72 from it.
Solution

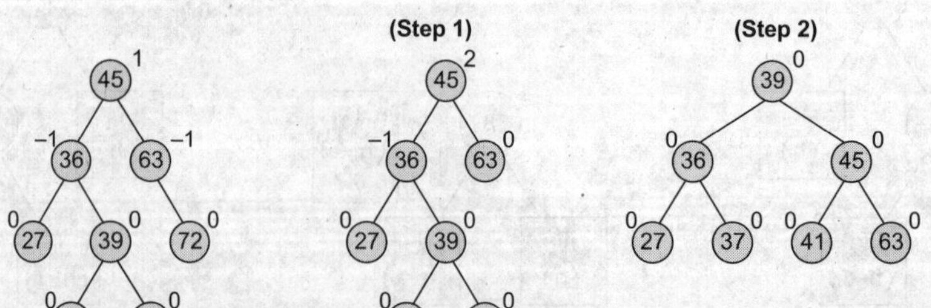

Figure 10.53 AVL tree

Example 10.10 Delete nodes 52, 36, and 61 from the AVL tree given in Fig. 10.54.

Solution

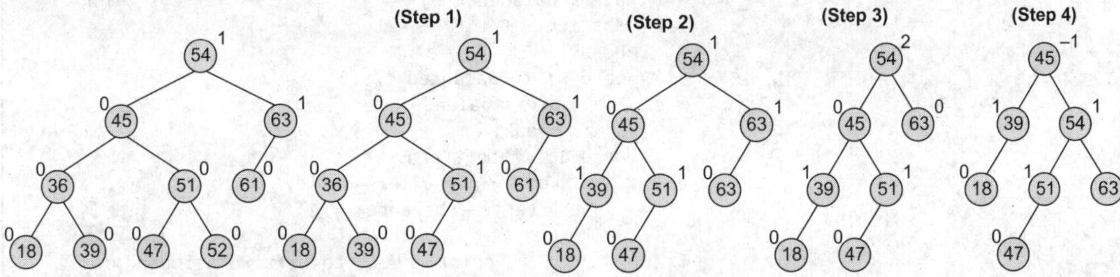

Figure 10.54 AVL tree

Programming Example

3. Write a program that shows insertion operation in an AVL tree.

```
#include <stdio.h>
typedef enum { FALSE ,TRUE } bool;
struct node
{
        int val;
        int balance;
        struct node *left_child;
        struct node *right_child;
};
struct node* search(struct node *ptr, int data)
{
        if(ptr!=NULL)
                if(data < ptr -> val)
                        ptr = search(ptr -> left_child,data);
                else if( data > ptr -> val)
                        ptr = search(ptr -> right_child, data);
        return(ptr);
}
struct node *insert (int data, struct node *ptr, bool *ht_inc)
{
        struct node *aptr;
        struct node *bptr;
        if(ptr==NULL)
        {
                ptr = (struct node *) malloc(sizeof(struct node));
                ptr -> val = data;
                ptr -> left_child = NULL;
                ptr -> right_child = NULL;
                ptr -> balance = 0;
                *ht_inc = TRUE;
                return (ptr);
        }
        if(data < ptr -> val)
        {
                ptr -> left_child = insert(data, ptr -> left_child, ht_inc);
                if(*ht_inc==TRUE)
                {
                        switch(ptr -> balance)
```

```
                        {
                              case -1: /* Right heavy */
                              ptr -> balance = 0;
                              *ht_inc = FALSE;
                              break;
                              case 0: /* Balanced */
                                    ptr -> balance = 1;
                                    break;
                              case 1: /* Left heavy */
                                    aptr = ptr -> left_child;
                                    if(aptr -> balance == 1)
                                    {
                                          printf("Left to Left Rotation\n");
                                          ptr -> left_child= aptr -> right_child;
                                          aptr -> right_child = ptr;
                                          ptr -> balance = 0;
                                          aptr -> balance=0;
                                          ptr = aptr;
                                    }
                                    else
                                    {
                                          printf("Left to right rotation\n");
                                          bptr = aptr -> right_child;
                                          aptr -> right_child = bptr -> left_child;
                                          bptr -> left_child = aptr;
                                          ptr -> left_child = bptr -> right_child;
                                          bptr -> right_child = ptr;
                                          if(bptr -> balance == 1 )
                                                ptr -> balance = -1;
                                          else
                                                ptr -> balance = 0;
                                          if(bptr -> balance == -1)
                                                aptr -> balance = 1;
                                          else
                                                aptr -> balance = 0;
                                          bptr -> balance=0;
                                          ptr = bptr;
                                    }
                                    *ht_inc = FALSE;
                        }
                  }
            }
            if(data > ptr -> val)
            {
                  ptr -> right_child = insert(data, ptr -> right_child, ht_inc);
                  if(*ht_inc==TRUE)
                  {
                        switch(ptr -> balance)
                        {
                              case 1: /* Left heavy */
                                    ptr -> balance = 0;
                                    *ht_inc = FALSE;
                                    break;
                              case 0: /* Balanced */
                                    ptr -> balance = -1;
                                    break;
                              case -1: /* Right heavy */
                                    aptr = ptr -> right_child;
                                    if(aptr -> balance == -1)
```

```
                                        {
                                                printf("Right to Right Rotation\n");
                                                ptr -> right_child= aptr -> left_child;
                                                aptr -> left_child = ptr;
                                                ptr -> balance = 0;
                                                aptr -> balance=0;
                                                ptr = aptr;
                                        }
                                        else
                                        {
                                                printf("Right to Left Rotation\n");
                                                bptr = aptr -> left_child;
                                                aptr -> left_child = bptr -> right_child;
                                                bptr -> right_child = aptr;
                                                ptr -> right_child = bptr -> left_child;
                                                bptr -> left_child = bptr;
                                                if(bptr -> balance == -1)
                                                        ptr -> balance = 1;
                                                else
                                                        ptr -> balance = 0;
                                                if(bptr -> balance == 1)
                                                        aptr -> balance = -1;
                                                else
                                                        aptr -> balance = 0;
                                                bptr -> balance=0;
                                                ptr = bptr;
                                        }/*End of else*/
                                        *ht_inc = FALSE;
                                }
                        }
                }
                return(ptr);
        }
        void display(struct node *ptr, int level)
        {
                int i;
                if ( ptr!=NULL )
                {
                        display(ptr -> right_child, level+1);
                        printf("\n");
                        for (i = 0; i < level; i++)
                                printf(" ");
                        printf("%d", ptr -> val);
                        display(ptr -> left_child, level+1);
                }
        }
        void inorder(struct node *ptr)
        {
                if(ptr!=NULL)
                {
                        inorder(ptr -> left_child);
                        printf("%d ",ptr -> val);
                        inorder(ptr -> right_child);
                }
        }
        main()
        {
                bool ht_inc;
                int data ;
```

```
        int option;
        struct node *root = (struct node *)malloc(sizeof(struct node));
        root = NULL;
        while(1)
        {
                printf("1.Insert\n");
                printf("2.Display\n");
                printf("3.Quit\n");
                printf("Enter your option : ");
                scanf("%d",&option);
                switch(option)
                {
                        case 1:
                                printf("Enter the value to be inserted : ");
                                scanf("%d", &data);
                                        if( search(root,data) == NULL )
                                                root = insert(data, root, &ht_inc);
                                                else
                                                printf("Duplicate value ignored\n");
                                        break;
                        case 2:
                                if(root==NULL)
                                {
                                        printf("Tree is empty\n");
                                        continue;
                                }
                                printf("Tree is :\n");
                                display(root, 1);
                                printf("\n\n");
                                printf("Inorder Traversal is: ");
                                inorder(root);
                                printf("\n");
                                break;
                        case 3:
                                exit(1);
                                default:
                                        printf("Wrong option\n");
                                }
                }
        }
```

10.5 RED-BLACK TREES

A red-black tree is a self-balancing binary search tree that was invented in 1972 by Rudolf Bayer who called it the 'symmetric binary B-tree'. Although a red-black tree is complex, it has good worst-case running time for its operations and is efficient to use as searching, insertion, and deletion can all be done in `O(log n)` time, where `n` is the number of nodes in the tree. Practically, a red-black tree is a binary search tree which inserts and removes intelligently, to keep the tree reasonably balanced. A special point to note about the red-black tree is that in this tree, no data is stored in the leaf nodes.

10.5.1 Properties of Red-Black Trees

A red-black tree is a binary search tree in which every node has a colour which is either red or black. Apart from the other restrictions of a binary search tree, the red-black tree has the following additional requirements:

1. The colour of a node is either red or black.
2. The colour of the root node is always black.

3. All leaf nodes are black.
4. Every red node has both the children coloured in black.
5. Every simple path from a given node to any of its leaf nodes has an equal number of black nodes.

Look at Fig. 10.55 which shows a red-black tree.

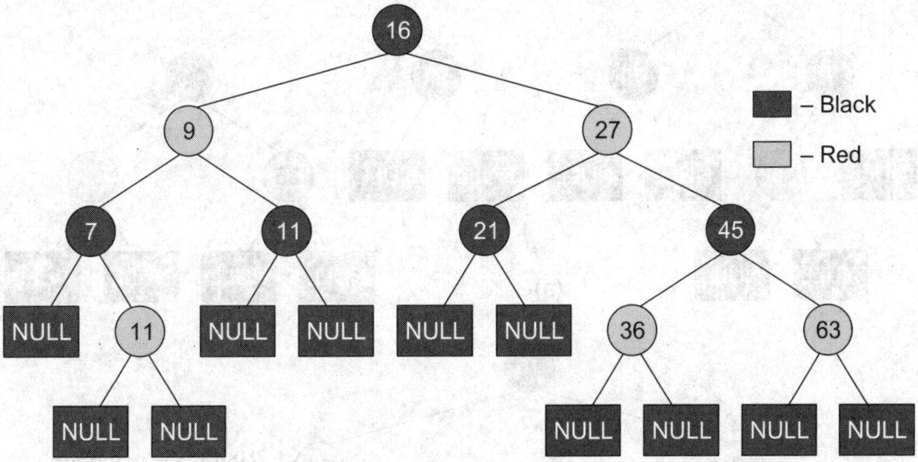

Figure 10.55 Red-black tree

These constraints enforce a critical property of red-black trees. *The longest path from the root node to any leaf node is no more than twice as long as the shortest path from the root to any other leaf in that tree.*

This results in a roughly balanced tree. Since operations such as insertion, deletion, and searching require worst-case times proportional to the height of the tree, this theoretical upper bound on the height allows red-black trees to be efficient in the worst case, unlike ordinary binary search trees.

To understand the importance of these properties, it suffices to note that according to property 4, no path can have two red nodes in a row. The shortest possible path will have all black nodes, and the longest possible path would alternately have a red and a black node. Since all maximal paths have the same number of black nodes (property 5), *no path is more than twice as long as any other path.*

Figure 10.56 shows some binary search trees that are not red-black trees.

10.5.2 Operations on Red-Black Trees

Preforming a read-only operation (like traversing the nodes in a tree) on a red-black tree requires no modification from those used for binary search trees. Remember that every red-black tree is a special case of a binary search tree. However, insertion and deletion operations may violate the properties of a red-black tree. Therefore, these operations may create a need to restore the red-black properties that may require a small number of (`O(log n)` or amortized `O(1)`) colour changes.

Inserting a Node in a Red-Black Tree

The insertion operation starts in the same way as we add a new node in the binary search tree. However, in a binary search tree, we always add the new node as a leaf, while in a red-black tree, leaf nodes contain no data. So instead of adding the new node as a leaf node, we add a red interior node that has two black leaf nodes. Note that the colour of the new node is red and its leaf nodes are coloured in black.

Once a new node is added, it may violate some properties of the red-black tree. So in order to restore their property, we check for certain cases and restore the property depending on the case that turns up after insertion. But before learning these cases in detail, first let us discuss certain important terms that will be used.

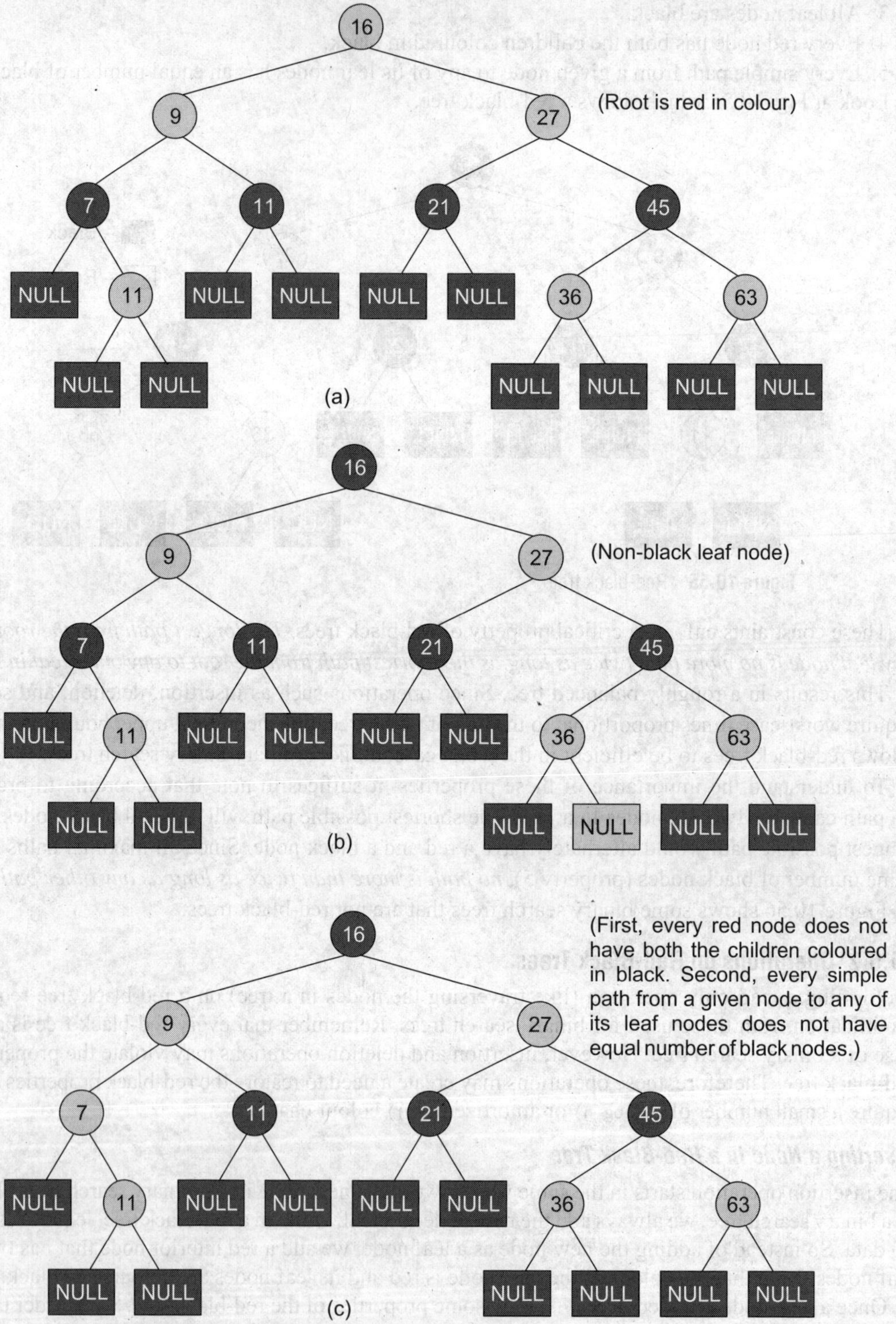

Figure 10.56 Trees

Grandparent node (G) of a node (N) refers to the parent of N's parent (P), as in human family trees. The C code to find a node's grandparent can be given as follows:

```
struct node * grand_parent(struct node *n)
{
        // No parent means no grandparent
        if ((n != NULL) && (n -> parent != NULL))
                return n -> parent -> parent;
        else
                return NULL;
}
```

Uncle node (U) of a node (N) refers to the sibling of N's parent (P), as in human family trees. The C code to find a node's uncle can be given as follows:

```
struct node *uncle(struct node *n)
{
        struct node *g;
        g = grand_parent(n);
        //With no grandparent, there cannot be any uncle
        if (g == NULL)
                return NULL;
        if (n -> parent == g -> left)
                return g -> right;
        else
                return g -> left;
}
```

When we insert a new node in a red-black tree, note the following:

- All leaf nodes are always black. So property 3 always holds true.
- Property 4 (both children of every red node are black) is threatened only by adding a red node, repainting a black node red, or a rotation.
- Property 5 (all paths from any given node to its leaf nodes has equal number of black nodes) is threatened only by adding a black node, repainting a red node black, or a rotation.

Case 1: The New Node N is Added as the Root of the Tree

In this case, N is repainted black, as the root of the tree is always black. Since N adds one black node to every path at once, Property 5 is not violated. The C code for case 1 can be given as follows:

```
void case1(struct node *n)
{
        if (n -> parent == NULL) // Root node
                n -> colour = BLACK;
        else
                case2(n);
}
```

Case 2: The New Node's Parent P is Black

In this case, both children of every red node are black, so Property 4 is not invalidated. Property 5 is also not threatened. This is because the new node N has two black leaf children, but because N is red, the paths through each of its children have the same number of black nodes. The C code to check for case 2 can be given as follows:

```
void case2(struct node *n)
{
        if (n->parent->colour == BLACK)
             return; /* Red black tree property is not violated*/
        else
             case3(n);
}
```

In the following cases, it is assumed that N *has a grandparent node* G, *because its parent* P *is red, and if it were the root, it would be black. Thus,* N *also has an uncle node* U *(irrespective of whether* U *is a leaf node or an internal node).*

Case 3: If Both the Parent (P) and the Uncle (U) are Red

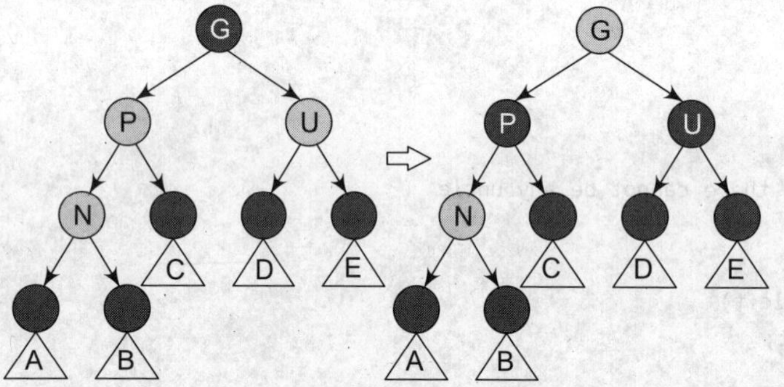

Figure 10.57 Insertion in Case 3

In this case, Property 5 which says all paths from any given node to its leaf nodes have an equal number of black nodes is violated. Insertion in the third case is illustrated in Fig. 10.57.

In order to restore Property 5, both nodes (P and U) are repainted black and the grandparent G is repainted red. Now, the new red node N has a black parent. Since any path through the parent or uncle must pass through the grandparent, the number of black nodes on these paths has not changed.

However, the grandparent G may now violate Property 2 which says that the root node is always black or Property 4 which states that both children of every red node are black. Property 4 will be violated when G has a red parent. In order to fix this problem, this entire procedure is recursively performed on G from Case 1. The C code to deal with Case 3 insertion is as follows:

```
void case3(struct node *n)
{
        struct node *u, *g;
        u = uncle (n);
        g = grand_parent(n);
        if ((u != NULL) && (u->colour == RED)) {
             n->parent->colour = BLACK;
             u->colour = BLACK;
             g->colour = RED;
             case1(g);
        }
        else {
             insert_case4(n);
        }
}
```

Note In the remaining cases, we assume that the parent node P is the left child of its parent. If it is the right child, then interchange left and right in cases 4 and 5.

Case 4: The Parent P is Red but the Uncle U is Black and N is the Right Child of P and P is the Left Child of G

In order to fix this problem, a left rotation is done to switch the roles of the new node N and its parent P. After the rotation, note that in the C code, we have re-labelled N and P and then, case 5 is called to deal with the new node's parent. This is done because Property 4 which says both children of every red node

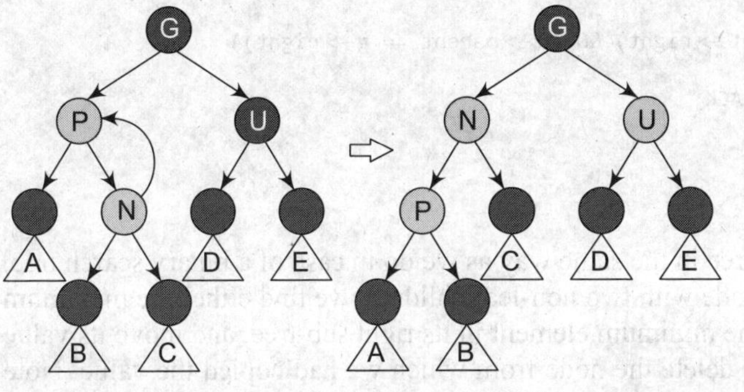

Figure 10.58 Insertion in Case 4

should be black is still violated. Figure 10.58 illustrates Case 4 insertion.

Note that in case N is the left child of P and P is the right child of G, we have to perform a right rotation. In the C code that handles Case 4, we check for P and N and then, perform either a left or a right rotation.

```
void case4(struct node *n)
{
        struct node *g = grand_
parent(n);
        if ((n == n->parent->right)
&& (n->parent == g->left))
        {
                rotate_left(n->parent);
                n = n->left;
        }
        else if ((n == n->parent->left) && (n->parent == g->right))
        {
                rotate_right(n->parent);
                n = n->right;
        }
        case5(n);
}
```

Case 5: The Parent P is Red but the Uncle U is Black and the New Node N is the Left Child of P, and P is the Left Child of its Parent G.

In order to fix this problem, a right rotation on G (the grandparent of N) is performed. After this rotation, the former parent P is now the parent of both the new node N and the former grandparent G.

We know that the colour of G is black (because otherwise its former child P could not have been red), so now switch the colours of P and G so that the resulting tree satisfies Property 4 which states that both children of a red node are black. Case 5 insertion is illustrated in Fig. 10.59.

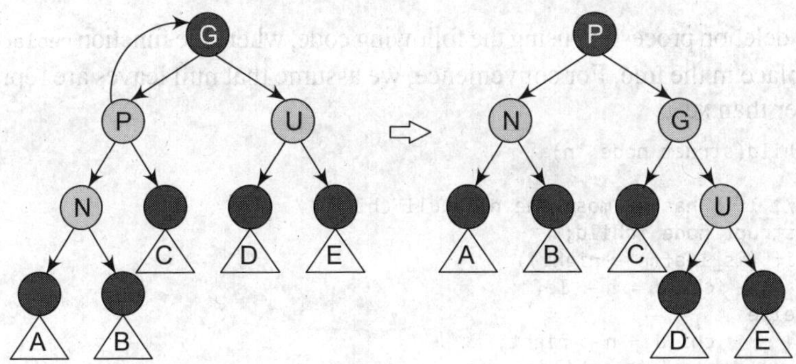

Figure 10.59 Insertion in case 5

Note that in case N is the right child of P and P is the right child of G, we perform a left rotation. In the C code that handles Case 5, we check for P and N and then, perform either a left or a right rotation.

```
void case5(struct node *n)
{
        struct node *g;
        g = grandparent(n);
        if ((n == n->parent->left) && (n->parent == g->left))
```

```
            rotate_right(g);
        else if ((n == n->parent->right) && (n->parent == g->right))
            rotate_left(g);
        n->parent->colour = BLACK;
        g->colour = RED;
}
```

Deleting a Node from a Red-Black Tree

We start deleting a node from a red-black tree in the same way as we do in case of a binary search tree. In a binary search tree, when we delete a node with two non-leaf children, we find either the maximum element in its left sub-tree of the node or the minimum element in its right sub-tree, and move its value into the node being deleted. After that, we delete the node from which we had copied the value. Note that this node must have less than two non-leaf children. Therefore, merely copying a value does not violate any red-black properties, but it just reduces the problem of deleting to the problem of deleting a node with at most one non-leaf child.

In this section, we will assume that we are deleting a node with at most one non-leaf child, which we will call its child. In case this node has both leaf children, then let one of them be its child.

While deleting a node, if its colour is red, then we can simply replace it with its child, which must be black. All paths through the deleted node will simply pass through one less red node, and both the deleted node's parent and child must be black, so none of the properties will be violated.

Another simple case is when we delete a black node that has a red child. In this case, property 4 and property 5 could be violated, so to restore them, just repaint the deleted node's child with black.

However, a complex situation arises when both the node to be deleted as well as its child is black. In this case, we begin by replacing the node to be deleted with its child. In the C code, we label the child node as (in its new position) `N`, and its sibling (its new parent's other child) as `S`. The C code to find the sibling of a node can be given as follows:

```
struct node *sibling(struct node *n)
{
        if (n == n->parent->left)
            return n->parent->right;
        else
            return n->parent->left;
}
```

We can start the deletion process by using the following code, where the function `replace_node` substitutes the `child` into `N's` place in the tree. For convenience, we assume that null leaves are represented by actual node objects, rather than `NULL`.

```
void delete_child(struct node *n)
{
        /* If N has at most one non-null child */
        struct node *child;
        if (is_leaf(n->right))
            child = n->left;
        else
            child = n->right;
        replace_node(n, child);
        if (n->colour == BLACK) {
            if (child->colour == RED)
                child->colour = BLACK;
            else
                del_case1(child);
        }
        free(n);
}
```

When both N and its parent P are black, then deleting P will cause paths which precede through N to have one fewer black nodes than the other paths. This will violate Property 5. Therefore, the tree needs to be rebalanced. There are several cases to consider, which are discussed below.

Case 1: N is the New Root

In this case, we have removed one black node from every path, and the new root is black, so none of the properties are violated.

```
void del_case1(struct node *n)
{
        if (n->parent != NULL)
                del_case2(n);
}
```

Note In cases 2, 5, and 6, we assume N is the left child of its parent P. If it is the right child, left and right should be interchanged throughout these three cases.

Case 2: Sibling S is Red

In this case, interchange the colours of P and S, and then rotate left at P. In the resultant tree, S will become N's grandparent. Figure 10.60 illustrates Case 2 deletion.

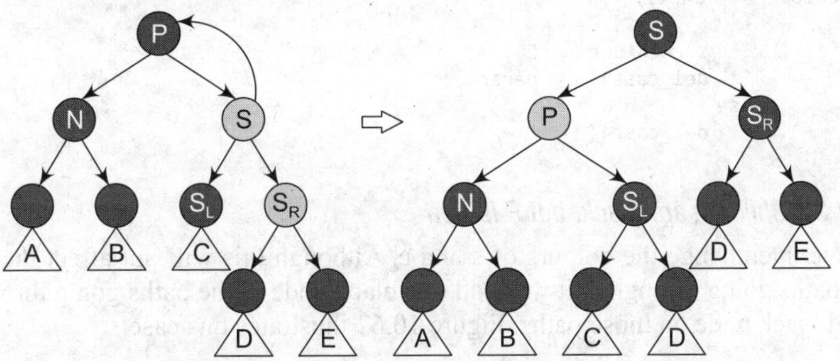

Figure 10.60 Deletion in case 2

The C code that handles case 2 deletion can be given as follows:

```
void del_case2(struct node *n)
{
        struct node *s;
        s = sibling(n);
        if (s->colour == RED)
        {
                if (n == n->parent->left)
                        rotate_left(n->parent);
                else
                        rotate_right(n->parent);
                n->parent->colour = RED;
                s->colour = BLACK;
        }
        del_case3(n);
}
```

Case 3: P, S, and S's Children are Black

In this case, simply repaint S with red. In the resultant tree, all the paths passing through S will have one less black node. Therefore, all the paths that pass through P now have one fewer black nodes than the paths that do not pass through P, so Property 5 is still violated. To fix this problem, we perform the rebalancing procedure on P, starting at Case 1. Case 3 is illustrated in Fig. 10.61.

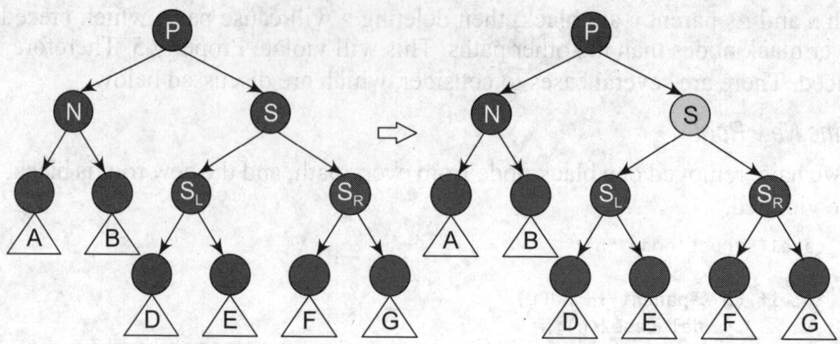

Figure 10.61 Insertion in case 3

The C code for Case 3 can be given as follows:

```
void del_case3(struct node *n)
{
        struct node *s;
        s = sibling(n);
        if ((n->parent->colour == BLACK) && (s->colour == BLACK) && (s->left->colour == BLACK) &&
(s -> right -> colour == BLACK))
        {
                s -> colour = RED;
                del_case1(n -> parent);
        } else
                del_case4(n);
}
```

Case 4: S and S's Children are Black, but P is Red

In this case, we interchange the colours of S and P. Although this will not affect the number of black nodes on the paths going through S, it will add one black node to the paths going through N, making up for the deleted black node on those paths. Figure 10.62 illustrates this case.

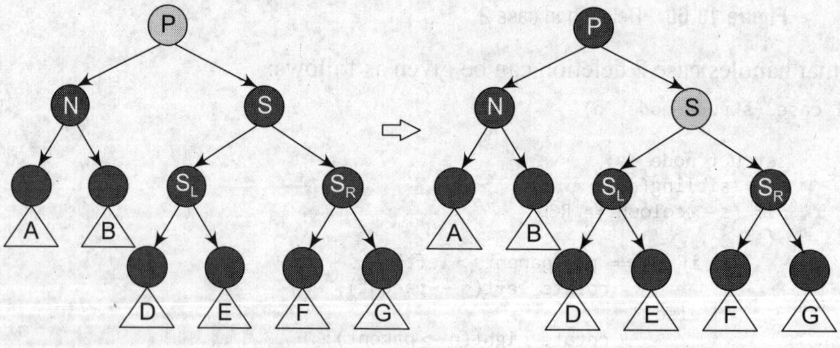

Figure 10.62 Insertion in case 4

The C code to handle Case 4 is as follows:

```
void del_case4(struct node *n)
{
        struct node *s;
        s = sibling(n);
        if ((n -> parent -> color == RED) && (s -> colour == BLACK) &&
(s -> left -> colour == BLACK) && (s -> right -> colour == BLACK))
        {
                s -> colour = RED;
```

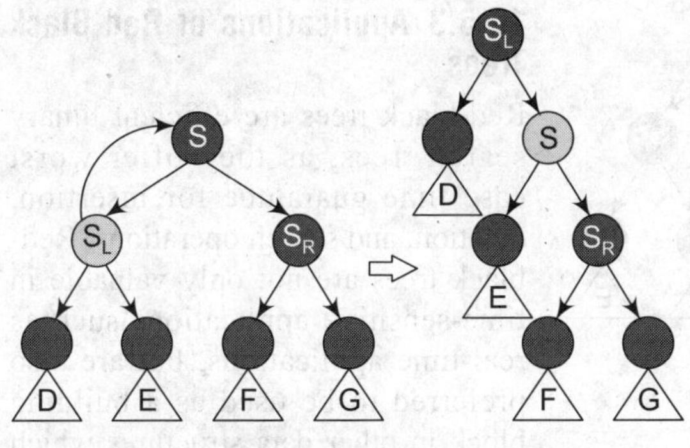

Figure 10.63 Insertion in case 5

The C code to handle case 5 is given as follows:

```
                n->parent->colour = BLACK;
        } else
                del_case5(n);
}
```

Case 5: N is the Left Child of P and S is Black, S's Left Child is Red, S's Right Child is Black.

In this case, perform a right rotation at `S`. After the rotation, `S`'s left child becomes `S`'s parent and `N`'s new sibling. Also, interchange the colours of `S` and its new parent.

Note that now all paths still have equal number of black nodes, but `N` has a black sibling whose right child is red, so we fall into Case 6. Refer Fig. 10.63.

```
void del_case5(struct node *n)
{
        struct node *s;
        s = sibling(n);
        if (s -> colour == BLACK)
        {
        /* the following code forces the red to be on the left of the left of the parent,
or right of the right, to be correctly operated in case 6. */
                if ((n == n -> parent -> left) && (s -> right -> colour == BLACK) && (s -> left
-> colour == RED))
                        rotate_right(s);
                else if ((n == n -> parent -> right) && (s -> left -> colour == BLACK) && (s ->
right -> colour == RED))
                        rotate_left(s);
                s -> colour = RED;
                s -> right -> colour = BLACK;
        }
        del_case6(n);
}
```

Case 6: S is Black, S's Right Child is Red, and N is the Left Child of its Parent P

In this case, a left rotation is done at `P` to make `S` the parent of `P` and `S`'s right child. After the rotation, the colours of `P` and `S` are interchanged and `S`'s right child is coloured black. Once these steps are followed, you will observe that property 4 and property 5 remain valid. Case 6 is explained in Fig. 10.64.

The C code to fix Case 6 can be given as follows:

```
Void del_case6(struct node *n)
{
        struct node *s;
        s = sibling(n);
        s -> colour = n -> parent -> colour;
        n -> parent -> colour = BLACK;
        if (n == n -> parent -> left) {
                s -> right -> colour = BLACK;
                rotate_left(n -> parent);
        } else {
                s -> left -> colour = BLACK;
                rotate_right(n -> parent);
        }
}
```

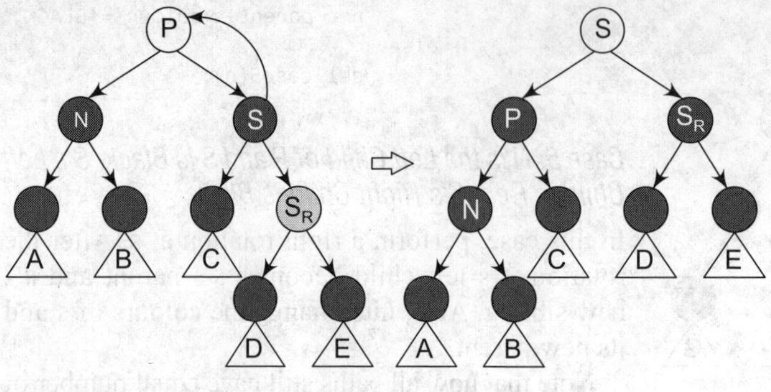

Figure 10.64 Insertion in case 6

10.5.3 Applications of Red-Black Trees

Red-black trees are efficient binary search trees, as they offer worst case time guarantee for insertion, deletion, and search operations. Red-black trees are not only valuable in time-sensitive applications such as real-time applications, but are also preferred to be used as a building block in other data structures which provide worst-case guarantee.

AVL trees also support `O(log n)` search, insertion, and deletion operations, but they are more rigidly balanced than red-black trees, thereby resulting in slower insertion and removal but faster retrieval of data.

10.6 SPLAY TREES

Splay trees were invented by Daniel Sleator and Robert Tarjan. A splay tree is a self-balancing binary search tree with an additional property that recently accessed elements can be re-accessed fast. It is said to be an efficient binary tree because it performs basic operations such as insertion, search, and deletion in `O(log(n))` amortized time. For many non-uniform sequences of operations, splay trees perform better than other search trees, even when the specific pattern of the sequence is unknown.

A splay tree consists of a binary tree, with no additional fields. When a node in a splay tree is accessed, it is rotated or 'splayed' to the root, thereby changing the structure of the tree. Since the most frequently accessed node is always moved closer to the starting point of the search (or the root node), these nodes are therefore located faster. A simple idea behind it is that if an element is accessed, it is likely that it will be accessed again.

In a splay tree, operations such as insertion, search, and deletion are combined with one basic operation called *splaying*. Splaying the tree for a particular node rearranges the tree to place that node at the root. A technique to do this is to first perform a standard binary tree search for that node and then use rotations in a specific order to bring the node on top.

Advantages of Splay tree

- Unlike the AVL trees and Red Black trees, the splay tree does not store any additional information. AVL trees store the balance factor of each node that requires extra space, and Red-Black trees store one extra bit of information that denotes the color of the node (Red or Black).
- Splay tree is the fastest variation of BST and for this reason it is used in **Windows NT and GCC compilers**.
- It provides better performance as the frequently accessed nodes will move nearer to the root node. This facilitates quick access of frequently used elements. Due to this feature, splay tree is used for implementing cache which is a fast memory that supports quick retrieval of recently accessed data.

Disadvantages of Splay tree

- The major drawback of the splay tree is that it is not strictly balanced.
- Since splay trees are roughly balanced, at times they form a linear structure taking O(n) time complexity.

Applications of Splay tree

- Splay trees are used in Windows NT (in the virtual memory, networking, and file system code)
- gcc compiler and GNU C++ library

- sed string editor
- Systems network routers
- The most popular implementation of Unix malloc
- Linux loadable kernel modules

10.6.1 Operations on Splay Trees

In this section, we will discuss the four main operations that are performed on a splay tree. These include splaying, insertion, search, and deletion.

Splaying

When we access a node `N`, splaying is performed on `N` to move it to the root. To perform a splay operation, certain *splay steps* are performed where each step moves `N` closer to the root. Splaying a particular node of interest after every access ensures that the recently accessed nodes are kept closer to the root and the tree remains roughly balanced, so that the desired amortized time bounds can be achieved.

Each splay step depends on three factors:

- Whether `N` is the left or right child of its parent `P`,
- Whether `P` is the root or not, and if not,
- Whether `P` is the left or right child of its parent, `G` (`N`'s grandparent).

Depending on these three factors, we have one splay step based on each factor.

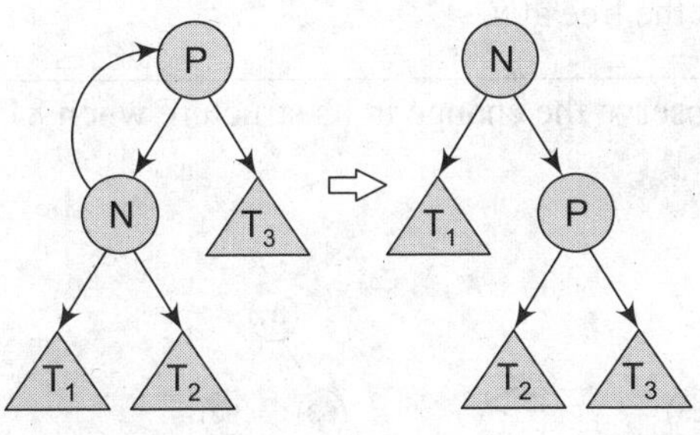

Figure 10.65 Zig step

Zig step The `zig` operation is done when `P` (the parent of `N`) is the root of the splay tree. In the `zig` step, the tree is rotated on the edge between `N` and `P`. `zig` step is usually performed as the last step in a splay operation and only when `N` has an odd depth at the beginning of the operation. Refer Fig. 10.65.

Zig-zig step The `zig-zig` operation is performed when `P` is not the root. In addition to this, `N` and `P` are either both right or left children of their parents. Figure 10.66 shows the case where `N` and `P` are the left children. During the `zig-zig` step, first the tree is rotated on the edge joining `P` and its parent `G`, and then again rotated on the edge joining `N` and `P`.

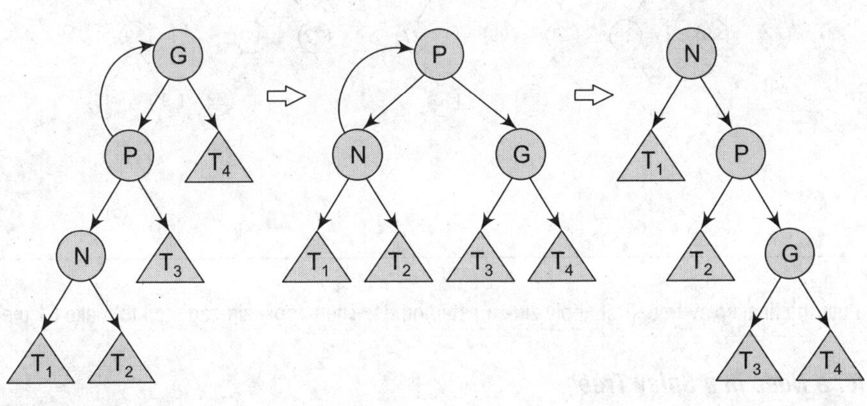

Figure 10.66 Zig-zig step

Zig-zag step The `zig-zag` operation is performed when `P` is not the root. In addition to this, `N` is the right child of `P` and `P` is the left child of `G` or vice versa. In `zig-zag` step, the tree is first rotated on the edge between `N` and `P`, and then rotated on the edge between `N` and `G`. Refer Fig.10.67.

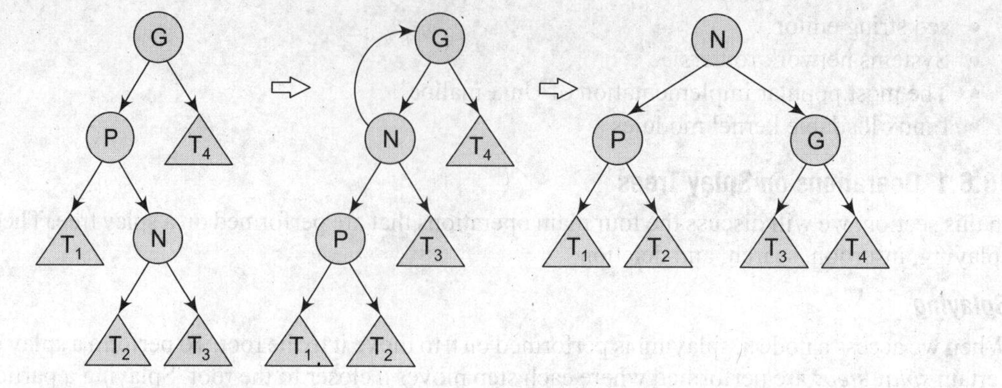

Figure 10.67 Zig-zag step

Inserting a Node in a Splay Tree

Although the process of inserting a new node `N` into a splay tree begins in the same way as we insert a node in a binary search tree, but after the insertion, `N` is made the new root of the splay tree. The steps performed to insert a new node `N` in a splay tree can be given as follows:

Step 1 Search `N` in the splay tree. If the search is successful, splay at the node `N`.

Step 2 If the search is unsuccessful, add the new node `N` in such a way that it replaces the `NULL` pointer reached during the search by a pointer to a new node `N`. Splay the tree at `N`.

Example 10.11 Consider the splay tree given on the left. Observe the change in its structure when 81 is added to it.

Solution

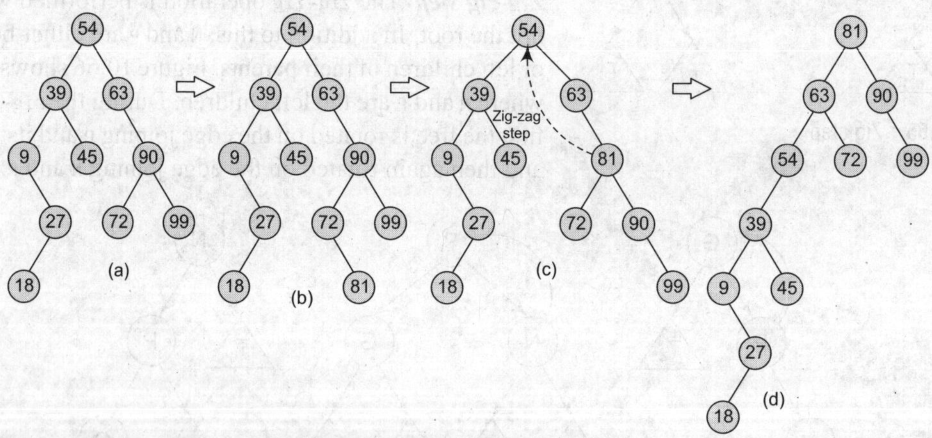

Note To get the final splay tree, first apply zig-zag step on 81. Then apply zig-zag step to make 81 the root node.

Searching for a Node in a Splay Tree

If a particular node `N` is present in the splay tree, then a pointer to `N` is returned; otherwise a pointer to the null node is returned. The steps performed to search a node `N` in a splay tree include:

- Search down the root of the splay tree looking for `N`.

Example 10.12 Consider the splay tree given in Fig. 10.68. Observe the change in its structure when a node containing 81 is searched in the tree.

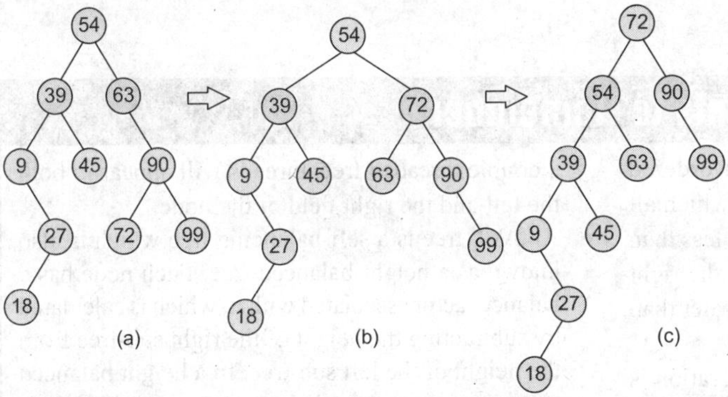

Figure 10.69 Splay tree

Example 10.13 Consider the splay tree at the left. When we delete node 39 from it, the new structure of the tree can be given as shown in the right side of Fig. 10.70(a).

After splaying the tree at P, the resultant tree will be as shown in Fig. 10.70(b):

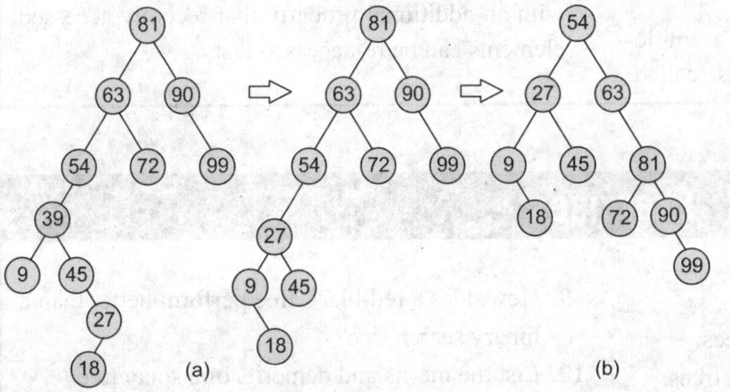

Figure 10.70 (a) Splay tree (b) Splay tree

- If the search is successful, and we reach N, then splay the tree at N and return a pointer to N.
- If the search is unsuccessful, i.e., the splay tree does not contain N, then we reach a null node. Splay the tree at the last non-null node reached during the search and return a pointer to null.

Deleting a Node from a Splay Tree

To delete a node N from a splay tree, we perform the following steps:

- Search for N that has to be deleted. If the search is unsuccessful, splay the tree at the last non-null node encountered during the search.
- If the search is successful and N is not the root node, then let P be the parent of N. Replace N by an appropriate descendent of P (as we do in binary search tree). Finally splay the tree at P.

10.6.2 Advantages and Disadvantages of Splay Trees

The advantages of using a splay tree are:

- A splay tree gives good performance for search, insertion, and deletion operations. This advantage centres on the fact that the splay tree is a self-balancing and a self-optimizing data structure in which the frequently accessed nodes are moved closer to the root so that they can be accessed quickly. This advantage is particularly useful for implementing caches and garbage collection algorithms.
- Splay trees are considerably simpler to implement than the other self-balancing binary search trees, such as red-black trees or AVL trees, while their average-case performance is just as efficient.
- Splay trees minimize memory requirements as they do not store any book-keeping data.
- Unlike other types of self-balancing trees, splay trees provide good performance (amortized O(log n)) with nodes containing identical keys.

However, the demerits of splay trees include:

- While sequentially accessing all the nodes of a tree in a sorted order, the resultant tree becomes completely unbalanced. This takes n accesses of the tree in which each access takes O(log n) time. For example, re-accessing the first node triggers an operation that in turn takes O(n) operations to rebalance the tree before returning the first node. Although this creates a significant delay for the

final operation, the amortized performance over the entire sequence is still `O(log n)`.
- For uniform access, the performance of a splay tree will be considerably worse than a somewhat balanced simple binary search tree. For uniform access, unlike splay trees, these other data structures provide worst-case time guarantees and can be more efficient to use.

Points to Remember

- A binary search tree, also known as an ordered binary tree, is a variant of binary tree in which all the nodes in the left sub-tree have a value less than that of the root node and all the nodes in the right sub-tree have a value either equal to or greater than the root node.
- The average running time of a search operation is $O(\log_2 n)$. However, in the worst case, a binary search tree will take `O(n)` time to search an element from the tree.
- Mirror image of a binary search tree is obtained by interchanging the left sub-tree with the right sub-tree at every node of the tree.
- In a threaded binary tree, null entries can be replaced to store a pointer to either the in-order predecessor or in-order successor of a node.
- A one-way threaded tree is also called a single threaded tree. In a two-way threaded tree, also called a double threaded tree, threads will appear in both the left and the right field of the node.
- An AVL tree is a self-balancing tree which is also known as a height-balanced tree. Each node has a balance factor associated with it, which is calculated by subtracting the height of the right sub-tree from the height of the left sub-tree. In a height balanced tree, every node has a balance factor of either 0, 1, or –1.
- A red-black tree is a self-balancing binary search tree which is also called as a 'symmetric binary B-tree'. Although a red-black tree is complex, it has good worst case running time for its operations and is efficient to use, as searching, insertion, and deletion can all be done in `O(log n)` time.
- A splay tree is a self-balancing binary search tree with an additional property that recently accessed elements can be re-accessed fast.

Exercises

Review Questions

1. Explain the concept of binary search trees.
2. Explain the operations on binary search trees.
3. How does the height of a binary search tree affect its performance?
4. How many nodes will a complete binary tree with 27 nodes have in the last level? What will be the height of the tree?
5. Write a short note on threaded binary trees.
6. Why are threaded binary trees called efficient binary trees? Give the merits of using a threaded binary tree.
7. Discuss the advantages of an AVL tree.
8. How is an AVL tree better than a binary search tree?
9. How does a red-black tree perform better than a binary search tree?
10. List the merits and demerits of a splay tree.
11. Create a binary search tree with the input given below:

    98, 2, 48, 12, 56, 32, 4, 67, 23, 87, 23, 55, 46

    (a) Insert 21, 39, 45, 54, and 63 into the tree

    (b) Delete values 23, 56, 2, and 45 from the tree
12. Consider the binary search tree given below. Now do the following operations:
    - Find the result of in-order, pre-order, and post-order traversals.
    - Show the deletion of the root node
    - Insert 11, 22, 33, 44, 55, 66, and 77 in the tree

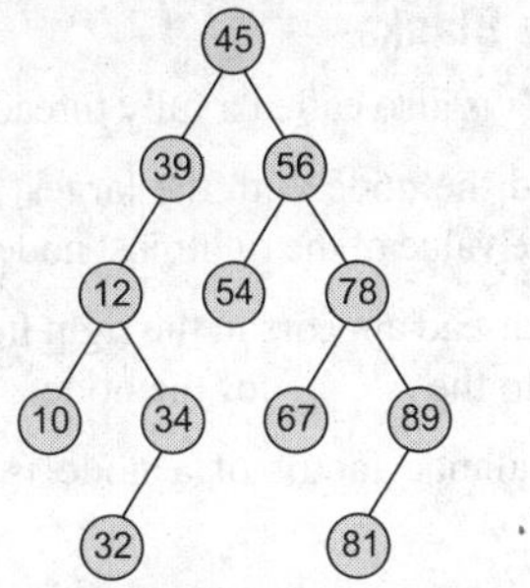

13. Consider the AVL tree given below and insert 18, 81, 29, 15, 19, 25, 26, and 1 in it.
Delete nodes 39, 63, 15, and 1 from the AVL tree formed after solving the above question.

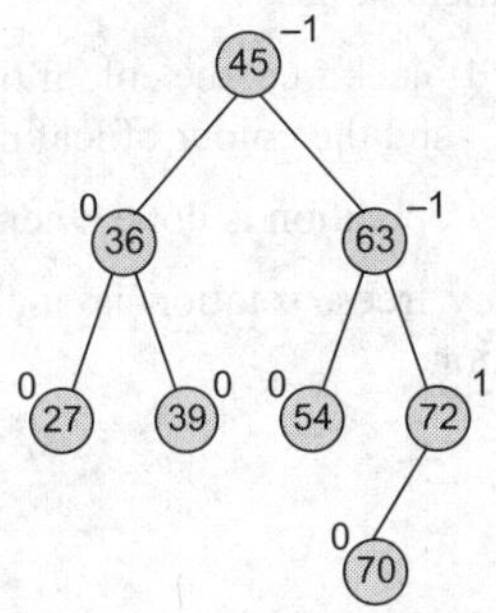

14. Discuss the properties of a red-black tree. Explain the insertion cases.
15. Explain splay trees in detail with relevant examples.
16. Provide the memory representation of the binary tree given below:
    - Find the result of one-way in-order, one-way pre-order, and two-way in-order threading of the tree.
    - In each case, draw the tree and also give its memory representation.

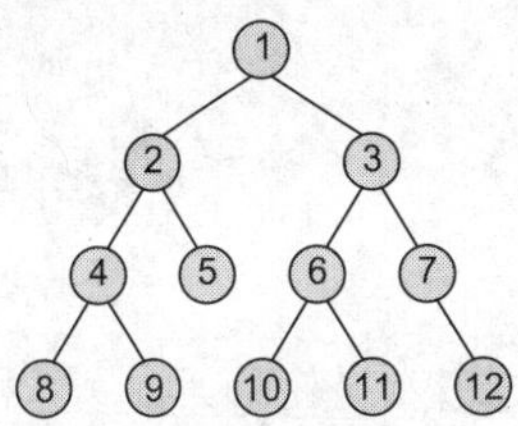

17. Balance the AVL trees given below.

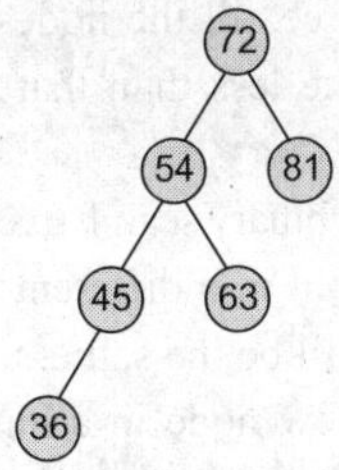

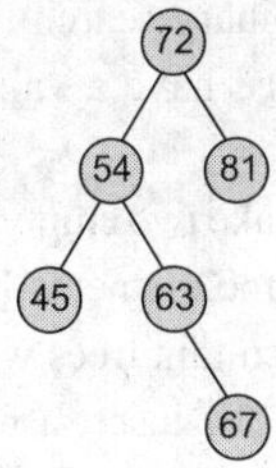

18. Create an AVL tree using the following sequence of data: 16, 27, 9, 11, 36, 54, 81, 63, 72.
19. Draw all possible binary search trees of 7, 9, and 11.

Programming Exercises

1. Write a program to insert and delete values from a binary search tree.
2. Write a program to count the number of nodes in a binary search tree.

Multiple-choice Questions

1. In the worst case, a binary search tree will take how much time to search an element?
   (a) `O(n)` (b) `O(log n)`
   (c) `O(n²)` (d) `O(n log n)`
2. How much time does an AVL tree take to perform search, insert, and delete operations in the average case as well as the worst case?
   (a) `O(n)` (b) `O(log n)`
   (c) `O(n²)` (d) `O(n log n)`
3. When the left sub-tree of the tree is one level higher than that of the right sub-tree, then the balance factor is
   (a) 0 (b) 1
   (c) –1 (d) 2
4. Which rotation is done when the new node is inserted in the right sub-tree of the right sub-tree of the critical node?
   (a) LL (b) LR
   (c) RL (d) RR
5. When a node N is accessed it is splayed to make it the
   (a) Root node (b) Parent node
   (c) Child node (d) Sibling node

True or False

1. In a binary search tree, all the nodes in the left sub-tree have a value less than that of the root node.
2. If we take two empty binary search trees and insert the same elements but in a different order, then the resultant trees will be the same.
3. When we insert a new node in a binary search tree, it will be added as an internal node.
4. Mirror image of a binary search tree is obtained by interchanging the left sub-tree with the right sub-tree at every node of the tree.
5. If the thread appears in the right field, then it will point to the in-order successor of the node.
6. If the node to be deleted is present in the left sub-tree of `A`, then `R` rotation is applied.
7. Height of an AVL tree is limited to `O(log n)`.
8. Critical node is the nearest ancestor node on the path from the root to the inserted node whose balance factor is –1, 0, or 1.
9. RL rotation is done when the new node is inserted in the right sub-tree of the right sub-tree of the critical node.
10. In a red-black tree, some leaf nodes can be red.

Fill in the Blanks

1. ______ is also called a fully threaded binary tree.
2. To find the node with the largest value, we will find the value of the rightmost node of the ______.
3. If the thread appears in the right field, then it will point to the ______ of the node.
4. The balance factor of a node is calculated by ______.
5. Balance factor –1 means ______.
6. Searching an AVL tree takes ______ time.
7. ______ rotation is done when the new node is inserted in the left sub-tree of the left sub-tree of the critical node.
8. In a red-black tree, the colour of the root node is ______ and the colour of leaf node is ______.
9. The zig operation is done when ______.
10. In splay trees, rotation is analogous to ______ operation.

CHAPTER 11

Multi-way Search Trees

LEARNING OBJECTIVE

In this chapter we will study about multi-way search trees which are quite different from other binary search trees. Though the concept is similar to normal binary search trees, but M-way search trees can store more than one key values in a single node. The chapter starts with a general description of M-way search trees, and then discusses in detail M-way search trees such as B trees, B+ trees, and 2-3 trees.

11.1 INTRODUCTION

We have discussed that every node in a binary search tree contains one value and two pointers, *left* and *right*, which point to the node's left and right sub-trees, respectively. The structure of a binary search tree node is shown in Fig. 11.1.

The same concept is used in an *M-way* search tree which has `M - 1` values per node and `M` sub-trees. In such a tree, `M` is called the degree of the tree. Note that in a binary search tree `M = 2`, so it has one value and two sub-trees. In other words, every internal node of an M-way search tree consists of pointers to `M` sub-trees and contains `M - 1` keys, where `M > 2`.

Pointer to left sub-tree	Value or Key of the node	Pointer to right sub-tree

Figure 11.1 Structure of a binary search tree node

The structure of an M-way search tree node is shown in Fig. 11.2.

P_0	K_0	P_1	K_1	P_2	K_2	......	P_{n-1}	K_{n-1}	P_n

Figure 11.2 Structure of an M-way search tree node

In the structure shown, P_0, P_1, P_2, ..., P_n are pointers to the node's sub-trees and K_0, K_1, K_2, ..., K_{n-1} are the key values of the node. All the key values are stored in ascending order. That is, $K_i < K_{i+1}$ for $0 \le i \le n-2$.

In an M-way search tree, it is not compulsory that every node has exactly `M-1` values and `M` sub-trees. Rather, the node can have anywhere from 1 to `M-1` values, and the number of sub-trees can vary from 0 (for a leaf node) to `i + 1`, where `i` is the number of key values in the node. `M` is thus a fixed upper limit that defines how many key values can be stored in the node.

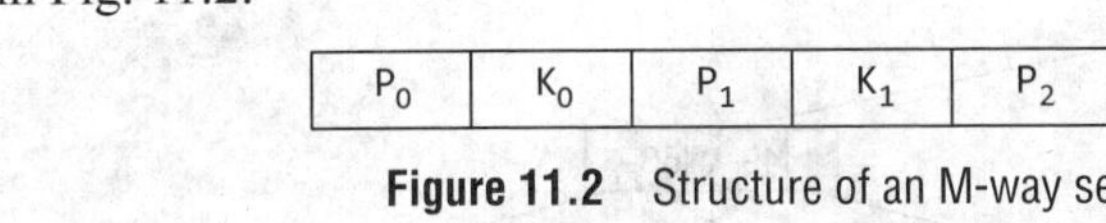

Figure 11.3 M-way search tree of order 3

Consider the M-way search tree shown in Fig. 11.3. Here `M = 3`. So a node can store a maximum of two key values and can contain pointers to three sub-trees.

In our example, we have taken a very small value of M so that the concept becomes easier for the reader, but in practice, M is usually very large. Using a 3-way search tree, let us lay down some of the basic properties of an M-way search tree.

- Note that the key values in the sub-tree pointed by P_0 are less than the key value K_0. Similarly, all the key values in the sub-tree pointed by P_1 are less than K_1, so on and so forth. Thus, the generalized rule is that all the key values in the sub-tree pointed by P_i are less than K_i, where $0 \le i \le n-1$.
- Note that the key values in the sub-tree pointed by P_1 are greater than the key value K_0. Similarly, all the key values in the sub-tree pointed by P_2 are greater than K_1, so on and so forth. Thus, the generalized rule is that all the key values in the sub-tree pointed by P_i are greater than K_{i-1}, where $0 \le i \le n-1$.

In an M-way search tree, every sub-tree is also an M-way search tree and follows the same rules.

11.2 B TREES

A B tree is a specialized M-way tree developed by Rudolf Bayer and Ed McCreight in 1970 that is widely used for disk access. A B tree of order m can have a maximum of m-1 keys and m pointers to its sub-trees. A B tree may contain a large number of key values and pointers to sub-trees. Storing a large number of keys in a single node keeps the height of the tree relatively small.

A B tree is designed to store sorted data and allows search, insertion, and deletion operations to be performed in logarithmic amortized time. A B tree of order m (the maximum number of children that each node can have) is a tree with all the properties of an M-way search tree. In addition it has the following properties:

1. Every node in the B tree has at most (maximum) m children.
2. Every node in the B tree except the root node and leaf nodes has at least (minimum) m/2 children. This condition helps to keep the tree bushy so that the path from the root node to the leaf is very short, even in a tree that stores a lot of data.
3. The root node has at least two children if it is not a terminal (leaf) node.
4. All leaf nodes are at the same level.

An internal node in the B tree can have n number of children, where $0 \le n \le m$. It is not necessary that every node has the same number of children, but the only restriction is that the node should have at least m/2 children. As B tree of order 4 is given in Fig. 11.4.

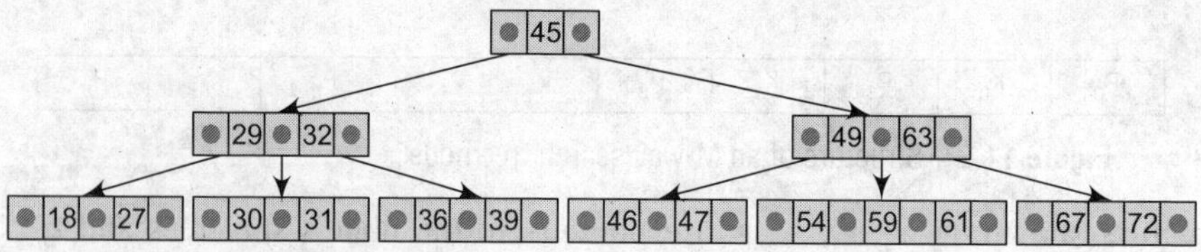

Figure 11.4 B tree of order 4

While performing insertion and deletion operations in a B tree, the number of child nodes may change. So, in order to maintain a minimum number of children, the internal nodes may be joined or split. We will discuss search, insertion, and deletion operations in this section.

11.2.1 Searching for an Element in a B Tree

Searching for an element in a B tree is similar to that in binary search trees. Consider the B tree given in Fig. 11.4. To search for 59, we begin at the root node. The root node has a value 45 which is less than 59. So, we traverse in the right sub-tree. The right sub-tree of the root node has two key values, 49 and 63. Since $49 \le 59 \le 63$, we traverse the right sub-tree of 49, that is, the left sub-tree of 63. This sub-tree has three values, 54, 59, and 61. On finding the value 59, the search is successful.

Take another example. If you want to search for 9, then we traverse the left sub-tree of the root node. The left sub-tree has two key values, 29 and 32. Again, we traverse the left sub-tree of 29. We find that it has two key values, 18 and 27. There is no left sub-tree of 18, hence the value 9 is not stored in the tree.

Since the running time of the search operation depends upon the height of the tree, the algorithm to search for an element in a B tree takes $O(\log_t n)$ time to execute.

11.2.2 Inserting a New Element in a B Tree

In a B tree, all insertions are done at the leaf node level. A new value is inserted in the B tree using the algorithm given below.

1. Search the B tree to find the leaf node where the new key value should be inserted.
2. If the leaf node is not full, that is, it contains less than `m-1` key values, then insert the new element in the node keeping the node's elements ordered.
3. If the leaf node is full, that is, the leaf node already contains `m-1` key values, then
    (a) insert the new value in order into the existing set of keys,
    (b) split the node at its median into two nodes (note that the split nodes are half full), and
    (c) push the median element up to its parent's node. If the parent's node is already full, then split the parent node by following the same steps.

Example 11.1 Look at the B tree of order 5 given below and insert 8, 9, 39, and 4 into it.

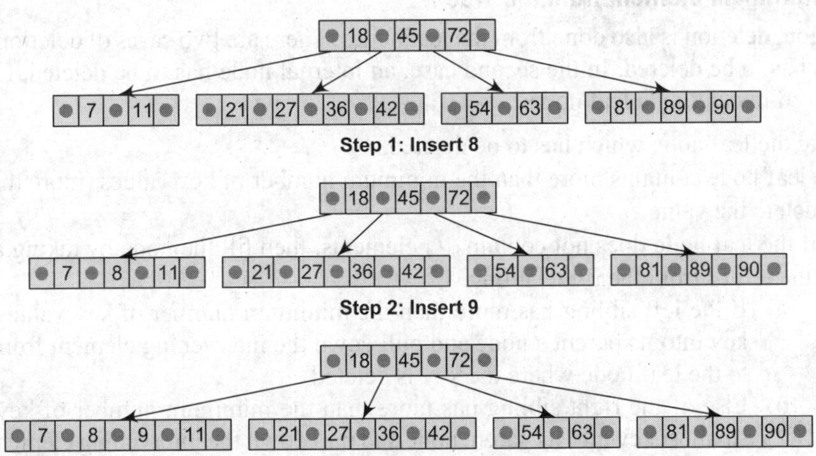

Figure 11.5(a)

Till now, we have easily inserted 8 and 9 in the tree because the leaf nodes were not full. But now, the node in which 39 should be inserted is already full as it contains four values. Here we split the nodes to form two separate nodes. But before splitting, arrange the key values in order (including the new value). The ordered set of values is given as 21, 27, 36, 39, and 42. The median value is 36, so push 36 into its parent's node and split the leaf nodes.

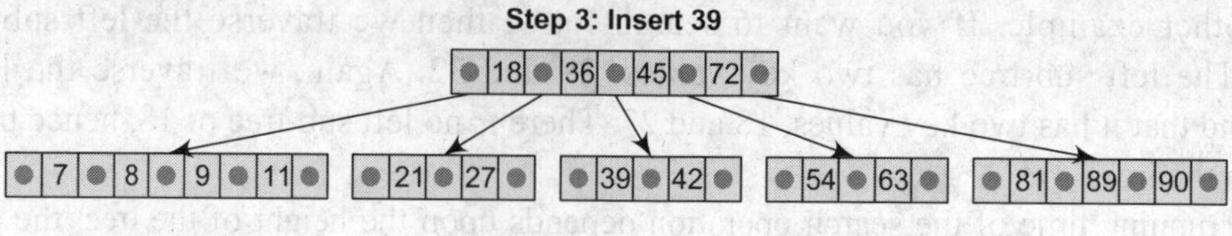

Figure 11.5(b)

Now the node in which 4 should be inserted is already full as it contains four key values. Here we split the nodes to form two separate nodes. But before splitting, we arrange the key values in order (including the new value). The ordered set of values is given as 4, 7, 8, 9, and 11. The median value is 8, so we push 8 into its parent's node and split the leaf nodes. But again, we see that the parent's node is already full, so we split the parent node using the same procedure.

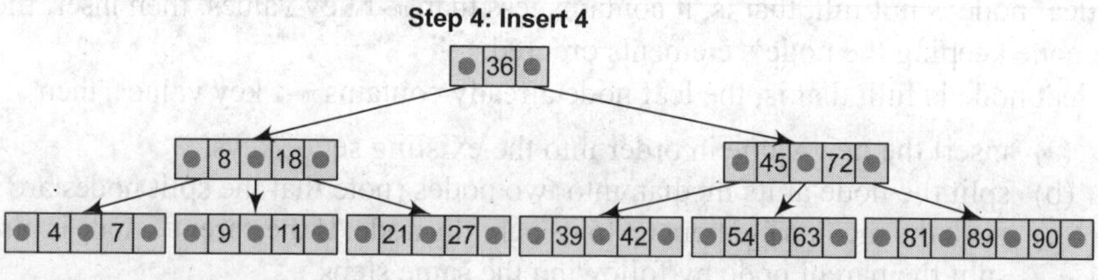

Figure 11.5(c) B tree

11.2.3 Deleting an Element from a B Tree

Like insertion, deletion is also done from the leaf nodes. There are two cases of deletion. In the first case, a leaf node has to be deleted. In the second case, an internal node has to be deleted. Let us first see the steps involved in deleting a leaf node.

1. Locate the leaf node which has to be deleted.
2. If the leaf node contains more than the minimum number of key values (more than `m/2` elements), then delete the value.
3. Else if the leaf node does not contain `m/2` elements, then fill the node by taking an element either from the left or from the right sibling.
   (a) If the left sibling has more than the minimum number of key values, push its largest key into its parent's node and pull down the intervening element from the parent node to the leaf node where the key is deleted.
   (b) Else, if the right sibling has more than the minimum number of key values, push its smallest key into its parent node and pull down the intervening element from the parent node to the leaf node where the key is deleted.
4. Else, if both left and right siblings contain only the minimum number of elements, then create a new leaf node by combining the two leaf nodes and the intervening element of the parent node (ensuring that the number of elements does not exceed the maximum number of elements a node can have, that is, `m`). If pulling the intervening element from the parent node leaves it with less than the minimum number of keys in the node, then propagate the process upwards, thereby reducing the height of the B tree.

To delete an internal node, promote the successor or predecessor of the key to be deleted to occupy the position of the deleted key. This predecessor or successor will always be in the leaf node. So the processing will be done as if a value from the leaf node has been deleted.

Example 11.2 Consider the following B tree of order 5 and delete values 93, 201, 180, and 72 from it (Fig. 11.6(a)).

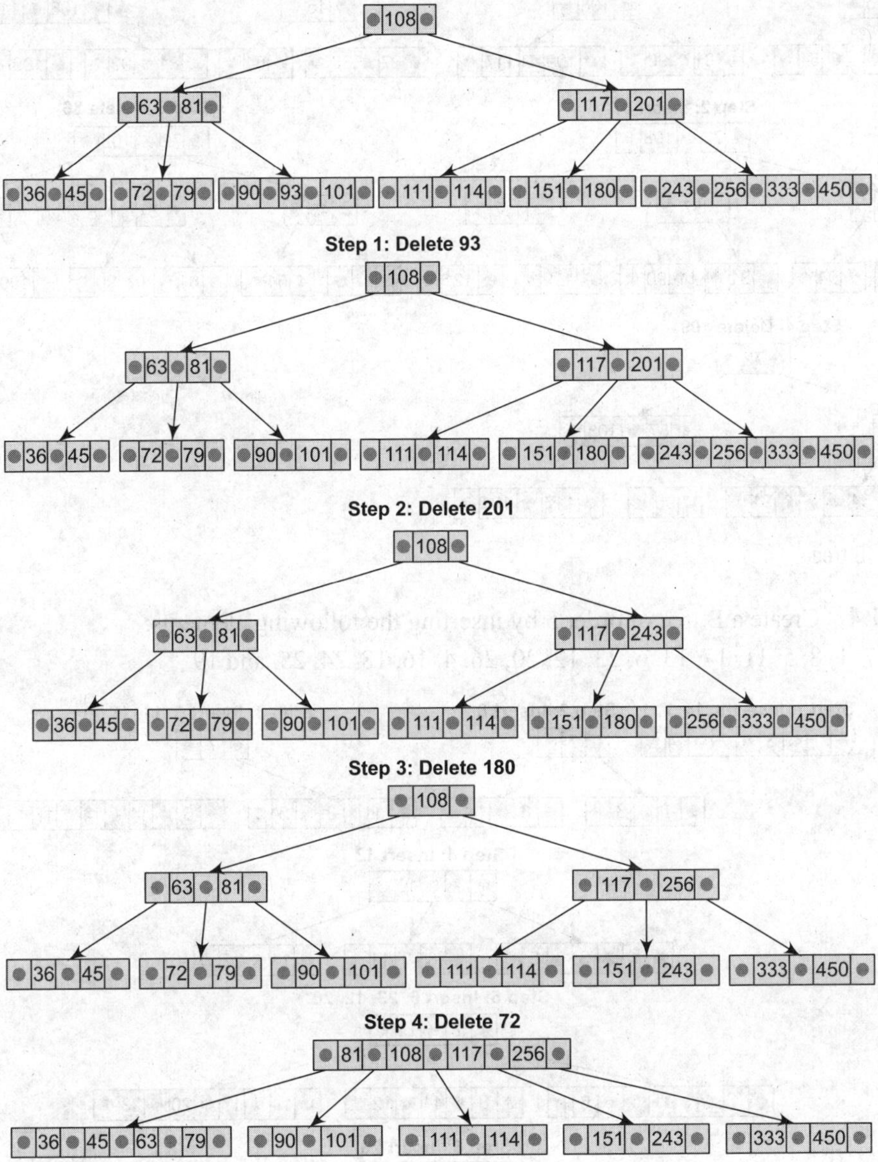

Figure 11.6 B tree

Example 11.3 Consider the B tree of order 3 given below and perform the following operations: (a) insert 121, 87 and then (b) delete 36, 109.

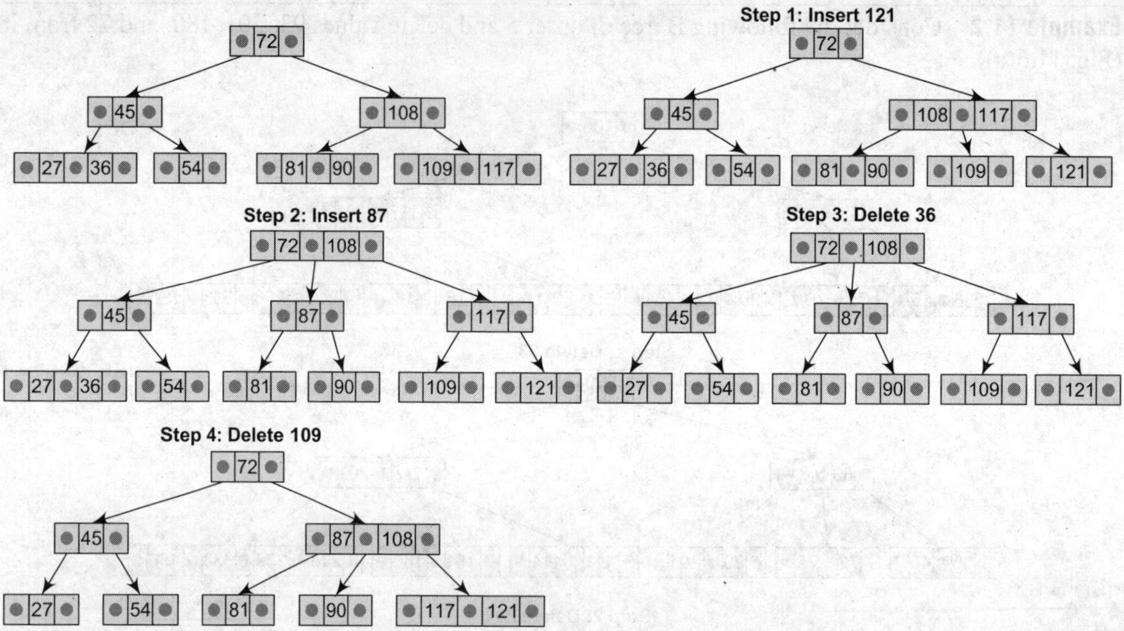

Figure 11.7 B tree

Example 11.4 Create a B tree of order 5 by inserting the following elements:
3, 14, 7, 1, 8, 5, 11, 17, 13, 6, 23, 12, 20, 26, 4, 16, 18, 24, 25, and 19.

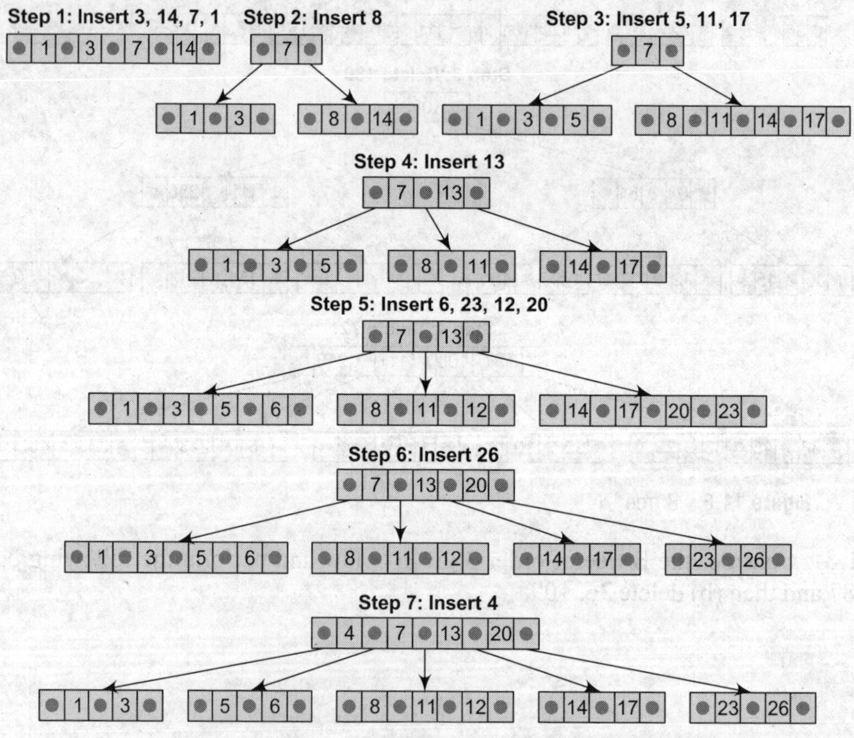

(Contd)

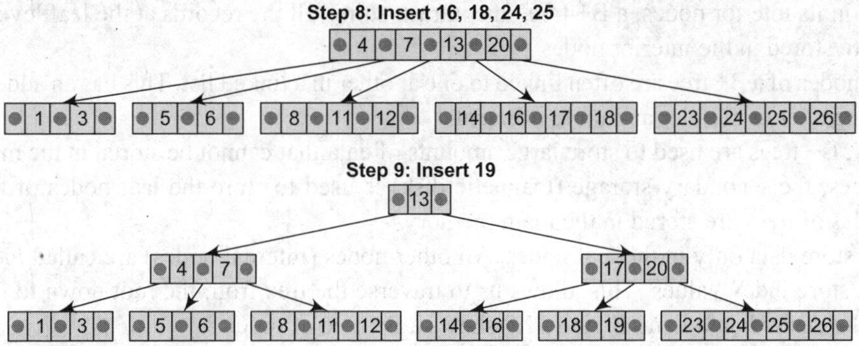

Figure 11.8 B tree

11.2.4 Applications of B Trees

A database is a collection of related data. The prime reason for using a database is that it stores organized data to facilitate its users to update, retrieve, and manage the data. The data stored in the database may include names, addresses, pictures, and numbers. For example, a teacher may wish to maintain a database of all the students that includes the names, roll numbers, date of birth, and marks obtained by every student.

Nowadays, databases are used in every industry to store hundreds of millions of records. In the real world, it is not uncommon for a database to store gigabytes and terabytes of data. For example, a telecommunication company maintains a customer billing database with more than 50 billion rows that contains terabytes of data.

We know that primary memory is very expensive and is capable of storing very little data as compared to secondary memory devices like magnetic disks. Also, RAM is volatile in nature and we cannot store all the data in primary memory. We have no other option but to store data on secondary storage devices. But accessing data from magnetic disks is 10,000 to 1,000,000 times slower than accessing it from the main memory. So, B trees are often used to index the data and provide fast access.

Consider a situation in which we have to search an un-indexed and unsorted database that contains `n` key values. The worst case running time to perform this operation would be `O(n)`. In contrast, if the data in the database is indexed with a B tree, the same search operation will run in `O(log n)`. For example, searching for a single key on a set of one million keys will at most require 1,000,000 comparisons. But if the same data is indexed with a B tree of order 10, then only 114 comparisons will be required in the worst case.

Hence, we see that indexing large amounts of data can provide significant boost to the performance of search operations.

When we use B trees or generalized M-way search trees, the value of `m` or the order of B trees is often very large. Typically, it varies from 128–512. This means that a single node in the tree can contain 127–511 keys and 128–512 pointers to child nodes.

We take a large value of `m` mainly because of three reasons:

1. Disk access is very slow. We should be able to fetch a large amount of data in one disk access.
2. Disk is a block-oriented device. That is, data is organized and retrieved in terms of blocks. So while using a B tree (generalized M-way search tree), a large value of `m` is used so that one single node of the tree can occupy the entire block. In other words, `m` represents the maximum number of data items that can be stored in a single block. `m` is maximized to speed up processing. More the data stored in a block, lesser the time needed to move it into the main memory.
3. A large value minimizes the height of the tree. So, search operation becomes really fast.

11.3 B+ TREES

A B+ tree is a variant of a B tree which stores sorted data in a way that allows for efficient insertion, retrieval, and removal of records, each of which is identified by a *key*. While a B tree can store both keys and records in its interior nodes, a B+ tree, in contrast, stores all the records at the leaf level of the tree; only keys are stored in the interior nodes.

The leaf nodes of a B+ tree are often linked to one another in a linked list. This has an added advantage of making the queries simpler and more efficient.

Typically, B+ trees are used to store large amounts of data that cannot be stored in the main memory. With B+ trees, the secondary storage (magnetic disk) is used to store the leaf nodes of trees and the internal nodes of trees are stored in the main memory.

B+ trees store data only in the leaf nodes. All other nodes (internal nodes) are called *index nodes* or *i-nodes* and store index values. This allows us to traverse the tree from the root down to the leaf node that stores the desired data item. Figure 11.9 shows a B+ tree of order 3.

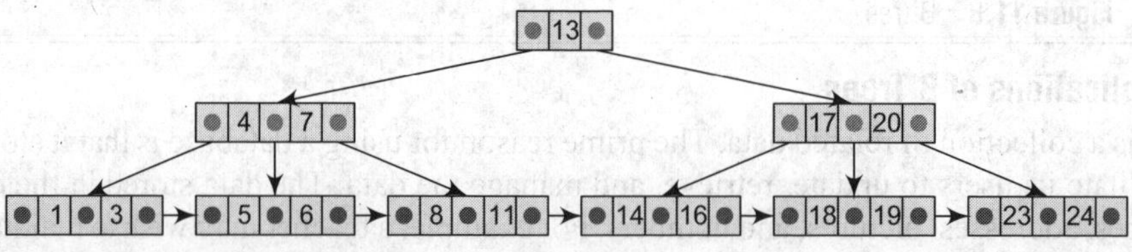

Figure 11.9 B+ tree of order 3

Many database systems are implemented using B+ tree structure because of its simplicity. Since all the data appear in the leaf nodes and are ordered, the tree is always balanced and makes searching for data efficient.

A B+ tree can be thought of as a multi-level index in which the leaves make up a dense index and the non-leaf nodes make up a sparse index. The advantages of B+ trees can be given as follows:

1. Records can be fetched in equal number of disk accesses
2. It can be used to perform a wide range of queries easily as leaves are linked to nodes at the upper level
3. Height of the tree is less and balanced
4. Supports both random and sequential access to records
5. Keys are used for indexing

Comparison Between B Trees and B+ Trees

Table 11.1 shows the comparison between B trees and B+ trees.

Table 11.1 Comparison between B trees and to B+ trees

B Tree	B+ Tree
1. Search keys are not repeated	1. Stores redundant search key
2. Data is stored in internal or leaf nodes	2. Data is stored only in leaf nodes
3. Searching takes more time as data may be found in a leaf or non-leaf node	3. Searching data is very easy as the data can be found in leaf nodes only
4. Deletion of non-leaf nodes is very complicated	4. Deletion is very simple because data will be in the leaf node
5. Leaf nodes cannot be stored using linked lists	5. Leaf node data are ordered using sequential linked lists
6. The structure and operations are complicated	6. The structure and operations are simple

Advantages of B+ Tree

- Records can be fetched in equal number of disk accesses.
- When compared with B tree, the height of a B+ tree remains balanced and less.
- Data in a B+ tree can be accessed sequentially as well as directly.

- Keys of the B+ tree are used for indexing.
- Supports faster search queries as the data is stored only on the leaf nodes.

Applications of B+ Tree

- They are used in multi-level Indexing
- Supports faster operations like insertion, deletion, search
- Used for database indexing
- Used to store large amount of data which cannot be stored in the main memory. Since size of main memory is limited, the internal nodes act as keys to access records of the B+ tree. While internal nodes are stored in the main memory, leaf nodes are stored in the secondary memory.

11.3.1 Inserting a New Element in a B+ Tree

A new element is simply added in the leaf node if there is space for it. But if the data node in the tree where insertion has to be done is full, then that node is split into two nodes. This calls for adding a new index value in the parent index node so that future queries can arbitrate between the two new nodes.

However, adding the new index value in the parent node may cause it, in turn, to split. In fact, all the nodes on the path from a leaf to the root may split when a new value is added to a leaf node. If the root node splits, a new leaf node is created and the tree grows by one level.
The steps to insert a new node in a B+ Tree are summarized in Fig. 11.10.

Step 1:	Insert the new node as the leaf node.
Step 2:	If the leaf node overflows, split the node and copy the middle element to next index node.
Step 3:	If the index node overflows, split that node and move the middle element to next index page.

Figure 11.10 Algorithm for inserting a new node in a B+ tree

Example 11.5 Consider the B+ tree of order 4 given and insert 33 in it.

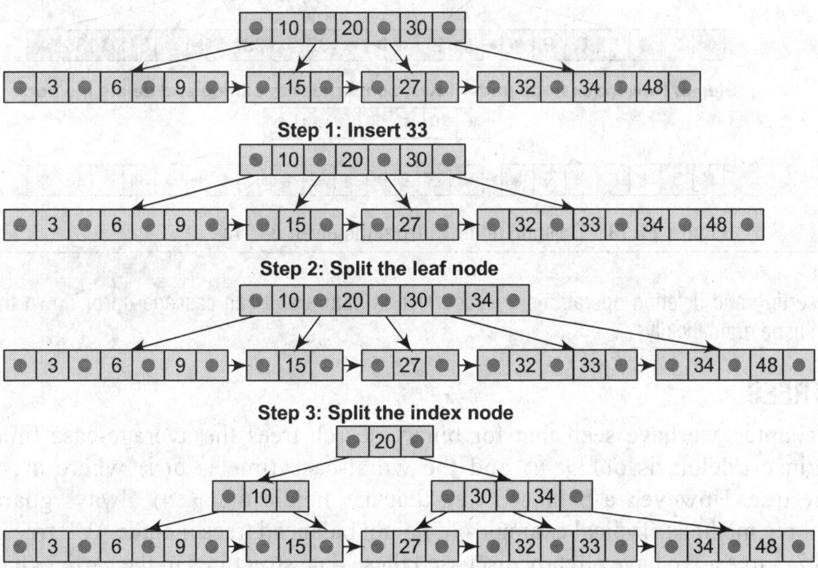

Figure 11.11 Inserting node 33 in the given B+ Tree

11.3.2 Deleting an Element from a B+ Tree

As in B trees, deletion is always done from a leaf node. If deleting a data element leaves that node empty, then the neighbouring nodes are examined and merged with the *underfull* node.

This process calls for the deletion of an index value from the parent index node which, in turn, may cause it to become empty. Similar to the insertion process, deletion may cause a merge-delete wave to run from a leaf node all the way up to the root. This leads to shrinking of the tree by one level.

The steps to delete a node from a B+ tree are summarized in Fig. 11.12.

Step 1: Delete the key and data from the leaves.
Step 2: If the leaf node underflows, merge that node with the sibling and delete the key in between them.
Step 3: If the index node underflows, merge that node with the sibling and move down the key in between them.

Figure 11.12 Algorithm for deleting a node from a B+ Tree

Example 11.6 Consider the B+ tree of order 4 given below and delete node 15 from it.

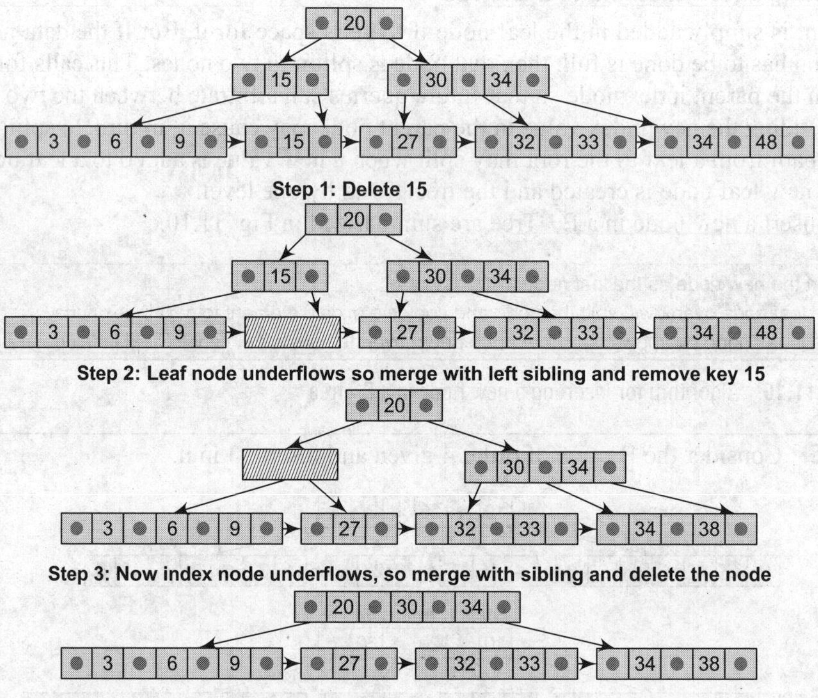

Figure 11.13 Deleting node 15 from the given B+ Tree

Note Insertion and deletion operations are recursive in nature and can cascade up or down the B+tree, thereby affecting its shape dramatically.

11.4 2-3 TREES

In the last chapter, we have seen that for binary search trees the average-case time for operations like search/insert/delete is `O(log N)` and the worst-case time is `O(N)` where `N` is the number of nodes in the tree. However, a balanced tree that has height `O(log N)` always guarantees `O(log N)` time for all three methods. Typical examples of height balanced trees include AVL trees, red-black trees, B trees, and 2-3 trees. We have already discussed these data structures in the earlier chapter and section; now we will discuss 2-3 trees.

In a 2-3 tree, each interior node has either two or three children.

- Nodes with two children are called 2-nodes. The 2-nodes have one data value and two children
- Nodes with three children are called 3-nodes. The 3-nodes have two data values and three children (left child, middle child, and a right child)

This means that a 2-3 tree is not a binary tree. In this tree, all the leaf nodes are at the same level (bottom level). Look at Fig. 11.14 which shows a 2-3 tree.

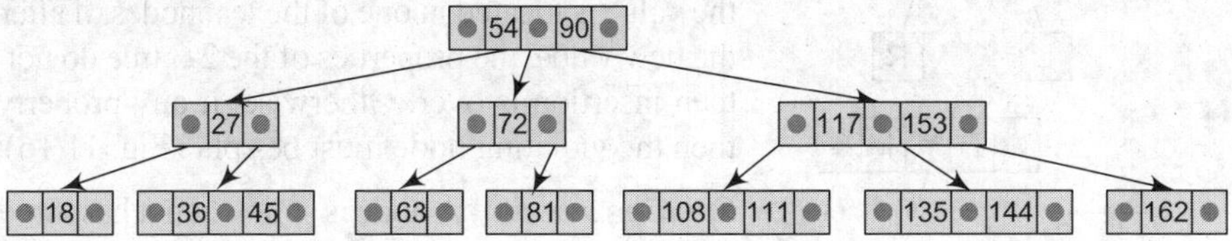

Figure 11.14 2-3 Tree

11.4.1 Searching for an Element in a 2-3 Tree

The search operation is used to determine whether a data value x is present in a 2-3 tree T. The process of searching a value in a 2-3 tree is very similar to searching a value in a binary search tree.

The search for a data value x starts at the root. If k_1 and k_2 are the two values stored in the root node, then

- if $x < k_1$, move to the left child.
- if $x \geq k_1$ and the node has only two children, move to the right child.
- if $x \geq k_1$ and the node has three children, then move to the middle child if $x < k_2$ else to the right child if $x \geq k_2$.

At the end of the process, the node with data value x is reached if and only if x is at this leaf.

Example 11.7 Consider the 2-3 tree in Fig. 11.14 and search 63 in the tree.

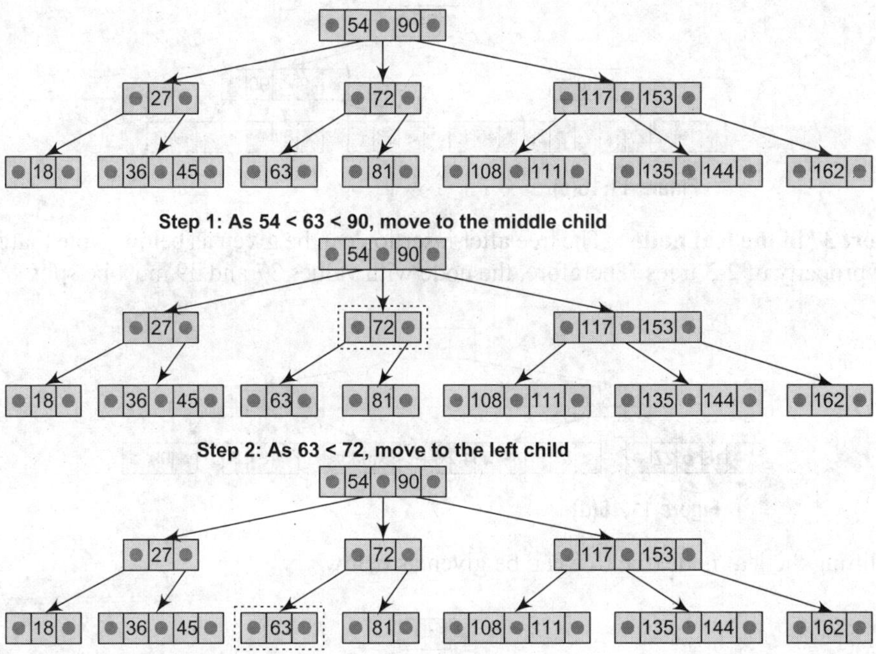

Figure 11.15 Searching for element 63 in the 2-3 tree of Fig. 11.14

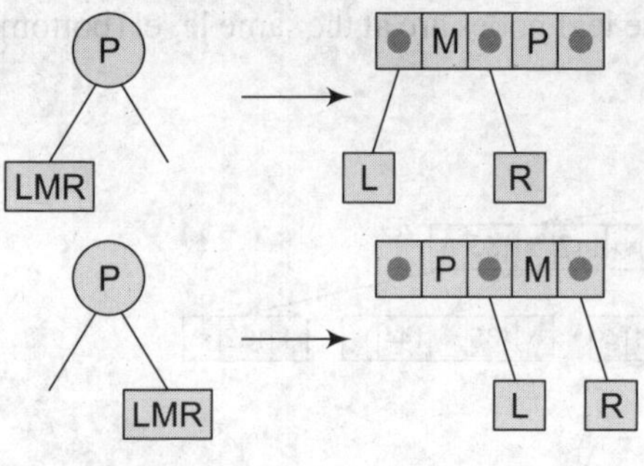

Figure 11.16(a)

11.4.2 Inserting a New Element in a 2-3 Tree

To insert a new value in the 2-3 tree, an appropriate position of the value is located in one of the leaf nodes. If after insertion of the new value, the properties of the 2-3 tree do not get violated then insertion is over. Otherwise, if any property is violated then the violating node must be split (Fig. 11.16).

Splitting a node A node is split when it has three data values and four children. Here, P is the parent and L, M, R denote the left, middle, and right children.

Example 11.8 Consider the 2-3 tree given below and insert the following data values into it: 39, 37, 42, 47.

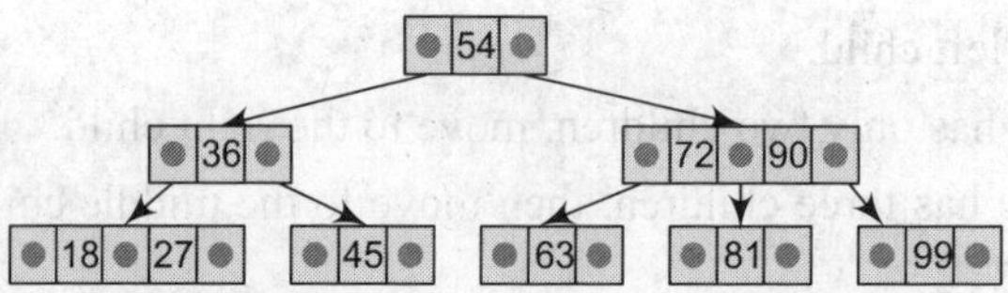

Figure 11.16(b)

Step 1: Insert 39 in the leaf node The tree after insertion can be given as

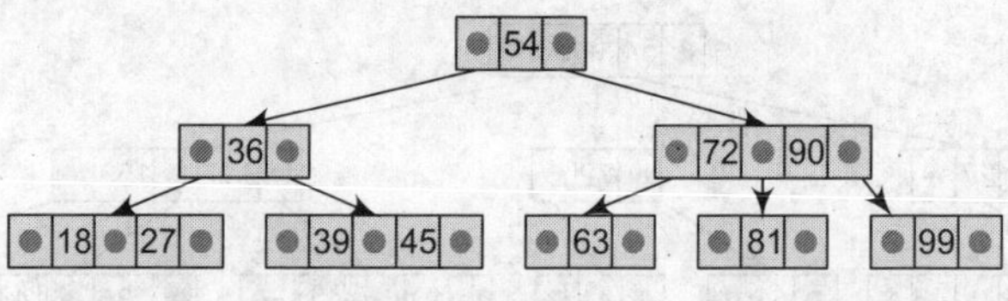

Figure 11.16(c)

Step 2: Insert 37 in the leaf node The tree after insertion can be given as below. Note that inserting 37 violates the property of 2-3 trees. Therefore, the node with values 37 and 39 must be split.

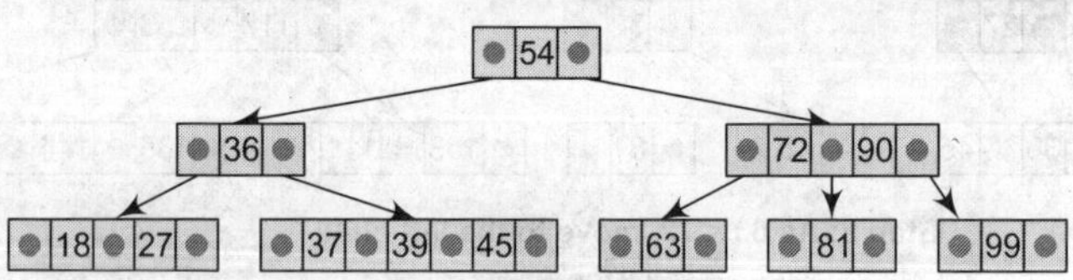

Figure 11.16(d)

After splitting the leaf node, the tree can be given as below.

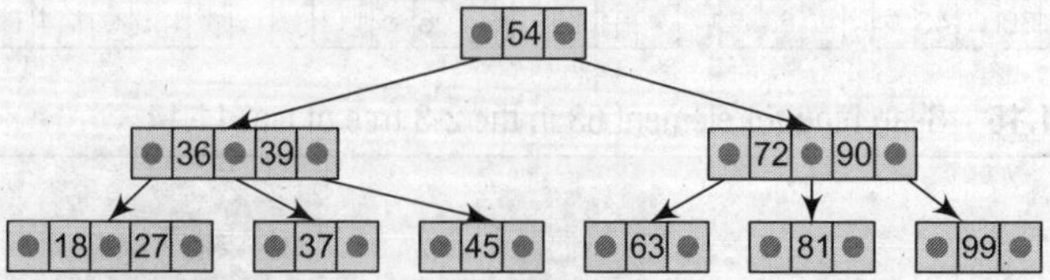

Figure 11.16(e)

Step 3: Insert 42 in the leaf node The tree after insertion can be given as follows.

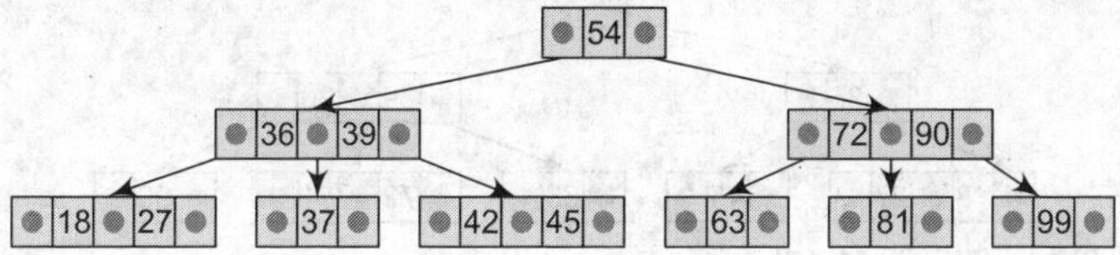

Figure 11.16(f)

Step 4: Insert 47 in the leaf node The tree after insertion can be given as follows.

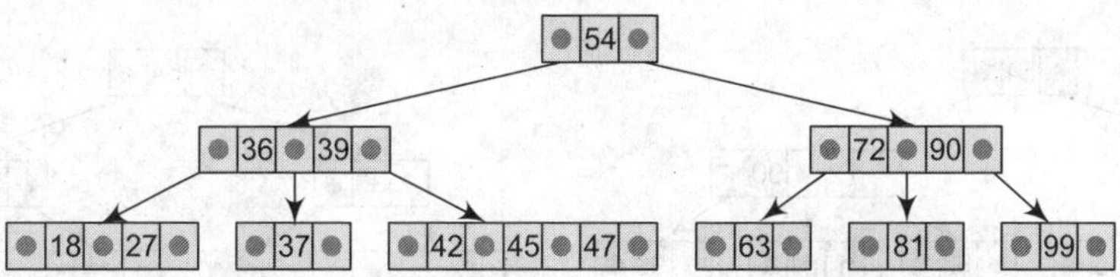

Figure 11.16(g)

The leaf node has three data values. Therefore, the node is violating the properties of the tree and must be split.

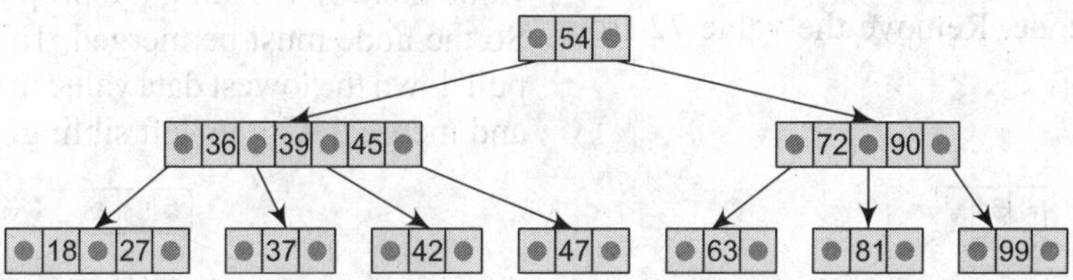

Figure 11.16(h)

The parent node has three data values. Therefore, the node is violating the properties of the tree and must be split.

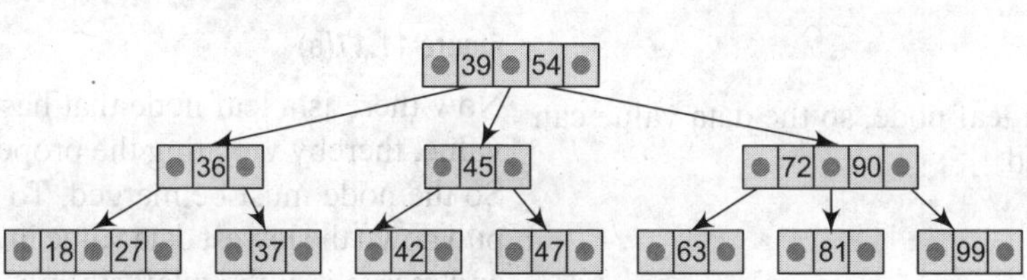

Figure 11.16(i) Inserting values in the given 2-3 Tree

11.4.3 Deleting an Element from a 2-3 Tree

In the deletion process, a specified data value is deleted from the 2-3 tree. If deleting a value from a node violates the property of a tree, that is, if a node is left with less than one data value then two nodes must be merged together to preserve the general properties of a 2-3 tree.

In insertion, the new value had to be added in any of the leaf nodes but in deletion it is not necessary that the value has to be deleted from a leaf node. The value can be deleted from any of the nodes. To delete a value `x`, it is replaced by its in-order successor and then removed. If a node becomes empty after deleting a value, it is then merged with another node to restore the property of the tree.

Example 11.9 Consider the 2-3 tree given below and delete the following values from it: 69, 72, 99, 81.

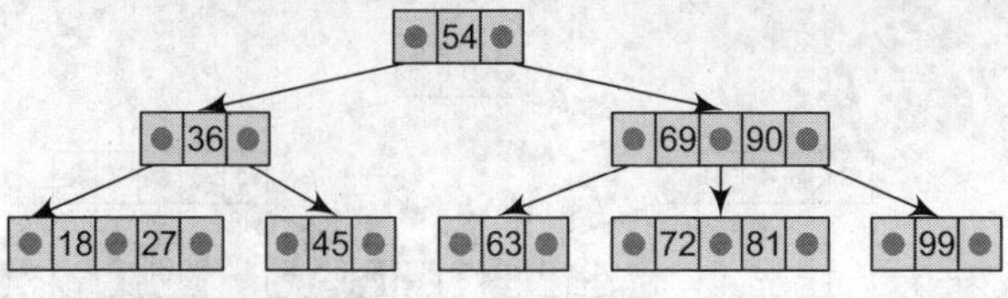

Figure 11.17(a)

To delete 69, swap it with its in-order successor, that is, 72. 69 now comes in the leaf node. Remove the value 69 from the leaf node.

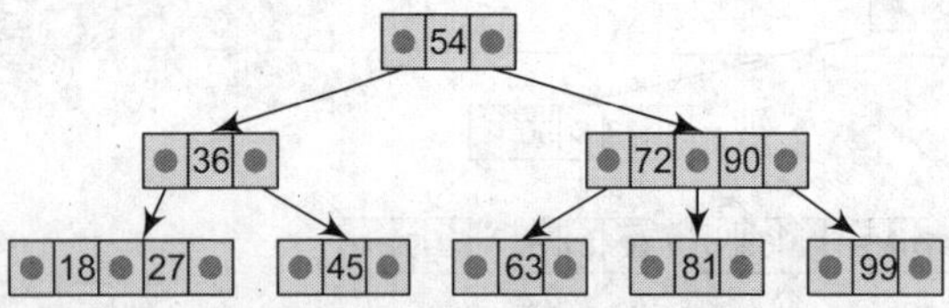

Figure 11.17(b)

72 is an internal node. To delete this value swap 72 with its in-order successor 81 so that 72 now becomes a leaf node. Remove the value 72 from the leaf node.

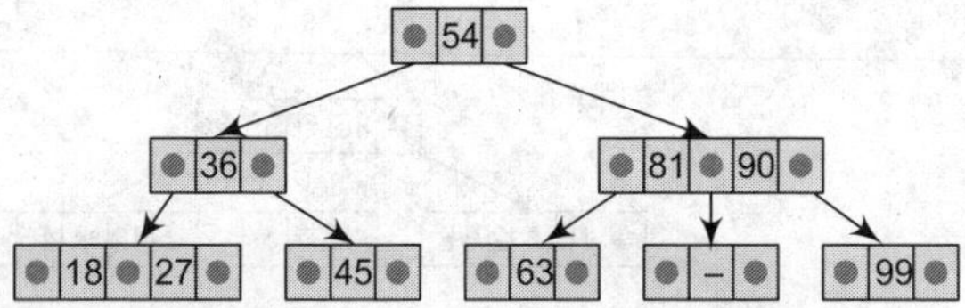

Figure 11.17(c)

Now there is a leaf node that has less than 1 data value thereby violating the property of a 2-3 tree. So the node must be merged. To merge the node, pull down the lowest data value in the parent's node and merge it with its left sibling.

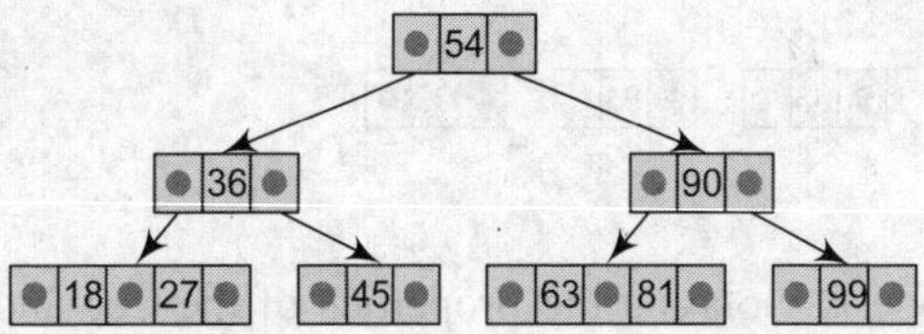

Figure 11.17(d)

99 is present in a leaf node, so the data value can be easily removed.

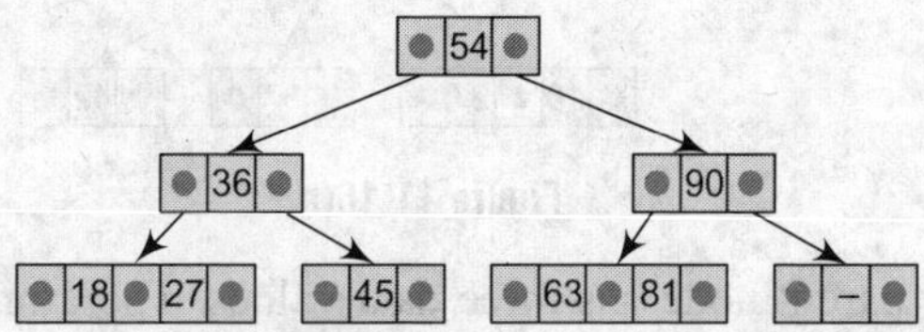

Figure 11.17(e)

Now there is a leaf node that has less than 1 data value, thereby violating the property of a 2-3 tree. So the node must be merged. To merge the node, pull down the lowest data value in the parent's node and merge it with its left sibling.

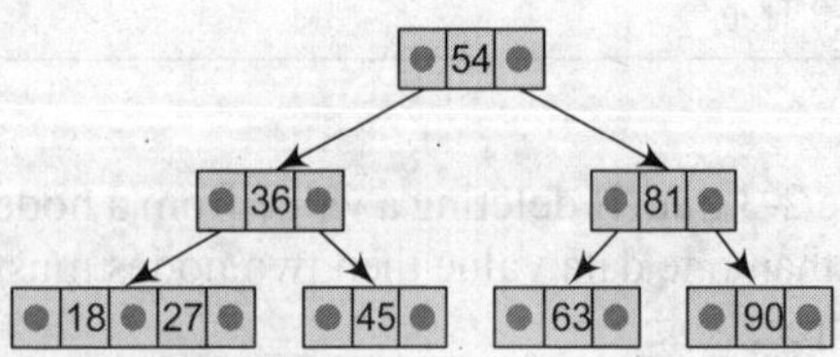

Figure 11.17(f)

81 is an internal node. To delete this value swap 81 with its in-order successor 90 so that 81 now becomes a leaf node. Remove the value 81 from the leaf node.

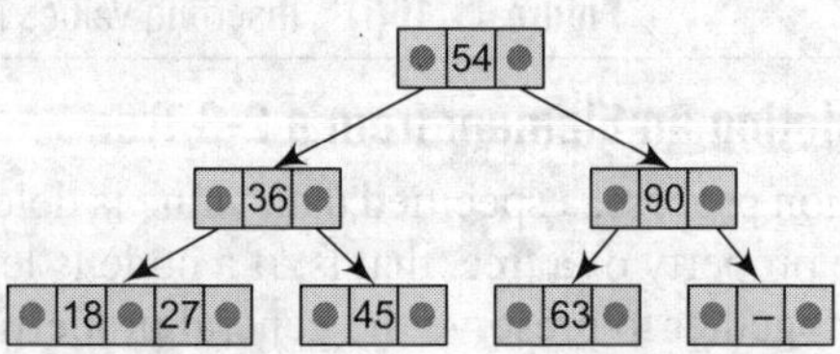

Figure 11.17(g)

Now there is a leaf node that has less than 1 data value, thereby violating the property of a 2-3 tree. So the node must be merged. To merge the node, pull down the lowest data value in the parent's node and merge it with its left sibling.

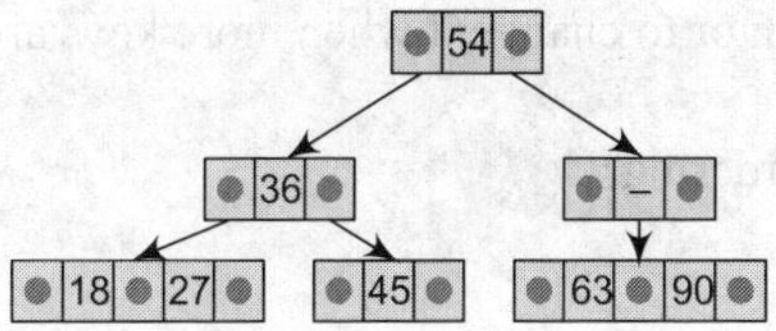

Figure 11.17(h)

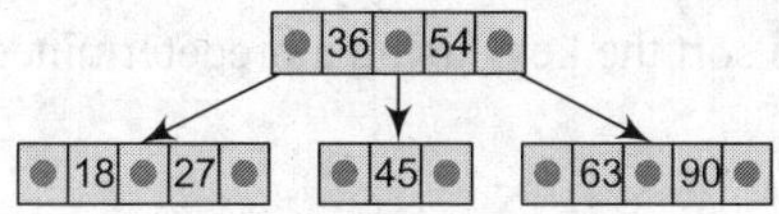

Figure 11.17(i) Deleting values from the given 2-3 tree

An internal node cannot be empty, so now pull down the lowest data value from the parent's node and merge the empty node with its left sibling.

11.5 TRIE

The term *trie* has been taken from the word 'retrieval'. A trie is an ordered tree data structure, which was introduced in the 1960s by Edward Fredkin. Trie stores keys that are usually strings. It is basically a *k-ary* position tree.

In contrast to binary search trees, nodes in a trie do not store the keys associated with them. Rather, a node's position in the tree represents the key associated with that node. All the descendants of a node have a common prefix of the string associated with that node, and the root is associated with the empty string. Figure 11.18 shows a trie.

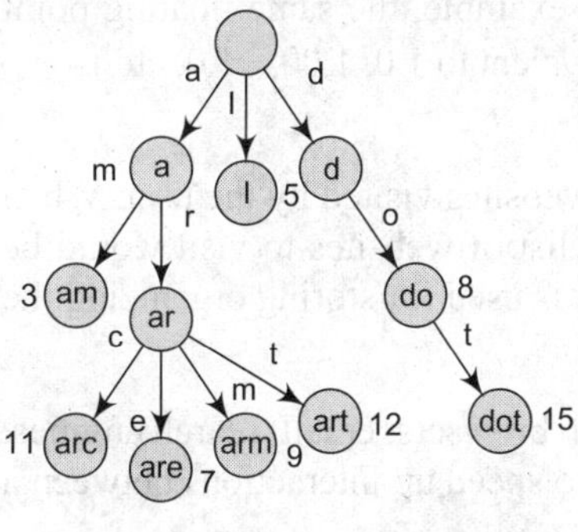

Figure 11.18 Trie data structure

In the given tree, keys are listed in the nodes and the values below them. Note that each complete English word is assigned an arbitrary integer value. We can find each of these words by traversing the various branches in the tree until a leaf node is encountered. Any path from the root to a leaf represents a word.

Advantages Relative to Binary Search Tree

When compared with a binary search tree, the trie data structure has the following advantages.

Faster search Searching for keys is faster, as searching a key of length `m` takes `O(m)` time in the worst case. On the other hand, a binary search tree performs `O(logn)` comparisons of keys, where `n` is the number of nodes in the tree. Since search time depends on the height of the tree which is logarithmic in the number of keys (if the tree is balanced), the worst case may take `O(m log n)` time. In addition to this, `m` approaches `log(n)` in the worst case. Hence, a trie data structure provides a faster search mechanism.

Less space Trie occupies less space, especially when it contains a large number of short strings. Since keys are not stored explicitly and nodes are shared between the keys with common initial subsequences, a trie calls for less space as compared to a binary search tree.

Longest prefix-matching Trie facilitates the longest-prefix matching which enables us to find the key sharing the longest possible prefix of all unique characters. Since trie provides more advantages, it can be thought of as a good replacement for binary search trees.

Advantages Relative to Hash Table

Trie can also be used to replace a *hash table* as it provides the following advantages:

- Searching for data in a trie is faster in the worst case, `O(m)` time, compared to an imperfect hash table, discussed in Chapter 15, which may have numerous key collisions. Trie is free from collision of keys problem.

- Unlike a hash table, there is no need to choose a hash function or to change it when more keys are added to a trie.
- A trie can sort the keys using a predetermined alphabetical ordering.

Disadvantages

The disadvantages of having a trie are listed below:

- In some cases, tries can be slower than hash tables while searching data. This is true in cases when the data is directly accessed on a hard disk drive or some other secondary storage device that has high random access time as compared to the main memory.
- All the key values cannot be easily represented as strings. For example, the same floating point number can be represented as a string in multiple ways (1 is equivalent to 1.0, 1.00, +1.0, etc.).

Applications of Trie Data Structure

Browser History: Every web browser keeps a track of the history of websites visited by the user. When the prefix of a previously visited URL is typed in the address bar, a list of websites to visit would be suggested to the user. To provide the suggested list, trie data structure is used for storing organizing the number of visits to a website.

AutoComplete: The Auto Complete feature is extensively used by web browsers, email, search engines, code editors, command-line interpreters (CLI), and word processors to speed up interactions between a user and the application and give a great user experience.

Trie provides alphabetical ordering of data by keys and is the fastest data structure to give auto-complete suggestions. Even in the worst case, it is O(n) (where n is the string length) times faster than the hashing techniques and eliminates issues related to key collisions.

Thus, trie provides a simple way to find an alternative word to complete the word by providing an alphabetical filter of entries by the key of the node. Pointers are then traced to get the node that represents the string entered by the user.

Auto-complete functionality is widely used on text editors, mobile applications, and the Internet. It provides a simple way to find an alternative word to complete the word for the following reasons.

- It provides an alphabetical filter of entries by the key of the node.
- We trace pointers only to get the node that represents the string entered by the user.
- As soon as you start typing, it tries to complete your input.

Spell Checkers/ Auto-correct: It is a 3-step process that includes,

- Checking for the word in the data dictionary.
- Generating potential suggestions.
- Sorting the suggestions with higher priority on top.

Trie data structure stores the data dictionary and supports quick and easy searching of words from that dictionary. It then provides the list of valid/ relevant words for the suggestion.

Longest Prefix Matching Algorithm: Also known as Maximum Prefix Length Match, the algorithm is used in IP networking by the routing devices. To optimize network route, trie data structure is used to speed up the lookup process. Multiple Bit trie schemes are now used to speed up the performance of lookups of multiple bits.

Disadvantages of Trie Data Structure

- It takes more memory to store all the strings. For each node, there are too many node pointers which in the worst case may be equal to the number of characters.
- An efficiently constructed hash table performs lookup operation in O(1) time which is better than that of trie that has O(l) time complexity where l is the length of the string.

Applications of Trie Data Structure

Tries are commonly used to store a dictionary (for example, on a mobile telephone). These applications take advantage of a trie's ability to quickly search, insert, and delete the entries. Tries are also used to implement approximate matching algorithms, including those used in spell-checking software.

Points to Remember

- An M-way search tree has `M - 1` values per node and `M` sub-trees. In such a tree, `M` is called the degree of the tree. M-way search tree consists of pointers to `M` sub-trees and contains `M - 1` keys, where `M > 2`.
- A B tree of order `m` can have a maximum of `m-1` keys and `m` pointers to its sub-trees. A B tree may contain a large number of key values and pointers to its sub-trees.
- A B+ tree is a variant of B tree which stores sorted data in a way that allows for efficient insertion, retrieval, and removal of records, each of which is identified by a key. B+ tree record data at the leaf level of the tree; only keys are stored in interior nodes.
- A trie is an ordered tree data structure which stores keys that are usually strings. It is basically a k-ary position tree.
- In contrast to binary search trees, nodes in a trie do not store the keys associated with them. Rather, a node's position in the tree represents the key associated with that node.
- In a 2-3 tree, each interior node has either two or three children. This means that a 2-3 tree is not a binary tree.

Exercises

Review Questions

1. Why is a large value of `m` needed in a B tree?
2. Compare B trees with B+ trees.
3. In what conditions will you prefer a B+ tree over a B tree?
4. Write a short note on trie data structure.
5. Compare binary search trees with trie. Also, list the merits and demerits of using the trie data structure.
6. Compare hash tables with trie.
7. Give a brief summary of M-way search trees.
8. Consider the B tree given below
   (a) Insert 1, 5, 7, 11, 13, 15, 17, and 19 in the tree.
   (b) Delete 30, 59, and 67 from the tree.
9. Write an essay on B+ trees.
10. Create a B+ tree of order 5 for the following data arriving in sequence:
    90, 27, 7, 9, 18, 21, 3, 4, 16, 11, 21, 72

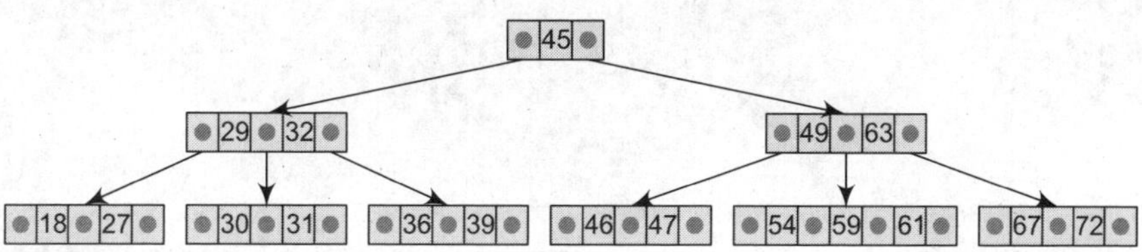

(B tree for Q.8)

11. List down the applications of B trees.
12. B trees of order 2 are full binary trees. Justify this statement.
13. Consider the 3-way search tree given below. Insert 23, 45, 67, 87, 54, 32, and 11 in the tree. Then, delete 9, 36, and 54 from it.

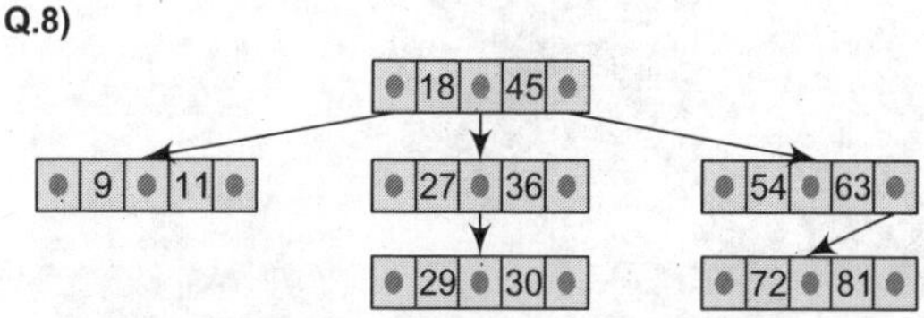

(3-way search tree for Q.13)

Multiple-choice Questions

1. Every internal node of an M-way search tree consists of pointers to M sub-trees and contains how many keys?
   (a) M (b) M–1
   (c) 2 (d) M+1
2. Every node in a B tree has at most ______ children.
   (a) M (b) M–1
   (c) 2 (d) M+1
3. Which data structure is commonly used to store a dictionary?
   (a) Binary Tree (b) Splay tree
   (c) Trie (d) Red black tree
4. In M-way search tree, M stands for
   (a) Internal nodes (b) External nodes
   (c) Degree of node (d) Leaf nodes
5. In best case, searching a value in a binary search tree may take
   (a) O(n) (b) O(n log n)
   (c) O(log n) (d) O(n^2)

True or False

1. All leaf nodes in the B tree are at the same level.
2. A B+ tree stores data only in the i-nodes.
3. B tree stores unsorted data.
4. Every node in the B-tree has at most (maximum) m–1 children.
5. The leaf nodes of a B tree are often linked to one another.
6. B+ tree stores redundant search key.
7. A trie is an ordered tree data structure.
8. A trie uses more space as compared to a binary search tree.
9. External nodes are called index nodes.

Fill in the Blanks

1. An M-way search tree consists of pointers to ______ sub-trees and contains ______ keys.
2. A B-tree of order ______ can have a maximum of ______ keys and m pointers to its sub-trees.
3. Every node in the B-tree except the root node and leaf nodes have at least ______ children.
4. In ______ data is stored in internal or leaf nodes.
5. A balanced tree that has height O(log N) always guarantees ______ time for all three methods.

CHAPTER 12

Heaps

LEARNING OBJECTIVE

A heap is a specialized tree-based data structure. There are several variants of heaps which are the prototypical implementations of priority queues. We have already discussed priority queues in Chapter 8. Heaps are also crucial in several efficient graph algorithms. In this chapter, we will discuss three types of heaps—binary heaps, binomial heaps, and Fibonacci heaps.

12.1 BINARY HEAPS

A binary heap is a complete binary tree in which every node satisfies the heap property which states that:

```
If B is a child of A, then key(A) ≥ key(B)
```

This implies that elements at every node will be either greater than or equal to the element at its left and right child. Thus, the root node has the highest key value in the heap. Such a heap is commonly known as a *max-heap*.

Alternatively, elements at every node will be either less than or equal to the element at its left and right child. Thus, the root has the lowest key value. Such a heap is called a *min-heap*.

Figure 12.1 shows a binary min heap and a binary max heap. The properties of binary heaps are given as follows:

- Since a heap is defined as a complete binary tree, all its elements can be stored sequentially in an array. It follows the same rules as that of a complete binary tree. That is, if an element is at position `i` in the array, then its left child is stored at position `2i` and its right child at position `2i+1`. Conversely, an element at position `i` has its parent stored at position `i/2`.
- Being a complete binary tree, all the levels of the tree except the last level are completely filled.
- The height of a binary tree is given as $\log_2 n$, where `n` is the number of elements.
- Heaps (also known as partially ordered trees) are a very popular data structure for implementing priority queues.

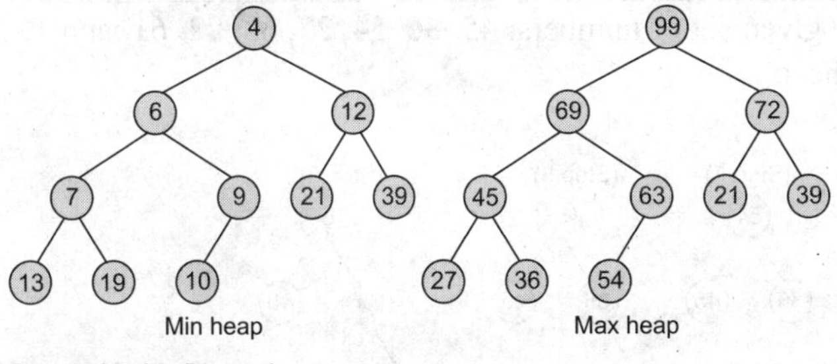

Figure 12.1 Binary heaps

A binary heap is a useful data structure in which elements can be added randomly but only the element with the highest value is removed in case of max heap and lowest value in case of min heap. A binary tree is an efficient data structure, but a binary heap is more space efficient and simpler.

12.1.1 Inserting a New Element in a Binary Heap

Consider a max heap H with n elements. Inserting a new value into the heap is done in the following two steps:

1. Add the new value at the bottom of H in such a way that H is still a complete binary tree but not necessarily a heap.
2. Let the new value rise to its appropriate place in H so that H now becomes a heap as well.

To do this, compare the new value with its parent to check if they are in the correct order. If they are, then the procedure halts, else the new value and its parent's value are swapped and Step 2 is repeated.

Example 12.1 Consider the max heap given in Fig. 12.2 and insert 99 in it.

Solution

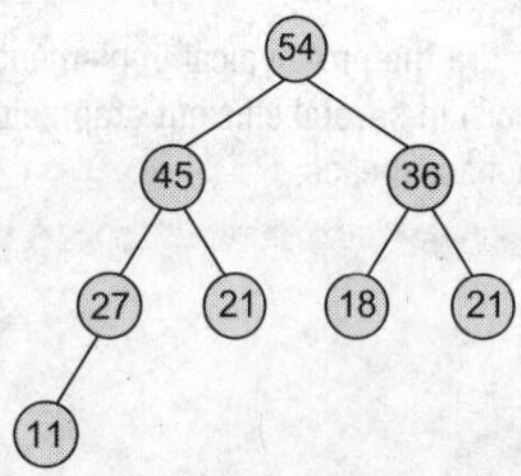

Figure 12.2 Binary heap

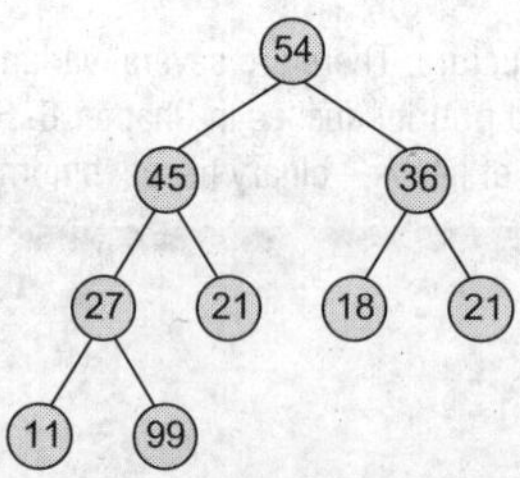

Figure 12.3 Binary heap after insertion of 99

The first step says that insert the element in the heap so that the heap is a complete binary tree. So, insert the new value as the right child of node 27 in the heap. This is illustrated in Fig. 12.3.

Now, as per the second step, let the new value rise to its appropriate place in H so that H becomes a heap as well. Compare 99 with its parent node value. If it is less than its parent's value, then the new node is in its appropriate place and H is a heap. If the new value is greater than that of its parent's node, then swap the two values. Repeat the whole process until H becomes a heap. This is illustrated in Fig. 12.4.

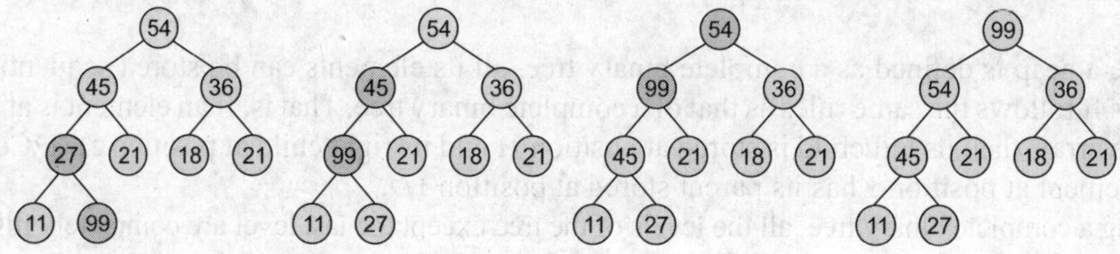

Figure 12.4 Heapify the binary heap

Example 12.2 Build a max heap H from the given set of numbers: 45, 36, 54, 27, 63, 72, 61, and 18. Also draw the memory representation of the heap.

Solution

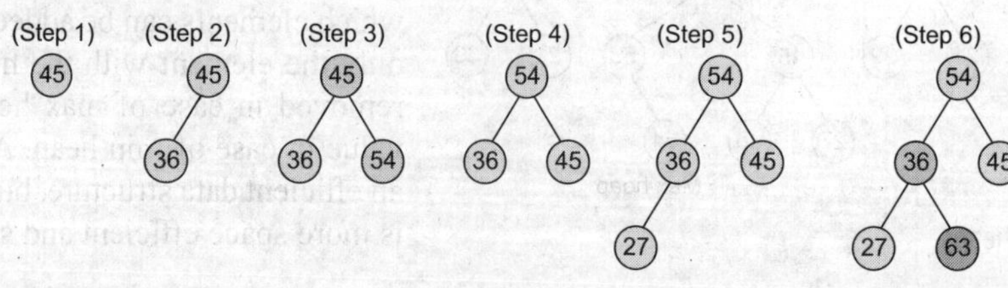

(Contd)

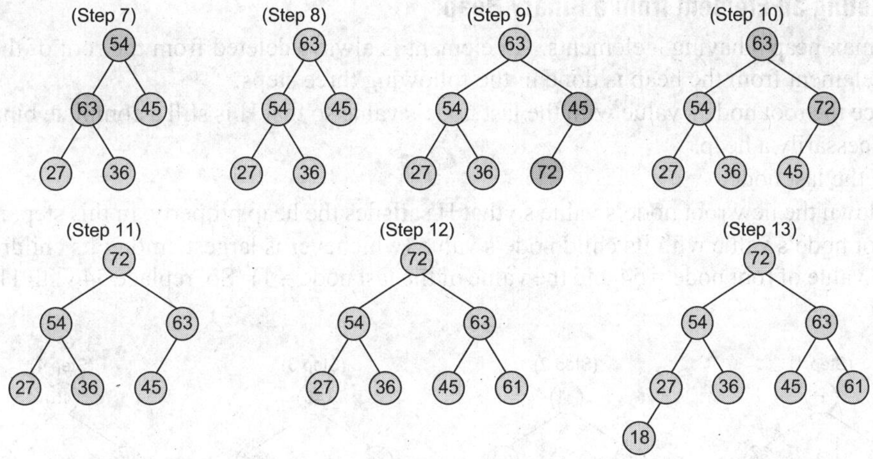

Figure 12.5 (Contd)

The memory representation of H can be given as shown in Fig. 12.6.

HEAP[1]	HEAP[2]	HEAP[3]	HEAP[4]	HEAP[5]	HEAP[6]	HEAP[7]	HEAP[8]	HEAP[9]	HEAP[10]
72	54	63	27	36	45	61	18		

Figure 12.6 Memory representation of binary heap H

```
Step 1: [Add the new value and set its POS]
        SET N = N + 1, POS = N
Step 2: SET HEAP[N] = VAL
Step 3: [Find appropriate location of VAL]
        Repeat Steps 4 and 5 while POS > 1
Step 4:     SET PAR = POS/2
Step 5:     IF HEAP[POS] <= HEAP[PAR],
            then Goto Step 6.
            ELSE
                  SWAP HEAP[POS], HEAP[PAR]
                  POS = PAR
            [END OF IF]
      [END OF LOOP]
Step 6: RETURN
```

Figure 12.7 Algorithm to insert an element in a max heap

After discussing the concept behind inserting a new value in the heap, let us now look at the algorithm to do so as shown in Fig. 12.7. We assume that H with n elements is stored in array HEAP. VAL has to be inserted in HEAP. The location of VAL as it rises in the heap is given by POS, and PAR denotes the location of the parent of VAL.

Note that this algorithm inserts a single value in the heap. In order to build a heap, use this algorithm in a loop. For example, to build a heap with 9 elements, use a `for` loop that executes 9 times and in each pass, a single value is inserted.

The complexity of this algorithm in the average case is `O(1)`. This is because a binary heap has `O(log n)` height. Since approximately 50% of the elements are leaves and 75% are in the bottom two levels, the new element to be inserted will only move a few levels upwards to maintain the heap.

In the worst case, insertion of a single value may take `O(log n)` time and, similarly, to build a heap of n elements, the algorithm will execute in `O(n log n)` time.

Example 12.3 Consider the max heap H shown in Fig. 12.8 and delete the root node's value.

Solution

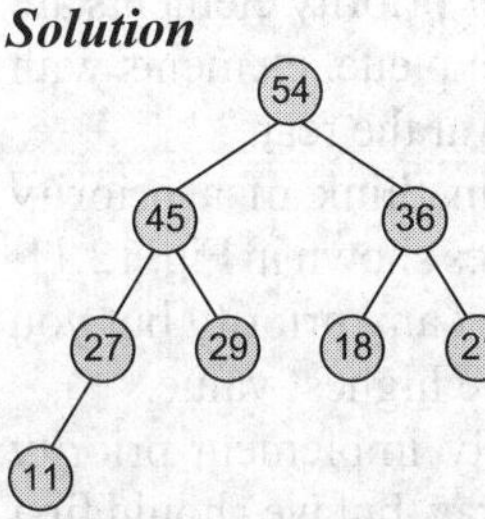

Figure 12.8 Binary heap

12.1.2 Deleting an Element from a Binary Heap

Consider a max heap H having n elements. An element is always deleted from the root of the heap. So, deleting an element from the heap is done in the following three steps:

1. Replace the root node's value with the last node's value so that H is still a complete binary tree but not necessarily a heap.
2. Delete the last node.
3. Sink down the new root node's value so that H satisfies the heap property. In this step, interchange the root node's value with its child node's value (whichever is largest among its children).

Here, the value of root node = 54 and the value of the last node = 11. So, replace 54 with 11 and delete the last node.

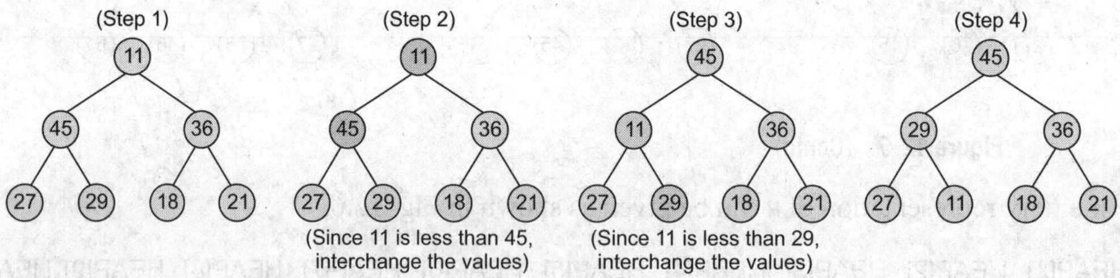

Figure 12.9 Binary heap

After discussing the concept behind deleting the root element from the heap, let us look at the algorithm given in Fig. 12.10. We assume that heap H with n elements is stored using a sequential array called HEAP. LAST is the last element in the heap and PTR, LEFT, and RIGHT denote the position of LAST and its left and right children respectively as it moves down the heap.

12.1.3 Applications of Binary Heaps

Binary heaps are mainly applied for

1. Sorting an array using heapsort algorithm. We will discuss heapsort algorithm in Chapter 14.
2. Implementing priority queues.

```
Step 1: [Remove the last node from the heap]
        SET LAST = HEAP[N], SET N = N - 1
Step 2: [Initialization]
        SET PTR = 1, LEFT = 2, RIGHT = 3
Step 3: SET HEAP[PTR] = LAST
Step 4: Repeat Steps 5 to 7 while LEFT <= N
Step 5: IF HEAP[PTR] >= HEAP[LEFT] AND
         HEAP[PTR] >= HEAP[RIGHT]
              Go to Step 8
        [END OF IF]
Step 6: IF HEAP[RIGHT] <= HEAP[LEFT]
              SWAP HEAP[PTR], HEAP[LEFT]
              SET PTR = LEFT
        ELSE
              SWAP HEAP[PTR], HEAP[RIGHT]
              SET PTR = RIGHT
        [END OF IF]
Step 7: SET LEFT = 2 * PTR and RIGHT = LEFT + 1
        [END OF LOOP]
Step 8: RETURN
```

Figure 12.10 Algorithm to delete the root element from a max heap

12.1.4 Binary Heap Implementation of Priority Queues

In Chapter 8, we learned about priority queues. We have also seen how priority queues can be implemented using linked lists. A priority queue is similar to a queue in which an item is dequeued (or removed) from the front. However, unlike a regular queue, in a priority queue the logical order of elements is determined by their priority. While the higher priority elements are added at the front of the queue, elements with lower priority are added at the rear.

Conceptually, we can think of a priority queue as a bag of priorities shown in Fig. 12.11. In this bag you can insert any priority but you can take out one with the highest value.

Though we can easily implement priority queues using a linear array, but we should first consider the time required to insert an element

Figure 12.11 Priority queue visualization

in the array and then sort it. We need `O(n)` time to insert an element and at least `O(n log n)` time to sort the array. Therefore, a better way to implement a priority queue is by using a binary heap which allows both enqueue and dequeue of elements in `O(log n)` time.

12.2 BINOMIAL HEAPS

A binomial heap `H` is a set of binomial trees that satisfy the binomial heap properties. First, let us discuss what a binomial tree is.

A *binomial tree* is an ordered tree that can be recursively defined as follows:

- A binomial tree of order 0 has a single node.
- A binomial tree of order `i` has a root node whose children are the root nodes of binomial trees of order `i-1`, `i-2`, . . ., `2`, `1`, and `0`.
- A binomial tree B_i has 2^i nodes.
- The height of a binomial tree B_i is `i`.

Look at Fig. 12.12 which shows a few binomial trees of different orders. We can construct a binomial tree B_i from two binomial trees of order B_{i-1} by linking them together in such a way that the root of one is the leftmost child of the root of another.

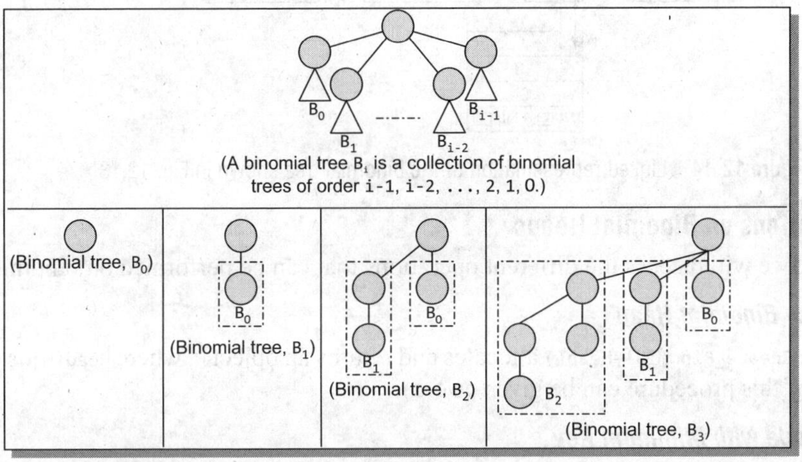

Figure 12.12 Binomial trees

A *binomial heap* `H` is a collection of binomial trees that satisfy the following properties:

- Every binomial tree in `H` satisfies the minimum heap property (i.e., the key of a node is either greater than or equal to the key of its parent).
- There can be one or zero binomial trees for each order including zero order.

According to the first property, the root of a heap-ordered tree contains the smallest key in the tree. The second property, on the other hand, implies that a binomial heap `H` having `N` nodes contains at most `log (N + 1)` binomial trees.

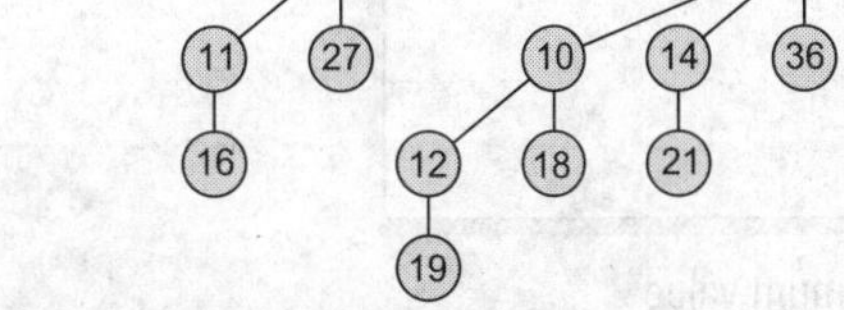

Figure 12.13 Binomial heap

12.2.1 Linked Representation of Binomial Heaps

Each node in a binomial heap `H` has a `val` field that stores its value. In addition, each node `N` has following pointers:

- `P[N]` that points to the parent of `N`

- `Child[N]` that points to the leftmost child
- `Sibling[N]` that points to the sibling of `N` which is immediately to its right

If `N` is the root node, then `P[N] = NULL`. If `N` has no children, then `Child[N] = NULL`, and if `N` is the rightmost child of its parent, then `Sibling[N] = NIL`.

In addition to this, every node `N` has a degree field which stores the number of children of `N`. Look at the binomial heap shown in Fig. 12.13. Figure 12.14 shows its corresponding linked representation.

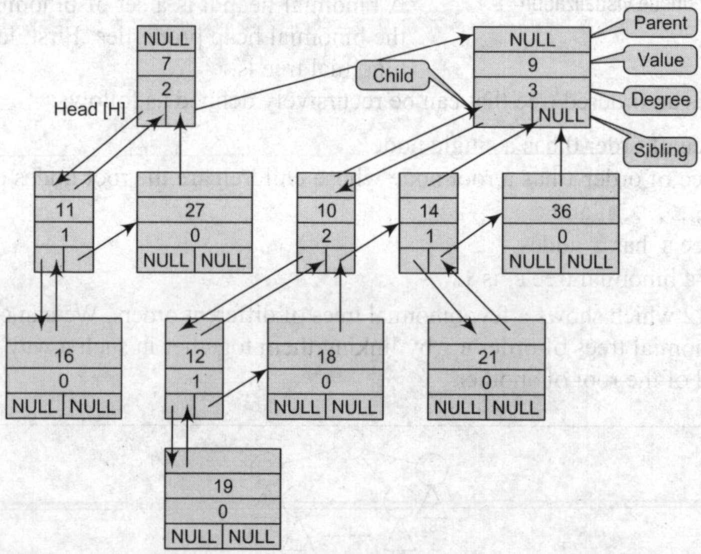

Figure 12.14 Linked representation of the binomial tree shown in Fig. 12.13

12.2.2 Operations on Binomial Heaps

In this section, we will discuss the different operations that can be performed on binomial heaps.

Creating a New Binomial Heap

The procedure `Create_Binomial-Heap()` allocates and returns an object `H`, where `Head[H]` is set to `NULL`. The running time of this procedure can be given as `O(1)`.

Finding the Node with Minimum Key

The procedure `Min_Binomial-Heap()` returns a pointer to the node which has the minimum value in the binomial heap `H`. The algorithm for `Min_Binomial-Heap()` is shown in Fig. 12.15.

```
Min_Binomial-Heap(H)

Step 1: [INITIALIZATION] SET Y = NULL, X = Head[H] and Min = ∞
Step 2: REPEAT Steps 3 and 4 While X ≠ NULL
Step 3:         IF Val[X] < Min
                    SET Min = Val[X]
                    SET Y = X
                [END OF IF]
Step 4:         SET X = Sibling[X]
            [END OF LOOP]
Step 5: RETURN Y
```

Figure 12.15 Algorithm to find the node with minimum value

We have already discussed that a binomial heap is heap-ordered; therefore, the node with the minimum value in a particular binomial tree will appear as a root node in the binomial heap. Thus, the `Min_ Binomial-Heap()` procedure checks all roots. Since there are at most `log (n + 1)` roots to check, the running time of this procedure is `O(log n)`.

Example 12.4 Consider the binomial heap given below and see how the procedure works in this case.

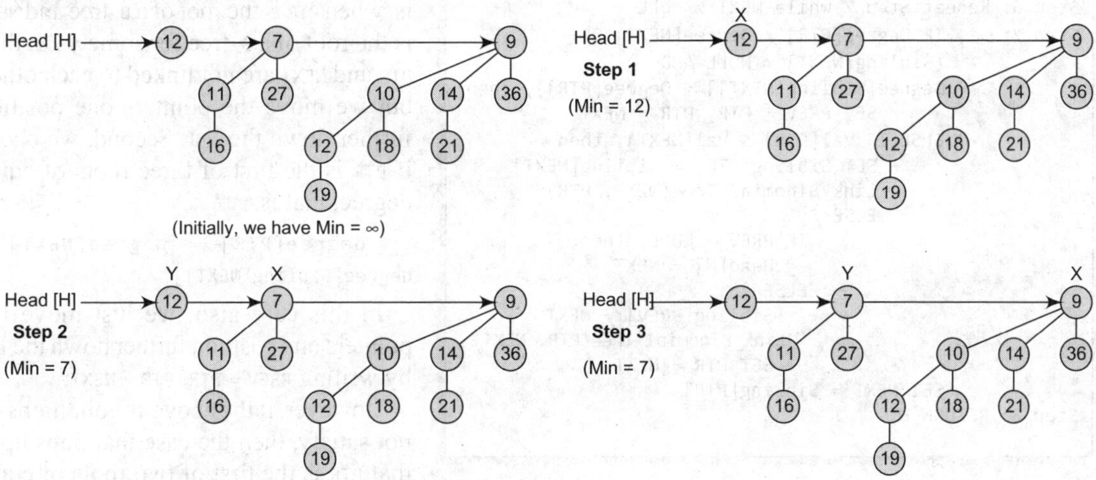

Figure 12.16 Binomial heap

```
Link_Binomial-Tree(Y, Z)

Step 1: SET Parent[Y] = Z
Step 2: SET Sibling[Y] = Child[Z]
Step 3: SET Child[Z] = Y
Step 4: Set Degree[Z] = Degree[Z]+ 1
Step 5: END
```

Figure 12.17 Algorithm to link two binomial trees

Uniting Two Binomial Heaps

The procedure of uniting two binomial heaps is used as a subroutine by other operations. The `Union_Binomial-Heap()` procedure links together binomial trees whose roots have the same degree. The algorithm to link B_{i-1} tree rooted at node `Y` to the B_{i-1} tree rooted at node `Z`, making `Z` the parent of `Y`, is shown in Fig. 12.17.

The `Link_Binomial-Tree()` procedure makes `Y` the new head of the linked list of node `Z`'s children in `O(1)` time.

The algorithm to unite two binomial heaps H_1 and H_2 is given in Fig. 12.18.

The algorithm destroys the original representations of heaps H_1 and H_2. Apart from `Link_Binomial-Tree()`, it uses another procedure `Merge_Binomial-Heap()` which is used to merge the root lists of H_1 and H_2 into a single linked list that is sorted by degree into a monotonically increasing order.

In the algorithm, Steps 1 to 3 merge the root lists of binomial heaps H_1 and H_2 into a single root list `H` in such a way that H_1 and H_2 are sorted strictly by increasing degree. `Merge_Binomial-Heap()` returns a root list `H` that is sorted by monotonically increasing degree. If there are `m` roots in the root lists of H_1 and H_2, then `Merge_Binomial-Heap()` runs in `O(m)` time. This procedure repeatedly examines the roots at the heads of the two root lists and appends the root with the lower degree to the output root list, while removing it from its input root list.

Step 4 of the algorithm checks if there is at least one root in the heap `H`. The algorithm proceeds only if `H` has at least one root. In Step 5, we initialize three pointers: `PTR` which points to the root that is currently being examined, `PREV` which points to the root preceding `PTR` on the root list, and `NEXT` which points to the root following `PTR` on the root list.

```
Union_Binomial-Heap(H1, H2)

Step 1: SET H = Create_Binomial-Heap()
Step 2: SET Head[H] = Merge_Binomial-Heap(H1, H2)
Step 3: Free the memory occupied by H1 and H2
Step 4: IF Head[H] = NULL, then RETURN H
Step 5: SET PREV = NULL, PTR = Head[H] and NEXT =
        Sibling[PTR]
Step 6: Repeat Step 7 while NEXT ≠ NULL
Step 7:       IF Degree[PTR] ≠ Degree[NEXT] OR
              (Sibling[NEXT] ≠ NULL AND
              Degree[Sibling[NEXT]] = Degree[PTR]), then
                    SET PREV = PTR, PTR = NEXT
              ELSE IF Val[PTR] ≤ Val[NEXT], then
                    SET Sibling[PTR] = Sibling[NEXT]
                    Link_Binomial-Tree(NEXT, PTR)
                    ELSE
                          IF PREV = NULL, then
                             Head[H] = NEXT
                          ELSE
                             Sibling[PREV] = NEXT
                            Link_Binomial-Tree(PTR, NEXT)
                             SET PTR = NEXT
              SET NEXT = Sibling[PTR]
Step 8: RETURN H
```

Figure 12.18 Algorithm to unite two binomial heaps

In Step 6, we have a `while` loop in which at each iteration, we decide whether to link `PTR` to `NEXT` or `NEXT` to `PTR` depending on their degrees and possibly the degree of `sibling[NEXT]`.

In Step 7, we check for two conditions. First, if `degree[PTR] ≠ degree[NEXT]`, that is, when `PTR` is the root of a B_i tree and `NEXT` is the root of a B_j tree for some `j > i`, then `PTR` and `NEXT` are not linked to each other, but we move the pointers one position further down the list. Second, we check if `PTR` is the first of three roots of equal degree, that is,

`degree[PTR] = degree[NEXT] = degree[Sibling[NEXT]]`

In this case also, we just move the pointers one position further down the list by writing `PREV = PTR, PTR = NEXT`.

However, if the above `IF` conditions do not satisfy, then the case that pops up is that `PTR` is the first of two roots of equal degree, that is,

`degree[PTR] = degree[NEXT] ≠ degree[Sibling[NEXT]]`

In this case, we link either `PTR` with `NEXT` or `NEXT` with `PTR` depending on whichever has the smaller key. Of course, the node with the smaller key will be the root after the two nodes are linked.

The running time of `Union_Binomial-Heap()` can be given as `O(log n)`, where `n` is the total number of nodes in binomial heaps H_1 and H_2. If H_1 contains n_1 nodes and H_2 contains n_2 nodes, then H_1 contains at most $\log(n_1 + 1)$ roots and H_2 contains at most $\log(n_2 + 1)$ roots, so H contains at most $(\log n_2 + \log n_1 + 2) \leq (2 \log n + 2) = O(\log n)$ roots when we call `Merge_Binomial-Heap()`. Since, $n = n_1 + n_2$, the `Merge_Binomial-Heap()` takes `O(log n)` to execute. Each iteration of the `while` loop takes `O(1)` time, and because there are at most $(\log n_1 + \log n_2 + 2)$ iterations, the total time is thus `O(log n)`.

Example 12.5 Unite the binomial heaps given below.

Solution

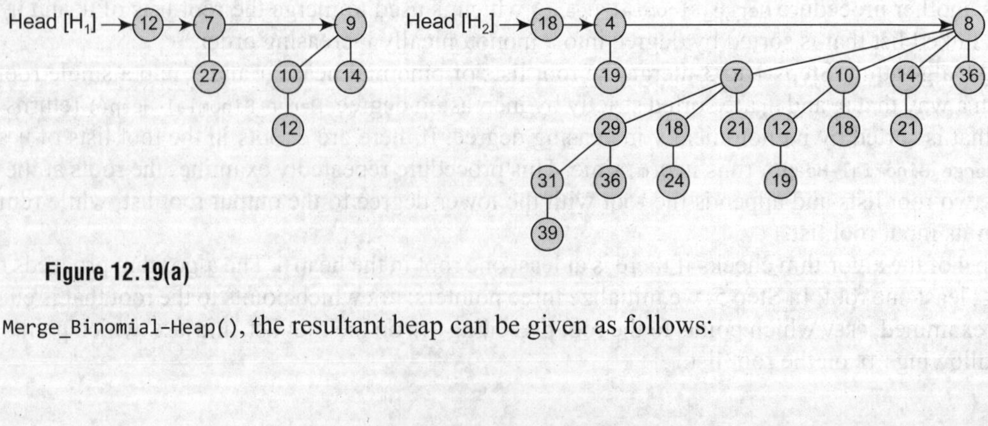

Figure 12.19(a)

After `Merge_Binomial-Heap()`, the resultant heap can be given as follows:

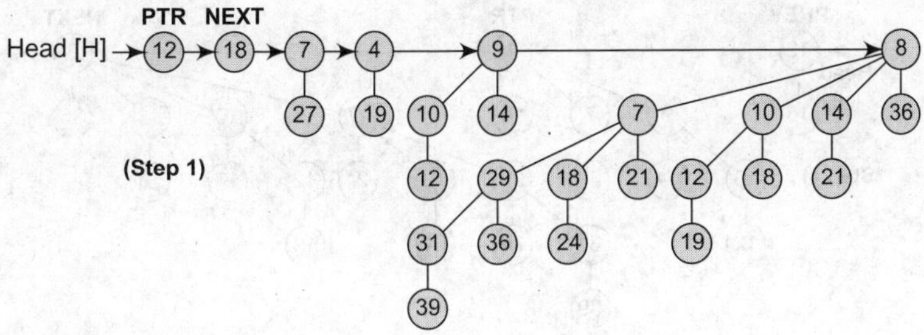

Figure 12.19(b)

Link NEXT to PTR, making PTR the parent of the node pointed by NEXT.

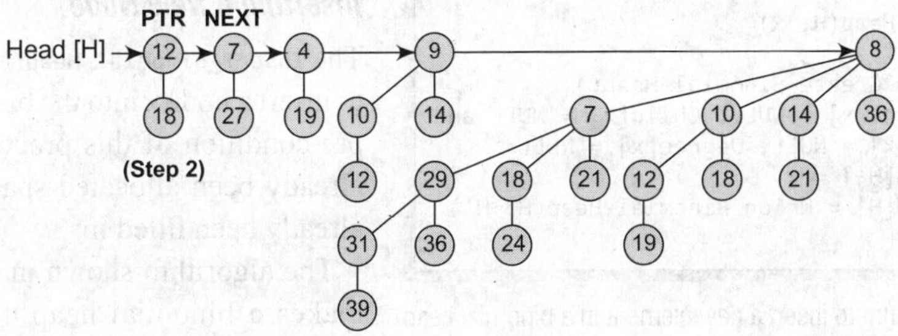

Figure 12.19(c)

Now PTR is the first of the three roots of equal degree, that is, `degree[PTR] = degree[NEXT] = degree[sibling[NEXT]]`. Therefore, move the pointers one position further down the list by writing PREV = PTR, PTR = NEXT, and NEXT = sibling[PTR].

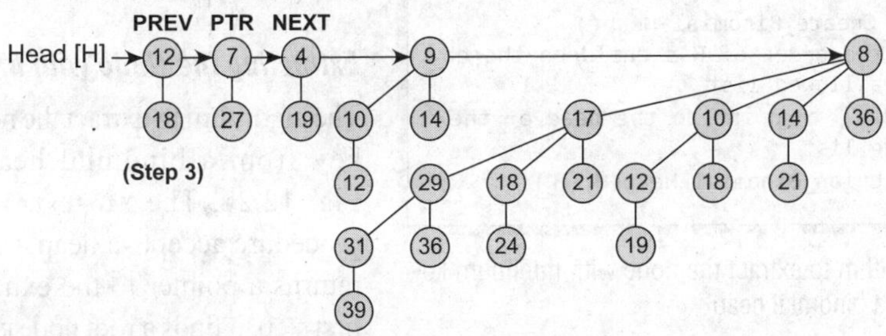

Figure 12.19(d)

Link PTR to NEXT, making NEXT the parent of the node pointed by PTR.

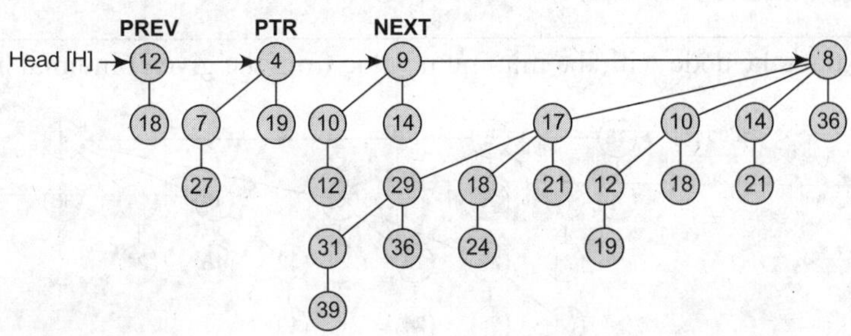

Figure 12.19(e)

Link NEXT to PTR, making PTR the parent of the node pointed by NEXT.

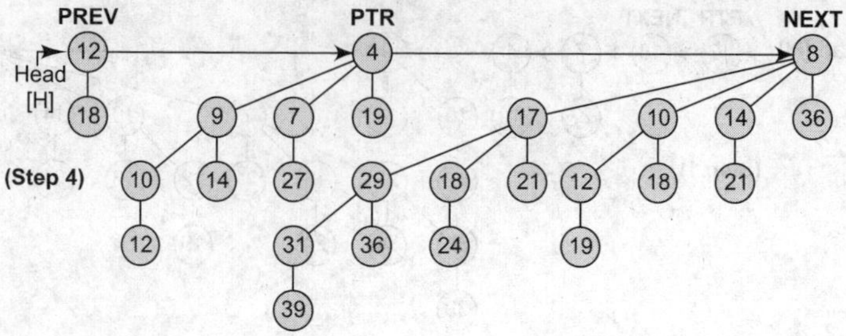

Figure 12.19(f) Binomial heap

```
Insert_Binomial-Heap(H, x)

Step 1: SET H' = Create_Binomial-Heap()
Step 2: SET Parent[x] = NULL, Child[x] = NULL and
        Sibling[x] = NULL, Degree[x] = NULL
Step 3: SET Head[H'] = x
Step 4: SET Head[H] = Union_Binomial-Heap(H, H')
Step 5: END
```

Figure 12.20 Algorithm to insert a new element in a binomial heap

```
Min-Extract_Binomial Heap (H)

Step 1: Find the root R having minimum value in
        the root list of H
Step 2: Remove R from the root list of H
Step 3: SET H′ = Create_Binomial-Heap()
Step 4: Reverse the order of R's children thereby
        forming a linked list
Step 5: Set head[H′] to point to the head of the
        resulting list
Step 6: SET H = Union_Binomial-Heap(H, H′)
```

Figure 12.21 Algorithm to extract the node with minimum key from a binomial heap

Inserting a New Node

The `Insert_Binomial-Heap()` procedure is used to insert a node `x` into the binomial heap `H`. The pre-condition of this procedure is that `x` has already been allocated space and `val[x]` has already been filled in.

The algorithm shown in Fig. 12.20 simply makes a binomial heap `H′` in `O(1)` time. `H′` contains just one node which is `x`. Finally, the algorithm unites `H′` with the `n`-node binomial heap `H` in `O(log n)` time. Note that the memory occupied by `H′` is freed in the `Union_Binomial-Heap(H, H′)` procedure.

Extracting the Node with Minimum Key

The algorithm to extract the node with minimum key from a binomial heap `H` is shown in Fig. 12.21. The `Min-Extract_Binomial-Heap` procedure accepts a heap `H` as a parameter and returns a pointer to the extracted node. In the first step, it finds a root node `R` with the minimum value and removes it from the root list of `H`. Then, the order of `R`'s children is reversed and they are all added to the root list of `H′`. Finally, `Union_Binomial-Heap (H, H′)` is called to unite the two heaps and `R` is returned. The algorithm `Min-Extract_Binomial-Heap()` runs in `O(log n)` time, where `n` is the number of nodes in `H`.

Example 12.6 Extract the node with the minimum value from the given binomial heap.

Solution

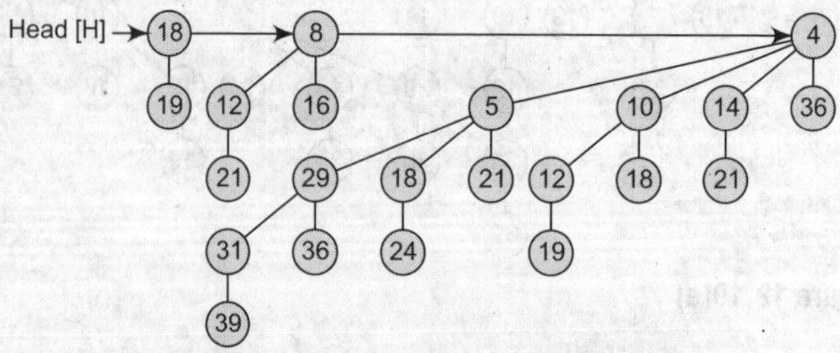

(Contd)

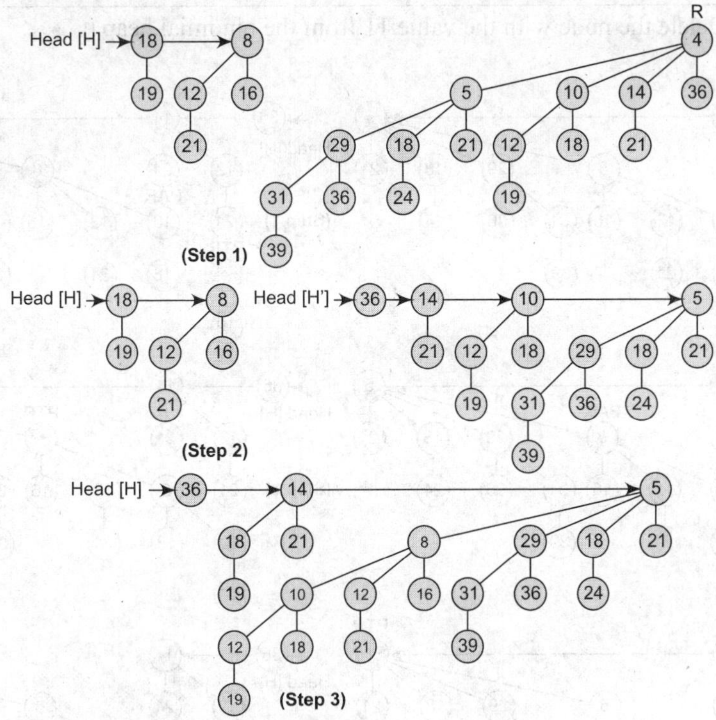

Figure 12.22 (Contd) Binomial heap

```
Binomial-Heap_Decrease_Val(H, x, k)

Step 1: IF Val[x] < k, then Print " ERROR"
Step 2: SET Val[x] = k
Step 3: SET PTR = x and PAR = Parent[PTR]
Step 4: Repeat while PAR ≠ NULL and Val[PTR] < Val[PAR]
Step 5:             SWAP ( Val[PTR], Val[PAR] )
Step 6:             SET PTR = PAR and PAR = Parent [PTR]
        [END OF LOOP]
Step 7: END
```

Figure 12.23 Algorithm to decrease the value of a node x in a binomial heap H

Decreasing the Value of a Node

The algorithm to decrease the value of a node `x` in a binomial heap `H` is given in Fig. 12.23. In the algorithm, the value of the node is overwritten with a new value `k`, which is less than the current value of the node.

In the algorithm, we first ensure that the new value is not greater than the current value and then assign the new value to the node.

We then go up the tree with `PTR` initially pointing to node `x`. In each iteration of the `while` loop, `val[PTR]` is compared with the value of its parent `PAR`. However, if either `PTR` is the root or `key[PTR]` ≥ `key[PAR]`, then the binomial tree is heap-ordered. Otherwise, node `PTR` violates heap-ordering, so its key is exchanged with that of its parent. We set `PTR = PAR` and `PAR = Parent[PTR]` to move up one level in the tree and continue the process.

```
Binomial-Heap_Delete-Node(H, x)

Step 1: Binomial-Heap_Decrease_Val(H, x, -∞)
Step 2: Min-Extract_Binomial-Heap(H)
Step 3: END
```

Figure 12.24 Algorithm to delete a node from a bionomial heap

The `Binomial-Heap_Decrease_Val` procedure takes `O(log n)` time as the maximum depth of node `x` is `log n`, so the `while` loop will iterate at most `log n` times.

Example 12.7 Delete the node with the value 11 from the binomial heap H.

Solution

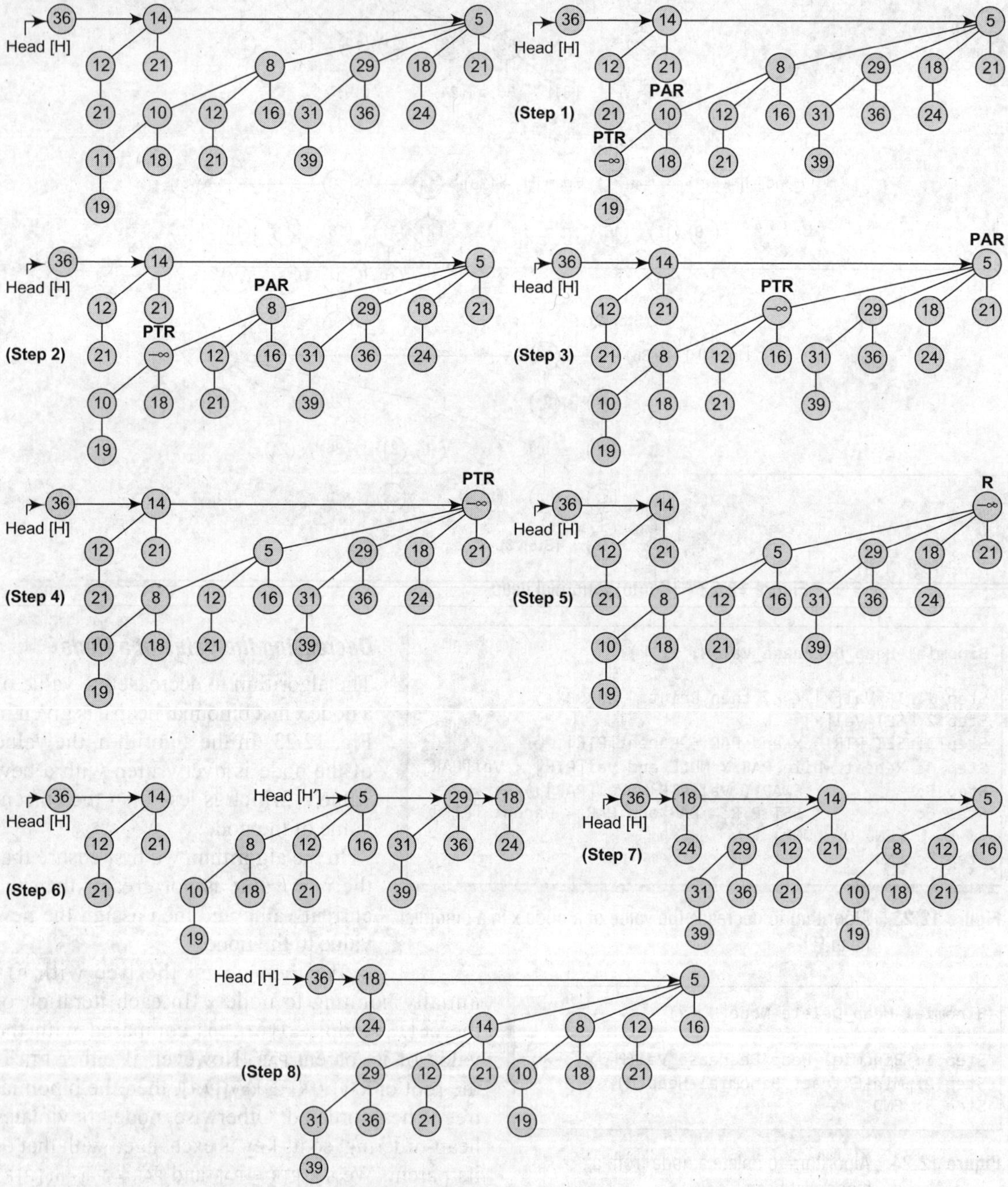

Figure 12.25 Binomial heap

Deleting a Node

Once we have understood the `Binomial-Heap_Decrease_Val` procedure, it becomes easy to delete a node x's value from the binomial heap H in `O(log n)` time. To start with the algorithm, we set the value of x to – ∞. Assuming that there is no node in the heap that has a value less than – ∞, the algorithm to delete a node from a binomial heap can be given as shown in Fig. 12.24.

The `Binomial-Heap_Delete-Node` procedure sets the value of x to – ∞, which is a unique minimum value in the entire binomial heap. The `Binomial-Heap_Decrease_Val` algorithm bubbles this key upto a root and then this root is removed from the heap by making a call to the `Min-Extract_Binomial-Heap` procedure. The `Binomial-Heap_Delete-Node` procedure takes `O(log n)` time.

12.3 FIBONACCI HEAPS

In the last section, we have seen that binomial heaps support operations such as insert, extract-minimum, decrease-value, delete, and union in `O(log n)` worst-case time. In this section, we will discuss Fibonacci heaps which support the same operations but have the advantage that operations that do not involve deleting an element run in `O(1)` amortized time. So, theoretically, Fibonacci heaps are especially desirable when the number of extract-minimum and delete operations is small relative to the number of other operations performed. This situation arises in many applications, where algorithms for graph problems may call the decrease-value once per edge. However, the programming complexity of Fibonacci heaps makes them less desirable to use.

A Fibonacci heap is a collection of trees. It is loosely based on binomial heaps. If neither the decrease-value nor the delete operation is performed, each tree in the heap is like a binomial tree. Fibonacci heaps differ from binomial heaps as they have a more relaxed structure, allowing improved asymptotic time bounds.

12.3.1 Structure of Fibonacci Heaps

Although a Fibonacci heap is a collection of heap-ordered trees, the trees in a Fibonacci heap are not constrained to be binomial trees. That is, while the trees in a binomial heap are ordered, those within Fibonacci heaps are rooted but unordered.

Look at the Fibonacci heap given in Fig. 12.26. The figure shows that each node in the Fibonacci heap contains the following pointers:

- a pointer to its parent, and
- a pointer to any one of its children.

Note that the children of each node are linked together in a circular doubly linked list which is known as the child list of that node. Each child x in a child list contains pointers to its left and right siblings. If node x is the only child of its parent, then `left[x] = right[x] = x` (refer Fig. 12.25).

Circular doubly linked lists provide an added advantage, as they allow a node to be removed in `O(1)` time. Also, given two circular doubly linked lists, the lists can be concatenated to form one list in `O(1)` time.

Apart from this information, every node will store two other fields. First, the number of children in the child list of node x is stored in `degree[x]`. Second, a boolean value `mark[x]` indicates whether node x has lost a child since the last time x was made the child of another node. Of course, the newly created nodes are unmarked. Also, when the node x is made the child of another node, it becomes unmarked.

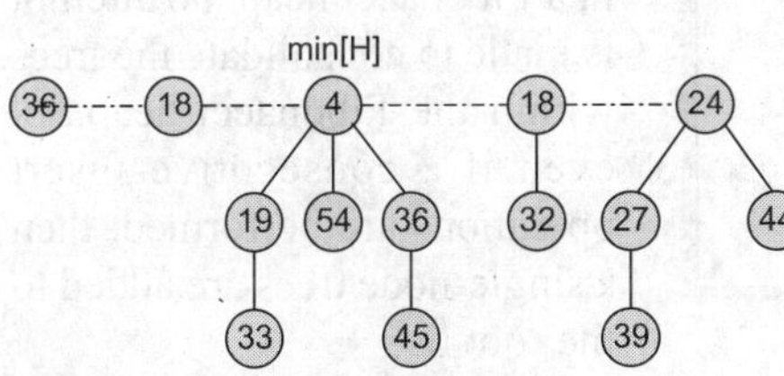

Figure 12.26 Fibonacci heap

Fibonacci heap H is generally accessed by a pointer called `min[H]` which points to the root that has a minimum value. If the Fibonacci heap H is empty, then `min[H] = NULL`.

As seen in Fig. 12.27, roots of all the trees in a Fibonacci heap are linked together using their left and right pointers into a circular doubly linked list called the *root list* of the Fibonacci heap. Also note that the order of the trees within a root list is arbitrary.

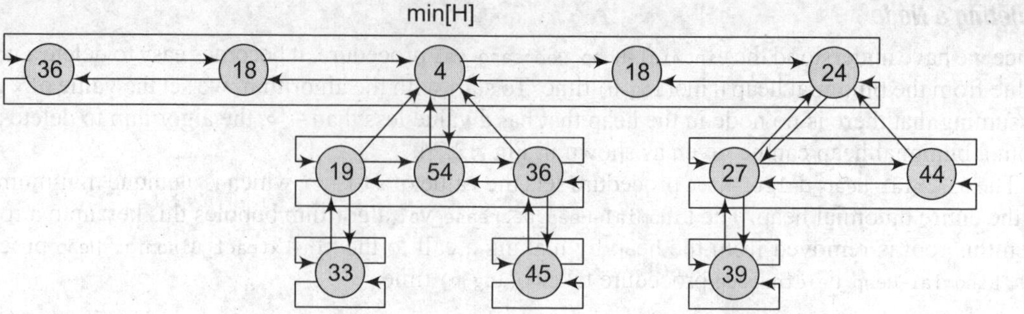

Figure 12.27 Linked representation of the Fibonacci heap shown in Fig. 12.24

In a Fibonacci heap `H`, the number of nodes in `H` is stored in `n[H]` and the degree of nodes is stored in `D(n)`.

12.3.2 Operations on Fibonacci Heaps

In this section, we will discuss the operations that can be implemented on Fibonacci heaps. If we perform operations such as create-heap, insert, find extract-minimum, and union, then each Fibonacci heap is simply a collection of unordered binomial trees. An *unordered binomial tree* U_0 consists of a single node, and an unordered binomial tree U_i consists of two unordered binomial trees U_{i-1} for which the root of one is made into a child of the root of another. All the properties of a binomial tree also hold for unordered binomial trees but for an unordered binomial tree U_i, the root has degree `i`, which is greater than that of any other node. The children of the root are roots of sub-trees $U_0, U_1, \ldots, U_{i-1}$ in some order. Thus, if an `n`-node Fibonacci heap is a collection of unordered binomial trees, then `D(n) = log n`. The underlying principle of operations on Fibonacci heaps is to delay the work as long as possible.

Creating a New Fibonacci Heap

To create an empty Fibonacci heap, the `Create_Fib-Heap` procedure allocates and returns the Fibonacci heap object `H`, where `n[H] = 0` and `min[H] = NULL`. The amortized cost of `Create_Fib-Heap` is equal to `O(1)`.

Inserting a New Node

The algorithm to insert a new node in an already existing Fibonacci heap is shown in Fig. 12.28.

In Steps 1 and 2, we first initialize the structural fields of node `x`, making it its own circular doubly linked list. Step 3 adds `x` to the root list of `H` in `O(1)` actual time. Now, `x` becomes an unordered binomial tree in the Fibonacci heap. In Step 4, the pointer to the minimum node of Fibonacci heap `H` is updated. Finally, we increment the number of nodes in `H` to reflect the addition of the new node.

```
Insert_Fib-Heap(H, x)

Step 1: [INITIALIZATION] SET Degree[x] = 0, Parent[x] = NULL,
        Child[x] = NULL, mark[x] = False
Step 2: SET Left[x] = x and Right[x] = x
Step 3: Concatenate the root list containing x with the
        root list of H
Step 4: IF min[H] = NULL OR Val[x] < Val[min[H]], then
            SET min[H] = x
        [END OF IF]
Step 5: SET n[H] = n[H]+ 1
Step 6: END
```

Figure 12.28 Algorithm to insert a new node in a Fibonacci heap

Note that unlike the insert operation in the case of a binomial heap, when we insert a node in a Fibonacci heap, no attempt is made to consolidate the trees within the Fibonacci heap.So, even if `k` consecutive insert operations are performed, then `k` single-node trees are added to the root list.

Example 12.8 Insert node 16 in the Fibonacci heap given below.

Solution

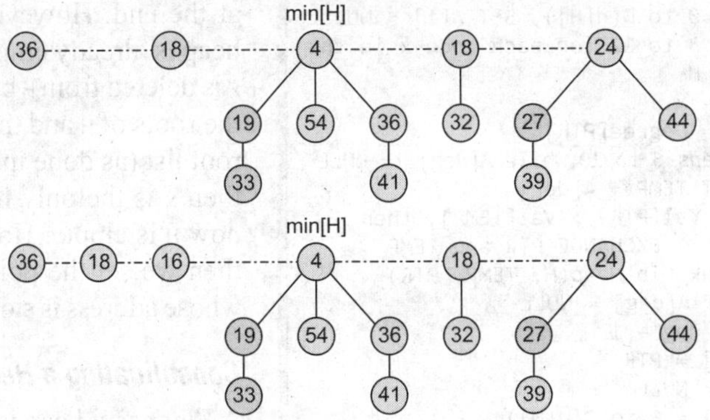

Figure 12.29 Fibonacci heap

```
Union_Fib-Heap(H1, H2)

Step 1: H = Create_Fib-Heap()
Step 2: SET min[H] = min[H1]
Step 3: Concatenate root list of H2 with that of H
Step 4: IF (min[H1] = NULL) OR (min[H2] != NULL
         and min[H2] < min[H1]), then
                     SET min[H] = min[H2]
        [END OF IF]
Step 5: SET n[H] = n[H1] + n[H2]
Step 6: Free H1 and H2
Step 7: RETURN H
```

Figure 12.30 Algorithm to unite two Fibonacci heaps

```
Extract-Min_Fib-Heap(H)

Step 1: SET x = min[H]
Step 2: IF x != NULL, then
           For each child PTR of x
                  Add PTR to the root list of H and
                  Parent[PTR] = NULL
           Remove x from the root list of H
        [END OF IF]
Step 3: IF x = Right[x], then
           SET min[H] = NULL
        ELSE
           SET min[H] = Right[x]
           Consolidate(H)
        [END OF IF]
Step 4: SET n[H] = n[H] - 1
Step 5: RETURN x
```

Figure 12.31 Algorithm to extract the node with minimum key

Finding the Node with Minimum Key

Fibonacci heaps maintain a pointer `min[H]` that points to the root having the minimum value. Therefore, finding the minimum node is a straightforward task that can be performed in just `O(1)` time.

Uniting Two Fibonacci Heaps

The algorithm given in Fig. 12.30 unites two Fibonacci heaps H_1 and H_2.

In the algorithm, we first concatenate the root lists of H_1 and H_2 into a new root list H. Then, the minimum node of H is set and the total number of nodes in H is updated. Finally, the memory occupied by H_1 and H_2 is freed and the resultant heap H is returned.

Extracting the Node with Minimum Key

The process of extracting the node with minimum value from a Fibonacci heap is the most complicated operation of all the operations that we have discussed so far. Till now, we had been delaying the work of consolidating the trees, but in this operation, we will finally implement the consolidation process. The algorithm to extract the node with minimum value is given in Fig. 12.31.

In the `Extract-Min_Fib-Heap` algorithm, we first make a root out of each of the minimum node's children and then remove the minimum node from the root list of H. Finally, the root list of the resultant Fibonacci heap H is consolidated by linking the roots of equal degree until at most one root remains of each degree.

```
Consolidate(H)

Step 1: Repeat for i=0 to D(n[H]), SET A[i] = NULL
Step 2: Repeat Steps 3 to 12 for each node x in the
        root list of H
Step 3:      SET PTR = x
Step 4:      SET deg = Degree[PTR]
Step 5:     Repeat Steps 6 to 10 while A[deg] != NULL
Step 6:             SET TEMP = A[deg]
Step 7:             IF Val[PTR] > Val[TEMP], then
Step 8:                    EXCHANGE PTR and TEMP
Step 9:             Link_Fib-Heap(H, TEMP, PTR)
Step 10:            SET A[deg] = NULL
Step 11:    SET deg = deg + 1
Step 12:    SET A[deg] = PTR
Step 13: SET min[H] = NULL
Step 14: Repeat for i = 0 to D(n(H])
Step 15:      IF A[i] != NULL, then
Step 16:            Add A[i] to the root list of H
Step 17:            IF min[H] = NULL OR Val[A[i]] <
                    Val[min[H]], then
Step 18:      SET min[H] = A[i]
Step 19: END
```

Figure 12.32 Algorithm to consolidate a Fibonacci heap

```
Link_Fib-Heap (H, x, y)

Step 1: Remove node y from the root list of H
Step 2: Make x the parent of y
Step 3: Increment the degree of x
Step 4: SET mark[y] = FALSE
Step 5: END
```

Figure 12.33 Algorithm to link two Fibonacci heaps

Note that in Step 1, we save a pointer `x` to the minimum node; this pointer is returned at the end. However, if `x = NULL`, then the heap is already empty. Otherwise, the node `x` is deleted from `H` by making all its children the roots of `H` and then removing `x` from the root list (as done in Step 2). If `x = right[x]`, then `x` is the only node on the root list, so now `H` is empty. However, if `x != Right[x]`, then we set the pointer `min[H]` to the node whose address is stored in the right field of `x`.

Consolidating a Heap

A Fibonacci heap is consolidated to reduce the number of trees in the heap. While consolidating the root list of `H`, the following steps are repeatedly executed until every root in the root list has a distinct *degree* value.

- Find two roots `x` and `y` in the root list that has the same degree and where `Val[x]` ≤ `Val[y]`.
- Link y to x. That is, remove y from the root list of H and make it a child of x. This operation is actually done in the Link_Fib–Heap procedure. Finally, degree[x] is incremented and the mark on y, if any, is cleared.

In the consolidate algorithm shown in Fig. 12.32, we have used an auxiliary array `A[0...D(n[H])]`, such that if `A[i] = x`, then `x` is currently a node in the root list of `H` and `degree[x]= i`.

In Step 1, we set every entry in the array `A` to `NULL`. When Step 1 is over, we get a tree that is rooted at some node `x`. Initially, the array entry `A[degree[x]]` is set to point to `x`. In the `for` loop, each root node in `H` is examined. In each iteration of the `while` loop, `A[d]` points to some root `TEMP` because `d = degree[PTR] = degree[TEMP]`, so these two nodes must be linked with each other. Of course, the node with the smaller key becomes the parent of the other as a result of the link operation and so if need arises, we exchange the pointers to `PTR` and `TEMP`.

Next, we link `TEMP` to `PTR` using the `Link_Fib-Heap` procedure. The `Link_Fib-Heap` procedure (Fig. 12.33) increments the degree of `x` but leaves the degree of `y` unchanged. Since node `y` is no longer a root, the pointer to it in array `A` is removed in Step 10. Note that the value of degree of `x` is incremented in the `Link_Fib-Heap` procedure, so Step 13 restores the value of `d = degree[x]`. The `while` loop is repeated until `A[d] = NULL`, that is until no other root with the same degree as `x` exists in the root list of `H`.

Example 12.9 Remove the minimum node from the Fibonacci heap given below.

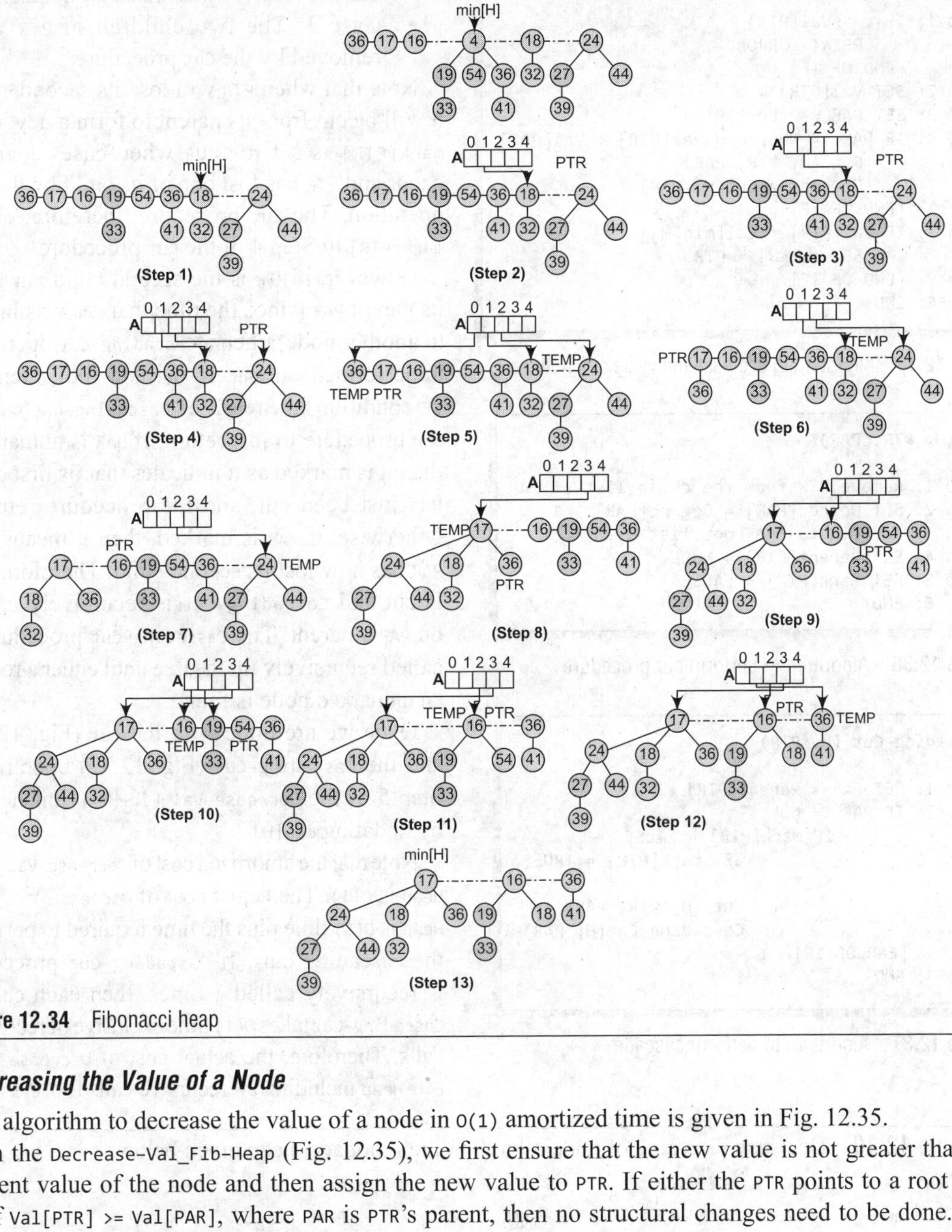

Figure 12.34 Fibonacci heap

Decreasing the Value of a Node

The algorithm to decrease the value of a node in `O(1)` amortized time is given in Fig. 12.35.

In the `Decrease-Val_Fib-Heap` (Fig. 12.35), we first ensure that the new value is not greater than the current value of the node and then assign the new value to `PTR`. If either the `PTR` points to a root node or if `Val[PTR] >= Val[PAR]`, where `PAR` is `PTR`'s parent, then no structural changes need to be done. This condition is checked in Step 4.

However, if the `IF` condition in Step 4 evaluates to a false value, then the heap order has been violated and a series of changes may occur. First, we call the `Cut` procedure to disconnect (or cut) any link between `PTR` and its `PAR`, thereby making `PTR` a root.

If `PTR` is a node that has undergone the following history, then the importance of the `mark` field can be understood as follows:

```
Decrease-Val_Fib-Heap (H, PTR, v)

Step 1: IF v > Val[PTR]
              PRINT "ERROR"
        [END OF IF]
Step 2: SET Val[PTR] = v
Step 3: SET PAR = Parent[PTR]
Step 4: IF PAR != NULL and Val[PTR] < Val[PAR]
              Cut (H, PTR, PAR)
              Cascading-Cut(H, PAR)
        [END OF IF]
Step 5: IF Val[PTR] < Val[min[H]]
              SET min[H] = PTR
        [END OF IF]
Step 6: END
```

Figure 12.35 Algorithm to decrease the value of a node

```
Cut(H, PTR, PAR)

Step 1: Remove PTR from the child list of PAR
Step 2: SET Degree[PAR] = Degree[PAR] - 1
Step 3: Add PTR to the root list of H
Step 4: SET Parent[PTR] = NULL
Step 5: SET Mark[PTR] = FALSE
Step 6: END
```

Figure 12.36 Algorithm to perform cut procedure

```
Cascading-Cut (H, PTR)

Step 1: SET PAR = Parent[PTR]
Step 2: IF PAR != NULL
              IF mark[PTR] = FALSE
                    SET mark[PTR] = TRUE
              ELSE
                    Cut (H, PTR, PAR)
                    Cascading-Cut(H, PAR)
        [END OF IF]
Step 3: END
```

Figure 12.37 Algorithm to perform cascade

- Case 1: `PTR` was a root node.
- Case 2: Then `PTR` was linked to another node.
- Case 3: The two children of `PTR` were removed by the `Cut` procedure.

Note that when `PTR` will lose its second child, it will be cut from its parent to form a new root. `mark[PTR]` is set to `TRUE` when cases 1 and 2 occur and `PTR` has lost one of its child by the `Cut` operation. The `Cut` procedure, therefore, clears `mark[PTR]` in Step 4 of the `Cut` procedure.

However, if `PTR` is the second child cut from its parent `PAR` (since the time that `PAR` was linked to another node), then a `Cascading-Cut` operation is performed on `PAR`. If `PAR` is a root, then the `IF` condition in Step 2 of `Cascading-Cut` causes the procedure to just return. If `PAR` is unmarked, then it is marked as it indicates that its first child has just been cut, and the procedure returns. Otherwise, if `PAR` is marked, then it means that `PAR` has now lost its second child. Therefore, `PTR` is cut and `Cascading-Cut` is recursively called on `PAR`'s parent. The `Cascading-Cut` procedure is called recursively up the tree until either a root or an unmarked node is found.

Once we are done with the `Cut` (Fig. 12.36) and the `Cascading-Cut` (Fig. 12.37) operations, Step 5 of the `Decrease-Val_Fib-Heap` finishes up by updating `min[H]`.

Note that the amortized cost of `Decrease-Val_Fib-Heap` is `O(1)`. The actual cost of `Decrease-Val_Fib-Heap` is `O(1)` time plus the time required to perform the cascading cuts. If `Cascading-Cut` procedure is recursively called `c` times, then each call of `Cascading-Cut` takes `O(1)` time exclusive of recursive calls. Therefore, the actual cost of `Decrease-Val_Fib-Heap` including all recursive calls is `O(c)`.

Example 12.10 Decrease the value of node 39 to 9 in the Fibonacci heap given below.

Solution

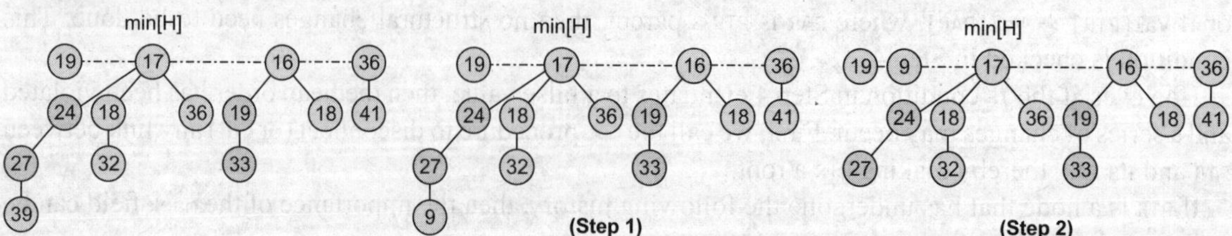

(Contd)

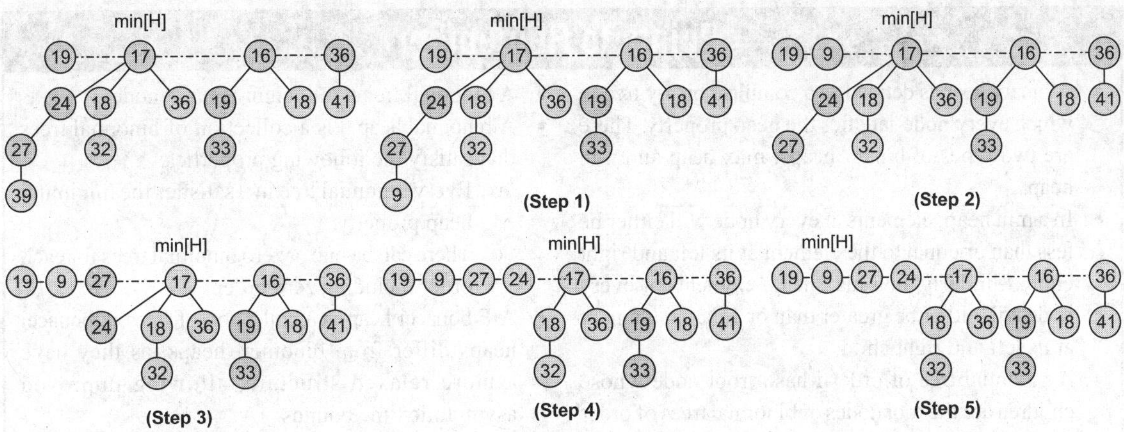

Figure 12.38 (Contd) Fibonacci heap

```
Del_Fib-Heap (H, x)

Step 1: DECREASE-VAL_FIB-HEAP(H, x, -∞)
Step 2: EXTRACT-MIN_FIB-HEAP(H)
Step 3: END
```

Figure 12.39 Algorithm to delete a node from a Fibonacci heap

Deleting a Node

A node from a Fibonacci heap can be very easily deleted in `O(D(n))` amortized time. The procedure to delete a node is given in Fig. 12.39.

`Del_Fib-Heap` assigns a minimum value to `x`. The node `x` is then removed from the Fibonacci heap by making a call to the `Extract-Min_Fib-Heap` procedure. The amortized time of the delete procedure is the sum of the `O(1)` amortized time of `Decrease-Val_Fib-Heap` and the `O(D(n))` amortized time of `Extract-Min_Fib-Heap`.

12.4 COMPARISON OF BINARY, BINOMIAL, AND FIBONACCI HEAPS

Table 12.1 makes a comparison of the operations that are commonly performed on heaps.

Table 12.1 Comparison of binary, binomial, and Fibonacci heaps

Operation	Description	Time complexity in Big O Notation		
		Binary	Binomial	Fibonacci
Create Heap	Creates an empty heap	O(n)	O(n)	O(n)
Find Min	Finds the node with minimum value	O(1)	O(log n)	O(n)
Delete Min	Deletes the node with minimum value	O(log n)	O(log n)	O(log n)
Insert	Inserts a new node in the heap	O(log n)	O(log n)	O(1)
Decrease Value	Decreases the value of a node	O(log n)	O(log n)	O(1)
Union	Unites two heaps into one	O(n)	O(log n)	O(1)

12.5 APPLICATIONS OF HEAPS

Heaps are preferred for applications that include:

- ***Heap sort*** It is one of the best sorting methods that has no quadratic worst-case scenarios. Heap sort algorithm is discussed in Chapter 14.
- ***Selection algorithms*** These algorithms are used to find the minimum and maximum values in linear or sub-linear time.
- ***Graph algorithms*** Heaps can be used as internal traversal data structures. This guarantees that runtime is reduced by an order of polynomial. Heaps are therefore used for implementing Prim's minimal spanning tree algorithm and Dijkstra's shortest path problem.

Points to Remember

- A binary heap is defined as a complete binary tree in which every node satisfies the heap property. There are two types of binary heaps: max heap and min heap.
- In a min heap, elements at every node will either be less than or equal to the element at its left and right child. Similarly, in a max heap, elements at every node will either be greater than or equal to element at its left and right child.
- A binomial tree of order i has a root node whose children are the root nodes of binomial trees of order `i-1, i-2, ..., 2, 1, 0`.
- A binomial tree B_i of height `i` has 2^i nodes.
- A binomial heap `H` is a collection of binomial trees that satisfy the following properties:
  - o Every binomial tree in `H` satisfies the minimum heap property.
  - o There can be one or zero binomial trees for each order including zero order.
- A Fibonacci heap is a collection of trees. Fibonacci heaps differ from binomial heaps, as they have a more relaxed structure, allowing improved asymptotic time bounds.

Exercises

Review Questions

1. Define a binary heap.
2. Differentiate between a min-heap and a max-heap.
3. Compare binary trees with binary heaps.
4. Explain the steps involved in inserting a new value in a binary heap with the help of a suitable example.
5. Explain the steps involved in deleting a value from a binary heap with the help of a suitable example.
6. Discuss the applications of binary heaps.
7. Form a binary max-heap and a min-heap from the following sequence of data:
   50, 40, 35, 25, 20, 27, 33.
8. Heaps are excellent data structures to implement priority queues. Justify this statement.
9. Define a binomial heap. Draw its structure.
10. Differentiate among binary, binomial, and Fibonacci heaps.
11. Explain the operations performed on a Fibonacci heap.
12. Why are Fibonacci heaps preferred over binary and binomial heaps?
13. Analyse the complexity of the algorithm to unite two binomial heaps.
14. The running time of the algorithm to find the minimum key in a binomial heap is `O(log n)`. Comment.
15. Discuss the process of inserting a new node in a binomial heap. Explain with the help of an example.
16. The algorithm `Min-Extract_Binomial-Heap()` runs in `O(log n)` time where `n` is the number of nodes in `H`. Justify this statement.
17. Explain how an existing node is deleted from a binomial heap with the help of a relevant example.
18. Explain the process of inserting a new node in a Fibonacci heap.
19. Write down the algorithm to unite two Fibonacci heaps.
20. What is the procedure to extract the node with the minimum value from a Fibonacci heap? Give the algorithm and analyse its complexity.
21. Consider the figure given below and state whether it is a heap or not.

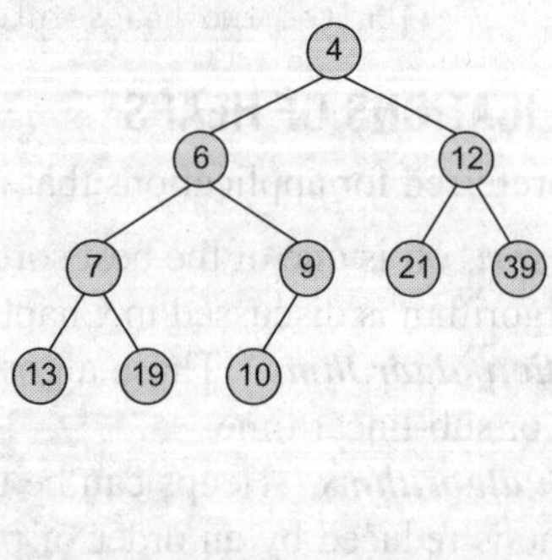

22. Reheap the following structure to make it a heap.

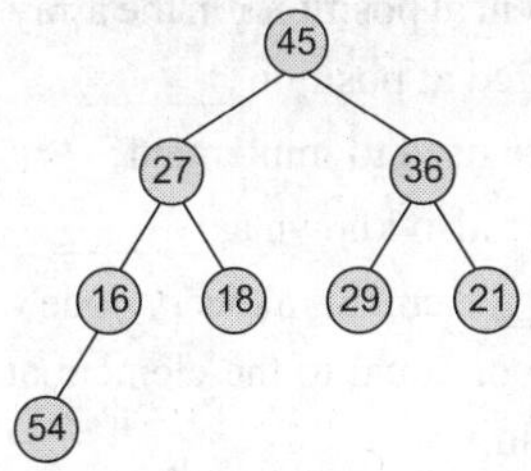

23. Show the array implementation of the following heap.

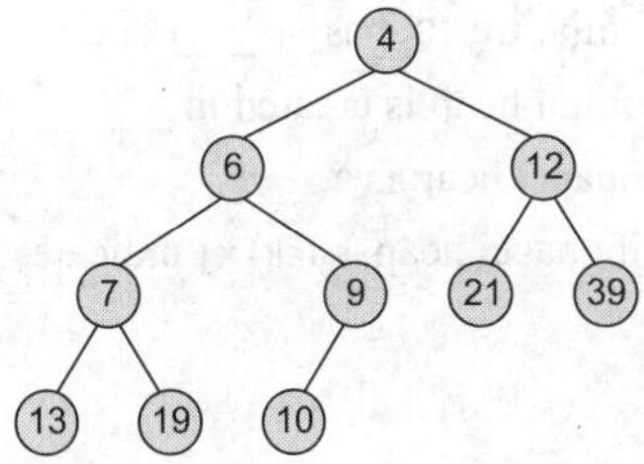

24. Given the following array structure, draw the heap.

45	27	36	18	16	21	23	10

Also, find out
(a) the parent of nodes 10, 21, and 23, and
(b) index of left and right child of node 23.

25. Which of the following sequences represents a binary heap?
(a) 40, 33, 35, 22, 12, 16, 5, 7
(b) 44, 37, 20, 22, 16, 32, 12
(c) 15, 15, 15, 15, 15, 15

26. A heap sequence is given as: 52, 32, 42, 22, 12, 27, 37, 12, 7. Which element will be deleted when the deletion algorithm is called thrice?

27. Show the resulting heap when values 35, 24, and 10 are added to the heap of the above question.

28. Draw a heap that is also a binary search tree.

29. Analyse the complexity of heapify algorithm.

30. Consider the Fibonacci heap given below and then decrease the value of node 33 to 9. Insert a new node with value 5 and finally delete node 19 from it.

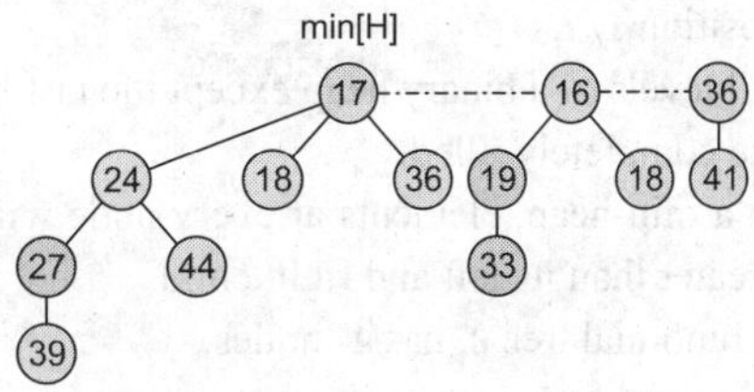

Multiple-choice Questions

1. The height of a binary heap with n nodes is equal to
(a) O(n) (b) O(log n)
(c) O(n log n) (d) $O(n^2)$

2. An element at position i in an array has its left child stored at position
(a) 2i (b) 2i + 1
(c) i/2 (d) i/2 + 1

3. In the worst case, how much time does it take to build a binary heap of n elements?
(a) O(n) (b) O(log n)
(c) O(n log n) (d) $O(n^2)$

4. The height of a binomial tree B_i is
(a) 2i (b) 2i + 1
(c) i/2 (d) i

5. How many nodes does a binomial tree of order 0 have?
(a) 0 (b) 1
(c) 2 (d) 3

6. The running time of `Link_Binomial-Tree()` procedure is
(a) O(n) (b) O(log n)
(c) O(n log n) (d) O(1)

7. In a Fibonacci heap, how much time does it take to find the minimum node?
(a) O(n) (b) O(log n)
(c) O(n log n) (d) O(1)

True or False

1. A binary heap is a complete binary tree.
2. In a min heap, the root node has the highest key value in the heap.
3. An element at position `i` has its parent stored at position `i/2`.
4. All levels of a binary heap except the last level are completely filled.
5. In a min-heap, elements at every node will be greater than its left and right child.
6. A binomial tree B_i has `2i` nodes.
7. Binomial heaps are ordered.
8. Fibonacci heaps are rooted and ordered.
9. The running time of `Min_Binomial-Heap()` procedure is `O(log n)`.
10. If there are `m` roots in the root lists of H_1 and H_2, then `Merge_Binomial-Heap()` runs in `O(m log m)` time.
11. Fibonacci heaps are preferred over binomial heaps.

Fill in the Blanks

1. An element at position `i` in the array has its right child stored at position ______.
2. Heaps are used to implement ______.
3. Heaps are also known as ______.
4. In ______, elements at every node will either be less than or equal to the element at its left and right child.
5. An element is always deleted from the ______.
6. The height of a binomial tree B_i is ______.
7. A binomial heap is defined as ______.
8. A binomial tree B_i has ______ nodes.
9. A binomial heap is created in ______ time.
10. A Fibonacci heap is a ______.
11. In a Fibonacci heap, `mark[x]` indicates ______.

CHAPTER 13

Graphs

LEARNING OBJECTIVE

In this chapter, we will discuss another non-linear data structure called graphs. We will discuss the representation of graphs in the memory as well as the different operations that can be performed on them. Last but not the least, we will discuss some of the real-world applications of graphs.

13.1 INTRODUCTION

A graph is an abstract data structure that is used to implement the mathematical concept of graphs. It is basically a collection of vertices (also called nodes) and edges that connect these vertices. A graph is often viewed as a generalization of the tree structure, where instead of having a purely parent-to-child relationship between tree nodes, any kind of complex relationship can exist.

Why are Graphs Useful?

Graphs are widely used to model any situation where entities or things are related to each other in pairs. For example, the following information can be represented by graphs:

- *Family trees* in which the member nodes have an edge from parent to each of their children.
- *Transportation networks* in which nodes are airports, intersections, ports, etc. The edges can be airline flights, one-way roads, shipping routes, etc.

Definition

A graph `G` is defined as an ordered set `(V, E)`, where `V(G)` represents the set of vertices and `E(G)` represents the edges that connect these vertices.

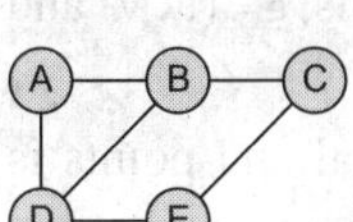

Figure 13.1 Undirected graph

Figure 13.1 shows a graph with `V(G) = {A, B, C, D and E}` and `E(G) = {(A, B), (B, C), (A, D), (B, D), (D, E), (C, E)}`. Note that there are five vertices or nodes and six edges in the graph.

A graph can be directed or undirected. In an undirected graph, edges do not have any direction associated with them. That is, if an edge is drawn between nodes `A` and `B`, then the nodes can be traversed from `A` to `B` as well as from `B` to `A`. Figure 13.1 shows an undirected graph because it does not give any information about the direction of the edges.

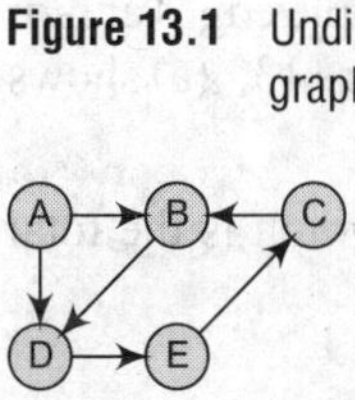

Figure 13.2 Directed graph

Look at Fig. 13.2 which shows a directed graph. In a directed graph, edges form an ordered pair. If there is an edge from `A` to `B`, then there is a path from `A` to `B` but not from `B` to `A`. The edge `(A, B)` is said to initiate from node `A` (also known as initial node) and terminate at node `B` (terminal node).

13.2 Graph Terminology

Adjacent nodes or neighbours For every edge, `e = (u, v)` that connects nodes `u` and `v`, the nodes `u` and `v` are the end-points and are said to be the adjacent nodes or neighbours.

Degree of a node Degree of a node `u`, `deg(u)`, is the total number of edges containing the node `u`. If `deg(u) = 0`, it means that `u` does not belong to any edge and such a node is known as an isolated node.

Regular graph It is a graph where each vertex has the same number of neighbours. That is, every node has the same degree. A regular graph with vertices of degree `k` is called a `k-regular graph` or a regular graph of degree `k`. Figure 13.3 shows regular graphs.

Path A path `P` written as $P = \{v_0, v_1, v_2, \ldots, v_n\}$, of length `n` from a node `u` to `v` is defined as a sequence of `(n+1)` nodes. Here, $u = v_0$, $v = v_n$ and v_{i-1} is adjacent to v_i for `i = 1, 2, 3, ..., n`.

Closed path A path `P` is known as a closed path if the edge has the same end-points. That is, if $v_0 = v_n$.

Simple path A path `P` is known as a simple path if all the nodes in the path are distinct with an exception that v_0 may be equal to v_n. If $v_0 = v_n$, then the path is called a closed simple path.

Cycle A path in which the first and the last vertices are same. A *simple cycle* has no repeated edges or vertices (except the first and last vertices).

Connected graph A graph is said to be connected if for any two vertices `(u, v)` in `V` there is a path from `u` to `v`. That is to say that there are no isolated nodes in a connected graph. A connected graph that does not have any cycle is called a tree. Therefore, a tree is treated as a special graph (Refer Fig. 13.4(b)).

Complete graph A graph `G` is said to be complete if all its nodes are fully connected. That is, there is a path from one node to every other node in the graph. A complete graph has `n(n-1)/2` edges, where `n` is the number of nodes in `G`.

Clique In an undirected graph `G = (V, E)`, clique is a subset of the vertex set $C \subseteq V$, such that for every two vertices in `C`, there is an edge that connects two vertices.

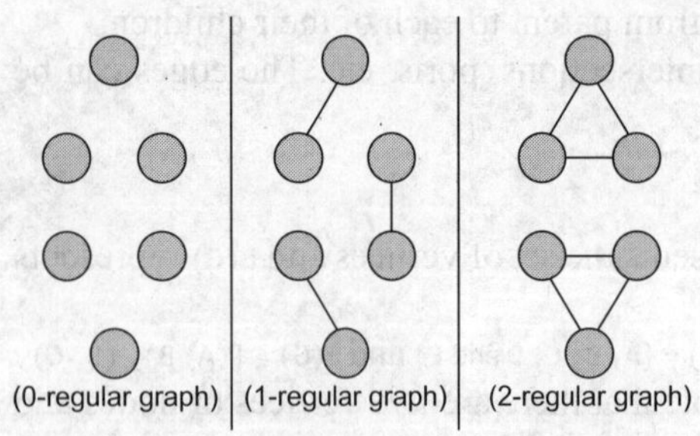

Figure 13.3 Regular graphs

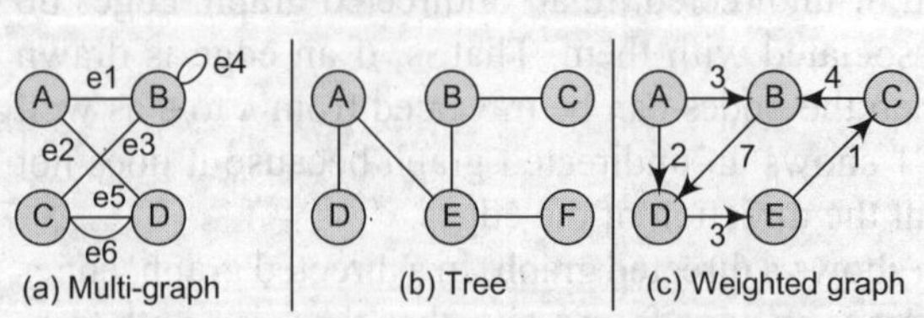

Figure 13.4 Multi-graph, tree, and weighted graph

Labelled graph or weighted graph A graph is said to be labelled if every edge in the graph is assigned some data. In a weighted graph, the edges of the graph are assigned some weight or length. The weight of an edge denoted by `w(e)` is a positive value which indicates the cost of traversing the edge. Figure 13.4(c) shows a weighted graph.

Multiple edges Distinct edges which connect the same end-points are called multiple edges. That is, `e = (u, v)` and `e' = (u, v)` are known as multiple edges of `G`.

Loop An edge that has identical end-points is called a loop. That is, `e = (u, u)`.

Multi-graph A graph with multiple edges and/or loops is called a multi-graph. Figure 13.4(a) shows a multi-graph.

Size of a graph The size of a graph is the total number of edges in it.

13.3 DIRECTED GRAPHS

A directed graph G, also known as a *digraph*, is a graph in which every edge has a direction assigned to it. An edge of a directed graph is given as an ordered pair (u, v) of nodes in G. For an edge (u, v),

- The edge begins at u and terminates at v.
- u is known as the origin or initial point of e. Correspondingly, v is known as the destination or terminal point of e.
- u is the predecessor of v. Correspondingly, v is the successor of u.
- Nodes u and v are adjacent to each other.

13.3.1 Terminology of a Directed Graph

Out-degree of a node The out-degree of a node u, written as outdeg(u), is the number of edges that originate at u.

In-degree of a node The in-degree of a node u, written as indeg(u), is the number of edges that terminate at u.

Degree of a node The degree of a node, written as deg(u), is equal to the sum of in-degree and out-degree of that node. Therefore, deg(u) = indeg(u) + outdeg(u).

Isolated vertex A vertex with degree zero. Such a vertex is not an end-point of any edge.

Pendant vertex (also known as leaf vertex) A vertex with degree one.

Cut vertex A vertex which when deleted would disconnect the remaining graph.

Source A node u is known as a source if it has a positive out-degree but a zero in-degree.

Sink A node u is known as a sink if it has a positive in-degree but a zero out-degree.

Reachability A node v is said to be reachable from node u, if and only if there exists a (directed) path from node u to node v. For example, if you consider the directed graph given in Fig. 13.5(a), you will observe that node D is reachable from node A.

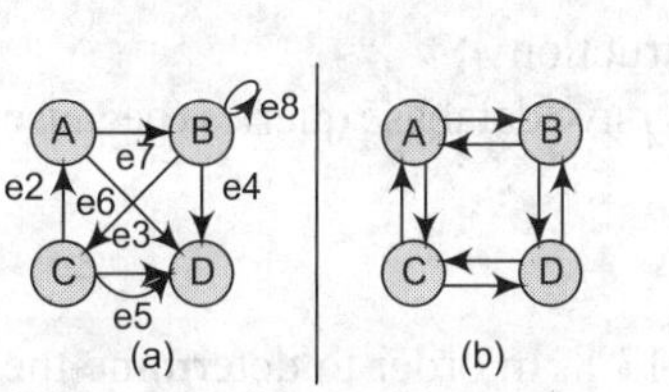

Figure 13.5 (a) Directed acyclic graph and (b) strongly connected directed acyclic graph

Strongly connected directed graph A digraph is said to be strongly connected if and only if there exists a path between every pair of nodes in G. That is, if there is a path from node u to v, then there must be a path from node v to u.

Unilaterally connected graph A digraph is said to be unilaterally connected if there exists a path between any pair of nodes u, v in G such that there is a path from u to v or a path from v to u, but not both.

Weakly connected digraph A directed graph is said to be weakly connected if it is connected by ignoring the direction of edges. That is, in such a graph, it is possible to reach any node from any other node by traversing edges in any direction (may not be in the direction they point). The nodes in a weakly connected directed graph must have either out-degree or in-degree of at least 1.

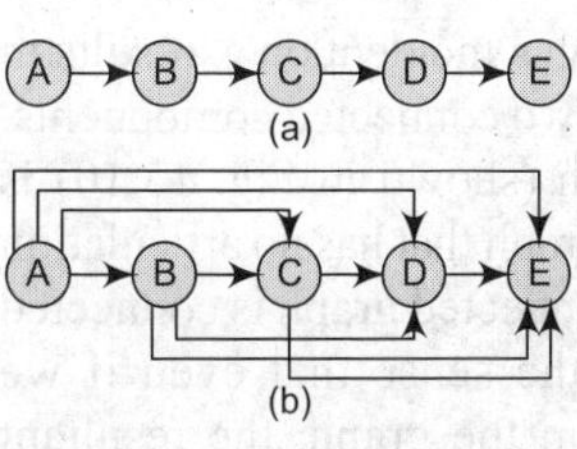

Figure 13.6 (a) A graph G and its (b) transitive closure G*

Parallel/Multiple edges Distinct edges which connect the same end-points are called multiple edges. That is, e = (u, v) and e' = (u, v) are known as multiple edges of G. In Fig. 13.5(a), e3 and e5 are multiple edges connecting nodes C and D.

Simple directed graph A directed graph G is said to be a simple directed graph if and only if it has no parallel edges. However, a simple directed graph may contain cycles with an exception that it cannot have more than one loop at a given node.

The graph G given in Fig. 13.5(a) is a directed graph in which there are four nodes and eight edges. Note that edges e3 and e5 are parallel since they begin at C and end at D. The edge e8 is a loop since it originates and terminates at the same node. The sequence of nodes, A, B, D, and C, does not form a path because (D, C) is not an edge. Although there is a path from node C to D, there is no way from D to C.

In the graph, we see that there is no path from node D to any other node in G, so the graph is not strongly connected. However, G is said to be unilaterally connected. We also observe that node D is a sink since it has a positive in-degree but a zero out-degree.

13.3.2 Transitive Closure of a Directed Graph

A transitive closure of a graph is constructed to answer reachability questions. That is, is there a path from a node A to node E in one or more hops? A binary relation indicates only whether the node A is connected to node B, whether node B is connected to node C, etc. But once the transitive closure is constructed as shown in Fig. 13.6, we can easily determine in O(1) time whether node E is reachable from node A or not. Like the adjacency list, discussed in Section 13.5.2, transitive closure is also stored as a matrix T, so if T[1][5] = 1, then node 5 can be reached from node 1 in one or more hops.

Definition

For a directed graph G = (V,E), where V is the set of vertices and E is the set of edges, the transitive closure of G is a graph G* = (V,E*). In G*, for every vertex pair v, w in V there is an edge (v, w) in E* if and only if there is a valid path from v to w in G.

Where and Why is it Needed?

Finding the transitive closure of a directed graph is an important problem in the following computational tasks:

- Transitive closure is used to find the reachability analysis of transition networks representing distributed and parallel systems.
- It is used in the construction of parsing automata in compiler construction.
- Recently, transitive closure computation is being used to evaluate recursive database queries (because almost all practical recursive queries are transitive in nature).

Algorithm

The algorithm to find the transitive closure of a graph G is given in Fig. 13.8. In order to determine the transitive closure of a graph, we define a matrix t where $t^k_{ij} = 1$, for i, j, k = 1, 2, 3, ... n if there exists a path in G from the vertex i to vertex j with intermediate vertices in the set (1, 2, 3, ..., k) and 0 otherwise. That is, G* is constructed by adding an edge (i, j) into E* if and only if $t^k_{ij} = 1$. Look at Fig. 13.7 which shows the relation between k and T^k_{ij}.

13.4 BI-CONNECTED COMPONENTS

A vertex v of G is called an articulation point, if removing v along with the edges incident on v, results in a graph that has at least two connected components.

When k = 0	$T^0_{ij} = \begin{cases} 0 \text{ if } (i, j) \text{ is not in } E \\ 1 \text{ if } (i, j) \text{ is in } E \end{cases}$
When k ≥ 1	$T^k_{ij} = T^{k-1}_{ij} \vee (T^{k-1}_{ik} \wedge T^{k-1}_{kj})$

Figure 13.7 Relation between k and T^k_{ij}

A bi-connected graph (shown in Fig. 13.10) is defined as a connected graph that has no articulation vertices. That is, a bi-connected graph is connected and non-separable in the sense that even if we remove any vertex from the graph, the resultant graph is still connected. By definition,

```
Transitive_Closure(A, t, n)

Step 1: SET i=1, j=1, k=1
Step 2: Repeat Steps 3 and 4 while i<=n
Step 3:     Repeat Step 4 while j<=n
Step 4:         IF (A[i][j] = 1)
                   SET t[i][j] = 1
                ELSE
                   SET t[i][j] = 0
            INCREMENT j
            [END OF LOOP]
        INCREMENT i
        [END OF LOOP]
Step 5: Repeat Steps 6 to 11 while k<=n
Step 6:     Repeat Steps 7 to 10 while i<=n
Step 7:         Repeat Steps 8 and 9 while j<=n
Step 8:            SET t[i,j] = t[i][j] V (t[i][k] Λ t[k][j])
Step 9:            INCREMENT j
                [END OF LOOP]
Step 10:     INCREMENT i
            [END OF LOOP]
Step 11:    INCREMENT k
            [END OF LOOP]
Step 12: END
```

Figure 13.8 Algorithm to find the transitive enclosure of a graph G

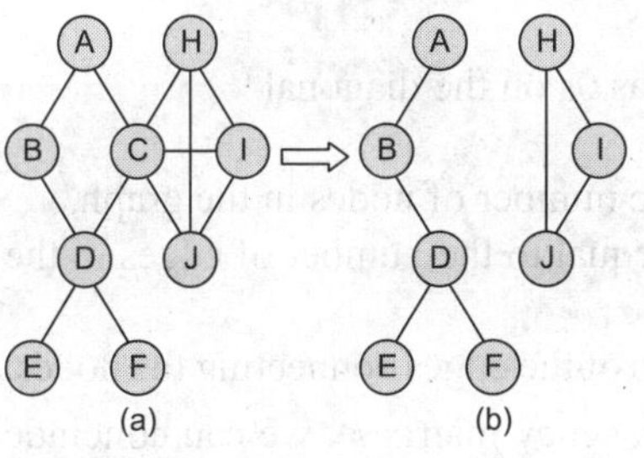

Figure 13.9 Non bi-connected graph

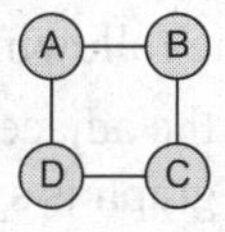

Figure 13.10 Bi-connected graph

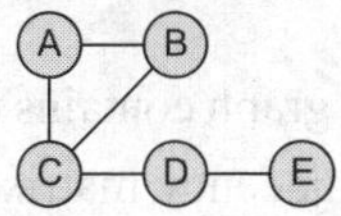

Figure 13.11 Graph with bridges

- A bi-connected undirected graph is a connected graph that cannot be broken into disconnected pieces by deleting any single vertex.
- In a bi-connected directed graph, for any two vertices v and w, there are two directed paths from v to w which have no vertices in common other than v and w.

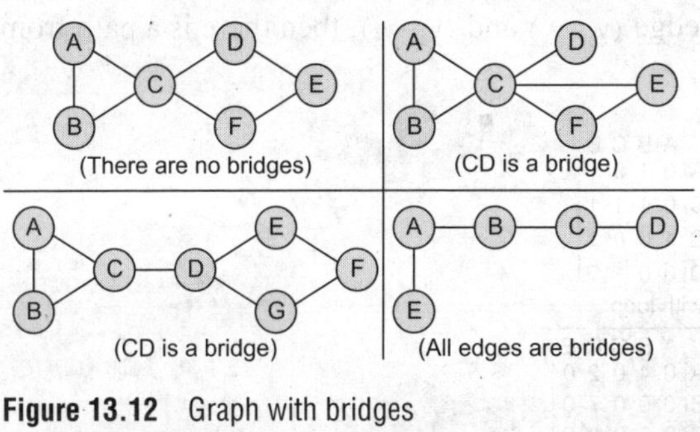

Figure 13.12 Graph with bridges

Note that the graph shown in Fig. 13.9(a) is not a bi-connected graph, as deleting vertex C from the graph results in two disconnected components of the original graph (Fig. 13.9(b)).

As for vertices, there is a related concept for edges. An edge in a graph is called a *bridge* if removing that edge results in a disconnected graph. Also, an edge in a graph that does not lie on a cycle is a bridge. This means that a bridge has at least one articulation point at its end, although it is not necessary that the articulation point is linked to a bridge. Look at the graph shown in Fig. 13.11.

In the graph, CD and DE are bridges. Consider some more examples shown in Fig. 13.12.

$$a_{ij} = \begin{cases} 1 & \text{[if } v_i \text{ is adjacent to } v_j \text{, that is there is an edge } (v_i, v_j)\text{]A} \\ 0 & \text{[otherwise]} \end{cases}$$

Figure 13.13 Adjacency matrix entry

13.5 REPRESENTATION OF GRAPHS

There are three common ways of storing graphs in the computer's memory. They are:

- *Sequential representation* by using an adjacency matrix.
- *Linked representation* by using an adjacency list that stores the neighbours of a node using a linked list.
- *Adjacency multi-list* which is an extension of linked representation.

In this section, we will discuss both these schemes in detail.

13.5.1 Adjacency Matrix Representation

An adjacency matrix is used to represent which nodes are adjacent to one another. By definition, two nodes are said to be adjacent if there is an edge connecting them.

In a directed graph G, if node v is adjacent to node u, then there is definitely an edge from u to v. That is, if v is adjacent to u, we can get from u to v by traversing one edge. For any graph G having n nodes, the adjacency matrix will have the dimension of $n \times n$.

In an adjacency matrix, the rows and columns are labelled by graph vertices. An entry a_{ij} in the adjacency matrix will contain 1, if vertices v_i and v_j are adjacent to each other. However, if the nodes are not adjacent, a_{ij} will be set to zero. It is summarized in Fig. 13.13.

Since an adjacency matrix contains only 0s and 1s, it is called a *bit matrix* or a *Boolean matrix*. The entries in the matrix depend on the ordering of the nodes in G. Therefore, a change in the order of nodes will result in a different adjacency matrix. Figure 13.14 shows some graphs and their corresponding adjacency matrices.

From the above examples, we can draw the following conclusions:

- For a simple graph (that has no loops), the adjacency matrix has 0s on the diagonal.
- The adjacency matrix of an undirected graph is symmetric.
- The memory use of an adjacency matrix is $O(n^2)$, where n is the number of nodes in the graph.
- Number of 1s (or non-zero entries) in an adjacency matrix is equal to the number of edges in the graph.
- The adjacency matrix for a weighted graph contains the weights of the edges connecting the nodes.

Now let us discuss the powers of an adjacency matrix. From adjacency matrix A^1, we can conclude that an entry 1 in the ith row and jth column means that there exists a path of length 1 from v_i to v_j. Now consider, A^2, A^3, and A^4.

$$(a_{ij})^2 = \sum a_{ik} a_{kj}$$

Any entry $a_{ij} = 1$ if $a_{ik} = a_{kj} = 1$. That is, if there is an edge (v_i, v_k) and (v_k, v_j), then there is a path from v_i to v_j of length 2.

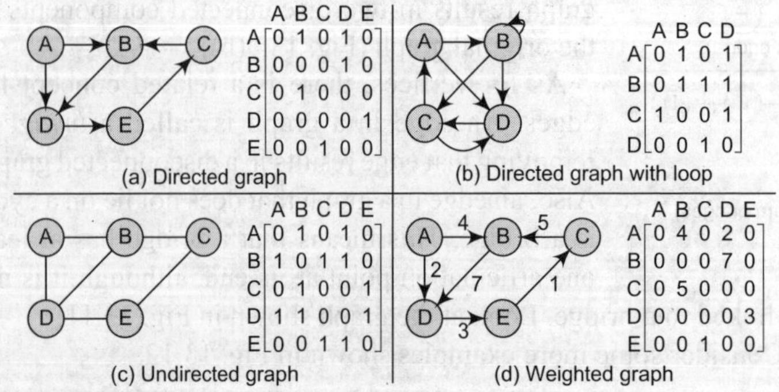

Figure 13.14 Graphs and their corresponding adjacency matrices

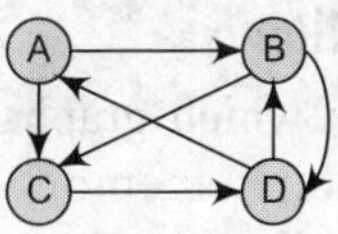

$$\begin{array}{c|cccc} & A & B & C & D \\ \hline A & 0 & 1 & 1 & 0 \\ B & 0 & 0 & 1 & 1 \\ C & 0 & 0 & 0 & 1 \\ D & 1 & 1 & 0 & 0 \end{array}$$

Figure 13.15 Directed graph with its adjacency matrix

Similarly, every entry in the `ith` row and `jth` column of A^3 gives the number of paths of length 3 from node v_i to v_j.

In general terms, we can conclude that every entry in the `ith` row and `jth` column of A^n (where `n` is the number of nodes in the graph) gives the number of paths of length `n` from node v_i to v_j. Consider a directed graph given in Fig. 13.15. Given its adjacency matrix `A`, let us calculate A^2, A^3, and A^4.

$$A^2 = A^1 \times A^1$$

$$A^2 = \begin{bmatrix} 0 & 1 & 1 & 0 \\ 0 & 0 & 1 & 1 \\ 0 & 0 & 0 & 1 \\ 1 & 1 & 0 & 0 \end{bmatrix} \times \begin{bmatrix} 0 & 1 & 1 & 0 \\ 0 & 0 & 1 & 1 \\ 0 & 0 & 0 & 1 \\ 1 & 1 & 0 & 0 \end{bmatrix} = \begin{bmatrix} 0 & 0 & 1 & 2 \\ 1 & 1 & 0 & 1 \\ 1 & 1 & 0 & 0 \\ 1 & 1 & 2 & 1 \end{bmatrix}$$

$$A^3 = \begin{bmatrix} 0 & 0 & 1 & 2 \\ 1 & 1 & 0 & 1 \\ 1 & 1 & 0 & 0 \\ 1 & 1 & 2 & 1 \end{bmatrix} \times \begin{bmatrix} 0 & 1 & 1 & 0 \\ 0 & 0 & 1 & 1 \\ 0 & 0 & 0 & 1 \\ 1 & 1 & 0 & 0 \end{bmatrix} = \begin{bmatrix} 2 & 2 & 0 & 1 \\ 1 & 2 & 2 & 1 \\ 0 & 1 & 2 & 1 \\ 1 & 2 & 2 & 3 \end{bmatrix}$$

$$A^4 = \begin{bmatrix} 2 & 2 & 0 & 1 \\ 1 & 2 & 2 & 1 \\ 0 & 1 & 2 & 1 \\ 1 & 2 & 2 & 3 \end{bmatrix} \times \begin{bmatrix} 0 & 1 & 1 & 0 \\ 0 & 0 & 1 & 1 \\ 0 & 0 & 0 & 1 \\ 1 & 1 & 0 & 0 \end{bmatrix} = \begin{bmatrix} 1 & 3 & 4 & 2 \\ 1 & 2 & 3 & 4 \\ 1 & 1 & 1 & 3 \\ 3 & 4 & 3 & 4 \end{bmatrix}$$

Now, based on the above calculations, we define matrix `B` as:

$$B^r = A^1 + A^2 + A^3 + \ldots + A^r$$

An entry in the `ith` row and `jth` column of matrix B^r gives the number of paths of length `r` or less than `r` from vertex v_i to v_j. The main goal to define matrix `B` is to obtain the path matrix `P`. The path matrix `P` can be calculated from `B` by setting an entry $P_{ij} = 1$, if B_{ij} is non-zero and $P_{ij} = 0$, if otherwise. The path matrix is used to show whether there exists a simple path from node v_i to v_j or not. This is shown in Fig. 13.16.

Let us now calculate matrix `B` and matrix `P` using the above discussion.

$$B = \begin{bmatrix} 0 & 1 & 1 & 0 \\ 0 & 0 & 1 & 1 \\ 0 & 0 & 0 & 1 \\ 1 & 1 & 0 & 0 \end{bmatrix} + \begin{bmatrix} 0 & 0 & 1 & 2 \\ 1 & 1 & 0 & 1 \\ 1 & 1 & 0 & 0 \\ 1 & 1 & 2 & 1 \end{bmatrix} + \begin{bmatrix} 2 & 2 & 0 & 1 \\ 1 & 2 & 2 & 1 \\ 0 & 1 & 2 & 1 \\ 1 & 2 & 2 & 3 \end{bmatrix} + \begin{bmatrix} 1 & 3 & 4 & 2 \\ 1 & 2 & 3 & 4 \\ 1 & 1 & 1 & 3 \\ 3 & 4 & 3 & 4 \end{bmatrix} = \begin{bmatrix} 3 & 6 & 6 & 5 \\ 3 & 5 & 6 & 7 \\ 2 & 3 & 3 & 5 \\ 6 & 8 & 7 & 8 \end{bmatrix}$$

Now the path matrix P can be given as:

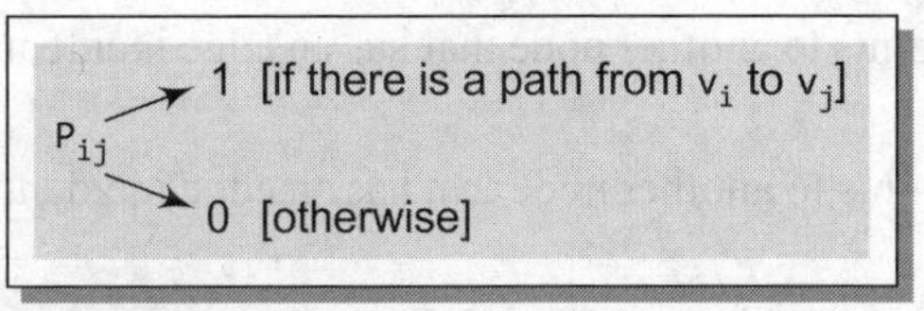

$$P = \begin{bmatrix} 1 & 1 & 1 & 1 \\ 1 & 1 & 1 & 1 \\ 1 & 1 & 1 & 1 \\ 1 & 1 & 1 & 1 \end{bmatrix}$$

Figure 13.16 Path matrix entry

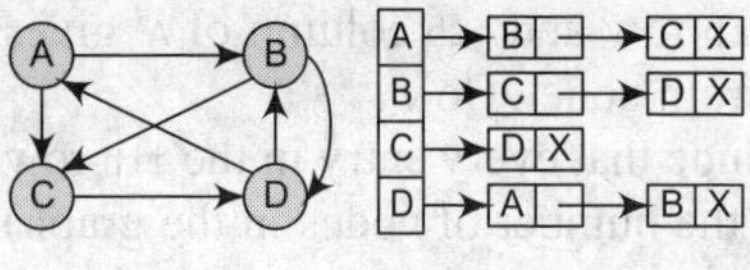

Figure 13.17 Graph G and its adjacency list

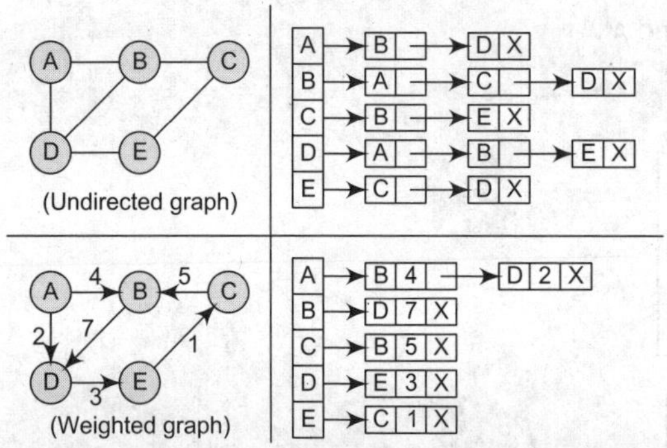

Figure 13.18 Adjacency list for an undirected graph and a weighted graph

13.5.2 Adjacency List Representation

An adjacency list is another way in which graphs can be represented in the computer's memory. This structure consists of a list of all nodes in G. Furthermore, every node is in turn linked to its own list that contains the names of all other nodes that are adjacent to it.

The key advantages of using an adjacency list are:

- It is easy to follow and clearly shows the adjacent nodes of a particular node.
- It is often used for storing graphs that have a small-to-moderate number of edges. That is, an adjacency list is preferred for representing sparse graphs in the computer's memory; otherwise, an adjacency matrix is a good choice.
- Adding new nodes in G is easy and straightforward when G is represented using an adjacency list. Adding new nodes in an adjacency matrix is a difficult task, as the size of the matrix needs to be changed and existing nodes may have to be reordered.

Consider the graph given in Fig. 13.17 and see how its adjacency list is stored in the memory.

For a directed graph, the sum of the lengths of all adjacency lists is equal to the number of edges in G. However, for an undirected graph, the sum of the lengths of all adjacency lists is equal to twice the number of edges in G because an edge (u, v) means an edge from node u to v as well as an edge from v to u. Adjacency lists can also be modified to store weighted graphs. Let us now see an adjacency list for an undirected graph as well as a weighted graph. This is shown in Fig. 13.18.

13.5.3 Adjacency Multi-list Representation

Graphs can also be represented using multi-lists which can be said to be modified version of adjacency lists. Adjacency multi-list is an edge-based rather than a vertex-based representation of graphs. A multi-list representation basically consists of two parts—a directory of nodes' information and a set of linked lists storing information about edges. While there is a single entry for each node in the node directory, every node, on the other hand, appears in two adjacency lists (one for the node at each end of the edge). For example, the directory entry for node *i* points to the adjacency list for node *i*. This means that the nodes are shared among several lists.

In a multi-list representation, the information about an edge (v_i, v_j) of an undirected graph can be stored using the following attributes:

M: A single bit field to indicate whether the edge has been examined or not.

v_i: A vertex in the graph that is connected to vertex v_j by an edge.

v_j: A vertex in the graph that is connected to vertex v_i by an edge.

Link i for v_i: A link that points to another node that has an edge incident on v_i.

Link j for v_i: A link that points to another node that has an edge incident on v_j.

Consider the undirected graph given in Fig. 13.19.

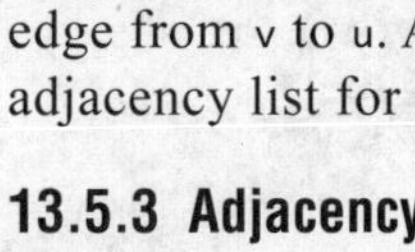

Figure 13.19 Undirected graph

The adjacency multi-list for the graph can be given as:

Edge 1		0	1	Edge 2	Edge 3
Edge 2		0	2	NULL	Edge 4
Edge 3		1	3	NULL	Edge 4
Edge 4		2	3	NULL	Edge 5
Edge 5		3	4	NULL	Edge 6
Edge 6		4	5	Edge 7	NULL
Edge 7		4	6	NULL	NULL

Using the adjacency multi-list given above, the adjacency list for vertices can be constructed as shown below:

VERTEX	LIST OF EDGES
0	Edge 1, Edge 2
1	Edge 1, Edge 3
2	Edge 2, Edge 4
3	Edge 3, Edge 4, Edge 5
4	Edge 5, Edge 6, Edge 7
5	Edge 6
6	Edge 7

Programming Example

1. Write a program to create a graph of *n* vertices using an adjacency list. Also write the code to read and print its information and finally to delete the graph.

```
#include <stdio.h>
#include <malloc.h>
struct node
{
        char vertex;
        struct node *next;
};
struct node *gnode;
void displayGraph(struct node *adj[], int no_of_nodes);
void deleteGraph(struct node *adj[], int no_of_nodes);
void createGraph(struct node *adj[], int no_of_nodes);
int main()
{
        struct node *Adj[10];
        int i, no_of_nodes;
```

```
        printf("\n Enter the number of nodes in G: ");
        scanf("%d", &no_of_nodes);
        for(i = 0; i < no_of_nodes; i++)
                Adj[i] = NULL;
        createGraph(Adj, no_of_nodes);
        printf("\n The graph is: ");
        displayGraph(Adj, no_of_nodes);
        deleteGraph(Adj, no_of_nodes);
        return 0;
}
void createGraph(struct node *Adj[], int no_of_nodes)
{
        struct node *new_node, *last;
        int i, j, n, val;
        for(i = 0; i < no_of_nodes; i++)
        {
                last = NULL;
                printf("\n Enter the number of neighbours of %d: ", i);
                scanf("%d", &n);
                for(j = 1; j <= n; j++)
                {
                        printf("\n Enter the neighbour %d of %d: ", j, i);
                        scanf("%d", &val);
                        new_node = (struct node *) malloc(sizeof(struct node));
                        new_node -> vertex = val;
                        new_node -> next = NULL;
                        if (Adj[i] == NULL)
                                Adj[i] = new_node;
                        else
                                last -> next = new_node;
                        last = new_node;
                }
        }
}
void displayGraph (struct node *Adj[], int no_of_nodes)
{
        struct node *ptr;
        int i;
        for(i = 0; i < no_of_nodes; i++)
        {
                ptr = Adj[i];
                printf("\n The neighbours of node %d are:", i);
                while(ptr != NULL)
                {
                        printf("\t%d", ptr -> vertex);
                        ptr = ptr -> next;
                }
        }
}
void deleteGraph (struct node *Adj[], int no_of_nodes)
{
        int i;
        struct node *temp, *ptr;
        for(i = 0; i <= no_of_nodes; i++)
        {
                ptr = Adj[i];
                while(ptr != NULL)
                {
                        temp = ptr;
                        ptr = ptr -> next;
```

```
                    free(temp);
                }
                Adj[i] = NULL;
            }
        }
```

Output

```
Enter the number of nodes in G: 3
Enter the number of neighbours of 0: 1
Enter the neighbour 1 of 0: 2
Enter the number of neighbours of 1: 2
Enter the neighbour 1 of 1: 0
Enter the neighbour 2 of 1: 2
Enter the number of neighbours of 2: 1
Enter the neighbour 1 of 2: 1
The neighbours of node 0 are: 1
The neighbours of node 1 are: 0 2
The neighbours of node 2 are: 0
```

Note If the graph in the above program had been a weighted graph, then the structure of the node would have been:

```
typedef struct node
{
        int vertex;
        int weight;
        struct node *next;
};
```

13.6 GRAPH TRAVERSAL ALGORITHMS

In this section, we will discuss how to traverse graphs. By traversing a graph, we mean the method of examining the nodes and edges of the graph. There are two standard methods of graph traversal which we will discuss in this section. These two methods are:

1. Breadth-first search
2. Depth-first search

While breadth-first search uses a queue as an auxiliary data structure to store nodes for further processing, the depth-first search scheme uses a stack. But both these algorithms make use of a variable STATUS. During the execution of the algorithm, every node in the graph will have the variable STATUS set to 1 or 2, depending on its current state. Table 13.1 shows the value of STATUS and its significance.

Table 13.1 Value of status and its significance

Status	State of the node	Description
1	Ready	The initial state of the node N
2	Waiting	Node N is placed on the queue or stack and waiting to be processed
3	Processed	Node N has been completely processed

13.6.1 Breadth-first Search Algorithm

Breadth-first search (BFS) is a graph search algorithm that begins at the root node and explores all the neighbouring nodes. Then for each of those nearest nodes, the algorithm (Fig. 13.20) explores their unexplored neighbour nodes, and so on, until it finds the goal.

```
Step 1: SET STATUS = 1 (ready state)
        for each node in G
Step 2: Enqueue the starting node A
        and set its STATUS = 2
        (waiting state)
Step 3: Repeat Steps 4 and 5 until
        QUEUE is empty
Step 4: Dequeue a node N. Process it
        and set its STATUS = 3
        (processed state).
Step 5: Enqueue all the neighbours of
        N that are in the ready state
        (whose STATUS = 1) and set
        their STATUS = 2
        (waiting state)
        [END OF LOOP]
Step 6: EXIT
```

Figure 13.20 Algorithm for breadth-first search

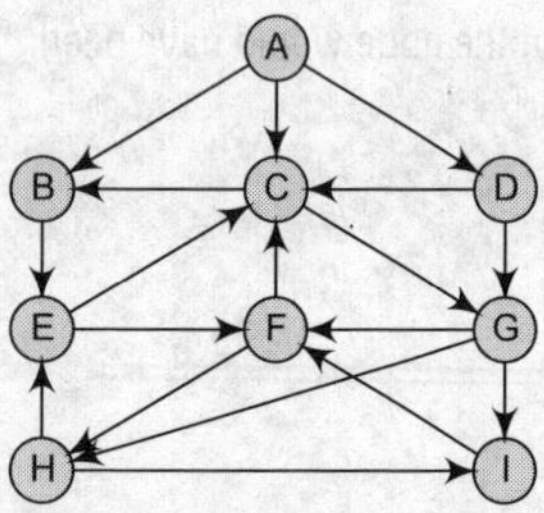

Adjacency lists
A: B, C, D
B: E
C: B, G
D: C, G
E: C, F
F: C, H
G: F, H, I
H: E, I
I: F

Figure 13.21 Graph G and its adjacency list

That is, we start examining the node A and then all the neighbours of A are examined. In the next step, we examine the neighbours of neighbours of A, so on and so forth. This means that we need to track the neighbours of the node and guarantee that every node in the graph is processed and no node is processed more than once. This is accomplished by using a queue that will hold the nodes that are waiting for further processing and a variable STATUS to represent the current state of the node.

Example 13.1 Consider the graph G given in Fig. 13.21. The adjacency list of G is also given. Assume that G represents the daily flights between different cities and we want to fly from city A to I with minimum stops. That is, find the minimum path P from A to I given that every edge has a length of 1.

Solution

The minimum path P can be found by applying the breadth-first search algorithm that begins at city A and ends when I is encountered. During the execution of the algorithm, we use two arrays:
QUEUE and ORIG. While QUEUE is used to hold the nodes that have to be processed, ORIG is used to keep track of the origin of each edge. Initially, FRONT = REAR = -1. The algorithm for this is as follows:

(a) Add A to QUEUE and add NULL to ORIG.

FRONT = 0	QUEUE = A
REAR = 0	ORIG = \0

(b) Dequeue a node by setting FRONT = FRONT + 1 (remove the FRONT element of QUEUE) and enqueue the neighbours of A. Also, add A as the ORIG of its neighbours.

FRONT = 1	QUEUE = A	B	C	D
REAR = 3	ORIG = \0	A	A	A

(c) Dequeue a node by setting FRONT = FRONT + 1 and enqueue the neighbours of B. Also, add B as the ORIG of its neighbours.

FRONT = 2	QUEUE = A	B	C	D	E
REAR = 4	ORIG = \0	A	A	A	B

(d) Dequeue a node by setting FRONT = FRONT + 1 and enqueue the neighbours of C. Also, add C as the ORIG of its neighbours. Note that C has two neighbours B and G. Since B has already been added to the queue and it is not in the Ready state, we will not add B and only add G.

FRONT = 3	QUEUE = A	B	C	D	E	G
REAR = 5	ORIG = \0	A	A	A	B	C

(e) Dequeue a node by setting FRONT = FRONT + 1 and enqueue the neighbours of D. Also, add D as the ORIG of its neighbours. Note that D has two neighbours C and G. Since both of them have already been added to the queue and they are not in the Ready state, we will not add them again.

FRONT = 4	QUEUE = A	B	C	D	E	G
REAR = 5	ORIG = \0	A	A	A	B	C

(f) Dequeue a node by setting FRONT = FRONT + 1 and enqueue the neighbours of E. Also, add E as the ORIG of its neighbours. Note that E has two neighbours C and F. Since C has already been added to the queue and it is not in the Ready state, we will not add C and add only F.

FRONT = 5	QUEUE = A	B	C	D	E	G	F
REAR = 6	ORIG = \0	A	A	A	B	C	E

(g) Dequeue a node by setting FRONT = FRONT + 1 and enqueue the neighbours of G. Also, add G as the ORIG of its neighbours. Note that G has three neighbours F, H, and I.

FRONT = 6	QUEUE = A	B	C	D	E	G	F	H	I
REAR = 9	ORIG = \0	A	A	A	B	C	E	G	G

Since F has already been added to the queue, we will only add H and I. As I is our final destination, we stop the execution of this algorithm as soon as it is encountered and added to the QUEUE. Now, backtrack from I using ORIG to find the minimum path P. Thus, we have P as A –> C –> G –> I.

Features of Breadth-First Search Algorithm

Space complexity In the breadth-first search algorithm, all the nodes at a particular level must be saved until their child nodes in the next level have been generated. The space complexity is therefore proportional to the number of nodes at the deepest level of the graph. Given a graph with branching factor b (number of children at each node) and depth d, the asymptotic space complexity is the number of nodes at the deepest level $O(b^d)$.

If the number of vertices and edges in the graph are known ahead of time, the space complexity can also be expressed as $O(|E| + |V|)$, where $|E|$ is the total number of edges in G and $|V|$ is the number of nodes or vertices.

Time complexity In the worst case, breadth-first search has to traverse through all paths to all possible nodes, thus the time complexity of this algorithm asymptotically approaches $O(b^d)$. However, the time complexity can also be expressed as $O(|E| + |V|)$, since every vertex and every edge will be explored in the worst case.

Completeness Breadth-first search is said to be a complete algorithm because if there is a solution, breadth-first search will find it regardless of the kind of graph. But in case of an infinite graph where there is no possible solution, it will diverge.

Optimality Breadth-first search is optimal for a graph that has edges of equal length, since it always returns the result with the fewest edges between the start node and the goal node. But generally, in real-world applications, we have weighted graphs that have costs associated with each edge, so the goal next to the start does not have to be the cheapest goal available.

Applications of Breadth-First Search Algorithm

Breadth-first search can be used to solve many problems such as:

- Finding all connected components in a graph G.
- Finding all nodes within an individual connected component.
- Finding the shortest path between two nodes, u and v, of an unweighted graph.
- Finding the shortest path between two nodes, u and v, of a weighted graph.

Programming Example

2. Write a program to implement the breadth-first search algorithm.

```
#include <stdio.h>
#define MAX 10
void breadth_first_search(int adj[][MAX],int visited[],int start)
{
        int queue[MAX],rear = -1,front = -1, i;
        queue[++rear] = start;
        visited[start] = 1;
        while(rear != front)
        {
                start = queue[++front];
                if(start == 4)
                        printf("5\t");
                else
                        printf("%c \t",start + 65);
                for(i = 0; i < MAX; i++)
                {
                        if(adj[start][i] == 1 && visited[i] == 0)
                        {
                                queue[++rear] = i;
                                visited[i] = 1;
                        }
                }
        }
}
int main()
{
        int visited[MAX] = {0};
        int adj[MAX][MAX], i, j;
        printf("\n Enter the adjacency matrix: ");
        for(i = 0; i < MAX; i++)
                for(j = 0; j < MAX; j++)
                        scanf("%d", &adj[i][j]);
        breadth_first_search(adj,visited,0);
        return 0;
}
```

Output

```
Enter the adjacency matrix:
0 1 0 1 0
1 0 1 1 0
0 1 0 0 1
1 1 0 0 1
0 0 1 1 0
A B D C E
```

13.6.2 Depth-first Search Algorithm

The depth-first search algorithm (Fig. 13.22) progresses by expanding the starting node of G and then going deeper and deeper until the goal node is found, or until a node that has no children is encountered. When a dead-end is reached, the algorithm backtracks, returning to the most recent node that has not been completely explored.

In other words, depth-first search begins at a starting node A which becomes the current node. Then, it examines each node N along a path P which begins at A. That is, we process a neighbour of A, then a neighbour of neighbour of A, and so on. During the execution of the algorithm, if we reach a path that has a node N that has already been processed, then we backtrack to the current node. Otherwise, the unvisited (unprocessed) node becomes the current node.

```
Step 1: SET STATUS = 1 (ready state) for each node in G
Step 2: Push the starting node A on the stack and set
        its STATUS = 2 (waiting state)
Step 3: Repeat Steps 4 and 5 until STACK is empty
Step 4:    Pop the top node N. Process it and set its
           STATUS = 3 (processed state)
Step 5:    Push on the stack all the neighbours of N that
           are in the ready state (whose STATUS = 1) and
           set their STATUS = 2 (waiting state)
        [END OF LOOP]
Step 6: EXIT
```

Figure 13.22 Algorithm for depth-first search

The algorithm proceeds like this until we reach a dead-end (end of path P). On reaching the dead-end, we backtrack to find another path P′. The algorithm terminates when backtracking leads back to the starting node A. In this algorithm, edges that lead to a new vertex are called *discovery edges* and edges that lead to an already visited vertex are called *back edges*.

Observe that this algorithm is similar to the in-order traversal of a binary tree. Its implementation is similar to that of the breadth-first search algorithm but here we use a stack instead of a queue. Again, we use a variable STATUS to represent the current state of the node.

Example 13.2 Consider the graph G given in Fig. 13.23. The adjacency list of G is also given. Suppose we want to print all the nodes that can be reached from the node H (including H itself). One alternative is to use a depth-first search of G starting at node H. The procedure can be explained here.

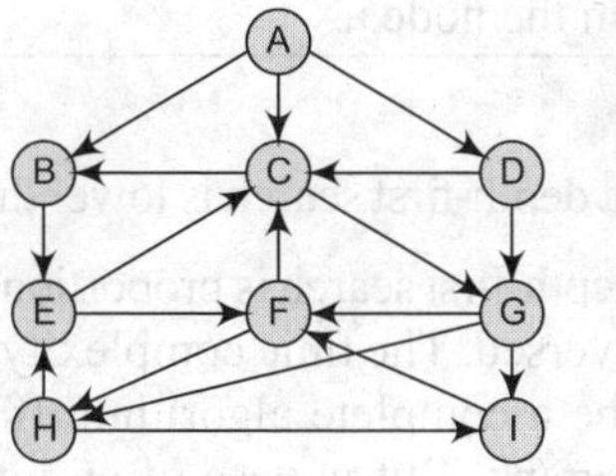

Adjacency lists
A: B, C, D
B: E
C: B, G
D: C, G
E: C, F
F: C, H
G: F, H, I
H: E, I
I: F

Figure 13.23 Graph G and its adjacency list

Solution

(a) Push H onto the stack.

STACK: H

(b) Pop and print the top element of the STACK, that is, H. Push all the neighbours of H onto the stack that are in the ready state. The STACK now becomes

PRINT: H   STACK: E, I

(c) Pop and print the top element of the STACK, that is, I. Push all the neighbours of I onto the stack that are in the ready state. The STACK now becomes

PRINT: I   STACK: E, F

(d) Pop and print the top element of the STACK, that is, F. Push all the neighbours of F onto the stack that are in the ready state. (Note F has two neighbours, C and H. But only C will be added, as H is not in the ready state.) The STACK now becomes

PRINT: F   STACK: E, C

(e) Pop and print the top element of the STACK, that is, C. Push all the neighbours of C onto the stack that are in the ready state. The STACK now becomes

PRINT: C   STACK: E, B, G

(f) Pop and print the top element of the STACK, that is, G. Push all the neighbours of G onto the stack that are in the ready state. Since there are no neighbours of G that are in the ready state, no push operation is performed. The STACK now becomes

PRINT: G   STACK: E, B

(g) Pop and print the top element of the STACK, that is, B. Push all the neighbours of B onto the stack that are in the ready state. Since there are no neighbours of B that are in the ready state, no push operation is performed. The STACK now becomes

PRINT: B   STACK: E

(h) Pop and print the top element of the STACK, that is, E. Push all the neighbours of E onto the stack that are in the ready state. Since there are no neighbours of E that are in the ready state, no push operation is performed. The STACK now becomes empty.

PRINT: E   STACK:

Since the STACK is now empty, the depth-first search of G starting at node H is complete and the nodes which were printed are:

```
H, I, F, C, G, B, E
```

These are the nodes which are reachable from the node H.

Features of Depth-First Search Algorithm

Space complexity The space complexity of a depth-first search is lower than that of a breadth-first search.

Time complexity The time complexity of a depth-first search is proportional to the number of vertices plus the number of edges in the graphs that are traversed. The time complexity can be given as (O(|V| + |E|)).

Completeness Depth-first search is said to be a complete algorithm. If there is a solution, depth-first search will find it regardless of the kind of graph. But in case of an infinite graph, where there is no possible solution, it will diverge.

Applications of Depth-First Search Algorithm

Depth-first search is useful for:

- Finding a path between two specified nodes, u and v, of an unweighted graph.
- Finding a path between two specified nodes, u and v, of a weighted graph.
- Finding whether a graph is connected or not.
- Computing the spanning tree of a connected graph.

Programming Example

3. Write a program to implement the depth-first search algorithm.

```
#include <stdio.h>
#define MAX 5
void depth_first_search(int adj[][MAX],int visited[],int start)
{
          int stack[MAX];
          int top = -1, i;
          printf("%c-",start + 65);
          visited[start] = 1;
          stack[++top] = start;
          while(top != -1)
          {
                    start = stack[top];
                    for(i = 0; i < MAX; i++)
                    {
                              if(adj[start][i] && visited[i] == 0)
                              {
                                        stack[++top] = i;
                                        printf("%c-", i + 65);
                                        visited[i] = 1;
                                        break;
                              }
                    }
                    if(i == MAX)
                    top--;
          }
}
int main()
{
          int adj[MAX][MAX];
          int visited[MAX] = {0}, i, j;
          printf("\n Enter the adjacency matrix: ");
          for(i = 0; i < MAX; i++)
                    for(j = 0; j < MAX; j++)
                              scanf("%d", &adj[i][j]);
          printf("DFS Traversal: ");
          depth_first_search(adj,visited,0);
          printf("\n");
          return 0;
}
```

Output

```
Enter the adjacency matrix:
0 1 0 1 0
1 0 1 1 0
0 1 0 0 1
1 1 0 0 1
0 0 1 1 0
DFS Traversal: A -> C -> E ->
```

13.7 TOPOLOGICAL SORTING

Topological sort of a directed acyclic graph (DAG) G is defined as a linear ordering of its nodes in which each node comes before all nodes to which it has outbound edges. Every DAG has one or more number of topological sorts.

Example 13.3 Consider three DAGs shown in Fig. 13.24 and their possible topological sorts.

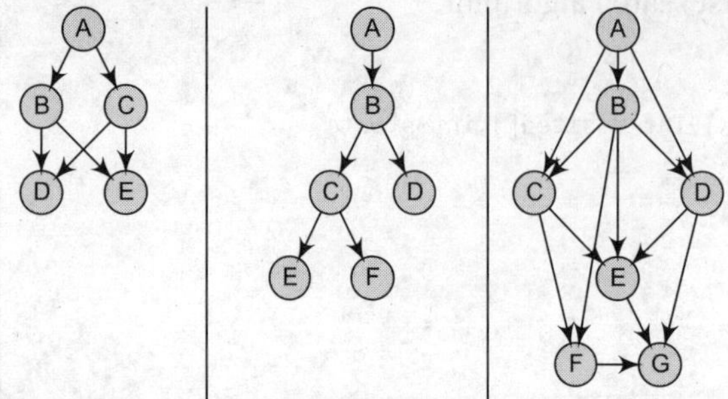

Topological sort can be given as:	Topological sort can be given as:	Topological sort can be given as:
• A, B, C, D, E	• A, B, D, C, E, F	• A, B, C, F, D, E, C
• A, B, C, E, D	• A, B, D, C, F, E	• A, B, C, D, E, F, G
• A, C, B, D, E	• A, B, C, D, E, F	• A, B, C, D, F, E, G
• A, C, B, E, D	• A, B, C, D, F, E	• A, B, D, C, E, F, G
	....	....
	• A, B, F, E, D	• A, B, D, C, F, E, G

Figure 13.24 Topological sort

One main property of a DAG is that more the number of edges in a DAG, fewer the number of topological orders it has. This is because each edge `(u, v)` forces node `u` to occur before `v`, which restricts the number of valid permutations of the nodes.

A topological sort of a DAG `G` is an ordering of the vertices of `G` such that if `G` contains an edge `(u, v)`, then `u` appears before `v` in the ordering. Note that topological sort is possible only on directed acyclic graphs that do not have any cycles. For a DAG that contains cycles, no linear ordering of its vertices is possible.

In simple words, a topological ordering of a DAG `G` is an ordering of its vertices such that any directed path in `G` traverses the vertices in increasing order.

Topological sorting is widely used in scheduling applications, jobs, or tasks. The jobs that have to be completed are represented by nodes, and there is an edge from node `u` to `v` if job `u` must be completed before job `v` can be started. A topological sort of such a graph gives an order in which the given jobs must be performed.

Algorithm

The algorithm for the topological sort of a graph (Fig. 13.25) that has no cycles focuses on selecting a node `N` with zero in-degree, that is, a node that has no predecessor. The two main steps involved in the topological sort algorithm include:

- Selecting a node with zero in-degree
- Deleting N from the graph along with its edges

```
Step 1: Find the in-degree INDEG(N) of every node
        in the graph
Step 2: Enqueue all the nodes with a zero in-degree
Step 3: Repeat Steps 4 and 5 until the QUEUE is empty
Step 4:   Remove the front node N of the QUEUE by setting
          FRONT = FRONT + 1
Step 5:   Repeat for each neighbour M of node N:
            a) Delete the edge from N to M by setting
               INDEG(M) = INDEG(M) - 1
            b) IF INDEG(M) = 0, then Enqueue M, that is,
               add M to the rear of the queue
          [END OF INNER LOOP]
      [END OF LOOP]
Step 6: Exit
```

Figure 13.25 Algorithm for topological sort

We will use a `QUEUE` to hold the nodes with zero in-degree. The order in which the nodes will be deleted from the graph will depend on the sequence in which the nodes are inserted in the `QUEUE`. Then, we will use a variable `INDEG`, where `INDEG(N)` will represent the in-degree of node `N`.

Notes
1. The in-degree can be calculated in two ways—either by counting the incoming edges from the graph or traversing through the adjacency list.
2. The running time of the algorithm for topological sorting can be given linearly as the number of nodes plus the number of edges O(|V|+|E|).

Example 13.4 Consider a directed acyclic graph G given in Fig. 13.26. We use the algorithm given above to find a topological sort T of G. The steps are given as below:

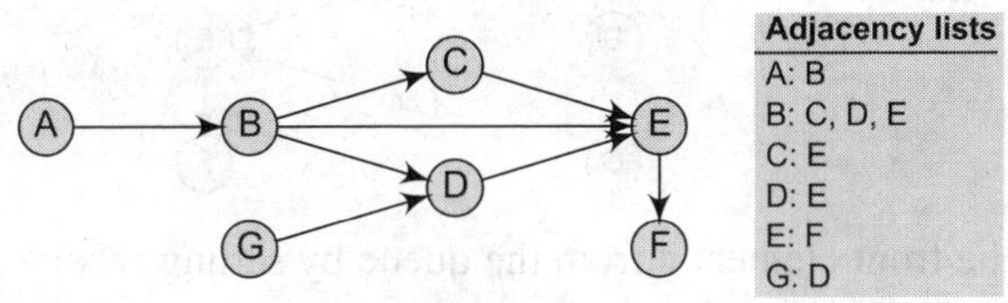

Figure 13.26 Graph G

Step 1: Find the in-degree INDEG(N) of every node in the graph
INDEG(A) = 0 INDEG(B) = 1 INDEG(C) = 1 INDEG(D) = 2
INDEG(E) = 3 INDEG(F) = 1 INDEG(G) = 0

Step 2: Enqueue all the nodes with a zero in-degree
FRONT = 1 REAR = 2 QUEUE = A, G

Step 3: Remove the front element A from the queue by setting FRONT = FRONT + 1, so
FRONT = 2 REAR = 2 QUEUE = A, G

Step 4: Set INDEG(B) = INDEG(B) – 1, since B is the neighbour of A. Note that INDEG(B) is 0, so add it on the queue. The queue now becomes
FRONT = 2 REAR = 3 QUEUE = A, G, B

Delete the edge from A to B. The graph now becomes as shown in the figure below

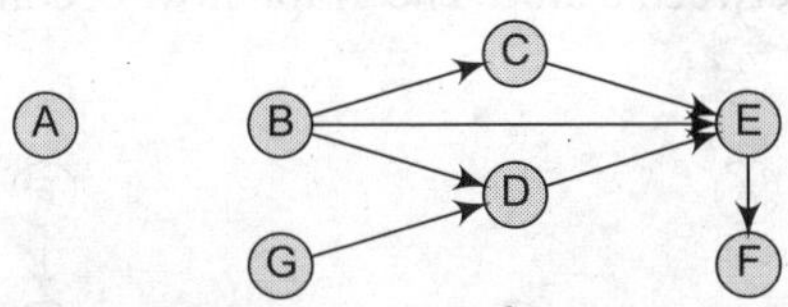

Step 5: Remove the front element B from the queue by setting FRONT = FRONT + 1, so
FRONT = 2 REAR = 3 QUEUE = A, G, B

Step 6: Set INDEG(D) = INDEG(D) – 1, since D is the neighbour of G. Now,
INDEG(C) = 1 INDEG(D) = 1 INDEG(E) = 3 INDEG(F) = 1

Delete the edge from G to D. The graph now becomes as shown in the figure below

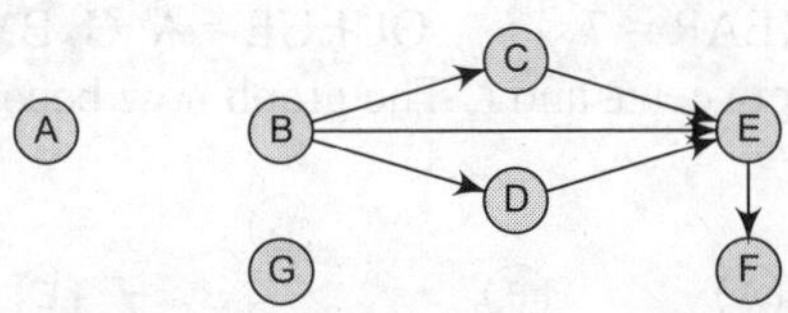

Step 7: Remove the front element B from the queue by setting FRONT = FRONT + 1, so
FRONT = 4 REAR = 3 QUEUE = A, G, B

Step 8: Set INDEG(C) = INDEG(C) – 1, INDEG(D) = INDEG(D) – 1, INDEG(E) = INDEG(E) – 1, since C, D, and E are the neighbours of B. Now,
INDEG(C) = 0, INDEG(D) = 1 and INDEG(E) = 2

Step 9: Since the in-degree of node C and D is zero, add C and D at the rear of the queue. The queue can be given as below:

FRONT = 4 REAR = 5 QUEUE = A, G, B, C, D

The graph now becomes as shown in the figure below

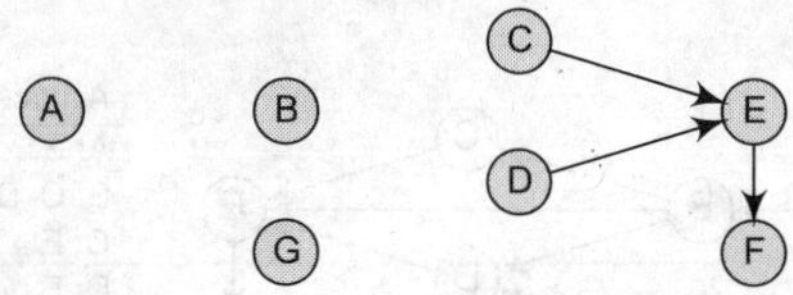

Step 10: Remove the front element C from the queue by setting `FRONT = FRONT + 1`, so

FRONT = 5 REAR = 5 QUEUE = A, G, B, C, D

Step 11: Set INDEG(E) = INDEG(E) – 1, since E is the neighbour of C. Now, INDEG(E) = 1

The graph now becomes as shown in the figure below

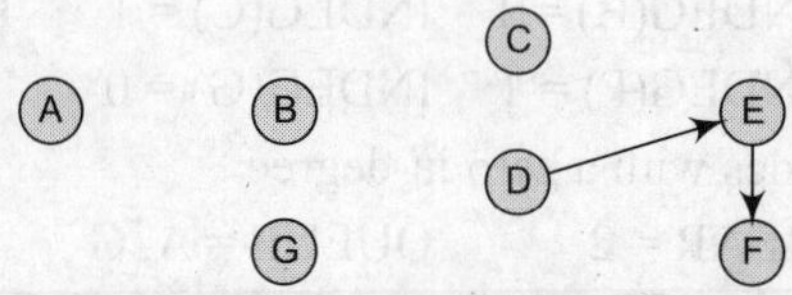

Step 12: Remove the front element D from the queue by setting `FRONT = FRONT + 1`, so

FRONT = 6 REAR = 5 QUEUE = A, B, G, C, D

Step 13: Set INDEG(E) = INDEG(E) – 1, since E is the neighbour of D. Now, INDEG(E) = 0, so add E to the queue. The queue now becomes.

FRONT = 6 REAR = 6 QUEUE = A, G, B, C, D, E

Step 14: Delete the edge between D an E. The graph now becomes as shown in the figure below

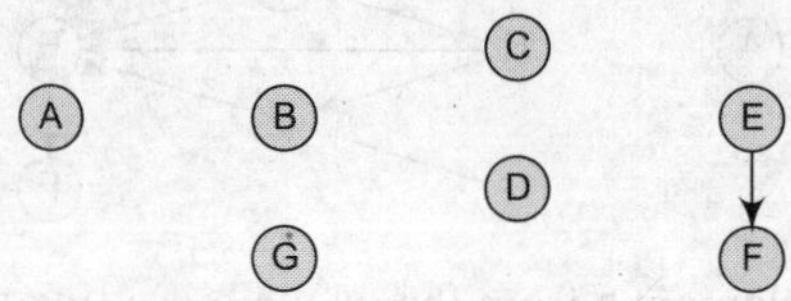

Step 15: Remove the front element D from the queue by setting `FRONT = FRONT + 1`, so

FRONT = 7 REAR = 6 QUEUE = A, G, B, C, D, E

Step 16: Set INDEG(F) = INDEG(F) – 1, since F is the neighbour of E. Now INDEG(F) = 0, so add F to the queue. The queue now becomes,

FRONT = 7 REAR = 7 QUEUE = A, G, B, C, D, E, F

Step 17: Delete the edge between E and F. The graph now becomes as shown in the figure below

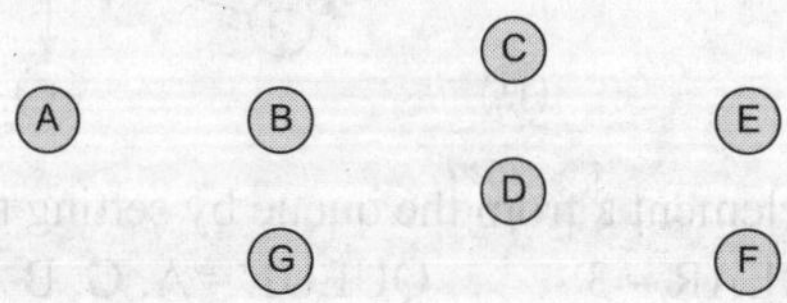

There are no more edges in the graph and all the nodes have been added to the queue, so the topological sort T of G can be given as: A, G, B, C, D, E, F. When we arrange these nodes in a sequence, we find that if there is an edge from u to v, then u appears before v.

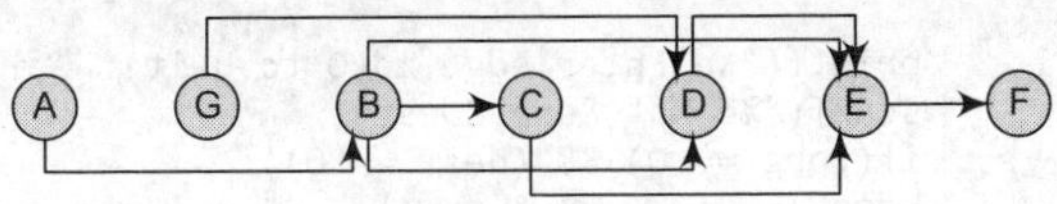

Figure 13.27 Topological sort of G

Programming Example

4. Write a program to implement topological sorting.

```
#include <stdio.h>
#define MAX 10
int n,adj[MAX][MAX];
int front = -1,rear = -1,queue[MAX];
void create_graph(void);
void display();
void insert_queue(int);
int delete_queue(void);
int find_indegree(int);
void main()
{
        int node,j = 0,del_node, I;
        int topsort[MAX],indeg[MAX];
        create_graph();
        printf("\n The adjacency matrix is:");
        display();
/*Find the in-degree of each node*/
for(node = 1; node <= n; node++)
{
        indeg[node] = find_indegree(node);
        if( indeg[node] == 0 )
                insert_queue(node);
}
while(front <= rear) /*Continue loop until queue is empty */
{
        del_node = delete_queue();
        topsort[j] = del_node; /*Add the deleted node to topsort*/
        j++;
/*Delete the del_node edges */
for(node = 1; node <= n; node++)
{
        if(adj[del_node][node] == 1 )
        {
                adj[del_node][node] = 0;
                indeg[node] = indeg[node] -1;
                if(indeg[node] == 0)
                insert_queue(node);
        }
    }
}
printf("The topological sorting can be given as :\n");
for(node=0;i<j;node++)
        printf("%d",topsort[node]);
}
void create_graph()
{
        int i,max_edges,org,dest;
```

```
        printf("\n Enter the number of vertices: ");
        scanf("%d",&n);
        max_edges = n*(n - 1);
        for(i = 1; i <= max_edges; i++)
        {
                printf("\n Enter edge %d(0 to quit): ",i);
                scanf("%d %d",&org,&dest);
                if((org == 0) && (dest == 0))
                break;
                if( org > n || dest > n || org <= 0 || dest <= 0)
                {
                        printf("\n Invalid edge");
                        i--;
                }
                else
                        adj[org][dest] = 1;
        }
}
void display()
{
        int i,j;
        for(i=1;i<=n;i++)
        {
                printf("\n");
                for(j=1;j<=n;j++)
                        printf("%3d",adj[i][j]);
        }
}
void insert_queue(int node)
{
        if (rear==MAX-1)
                printf("\n OVERFLOW ");
        else
        {
                if (front == -1) /*If queue is initially empty */
                        front=0;
                queue[++rear] = node ;
        }
}
int delete_queue()
{
        int del_node;
        if (front == -1 || front > rear)
        {
                printf("\n UNDERFLOW ");
                return ;
        }
        else
        {
                del_node = queue[front++];
                return del_node;
        }
}
int find_indegree(int node)
{
                int i,in_deg = 0;
                for(i = 1; i <= n; i++)
                {
                        if( adj[i][node] == 1 )
                                in_deg++;
                }
                return in_deg;
}
```

Output

```
Enter number of vertices: 7
Enter edge 1(0 to quit): 1 2
Enter edge 2(0 to quit): 2 3
Enter edge 3(0 to quit): 2 5
Enter edge 4(0 to quit): 2 4
Enter edge 5(0 to quit): 3 5
Enter edge 6(0 to quit): 4 5
Enter edge 7(0 to quit): 5 6
Enter edge 8(0 to quit): 7 4
The topological sorting can be given as:
1 7 2 3 4 5 6
```

13.8 SHORTEST PATH ALGORITHMS

In this section, we will discuss three different algorithms to calculate the shortest path between the vertices of a graph G. These algorithms include:

- Minimum spanning tree
- Dijkstra's algorithm
- Warshall's algorithm

While the first two use an adjacency list to find the shortest path, Warshall's algorithm uses an adjacency matrix to do the same.

13.8.1 Minimum Spanning Trees

A spanning tree of a connected, undirected graph G is a sub-graph of G which is a tree that connects all the vertices together. A graph G can have many different spanning trees. We can assign *weights* to each edge (which is a number that represents how unfavourable the edge is), and use it to assign a weight to a spanning tree by calculating the sum of the weights of the edges in that spanning tree. A *minimum spanning tree* (MST) is defined as a spanning tree with weight less than or equal to the weight of every other spanning tree. In other words, a minimum spanning tree is a spanning tree that has weights associated with its edges, and the total weight of the tree (the sum of the weights of its edges) is at a minimum.

An Analogy

Take an analogy of a cable TV company laying cable in a new neighbourhood. If it is restricted to bury the cable only along particular paths, then we can make a graph that represents the points that are connected by those paths. Some paths may be more expensive (due to their length or the depth at which the cable should be buried) than the others. We can represent these paths by edges with larger weights.

Therefore, a spanning tree for such a graph would be a subset of those paths that has no cycles but still connects to every house. Many distinct spanning trees can be obtained from this graph, but a minimum spanning tree would be the one with the lowest total cost.

Properties

Possible multiplicity There can be multiple minimum spanning trees of the same weight. Particularly, if all the weights are the same, then every spanning tree will be minimum.

Uniqueness When each edge in the graph is assigned a different weight, then there will be only one unique minimum spanning tree.

Minimum-cost subgraph If the edges of a graph are assigned *non-negative* weights, then a minimum spanning tree is in fact the minimum-cost subgraph or a tree that connects all vertices.

Cycle property If there exists a cycle C in the graph G that has a weight larger than that of other edges of C, then this edge cannot belong to an MST.

Usefulness Minimum spanning trees can be computed quickly and easily to provide optimal solutions. These trees create a sparse subgraph that reflects a lot about the original graph.

Simplicity The minimum spanning tree of a weighted graph is nothing but a spanning tree of the graph which comprises of `n-1` edges of minimum total weight. Note that for an unweighted graph, any spanning tree is a minimum spanning tree.

Example 13.5 Consider an unweighted graph `G` given below (Fig. 13.28). From `G`, we can draw many distinct spanning trees. Eight of them are given here. For an unweighted graph, every spanning tree is a minimum spanning tree.

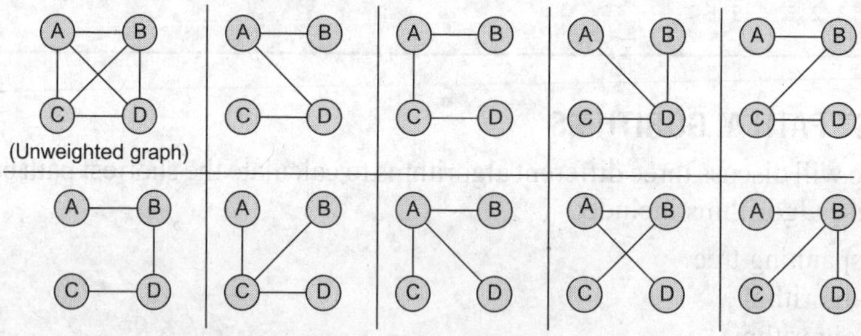

Figure 13.28 Unweighted graph and its spanning trees

Example 13.6 Consider a weighted graph `G` shown in Fig. 13.29. From `G`, we can draw three distinct spanning trees. But only a single minimum spanning tree can be obtained, that is, the one that has the minimum weight (cost) associated with it.

Of all the spanning trees given in Fig. 13.29, the one that is highlighted is called the minimum spanning tree, as it has the lowest cost associated with it.

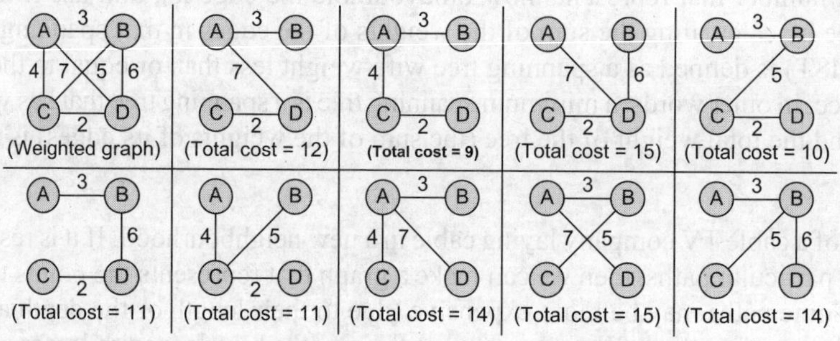

Figure 13.29 Weighted graph and its spanning trees

Applications of Minimum Spanning Trees

1. MSTs are widely used for designing networks. For instance, people separated by varying distances wish to be connected together through a telephone network. A minimum spanning tree is used to determine the least costly paths with no cycles in this network, thereby providing a connection that has the minimum cost involved.
2. MSTs are used to find airline routes. While the vertices in the graph denote cities, edges represent the routes between these cities. No doubt, more the distance between the cities, higher will be the amount charged. Therefore, MSTs are used to optimize airline routes by finding the least costly path with no cycles.
3. MSTs are also used to find the cheapest way to connect terminals, such as cities, electronic components or computers via roads, airlines, railways, wires or telephone lines.
4. MSTs are applied in routing algorithms for finding the most efficient path.

```
Step 1: Select a starting vertex
Step 2: Repeat Steps 3 and 4 until there are fringe vertices
Step 3:     Select an edge e connecting the tree vertex and
            fringe vertex that has minimum weight
Step 4:     Add the selected edge and the vertex to the
            minimum spanning tree T
        [END OF LOOP]
Step 5: EXIT
```

Figure 13.30 Prim's algorithm

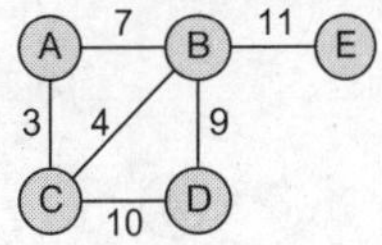

Figure 13.31 Graph G

13.8.2 Prim's Algorithm

Prim's algorithm is a greedy algorithm that is used to form a minimum spanning tree for a connected weighted undirected graph. In other words, the algorithm builds a tree that includes every vertex and a subset of the edges in such a way that the total weight of all the edges in the tree is minimized. For this, the algorithm maintains three sets of vertices which can be given as below:

- ***Tree vertices*** Vertices that are a part of the minimum spanning tree T.
- ***Fringe vertices*** Vertices that are currently not a part of T, but are adjacent to some tree vertex.
- ***Unseen vertices*** Vertices that are neither tree vertices nor fringe vertices fall under this category.

The steps involved in the Prim's algorithm are shown in Fig. 13.30.

- Choose a starting vertex.
- Branch out from the starting vertex and during each iteration, select a new vertex and an edge. Basically, during each iteration of the algorithm, we have to select a vertex from the fringe vertices in such a way that the edge connecting the tree vertex and the new vertex has the minimum weight assigned to it.

The running time of Prim's algorithm can be given as O(E log V) where E is the number of edges and V is the number of vertices in the graph.

Example 13.7 Construct a minimum spanning tree of the graph given in Fig. 13.31.

Step 1: Choose a starting vertex A.

Step 2: Add the fringe vertices (that are adjacent to A). The edges connecting the vertex and fringe vertices are shown with dotted lines.

Step 3: Select an edge connecting the tree vertex and the fringe vertex that has the minimum weight and add the selected edge and the vertex to the minimum spanning tree T. Since the edge connecting A and C has less weight, add C to the tree. Now C is not a fringe vertex but a tree vertex.

Step 4: Add the fringe vertices (that are adjacent to C).

Step 5: Select an edge connecting the tree vertex and the fringe vertex that has the minimum weight and add the selected edge and the vertex to the minimum spanning tree T. Since the edge connecting C and B has less weight, add B to the tree. Now B is not a fringe vertex but a tree vertex.

Step 6: Add the fringe vertices (that are adjacent to B).

Step 7: Select an edge connecting the tree vertex and the fringe vertex that has the minimum weight and add the selected edge and the vertex to the minimum spanning tree T. Since the edge connecting B and D has less weight, add D to the tree. Now D is not a fringe vertex but a tree vertex.

Step 8: Note, now node E is not connected, so we will add it in the tree because a minimum spanning tree is one in which all the n nodes are connected with n-1 edges that have minimum weight. So, the minimum spanning tree can now be given as,

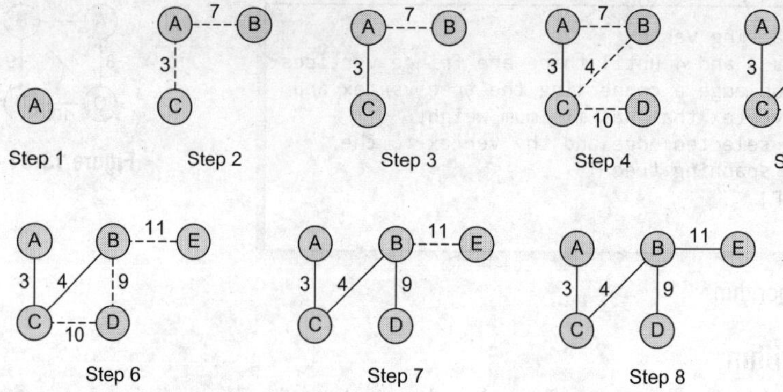

Example 13.8 Construct a minimum spanning tree of the graph given in Fig. 13.32. Start the Prim's algorithm from vertex D.

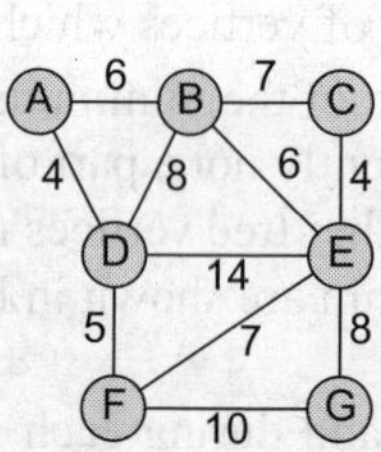

Figure 13.32 Graph G

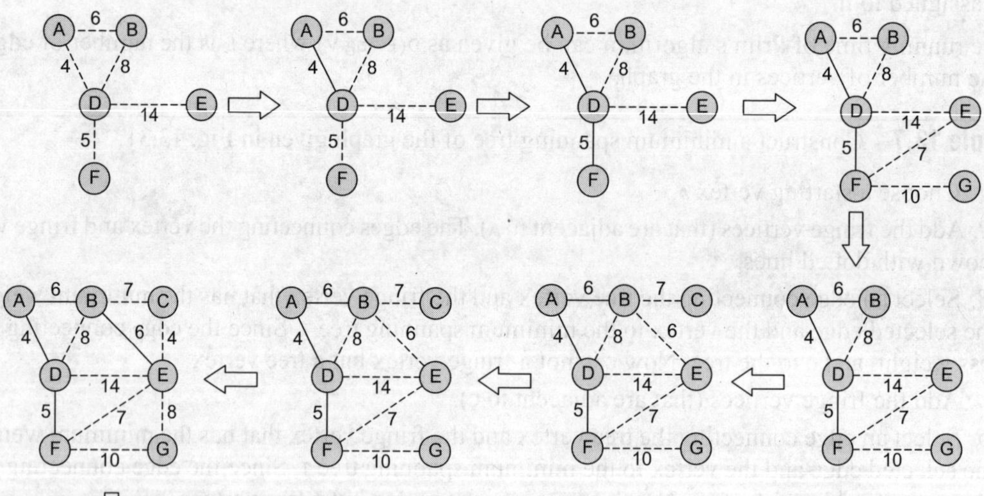

13.8.3 Kruskal's Algorithm

Kruskal's algorithm is used to find the minimum spanning tree for a connected weighted graph. The algorithm aims to find a subset of the edges that forms a tree that includes every vertex. The total weight of all the edges in the tree is minimized. However, if the graph is not connected, then it finds a *minimum spanning forest*. Note that a forest is a collection of trees. Similarly, a minimum spanning forest is a collection of minimum spanning trees.

Kruskal's algorithm is an example of a greedy algorithm, as it makes the locally optimal choice at each stage with the hope of finding the global optimum. The algorithm is shown in Fig. 13.33.

```
Step 1: Create a forest in such a way that each graph is a separate
        tree.
Step 2: Create a priority queue Q that contains all the edges of the
        graph.
Step 3: Repeat Steps 4 and 5 while Q is NOT EMPTY
Step 4:        Remove an edge from Q
Step 5: IF the edge obtained in Step 4 connects two different trees,
        then Add it to the forest (for combining two trees into one
        tree).
        ELSE
               Discard the edge
Step 6: END
```

Figure 13.33 Kruskal's algorithm

In the algorithm, we use a priority queue `Q` in which edges that have minimum weight takes a priority over any other edge in the graph. When the Kruskal's algorithm terminates, the forest has only one component and forms a minimum spanning tree of the graph. The running time of Kruskal's algorithm can be given as `O(E log V)`, where `E` is the number of edges and `V` is the number of vertices in the graph.

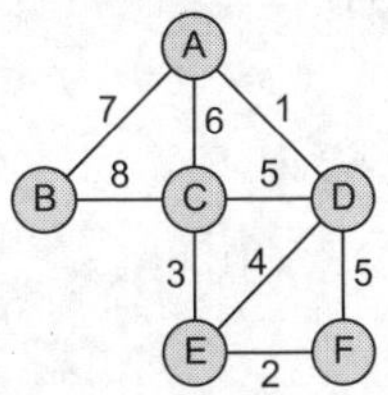

Figure 13.34

Example 13.9 Apply Kruskal's algorithm on the graph given in Fig. 13.34.

Initially, we have F = {{A}, {B}, {C}, {D}, {E}, {F}}

MST = {}

Q = {(A, D), (E, F), (C, E), (E, D), (C, D), (D, F), (A, C), (A, B), (B, C)}

Step 1: Remove the edge `(A, D)` from `Q` and make the following changes:

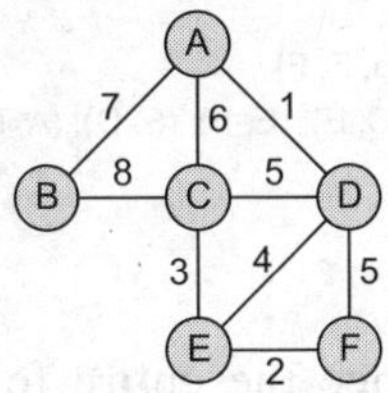

F = {{A, D}, {B}, {C}, {E}, {F}}

MST = {A, D}

Q = {(E, F), (C, E), (E, D), (C, D), (D, F), (A, C), (A, B), (B, C)}

Step 2: Remove the edge `(E, F)` from `Q` and make the following changes:

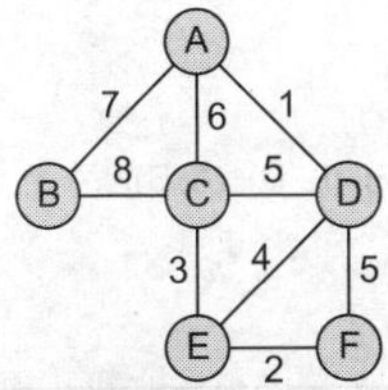

F = {{A, D}, {B}, {C}, {E, F}}

MST = {(A, D), (E, F)}

Q = {(C, E), (E, D), (C, D), (D, F), (A, C), (A, B), (B, C)}

Step 3: Remove the edge `(C, E)` from `Q` and make the following changes:

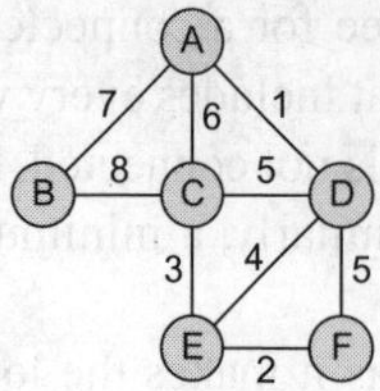

F = {{A, D}, {B}, {C, E, F}}
MST = {(A, D), (C, E), (E, F)}
Q = {(E, D), (C, D), (D, F), (A, C), (A, B), (B, C)}

Step 4: Remove the edge `(E, D)` from `Q` and make the following changes:

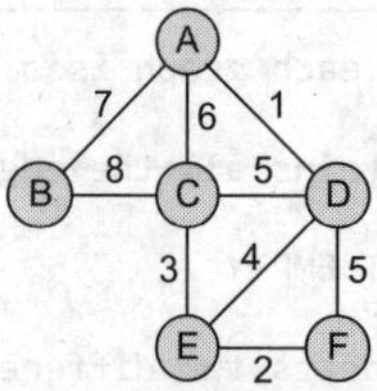

F = {{A, C, D, E, F}, {B}}
MST = {(A, D), (C, E), (E, F), (E, D)}
Q = {(C, D), (D, F), (A, C), (A, B), (B, C)}

Step 5: Remove the edge `(C, D)` from `Q`. Note that this edge does not connect different trees, so simply discard this edge. Only an edge connecting `(A, D, C, E, F)` to `B` will be added to the MST. Therefore,

F = {{A, C, D, E, F}, {B}}
MST = {(A, D), (C, E), (E, F), (E, D)}
Q = {(D, F), (A, C), (A, B), (B, C)}

Step 6: Remove the edge `(D, F)` from `Q`. Note that this edge does not connect different trees, so simply discard this edge. Only an edge connecting `(A, D, C, E, F)` to `B` will be added to the MST.

F = {{A, C, D, E, F}, {B}}
MST = {(A, D), (C, E), (E, F), (E, D)}
Q = {(A, C), (A, B), (B, C)}

Step 7: Remove the edge `(A, C)` from `Q`. Note that this edge does not connect different trees, so simply discard this edge. Only an edge connecting `(A, D, C, E, F)` to `B` will be added to the MST.

F = {{A, C, D, E, F}, {B}}
MST = {(A, D), (C, E), (E, F), (E, D)}
Q = {(A, B), (B, C)}

Step 8: Remove the edge `(A, B)` from `Q` and make the following changes:

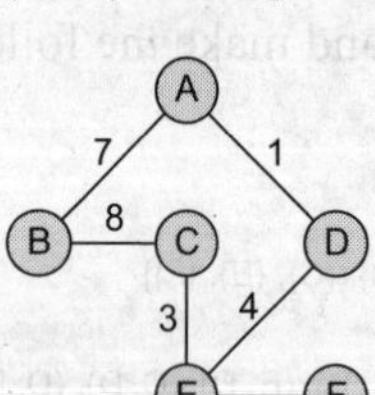

F = {A, B, C, D, E, F}
MST = {(A, D), (C, E), (E, F), (E, D), (A, B)}
Q = {(B, C)}

Step 9: The algorithm continues until `Q` is empty. Since the entire forest has become one tree, all the remaining edges will simply be discarded. The resultant MS can be given as shown below.

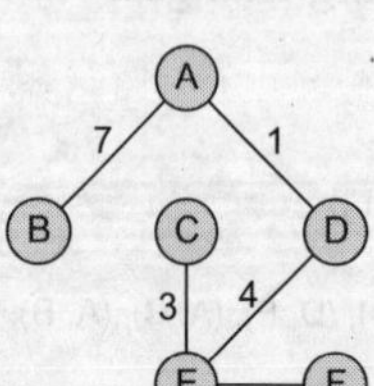

F = {A, B, C, D, E, F}
MST = {(A, D), (C, E), (E, F), (E, D), (A, B)}
Q = {}

Programming Example

5. Write a program which finds the cost of a minimum spanning tree.

```
#include<stdio.h>
#define MAX 10
int adj[MAX][MAX], tree[MAX][MAX], n;
void readmatrix()
{
        int i, j;
        printf("\n Enter the number of nodes in the Graph : ");
        scanf("%d", &n);
        printf("\n Enter the adjacency matrix of the Graph");
        for (i = 1; i <= n; i++)
                for (j = 1; j <= n; j++)
                        scanf("%d", &adj[i][j]);
}
int spanningtree(int src)
{
        int visited[MAX], d[MAX], parent[MAX];
        int i, j, k, min, u, v, cost;
        for (i = 1; i <= n; i++)
        {
                d[i] = adj[src][i];
                visited[i] = 0;
                parent[i] = src;
        }
        visited[src] = 1;
        cost = 0;
        k = 1;
        for (i = 1; i < n; i++)
        {
                min = 9999;
                for (j = 1; j <= n; j++)
                {
                        if (visited[j]==0 && d[j] < min)
                        {
                                min = d[j];
                                u = j;
                                cost += d[u];
                        }
                }
                visited[u] = 1;
                //cost = cost + d[u];
                tree[k][1] = parent[u];
                tree[k++][2] = u;
                for (v = 1; v <= n; v++)
                        if (visited[v]==0 && (adj[u][v] < d[v]))
                        {
                                d[v] = adj[u][v];
                                parent[v] = u;
                        }
        }
        return cost;
}
void display(int cost)
{
        int i;
        printf("\n The Edges of the Mininum Spanning Tree are");
        for (i = 1; i < n; i++)
```

```
                    printf(" %d %d \n", tree[i][1], tree[i][2]);
            printf("\n The Total cost of the Minimum Spanning Tree is : %d", cost);
    }
    main()
    {
            int source, treecost;
            readmatrix();
            printf("\n Enter the Source : ");
            scanf("%d", &source);
            treecost = spanningtree(source);
            display(treecost);
            return 0;
    }
```

Output

```
Enter the number of nodes in the Graph : 4
Enter the adjacency matrix : 0      1       1       0
0       0       0       1
0       1       0       0
1       0       1       0
Enter the source : 1
The edges of the Minimum Spanning Tree are    1    4
4       2
2       3
The total cost of the Minimum Spanning Tree is : 1
```

13.8.4 Dijkstra's Algorithm

Dijkstra's algorithm, given by a Dutch scientist Edsger Dijkstra in 1959, is used to find the shortest path tree. This algorithm is widely used in network routing protocols, most notably IS-IS and OSPF (Open Shortest Path First).

Given a graph G and a source node A, the algorithm is used to find the shortest path (one having the lowest cost) between A (source node) and every other node. Moreover, Dijkstra's algorithm is also used for finding the costs of the shortest paths from a source node to a destination node.

For example, if we draw a graph in which nodes represent the cities and weighted edges represent the driving distances between pairs of cities connected by a direct road, then Dijkstra's algorithm when applied gives the shortest route between one city and all other cities.

Algorithm

Dijkstra's algorithm is used to find the length of an *optimal* path between two nodes in a graph. The term *optimal* can mean anything, shortest, cheapest, or fastest. If we start the algorithm with an initial node, then the distance of a node Y can be given as the distance from the initial node to that node. Figure 13.35 explains the Dijkstra's algorithm.

Dijkstra's algorithm labels every node in the graph where the labels represent the distance (cost) from the source node to that node. There are two kinds of labels: *temporary* and *permanent*. Temporary labels are assigned to nodes that have not been reached, while permanent labels are given to nodes that have been reached and their distance (cost) to the source node is known. A node must be a permanent label or a temporary label, but not both.

The execution of this algorithm will produce either of the following two results:

1. If the destination node is labelled, then the label will in turn represent the distance from the source node to the destination node.
2. If the destination node is not labelled, then there is no path from the source to the destination node.

```
1. Select the source node also called the initial node
2. Define an empty set N that will be used to hold nodes to which a shortest
   path has been found.
3. Label the initial node with 0, and insert it into N.
4. Repeat Steps 5 to 7 until the destination node is in N or there are no more
   labelled nodes in N.
5. Consider each node that is not in N and is connected by an edge from
   the newly inserted node.
6. (a) If the node that is not in N has no label then SET the label of the
       node = the label of the newly inserted node + the length of the edge.
   (b) Else if the node that is not in N was already labelled, then SET its new
       label = minimum (label of newly inserted vertex + length of edge, old
       label)
7. Pick a node not in N that has the smallest label assigned to it and add it
   to N.
```

Figure 13.35 Dijkstra's algorithm

Example 13.10 Consider the graph G given in Fig. 13.36. Taking D as the initial node, execute the Dijkstra's algorithm on it.

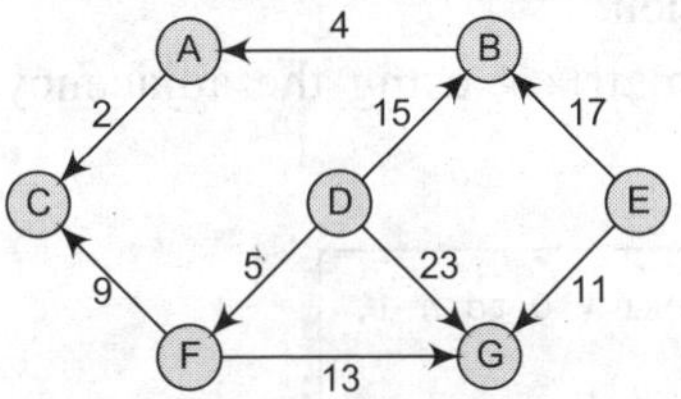

Figure 13.36 Graph G

Step 1: Set the label of D = 0 and N = {D}.

Step 2: Label of D = 0, B = 15, G = 23, and F = 5. Therefore, N = {D, F}.

Step 3: Label of D = 0, B = 15, G has been re-labelled 18 because minimum (5 + 13, 23) = 18, C has been re-labelled 14 (5 + 9). Therefore, N = {D, F, C}.

Step 4: Label of D = 0, B = 15, G = 18. Therefore, N = {D, F, C, B}.

Step 5: Label of D = 0, B = 15, G = 18 and A = 19 (15 + 4). Therefore, N = {D, F, C, B, G}.

Step 6: Label of D = 0 and A = 19. Therefore, N = {D, F, C, B, G, A}

Note that we have no labels for node E; this means that E is not reachable from D. Only the nodes that are in N are reachable from B.

The running time of Dijkstra's algorithm can be given as $O(|V|^2+|E|)=O(|V|^2)$ where V is the set of vertices and E in the graph.

Difference between Dijkstra's Algorithm and Minimum Spanning Tree

Minimum spanning tree algorithm is used to traverse a graph in the most efficient manner, but Dijkstra's algorithm calculates the distance from a given vertex to every other vertex in the graph.

Dijkstra's algorithm is very similar to Prim's algorithm. Both the algorithms begin at a specific node and extend outward within the graph, until all other nodes in the graph have been reached. The point where these algorithms differ is that while Prim's algorithm stores a minimum cost edge, Dijkstra's algorithm stores the total cost from a source node to the current node. Moreover, Dijkstra's algorithm is used to store the summation of minimum cost edges, while Prim's algorithm stores at most one minimum cost edge.

13.8.5 Warshall's Algorithm

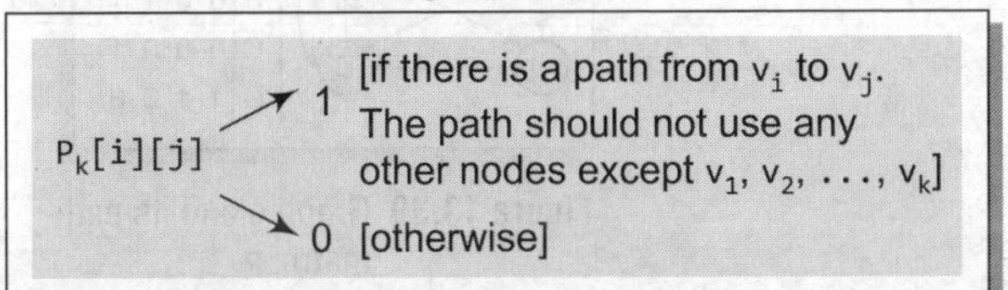

Figure 13.37 Path matrix entry

If a graph G is given as G=(V, E), where V is the set of vertices and E is the set of edges, the path matrix of G can be found as, $P = A + A^2 + A^3 + \dots + A^n$. This is a lengthy process, so Warshall has given a very efficient algorithm to calculate the path matrix. Warshall's algorithm defines matrices $P_0, P_1, P_2, \dots, P_n$ as given in Fig. 13.37.

This means that if $P_0[i][j] = 1$, then there exists an edge from node v_i to v_j.

If $P_1[i][j] = 1$, then there exists an edge from v_i to v_j that does not use any other vertex except v_1.

If $P_2[i][j] = 1$, then there exists an edge from v_i to v_j that does not use any other vertex except v_1 and v_2.

Note that P_0 is equal to the adjacency matrix of G. If G contains n nodes, then $P_n = P$ which is the path matrix of the graph G.

From the above discussion, we can conclude that $P_k[i][j]$ is equal to 1 only when either of the two following cases occur:

- There is a path from v_i to v_j that does not use any other node except $v_1, v_2, ..., v_{k-1}$. Therefore, $P_{k-1}[i][j] = 1$.
- There is a path from v_i to v_k and a path from v_k to v_j where all the nodes use $v_1, v_2, \ldots, v_{k-1}$. Therefore,

$$P_{k-1}[i][k] = 1 \text{ AND } P_{k-1}[k][j] = 1$$

Hence, the path matrix P_n can be calculated with the formula given as:

$$P_k[i][j] = P_{k-1}[i][j] \vee (P_{k-1}[i][k] \wedge P_{k-1}[k][j])$$

where $\vee$ indicates logical OR operation and $\wedge$ indicates logical AND operation.

Figure 13.38 shows the Warshall's algorithm to find the path matrix P using the adjacency matrix A.

```
Step 1: [INITIALIZE the Path Matrix] Repeat Step 2 for I = 0 to n-1,
        where n is the number of nodes in the graph
Step 2:     Repeat Step 3 for J = 0 to n-1
Step 3:           IF A[I][J] = 0, then SET P[I][J] = 0
                  ELSE P[I][J] = 1
            [END OF LOOP]
      [END OF LOOP]
Step 4: [Calculate the path matrix P] Repeat Step 5 for K = 0 to n-1
Step 5:     Repeat Step 6 for I = 0 to n-1
Step 6:           Repeat Step 7 for J=0 to n-1
Step 7:                  SET PK[I][J] = PK-1[I][J] V (PK-1[I][K]
                         Λ PK-1[K][J])
Step 8: EXIT
```

Figure 13.38 Warshall's algorithm

Example 13.11 Consider the graph in Fig. 13.39 and its adjacency matrix A. We can straightaway calculate the path matrix P using the Warshall's algorithm.

The path matrix P can be given in a single step as:

$$P = \begin{array}{c} \\ A \\ B \\ C \\ D \end{array} \begin{array}{c} \begin{array}{cccc} A & B & C & D \end{array} \\ \begin{pmatrix} 1 & 1 & 1 & 1 \\ 1 & 1 & 1 & 1 \\ 1 & 1 & 1 & 1 \\ 1 & 1 & 1 & 1 \end{pmatrix} \end{array}$$

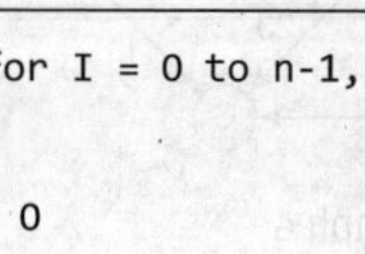

$$\begin{array}{c} \\ A \\ B \\ C \\ D \end{array} \begin{array}{c} \begin{array}{cccc} A & B & C & D \end{array} \\ \begin{pmatrix} 0 & 1 & 1 & 0 \\ 0 & 0 & 1 & 1 \\ 0 & 0 & 0 & 1 \\ 1 & 1 & 0 & 0 \end{pmatrix} \end{array}$$

Figure 13.39 Graph G and its path matrix P

Thus, we see that calculating A, A2, A3, A4, . . ., A5 to calculate P is a very slow and inefficient technique as compared to the Warshall's technique.

Programming Example

6. Write a program to implement Warshall's algorithm to find the path matrix.

```
#include <stdio.h>
void read (int mat[5][5], int n);
void display (int mat[5][5], int n);
void mul(int mat[5][5], int n);
int main()
{
        int adj[5][5], P[5][5], n, i, j, k;
        printf("\n Enter the number of nodes in the graph : ");
        scanf("%d", &n);
        printf("\n Enter the adjacency matrix : ");
        read(adj, n);
        printf("\n The adjacency matrix is : ");
        display(adj, n);
        for(i=0;i<n;i++)
        {
                for(j=0;j<n;j++)
                {
                        if(adj[i][j] == 0)
                                P[i][j] = 0;
                        else
                                P[i][j] = 1;
                }
        }
        for(k=0; k<n;k++)
        {
                for(i=0;i<n;i++)
                {
                        for(j=0;j<n;j++)
                        P[i][j] = P[i][j] | ( P[i][k] & P[k][j]);
                }
        }
        printf("\n The Path Matrix is :");
        display (P, n);
        return 0;
}
void read(int mat[5][5], int n)
{
        int i, j;
        for(i=0;i<n;i++)
        {
                for(j=0;j<n;j++)
                {
                        printf("\n mat[%d][%d] = ", i, j);
                        scanf("%d", &mat[i][j]);
                }
        }
}
void display(int mat[5][5], int n)
{
        int i, j;
        for(i=0;i<n;i++)
        printf("\n");
                for(j=0;j<n;j++)
                        printf("%d\t", mat[i][j]);

}
```

Output

```
The adjacency matrix is
0       1       1.      0
0       0       1       1
0       0       0       1
1       1       0       0
The Path Matrix is
1       1       1       1
1       1       1       1
1       1       1       1
1       1       1       1
```

13.8.6 Modified Warshall's Algorithm

Warshall's algorithm can be modified to obtain a matrix that gives the shortest paths between the nodes in a graph G. As an input to the algorithm, we take the adjacency matrix A of G and replace all the values of A which are zero by infinity (∞). Infinity (∞) denotes a very large number and indicates that there is no path between the vertices. In Warshall's modified algorithm, we obtain a set of matrices Q_0, Q_1, Q_2, . . ., Q_m using the formula given below.

$$Q_k[i][j] = \text{Minimum}(\ M_{k-1}[i][j],\ M_{k-1}[i][k] + M_{k-1}[k][j])$$

Q_0 is exactly the same as A with a little difference that every element having a zero value in A is replaced by (∞) in Q_0. Using the given formula, the matrix Q_n will give the path matrix that has the shortest path between the vertices of the graph. Warshall's modified algorithm is shown in Fig. 13.40.

```
Step 1: [Initialize the Shortest Path Matrix, Q] Repeat Step 2 for I = 0
        to n-1, where n is the number of nodes in the graph
Step 2:     Repeat Step 3 for J = 0 to n-1
Step 3:           IF A[I][J] = 0, then SET Q[I][J] = Infinity (or 9999)
                  ELSE Q[I][J] = A[I][j]
            [END OF LOOP]
      [END OF LOOP]
Step 4: [Calculate the shortest path matrix Q] Repeat Step 5 for K = 0
        to n-1
Step 5:     Repeat Step 6 for I = 0 to n-1
Step 6:           Repeat Step 7 for J=0 to n-1
Step 7:                 IF Q[I][J] <= Q[I][K] + Q[K][J]
                        SET Q[I][J] = Q[I][J]
                  ELSE SET Q[I][J] = Q[I][K] + Q[K][J]
                  [END OF IF]
            [END OF LOOP]
      [END OF LOOP]
      [END OF LOOP]
Step 8: EXIT
```

Figure 13.40 Modified Warshall's algorithm

Example 13.12 Consider the unweighted graph G given in Fig. 13.41 and apply Warshall's algorithm to it.

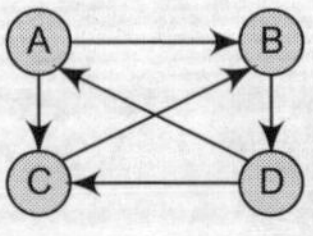

$$\begin{pmatrix} 0 & 1 & 1 & 0 \\ 0 & 0 & 0 & 1 \\ 0 & 1 & 0 & 0 \\ 1 & 0 & 1 & 0 \end{pmatrix}$$

Figure 13.41 Graph G

$$\mathbf{Q0} = \begin{bmatrix} 9999 & 1 & 1 & 9999 \\ 9999 & 9999 & 9999 & 1 \\ 9999 & 1 & 9999 & 9999 \\ 1 & 9999 & 1 & 9999 \end{bmatrix} \qquad \mathbf{Q1} = \begin{bmatrix} 9999 & 1 & 1 & 9999 \\ 9999 & 9999 & 9999 & 1 \\ 9999 & 1 & 9999 & 9999 \\ 1 & 2 & 1 & 9999 \end{bmatrix}$$

$$Q2 = \begin{bmatrix} 9999 & 1 & 1 & 2 \\ 9999 & 9999 & 9999 & 1 \\ 9999 & 1 & 9999 & 2 \\ 1 & 2 & 9999 & 3 \end{bmatrix} \quad Q3 = \begin{bmatrix} 9999 & 1 & 1 & 2 \\ 9999 & 9999 & 9999 & 1 \\ 9999 & 1 & 9999 & 2 \\ 1 & 2 & 9999 & 3 \end{bmatrix} \quad Q4 = Q \begin{bmatrix} 3 & 1 & 1 & 2 \\ 2 & 3 & 2 & 1 \\ 3 & 1 & 3 & 2 \\ 1 & 2 & 1 & 3 \end{bmatrix}$$

Example 13.13 Consider a weighted graph G given in Fig. 13.42 and apply Warshall's shortest path algorithm to it.

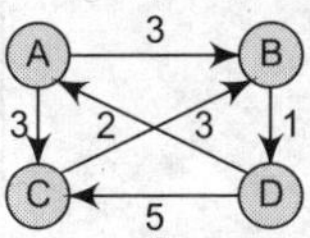

$$\begin{pmatrix} 0 & 3 & 3 & 0 \\ 0 & 0 & 0 & 1 \\ 0 & 3 & 0 & 0 \\ 2 & 0 & 5 & 0 \end{pmatrix}$$

Figure 13.42 Graph G

$$Q0 = \begin{bmatrix} 9999 & 3 & 3 & 9999 \\ 9999 & 9999 & 9999 & 1 \\ 9999 & 3 & 9999 & 9999 \\ 2 & 9999 & 5 & 9999 \end{bmatrix}$$

$$Q1 = \begin{bmatrix} 9999 & 3 & 3 & 9999 \\ 9999 & 9999 & 9999 & 1 \\ 9999 & 3 & 9999 & 9999 \\ 2 & 5 & 5 & 9999 \end{bmatrix} \quad Q2 = \begin{bmatrix} 9999 & 3 & 3 & 4 \\ 9999 & 9999 & 9999 & 1 \\ 9999 & 3 & 9999 & 4 \\ 2 & 5 & 5 & 6 \end{bmatrix}$$

$$Q3 = \begin{bmatrix} 9999 & 3 & 3 & 4 \\ 9999 & 9999 & 9999 & 1 \\ 9999 & 3 & 9999 & 6 \\ 2 & 5 & 5 & 6 \end{bmatrix} \quad Q4 = Q \begin{bmatrix} 6 & 3 & 3 & 4 \\ 3 & 6 & 6 & 1 \\ 6 & 3 & 9 & 4 \\ 2 & 5 & 5 & 6 \end{bmatrix}$$

Programming Example

7. Write a program to implement Warshall's modified algorithm to find the shortest path.

```
#include <stdio.h>
#define INFINITY 9999
void read (int mat[5][5], int n);
void display(int mat[5][5], int n);
int main()
{
          int adj[5][5], Q[5][5], n, i, j, k;
          printf("\n Enter the number of nodes in the graph : ");
          scanf("%d", &n);
          printf("\n Enter the adjacency matrix : ");
          read(adj, n);
          printf("\n The adjacency matrix is : ");
          display(adj, n);
          for(i=0;i<n;i++)
          {
                    for(j=0;j<n;j++)
                    {
                              if(adj[i][j] == 0)
```

```
                                        Q[i][j] = INFINITY;
                                else
                                        Q[i][j] = adj[i][j];
                        }
                }
                for(k=0; k<n;k++)
                {
                        for(i=0;i<n;i++)
                        {
                                for(j=0;j<n;j++)
                                {
                                        if(Q[i][j] <= Q[i][k] + Q[k][j])
                                                Q[i][j] = Q[i][j];
                                        else
                                                Q[i][j] = Q[i][k] + Q[k][j];
                                }
                        }
                        printf("\n\n");
                        display(Q, n);
                }
                return 0;
        }
        void read(int mat[5][5], int n)
        {
                int i, j;
                for(i=0;i<n;i++)
                {
                        for(j=0;j<n;j++)
                        {
                                printf("\n mat[%d][%d] = ", i, j);
                                scanf("%d", &mat[i][j]);
                        }
                }
        }
        void display(int mat[5][5], int n)
        {
                int i, j;
                for(i=0;i<n;i++)
                {printf("\n");
                        for(j=0;j<n;j++)
                                printf("%d\t", mat[i][j]);
                }
        }
```

Output

```
6       3       3       4
3       6       6       1
6       3       9       4
1       5       5       6
```

13.9 APPLICATIONS OF GRAPHS

Graphs are constructed for various types of applications such as:

- In circuit networks where points of connection are drawn as vertices and component wires become the edges of the graph.
- In transport networks where stations are drawn as vertices and routes become the edges of the graph.

- In maps that draw cities/states/regions as vertices and adjacency relations as edges.
- In program flow analysis where procedures or modules are treated as vertices and calls to these procedures are drawn as edges of the graph.
- Once we have a graph of a particular concept, they can be easily used for finding shortest paths, project planning, etc.
- In flowcharts or control-flow graphs, the statements and conditions in a program are represented as nodes and the flow of control is represented by the edges.
- In state transition diagrams, the nodes are used to represent states and the edges represent legal moves from one state to the other.
- Graphs are also used to draw activity network diagrams. These diagrams are extensively used as a project management tool to represent the interdependent relationships between groups, steps, and tasks that have a significant impact on the project.

An Activity Network Diagram (AND) also known as an Arrow Diagram or a PERT (Program Evaluation Review Technique) is used to identify time sequences of events which are pivotal to objectives. It is also helpful when a project has multiple activities which need simultaneous management. ANDs help the project development team to create a realistic project schedule by drawing graphs that exhibit:

- the total amount of time needed to complete the project
- the sequence in which activities must be performed
- the activities that can be performed simultaneously
- the critical activities that must be monitored on a regular basis.

A sample AND is shown in Fig. 13.43.

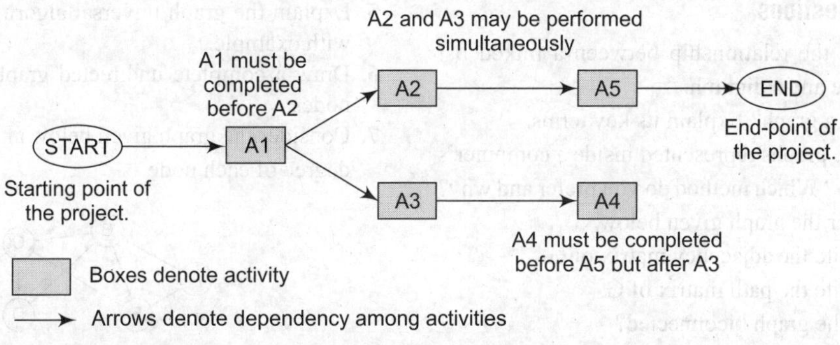

Figure 13.43 Activity network diagram

Points to Remember

- A graph is basically a collection of vertices (also called nodes) and edges that connect these vertices.
- Degree of a node u is the total number of edges containing the node u. When the degree of a node is zero, it is also called an isolated node. A path P is known as a closed path if the edge has the same end-points. A closed simple path with length 3 or more is known as a cycle.
- A graph in which there exists a path between any two of its nodes is called a connected graph. An edge that has identical end-points is called a loop. The size of a graph is the total number of edges in it.
- The out-degree of a node is the number of edges that originate at u.
- The in-degree of a node is the number of edges that terminate at u. A node u is known as a sink if it has a positive in-degree but a zero out-degree.
- A transitive closure of a graph is constructed to answer reachability questions.

- Since an adjacency matrix contains only 0s and 1s, it is called a bit matrix or a Boolean matrix. The memory use of an adjacency matrix is $O(n^2)$, where n is the number of nodes in the graph.
- Topological sort of a directed acyclic graph G is defined as a linear ordering of its nodes in which each node comes before all the nodes to which it has outbound edges. Every DAG has one or more number of topological sorts.
- A vertex v of G is called an articulation point if removing v along with the edges incident to v results in a graph that has at least two connected components.
- A biconnected graph is defined as a connected graph that has no articulation vertices.
- Breadth-first search is a graph search algorithm that begins at the root node and explores all the neighbouring nodes. Then for each of those nearest nodes, the algorithm explores their unexplored neighbour nodes, and so on, until it finds the goal.
- The depth-first search algorithm progresses by expanding the starting node of G and thus going deeper and deeper until a goal node is found, or until a node that has no children is encountered.
- A spanning tree of a connected, undirected graph G is a sub-graph of G which is a tree that connects all the vertices together.
- Kruskal's algorithm is an example of a greedy algorithm, as it makes the locally optimal choice at each stage with the hope of finding the global optimum.
- Dijkstra's algorithm is used to find the length of an optimal path between two nodes in a graph.

Exercises

Review Questions

1. Explain the relationship between a linked list structure and a digraph.
2. What is a graph? Explain its key terms.
3. How are graphs represented inside a computer's memory? Which method do you prefer and why?
4. Consider the graph given below.
   (a) Write the adjacency matrix of G.
   (b) Write the path matrix of G.
   (c) Is the graph biconnected?
   (d) Is the graph complete?
   (e) Find the shortest path matrix using Warshall's algorithm.

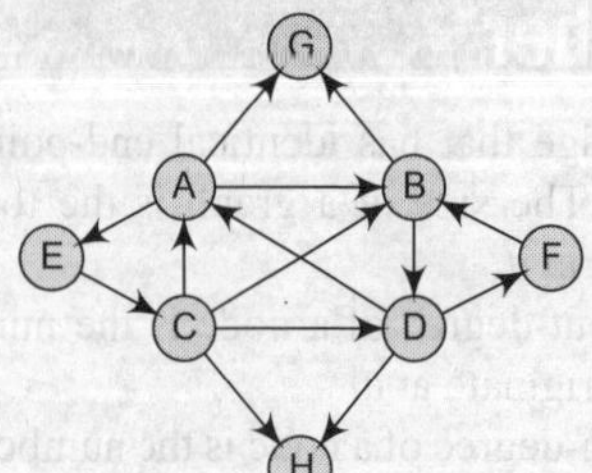

5. Explain the graph traversal algorithms in detail with example.
6. Draw a complete undirected graph having five nodes.
7. Consider the graph given below and find out the degree of each node.

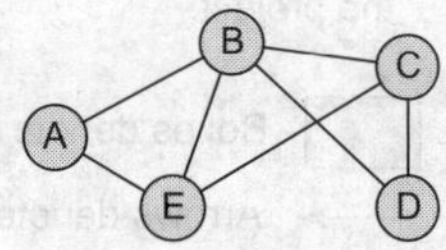

8. Consider the graph given below. State all the simple paths from A to D, B to D, and C to D. Also, find out the in-degree and out-degree of each node. Is there any source or sink in the graph?

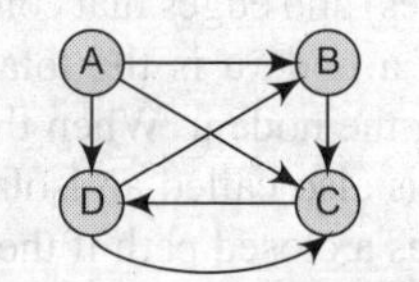

9. Consider the graph given below. Find out its depth-first and breadth-first traversal scheme.

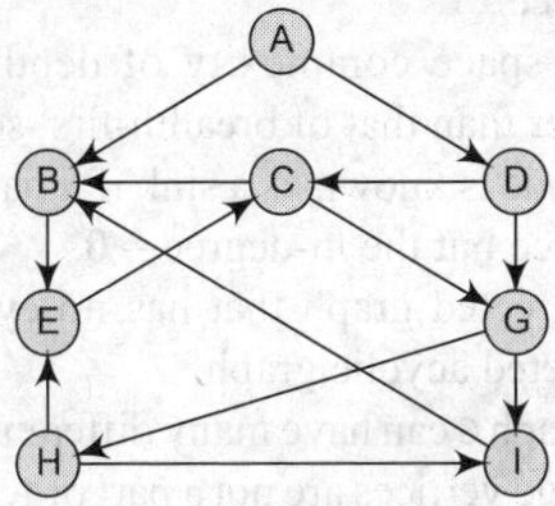

10. Differentiate between depth-first search and breadth-first search traversal of a graph.

11. Explain the topological sorting of a graph `G`.

12. Define spanning tree.

13. When is a spanning tree called a minimum spanning tree? Take a weighted graph of your choice and find out its minimum spanning tree.

14. Explain Prim's algorithm.

15. Write a brief note on Kruskal's algorithm.

16. Write a short note on Dijkstra's algorithm.

17. Differentiate between Dijkstra's algorithm and minimum spanning tree algorithm.

18. Consider the graph given below. Find the minimum spanning tree of this graph using (a) Prim's algorithm, (b) Kruskal's algorithm, and (c) Dijkstra's algorithm.

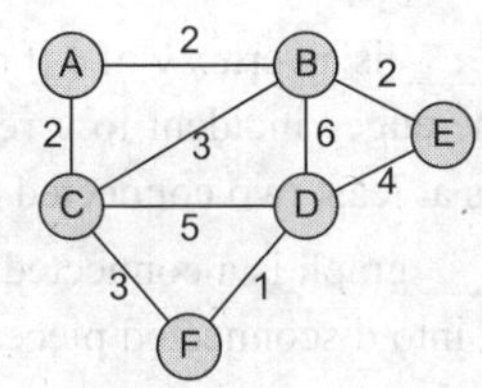

19. Briefly discuss Warshall's algorithm. Also, discuss its modified version.

20. Show the working of Floyd-Warshall's algorithm to find the shortest paths between all pairs of nodes in the following graph.

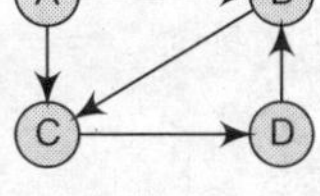

21. Write a short note on transitive closure of a graph.

22. Given the adjacency matrix of a graph, write a program to calculate the degree of a node `N` in the graph.

23. Given the adjacency matrix of a graph, write a program to calculate the in-degree and the out-degree of a node `N` in the graph.

24. Given the adjacency matrix of a graph, write a function `isFullConnectedGraph` which returns 1 if the graph is fully connected and 0 otherwise.

25. In which kind of graph do we use topological sorting?

26. Consider the graph given below and show its adjacency list in the memory.

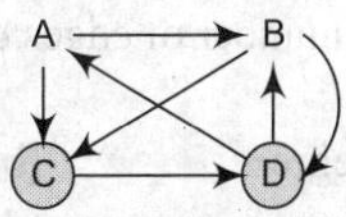

27. Consider the graph given in Question 26 and show the changes in the graph as well as its adjacency list when node `E` and edges `(A, E)` and `(C, E)` are added to it. Also, delete edge `(B, D)` from the graph.

28. Given the following adjacency matrix, draw the weighted graph.

$$\begin{pmatrix} 0 & 4 & 0 & 2 & 0 \\ 0 & 0 & 0 & 7 & 0 \\ 0 & 5 & 0 & 0 & 0 \\ 0 & 0 & 0 & 0 & 3 \\ 0 & 0 & 1 & 0 & 0 \end{pmatrix}$$

29. Consider five cities: (1) New Delhi, (2) Mumbai, (3) Chennai, (4) Bangalore, and (5) Kolkata, and a list of flights that connect these cities as shown in the following table. Use the given information to construct a graph.

Flight No.	Origin	Destination
101	2	3
102	3	2
103	5	3
104	3	4
105	2	5
106	5	2

107	5	1
108	1	4
109	5	4
110	4	5

Programming Exercises

1. Write a program to create and print a graph.
2. Write a program to determine whether there is at least one path from the source to the destination.

Multiple-choice Questions

1. An edge that has identical end-points is called a
   (a) Multi-path (b) Loop
   (c) Cycle (d) Multi-edge
2. The total number of edges containing the node u is called
   (a) In-degree (b) Out-degree
   (c) Degree (d) None of these
3. A graph in which there exists a path between any two of its nodes is called
   (a) Complete graph (b) Connected graph
   (c) Digraph (d) In-directed graph
4. The number of edges that originate at u are called
   (a) In-degree (b) Out-degree
   (c) Degree (d) source
5. The memory use of an adjacency matrix is
   (a) `O(n)` (b) `O(n²)`
   (c) `O(n³)` (d) `O(log n)`
6. The term optimal can mean
   (a) Shortest (b) Cheapest
   (c) Fastest (d) All of these
7. How many articulation vertices does a biconnected graph contain?
   (a) 0 (b) 1
   (c) 2 (d) 3

True or False

1. Graph is a linear data structure.
2. In-degree of a node is the number of edges leaving that node.
3. The size of a graph is the total number of vertices in it.
4. A sink has a zero in-degree but a positive out-degree.
5. The space complexity of depth-first search is lower than that of breadth-first search.
6. A node is known as a sink if it has a positive out-degree but the in-degree = 0.
7. A directed graph that has no cycles is called a directed acyclic graph.
8. A graph `G` can have many different spanning trees.
9. Fringe vertices are not a part of `T`, but are adjacent to some tree vertex.
10. Kruskal's algorithm is an example of a greedy algorithm.

Fill in the Blanks

1. ______ has a zero degree.
2. In-degree of a node is the number of edges that ______ at `u`.
3. Adjacency matrix is also known as a ______.
4. A path `P` is known as a ______ path if the edge has the same end-points.
5. A graph with multiple edges and/or a loop is called a ______.
6. Vertices that are a part of the minimum spanning tree `T` are called ______.
7. A ______ of a graph is constructed to answer reachability questions.
8. An ______ is a vertex `v` of `G` if removing `v` along with the edges incident to `v` results in a graph that has at least two connected components.
9. A ______ graph is a connected graph that is not broken into disconnected pieces by deleting any single vertex.
10. An edge is called a ______ if removing that edge results in a disconnected graph.

CHAPTER 14

Searching and Sorting

LEARNING OBJECTIVE

Searching and sorting are two of the most common operations in computer science. Searching refers to finding the position of a value in a collection of values. Sorting refers to arranging data in a certain order. The two commonly used orders are numerical order and alphabetical order. In this chapter, we will discuss the different techniques of searching and sorting arrays of numbers or characters.

14.1 INTRODUCTION TO SEARCHING

Searching means to find whether a particular value is present in an array or not. If the value is present in the array, then searching is said to be successful and the searching process gives the location of that value in the array. However, if the value is not present in the array, the searching process displays an appropriate message and in this case searching is said to be unsuccessful.

There are two popular methods for searching the array elements: *linear search* and *binary search*. The algorithm that should be used depends entirely on how the values are organized in the array. For example, if the elements of the array are arranged in ascending order, then binary search should be used, as it is more efficient for sorted lists in terms of complexity. We will discuss all these methods in detail in this section.

14.2 LINEAR SEARCH

Linear search, also called as *sequential search*, is a very simple method used for searching an array for a particular value. It works by comparing the value to be searched with every element of the array one by one in a sequence until a match is found. Linear search is mostly used to search an unordered list of elements (array in which data elements are not sorted). For example, if an array A[] is declared and initialized as,

```
int A[] = {10, 8, 2, 7, 3, 4, 9, 1, 6, 5};
```

and the value to be searched is VAL = 7, then searching means to find whether the value '7' is present in the array or not. If yes, then it returns the position of its occurrence. Here, POS = 3 (index starting from 0).

Figure 14.1 shows the algorithm for linear search.

In Steps 1 and 2 of the algorithm, we initialize the value of POS and I. In Step 3, a while loop is executed that would be executed till I is less than N (total number of elements in the array). In Step 4, a check is made to see if a match is found between the current array element and VAL. If a match is found, then the position of the array element is printed,

```
LINEAR_SEARCH(A, N, VAL)
Step 1: [INITIALIZE] SET POS = -1
Step 2: [INITIALIZE] SET I = 1
Step 3:      Repeat Step 4 while I<=N
Step 4:            IF A[I] = VAL
                         SET POS = I
                         PRINT POS
                         Go to Step 6
                   [END OF IF]
                    SET I = I + 1
             [END OF LOOP]
Step 5: IF POS = -1
        PRINT "VALUE IS NOT PRESENT
        IN THE ARRAY"
        [END OF IF]
Step 6: EXIT
```

Figure 14.1 Algorithm for linear search

else the value of I is incremented to match the next element with VAL. However, if all the array elements have been compared with VAL and no match is found, then it means that VAL is not present in the array.

Complexity of Linear Search Algorithm

Linear search executes in O(n) time where n is the number of elements in the array. Obviously, the best case of linear search is when VAL is equal to the first element of the array. In this case, only one comparison will be made. Likewise, the worst case will happen when either VAL is not present in the array or it is equal to the last element of the array. In both the cases, n comparisons will have to be made. However, the performance of the linear search algorithm can be improved by using a sorted array.

Programming Example

1. Write a program to search an element in an array using the linear search technique.

```
#include <stdio.h>
#include <stdlib.h>
#define size 20
int main(int argc, char *argv[]) {
        int arr[size], num, i, n, found = 0, pos = -1;
        printf("\n Enter the number of elements in the array : ");
        scanf("%d", &n);
        printf("\n Enter the elements: ");
        for(i=0;i<n;i++)
        {
                scanf("%d", &arr[i]);
        }
        printf("\n Enter the number that has to be searched : ");
        scanf("%d", &num);
        for(i=0;i<n;i++)
        {
                if(arr[i] == num)
                {
                        found =1;
                        pos=i;
                        printf("\n %d is found in the array at position= %d",
num,i+1);
                        break;
                }
        }
        if (found == 0)
        printf("\n %d does not exist in the array", num);
        return 0;
}
```

14.3 BINARY SEARCH

Binary search is a searching algorithm that works efficiently with a sorted list. The mechanism of binary search can be better understood by an analogy of a telephone directory. When we are searching for a particular name in a directory, we first open the directory from the middle and then decide whether to look for the name in the first part of the directory or in the second part of the directory. Again, we open some page in the middle and the whole process is repeated until we finally find the right name.

Take another analogy. How do we find words in a dictionary? We first open the dictionary somewhere in the middle. Then, we compare the first word on that page with the desired word whose meaning we are looking for. If the desired word comes before the word on the page, we look in the first half of the dictionary, else we look in the second half. Again, we open a page in the first half of the dictionary and compare the first word on that page with the desired word and repeat the same procedure until we finally get the word. The same mechanism is applied in the binary search.

Now, let us consider how this mechanism is applied to search for a value in a sorted array. Consider an array `A[]` that is declared and initialized as

```
int A[] = {0, 1, 2, 3, 4, 5, 6, 7, 8, 9, 10};
```

and the value to be searched is `VAL = 9`. The algorithm will proceed in the following manner.

```
BEG = 0, END = 10, MID = (0 + 10)/2 = 5
```

Now, `VAL = 9` and `A[MID] = A[5] = 5`

`A[5]` is less than `VAL`, therefore, we now search for the value in the second half of the array. So, we change the values of `BEG` and `MID`.

Now, `BEG = MID + 1 = 6, END = 10, MID = (6 + 10)/2 =16/2 = 8`

```
VAL = 9 and A[MID] = A[8] = 8
```

`A[8]` is less than `VAL`, therefore, we now search for the value in the second half of the segment. So, again we change the values of `BEG` and `MID`.

Now, `BEG = MID + 1 = 9, END = 10, MID = (9 + 10)/2 = 9`

Now, `VAL = 9` and `A[MID] = 9`.

In this algorithm, we see that `BEG` and `END` are the beginning and ending positions of the segment that we are looking to search for the element. `MID` is calculated as `(BEG + END)/2`. Initially, `BEG = lower_bound` and `END = upper_bound`. The algorithm will terminate when `A[MID] = VAL`. When the algorithm ends, we will set `POS = MID`. `POS` is the position at which the value is present in the array.

However, if `VAL` is not equal to `A[MID]`, then the values of `BEG`, `END`, and `MID` will be changed depending on whether `VAL` is smaller or greater than `A[MID]`.

(a) If `VAL < A[MID]`, then `VAL` will be present in the left segment of the array. So, the value of `END` will be changed as `END = MID - 1`.

(b) If `VAL > A[MID]`, then `VAL` will be present in the right segment of the array. So, the value of `BEG` will be changed as `BEG = MID + 1`.

Finally, if `VAL` is not present in the array, then eventually, `END` will be less than `BEG`. When this happens, the algorithm will terminate and the search will be unsuccessful.

Figure 14.2 shows the algorithm for binary search.

In Step 1, we initialize the value of variables, `BEG`, `END`, and `POS`. In Step 2, a `while` loop is executed until `BEG` is less than or equal to `END`. In Step 3, the value of `MID` is calculated. In Step 4, we check if the array value at `MID` is equal to `VAL` (item to be searched in the array). If a match is found, then the value of `POS` is printed and the algorithm exits. However, if a match is not found, and if the value of `A[MID]` is greater than `VAL`, the value of `END` is modified, otherwise if `A[MID]` is greater than `VAL`, then the value of `BEG` is altered. In Step 5, if the value of `POS = -1`, then `VAL` is not present in the array and an appropriate message is printed on the screen before the algorithm exits.

```
BINARY_SEARCH(A, lower_bound, upper_bound, VAL)
Step 1: [INITIALIZE] SET BEG = lower_bound
        END = upper_bound, POS = - 1
Step 2: Repeat Steps 3 and 4 while BEG <= END
Step 3:           SET MID = (BEG + END)/2
Step 4:           IF A[MID] = VAL
                        SET POS = MID
                        PRINT POS
                        Go to Step 6
                  ELSE IF A[MID] > VAL
                        SET END = MID - 1
                  ELSE
                        SET BEG = MID + 1
                  [END OF IF]
        [END OF LOOP]
Step 5: IF POS = -1
              PRINT "VALUE IS NOT PRESENT IN THE ARRAY"
        [END OF IF]
Step 6: EXIT
```

Figure 14.2 Algorithm for binary search

Complexity of Binary Search Algorithm

The complexity of the binary search algorithm can be expressed as `f(n)`, where `n` is the number of elements in the array. The complexity of the algorithm is calculated depending on the number of comparisons that are made. In the binary search algorithm, we see that with each comparison, the size of the segment where search has to be made is reduced to half. Thus, we can say that, in order to locate a particular value in the array, the total number of comparisons that will be made is given as

$$2^{f(n)} > n \text{ or } f(n) = \log_2 n$$

Programming Example

2. Write a program to search an element in an array using binary search.

```
##include <stdio.h>
#include <stdlib.h>
#define size 10
int smallest(int arr[], int k, int n);
void selection_sort(int arr[], int n);
int main(int argc, char *argv[]) {
          int arr[size], num, i, n, beg, end, mid, found=0;
          printf("\n Enter the number of elements in the array: ");
          scanf("%d", &n);
          printf("\n Enter the elements: ");
          for(i=0;i<n;i++)
          {
                    scanf("%d", &arr[i]);
          }
          selection_sort(arr, n);
          printf("\n The sorted array is: \n");
          for(i=0;i<n;i++)
          printf(" %d\t", arr[i]);
          printf("\n\n Enter the number that has to be searched: ");
          scanf("%d", &num);
          beg = 0, end = n-1;
          while(beg<=end)
          {
                    mid = (beg + end)/2;
                    if (arr[mid] == num)
                    {
                              printf("\n %d is present in the array at position %d", num,
mid+1);
                              found =1;
                              break;
                    }
                    else if (arr[mid]>num)
                    end = mid-1;
                    else
                    beg = mid+1;
          }
          if (beg > end && found == 0)
          printf("\n %d does not exist in the array", num);
          return 0;
}

int smallest(int arr[], int k, int n)
{
          int pos = k, small=arr[k], i;
          for(i=k+1;i<n;i++)
          {
                    if(arr[i]< small)
                    {
                              small = arr[i];
```

```
                    pos = i;
            }
        }
        return pos;
}
void selection_sort(int arr[],int n)
{
        int k, pos, temp;
        for(k=0;k<n;k++)
        {
                pos = smallest(arr, k, n);
                temp = arr[k];
                arr[k] = arr[pos];
                arr[pos] = temp;
        }
}
```

14.4 INTERPOLATION SEARCH

Interpolation search, also known as extrapolation search, is a searching technique that finds a specified value in a sorted array. The concept of interpolation search is similar to how we search for names in a telephone book or for keys by which a book's entries are ordered. For example, when looking for a name "Bharat" in a telephone directory, we know that it will be near the extreme left, so applying a binary search technique by dividing the list in two halves each time is not a good idea. We must start scanning the extreme left in the first pass itself.

In each step of interpolation search, the remaining search space for the value to be found is calculated. The calculation is done based on the values at the bounds of the search space and the value to be searched. The value found at this estimated position is then compared with the value being searched for. If the two values are equal, then the search is complete.

However, in case the values are not equal then depending on the comparison, the remaining search space is reduced to the part before or after the estimated position. Thus, we see that interpolation search is similar to the binary search technique. However, the important difference between the two techniques is that binary search always selects the middle value of the remaining search space. It discards half of the values based on the comparison between the value found at the estimated position and the value to be searched. But in interpolation search, interpolation is used to find an item near the one being searched for, and then linear search is used to find the exact item.

The algorithm for interpolation search is given in Fig. 14.3.

Figure 14.4 helps us to visualize how the search space is divided in case of binary search and interpolation search.

```
INTERPOLATION_SEARCH (A, lower_bound, upper_bound, VAL)

Step 1: [INITIALIZE] SET LOW = lower_bound,
        HIGH = upper_bound, POS = -1
Step 2:    Repeat Steps 3 to 4 while LOW <= HIGH
Step 3:         SET MID = LOW + (HIGH - LOW) ×
                ((VAL - A[LOW]) / (A[HIGH] - A[LOW]))
Step 4:         IF VAL = A[MID]
                  POS = MID
                  PRINT POS
                  Go to Step 6
                 ELSE IF VAL < A[MID]
                   SET HIGH = MID - 1
                  ELSE
                   SET LOW = MID + 1
                [END OF IF]
        [END OF LOOP]
Step 5: IF POS = -1
              PRINT "VALUE IS NOT PRESENT IN THE ARRAY"
        [END OF IF]
Step 6: EXIT
```

Figure 14.3 Algorithm for interpolation search

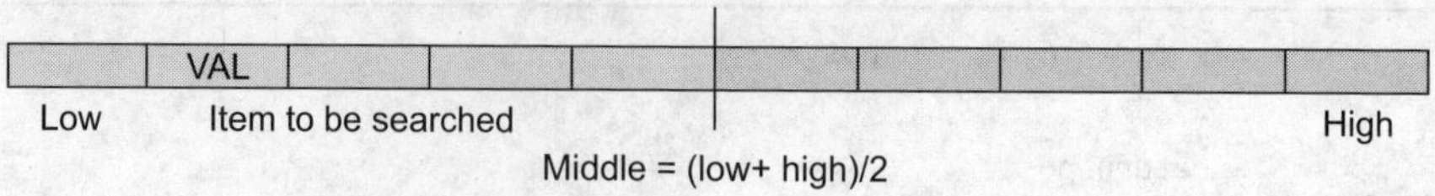

(a) Binary search divides the list into two equal halves

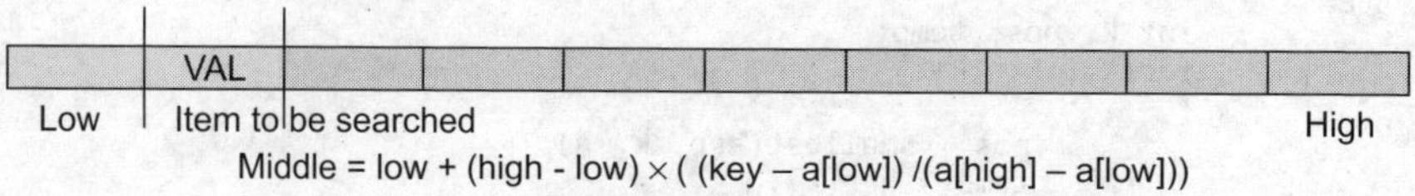

(b) Interpolation search divides the list into two equal halves

Figure 14.4 Difference between binary search and interpolation search

Complexity of Interpolation Search Algorithm

When `n` elements of a list to be sorted are uniformly distributed (average case), interpolation search makes about `log(log n)` comparisons. However, in the worst case, that is when the elements increase exponentially, the algorithm can make up to `O(n)` comparisons.

Example 14.1 Given a list of numbers `a[] = {1, 3, 5, 7, 9, 11, 13, 15, 17, 19, 21}`. Search for value 19 using interpolation search technique.

Solution

```
Low = 0, High = 10, VAL = 19, a[Low] = 1, a[High] = 21
Middle = Low + (High – Low)×((VAL – a[Low]) /(a[High] – a[Low] ))
       = 0 +(10 – 0) × ((19 – 1) / (21 – 1) )
       = 0 + 10 × 0.9 = 9
a[middle] = a[9] = 19 which is equal to value to be searched.
```

Programming Example

3. Write a program to search an element in an array using interpolation search.

```
#include <stdio.h>
#define MAX 20
int interpolation_search(int a[], int low, int high, int val)
{
        int mid;
        while(low <= high)
        {
                mid = low + (high – low)*((val – a[low]) / (a[high] – a[low]));
                if(val == a[mid])
                     return mid;
                if(val < a[mid])
                     high = mid – 1;
                else
                     low = mid + 1;
        }
        return –1;
}
int main()
{
        int arr[MAX], i, n, val, pos;
        printf("\n Enter the number of elements in the array : ");
        scanf("%d", &n);
```

```
        printf("\n Enter the elements : ");
        for(i = 0; i <n; i++)
                scanf("%d", &arr[i]);
        printf("\n Enter the value to be searched : ");
        scanf("%d", &val);
        pos = interpolation_search(arr, 0, n-1, val);
        if(pos == -1)
                printf("\n %d is not found in the array", val);
        else
                printf("\n %d is found at position %d", val, pos);
        getchar();
        return 0;
}
```

14.5 JUMP SEARCH

When we have an already sorted list, then the other efficient algorithm to search for a value is jump search or block search. In jump search, it is not necessary to scan all the elements in the list to find the desired value. We just check an element and if it is less than the desired value, then some of the elements following it are skipped by jumping ahead. After moving a little forward again, the element is checked. If the checked element is greater than the desired value, then we have a boundary and we are sure that the desired value lies between the previously checked element and the currently checked element. However, if the checked element is less than the value being searched for, then we again make a small jump and repeat the process.

Once the boundary of the value is determined, a linear search is done to find the value and its position in the array. For example, consider an array `a[] = {1,2,3,4,5,6,7,8,9}`. The length of the array is 9. If we have to find value 8 then following steps are performed using the jump search technique.

`Step 1: First three elements are checked. Since 3 is smaller than 8, we will have to make a jump ahead`

1	2	3	4	5	6	7	8	9

`Step 2: Next three elements are checked. Since 6 is smaller than 8, we will have to make a jump ahead`

1	2	3	4	5	6	7	8	9

`Step 3: Next three elements are checked. Since 9 is greater than 8, the desired value lies within the current boundary`

1	2	3	4	5	6	7	8	9

`Step 4: A linear search is now done to find the value in the array.`

The algorithm for jump search is given in Fig. 14.5.

Advantage of Jump Search over Linear Search

Suppose we have a sorted list of 1000 elements where the elements have values `0, 1, 2, 3, 4, …, 999`, then sequential search will find the value 674 in exactly 674 iterations. But with jump search, the same value can be found in 44 iterations. Hence, jump search performs far better than a linear search on a sorted list of elements.

Advantage of Jump Search over Binary Search

No doubt, binary search is very easy to implement and has a complexity of `O(log n)`, but in case of a list having very large number of elements, jumping to the middle of the list to make comparisons is not a

```
JUMP_SEARCH (A, lower_bound, upper_bound, VAL, N)
Step 1: [INITIALIZE] SET STEP = sqrt(N), I = 0, LOW = lower_bound, HIGH = upper_bound, POS = -1
Step 2: Repeat Step 3 while I < STEP
Step 3:         IF VAL < A[STEP]
            SET HIGH = STEP - 1
                ELSE
            SET LOW = STEP + 1
           [END OF IF]
           SET I = I + 1
    [END OF LOOP]
Step 4: SET I = LOW
Step 5: Repeat Step 6 while I <= HIGH
Step 6:         IF A[I] = Val
                          POS =  I
                  PRINT POS
                  Go to Step 8
             [END OF IF]
             SET I = I + 1
    [END OF LOOP]
Step 7:           IF POS = -1
          PRINT "VALUE IS NOT PRESENT IN THE ARRAY"
    [END OF IF]
Step 8: EXIT
```

Figure 14.5 Algorithm for jump search

good idea because if the value being searched is at the beginning of the list then one (or even more) large step(s) in the backward direction would have to be taken. In such cases, jump search performs better as we have to move little backward that too only once. Hence, when jumping back is slower than jumping forward, the jump search algorithm always performs better.

How to Choose the Step Length?

For the jump search algorithm to work efficiently, we must define a fixed size for the step. If the step size is 1, then algorithm is same as linear search. Now, in order to find an appropriate step size, we must first try to figure out the relation between the size of the list (n) and the size of the step (k). Usually, k is calculated as $\sqrt{n}$.

Further Optimization of Jump Search

Till now, we were dealing with lists having small number of elements. But in real-world applications, lists can be very large. In such large lists searching the value from the beginning of the list may not be a good idea. A better option is to start the search from the k-th element as shown in the figure below.

1 2 3 4 5 6 7 8 9 10 11 12 13 14 15 16 17 18 19 20 21 ....

Searching can start from somewhere middle in the list rather than from the beginning to optimize performance.

We can also improve the performance of jump search algorithm by repeatedly applying jump search. For example, if the size of the list is 10,00,000 (n). The jump interval would then be $\sqrt{n} = \sqrt{1000000} = 1000$. Now, even the identified interval has 1000 elements and is again a large list. So, jump search can be applied again with a new step size of $\sqrt{1000} \approx 31$. Thus, every time we have a desired interval with a large number of values, the jump search algorithm can be applied again but with a smaller step. However, in this case, the complexity of the algorithm will no longer be $O(\sqrt{n})$ but will approach a logarithmic value.

Complexity of Jump Search Algorithm

Jump search works by jumping through the array with a step size (optimally chosen to be √n) to find the interval of the value. Once this interval is identified, the value is searched using the linear search technique. Therefore, the complexity of the jump search algorithm can be given as `O(√n)`.

Programming Example

4. Write a program to search an element in an array using jump search.

```
#include <stdio.h>
#include <math.h>
#define MAX 20
int jump_search(int a[], int low, int high, int val, int n)
{
        int step, i;
        step = sqrt(n);
        for(i=0;i<step;i++)
        {
                if(val < a[step])
                        high = step - 1;
                else
                        low = step + 1;
        }
        for(i=low;i<=high;i++)
        {
             if(a[i]==val)
                  return i;
        }
        return -1;
}

int main()
{
        int arr[MAX], i, n, val, pos;
        printf("\n Enter the number of elements in the array : ");
        scanf("%d", &n);
        printf("\n Enter the elements : ");
        for(i = 0; i <n; i++)
                scanf("%d", &arr[i]);
        printf("\n Enter the value to be searched : ");
        scanf("%d", &val);
        pos = jump_search(arr, 0, n-1, val, n);
        if(pos == -1)
                printf("\n %d is not found in the array", val);
        else
                printf("\n %d is found at position %d", val, pos);
        getchar();
        return 0;
}
```

Fibonacci Search

We are all well aware of the Fibonacci series in which the first two terms are 0 and 1 and then each successive term is the sum of previous two terms. In the Fibonacci series given below, each number is called a Fibonacci number.

0, 1, 1, 2, 3, 5, 8, 13, 21, 34, 55, 89, ...

The same series and concept can be used to search for a given value in a list of numbers. Such a search algorithm which is based on Fibonacci numbers is called Fibonacci search and was developed by Kiefer in 1953. The search follows a divide-and-conquer technique and narrows down possible locations with the help of Fibonacci numbers.

Fibonacci search is similar to binary search. It also works on a sorted list and has a run time complexity of `O(log n)`. However, unlike the binary search algorithm, Fibonacci search does not divide the list into two equal halves rather it subtracts a Fibonacci number from the index to reduce the size of the list to be searched. So, the key advantage of Fibonacci search over binary search is that comparison dispersion is low.

14.6 INTRODUCTION TO SORTING

Sorting means arranging the elements of an array so that they are placed in some relevant order which may be either ascending or descending. That is, if `A` is an array, then the elements of `A` are arranged in a sorted order (ascending order) in such a way that `A[0] < A[1] < A[2] < ...... < A[N]`.

For example, if we have an array that is declared and initialized as

```
int A[] = {21, 34, 11, 9, 1, 0, 22};
```

Then the sorted array (ascending order) can be given as:

```
A[] = {0, 1, 9, 11, 21, 22, 34;
```

A sorting algorithm is defined as an algorithm that puts the elements of a list in a certain order, which can be either numerical order, lexicographical order, or any user-defined order. Efficient sorting algorithms are widely used to optimize the use of other algorithms like search and merge algorithms which require sorted lists to work correctly. There are two types of sorting:

- ***Internal sorting*** which deals with sorting the data stored in the computer's memory
- ***External sorting*** which deals with sorting the data stored in files. External sorting is applied when there is voluminous data that cannot be stored in the memory.

14.6.1 Sorting on Multiple Keys

Many a times, when performing real-world applications, it is desired to sort arrays of records using multiple keys. This situation usually occurs when a single key is not sufficient to uniquely identify a record. For example, in a big organization we may want to sort a list of employees on the basis of their departments first and then according to their names in alphabetical order.

Other examples of sorting on multiple keys can be

- Telephone directories in which names are sorted by location, category (business or residential), and then in an alphabetical order.
- In a library, the information about books can be sorted alphabetically based on titles and then by authors' names.
- Customers' addresses can be sorted based on the name of the city and then the street.

Note Data records can be sorted based on a property. Such a component or property is called a **sort key**. A sort key can be defined using two or more sort keys. In such a case, the first key is called the **primary sort key**, the second is known as the **secondary sort key**, etc.

Consider the data records given below:

Name	Department	Salary	Phone Number
Janak	Telecommunications	1000000	9812345678
Raj	Computer Science	890000	9910023456
Aditya	Electronics	900000	7838987654
Huma	Telecommunications	1100000	9654123456
Divya	Computer Science	750000	9350123455

Now if we take department as the primary key and name as the secondary key, then the sorted order of records can be given as:

Name	Department	Salary	Phone Number
Divya	Computer Science	750000	9350123455
Raj	Computer Science	890000	9910023456
Aditya	Electronics	900000	7838987654
Huma	Telecommunications	1100000	9654123456
Janak	Telecommunications	1000000	9812345678

Observe that the records are sorted based on department. However, within each department the records are sorted alphabetically based on the names of the employees.

14.6.2 Practical Considerations for Internal Sorting

As mentioned above, records can be sorted either in ascending or descending order based on a field often called as the sort key. The list of records can be either stored in a contiguous and randomly accessible data structure (array) or may be stored in a dispersed and only sequentially accessible data structure like a linked list. But irrespective of the underlying data structure used to store the records, the logic to sort the records will be same and only the implementation details will differ.

When analysing the performance of different sorting algorithms, the practical considerations would be the following:

- Number of sort key comparisons that will be performed
- Number of times the records in the list will be moved
- Best case performance
- Worst case performance
- Average case performance
- Stability of the sorting algorithm where stability means that equivalent elements or records retain their relative positions even after sorting is done

14.7 BUBBLE SORT

Bubble sort is a very simple method that sorts the array elements by repeatedly moving the largest element to the highest index position of the array segment (in case of arranging elements in ascending order). In *bubble sorting*, consecutive adjacent pairs of elements in the array are compared with each other. If the element at the lower index is greater than the element at the higher index, the two elements are interchanged so that the element is placed before the bigger one. This process will continue till the list of unsorted elements exhausts.

This procedure of sorting is called bubble sorting because elements 'bubble' to the top of the list. Note that at the end of the first pass, the largest element in the list will be placed at its proper position (i.e., at the end of the list).

Note If the elements are to be sorted in descending order, then in first pass the smallest element is moved to the highest index of the array.

Technique

The basic methodology of the working of bubble sort is given as follows:

(a) In Pass 1, `A[0]` and `A[1]` are compared, then `A[1]` is compared with `A[2]`, `A[2]` is compared with `A[3]`, and so on. Finally, `A[N-2]` is compared with `A[N-1]`. Pass 1 involves `n-1` comparisons and places the biggest element at the highest index of the array.

(b) In Pass 2, `A[0]` and `A[1]` are compared, then `A[1]` is compared with `A[2]`, `A[2]` is compared with `A[3]`, and so on. Finally, `A[N-3]` is compared with `A[N-2]`. Pass 2 involves `n-2` comparisons and places the second biggest element at the second highest index of the array.

(c) In Pass 3, `A[0]` and `A[1]` are compared, then `A[1]` is compared with `A[2]`, `A[2]` is compared with `A[3]`, and so on. Finally, `A[N-4]` is compared with `A[N-3]`. Pass 3 involves `n-3` comparisons and places the third biggest element at the third highest index of the array.

(d) In Pass `n-1`, `A[0]` and `A[1]` are compared so that `A[0]<A[1]`. After this step, all the elements of the array are arranged in ascending order.

Example 14.2 To discuss bubble sort in detail, let us consider an array `A[]` that has the following elements:

```
A[] = {30, 52, 29, 87, 63, 27, 19, 54}
```

Pass 1:

```
(a) Compare 30 and 52. Since 30 < 52, no swapping is done.
(b) Compare 52 and 29. Since 52 > 29, swapping is done.
    30, 29, 52, 87, 63, 27, 19, 54
(c) Compare 52 and 87. Since 52 < 87, no swapping is done.
(d) Compare 87 and 63. Since 87 > 63, swapping is done.
    30, 29, 52, 63, 87, 27, 19, 54
(e) Compare 87 and 27. Since 87 > 27, swapping is done.
    30, 29, 52, 63, 27, 87, 19, 54
(f) Compare 87 and 19. Since 87 > 19, swapping is done.
    30, 29, 52, 63, 27, 19, 87, 54
(g) Compare 87 and 54. Since 87 > 54, swapping is done.
    30, 29, 52, 63, 27, 19, 54, 87
```

Observe that after the end of the first pass, the largest element is placed at the highest index of the array. All the other elements are still unsorted.

Pass 2:

```
(a) Compare 30 and 29. Since 30 > 29, swapping is done.
    29, 30, 52, 63, 27, 19, 54, 87
(b) Compare 30 and 52. Since 30 < 52, no swapping is done.
(c) Compare 52 and 63. Since 52 < 63, no swapping is done.
(d) Compare 63 and 27. Since 63 > 27, swapping is done.
    29, 30, 52, 27, 63, 19, 54, 87
(e) Compare 63 and 19. Since 63 > 19, swapping is done.
    29, 30, 52, 27, 19, 63, 54, 87
(f) Compare 63 and 54. Since 63 > 54, swapping is done.
    29, 30, 52, 27, 19, 54, 63, 87
```

Observe that after the end of the second pass, the second largest element is placed at the second highest index of the array. All the other elements are still unsorted.

Pass 3:

```
(a) Compare 29 and 30. Since 29 < 30, no swapping is done.
(b) Compare 30 and 52. Since 30 < 52, no swapping is done.
(c) Compare 52 and 27. Since 52 > 27, swapping is done.
    29, 30, 27, 52, 19, 54, 63, 87
(d) Compare 52 and 19. Since 52 > 19, swapping is done.
    29, 30, 27, 19, 52, 54, 63, 87
(e) Compare 52 and 54. Since 52 < 54, no swapping is done.
```

Observe that after the end of the third pass, the third largest element is placed at the third highest index of the array. All the other elements are still unsorted.

Pass 4:

```
(a) Compare 29 and 30. Since 29 < 30, no swapping is done.
(b) Compare 30 and 27. Since 30 > 27, swapping is done.
    29, 27, 30, 19, 52, 54, 63, 87
(c) Compare 30 and 19. Since 30 > 19, swapping is done.
    29, 27, 19, 30, 52, 54, 63, 87
(d) Compare 30 and 52. Since 30 < 52, no swapping is done.
```

Observe that after the end of the fourth pass, the fourth largest element is placed at the fourth highest index of the array. All the other elements are still unsorted.

```
Pass 5:
        (a) Compare 29 and 27. Since 29 > 27, swapping is done.
            27, 29, 19, 30, 52, 54, 63, 87
        (b) Compare 29 and 19. Since 29 > 19, swapping is done.
            27, 19, 29, 30, 52, 54, 63, 87
        (c) Compare 29 and 30. Since 29 < 30, no swapping is done.
```

Observe that after the end of the fifth pass, the fifth largest element is placed at the fifth highest index of the array. All the other elements are still unsorted.

```
Pass 6:
        (a) Compare 27 and 19. Since 27 > 19, swapping is done.
            19, 27, 29, 30, 52, 54, 63, 87
        (b) Compare 27 and 29. Since 27 < 29, no swapping is done.
```

Observe that after the end of the sixth pass, the sixth largest element is placed at the sixth largest index of the array. All the other elements are still unsorted.

```
Pass 7:
        (a) Compare 19 and 27. Since 19 < 27, no swapping is done.
```

Observe that the entire list is sorted now.

Figure 14.6 shows the algorithm for bubble sort. In this algorithm, the outer loop is for the total number of passes which is `N-1`. The inner loop will be executed for every pass. However, the frequency of the inner loop will decrease with every pass because after every pass, one element will be in its correct position. Therefore, for every pass, the inner loop will be executed `N-I` times, where `N` is the number of elements in the array and `I` is the count of the pass.

Complexity of Bubble Sort

The complexity of any sorting algorithm depends upon the number of comparisons. In bubble sort, we have seen that there are `N-1` passes in total. In the first pass, `N-1` comparisons are made to place the highest element in its correct position. Then, in Pass 2, there are `N-2` comparisons and the second highest element is placed in its position. Therefore, to compute the complexity of bubble sort, we need to calculate the total number of comparisons. It can be given as:

$$f(n) = (n - 1) + (n - 2) + (n - 3) + ... + 3 + 2 + 1$$

$$f(n) = n (n - 1)/2$$

$$f(n) = n^2/2 + O(n) = O(n^2)$$

Therefore, the complexity of bubble sort algorithm is $O(n^2)$. It means the time required to execute bubble sort is proportional to n^2, where n is the total number of elements in the array.

```
BUBBLE_SORT(A, N)

Step 1: Repeat Step 2 For 1 = 0 to N-1
Step 2:        Repeat For J = 0 to N - I
Step 3:                IF A[J] > A[J + 1]
                       SWAP A[J] and A[J+1]
           [END OF INNER LOOP]
        [END OF OUTER LOOP]
Step 4: EXIT
```

Figure 14.6 Algorithm for bubble sort

Programming Example

5. Write a program to enter *n* numbers in an array. Redisplay the array with elements being sorted in ascending order.

```
#include <stdio.h>
int main()
{
        int i, n, temp, j, arr[10];
```

```
                printf("\n Enter the number of elements in the array : ");
                scanf("%d", &n);
                printf("\n Enter the elements: ");
                for(i=0;i<n;i++)
                {
                        scanf("%d", &arr [i]);
                }
                for(i=0;i<n;i++)
                {
                        for(j=0;j<n-i-1;j++)
                        {
                                if(arr[j] > arr[j+1])
                                {
                                        temp = arr[j];
                                        arr[j] = arr[j+1];
                                        arr[j+1] = temp;
                                }
                        }
                }
                printf("\n The array sorted in ascending order is :\n");
                for(i=0;i<n;i++)
                        printf("%d\t", arr[i]);
                return 0;
        }
        Output
        Enter the number of elements in the array : 10
        Enter the elements : 8    9    6    7    5    4    2    3    1    10
        The array sorted in ascending order is :
        1    2    3    4    5    6    7    8    9    10
```

Bubble Sort Optimization

Consider a case when the array is already sorted. In this situation no swapping is done but we still have to continue with all `n-1` passes. We may even have an array that will be sorted in 2 or 3 passes but we still have to continue with rest of the passes. So once we have detected that the array is sorted, the algorithm must not be executed further. This is the optimization over the original bubble sort algorithm. In order to stop the execution of further passes after the array is sorted, we can have a variable flag which is set to TRUE before each pass and is made FALSE when a swapping is performed. The code for the optimized bubble sort can be given as:

```
void bubble_sort(int *arr, int n)
{
        int i, j, temp, flag = 0;
    for(i=0; i<n; i++)
    {
      for(j=0; j<n–i-1; j++)
      {
         if(arr[j]>arr[j+1])
         {
            flag = 1;
            temp = arr[j+1];
            arr[j+1] = arr[j];
            arr[j] = temp;
         }
      }
     if(flag == 0)  // array is sorted
        return;
    }
}
```

Complexity of Optimized Bubble Sort Algorithm

In the best case, when the array is already sorted, the optimized bubble sort will take `O(n)` time. In the worst case, when all the passes are performed, the algorithm will perform slower than the original algorithm. In average case also, the performance will see an improvement. Compare it with the complexity of original bubble sort algorithm which takes `O(n²)` in all the cases.

14.8 INSERTION SORT

Insertion sort is a very simple sorting algorithm in which the sorted array (or list) is built one element at a time. We all are familiar with this technique of sorting, as we usually use it for ordering a deck of cards while playing bridge.

The main idea behind insertion sort is that it inserts each item into its proper place in the final list. To save memory, most implementations of the insertion sort algorithm work by moving the current data element past the already sorted values and repeatedly interchanging it with the preceding value until it is in its correct place.

Insertion sort is less efficient as compared to other more advanced algorithms such as quick sort, heap sort, and merge sort.

Technique

Insertion sort works as follows:

- The array of values to be sorted is divided into two sets. One that stores sorted values and another that contains unsorted values.
- The sorting algorithm will proceed until there are elements in the unsorted set.
- Suppose there are `n` elements in the array. Initially, the element with index 0 (assuming `LB = 0`) is in the sorted set. Rest of the elements are in the unsorted set.
- The first element of the unsorted partition has array index 1 (if `LB = 0`).
- During each iteration of the algorithm, the first element in the unsorted set is picked up and inserted into the correct position in the sorted set.

Example 14.3 Consider an array of integers given below. We will sort the values in the array using insertion sort.

Solution

39	9	45	63	18	81	108	54	72	36

39	9	45	63	18	81	108	54	72	36

A[0] is the only element in sorted list

9	39	45	63	18	81	108	54	72	36

(Pass 1)

9	39	45	63	18	81	108	54	72	36

(Pass 2)

9	39	45	63	18	81	108	54	72	36

(Pass 3)

9	18	39	45	63	81	108	54	72	36

(Pass 4)

9	18	39	45	63	81	108	54	72	36

(Pass 5)

9	18	39	45	63	81	108	54	72	36

(Pass 6)

9	18	39	45	54	63	81	108	72	36

(Pass 7)

9	18	39	45	54	63	72	81	108	36

(Pass 8)

9	18	36	39	45	54	63	72	81	108

(Pass 9)

Sorted   Unsorted

Initially, `A[0]` is the only element in the sorted set. In Pass 1, `A[1]` will be placed either before or after `A[0]`, so that the array `A` is sorted. In Pass 2, `A[2]` will be placed either before `A[0]`, in between `A[0]` and `A[1]`, or after `A[1]`. In Pass 3, `A[3]` will be placed in its proper place. In Pass `N-1`, `A[N-1]` will be placed in its proper place to keep the array sorted.

To insert an element `A[K]` in a sorted list `A[0]`, `A[1]`, `...`, `A[K-1]`, we need to compare `A[K]` with `A[K-1]`, then with `A[K-2]`, `A[K-3]`, and so on until we meet an element `A[J]` such that `A[J] <= A[K]`. In order to insert `A[K]` in its correct position, we need to move elements `A[K-1]`, `A[K-2]`, `...`, `A[J]` by one position and then `A[K]` is inserted at the `(J+1)`th location. The algorithm for insertion sort is given in Fig. 14.7.

In the algorithm, Step 1 executes a `for` loop which will be repeated for each element in the array. In Step 2, we store the value of the `K`th element in `TEMP`. In Step 3, we set the `J`th index in the array. In Step 4, a `for` loop is executed that will create space for the new element from the unsorted list to be stored in the list of sorted elements. Finally, in Step 5, the element is stored at the `(J+1)th` location.

Complexity of Insertion Sort

For insertion sort, the best case occurs when the array is already sorted. In this case, the running time of the algorithm has a linear running time (i.e., `O(n)`). This is because, during each iteration, the first element from the unsorted set is compared only with the last element of the sorted set of the array.

Similarly, the worst case of the insertion sort algorithm occurs when the array is sorted in the reverse order. In the worst case, the first element of the unsorted set has to be compared with almost every element in the sorted set. Furthermore, every iteration of the inner loop will have to shift the elements of the sorted set of the array before inserting the next element. Therefore, in the worst case, insertion sort has a quadratic running time (i.e., $O(n^2)$).

Even in the average case, the insertion sort algorithm will have to make at least `(K-1)/2` comparisons. Thus, the average case also has a quadratic running time.

Advantages of Insertion Sort

The advantages of this sorting algorithm are as follows:

- It is easy to implement and efficient to use on small sets of data.
- It can be efficiently implemented on data sets that are already substantially sorted.
- It performs better than algorithms like selection sort and bubble sort. Insertion sort algorithm is simpler than shell sort, with only a small trade-off in efficiency. It is over twice as fast as the bubble sort and almost 40 per cent faster than the selection sort.
- It requires less memory space (only `O(1)` of additional memory space).
- It is said to be online, as it can sort a list as and when it receives new elements.

Programming Example

6. Write a program to sort an array using insertion sort algorithm.

```
#include <stdio.h>
#define size 5
void insertion_sort(int arr[], int n);
void main()
{
        int arr[size], i, n;
        printf("\n Enter the number of elements in the array: ");
        scanf("%d", &n);
        printf("\n Enter the elements of the array: ");
        for(i=0;i<n;i++)
        {
                scanf("%d", &arr[i]);
        }
        insertion_sort(arr, n);
        printf("\n The sorted array is:  \n");
```

```
        for(i=0;i<n;i++)
        printf(" %d\t", arr[i]);
}
void insertion_sort(int arr[], int n)
{
        int i, j, temp;
        for(i=1;i<n;i++)
        {
                temp = arr[i];
                j = i-1;
                while((temp < arr[j]) && (j>=0))
                {
                        arr[j+1] = arr[j];
                        j--;
                }
                arr[j+1] = temp;
        }
}
```

Output

```
Enter the number of elements in the array : 5
Enter the elements of the array : 500 1 50 23 76
The sorted array is :
1    23    20    76    500    6    7    8    9    10
```

14.9 SELECTION SORT

Selection sort is a sorting algorithm that has a quadratic running time complexity of $O(n^2)$, thereby making it inefficient to be used on large lists. Although selection sort performs worse than insertion sort algorithm, it is noted for its simplicity and also has performance advantages over more complicated algorithms in certain situations. Selection sort is generally used for sorting files with very large objects (records) and small keys.

Technique

Consider an array ARR with N elements. Selection sort works as follows:

First find the smallest value in the array and place it in the first position. Then, find the second smallest value in the array and place it in the second position. Repeat this procedure until the entire array is sorted. Therefore,

- In Pass 1, find the position POS of the smallest value in the array and then swap ARR[POS] and ARR[0]. Thus, ARR[0] is sorted.
- In Pass 2, find the position POS of the smallest value in sub-array of N-1 elements. Swap ARR[POS] with ARR[1]. Now, ARR[0] and ARR[1] is sorted.
- In Pass N-1, find the position POS of the smaller of the elements ARR[N-2] and ARR[N-1]. Swap ARR[POS] and ARR[N-2] so that ARR[0], ARR[1], ..., ARR[N-1] is sorted.

Example 14.4 Sort the array given below using selection sort.

39	9	81	45	90	27	72	18

PASS	POS	ARR[0]	ARR[1]	ARR[2]	ARR[3]	ARR[4]	ARR[5]	ARR[6]	ARR[7]
1	1	9	39	81	45	90	27	72	18
2	7	9	18	81	45	90	27	72	39
3	5	9	18	27	45	90	81	72	39
4	7	9	18	27	39	90	81	72	45
5	7	9	18	27	39	45	81	72	90
6	6	9	18	27	39	45	72	81	90
7	6	9	18	27	39	45	72	81	90

The algorithm for selection sort is shown in Fig. 14.8. In the algorithm, during the Kth pass, we need to find the position POS of the smallest elements from ARR[K], ARR[K+1], ..., ARR[N]. To find the smallest element, we use a variable SMALL to hold the smallest value in the sub-array ranging from ARR[K] to ARR[N]. Then, swap ARR[K] with ARR[POS]. This procedure is repeated until all the elements in the array are sorted.

```
SMALLEST (ARR, K, N, POS)

Step 1: [INITIALIZE] SET SMALL = ARR[K]
Step 2: [INITIALIZE] SET POS = K
Step 3: Repeat for J = K+1 to N-1
            IF SMALL > ARR[J]
                  SET SMALL = ARR[J]
                  SET POS = J
            [END OF IF]
        [END OF LOOP]
Step 4: RETURN POS
```

```
SELECTION SORT(ARR, N)

Step 1: Repeat Steps 2 and 3 for K = 1
        to N-1
Step 2:     CALL SMALLEST(ARR, K, N, POS)
Step 3:     SWAP A[K] with ARR[POS]
       [END OF LOOP]
Step 4: EXIT
```

Figure 14.8 Algorithm for selection sort

Complexity of Selection Sort

Selection sort is a sorting algorithm that is independent of the original order of elements in the array. In Pass 1, selecting the element with the smallest value calls for scanning all n elements; thus, n-1 comparisons are required in the first pass. Then, the smallest value is swapped with the element in the first position. In Pass 2, selecting the second smallest value requires scanning the remaining n - 1 elements and so on. Therefore,

$$(n - 1) + (n - 2) + \dots + 2 + 1$$
$$= n(n - 1) / 2 = O(n^2) \text{ comparisons}$$

Advantages of Selection Sort

- It is simple and easy to implement.
- It can be used for small data sets.
- It is 60 per cent more efficient than bubble sort.

However, in case of large data sets, the efficiency of selection sort drops as compared to insertion sort.

Programming Example

7. Write a program to sort an array using selection sort algorithm.

```
#include <stdio.h>
#include <stdlib.h>
int smallest(int arr[], int k, int n);
void selection_sort(int arr[], int n);
void main(int argc, char *argv[]) {
        int arr[10], i, n;
        printf("\n Enter the number of elements in the array: ");
        scanf("%d", &n);
        printf("\n Enter the elements of the array: ");
        for(i=0;i<n;i++)
        {
                scanf("%d", &arr[i]);
        }
        selection_sort(arr, n);
        printf("\n The sorted array is: \n");
        for(i=0;i<n;i++)
        printf(" %d\t", arr[i]);
}
int smallest(int arr[], int k, int n)
{
        int pos = k, small=arr[k], i;
        for(i=k+1;i<n;i++)
        {
                if(arr[i]< small)
                {
                        small = arr[i];
                        pos = i;
                }
        }
        return pos;
}
void selection_sort(int arr[],int n)
{
        int k, pos, temp;
        for(k=0;k<n;k++)
        {
                pos = smallest(arr, k, n);
                temp = arr[k];
                arr[k] = arr[pos];
                arr[pos] = temp;
        }
}
```

14.10 MERGE SORT

Merge sort is a sorting algorithm that uses the divide, conquer, and combine algorithmic paradigm.

Divide means partitioning the n-element array to be sorted into two sub-arrays of n/2 elements. If A is an array containing zero or one element, then it is already sorted. However, if there are more elements in the array, divide A into two sub-arrays, A_1 and A_2, each containing about half of the elements of A.

Conquer means sorting the two sub-arrays recursively using merge sort.

Combine means merging the two sorted sub-arrays of size n/2 to produce the sorted array of n elements.

Merge sort algorithm focuses on two main concepts to improve its performance (running time):

- A smaller list takes fewer steps and thus less time to sort than a large list.
- As number of steps is relatively less, thus less time is needed to create a sorted list from two sorted lists rather than creating it using two unsorted lists.

The basic steps of a merge sort algorithm are as follows:

- If the array is of length 0 or 1, then it is already sorted.
- Otherwise, divide the unsorted array into two sub-arrays of about half the size.
- Use merge sort algorithm recursively to sort each sub-array.
- Merge the two sub-arrays to form a single sorted list.

Example 14.5 Sort the array given below using merge sort.

Solution

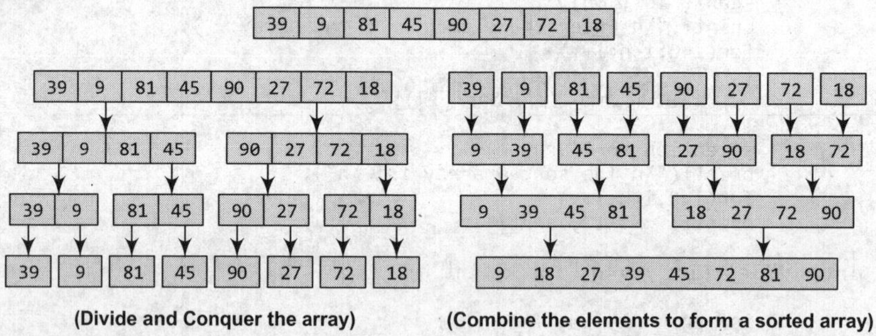

The merge sort algorithm (Fig. 14.9) uses a function `merge` which combines the sub-arrays to form a sorted array. While the merge sort algorithm recursively divides the list into smaller lists, the merge algorithm conquers the list to sort the elements in individual lists. Finally, the smaller lists are merged to form one list.

To understand the merge algorithm, consider the figure below which shows how we merge two lists to form one list. For ease of understanding, we have taken two sub-lists each containing four elements. The same concept can be utilized to merge four sub-lists containing two elements, or eight sub-lists having one element each.

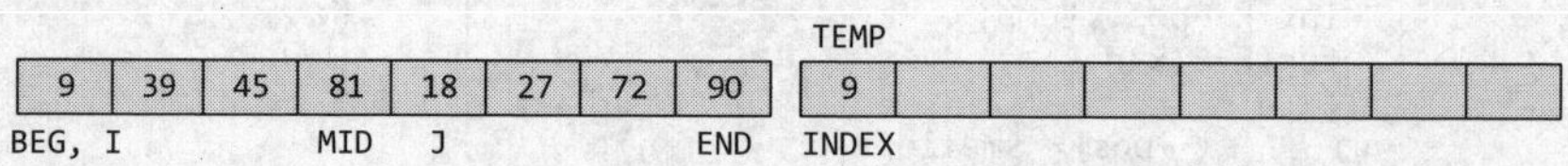

Compare `ARR[I]` and `ARR[J]`, the smaller of the two is placed in `TEMP` at the location specified by `INDEX` and subsequently the value `I` or `J` is incremented.

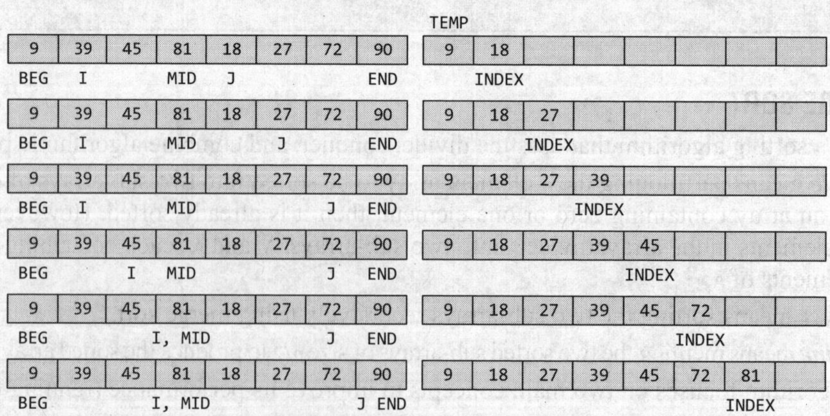

When `I` is greater than `MID`, copy the remaining elements of the right sub-array in `TEMP`.

9	39	45	81	18	27	72	90
BEG			MID	I			J END

9	18	27	39	45	72	81	90
							INDEX

```
MERGE (ARR, BEG, MID, END)

Step 1: [INITIALIZE] SET I = BEG, J = MID + 1, INDEX = 0
Step 2: Repeat while (I <= MID) AND (J<=END)
            IF ARR[I] < ARR[J]
                  SET TEMP[INDEX] = ARR[I]
                  SET I = I + 1
            ELSE
                  SET TEMP[INDEX] = ARR[J]
                  SET J = J + 1
            [END OF IF]
            SET INDEX = INDEX + 1
      [END OF LOOP]
Step 3: [Copy the remaining elements of right sub-array, if any]
            IF I > MID
               Repeat while J <= END
                  SET TEMP[INDEX] = ARR[J]
                  SET INDEX = INDEX + 1, SET J = J + 1
               [END OF LOOP]
      [Copy the remaining elements of left sub-array, if any]
            ELSE
               Repeat while I <= MID
                  SET TEMP[INDEX] = ARR[I]
                  SET INDEX = INDEX + 1, SET I = I + 1
               [END OF LOOP]
            [END OF IF]
Step 4: [Copy the contents of TEMP back to ARR] SET K=0
Step 5: Repeat while K < INDEX
               SET ARR[K] = TEMP[K]
               SET K = K + 1
      [END OF LOOP]
Step 6: END
```

Complexity of Merge Sort

```
MERGE_SORT(ARR, BEG, END)
Step 1: IF BEG < END
            SET MID = (BEG + END)/2
            CALL MERGE_SORT (ARR, BEG, MID)
            CALL MERGE_SORT (ARR, MID + 1, END)
            MERGE (ARR, BEG, MID, END)
        [END OF IF]
Step 2: END
```

Figure 14.9 Algorithm for merge sort

The running time of merge sort in the average case and the worst case can be given as `O(n log n)`. Although merge sort has an optimal time complexity, it needs an additional space of `O(n)` for the temporary array `TEMP`.

Programming Example

8. Write a program to implement merge sort.

```
#include <stdio.h>
#define size 100
void merge(int a[], int, int, int);
```

```
void merge_sort(int a[],int, int);
void main()
{
        int arr[size], i, n;
        printf("\n Enter the number of elements in the array : ");
        scanf("%d", &n);
        printf("\n Enter the elements of the array: ");
        for(i=0;i<n;i++)
        {
                scanf("%d", &arr[i]);
        }
        merge_sort(arr, 0, n-1);
        printf("\n The sorted array is: \n");
        for(i=0;i<n;i++)
        printf(" %d\t", arr[i]);
}
void merge(int arr[], int beg, int mid, int end)
{
        int i=beg, j=mid+1, index=beg, temp[size], k;
        while((i<=mid) && (j<=end))
        {
                if(arr[i] < arr[j])
                {
                        temp[index] = arr[i];
                        i++;
                }
                else
                {
                        temp[index] = arr[j];
                        j++;
                }
                index++;
        }
        if(i>mid)
        {
                while(j<=end)
                {
                        temp[index] = arr[j];
                        j++;
                        index++;
                }
        }
        else
        {
                while(i<=mid)
                {
                        temp[index] = arr[i];
                        i++;
                        index++;
                }
        }
        for(k=beg;k<index;k++)
        arr[k] = temp[k];
}
void merge_sort(int arr[], int beg, int end)
{
        int mid;
        if(beg<end)
        {
                mid = (beg+end)/2;
```

```
                merge_sort(arr, beg, mid);
                merge_sort(arr, mid+1, end);
                merge(arr, beg, mid, end);
            }
    }
```

14.11 QUICK SORT

Quick sort is a widely used sorting algorithm developed by C. A. R. Hoare that makes `O(n log n)` comparisons in the average case to sort an array of `n` elements. However, in the worst case, it has a quadratic running time given as `O(n²)`. Basically, the quick sort algorithm is faster than other `O(n log n)` algorithms, because its efficient implementation can minimize the probability of requiring quadratic time. Quick sort is also known as partition exchange sort.

Like merge sort, this algorithm works by using a divide-and-conquer strategy to divide a single unsorted array into two smaller sub-arrays.

The quick sort algorithm works as follows:

1. Select an element pivot from the array elements.
2. Rearrange the elements in the array in such a way that all elements that are less than the pivot appear before the pivot and all elements greater than the pivot element come after it (equal values can go either way). After such a partitioning, the pivot is placed in its final position. This is called the *partition* operation.
3. Recursively sort the two sub-arrays thus obtained. (One with sub-list of values smaller than that of the pivot element and the other having higher value elements.)

Like merge sort, the *base case* of the recursion occurs when the array has zero or one element because in that case the array is already sorted. After each iteration, one element (pivot) is always in its final position. Hence, with every iteration, there is one less element to be sorted in the array.

Thus, the main task is to find the pivot element, which will partition the array into two halves. To understand how we find the pivot element, follow the steps given below. (We take the first element in the array as pivot.)

Technique

Quick sort works as follows:

1. Set the index of the first element in the array to `loc` and `left` variables. Also, set the index of the last element of the array to the `right` variable.
   That is, `loc = 0`, `left = 0`, and `right = n-1` (where `n` in the number of elements in the array)
2. Start from the element pointed by right and scan the array from right to left, comparing each element on the way with the element pointed by the variable `loc`.
   That is, `a[loc]` should be less than `a[right]`.
   (a) If that is the case, then simply continue comparing until `right` becomes equal to `loc`. Once `right = loc`, it means the pivot has been placed in its correct position.
   (b) However, if at any point, we have `a[loc] > a[right]`, then interchange the two values and jump to Step 3.
   (c) Set `loc = right`
3. Start from the element pointed by `left` and scan the array from left to right, comparing each element on the way with the element pointed by `loc`.
   That is, `a[loc]` should be greater than `a[left]`.

(a) If that is the case, then simply continue comparing until `left` becomes equal to `loc`. Once `left = loc`, it means the pivot has been placed in its correct position.
(b) However, if at any point, we have `a[loc] < a[left]`, then interchange the two values and jump to Step 2.
(c) Set `loc = left`.

Example 14.6 Sort the elements given in the following array using quick sort algorithm

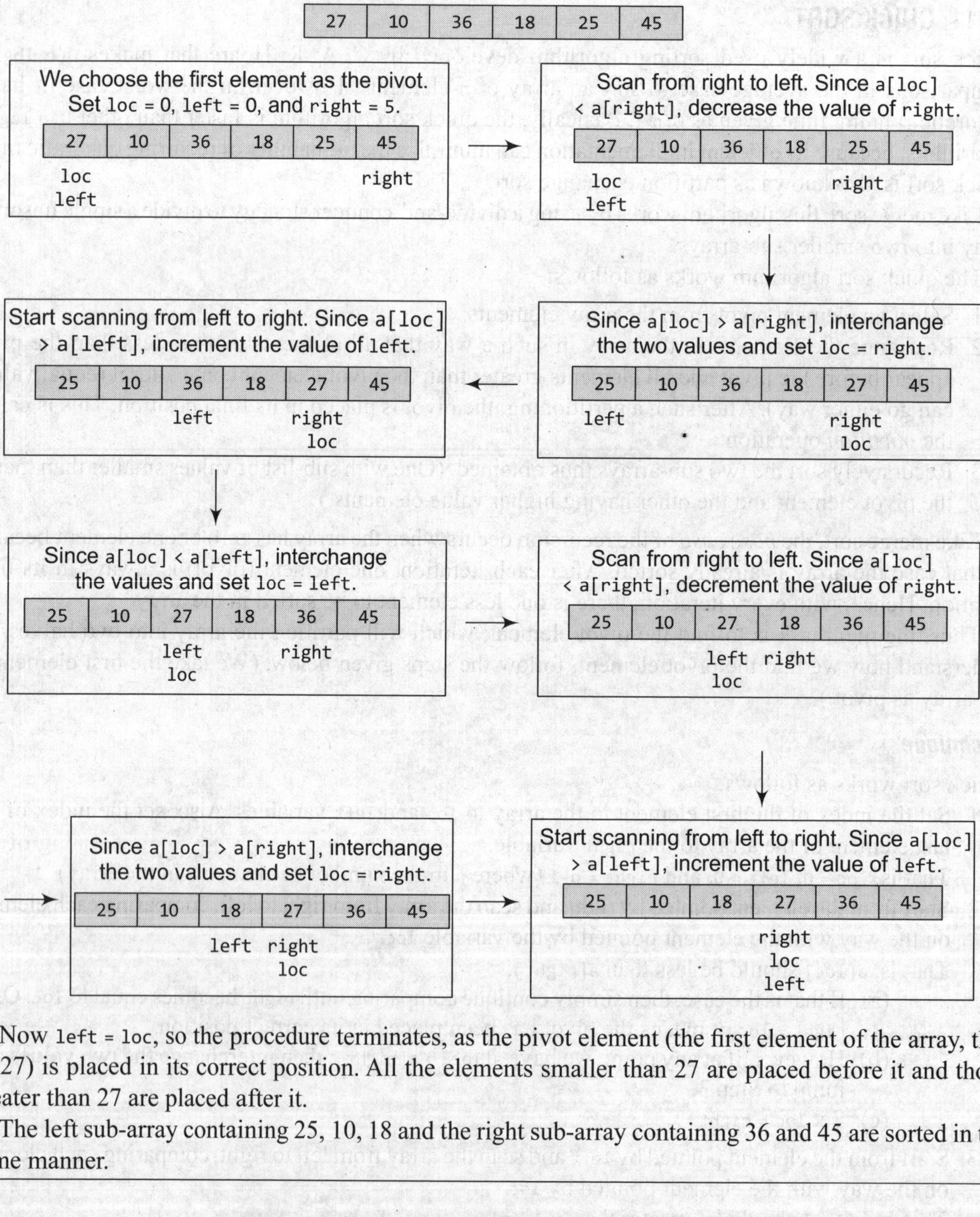

Now `left = loc`, so the procedure terminates, as the pivot element (the first element of the array, that is, 27) is placed in its correct position. All the elements smaller than 27 are placed before it and those greater than 27 are placed after it.

The left sub-array containing 25, 10, 18 and the right sub-array containing 36 and 45 are sorted in the same manner.

The quick sort algorithm (Fig. 14.10) makes use of a function `Partition` to divide the array into two sub-arrays.

```
PARTITION (ARR, BEG, END, LOC)

Step 1: [INITIALIZE] SET LEFT = BEG, RIGHT = END, LOC = BEG, FLAG = 0
Step 2: Repeat Steps 3 to 6 while FLAG = 0
Step 3: Repeat while ARR[LOC] <= ARR[RIGHT] AND LOC != RIGHT
              SET RIGHT = RIGHT - 1
        [END OF LOOP]
Step 4: IF LOC = RIGHT
              SET FLAG = 1
        ELSE IF ARR[LOC] > ARR[RIGHT]
              SWAP ARR[LOC] with  ARR[RIGHT]
              SET LOC = RIGHT
        [END OF IF]
Step 5: IF FLAG = 0
              Repeat while ARR[LOC] >= ARR[LEFT] AND LOC != LEFT
              SET LEFT = LEFT + 1
              [END OF LOOP]
Step 6:       IF LOC = LEFT
                     SET FLAG = 1
              ELSE IF ARR[LOC] < ARR[LEFT]
                     SWAP ARR[LOC] with  ARR[LEFT]
                     SET LOC = LEFT
              [END OF IF]
        [END OF IF]
Step 7: [END OF LOOP]
Step 8: END
```

```
QUICK_SORT (ARR, BEG, END)

Step 1: IF (BEG < END)
             CALL PARTITION (ARR, BEG, END, LOC)
             CALL QUICKSORT(ARR, BEG, LOC - 1)
             CALL QUICKSORT(ARR, LOC + 1, END)
        [END OF IF]
Step 2: END
```

Figure 14.10 Algorithm for quick sort

Complexity of Quick Sort

In the average case, the running time of quick sort can be given as O(n log n). The partitioning of the array which simply loops over the elements of the array once uses O(n) time.

In the best case, every time we partition the array, we divide the list into two nearly equal pieces. That is, the recursive call processes the sub-array of half the size. At the most, only log n nested calls can be made before we reach a sub-array of size 1. It means the depth of the call tree is O(log n). And because at each level, there can only be O(n), the resultant time is given as O(n log n) time.

Practically, the efficiency of quick sort depends on the element which is chosen as the pivot. Its worst-case efficiency is given as $O(n^2)$. The worst case occurs when the array is already sorted (either in ascending or descending order) and the left-most element is chosen as the pivot.

However, many implementations randomly choose the pivot element. The randomized version of the quick sort algorithm always has an algorithmic complexity of O(n log n).

Pros and Cons of Quick Sort

It is faster than other algorithms such as bubble sort, selection sort, and insertion sort. Quick sort can be used to sort arrays of small size, medium size, or large size. On the flip side, quick sort is complex and massively recursive.

Programming Example

9. Write a program to implement quick sort algorithm.

```
#include <stdio.h>
#define size 100
int partition(int a[], int beg, int end);
void quick_sort(int a[], int beg, int end);
void main()
{
        int arr[size], i, n;
        printf("\n Enter the number of elements in the array: ");
        scanf("%d", &n);
        printf("\n Enter the elements of the array: ");
        for(i=0;i<n;i++)
        {
                scanf("%d", &arr[i]);
        }
        quick_sort(arr, 0, n-1);
        printf("\n The sorted array is: \n");
        for(i=0;i<n;i++)
        printf(" %d\t", arr[i]);
}
int partition(int a[], int beg, int end)
{
        int left, right, temp, loc, flag;
        loc = left = beg;
        right = end;
        flag = 0;
        while(flag != 1)
        {
                while((a[loc] <= a[right]) && (loc!=right))
                right--;
                if(loc==right)
                flag =1;
                else if(a[loc]>a[right])
                {
                        temp = a[loc];
                        a[loc] = a[right];
                        a[right] = temp;
                        loc = right;
                }
                if(flag!=1)
                {
                        while((a[loc] >= a[left]) && (loc!=left))
                        left++;
                        if(loc==left)
                        flag =1;
                        else if(a[loc] <a[left])
                        {
                                temp = a[loc];
                                a[loc] = a[left];
```

```
                        a[left] = temp;
                        loc = left;
                    }
                }
            }
            return loc;
        }
        void quick_sort(int a[], int beg, int end)
        {
            int loc;
            if(beg<end)
            {
                loc = partition(a, beg, end);
                quick_sort(a, beg, loc-1);
                quick_sort(a, loc+1, end);
            }
        }
```

14.12 RADIX SORT

Radix sort is a linear sorting algorithm for integers and uses the concept of sorting names in alphabetical order. When we have a list of sorted names, the *radix* is 26 (or 26 buckets) because there are 26 letters in the English alphabet. So radix sort is also known as bucket sort. Observe that words are first sorted according to the first letter of the name. That is, 26 classes are used to arrange the names, where the first class stores the names that begin with A, the second class contains the names with B, and so on.

During the second pass, names are grouped according to the second letter. After the second pass, names are sorted on the first two letters. This process is continued till the nth pass, where n is the length of the name with maximum number of letters.

After every pass, all the names are collected in order of buckets. That is, first pick up the names in the first bucket that contains the names beginning with A. In the second pass, collect the names from the second bucket, and so on.

When radix sort is used on integers, sorting is done on each of the digits in the number. The sorting procedure proceeds by sorting the least significant to the most significant digit. While sorting the numbers, we have ten buckets, each for one digit (0, 1, 2, …, 9) and the number of passes will depend on the length of the number having maximum number of digts.

```
Algorithm for RadixSort (ARR, N)

Step 1: Find the largest number in ARR as LARGE
Step 2: [INITIALIZE] SET NOP = Number of digits in LARGE
Step 3: SET PASS = 0
Step 4: Repeat Step 5 while PASS <= NOP-1
Step 5:             SET I = 0 and INITIALIZE buckets
Step 6:             Repeat Steps 7 to 9 while I<N-1
Step 7:                   SET DIGIT  = digit at PASSth place in A[I]
Step 8:                   Add A[I] to the bucket numbered DIGIT
Step 9:                   INCEREMENT bucket count for bucket numbered DIGIT
                    [END OF LOOP]
Step 10:            Collect the numbers in the bucket
        [END OF LOOP]
Step 11: END
```

Figure 14.11 Algorithm for radix sort

Example 14.7 Sort the numbers given below using radix sort.

345, 654, 924, 123, 567, 472, 555, 808, 911

In the first pass, the numbers are sorted according to the digit at ones place. The buckets are pictured upside down as shown below.

Number	0	1	2	3	4	5	6	7	8	9
345						345				
654					654					
924					924					
123				123						
567								567		
472			472							
555						555				
808									808	
911		911								

After this pass, the numbers are collected bucket by bucket. The new list thus formed is used as an input for the next pass. In the second pass, the numbers are sorted according to the digit at the tens place. The buckets are pictured upside down.

Number	0	1	2	3	4	5	6	7	8	9
911		911								
472								472		
123			123							
654						654				
924			924							
345					345					
555						555				
567							567			
808	808									

In the third pass, the numbers are sorted according to the digit at the hundreds place. The buckets are pictured upside down.

Number	0	1	2	3	4	5	6	7	8	9
808									808	
911										911
123		123								
924										924
345				345						
654							654			
555						555				
567						567				
472					472					

The numbers are collected bucket by bucket. The new list thus formed is the final sorted result. After the third pass, the list can be given as

123, 345, 472, 555, 567, 654, 808, 911, 924.

Complexity of Radix Sort

To calculate the complexity of radix sort algorithm, assume that there are n numbers that have to be sorted and k is the number of digits in the largest number. In this case, the radix sort algorithm is called a total of k times. The inner loop is executed n times. Hence, the entire radix sort algorithm takes O(kn) time to execute. When radix sort is applied on a data set of finite size (very small set of numbers), then the algorithm runs in O(n) asymptotic time.

Pros and Cons of Radix Sort

Radix sort is a very simple algorithm. When programmed properly, radix sort is one of the fastest sorting algorithms for numbers or strings of letters.

But there are certain trade-offs for radix sort that can make it less preferable as compared to other sorting algorithms. Radix sort takes more space than other sorting algorithms. Besides the array of numbers, we need 10 buckets to sort numbers, 26 buckets to sort strings containing only characters, and at least 40 buckets to sort a string containing alphanumeric characters.

Another drawback of radix sort is that the algorithm is dependent on digits or letters. This feature compromises with the flexibility to sort input of any data type. For every different data type, the algorithm has to be rewritten. Even if the sorting order changes, the algorithm has to be rewritten. Thus, radix sort takes more time to write and writing a general purpose radix sort algorithm that can handle all kinds of data is not a trivial task.

Radix sort is a good choice for many programs that need a fast sort, but there are faster sorting algorithms available. This is the main reason why radix sort is not as widely used as other sorting algorithms.

Programming Example

10. Write a program to implement radix sort algorithm.

```
##include <stdio.h>
#define size 10
int largest(int arr[], int n);
void radix_sort(int arr[], int n);
void main()
{
        int arr[size], i, n;
        printf("\n Enter the number of elements in the array: ");
        scanf("%d", &n);
        printf("\n Enter the elements of the array: ");
        for(i=0;i<n;i++)
        {
                scanf("%d", &arr[i]);
        }
        radix_sort(arr, n);
        printf("\n The sorted array is: \n");
        for(i=0;i<n;i++)
        printf(" %d\t", arr[i]);
}
int largest(int arr[], int n)
{
        int large=arr[0], i;
        for(i=1;i<n;i++)
        {
                if(arr[i]>large)
                large = arr[i];
        }
        return large;
```

```
    }
    void radix_sort(int arr[], int n)
    {
            int bucket[size][size], bucket_count[size];
            int i, j, k, remainder, NOP=0, divisor=1, large, pass;
            large = largest(arr, n);
            while(large>0)
            {
                    NOP++;
                    large/=size;
            }
            for(pass=0;pass<NOP;pass++) // Initialize the buckets
            {
                    for(i=0;i<size;i++)
                    bucket_count[i]=0;
                    for(i=0;i<n;i++)
                    {
                            // sort the numbers according to the digit at passth place
                            remainder = (arr[i]/divisor)%size;
                            bucket[remainder][bucket_count[remainder]] = arr[i];
                            bucket_count[remainder] += 1;
                    }
                    // collect the numbers after PASS pass
                    i=0;
                    for(k=0;k<size;k++)
                    {
                            for(j=0;j<bucket_count[k];j++)
                            {
                                    arr[i] = bucket[k][j];
                                    i++;
                            }
                    }
                    divisor *= size;
            }
    }

    }
```

14.13 HEAP SORT

We have discussed binary heaps in Chapter 12. Therefore, we already know how to build a heap H from an array, how to insert a new element in an already existing heap, and how to delete an element from H. Now, using these basic concepts, we will discuss the application of heaps to write an efficient algorithm of heap sort (also known as tournament sort) that has a running time complexity of O(n log n).

```
HEAPSORT(ARR, N)

Step 1: [Build Heap H]
        Repeat for I = 0 to N-1
              CALL Insert_Heap(ARR, N, ARR[I])
        [END OF LOOP]
Step 2: (Repeatedly delete the root element)
        Repeat while N>O
              CALL Delete_Heap(ARR, N, VAL)
              SET N = N + 1
        [END OF LOOP]
Step 3: END
```

Figure 14.12 Algorithm for heap sort

Given an array ARR with n elements, the heap sort algorithm can be used to sort ARR in two phases:

- In phase 1, build a heap H using the elements of ARR.
- In phase 2, repeatedly delete the root element of the heap formed in phase 1.

In a max heap, we know that the largest value in H is always present at the root node. So in phase 2, when the root element is deleted, we are actually collecting the elements of ARR in decreasing order. The algorithm of heap sort is shown in Fig. 14.12.

Complexity of Heap Sort

Heap sort uses two heap operations: *insertion* and *root deletion*. Each element extracted from the root is placed in the last empty location of the array.

In phase 1, when we build a heap, the number of comparisons to find the right location of the new element in `H` cannot exceed the depth of `H`. Since `H` is a complete tree, its depth cannot exceed `m`, where `m` is the number of elements in heap `H`.

Thus, the total number of comparisons `g(n)` to insert `n` elements of `ARR` in `H` is bounded as:

```
g(n) <= n log n
```

Hence, the running time of the first phase of the heap sort algorithm is `O(n log n)`.

In phase 2, we have `H` which is a complete tree with `m` elements having left and right sub-trees as heaps. Assuming `L` to be the root of the tree, *reheaping* the tree would need 4 comparisons to move `L` one step down the tree `H`. Since the depth of `H` cannot exceed `O(log m)`, reheaping the tree will require a maximum of `4 log m` comparisons to find the right location of `L` in `H`.

Since `n` elements will be deleted from heap `H`, reheaping will be done `n` times. Therefore, the number of comparisons to delete `n` elements is bounded as:

```
h(n) <= 4n log n
```

Hence, the running time of the second phase of the heap sort algorithm is `O(n log n)`.

Each phase requires time proportional to `O(n log n)`. Therefore, the running time to sort an array of `n` elements in the worst case is proportional to `O(n log n)`.

Therefore, we can conclude that heap sort is a simple, fast, and stable sorting algorithm that can be used to sort large sets of data efficiently.

Programming Example

11. Write a program to implement heap sort algorithm.

```
#include <stdio.h>
#define MAX 10
void RestoreHeapUp(int *,int);
void RestoreHeapDown(int*,int,int);
int main()
{
          int Heap[MAX],n,i,j;
          printf("\n Enter the number of elements : ");
          scanf("%d",&n);
          printf("\n Enter the elements : ");
          for(i=1;i<=n;i++)
          {
                    scanf("%d",&Heap[i]);
                    RestoreHeapUp(Heap, i);   // Heapify
          }
          // Delete the root element and heapify the heap
          j=n;
          for(i=1;i<=j;i++)
          {
                    int temp;
                    temp=Heap[1];
                    Heap[1]= Heap[n];
                    Heap[n]=temp;
```

```
                n = n-1;          // The element Heap[n] is supposed to be deleted
                RestoreHeapDown(Heap,1,n); // Heapify
            }
            n=j;
            printf("\n The sorted elements are: ");
            for(i=1;i<=n;i++)
                printf("%4d",Heap[i]);
            return 0;
        }
        void RestoreHeapUp(int *Heap,int index)
        {
            int val = Heap[index];
            while( (index>1) && (Heap[index/2] < val) )// Check parent's value
            {
                Heap[index]=Heap[index/2];
                index /= 2;
            }
            Heap[index]=val;
        }
        void RestoreHeapDown(int *Heap,int index,int n)
        {
            int val = Heap[index];
            int j=index*2;
            while(j<=n)
            {
                if( (j<n) && (Heap[j] < Heap[j+1]))// Check sibling's value
                    j++;
                if(Heap[j] < Heap[j/2])   // Check parent's value
                break;
                Heap[j/2]=Heap[j];
                j=j*2;
            }
            Heap[j/2]val;
        }
```

14.14 SHELL SORT

Shell sort, invented by Donald Shell in 1959, is a sorting algorithm that is a generalization of insertion sort. While discussing insertion sort, we have observed two things:

- First, insertion sort works well when the input data is 'almost sorted'.
- Second, insertion sort is quite inefficient to use as it moves the values just one position at a time.

Shell sort is considered an improvement over insertion sort as it compares elements separated by a gap of several positions. This enables the element to take bigger steps towards its expected position. In Shell sort, elements are sorted in multiple passes and in each pass, data are taken with smaller and smaller gap sizes. However, the last step of Shell sort is a plain insertion sort. But by the time we reach the last step, the elements are already 'almost sorted', and hence it provides good performance.

If we take a scenario in which the smallest element is stored in the other end of the array, then sorting such an array with either bubble sort or insertion sort will execute in $O(n^2)$ time and take roughly n comparisons and exchanges to move this value all the way to its correct position. On the other hand, Shell sort first moves small values using giant step sizes, so a small value will move a long way towards its final position, with just a few comparisons and exchanges.

Technique

To visualize the way in which shell sort works, perform the following steps:

- *Step 1:* Arrange the elements of the array in the form of a table and sort the columns (using insertion sort).
- *Step 2:* Repeat Step 1, each time with smaller number of longer columns in such a way that at the end, there is only one column of data to be sorted.

Note that we are only visualizing the elements being arranged in a table, the algorithm does its sorting in-place.

Example 14.8 Sort the elements given below using shell sort.

63, 19, 7, 90, 81, 36, 54, 45, 72, 27, 22, 9, 41, 59, 33

Solution

Arrange the elements of the array in the form of a table and sort the columns.

```
63  19  7   90  81  36  54  45          Result:
72  27  22  9   41  59  33              63  19  7   9   41  36  33  45
                                        72  27  22  90  81  59  54
```

The elements of the array can be given as:

63, 19, 7, 9, 41, 36, 33, 45, 72, 27, 22, 90, 81, 59, 54

Repeat Step 1 with smaller number of long columns.

```
                                Result:
63  19  7   9   41              22  19  7   9   27
36  33  45  72  27              36  33  45  59  41
22  90  81  59  54              63  90  81  72  54
```

The elements of the array can be given as:

22, 19, 7, 9, 27, 36, 33, 45, 59, 41, 63, 90, 81, 72, 54

Repeat Step 1 with smaller number of long columns.

```
                        Result:
22  19  7               9   19  7
9   27  36              22  27  36
33  45  59              33  45  54
41  63  90              41  63  59
81  72  54              81  72  90
```

The elements of the array can be given as:

9, 19, 7, 22, 27, 36, 33, 45, 54, 41, 63, 59, 81, 72, 90

Finally, arrange the elements of the array in a single column and sort the column.

```
        Result:
9       7
19      9
7       19
22      22
27      27
36      33
33      36
45      41
```

```
54          45
41          54
63          59
59          63
81          72
72          81
90          90
```

Finally, the elements of the array can be given as:

```
7, 9, 19, 22, 27, 33, 36, 41, 45, 54, 59, 63, 72, 81, 90
```

The algorithm to sort an array of elements using shell sort is shown in Fig. 14.13. In the algorithm, we sort the elements of the array `Arr` in multiple passes. In each pass, we reduce the `gap_size` (visualize it as the number of columns) by a factor of half as done in Step 4. In each iteration of the `for` loop in Step 5, we compare the values of the array and interchange them if we have a larger value preceding the smaller one.

```
Shell_Sort(Arr, n)

Step 1: SET FLAG = 1, GAP_SIZE = N
Step 2: Repeat Steps 3 to 6 while FLAG = 1 OR GAP_SIZE > 1
Step 3:      SET FLAG = 0
Step 4:      SET GAP_SIZE = (GAP_SIZE + 1) / 2
Step 5:      Repeat Step 6 for I = 0 to I < (N - GAP_SIZE)
Step 6:            IF Arr[I + GAP_SIZE] > Arr[I]
                         SWAP Arr[I + GAP_SIZE], Arr[I]
                         SET FLAG = 0
Step 7: END
```

Figure 14.13 Algorithm for shell sort

Programming Example

12. Write a program to implement shell sort algorithm.

```
#include<stdio.h>
void main()
{
          int arr[10]={-1};
          int i, j, n, flag = 1, gap_size, temp;
          printf("\n Enter the number of elements in the array: ");
          scanf("%d", &n);
          printf("\n Enter %d numbers: ",n);
          for(i=0;i<n;i++)
          scanf("%d", &arr[i]);
          gap_size = n;
          while(flag == 1 || gap_size > 1)
          {
                    flag = 0;
                    gap_size = (gap_size + 1) / 2;
                    for(i=0; i< (n - gap_size); i++)
                    {
                              if( arr[i+gap_size] < arr[i])
```

```
                        {
                                temp = arr[i+gap_size];
                                arr[i+gap_size] = arr[i];
                                arr[i] = temp;
                                flag = 0;
                        }
                }
        }
        printf("\n The sorted array is: \n");
        for(i=0;i<n;i++){
                printf(" %d\t", arr[i]);
        }
}
```

14.15 TREE SORT

A tree sort is a sorting algorithm that sorts numbers by making use of the properties of binary search tree (discussed in Chapter 10). The algorithm first builds a binary search tree using the numbers to be sorted and then does an in-order traversal so that the numbers are retrieved in a sorted order. We will not discuss this topic in detail here because we assume that reader has already studied it in sufficient details in the Chapter 10.

Complexity of Tree Sort Algorithm

Let us study the complexity of tree sort algorithm in all three cases.

Best Case	Worst Case
• Inserting a number in a binary search tree takes O (log n) time. • So, the complete binary search tree with n numbers is built in O (n log n) time. • A binary tree is traversed in O (n) time. • Total time required = O (n log n) + O (n) = O (n log n)	• Occurs with an unbalanced binary search tree, i.e., when the numbers are already sorted. • Binary search tree with n numbers is built in $O(n^2)$ time. • A binary tree is traversed in O (n) time. • Total time required = $O(n^2) + O(n) = O(n^2)$. • The worst case can be improved by using a self-balancing binary search tree.

Programming Example

13. Write a program to implement tree sort algorithm.

```
#include <stdio.h>
#include <alloc.h>
struct tree
{
        struct tree *left;
        int num;
        struct tree *right;
} ;
void insert (struct tree **, int);
void inorder (struct tree *);
void main( )
{
        struct tree *t ;
        int arr[10];
```

```
        int i ;
        printf("\n Enter 10 elements : ");
        for(i=0;i<10;i++)
                scanf("%d", &arr[i]);
        t = NULL;
        printf ("\n The elements of the array are : \n" );
        for (i = 0 ; i <10 ; i++)
                printf ("%d\t", arr[i]);
        for (i = 0 ; i <10 ; i++)
                insert (&t, arr[i]);
        printf ("\n The sorted array is : \n");
        inorder (t );
        getchar( );
}
void insert (struct tree **tree_node, int num)
{
        if ( *tree_node == NULL )
        {
                *tree_node = malloc (sizeof ( struct tree ));
                ( *tree_node ) -> left = NULL;
                ( *tree_node ) -> num = num;
                ( *tree_node ) -> right = NULL;
        }
        else
        {
                if ( num < ( *tree_node ) -> num )
                        insert ( &( ( *tree_node ) -> left ), num );
                else
                        insert ( &( ( *tree_node ) -> right ), num );
        }
}
void inorder (struct tree *tree_node )
{
        if ( tree_node != NULL )
        {
                inorder ( tree_node -> left );
                printf ( "%d\t", tree_node -> num );
                inorder ( tree_node -> right );
        }
}
```

Table 14.1 Comparison of algorithms

Algorithm	Average Case	Worst Case
Bubble sort	$O(n^2)$	$O(n^2)$
Bucket sort	O(n.k)	$O(n^2.k)$
Selection sort	$O(n^2)$	$O(n^2)$
Insertion sort	$O(n^2)$	$O(n^2)$
Shell sort	–	$O(n \log^2 n)$
Merge sort	O(n log n)	O(n log n)
Heap sort	O(n log n)	O(n log n)
Quick sort	O(n log n)	$O(n^2)$

14.16 COMPARISON OF SORTING ALGORITHMS

Table 14.1 compares the average-case and worst-case time complexities of different sorting algorithms discussed so far.

14.17 EXTERNAL SORTING

External sorting is a sorting technique that can handle massive amounts of data. It is usually applied when the data being sorted does not fit into the main memory (RAM) and, therefore, a slower memory (usually a magnetic disk or even a magnetic tape) needs to be used. We will explain the concept of external sorting using an example discussed below.

Example 14.9 Let us consider we need to sort 700 MB of data using only 100 MB of RAM. The steps for sorting are given below.

Step 1: Read 100 MB of the data in RAM and sort this data using any conventional sorting algorithm like quick sort.

Step 2: Write the sorted data back to the magnetic disk.

Step 3: Repeat Steps 1 and 2 until all the data (in 100 MB chunks) is sorted. All these seven chunks that are sorted need to be merged into one single output file.

Step 4: Read the first 10 MB of each of the sorted chunks and call them input buffers. So, now we have 70 MB of data in the RAM. Allocate the remaining RAM for output buffer.

Step 5: Perform seven-way merging and store the result in the output buffer. If at any point of time, the output buffer becomes full, then write its contents to the final sorted file. However, if any of the 7 input buffers gets empty, fill it with the next 10 MB of its associated 100 MB sorted chunk or else mark the input buffer (sorted chunk) as exhausted if it does not has any more left with it. Make sure that this chunk is not used for further merging of data.

The external merge sorting can be visualized as given in Fig. 14.14.

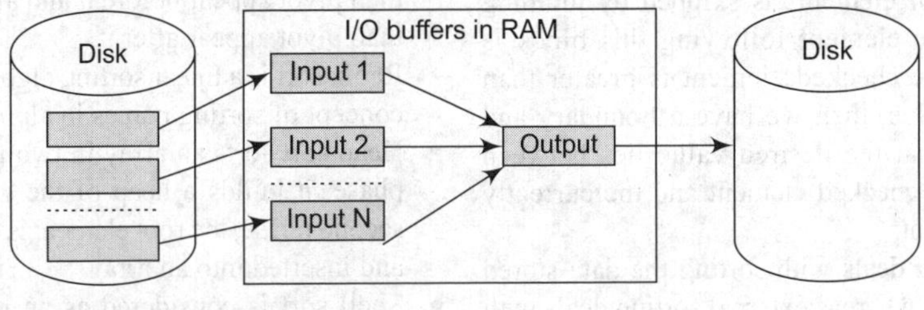

Figure 14.14 External merge sorting

Generalized External Merge Sort Algorithm

From the example above, we can now present a generalized merge sort algorithm for external sorting. If the amount of data to be sorted exceeds the available memory by a factor of K, then K chunks (also known as K run lists) of data are created. These K chunks are sorted and then a K-way merge is performed. If the amount of RAM available is given as X, then there will be K input buffers and 1 output buffer.

In the above example, a single-pass merge was used. But if the ratio of data to be sorted and available RAM is particularly large, a multi-pass sorting is used. We can first merge only the first half of the sorted chunks, then the other half, and finally merge the two sorted chunks. The exact number of passes depends on the following factors:

- Size of the data to be sorted when compared with the available RAM
- Physical characteristics of the magnetic disk such as transfer rate, seek time, etc.

Applications of External Sorting

External sorting is used to update a master file from a transaction file. For example, updating the EMPLOYEES file based on new hires, promotions, appraisals, and dismissals.

It is also used in database applications for performing operations like *Projection* and *Join*. Projection means selecting a subset of fields and join means joining two files on a common field to create a new file whose fields are the union of the fields of the two files. External sorting is also used to remove duplicate records.

Points to Remember

- Searching refers to finding the position of a value in a collection of values. Some of the popular searching techniques are linear search, binary search, interpolation search, and jump search.
- Linear search works by comparing the value to be searched with every element of the array one by one is a sequence until a match is found.
- Binary search works efficiently with a sorted list. In this algorithm, the value to be searched is compared with the middle element of the array segment.
- In each step of interpolation search, the search space for the value to be found is calculated. The calculation is done based on the values at the bounds of the search space and the value to be searched.
- Jump search is used with sorted lists. We first check an element and if it is less than the desired value, then a block of elements is skipped by jumping ahead, and the element following this block is checked. If the checked element is greater than the desired value, then we have a boundary and we are sure that the desired value lies between the previously checked element and the currently checked element.
- Internal sorting deals with sorting the data stored in the memory, whereas external sorting deals with sorting the data stored in files.
- In bubble sorting, consecutive adjacent pairs of elements in the array are compared with each other.
- Insertion sort works by moving the current data element past the already sorted values and repeatedly interchanging it with the preceding value until it is in the correct place.
- Selection sort works by finding the smallest value and placing it in the first position. It then finds the second smallest value and places it in the second position. This procedure is repeated until the whole array is sorted.
- Merge sort is a sorting algorithm that uses the divide, conquer, and combine algorithmic paradigm. *Divide* means partitioning the `n`-element array to be sorted into two sub-arrays of `n/2` elements in each sub-array. *Conquer* means sorting the two sub-arrays recursively using merge sort. *Combine* means merging the two sorted sub-arrays of size `n/2` each to produce a sorted array of `n` elements. The running time of merge sort in average case and worst case can be given as `O(n log n)`.
- Quick sort works by using a divide-and-conquer strategy. It selects a pivot element and rearranges the elements in such a way that all elements less than pivot appear before it and all elements greater than pivot appear after it.
- Radix sort is a linear sorting algorithm that uses the concept of sorting names in alphabetical order.
- Heap sort sorts an array in two phases. In the first phase, it builds a heap of the given array. In the second phase, the root element is deleted repeatedly and inserted into an array.
- Shell sort is considered as an improvement over insertion sort, as it compares elements separated by a gap of several positions.
- A tree sort is a sorting algorithm that sorts numbers by making use of the properties of binary search tree. The algorithm first builds a binary search tree using the numbers to be sorted and then does an in-order traversal so that the numbers are retrieved in a sorted order.

Exercises

Review Questions

1. Which technique of searching an element in an array would you prefer to use and in which situation?
2. Define sorting. What is the importance of sorting?
3. What are the different types of sorting techniques? Which sorting technique has the least worst case?
4. Explain the difference between bubble sort and quick sort. Which one is more efficient?
5. Sort the elements 77, 49, 25, 12, 9, 33, 56, 81 using
   (a) insertion sort (b) selection sort
   (c) bubble sort (d) merge sort
   (e) quick sort (f) radix sort
   (g) shell sort

6. Compare heap sort and quick sort.
7. Quick sort shows quadratic behaviour in certain situations. Justify.
8. If the following sequence of numbers is to be sorted using quick sort, then show the iterations of the sorting process.
   42, 34, 75, 23, 21, 18, 90, 67, 78
9. Sort the following sequence of numbers in descending order using heap sort.
   42, 34, 75, 23, 21, 18, 90, 67, 78
10. A certain sorting technique was applied to the following data set,
    45, 1, 27, 36, 54, 90
    After two passes, the rearrangement of the data set is given as below:
    1, 27, 45, 36, 54, 90
    Identify the sorting algorithm that was applied.
11. A certain sorting technique was applied to the following data set,
    81, 72, 63, 45, 27, 36
    After two passes, the rearrangement of the data set is given as below:
    27, 36, 80, 72, 63, 45
    Identify the sorting algorithm that was applied.
12. A certain sorting technique was applied to the following data set,
    45, 1, 63, 36, 54, 90
    After two passes, the rearrangement of the data set is given as below:
    1, 45, 63, 36, 54, 90
    Identify the sorting algorithm that was applied.
13. Write a recursive function to perform selection sort.
14. Compare the running time complexity of different sorting algorithms.
15. Discuss the advantages of insertion sort.

Programming Exercises

1. Write a program to implement bubble sort. Given the numbers 7, 1, 4, 12, 67, 33, and 45. How many swaps will be performed to sort these numbers using the bubble sort.
2. Write a program to implement a sort technique that works by repeatedly stepping through the list to be sorted.
3. Write a program to implement a sort technique in which the sorted array is built one entry at a time.
4. Write a program to implement an in-place comparison sort.
5. Write a program to implement a sort technique that works on the principle of divide and conquer strategy.
6. Write a program to implement partition-exchange sort.
7. Write a program to implement a sort technique which sorts the numbers based on individual digits.
8. Write a program to sort an array of integers in descending order using the following sorting techniques:
   (a) insertion sort (b) selection sort
   (c) bubble sort (d) merge sort
   (e) quick sort (f) radix sort
   (g) shell sort
9. Write a program to sort an array of floating point numbers in descending order using the following sorting techniques:
   (a) insertion sort (b) selection sort
   (c) bubble sort (d) merge sort
   (e) quick sort (f) radix sort
   (g) shell sort
10. Write a program to sort an array of names using the bucket sort.

Multiple-choice Questions

1. The worst case complexity is ______ when compared with the average case complexity of a binary search algorithm.
   (a) Equal (b) Greater
   (c) Less (d) None of these
2. The complexity of binary search algorithm is
   (a) O(n) (b) $O(n^2)$
   (c) O(n log n) (d) O(log n)
3. Which of the following cases occurs when searching an array using linear search the value to be searched is equal to the first element of the array?
   (a) Worst case (b) Average case
   (c) Best case (d) Amortized case
4. A card game player arranges his cards and picks them one by one. With which sorting technique can you compare this example?
   (a) Bubble sort (b) Selection sort
   (c) Merge sort (d) Insertion sort

5. Which of the following techniques deals with sorting the data stored in the computer's memory?
   (a) Insertion sort (b) Internal sort
   (c) External sort (d) Radix sort
6. In which sorting, consecutive adjacent pairs of elements in the array are compared with each other?
   (a) Bubble sort (b) Selection sort
   (c) Merge sort (d) Radix sort
7. Which term means sorting the two sub-arrays recursively using merge sort?
   (a) Divide (b) Conquer
   (c) Combine (d) All of these
8. Which sorting algorithm sorts by moving the current data element past the already sorted values and repeatedly interchanging it with the preceding value until it is in its correct place?
   (a) Insertion sort (b) Internal sort
   (c) External sort (d) Radix sort
9. Which algorithm uses the divide, conquer, and combine algorithmic paradigm?
   (a) Selection sort (b) Insertion sort
   (c) Merge sort (d) Radix sort
10. Quick sort is faster than
   (a) Selection sort (b) Insertion sort
   (c) Bubble sort (d) All of these
11. Which sorting algorithm is also known as tournament sort?
   (a) Selection sort (b) Insertion sort
   (c) Bubble sort (d) Heap sort

True or False

1. Binary search is also called sequential search.
2. Linear search is performed on a sorted array.
3. For insertion sort, the best case occurs when the array is already sorted.
4. Selection sort has a linear running time complexity.
5. The running time of merge sort in the average case and the worst case is `O(n log n)`.
6. The worst case running time complexity of quick sort is `O(n log n)`.
7. Heap sort is an efficient and a stable sorting algorithm.
8. External sorting deals with sorting the data stored in the computer's memory.
9. Insertion sort is less efficient than quick sort, heap sort, and merge sort.
10. The average case of insertion sort has a quadratic running time.
11. The partitioning of the array in quick sort is done in `O(n)` time.

Fill in the Blanks

1. Performance of the linear search algorithm can be improved by using a ______.
2. The complexity of linear search algorithm is ______.
3. Sorting means ______.
4. ______ sort shows the best average-case behaviour.
5. ______ deals with sorting the data stored in files.
6. `O(n²)` is the running time complexity of ______ algorithm.
7. In the worst case, insertion sort has a ______ running time.
8. ______ sort uses the divide, conquer, and combine algorithmic paradigm.
9. In the average case, quick sort has a running time complexity of ______.
10. The execution time of bucket sort in average case is ______.
11. The running time of merge sort in the average and the worst case is ______.
12. The efficiency of quick sort depends on ______.

CHAPTER 15

Hashing and Collision

LEARNING OBJECTIVE

In this chapter, we will discuss another data structure known as hash table. We will see what a hash table is and why do we prefer hash tables over simple arrays. We will also discuss hash functions, collisions, and the techniques to resolve collisions.

15.1 INTRODUCTION

In Chapter 14, we discussed two search algorithms: *linear search* and *binary search*. Linear search has a running time proportional to `O(n)`, while binary search takes time proportional to `O(log n)`, where `n` is the number of elements in the array. Binary search and binary search trees are efficient algorithms to search for an element. But what if we want to perform the search operation in time proportional to `O(1)`? In other words, is there a way to search an array in constant time, irrespective of its size?

There are two solutions to this problem. Let us take an example to explain the first solution. In a small company of 100 employees, each employee is assigned an `Emp_ID` in the range 0–99. To store the records in an array, each employee's `Emp_ID` acts as an index into the array where the employee's record will be stored as shown in Fig. 15.1.

In this case, we can directly access the record of any employee, once we know his `Emp_ID`, because the array index is the same as the `Emp_ID` number. But practically, this implementation is hardly feasible.

Let us assume that the same company uses a five-digit Emp_ID as the primary key. In this case, key values will range from 00000 to 99999. If we want to use the same technique as above, we need an array of size 100,000, of which only 100 elements will be used. This is illustrated in Fig. 15.2.

It is impractical to waste so much storage space just to ensure that each employee's record is in a unique and predictable location.

Key	Array of Employees' Records
Key 0 ⟶ [0]	Employee record with Emp_ID 0
Key 1 ⟶ [1]	Employee record with Emp_ID 1
Key 2 ⟶ [2]	Employee record with Emp_ID 2
....	....
....	....
Key 98 ⟶ [98]	Employee record with Emp_ID 98
Key 99 ⟶ [99]	Employee record with Emp_ID 99

Figure 15.1 Records of employees

Whether we use a two-digit primary key (`Emp_ID`) or a five-digit key, there are just 100 employees in the company. Thus, we will be using only 100 locations in the array. Therefore, in order to keep the array size down to the size that we will actually be using (100 elements), another good option is to use just the last two digits of the key to identify each employee. For example, the employee with `Emp_ID 79439` will be stored in the element of the array with index 39. Similarly, the employee with `Emp_ID 12345` will have his record stored in the array at the 45th location.

Key	Array of Employees' Records
Key 00000 ⟶ [0]	Employee record with Emp_ID 00000
....	....
Key n ⟶ [n]	Employee record with Emp_ID n
....	....
Key 99998 ⟶ [99998]	Employee record with Emp_ID 99998
Key 99999 ⟶ [99999]	Employee record with Emp_ID 99999

Figure 15.2 Records of employees with a five-digit Emp_ID

In the second solution, the elements are not stored according to the *value* of the key. So in this case, we need a way to convert a five-digit key number to a two-digit array index. We need a function which will do the transformation. In this case, we will use the term *hash table* for an array and the function that will carry out the transformation will be called a *hash function.*

15.2 HASH TABLES

Hash table is a data structure in which keys are mapped to array positions by a hash function. In the example discussed here we will use a hash function that extracts the last two digits of the key. Therefore, we map the keys to array locations or array indices. A value stored in a hash table can be searched in `O(1)` time by using a hash function which generates an address from the key (by producing the index of the array where the value is stored).

Figure 15.3 shows a direct correspondence between the keys and the indices of the array. This concept is useful when the total universe of keys is small and when most of the keys are actually used from the whole set of keys. This is equivalent to our first example, where there are 100 keys for 100 employees.

However, when the set `K` of keys that are actually used is smaller than the universe of keys `(U)`, a hash table consumes less storage space. The storage requirement for a hash table is `O(k)`, where `k` is the number of keys actually used.

In a hash table, an element with key `k` is stored at index `h(k)` and not `k`. It means a hash function `h` is used to calculate the index at which the element with key `k` will be stored. This process of mapping the keys to appropriate locations (or indices) in a hash table is called *hashing*.

Figure 15.4 shows a hash table in which each key from the set `K` is mapped to locations generated by using a hash function. Note that keys k_2 and k_6 point to the same memory location. This is known as *collision*. That is, when two or more keys map to the same memory location, a collision is said to occur.

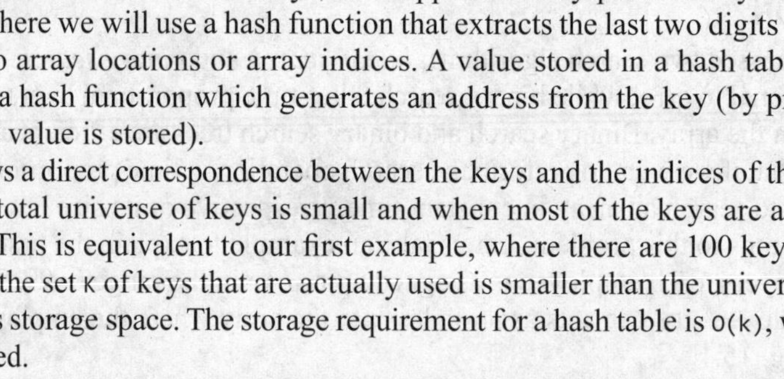

Figure 15.3 Direct relationship between key and index in the array

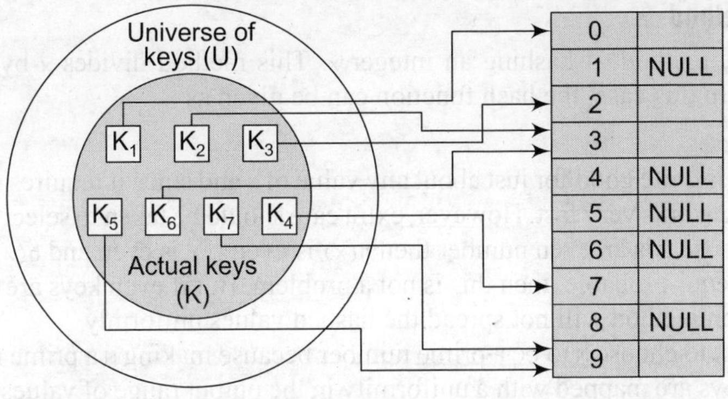

Figure 15.4 Relationship between keys and hash table index

Similarly, keys k_5 and k_7 also collide. The main goal of using a hash function is to reduce the range of array indices that have to be handled. Thus, instead of having U values, we just need K values, thereby reducing the amount of storage space required.

15.3 HASH FUNCTIONS

A hash function is a mathematical formula which, when applied to a key, produces an integer which can be used as an index for the key in the hash table. The main aim of a hash function is that elements should be relatively, randomly, and uniformly distributed. It produces a unique set of integers within some suitable range in order to reduce the number of collisions. In practice, there is no hash function that eliminates collisions completely. A good hash function can only minimize the number of collisions by spreading the elements uniformly throughout the array.

In this section, we will discuss the popular hash functions which help to minimize collisions. But before that, let us first look at the properties of a good hash function.

Properties of a Good Hash Function

Low cost The cost of executing a hash function must be small, so that using the hashing technique becomes preferable over other approaches. For example, if binary search algorithm can search an element from a sorted table of n items with $\log_2 n$ key comparisons, then the hash function must cost less than performing $\log_2 n$ key comparisons.

Determinism A hash procedure must be deterministic. This means that the same hash value must be generated for a given input value. However, this criteria excludes hash functions that depend on external variable parameters (such as the time of day) and on the memory address of the object being hashed (because address of the object may change during processing).

Uniformity A good hash function must map the keys as evenly as possible over its output range. This means that the probability of generating every hash value in the output range should roughly be the same. The property of uniformity also minimizes the number of collisions.

15.4 DIFFERENT HASH FUNCTIONS

In this section, we will discuss the hash functions which use numeric keys. However, there can be cases in real-world applications where we can have alphanumeric keys rather than simple numeric keys. In such cases, the ASCII value of the character can be used to transform it into its equivalent numeric key. Once this transformation is done, any of the hash functions given below can be applied to generate the hash value.

15.4.1 Division Method

It is the most simple method of hashing an integer x. This method divides x by M and then uses the remainder obtained. In this case, the hash function can be given as

```
h(x) = x mod M
```

The division method is quite good for just about any value of M and since it requires only a single division operation, the method works very fast. However, extra care should be taken to select a suitable value for M.

For example, suppose M is an even number then h(x) is even if x is even and h(x) is odd if x is odd. If all possible keys are equi-probable, then this is not a problem. But if even keys are more likely than odd keys, then the division method will not spread the hashed values uniformly.

Generally, it is best to choose M to be a prime number because making M a prime number increases the likelihood that the keys are mapped with a uniformity in the output range of values. M should also be not too close to the exact powers of 2. If we have

$$h(x) = x \bmod 2^k$$

then the function will simply extract the lowest k bits of the binary representation of x.

The division method is extremely simple to implement. The following code segment illustrates how to do this:

```
int const M = 97; // a prime number
int h (int x)
{ return (x % M); }
```

A potential drawback of the division method is that while using this method, consecutive keys map to consecutive hash values. On one hand, this is good as it ensures that consecutive keys do not collide, but on the other, it also means that consecutive array locations will be occupied. This may lead to degradation in performance.

Example 15.1 Calculate the hash values of keys 1234 and 5462.

Solution Setting M = 97, hash values can be calculated as:

```
h(1234) = 1234 % 97 = 70
h(5642) = 5642 % 97 = 16
```

15.4.2 Multiplication Method

The steps involved in the multiplication method are as follows:

Step 1: Choose a constant A such that 0 < A < 1.
Step 2: Multiply the key k by A.
Step 3: Extract the fractional part of kA.
Step 4: Multiply the result of Step 3 by the size of hash table (m).

Hence, the hash function can be given as:

$$h(k) = \lfloor m \, (kA \bmod 1) \rfloor$$

where (kA mod 1) gives the fractional part of kA and m is the total number of indices in the hash table.

The greatest advantage of this method is that it works practically with any value of A. Although the algorithm works better with some values, the optimal choice depends on the characteristics of the data being hashed. Knuth has suggested that the best choice of A is

" (sqrt5 - 1) /2 = 0.6180339887

Example 15.2 Given a hash table of size 1000, map the key 12345 to an appropriate location in the hash table.

Solution We will use A = 0.618033, m = 1000, and k = 12345

```
h(12345) = ⌊ 1000 (12345 × 0.618033 mod 1) ⌋
         = ⌊ 1000 (7629.617385 mod 1) ⌋
         = ⌊ 1000 (0.617385) ⌋
         = ⌊ 617.385 ⌋
         = 617
```

15.4.3 Mid-square Method

The mid-square method is a good hash function which works in two steps:

Step 1: Square the value of the key. That is, find k^2.

Step 2: Extract the middle r digits of the result obtained in Step 1.

The algorithm works well because most or all digits of the key value contribute to the result. This is because all the digits in the original key value contribute to produce the middle digits of the squared value. Therefore, the result is not dominated by the distribution of the bottom digit or the top digit of the original key value.

In the mid-square method, the same r digits must be chosen from all the keys. Therefore, the hash function can be given as:

```
h(k) = s
```

where s is obtained by selecting r digits from k^2.

Example 15.3 Calculate the hash value for keys 1234 and 5642 using the mid-square method. The hash table has 100 memory locations.

Solution Note that the hash table has 100 memory locations whose indices vary from 0 to 99. This means that only two digits are needed to map the key to a location in the hash table, so $r = 2$.

When $k = 1234$, $k^2 = 1522756$, h (1234) = 27

When $k = 5642$, $k^2 = 31832164$, h (5642) = 21

Observe that the 3rd and 4th digits starting from the right are chosen.

15.4.4 Folding Method

The folding method works in the following two steps:

Step 1: Divide the key value into a number of parts. That is, divide k into parts $k_1, k_2, \ldots, k_n$, where each part has the same number of digits except the last part which may have lesser digits than the other parts.

Step 2: Add the individual parts. That is, obtain the sum of $k_1 + k_2 + \ldots + k_n$. The hash value is produced by ignoring the last carry, if any.

Note that the number of digits in each part of the key will vary depending upon the size of the hash table. For example, if the hash table has a size of 1000, then there are 1000 locations in the hash table. To address these 1000 locations, we need at least three digits; therefore, each part of the key must have three digits except the last part which may have lesser digits.

Example 15.4 Given a hash table of 100 locations, calculate the hash value using folding method for keys 5678, 321, and 34567.

Solution

Since there are 100 memory locations to address, we will break the key into parts where each part (except the last) will contain two digits. The hash values can be obtained as shown below:

key	5678	321	34567
Parts	56 and 78	32 and 1	34, 56 and 7
Sum	134	33	97
Hash value	34 (ignore the last carry)	33	97

15.5 COLLISIONS

As discussed earlier in this chapter, collisions occur when the hash function maps two different keys to the same location. Obviously, two records cannot be stored in the same location. Therefore, a method used to solve the problem of collision, also called *collision resolution technique*, is applied. The two most popular methods of resolving collisions are:

1. Open addressing
2. Chaining

In this section, we will discuss both these techniques in detail.

15.5.1 Collision Resolution by Open Addressing

Once a collision takes place, open addressing or closed hashing computes new positions using a probe sequence and the next record is stored in that position. In this technique, all the values are stored in the hash table. The hash table contains two types of values: *sentinel values* (e.g., –1) and *data values*. The presence of a sentinel value indicates that the location contains no data value at present but can be used to hold a value.

When a key is mapped to a particular memory location, then the value it holds is checked. If it contains a sentinel value, then the location is free and the data value can be stored in it. However, if the location already has some data value stored in it, then other slots are examined systematically in the forward direction to find a free slot. If even a single free location is not found, then we have an `OVERFLOW` condition.

The process of examining memory locations in the hash table is called *probing*. Open addressing technique can be implemented using linear probing, quadratic probing, double hashing, and rehashing.

Linear Probing

The simplest approach to resolve a collision is linear probing. In this technique, if a value is already stored at a location generated by `h(k)`, then the following hash function is used to resolve the collision:

```
h(k, i) = [h′(k) + i] mod m
```

Where `m` is the size of the hash table, `h′(k) = (k mod m)`, and `i` is the probe number that varies from `0` to `m-1`.

Therefore, for a given key `k`, first the location generated by `[h′(k) mod m]` is probed because for the first time `i=0`. If the location is free, the value is stored in it, else the second probe generates the address of the location given by `[h′(k) + 1]mod m`. Similarly, if the location is occupied, then subsequent probes generate the address as `[h′(k) + 2]mod m`, `[h′(k) + 3]mod m`, `[h′(k) + 4]mod m`, `[h′(k) + 5]mod m`, and so on, until a free location is found.

> **Note** Linear probing is known for its simplicity. When we have to store a value, we try the slots: `[h′(k)] mod m`, `[h′(k) + 1]mod m`, `[h′(k) + 2]mod m`, `[h′(k) + 3]mod m`, `[h′(k) + 4]mod m`, `[h′(k) + 5]mod m`, and so no, until a vacant location is found.

Example 15.5 Consider a hash table of size 10. Using linear probing, insert the keys 72, 27, 36, 24, 63, 81, 92, and 101 into the table.

Let `h′(k)` = `k mod m, m = 10`

Initially, the hash table can be given as:

0	1	2	3	4	5	6	7	8	9
–1	–1	–1	–1	–1	–1	–1	–1	–1	–1

Step 1

```
          Key   = 72
    h(72, 0)    = (72 mod 10 + 0) mod 10
                = (2) mod 10
                = 2
```

Since `T[2]` is vacant, insert key 72 at this location.

0	1	2	3	4	5	6	7	8	9
–1	–1	72	–1	–1	–1	–1	–1	–1	–1

Step 2

```
         Key      = 27
    h(27, 0)      = (27 mod 10 + 0) mod 10
                  = (7) mod 10
                  = 7
```

Since `T[7]` is vacant, insert key 27 at this location.

0	1	2	3	4	5	6	7	8	9
–1	–1	72	–1	–1	–1	–1	27	–1	–1

Step 3

```
         Key      = 36
    h(36, 0)      = (36 mod 10 + 0) mod 10
                  = (6) mod 10
                  = 6
```

Since `T[6]` is vacant, insert key 36 at this location.

0	1	2	3	4	5	6	7	8	9
–1	–1	72	–1	–1	–1	36	27	–1	–1

Step 4

```
         Key      = 24
    h(24, 0)      = (24 mod 10 + 0) mod 10
                  = (4) mod 10
                  = 4
```

Since `T[4]` is vacant, insert key 24 at this location.

0	1	2	3	4	5	6	7	8	9
–1	–1	72	–1	24	–1	36	27	–1	–1

Step 5

```
         Key      = 63
    h(63, 0)      = (63 mod 10 + 0) mod 10
                  = (3) mod 10
                  = 3
```

Since `T[3]` is vacant, insert key 63 at this location.

0	1	2	3	4	5	6	7	8	9
–1	–1	72	63	24	–1	36	27	–1	–1

Step 6

```
         Key      = 81
    h(81, 0)      = (81 mod 10 + 0) mod 10
                  = (1) mod 10
                  = 1
```

Since `T[1]` is vacant, insert key 81 at this location.

0	1	2	3	4	5	6	7	8	9
0	81	72	63	24	–1	36	27	–1	–1

Step 7

```
        Key   = 92
h(92, 0)      = (92 mod 10 + 0) mod 10
              = (2) mod 10
              = 2
```

Now `T[2]` is occupied, so we cannot store the key 92 in `T[2]`. Therefore, try again for the next location. Thus probe, `i = 1`, this time.

```
        Key   = 92
h(92, 1)      = (92 mod 10 + 1) mod 10
              = (2 + 1) mod 10
              = 3
```

Now `T[3]` is occupied, so we cannot store the key 92 in `T[3]`. Therefore, try again for the next location. Thus probe, `i = 2`, this time.

```
        Key   = 92
h(92, 2)      = (92 mod 10 + 2) mod 10
              = (2 + 2) mod 10
              = 4
```

Now `T[4]` is occupied, so we cannot store the key 92 in `T[4]`. Therefore, try again for the next location. Thus probe, `i = 3`, this time.

```
        Key   = 92
h(92, 3)      = (92 mod 10 + 3) mod 10
              = (2 + 3) mod 10
              = 5
```

Since `T[5]` is vacant, insert key 92 at this location.

0	1	2	3	4	5	6	7	8	9
–1	81	72	63	24	92	36	27	–1	–1

Step 8

```
        Key   = 101
h(101, 0)     = (101 mod 10 + 0) mod 10
              = (1) mod 10
              = 1
```

Now `T[1]` is occupied, so we cannot store the key 101 in `T[1]`. Therefore, try again for the next location. Thus probe, `i = 1`, this time.

```
        Key   = 101
h(101, 1)     = (101 mod 10 + 1) mod 10
              = (1 + 1) mod 10
              = 2
```

`T[2]` is also occupied, so we cannot store the key in this location. The procedure will be repeated until the hash function generates the address of location 8 which is vacant and can be used to store the value in it.

Searching a Value using Linear Probing

The procedure for searching a value in a hash table is same as for storing a value in a hash table.

While searching for a value in a hash table, the array index is re-computed and the key of the element stored at that location is compared with the value that has to be searched. If a match is found, then the search operation is successful. The search time in this case is given as `O(1)`. If the key does not match, then the search function begins a sequential search of the array that continues until:

- the value is found, or
- the search function encounters a vacant location in the array, indicating that the value is not present, or
- the search function terminates because it reaches the end of the table and the value is not present.

In the worst case, the search operation may have to make `n-1` comparisons, and the running time of the search algorithm may take `O(n)` time. The worst case will be encountered when after scanning all the `n-1` elements, the value is either present at the last location or not present in the table.

Thus, we see that with the increase in the number of collisions, the distance between the array index computed by the hash function and the actual location of the element increases, thereby increasing the search time.

Pros and Cons

Linear probing finds an empty location by doing a linear search in the array beginning from position `h(k)`. Although the algorithm provides good memory caching through good locality of reference, the drawback of this algorithm is that it results in clustering, and thus there is a higher risk of more collisions where one collision has already taken place. The performance of linear probing is sensitive to the distribution of input values.

As the hash table fills, clusters of consecutive cells are formed and the time required for a search increases with the size of the cluster. In addition to this, when a new value has to be inserted into the table at a position which is already occupied, that value is inserted at the end of the cluster, which again increases the length of the cluster. Generally, an insertion is made between two clusters that are separated by one vacant location. But with linear probing, there are more chances that subsequent insertions will also end up in one of the clusters, thereby potentially increasing the cluster length by an amount much greater than one. More the number of collisions, higher the probes that are required to find a free location and lesser is the performance. This phenomenon is called *primary clustering*. To avoid primary clustering, other techniques such as quadratic probing and double hashing are used.

Quadratic Probing

In this technique, if a value is already stored at a location generated by `h(k)`, then the following hash function is used to resolve the collision:

$$h(k, i) = [h'(k) + c_1 i + c_2 i^2] \bmod m$$

where `m` is the size of the hash table, $h'(k) = (k \bmod m)$, `i` is the probe number that varies from `0` to `m-1`, and c_1 and c_2 are constants such that c_1 and $c_2 \neq 0$.

Quadratic probing eliminates the primary clustering phenomenon of linear probing because instead of doing a linear search, it does a quadratic search. For a given key `k`, first the location generated by $h'(k) \bmod m$ is probed. If the location is free, the value is stored in it, else subsequent locations probed are offset by factors that depend in a quadratic manner on the probe number `i`. Although quadratic probing performs better than linear probing, in order to maximize the utilization of the hash table, the values of c_1, c_2, and `m` need to be constrained.

Example 15.6 Consider a hash table of size 10. Using quadratic probing, insert the keys 72, 27, 36, 24, 63, 81, and 101 into the table. Take $c_1 = 1$ and $c_2 = 3$.

Solution

Let $h'(k) = k \bmod m$, $m = 10$

Initially, the hash table can be given as:

0	1	2	3	4	5	6	7	8	9
–1	–1	–1	–1	–1	–1	–1	–1	–1	–1

We have,

$$h(k, i) = [h'(k) + c_1 i + c_2 i^2] \bmod m$$

Step 1
```
Key       = 72
h(72, 0)  = [72 mod 10 + 1 X 0 + 3 X 0] mod 10
          = [72 mod 10] mod 10
          = 2 mod 10
          = 2
```
Since `T[2]` is vacant, insert the key 72 in `T[2]`. The hash table now becomes:

0	1	2	3	4	5	6	7	8	9
–1	–1	72	–1	–1	–1	–1	–1	–1	–1

Step 2
```
Key       = 27
h(27, 0)  = [27 mod 10 + 1 X 0 + 3 X 0] mod 10
          = [27 mod 10] mod 10
          = 7 mod 10
          = 7
```
Since `T[7]` is vacant, insert the key 27 in `T[7]`. The hash table now becomes:

0	1	2	3	4	5	6	7	8	9
–1	–1	72	–1	–1	–1	–1	27	–1	–1

Step 3
```
Key       = 36
h(36, 0)  = [36 mod 10 + 1 X 0 + 3 X 0] mod 10
          = [36 mod 10] mod 10
          = 6 mod 10
          = 6
```
Since `T[6]` is vacant, insert the key 36 in `T[6]`. The hash table now becomes:

0	1	2	3	4	5	6	7	8	9
–1	–1	72	–1	–1	–1	36	27	–1	–1

Step 4
```
Key       = 24
h(24, 0)  = [24 mod 10 + 1 X 0 + 3 X 0] mod 10
          = [24 mod 10] mod 10
          = 4 mod 10
          = 4
```
Since `T[4]` is vacant, insert the key 24 in `T[4]`. The hash table now becomes:

0	1	2	3	4	5	6	7	8	9
–1	–1	72	–1	24	–1	36	27	–1	–1

Step 5
```
Key       = 63
h(63, 0)  = [63 mod 10 + 1 X 0 + 3 X 0] mod 10
          = [63 mod 10] mod 10
          = 3 mod 10
          = 3
```
Since `T[3]` is vacant, insert the key 63 in `T[3]`. The hash table now becomes:

0	1	2	3	4	5	6	7	8	9
–1	–1	72	63	24	–1	36	27	–1	–1

Step 6 Key = 81

```
h(81,0) = [81 mod 10 + 1 X 0 + 3 X 0] mod 10
        = [81 mod 10] mod 10
        = 81 mod 10
        = 1
```

Since T[1] is vacant, insert the key 81 in T[1]. The hash table now becomes:

0	1	2	3	4	5	6	7	8	9
–1	81	72	63	24	–1	36	27	–1	–1

Step 7 Key = 101

```
h(101,0) = [101 mod 10 + 1 X 0 + 3 X 0] mod 10
         = [101 mod 10 + 0] mod 10
         = 1 mod 10
         = 1
```

Since T[1] is already occupied, the key 101 cannot be stored in T[1]. Therefore, try again for next location. Thus probe, i = 1, this time.

```
Key      = 101
h(101,0) = [101 mod 10 + 1 X 1 + 3 X 1] mod 10
         = [101 mod 10 + 1 + 3] mod 10
         = [101 mod 10 + 4] mod 10
         = [1 + 4] mod 10
         = 5 mod 10
         = 5
```

Since T[5] is vacant, insert the key 101 in T[5]. The hash table now becomes:

0	1	2	3	4	5	6	7	8	9
–1	81	72	63	24	101	36	27	–1	–1

Searching a Value using Quadratic Probing

While searching a value using the quadratic probing technique, the array index is re-computed and the key of the element stored at that location is compared with the value that has to be searched. If the desired key value matches with the key value at that location, then the element is present in the hash table and the search is said to be successful. In this case, the search time is given as O(1). However, if the value does not match, then the search function begins a sequential search of the array that continues until:

- the value is found, or
- the search function encounters a vacant location in the array, indicating that the value is not present, or
- the search function terminates because it reaches the end of the table and the value is not present.

In the worst case, the search operation may take n-1 comparisons, and the running time of the search algorithm may be O(n). The worst case will be encountered when after scanning all the n-1 elements, the value is either present at the last location or not present in the table.

Thus, we see that with the increase in the number of collisions, the distance between the array index computed by the hash function and the actual location of the element increases, thereby increasing the search time.

Pros and Cons

Quadratic probing resolves the primary clustering problem that exists in the linear probing technique. Quadratic probing provides good memory caching because it preserves some locality of reference. But linear probing does this task better and gives a better cache performance.

One of the major drawbacks of quadratic probing is that a sequence of successive probes may only explore a fraction of the table, and this fraction may be quite small. If this happens, then we will not be able to find an empty location in the table despite the fact that the table is by no means full. In Example 15.6 try to insert the key 92 and you will encounter this problem.

Although quadratic probing is free from primary clustering, it is still liable to what is known as *secondary clustering*. It means that if there is a collision between two keys, then the same probe sequence will be followed for both. With quadratic probing, the probability for multiple collisions increases as the table becomes full. This situation is usually encountered when the hash table is more than full.

Quadratic probing is widely applied in the Berkeley Fast File System to allocate free blocks.

Double Hashing

To start with, double hashing uses one hash value and then repeatedly steps forward an interval until an empty location is reached. The interval is decided using a second, independent hash function, hence the name *double hashing*. In double hashing, we use two hash functions rather than a single function. The hash function in the case of double hashing can be given as:

$$h(k, i) = [h_1(k) + ih_2(k)] \bmod m$$

where m is the size of the hash table, $h_1(k)$ and $h_2(k)$ are two hash functions given as $h_1(k) = k \bmod m$, $h_2(k) = k \bmod m'$, i is the probe number that varies from 0 to m-1, and m' is chosen to be less than m. We can choose m' = m-1 or m-2.

When we have to insert a key k in the hash table, we first probe the location given by applying $[h_1(k) \bmod m]$ because during the first probe, i = 0. If the location is vacant, the key is inserted into it, else subsequent probes generate locations that are at an offset of $[h_2(k) \bmod m]$ from the previous location. Since the offset may vary with every probe depending on the value generated by the second hash function, the performance of double hashing is very close to the performance of the ideal scheme of uniform hashing.

Pros and Cons

Double hashing minimizes repeated collisions and the effects of clustering. That is, double hashing is free from problems associated with primary clustering as well as secondary clustering.

Example 15.7 Consider a hash table of size = 10. Using double hashing, insert the keys 72, 27, 36, 24, 63, 81, 92, and 101 into the table. Take $h_1 = (k \bmod 10)$ and $h_2 = (k \bmod 8)$.

Solution

Let m = 10

Initially, the hash table can be given as:

0	1	2	3	4	5	6	7	8	9
–1	–1	–1	–1	–1	–1	–1	–1	–1	–1

We have,

$h(k, i) = [h_1(k) + ih_2(k)] \bmod m$

Step 1 Key = 72

$h(72, 0) = [72 \bmod 10 + (0 \times 72 \bmod 8)] \bmod 10$
$= [2 + (0 \times 0)] \bmod 10$
$= 2 \bmod 10$
$= 2$

Since T[2] is vacant, insert the key 72 in T[2]. The hash table now becomes:

0	1	2	3	4	5	6	7	8	9
–1	–1	72	–1	–1	–1	–1	–1	–1	–1

Step 2
```
Key       = 27
h(27, 0)  = [27 mod 10 + (0 × 27 mod 8)] mod 10
          = [7 + (0 × 3)] mod 10
          = 7 mod 10
          = 7
```

Since `T[7]` is vacant, insert the key 27 in `T[7]`. The hash table now becomes:

0	1	2	3	4	5	6	7	8	9
–1	–1	72	–1	–1	–1	–1	27	–1	–1

Step 3
```
Key       = 36
h(36, 0)  = [36 mod 10 + (0 × 36 mod 8)] mod 10
          = [6 + (0 × 4)] mod 10
          = 6 mod 10
          = 6
```

Since `T[6]` is vacant, insert the key 36 in `T[6]`. The hash table now becomes:

0	1	2	3	4	5	6	7	8	9
–1	–1	72	–1	–1	–1	36	27	–1	–1

Step 4
```
Key       = 24
h(24, 0)  = [24 mod 10 + (0 × 24 mod 8)] mod 10
          = [4 + (0 × 0)] mod 10
          = 4 mod 10
          = 4
```

Since `T[4]` is vacant, insert the key 24 in `T[4]`. The hash table now becomes:

0	1	2	3	4	5	6	7	8	9
–1	–1	72	–1	24	–1	36	27	–1	–1

Step 5
```
Key       = 63
h(63, 0)  = [63 mod 10 + (0 × 63 mod 8)] mod 10
          = [3 + (0 × 7)] mod 10
          = 3 mod 10
          = 3
```

Since `T[3]` is vacant, insert the key 63 in `T[3]`. The hash table now becomes:

0	1	2	3	4	5	6	7	8	9
–1	–1	72	63	24	–1	36	27	–1	–1

Step 6
```
Key       = 81
h(81, 0)  = [81 mod 10 + (0 × 81 mod 8)] mod 10
          = [1 + (0 × 1)] mod 10
          = 1 mod 10
          = 1
```

Since `T[1]` is vacant, insert the key 81 in `T[1]`. The hash table now becomes:

0	1	2	3	4	5	6	7	8	9
–1	81	72	63	24	–1	36	27	–1	–1

Step 7
```
        Key    = 92
h(92, 0)       = [92 mod 10 + (0 X 92 mod 8)] mod 10
               = [2 + (0 X 4)] mod 10
               = 2 mod 10
               = 2
```

Now `T[2]` is occupied, so we cannot store the key 92 in `T[2]`. Therefore, try again for the next location. Thus probe, `i = 1`, this time.

```
        Key    = 92
h(92, 1)       = [92 mod 10 + (1 X 92 mod 8)] mod 10
               = [2 + (1 X 4)] mod 10
               = (2 + 4) mod 10
               = 6 mod 10
               = 6
```

Now `T[6]` is occupied, so we cannot store the key 92 in `T[6]`. Therefore, try again for the next location. Thus probe, `i = 2`, this time.

```
        Key    = 92
h(92, 2)       = [92 mod 10 + (2 X 92 mod 8)] mod 10
               = [2 + (2 X 4)] mod 10
               = [2 + 8] mod 10
               = 10 mod 10
               = 0
```

Since `T[0]` is vacant, insert the key 92 in `T[0]`. The hash table now becomes:

0	1	2	3	4	5	6	7	8	9
92	81	72	63	24	–1	36	27	–1	–1

Step 8
```
        Key    = 101
h(101, 0)      = [101 mod 10 + (0 X 101 mod 8)] mod 10
               = [1 + (0 X 5)] mod 10
               = 1 mod 10
               = 1
```

Now `T[1]` is occupied, so we cannot store the key 101 in `T[1]`. Therefore, try again for the next location. Thus probe, `i = 1`, this time.

```
        Key    = 101
h(101, 1)      = [101 mod 10 + (1 X 101 mod 8)] mod 10
               = [1 + (1 X 5)] mod 10
               = [1 + 5] mod 10
               = 6
```

Now `T[6]` is occupied, so we cannot store the key 101 in `T[6]`. Therefore, try again for the next location with probe `i = 2`. Repeat the entire process until a vacant location is found. You will see that we have to probe many times to insert the key 101 in the hash table. Although double hashing is a very efficient algorithm, it always requires `m` to be a prime number. In our case `m=10`, which is not a prime number, hence, the degradation in performance. Had `m` been equal to 11, the algorithm would have worked very efficiently. Thus, we can say that the performance of the technique is sensitive to the value of `m`.

Rehashing

When the hash table becomes nearly full, the number of collisions increases, thereby degrading the performance of insertion and search operations. In such cases, a better option is to create a new hash table with size double of the original hash table.

All the entries in the original hash table will then have to be moved to the new hash table. This is done by taking each entry, computing its new hash value, and then inserting it in the new hash table.

Though rehashing seems to be a simple process, it is quite expensive and must therefore not be done frequently. Consider the hash table of size 5 given below. The hash function used is `h(x) = x % 5`. Rehash the entries into to a new hash table.

0	1	2	3	4
	26	31	43	17

Note that the new hash table is of 10 locations, double the size of the original table.

0	1	2	3	4	5	6	7	8	9

Now, rehash the key values from the old hash table into the new one using hash function—`h(x) = x % 10`.

0	1	2	3	4	5	6	7	8	9
	31		43			26	17		

Programming Example

1. Write a program to show searching using closed hashing.

```
int ht[10], i, found = 0, key;
void insert_val();
void search_val();
void delete_val();
void display();
int main()
{
      int option;
      for ( i = 0;i < 10;i++ ) //to initialize every element as '-1'
            ht[i] = -1;
      do
      {
            printf("\n MENU \n1.Insert \n2.Search \n3.Delete \n4.Display \n5.Exit");
                  printf( "\n Enter your option.");
                  scanf( "%d", &option);
                  switch (option)
                  {
                        case 1:
                              insert_val();
                              break;
                        case 2:
                              search_val();
                              break;
                        case 3:
                              delete_val();
                              break;
                        case 4:
                              display();
                              break;
```

```
                        default:
                                printf( "\nInvalid choice entry!!!\n" );
                                break;
                }
        }while (option!=5);
        return 0;
}
void insert_val()
{
        int val, f = 0;
        printf( "\nEnter the element to be inserted : " );
        scanf( "%d", &val );
        key = ( val % 10 ) - 1;
        if ( ht[key] == -1 )
        {
                ht[key] = val;
        }
        else
        {
                if ( key < 9 )
                {
                        for ( i = key + 1;i < 10;i++ )
                        {
                                if ( ht[i] == -1 )
                                {
                                        ht[i] = val;
                                        break;
                                }
                        }
                }
                for ( i = 0;i < key;i++ )
                {
                        if ( ht[i] == -1 )
                        {
                                ht[i] = val;
                                break;
                        }
                }
        }
}
void display()
{
        for (i = 0;i < 10;i++)
        printf( "\t%d", ht[ i ] );
}
void search_val()
{
        int val, flag = 0;
        printf( "\nEnter the element to be searched :: " );
        scanf( "%d", &val );
        key = ( val % 10 ) - 1;
        if ( ht[ key ] == val )
                flag = 1;
        else
        {
                for (i = key + 1;i < 10;i++)
```

```
                {
                        if(ht[i] == val)
                        {
                                flag = 1;
                                key = i;
                                break;
                        }
                }
        }
        if (flag == 0)
        {
                for (i = 0;i < key;i++)
                {
                        if (ht[ i ] == val)
                        {
                                flag = 1;
                                key = i;
                                break;
                        }
                }
        }
        if (flag == 1)
        {
                found=1;
                printf("\n The item searched was found at position %d !", key + 1 );
        }
        else
        {
                key = -1;
                printf( "\nThe item searched was not found in the hash table" );
        }
}
void delete_val()
{
        search_val();
        if (found==1)
        {
                if ( key != -1 )
                {
                        printf( "\nThe element deleted is %d ", ht[ key ] );
                        ht[ key ] = -1;
                }
        }
}
```

Output

```
MENU
1. Insert
2. Search
3. Delete
4. Display
5. Exit
Enter your option:  1
Enter the element to be inserted :1
Enter your option:  4
1 -1 -1 -1 -1 -1 -1 -1 -1 -1
 Enter your option:  5
```

15.5.2 Collision Resolution by Chaining

In chaining, each location in a hash table stores a pointer to a linked list that contains all the key values that were hashed to that location. That is, location l in the hash table points to the head of the linked list of all the key values that hashed to l. However, if no key value hashes to l, then location l in the hash table contains `NULL`. Figure 15.5 shows how the key values are mapped to a location in the hash table and stored in a linked list that corresponds to that location.

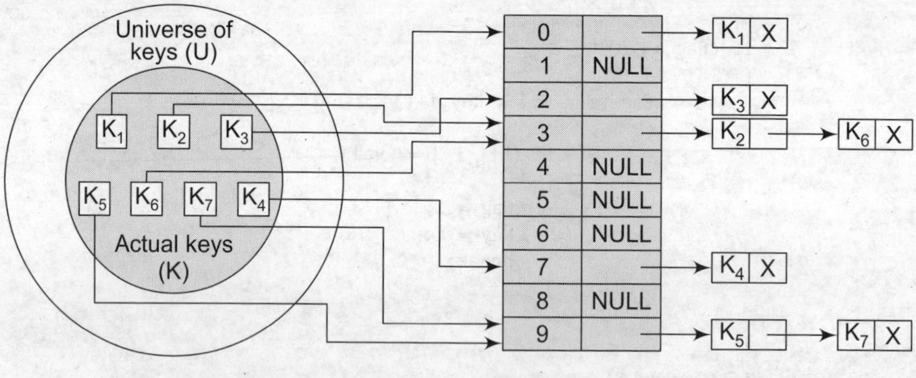

Figure 15.5 Keys being hashed to a chained hash table

Operations on a Chained Hash Table

Searching for a value in a chained hash table is as simple as scanning a linked list for an entry with the given key. Insertion operation appends the key to the end of the linked list pointed by the hashed location. Deleting a key requires searching the list and removing the element.

Chained hash tables with linked lists are widely used due to the simplicity of the algorithms to insert, delete, and search a key. The code for these algorithms is exactly the same as that for inserting, deleting, and searching a value in a single linked list that we have already studied in Chapter 6.

While the cost of inserting a key in a chained hash table is `O(1)`, the cost of deleting and searching a value is given as `O(m)` where `m` is the number of elements in the list of that location. Searching and deleting takes more time because these operations scan the entries of the selected location for the desired key.

In the worst case, searching a value may take a running time of `O(n)`, where n is the number of key values stored in the chained hash table. This case arises when all the key values are inserted into the linked list of the same location (of the hash table). In this case, the hash table is ineffective.

Table 15.1 gives the code to initialize a hash table as well as the codes to insert, delete and search a value in a chained hash table.

Example 15.8 Insert the keys 7, 24, 18, 52, 36, 54, 11, and 23 in a chained hash table of 9 memory locations. Use `h(k) = k mod m`.

In this case, `m=9`. Initially, the hash table can be given as:

0	NULL
1	NULL
2	NULL
3	NULL
4	NULL
5	NULL
6	NULL
7	NULL
8	NULL

Step 1:

```
Key = 7
h(k) = 7 mod 9
     = 7
```

Step 2:

```
Key = 24
h(k) = 24 mod 9
     = 6
```

Table 15.1 Codes to initialize, insert, delete, and search a value in a chained hash table

Struture of the node

```
typedef struct node_HT
{
    int value;
    struct node *next;
}node;
```

Code to initialize a chained hash table

```
/* Initializes m location in the chained
hash table.
The operation takes a running time of
O(m) */
void initializeHashTable (node *hash_ta-
ble[], int m)
{
    int i;
    for(i=0i<=m;i++)
        hash_table[i]=NULL;
```

Code to insert a value

```
/* The element is inserted at the beginning of
the linked list whose pointer to its head is
stored in the location given by h(k). The run-
ning time of the insert operation is O(1), as
the new key value is always added as the first
element of the list irrespective of the size of
the linked list as well as that of the chained
hash table. */
node *insert_value( node *hash_table[], int
val)
{
    node *new_node;
    new_node = (node *)malloc(sizeof(node));
    new_node value = val; new_node next = hash_
table[h(x)];
    hash_table[h(x)] = new_node;
}
```

Code to search a value

```
/* The element is searched in the linked
list whose pointer to its head is stored
in the location given by h(k). If search is
successful, the function returns a pointer
to the node in the linked list; otherwise
it returns NULL. The worst case running
time of the search operation is given as
order of size of the linked list. */
node *search_value(node *hash_table[],
int val)
{
    node *ptr;
    ptr = hash_table[h(x)];
    while ( (ptr!=NULL) && (ptr -> value
!= val))
        ptr = ptr -> next;
    if (ptr->value == val)
        return ptr;
else
        return NULL;
}
```

Code to delete a value

```
/* To delete a node from the linked list whose
head is stored at the location given by h(k) in
the hash table, we need to know the address of
the node's predecessor. We do this using a pointer
save. The running time complexity of the delete
operation is same as that of the search operation
because we need to search the predecessor of the
node so that the node can be removed without af-
fecting other nodes in the list. */
void delete_value (node *hash_table[], int val)
{
    node *save, *ptr;
    save = NULL;
    ptr = hash_table[h(x)];
    while ((ptr != NULL) && (ptr value != val))
    {
        save = ptr;
        ptr = ptr next;
    }
    if (ptr != NULL)
    {
        save next = ptr next;
        free (ptr);
    }
    else
        printf("\n VALUE NOT FOUND");
}
```

Create a linked list for location 7 and store the key value 7 in it as its only node.

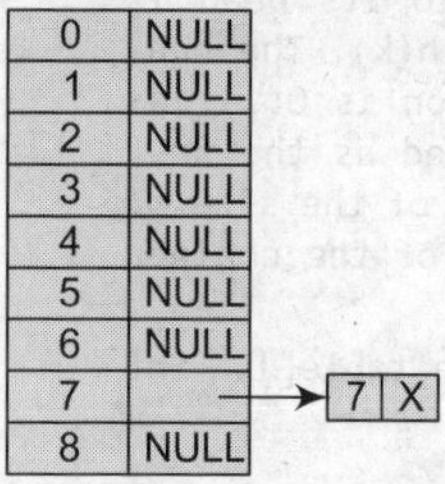

Create a linked list for location 6 and store the key value 24 in it as its only node.

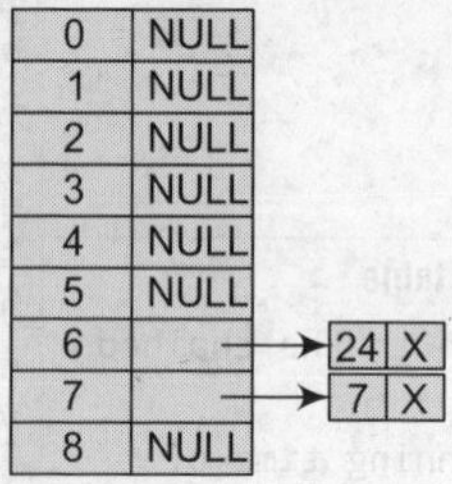

Step 3: Key = 18

h(k) = 18 mod 9 = 0

Create a linked list for location 0 and store the key value 18 in it as its only node.

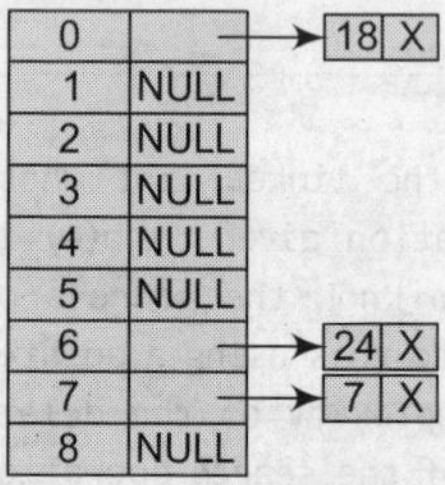

Step 4: Key = 52

h(k) = 52 mod 9 = 7

Insert 52 at the end of the linked list of location 7.

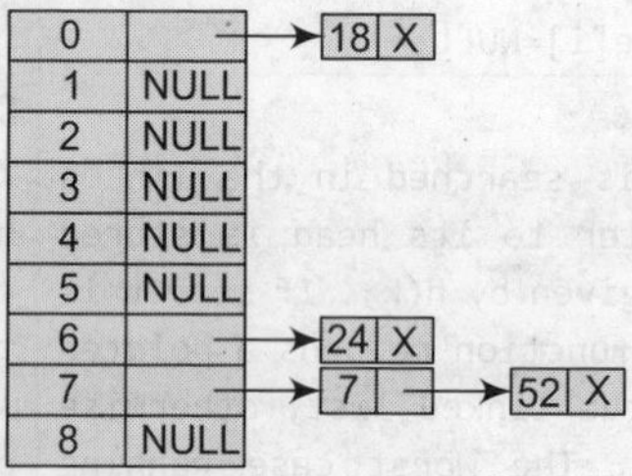

Step 5: Key = 36

h(k) = 36 mod 9 = 0

Insert 36 at the end of the linked list of location 0.

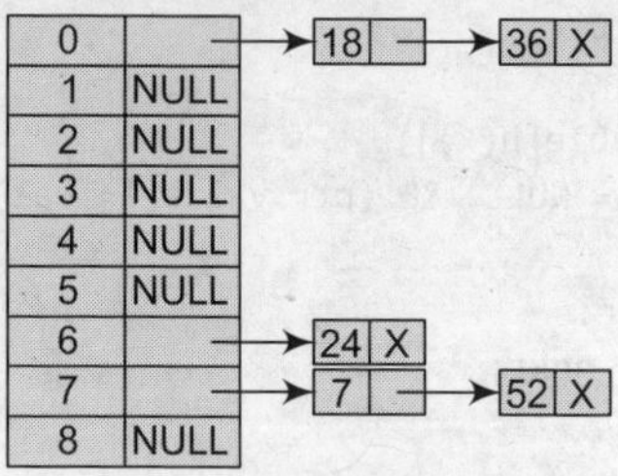

Step 6: Key = 54

h(k) = 54 mod 9 = 0

Insert 54 at the end of the linked list of location 0.

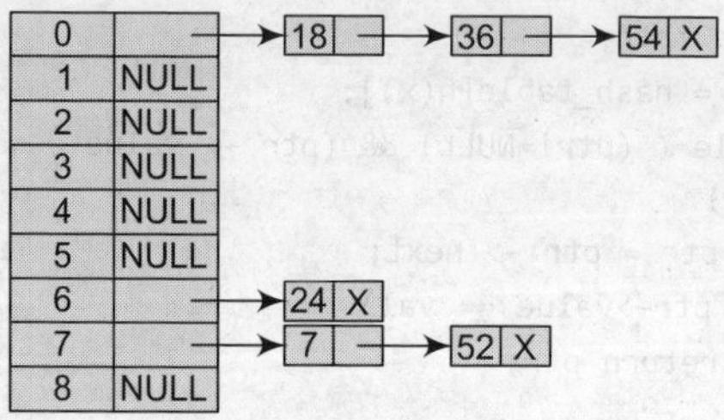

Step 7: Key = 11

h(k) = 11 mod 9 = 2

Create a linked list for location 2 and store the key value 11 in it as its only node.

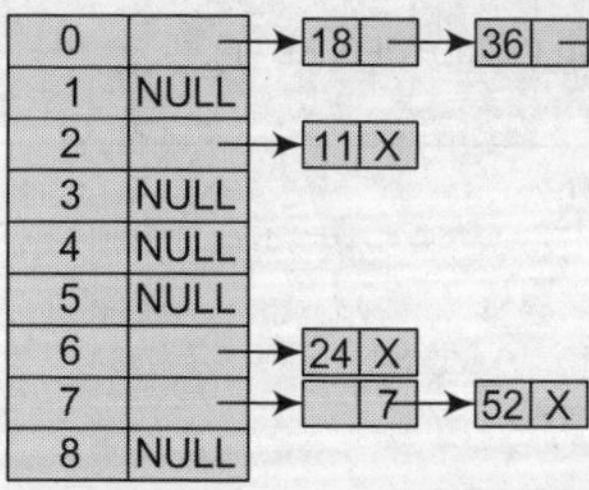

Step 8: Key = 23

h(k) = 23 mod 9 = 5

Create a linked list for location 5 and store the key value 23 in it as its only node.

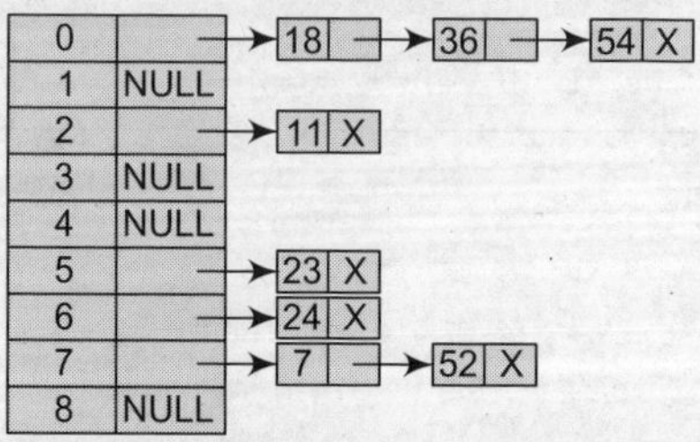

Pros and Cons

The main advantage of using a chained hash table is that it remains effective even when the number of key values to be stored is much higher than the number of locations in the hash table. However, with the increase in the number of keys to be stored, the performance of a chained hash table does degrade gradually (linearly). For example, a chained hash table with 1000 memory locations and 10,000 stored keys will give 5 to 10 times less performance as compared to a chained hash table with 10,000 locations. But a chained hash table is still 1000 times faster than a simple hash table.

The other advantage of using chaining for collision resolution is that its performance, unlike quadratic probing, does not degrade when the table is more than half full. This technique is absolutely free from clustering problems and thus provides an efficient mechanism to handle collisions.

However, chained hash tables inherit the disadvantages of linked lists. First, to store a key value, the space overhead of the next pointer in each entry can be significant. Second, traversing a linked list has poor cache performance, making the processor cache ineffective.

Bucket Hashing

In closed hashing, all the records are directly stored in the hash table. Each record with a key value `k` is stored in a location called its home position. The home position is calculated by applying some hash function.

In case the home position of the record with key `k` is already occupied by another record then the record will be stored in some other location in the hash table. This other location will be determined by the technique that is used for resolving collisions. Once the records are inserted, the same algorithm is again applied to search for a specific record.

One implementation of closed hashing groups the hash table into buckets where `M` slots of the hash table are divided into `B` *buckets*. Therefore, each bucket contains `M/B` slots. Now when a new record has to be inserted, the hash function computes the home position. If the slot is free, the record is inserted. Otherwise, the bucket's slots are sequentially searched until an open slot is found. In case, the entire bucket is full, the record is inserted into an *overflow bucket*. The overflow bucket has infinite capacity at the end of the table and is shared by all the buckets.

An efficient implementation of bucket hashing will be to use a hash function that evenly distributes the records amongst the buckets so that very few records have to be inserted in the overflow bucket.

When searching a record, first the hash function is used to determine the bucket in which the record can be present. Then the bucket is sequentially searched to find the desired record. If the record is not found and the bucket still has some empty slots, then it means that the search is complete and the desired record is not present in the hash table.

However, if the bucket is full and the record has not been found, then the overflow bucket is searched until the record is found or all the records in the overflow bucket have been checked. Obviously, searching the overflow bucket can be expensive if it has too many records.

15.6 PROS AND CONS OF HASHING

One advantage of hashing is that no extra space is required to store the index as in the case of other data structures. In addition, a hash table provides fast data access and an added advantage of rapid updates.

On the other hand, the primary drawback of using the hashing technique for inserting and retrieving data values is that it usually lacks locality and sequential retrieval by key. This makes insertion and retrieval of data values even more random.

All the more, choosing an effective hash function is more of an art than a science. It is not uncommon (in open-addressed hash tables) to create a poor hash function.

15.7 APPLICATIONS OF HASHING

Hash tables are widely used in situations where enormous amounts of data have to be accessed to quickly search and retrieve information. A few typical examples where hashing is used are given here.

Hashing is used for database indexing. Some database management systems store a separate file known as the index file. When data has to be retrieved from a file, the key information is first searched in the appropriate index file which references the exact record location of the data in the database file. This key information in the index file is often stored as a hashed value.

In many database systems, file and directory hashing is used in high-performance file systems. Such systems use two complementary techniques to improve the performance of file access. While one of these techniques is caching which saves information in the memory, the other is hashing which makes looking up the file location in the memory much quicker than most other methods.

Hashing technique is used to implement compiler symbol tables in C++. The compiler uses a symbol table to keep a record of all the user-defined symbols in a C++ program. Hashing facilitates the compiler to quickly look up variable names and other attributes associated with symbols. Hashing is also widely used for Internet search engines.

Real World Applications of Hashing

CD Databases For CDs, it is desirable to have a world-wide CD database so that when users put their disk in the CD player, they get a full table of contents on their own computer's screen. These tables are not stored on the disks themselves, i.e., the CD does not store any information about the songs, rather this information is downloaded from the database. The critical issue to solve here is that CDs have no ID numbers stored on them, so how will the computer know which CD has been put in the player? The only information that can be used is the track length, and the fact that every CD is different.

Basically, a big number is created from the track lengths, also known as a 'signature'. This signature is used to identify a particular CD. The signature is a value obtained by hashing. For example, a number of length of 8 or 10 hexadecimal. digits is made up; the number is then sent to the database, and that database looks for the closest match. The reason being that track length may not be measured exactly.

Drivers Licenses/Insurance Cards Like our CD example, even the driver's license numbers or insurance card numbers are created using hashing from data items that never change: date of birth, name, etc.

Sparse Matrix A sparse matrix is a two-dimensional array in which most of the entries contain a 0. That is, in a sparse array there are very few non-zero entries. Of course, we can store 2D array as it is, but this would lead to sheer wastage of valuable memory. So another possibility is to store the non-zero elements of the spare matrix as elements in a 1D array. That is by using hashing, we can store a two-dimensional array in a one-dimensional array. There is a one-to-one correspondence between the elements in the sparse matrix and the elements in the array. This concept is clearly visible in Fig. 15.6.

If the size of the sparse matrix is `n` × `n`, and there are `N` non-zero entries in it, then from the coordinates `(i,j)` of a matrix, we determine an index `k` in an array by a simple calculation. Thus, we have `k=h(i,j)` for some function `h`, called a hash function.

The size of the 1D array is proportional to `N`. This is far better from the size of the sparse matrix that required storage proportional to `n` × `n`. For example, if we have a triangular sparse matrix `A`, then an entry `A[i, j]` can be mapped to an entry in the 1D array by calculating the index using the hash function `h(i, j) = i(i-1)/2 + j`.

File Signatures File signatures provide a compact means of identifying files. We use a function, `h[x]`, the file signature, which is a property of the file. Although we can store files by name, signatures provide a compact identity to files.

Since a signature depends on the contents of a file, if any change is made to the file, then the signature will change. In this way, the signature of a file can be used as a quick verification to see if anyone has altered the file, or if it has lost a bit during transmission. Signatures are widely used for files that store marks of students.

Game Boards In the game board for tic-tac-toe or chess, a position in a game may be stored using a hash function.

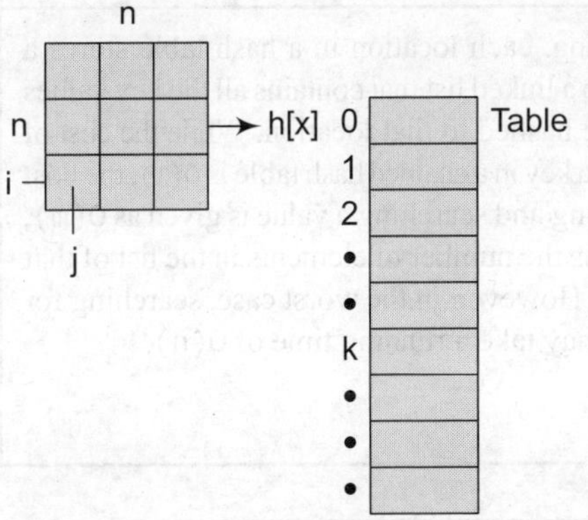

Figure 15.6 Sparse matrix

Graphics In graphics, a central problem is the storage of objects in a scene or view. For this, we organize our data by hashing. Hashing can be used to make a grid of appropriate size, an ordinary vertical–horizontal grid. (Note that a grid is nothing but a 2D array, and there is a one-to-one correspondence when we move from a 2D array to a 1D array.)

So, we store the grid as a 1D array as we did in the case of sparse matrices. All points that fall in one cell will be stored in the same place. If a cell contains three points, then these three points will be stored in the same entry. The mapping from the grid cell to the memory location is done by using a hash function. The key advantage of this method of storage is fast execution of operations like the nearest neighbour search.

Points to Remember

- Hash table is a data structure in which keys are mapped to array positions by a hash function. A value stored in a hash table can be searched in `O(1)` time using a hash function which generates an address from the key.
- The storage requirement for a hash table is `O(k)`, where `k` is the number of keys actually used. In a hash table, an element with key `k` is stored at index `h(k)`, not `k`. This means that a hash function `h` is used to calculate the index at which the element with key `k` will be stored. Thus, the process of mapping keys to appropriate locations (or indices) in a hash table is called hashing.
- Popular hash functions which use numeric keys are division method, multiplication method, mid square method, and folding method.
- Division method divides `x` by `M` and then uses the remainder obtained. A potential drawback of this method is that consecutive keys map to consecutive hash values.
- Multiplication method applies the hash function given as $h(x) = \lfloor m\,(kA \bmod 1) \rfloor$
- Mid square method works in two steps. First, it finds k^2 and then extracts the middle r digits of the result.
- Folding method works by first dividing the key value k into parts $k_1, k_2, \ldots, k_n$, where each part has the same number of digits except the last part which may have lesser digits than the other parts, and then obtaining the sum of $k_1 + k_2 + \ldots + k_n$. The hash value is produced by ignoring the last carry, if any.
- Collisions occur when a hash function maps two different keys to the same location. Therefore, a method used to solve the problem of collisions, also called *collision resolution technique*, is applied. The two most popular methods of resolving collisions are: (a) open addressing and (b) chaining.
- Once a collision takes place, open addressing computes new positions using a probe sequence and the next record is stored in that position. In this technique of collision resolution, all the values are stored in the hash table. The hash table will contain two types of values—either sentinel value (for example, –1) or a data value.
- Open addressing technique can be implemented using linear probing, quadratic probing, double hashing, and rehashing.
- In linear probing, if a value is already stored at a location generated by `h(k)`, then the following hash function is used to resolve the collision:

  $$h(k, i) = [h'(k) + i] \bmod m$$

  Though linear probing enables good memory caching, the drawback of this algorithm is that it results in primary clustering.
- In quadratic probing, if a value is already stored at a location generated by `h(k)`, then the following hash function is used to resolve the collision:

  $$h(k, i) = [h'(k) + c_1 i + c_2 i^2] \bmod m$$

  Quadratic probing eliminates primary clustering and provides good memory caching. But it is still liable to secondary clustering.
- In double hashing, we use two hash functions rather than a single function. The hash function in the case of double hashing can be given as:

  $$h(k, i) = [h_1(k) + i h_2(k)] \bmod m$$

The performance of double hashing is very close to the performance of the ideal scheme of uniform hashing. It minimizes repeated collisions and the effects of clustering.

- When the hash table becomes nearly full, the number of collisions increases, thereby degrading the performance of insertion and search operations. So in rehashing, all the entries in the original hash table are moved to the new hash table which is double the size of the original hash table.
- In chaining, each location in a hash table stores a pointer to a linked list that contains all the key values that were hashed to that location. While the cost of inserting a key in a chained hash table is `O(1)`, the cost for deleting and searching a value is given as `O(m)`, where `m` is the number of elements in the list of that location. However, in the worst case, searching for a value may take a running time of `O(n)`.

Exercises

Review Questions

1. Define a hash table.
2. What do you understand by a hash function? Give the properties of a good hash function.
3. How is a hash table better than a direct access table (array)?
4. Write a short note on the different hash functions. Give suitable examples.
5. Calculate hash values of keys: 1892, 1921, 2007, 3456 using different methods of hashing.
6. What is collision? Explain the various techniques to resolve a collision. Which technique do you think is better and why?
7. Consider a hash table with size = 10. Using linear probing, insert the keys 27, 72, 63, 42, 36, 18, 29, and 101 into the table.
8. Consider a hash table with size = 10. Using quadratic probing, insert the keys 27, 72, 63, 42, 36, 18, 29, and 101 into the table. Take $c_1 = 1$ and $c_2 = 3$.
9. Consider a hash table with size = 11. Using double hashing, insert the keys 27, 72, 63, 42, 36, 18, 29, and 101 into the table. Take $h_1 = k \bmod 10$ and $h_2 = k \bmod 8$.
10. What is hashing? Give its applications. Also, discuss the pros and cons of hashing.
11. Explain chaining with examples.
12. Write short notes on:
    Linear probing
    Quadratic probing
    Double hashing

Multiple-choice Questions

1. In a hash table, an element with key `k` is stored at index
   (a) `k` (b) `log k` (c) `h(k)` (d) k^2
2. In any hash function, `M` should be a
   (a) Prime number (b) Compositenumber
   (c) Even number (d) Odd number
3. In which of the following hash functions, do consecutive keys map to consecutive hash values?
   (a) Division method
   (b) Multiplication method
   (c) Folding method
   (d) Mid-square method
4. The process of examining memory locations in a hash table is called
   (a) Hashing (b) Collision
   (c) Probing (d) Addressing
5. Which of the following methods is applied in the Berkeley Fast File System to allocate free blocks?
   (a) Linear probing (b) Quadratic probing
   (c) Double hashing (d) Rehashing
6. Which open addressing technique is free from clustering problems?
   (a) Linear probing (b) Quadratic probing
   (c) Double hashing (d) Rehashing

True or False

1. Hash table is based on the property of locality of reference.
2. Binary search takes `O(n log n)` time to execute.
3. The storage requirement for a hash table is $O(k^2)$, where `k` is the number of keys.
4. Hashing takes place when two or more keys map to the same memory location.
5. A good hash function completely eliminates collision.
6. `M` should not be too close to exact powers of 2.
7. A sentinel value indicates that the location contains valid data.

8. Linear probing is sensitive to the distribution of input values.

9. A chained hash table is faster than a simple hash table.

Fill in the Blanks

1. In a hash table, keys are mapped to array positions by a ______.

2. ______ is the process of mapping keys to appropriate locations in a hash table.

3. In open addressing, hash table stores either of two values ______ and ______.

4. When there is no free location in the hash table then ______ occurs.

5. More the number of collisions, higher is the number of ______ to find free location ______ which eliminates primary clustering but not secondary clustering.

6. ______ eliminates primary clustering but not secondary clustering.

Coding Challenges

1. Given a string, write a function to find and return the first non-repeating character using a hash table.

2. Given an array of strings, group them such that all anagrams are together. Implement a function that takes an array of strings and returns a list of groups of anagrams using a hash table.

3. Implement a hash table and test it by inserting a large number of elements. Check for collisions and output the number of collisions encountered.

CHAPTER 16

Files and Their Organization

LEARNING OBJECTIVE

In this chapter, we will discuss the basic attributes of a file and the different ways in which files can be organized in the secondary memory. Then, we will learn about different indexing strategies that allow efficient and faster access to these files.

16.1 INTRODUCTION

Nowadays, most organizations use data collection applications which collect large amounts of data in one form or other. For example, when we seek admission in a college, a lot of data such as our name, address, phone number, the course in which we want to seek admission, aggregate of marks obtained in the last examination, and so on, are collected. Similarly, to open a bank account, we need to provide a lot of input. All these data were traditionally stored on paper documents, but handling these documents had always been a chaotic and difficult task.

Similarly, scientific experiments and satellites also generate enormous amounts of data. Therefore, in order to efficiently analyse all the data that has been collected from different sources, it has become a necessity to store the data in computers in the form of files.

In computer terminology, a file is a block of useful data which is available to a computer program and is usually stored on a persistent storage medium. Storing a file on a persistent storage medium like hard disk ensures the availability of the file for future use. These days, files stored on computers are a good alternative to paper documents that were once stored in offices and libraries.

16.2 DATA HIERARCHY

Every file contains data which can be organized in a hierarchy to present a systematic organization. The data hierarchy includes data items such as fields, records, files, and database. These terms are defined below.

- A *data field* is an elementary unit that stores a single fact. A data field is usually characterized by its type and size. For example, student's name is a data field that stores the name of students. This field is of type *character* and its size can be set to a maximum of 20 or 30 characters depending on the requirement.
- A *record* is a collection of related data fields which is seen as a single unit from the application point of view. For example, the student's record may contain data fields such as name, address, phone number, roll number, marks obtained, and so on.
- A *file* is a collection of related records. For example, if there are 60 students in a class, then there are 60 records. All these related records are stored in a file. Similarly, we can have a file of all the employees working in an organization, a file of all the customers of a company, a file of all the suppliers, so on and so forth.

- A *directory* stores information of related files. A directory organizes information so that users can find it easily. For example, consider Fig. 16.1 that shows how multiple related files are stored in a student directoy.

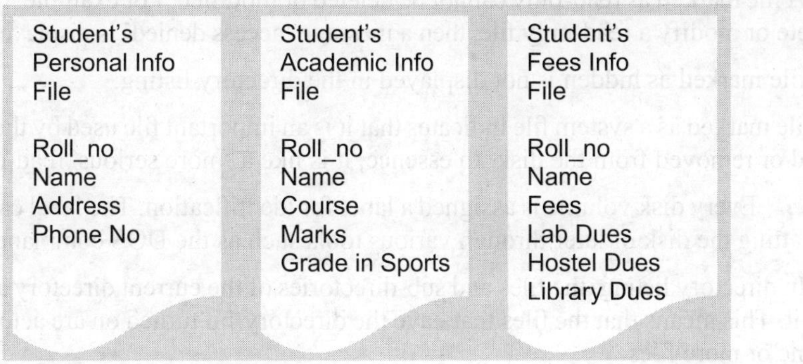

Figure 16.1 Student directory

16.3 FILE ATTRIBUTES

Every file in a computer system is stored in a directory. Each file has a list of attributes associated with it that gives the operating system and the application software information about the file and how it is intended to be used.

A software program which needs to access a file looks up the directory entry to discern the attributes of that file. For example, if a user attempts to write to a file that has been marked as a read-only file, then the program prints an appropriate message to notify the user that he is trying to write to a file that is meant only for reading.

Similarly, there is an attribute called *hidden*. When you execute the DIR command in DOS, then the files whose hidden attribute is set will not be displayed. These attributes are explained in this section.

File name It is a string of characters that stores the name of a file. File naming conventions vary from one operating system to the other.

File position It is a pointer that points to the position at which the next read/write operation will be performed.

File structure It indicates whether the file is a text file or a binary file. In the text file, the numbers (integer or floating point) are stored as a string of characters. A binary file, on the other hand, stores numbers in the same way as they are represented in the main memory.

File Access Method

It indicates whether the records in a file can be accessed sequentially or randomly. In sequential access mode, records are read one by one. That is, if 60 records of students are stored in the STUDENT file, then to read the record of 39th student, you have to go through the record of the first 38 students. However, in random access, records can be accessed in any order.

Table 16.1 Attribute flag

Attribute	Attribute Byte
Read-Only	00000001
Hidden	00000010
System	00000100
Volume Label	00001000
Directory	00010000
Archive	00100000

Attributes Flag

A file can have six additional attributes attached to it. These attributes are usually stored in a single byte, with each bit representing a specific attribute. If a particular bit is set to '1' then this means that the corresponding attribute is turned on. Table 16.1 shows the list of attributes and their position in the attribute flag or attribute byte.

If a system file is set as hidden and read-only, then its attribute byte can be given as 00000111. We will discuss all these attributes here in this section. Note that the directory is treated as a special file in the operating system. So, all these attributes are applicable to files as well as to directories.

Read-only A file marked as read-only cannot be deleted or modified. For example, if an attempt is made to either delete or modify a read-only file, then a message 'access denied' is displayed on the screen.

Hidden A file marked as hidden is not displayed in the directory listing.

System A file marked as a system file indicates that it is an important file used by the system and should not be altered or removed from the disk. In essence, it is like a 'more serious' read-only flag.

Volume Label Every disk volume is assigned a label for identification. The label can be assigned at the time of formatting the disk or later through various tools such as the DOS command LABEL.

Directory In directory listing, the files and sub-directories of the current directory are differentiated by a directory-bit. This means that the files that have the directory-bit turned on are actually sub-directories containing one or more files.

Archive The archive bit is used as a communication link between programs that modify files and those that are used for backing up files. Most backup programs allow the user to do an incremental backup. Incremental backup selects only those files for backup which have been modified since the last backup.

When the backup program takes the backup of a file, or in other words, when the program archives the file, it clears the archive bit (sets it to zero). Subsequently, if any program modifies the file, it turns on the archive bit (sets it to 1). Thus, whenever the backup program is run, it checks the archive bit to know whether the file has been modified since its last run. The backup program will archive only those files which were modified.

16.4 TEXT AND BINARY FILES

A *text file*, also known as a flat file or an ASCII file, is structured as a sequence of lines of alphabet, numerals, special characters, etc. However, the data in a text file, whether numeric or non-numeric, is stored using its corresponding ASCII code. The end of a text file is often denoted by placing a special character, called an end-of-file marker, after the last line in the text file.

A *binary file* contains any type of data encoded in binary form for computer storage and processing purposes. A binary file can contain text that is not broken up into lines. A binary file stores data in a format that is similar to the format in which the data is stored in the main memory. Therefore, a binary file is not readable by humans and it is up to the program reading the file to make sense of the data that is stored in the binary file and convert it into something meaningful (e.g., a fixed length of record).

Binary files contain formatting information that only certain applications or processors can understand. It is possible for humans to read text files which contain only ASCII text, while binary files must be run on an appropriate software or processor so that the software or processor can transform the data in order to make it readable. For example, only Microsoft Word can interpret the formatting information in a Word document.

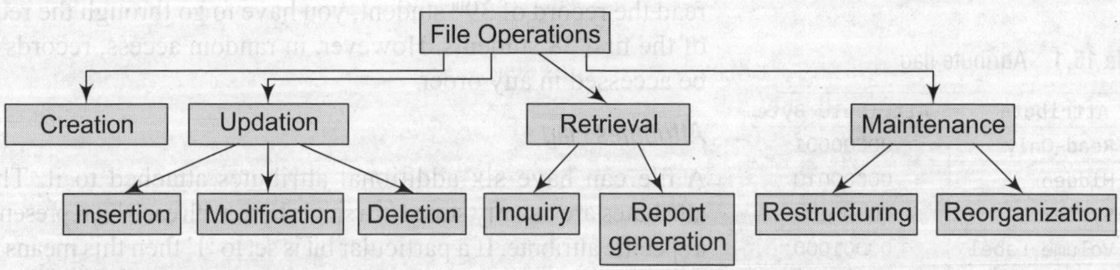

Figure 16.2 File operations

Although text files can be manipulated by any text editor, they do not provide efficient storage. In contrast, binary files provide efficient storage of data, but they can be read only through an appropriate program.

16.5 BASIC FILE OPERATIONS

The basic operations that can be performed on a file are given in Fig. 16.2.

Creating a File

A file is created by specifying its name and mode. Then the file is opened for writing records that are read from an input device. Once all the records have been written into the file, the file is closed. The file is now available for future read/write operations by any program that has been designed to use it in some way or the other.

Updating a File

Updating a file means changing the contents of the file to reflect a current picture of reality. A file can be updated in the following ways:

- Inserting a new record in the file. For example, if a new student joins the course, we need to add his record to the STUDENT file.
- Deleting an existing record. For example, if a student quits a course in the middle of the session, his record has to be deleted from the STUDENT file.
- Modifying an existing record. For example, if the name of a student was spelt incorrectly, then correcting the name will be a modification of the existing record.

Retrieving from a File

It means extracting useful data from a given file. Information can be retrieved from a file either for an inquiry or for report generation. An inquiry for some data retrieves low volume of data, while report generation may retrieve a large volume of data from the file.

Maintaining a File

It involves restructuring or re-organizing the file to improve the performance of the programs that access this file. Restructuring a file keeps the file organization unchanged and changes only the structural aspects of the file (for example, changing the field width or adding/deleting fields). On the other hand, file reorganization may involve changing the entire organization of the file. We will discuss file organization in detail in the next section.

16.6 FILE ORGANIZATION

We know that a file is a collection of related records. The main issue in file management is the way in which the records are organized inside the file because it has a significant effect on the system performance. Organization of records means the *logical* arrangement of records in the file and not the physical layout of the file as stored on a storage media.

Since choosing an appropriate file organization is a design decision, it must be done keeping the priority of achieving good performance with respect to the most likely usage of the file. Therefore, the following considerations should be kept in mind before selecting an appropriate file organization method:

- Rapid access to one or more records
- Ease of inserting/updating/deleting one or more records without disrupting the speed of accessing record(s)
- Efficient storage of records
- Using redundancy to ensure data integrity

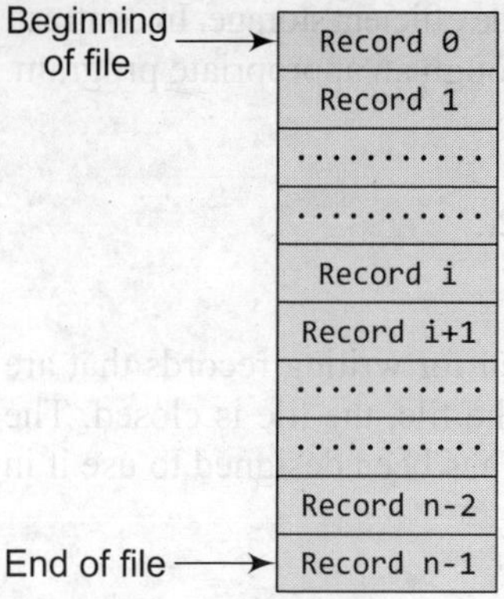

Figure 16.3 Sequential file organization

Although one may find that these requirements are in contradiction with each other, it is the designer's job to find a good compromise among them to get an adequate solution for the problem at hand. For example, the ease of addition of records can be compromised to get fast access to data.

In this section, we will discuss some of the techniques that are commonly used for file organization.

16.6.1 Sequential Organization

A sequentially organized file stores the records in the order in which they were entered. That is, the first record that was entered is written as the first record in the file, the second record entered is written as the second record in the file, and so on. As a result, new records are added only at the end of the file.

Sequential files can be read only sequentially, starting with the first record in the file. Sequential file organization is the most basic way to organize a large collection of records in a file. Figure 16.3 shows `n` records numbered from `0` to `n-1` stored in a sequential file.

Once we store the records in a file, we cannot make any changes to the records. We cannot even delete the records from a sequential file. In case we need to delete or update one or more records, we have to replace the records by creating a new file.

In sequential file organization, all the records have the same size and the same field format, and every field has a fixed size. The records are sorted based on the value of one field or a combination of two or more fields. This field is known as the *key*. Each key uniquely identifies a record in a file. Thus, every record has a different value for the key field. Records can be sorted in either ascending or descending order.

Sequential files are generally used to generate reports or to perform sequential reading of large amount of data which some programs need to do such as payroll processing of all the employees of an organization. Sequential files can be easily stored on both disks and tapes. Table 16.2 summarizes the features, advantages, and disadvantages of sequential file organization.

Table 16.2 Sequential file organization

Features	Advantages	Disadvantages
• Records are written in the order in which they are entered • Records are read and written sequentially • Deletion or updation of one or more records calls for replacing the original file with a new file that contains the desired changes • Records have the same size and the same field format • Records are sorted on a key value • Generally used for report generation or sequential reading	• Simple and easy to handle • No extra overheads involved • Sequential files can be stored on magnetic disks as well as magnetic tapes • Well suited for batch-oriented applications	• Records can be read only sequentially. If i^{th} record has to be read, then all the i-1 records must be read • Does not support update operation. A new file has to be created and the original file has to be replaced with the new file that contains the desired changes • Cannot be used for interactive applications

16.6.2 Relative File Organization

Relative file organization provides an effective way to access individual records directly. In a relative file organization, records are ordered by their *relative key*. It means the record number represents the location of the record relative to the beginning of the file. The record numbers range from `0` to `n-1`, where

Relative record number	Records stored in memory
0	Record 0
1	Record 1
2	FREE
3	FREE
4	Record 4
....	....
98	FREE
99	Record 99

Figure 16.4 Relative file organization

n is the number of records in the file. For example, the record with record number 0 is the first record in the file. The records in a relative file are of fixed length.

Therefore, in relative files, records are organized in ascending *relative record number*. A relative file can be thought of as a single dimension table stored on a disk, in which the relative record number is the index into the table. Relative files can be used for both random as well as sequential access. For sequential access, records are simply read one after another.

Relative files provide support for only one key, that is, the relative record number. This key must be numeric and must take a value between 0 and the current highest relative record number –1. This means that enough space must be allocated for the file to contain the records with relative record numbers between 0 and the highest record number –1. For example, if the highest relative record number is 1,000, then space must be allocated to store 1,000 records in the file.

Figure 16.4 shows a schematic representation of a relative file which has been allocated enough space to store 100 records. Although it has space to accommodate 100 records, not all the locations are occupied. The locations marked as `FREE` are yet to store records in them. Therefore, every location in the table either stores a record or is marked as `FREE`.

Relative file organization provides random access by directly jumping to the record which has to be accessed. If the records are of fixed length and we know the base address of the file and the length of the record, then any record `i` can be accessed using the following formula:

```
Address of ith record = base_address + (i-1) * record_length
```

Note that the base address of the file refers to the starting address of the file. We took `i-1` in the formula because record numbers start from 0 rather than 1.

Consider the base address of a file is 1000 and each record occupies 20 bytes, then the address of the 5th record can be given as:

```
1000 + (5-1) * 20
= 1000 + 80
= 1080
```

Table 16.3 summarizes the features, advantages, and disadvantages of relative file organization.

Table 16.3 Relative file organization

Features	Advantages	Disadvantages
• Provides an effective way to access individual records • The record number represents the location of the record relative to the beginning of the file • Records in a relative file are of fixed length • Relative files can be used for both random as well as sequential access • Every location in the table either stores a record or is marked as FREE	• Ease of processing • If the relative record number of the record that has to be accessed is known, then the record can be accessed instantaneously • Random access of records makes access to relative files fast • Allows deletions and updations in the same file • Provides random as well as sequential access of records with low overhead • New records can be easily added in the free locations based on the relative record number of the record to be inserted • Well suited for interactive applications	• Use of relative files is restricted to disk devices • Records can be of fixed length only • For random access of records, the relative record number must be known in advance

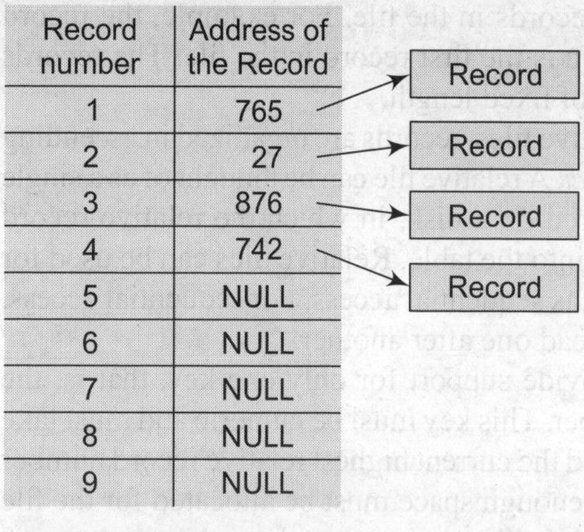

Figure 16.5 Indexed sequential file organization

16.6.3 Indexed Sequential File Organization

Indexed sequential file organization stores data for fast retrieval. The records in an indexed sequential file are of fixed length and every record is uniquely identified by a key field. We maintain a table known as the *index table* which stores the record number and the address of all the records. That is for every file, we have an index table. This type of file organization is called as indexed sequential file organization because physically the records may be stored anywhere, but the index table stores the address of those records.

The `ith` entry in the index table points to the `ith` record of the file. Initially, when the file is created, each entry in the index table contains `NULL`. When the `ith` record of the file is written, free space is obtained from the free space manager and its address is stored in the `ith` location of the index table.

Now, if one has to read the `4th` record, then there is no need to access the first three records. Address of the `4th` record can be obtained from the index table and the record can be straightaway read from the specified address (`742`, in our example). Conceptually, the index sequential file organization can be visualized as shown in Fig. 16.5.

An indexed sequential file uses the concept of both sequential as well as relative files. While the index table is read sequentially to find the address of the desired record, a direct access is made to the address of the specified record in order to access it randomly.

Indexed sequential files perform well in situations where sequential access as well as random access is made to the data. Indexed sequential files can be stored only on devices that support random access, for example, magnetic disks.

For example, take an example of a college where the details of students are stored in an indexed sequential file. This file can be accessed in two ways:

- *Sequentially*—to print the aggregate marks obtained by each student in a particular course or
- *Randomly*—to modify the name of a particular student.

Table 16.4 summarizes the features, advantages, and disadvantages of indexed sequential file organization.

Table 16.4 Indexed sequential file organization

Features	Advantages	Disadvantages
• Provides fast data retrieval • Records are of fixed length • Index table stores the address of the records in the file • The ith entry in the index table points to the ith record of the file • While the index table is read sequentially to find the address of the desired record, a direct access is made to the address of the specified record in order to access it randomly • Indexed sequential files perform well in situations where sequential access as well as random access is made to the data	• The key improvement is that the indices are small and can be searched quickly, allowing the database to access only the records it needs • Supports applications that require both batch and interactive processing • Records can be accessed sequentially as well as randomly • Updates the records in the same file	• Indexed sequential files can be stored only on disks • Needs extra space and overhead to store indices • Handling these files is more complicated than handling sequential files • Supports only fixed length records

16.7 INDEXING

An index for a file can be compared with a catalogue in a library. Like a library has card catalogues based on authors, subjects, or titles, a file can also have one or more indices.

Indexed sequential files are very efficient to use, but in real-world applications, these files are very large and a single file may contain millions of records. Therefore, in such situations, we require a more sophisticated indexing technique. There are several indexing techniques and each technique works well for a particular application. For a particular situation at hand, we analyse the indexing technique based on factors such as access type, access time, insertion time, deletion time, and space overhead involved. There are two kinds of indices:

- *Ordered indices* that are sorted based on one or more key values
- *Hash indices* that are based on the values generated by applying a *hash function*

16.7.1 Ordered Indices

Indices are used to provide fast random access to records. As stated above, a file may have multiple indices based on different key fields. An index of a file may be a primary index or a secondary index.

Primary Index

In a sequentially ordered file, the index whose search key specifies the sequential order of the file is defined as the primary index. For example, suppose records of students are stored in a STUDENT file in a sequential order starting from roll number 1 to roll number 60. Now, if we want to search a record for, say, roll number 10, then the student's roll number is the primary index. Indexed sequential files are a common example where a primary index is associated with the file.

Secondary Index

An index whose search key specifies an order different from the sequential order of the file is called as the secondary index. For example, if the record of a student is searched by his name, then the name is a secondary index. Secondary indices are used to improve the performance of queries on non-primary keys.

16.7.2 Dense and Sparse Indices

In a dense index, the index table stores the address of every record in the file. However, in a sparse index, the index table stores the address of only some of the records in the file. Although sparse indices are easy to fit in the main memory, a dense index would be more efficient to use than a sparse index if it fits in the memory. Figure 16.6 shows a dense index and a sparse index for an indexed sequential file.

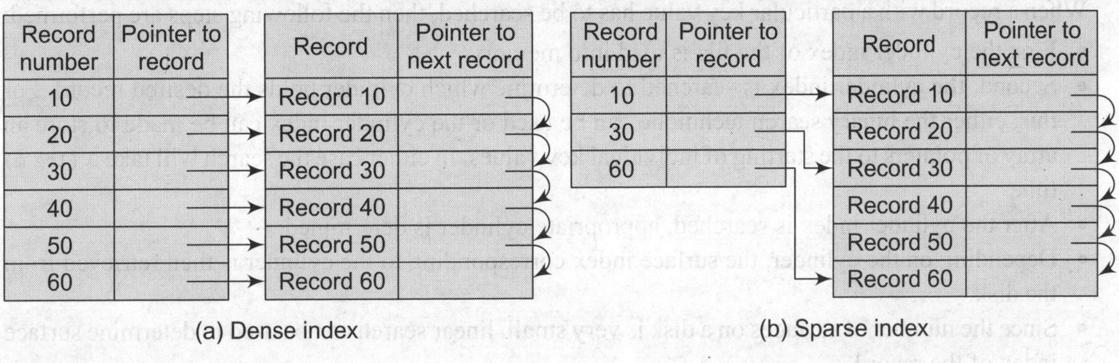

Figure 16.6 Dense index and sparse index

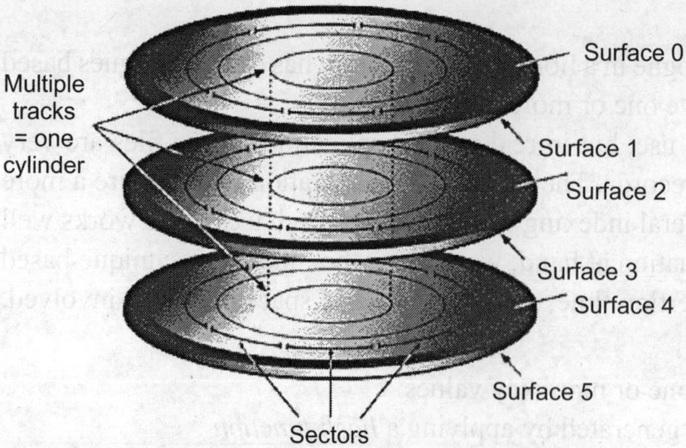

Figure 16.7 Physical and logical organization of disk

Note that the records need not be stored in consecutive memory locations. The pointer to the next record stores the address of the next record.

By looking at the dense index, it can be concluded directly whether the record exists in the file or not. This is not the case in a sparse index. In a sparse index, to locate a record, we first find an entry in the index table with the largest search key value that is either less than or equal to the search key value of the desired record. Then, we start at that record pointed to by that entry in the index table and then proceed searching the record using the sequential pointers in the file, until the desired record is obtained. For example, if we need to access record number 40, then record number 30 is the largest key value that is less than 40. So jump to the record pointed by record number 30 and move along the sequential pointer to reach record number 40.

Thus we see that sparse index takes more time to find a record with the given key. Dense indices are faster to use, while sparse indices require less space and impose less maintenance for insertions and deletions.

16.7.3 Cylinder Surface Indexing

Cylinder surface indexing is a very simple technique used only for the primary key index of a sequentially ordered file. In a sequentially ordered file, the records are stored sequentially in the increasing order of the primary key. The index file will contain two fields—cylinder index and several surface indices. Generally, there are multiple cylinders, and each cylinder has multiple surfaces. If the file needs `m` cylinders for storage then the cylinder index will contain `m` entries. Each cylinder will have an entry corresponding to the largest key value into that cylinder. If the disk has `n` usable surfaces, then each of the surface indices will have `n` entries. Therefore, the `ith` entry in the surface index for cylinder `j` is the largest key value on the `jth` track of the `ith` surface. Hence, the total number of surface index entries is `m.n`. The physical and logical organization of disk is shown in Fig. 16.7.

Note The number of cylinders in a disk is only a few hundred and the cylinder index occupies only one track.

When a record with a particular key value has to be searched, then the following steps are performed:

- First the cylinder index of the file is read into memory.
- Second, the cylinder index is searched to determine which cylinder holds the desired record. For this, either the binary search technique can be used or the cylinder index can be made to store an array of pointers to the starting of individual key values. In either case the search will take `O (log m)` time.
- After the cylinder index is searched, appropriate cylinder is determined.
- Depending on the cylinder, the surface index corresponding to the cylinder is then retrieved from the disk.
- Since the number of surfaces on a disk is very small, linear search can be used to determine surface index of the record.
- Once the cylinder and the surface are determined, the corresponding track is read and searched for the record with the desired key.

Hence, the total number of disk accesses is three—first, for accessing the cylinder index, second for accessing the surface index, and third for getting the track address. However, if track sizes are very large then it may not be a good idea to read the whole track at once. In such situations, we can also include sector addresses. But this would add an extra level of indexing and, therefore, the number of accesses needed to retrieve a record will then become four. In addition to this, when the file extends over several disks, a disk index will also be added.

The cylinder surface indexing method of maintaining a file and index is referred to as Indexed Sequential Access Method (ISAM). This technique is the most popular and simplest file organization in use for single key values. But with files that contain multiple keys, it is not possible to use this index organization for the remaining keys.

16.7.4 Multi-level Indices

In real-world applications, we have very large files that may contain millions of records. For such files, a simple indexing technique will not suffice. In such a situation, we use multi-level indices. To understand this concept, consider a file that has 10,000 records. If we use simple indexing, then we need an index table that can contain at least 10,000 entries to point to 10,000 records. If each entry in the index table occupies 4 bytes, then we need an index table of 4×10000 bytes = 40000 bytes. Finding such a big space consecutively is not always easy. So, a better scheme is to index the index table.

Figure 16.8 shows a two-level multi-indexing. We can continue further by having a three-level indexing and so on. But practically, we use two-level indexing. Note that two and higher-level indexing must always be sparse, otherwise multi-level indexing will lose its effectiveness. In the figure, the main index table stores pointers to three inner index tables. The inner index tables are sparse index tables that in turn store pointers to the records.

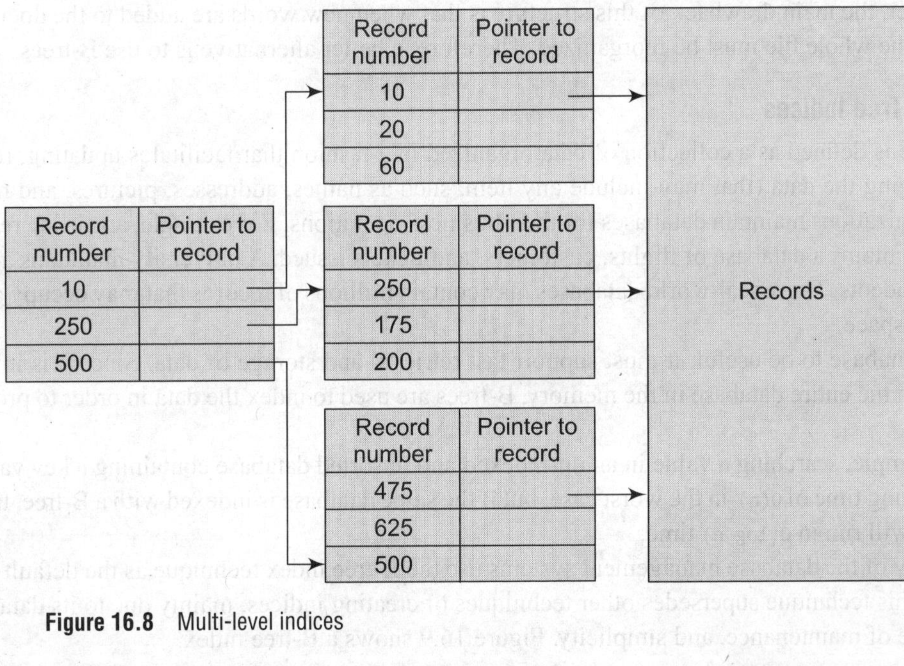

Figure 16.8 Multi-level indices

16.7.5 Inverted Indices

Inverted files are commonly used in document retrieval systems for large textual databases. An inverted file reorganizes the structure of an existing data file in order to provide fast access to all records having one field falling within the set limits.

For example, inverted files are widely used by bibliographic databases that may store author names, title words, journal names, etc. When a term or keyword specified in the inverted file is identified, the record number is given and a set of records corresponding to the search criteria are created.

Thus, for each keyword, an inverted file contains an inverted list that stores a list of pointers to all occurrences of that term in the main text. Therefore, given a keyword, the addresses of all the documents containing that keyword can easily be located.

There are two main variants of inverted indices:

- A record-level inverted index (also known as *inverted file index* or *inverted file*) stores a list of references to documents for each word
- A word-level inverted index (also known as *full inverted index* or *inverted list*) in addition to a list of references to documents for each word also contains the positions of each word within a document. Although this technique needs more time and space, it offers more functionality (like phrase searches)

Therefore, the inverted file system consists of an index file in addition to a document file (also known as *text file*). It is this index file that contains all the keywords which may be used as search terms. For each keyword, an address or reference to each location in the document where that word occurs is stored. There is no restriction on the number of pointers associated with each word.

For efficiently retrieving a word from the index file, the keywords are sorted in a specific order (usually alphabetically).

However, the main drawback of this structure is that when new words are added to the documents or text files, the whole file must be reorganized. Therefore, a better alternative is to use B-trees.

16.7.6 B-Tree Indices

A database is defined as a collection of data organized in a fashion that facilitates updating, retrieving, and managing the data (that may include any item, such as names, addresses, pictures, and numbers). Most organizations maintain databases for their business operations. For example, an airline reservation system maintains a database of flights, customers, and tickets issued. A university maintains a database of all its students. These real-world databases may contain millions of records that may occupy gigabytes of storage space.

For a database to be useful, it must support fast retrieval and storage of data. Since it is impractical to maintain the entire database in the memory, B-trees are used to index the data in order to provide fast access.

For example, searching a value in an un-indexed and unsorted database containing `n` key values may take a running time of `O(n)` in the worst case, but if the same database is indexed with a B-tree, the search operation will run in `O(log n)` time.

Majority of the database management systems use the B-tree index technique as the default indexing method. This technique supersedes other techniques of creating indices, mainly due to its data retrieval speed, ease of maintenance, and simplicity. Figure 16.9 shows a B-tree index.

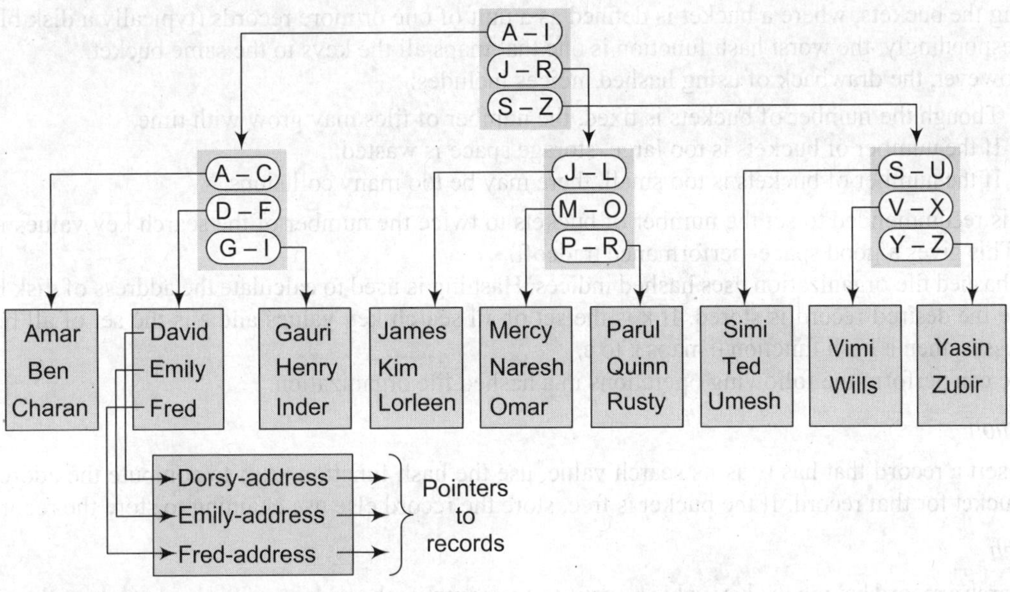

Figure 16.9 B-tree index

It forms a tree structure with the root at the top. The index consists of a B-tree (balanced tree) structure based on the values of the indexed column. In this example, the indexed column is *name* and the B-tree is created using all the existing names that are the values of the indexed column. The upper blocks of the tree contain index data pointing to the next lower block, thus forming a hierarchical structure. The lowest level blocks, also known as leaf blocks, contain pointers to the data rows stored in the table.

If a table has a column that has many unique values, then the selectivity of that column is said to be high. B-tree indices are most suitable for highly selective columns, but it causes a sharp increase in the size when the indices contain concatenation of multiple columns.

The B-tree structure has the following advantages:

- Since the leaf nodes of a B-tree are at the same depth, retrieval of any record from anywhere in the index takes approximately the same time.
- B-trees improve the performance of a wide range of queries that either search a value having an exact match or for a value within specified range.
- B-trees provide fast and efficient algorithms to insert, update, and delete records that maintain the key order.
- B-trees perform well for small as well as large tables. Their performance does not degrade as the size of a table grows.
- B-trees optimize costly disk access.

16.7.7 Hashed Indices

In the last chapter, we discussed hashing in detail. The same concept of hashing can be used to create hashed indices.

So far, we have studied that hashing is used to compute the address of a record by using a hash function on the search key value. If at any point of time, the hashed values map to the same address, then collision occurs and schemes to resolve these collisions are applied to generate a new address.

Choosing a good hash function is critical to the success of this technique. By a good hash function, we mean two things. First, a good hash function, irrespective of the number of search keys, gives an average-case lookup that is a small constant. Second, the function distributes records uniformly and randomly among the buckets, where a bucket is defined as a unit of one or more records (typically a disk block). Correspondingly, the worst hash function is one that maps all the keys to the same bucket.

However, the drawback of using hashed indices includes:

- Though the number of buckets is fixed, the number of files may grow with time.
- If the number of buckets is too large, storage space is wasted.
- If the number of buckets is too small, there may be too many collisions.

It is recommended to set the number of buckets to twice the number of the search key values in the file. This gives a good space–performance tradeoff.

A hashed file organization uses hashed indices. Hashing is used to calculate the address of disk block where the desired record is stored. If `K` is the set of all search key values and `B` is the set of all bucket addresses, then a hash function `H` maps `K` to `B`.

We can perform the following operations in a hashed file organization.

Insertion

To insert a record that has k_i as its search value, use the hash function $h(k_i)$ to compute the address of the bucket for that record. If the bucket is free, store the record else use chaining to store the record.

Search

To search a record having the key value k_i, use $h(k_i)$ to compute the address of the bucket where the record is stored. The bucket may contain one or several records, so check for every record in the bucket (by comparing k_i with the key of every record) to finally retrieve the desired record with the given key value.

Deletion

To delete a record with key value k_i, use $h(k_i)$ to compute the address of the bucket where the record is stored. The bucket may contain one or several records so check for every record in the bucket (by comparing k_i with the key of every record). Then delete the record as we delete a node from a linear linked list. We have already studied how to delete a record from a chained hash table in Chapter 15.

Note that in a hashed file organization, the secondary indices need to be organized using hashing.

Points to Remember

- A file is a block of useful information which is available to a computer program and is usually stored on a persistent storage medium.
- Every file contains data. This data can be organized in a hierarchy to present a systematic organization. The data hierarchy includes data items such as fields, records, files, and database.
- A data field is an elementary unit that stores a single fact. A record is a collection of related data fields which is seen as a single unit from the application point of view. A file is a collection of related records. A directory is a collection of related files.
- A database is defined as a collection of data organized in a fashion that facilitates updating, retrieving, and managing the data.
- There are two types of computer files—text files and binary files. A text file is structured as a sequence of lines of alphabet, numbers, special characters, etc. However, the data in a text file is stored using its corresponding ASCII code. Whereas in binary files, the data is stored in binary form, i.e., in the format it is stored in the memory.
- Each file has a list of attributes associated with it which can have one of two states—*on* or *off*. These attributes are: read-only, hidden, system, volume label, archive, and directory.
- A file marked as read-only cannot be deleted or modified.
- A hidden file is not displayed in the directory listing.
- A system file is used by the system and should not be altered or removed from the disk.

- The archive bit is useful for communication between programs that modify files and programs that are used for backing up files.
- A file that has the directory bit turned on is actually a sub-directory containing one or more files.
- File organization means the logical arrangement of records in the file. Files can be organized as sequential, relative, or index sequential.
- A sequentially organized file stores records in the order in which they were entered.
- In relative file organization, records in a file are ordered by their relative key. Relative files can be used for both random access as well as sequential access of data.
- In an indexed sequential file, every record is uniquely identified by a key field. We maintain a table known as the index table that stores record number and the address of the record in the file.
- There are several indexing techniques, and each technique works well for a particular application.
- In a dense index, index table stores the address of every record in the file. However, in a sparse index, index table stores address of only some of the records in the file.
- Cylinder surface indexing is a very simple technique which is used only for the primary key index of a sequentially ordered file.
- In multi-level indexing, we can create an index to the index itself. The original index is called the first-level index and the index to the index is called the second-level index.
- Inverted files are frequently used indexing technique in document retrieval systems for large textual databases. An inverted file reorganizes the structure of an existing data file in order to provide fast access to all records having one field falling within set limits.
- Majority of the database management systems use B-tree indexing technique. The index consists of a hierarchical structure with upper blocks containing indices pointing to the lower blocks and lowest level blocks containing pointers to the data records.
- Hashed file organization uses hashed indices. Hashing is used to calculate the address of disk block where the desired record is stored. If `K` is the set of all search key values and `B` is the set of bucket addresses, then a hash function `H` maps `K` to `B`.

Exercises

Review Questions

1. Why do we need files?
2. Explain the terms field, record, file organization, key, and index.
3. Define file. Explain all the file attributes.
4. How is archive attribute useful?
5. Differentiate between a binary file and a text file.
6. Explain the basic file operations.
7. What do you understand by the term file organization? Briefly summarize the different file organizations that are widely used today.
8. Write a brief note on indexing.
9. Differentiate between sparse index and dense index.
10. Explain the significance of multi-level indexing with an appropriate example.
11. What are inverted files? Why are they needed?
12. Give the merits and demerits of a B-tree index.

Multiple-choice Questions

1. Which of the following flags is cleared when a file is backed up?
   (a) Read-only
   (b) System
   (c) Hidden
   (d) Archive
2. Which is an important file used by the system and should not be altered or removed from the disk?
   (a) Hidden file
   (b) Archived file
   (c) System file
   (d) Read-only file
3. The data hierarchy can be given as
   (a) Fields, records, files and database
   (b) Records, files, fields and database
   (c) Database, files, records and fields
   (d) Fields, records, database, and files

4. Which of the following indexing techniques is used in document retrieval systems for large databases?
   (a) Inverted index
   (b) Multi-level indices
   (c) Hashed indices
   (d) B-tree index

True or False

1. When a backup program archives the file, it sets the archive bit to one.
2. In a text file, data is stored using ASCII codes.
3. A binary file is more efficient than a text file.
4. Maintenance of a file involves re-structuring or re-organization of the file.
5. Relative files can be used for both random access of data as well as sequential access.
6. In a sparse index, index table stores the address of every record in the file.
7. Higher level indexing must always be sparse.
8. B-tree indices are most suitable for highly selective columns.

Fill in the Blanks

1. ______ is a block of useful information.
2. A data field is usually characterized by its ______ and ______.
3. ______ is a collection of related data fields.
4. ______ is a pointer that points to the position at which next read/write operation will be performed.
5. ______ indicates whether the file is a text file or a binary file.
6. Index table stores ______ and ______ of the record in the file.
7. In a sequentially ordered file the index whose search key specifies the sequential order of the file is defined as the ______ index.
8. ______ files are frequently used indexing technique in document retrieval systems for large textual databases.
9. ______ is a collection of data organized in a fashion that facilitates updating, retrieving, and managing the data.

APPENDIX A

Memory Allocation in C Programs

C supports three kinds of memory allocation through the variables in C programs:

Static allocation When we declare a static or global variable, static allocation is done for the variable. Each static or global variable is allocated a fixed size of memory space. The number of bytes reserved for the variable cannot change during execution of the program.

Automatic allocation When we declare an automatic variable, such as a function argument or a local variable, automatic memory allocation is done. The space for an automatic variable is allocated when the compound statement containing the declaration is entered, and is freed when it exits from a compound statement.

Dynamic allocation A third important kind of memory allocation is known as *dynamic allocation.* In the following sections we will read about dynamic memory allocation using pointers.

Memory Usage

Before jumping into dynamic memory allocation, let us first understand how memory is used. Conceptually, memory is divided into two parts—program memory and data memory (Fig. A1).

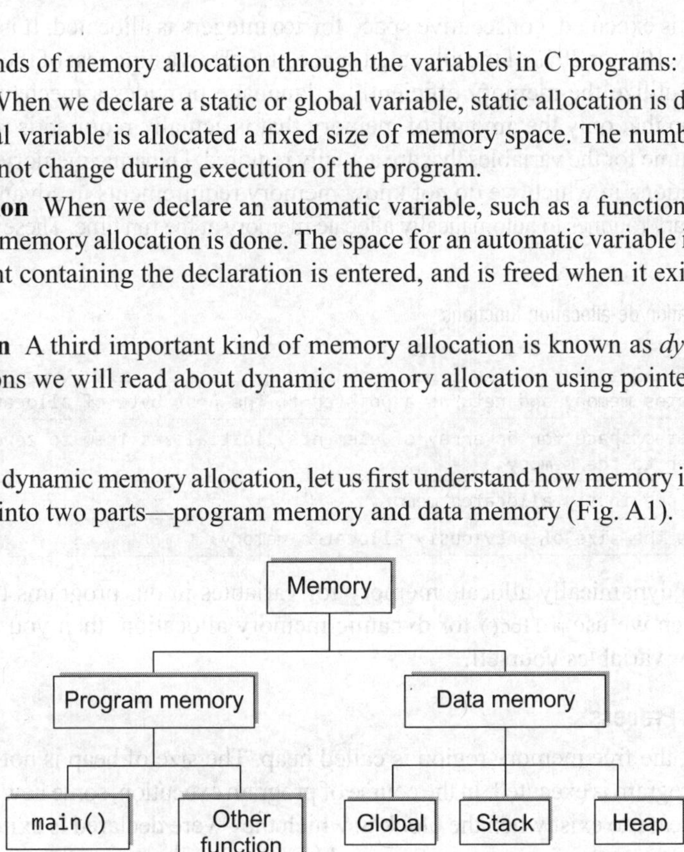

Figure A1 Memory usage

The program memory consists of memory used for the `main()` and other called functions in the program, whereas data memory consists of memory needed for permanent definitions such as global data, local data, constants, and dynamic memory data. The way in which `c` handles the memory requirements is a function of the operating system and the compiler.

When a program is being executed, its `main()` and all other functions are always kept in the memory. However, the local variables of the function are available in the memory only when they are active. When we studied recursive fun #include <conio.h> ctions, we have seen that the system stack is used to store a single copy of the function and multiple copies of the local variables.

Apart from the stack, we also have a memory pool known as heap. Heap memory is unused memory allocated to the program and available to be assigned during its execution. When we dynamically allocate memory for variables, heap acts as a memory pool from which memory is allocated to those variables.

However, this is just a conceptual view of memory and implementation of the memory is entirely in the hands of system designers.

Dynamic Memory Allocation

The process of allocating memory to the variables during execution of the program or at run time is known as *dynamic memory allocation*. `C` language has four library routines which allow this function. Till now whenever we needed an array we had declared a static array of fixed size as

```
int arr[100];
```

When this statement is executed, consecutive space for `100` integers is allocated. It is not uncommon that we may be using only 10% or 20% of the allocated space, thereby wasting rest of the space. To overcome this problem and to utilize the memory efficiently, `C` language provides a mechanism of dynamically allocating memory so that only the amount of memory that is actually required is reserved. We reserve space only at the run time for the variables that are actually required. Dynamic memory allocation gives best performance in situations in which we do not know memory requirements in advance.

`C` provides four library routines to automatically allocate memory at the run time. These routines are shown in Table A1.

Table A1 Memory allocation/de-allocation functions

Function	Task
`malloc()`	Allocates memory and returns a pointer to the first byte of allocated space
`calloc()`	Allocates space for an array of elements, initializes them to zero and returns a pointer to the memory
`free()`	Frees previously allocated memory
`realloc()`	Alters the size of previously allocated memory

When we have to dynamically allocate memory for variables in our programs then pointers are the only way to go. When we use `malloc()` for dynamic memory allocation, then you need to manage the memory allocated for variables yourself.

Memory Allocations Process

In computer science, the free memory region is called heap. The size of heap is not constant as it keeps changing when the program is executed. In the course of program execution, some new variables are created and some variables cease to exist when the block in which they were declared is exited. For this reason it is not uncommon to encounter memory overflow problems during dynamic allocation process. When an overflow condition occurs, the memory allocation functions mentioned above will return a null pointer.

Allocating a Block of Memory

Let us see how memory is allocated using the `malloc()`function. `malloc` is declared in `<stdlib.h>`, so we include this header file in any program that calls `malloc`. The `malloc` function reserves a block of memory of specified size and returns a pointer of type `void`. This means that we can assign it to any type of pointer. The general syntax of `malloc()` is

```
ptr =(cast-type*)malloc(byte-size);
```

where `ptr` is a pointer of type `cast-type`. `malloc()` returns a pointer (of cast type) to an area of memory with size `byte-size`.

For example,

```
arr=(int*)malloc(10*sizeof(int));
```

This statement is used to dynamically allocate memory equivalent to 10 times the area of `int` bytes. On successful execution of the statement the space is reserved and the address of the first byte of memory allocated is assigned to the pointer `arr` of type `int`.

Programming Tip

To use dynamic memory allocation functions, you must include the header file stdlib.h.

`calloc()` function is another function that reserves memory at the run time. It is normally used to request multiple blocks of storage each of the same size and then sets all bytes to `zero`. `calloc()` stands for contiguous memory allocation and is primarily used to allocate memory for arrays. The syntax of `calloc()` can be given as:

```
ptr=(cast-type*) calloc(n,elem-size);
```

The above statement allocates contiguous space for `n` blocks each of size `elem-size` bytes. The only difference between `malloc()` and `calloc()` is that when we use `calloc()`, all bytes are initialized to zero. `calloc()` returns a pointer to the first byte of the allocated region.

When we allocate memory using `malloc()` or `calloc()`, a `NULL` pointer will be returned if there is not enough space in the system to allocate. A `NULL` pointer, points definitely nowhere. It is a *not a pointer* marker; therefore, it is not a pointer you can use. Thus, whenever you allocate memory using `malloc()` or `calloc()`, you must check the returned pointer before using it. If the program receives a `NULL` pointer, it should at the very least print an error message and exit, or perhaps figure out some way of proceeding without the memory it asked for. But in any case, the program cannot go on to use the `NULL` pointer it got back from `malloc()/calloc()`.

A call to `malloc`, with an error check, typically looks something like this:

```
int *ip = malloc(100 * sizeof(int));
if(ip == NULL)
{
        printf("\n Memory could not be allocated");
        return;
}
```

Write a program to read and display values of an integer array. Allocate space dynamically for the array.

```
#include <stdio.h>
#include <stdlib.h>
int main()
{
        int i, n;
        int *arr;
        printf("\n Enter the number of elements ");
        scanf("%d", &n);
        arr = (int*)malloc(n * sizeof(int));
        if(arr == NULL)
        {
            printf("   \n Memory Allocation Failed");
            exit(0);
        }
        for(i=0;i<n;i++)
        {
            printf("\n Enter the value %d of the array: ", i);
            scanf("%d",&arr[i]);
        }
        printf("\n The array contains \n");
        for(i=0;i<n;i++)
            printf("%d", arr[i]);
        return 0;
}
```

Now let us also see how we can allocate memory using the `calloc` function. The `calloc()` function accepts two parameters—`num` and `size`, where `num` is the number of elements to be allocated and `size` is the size of elements. The following program demonstrates the use of `calloc()` to dynamically allocate space for an integer array.

```
#include <stdio.h>
#include <stdlib.h>
int main ()
{
          int i,n;
          int *arr;
          printf ("\n Enter the number of elements: ");
          scanf("%d",&n);
          arr = (int*) calloc(n,sizeof(int));
          if (arr==NULL)
              exit (1);
          printf("\n Enter the %d values to be stored in the array", n);
          for (i = 0; i < n; i++)
           scanf ("%d",&arr[i]);
          printf ("\n You have entered: ");
          for(i = 0; i < n; i++)
              printf ("%d",arr[i]);
          free(arr);
          return 0;
}
```

Releasing the Used Space

When a variable is allocated space during the compile time, then the memory used by that variable is automatically released by the system in accordance with its storage class. But when we dynamically allocate memory then it is our responsibility to release the space when it is not required. This is even more important when the storage space is limited. Therefore, if we no longer need the data stored in a particular block of memory and we do not intend to use that block for storing any other information, then as a good programming practice we must release that block of memory for future use, using the `free` function. The general syntax of the `free()`function is,

```
free(ptr);
```

where `ptr` is a pointer that has been created by using `malloc()` or `calloc()`. When memory is de-allocated using `free()`, it is returned back to the free list within the heap.

To Alter the Size of Allocated Memory

At times the memory allocated by using `calloc()` or `malloc()` might be insufficient or in excess. In both the situations we can always use `realloc()` to change the memory size already allocated by `calloc()` and `malloc()`. This process is called *reallocation of memory*. The general syntax for `realloc()` can be given as,

```
ptr = realloc(ptr,newsize);
```

The function `realloc()` allocates new memory space of size specified by `newsize` to the pointer variable `ptr`. It returns a pointer to the first byte of the memory block. The allocated new block may be or may not be at the same region. Thus, we see that `realloc()` takes two arguments. The first is the pointer referencing the memory and the second is the total number of bytes you want to reallocate. If you pass zero as the second argument, it will be equivalent to calling `free()`. Like `malloc()` and `calloc()`, `realloc` returns a void pointer if successful, else a `NULL` pointer is returned.

If `realloc()` was able to make the old block of memory bigger, it returns the same pointer. Otherwise, if `realloc()` has to go elsewhere to get enough contiguous memory then it returns a pointer to the new memory, after copying your old data there. However, if `realloc()` cannot find enough memory to satisfy the new request at all, it returns a null pointer. So again you must check before using that the pointer returned by the `realloc()` is not a null pointer.

```
/*Example program for reallocation*/
#include < stdio.h>
#include < stdlib.h>
#define NULL 0
int main()
{
        char *str;
        str = (char *)malloc(10);
        if(str==NULL)
        {
           printf("\n Memory could not be allocated");
           exit(1);
}
        strcpy(str,"Hi");
        printf("\n STR = %s", str);
        /*Reallocation*/
        str = (char *)realloc(str,20);
        if(str==NULL)
        {
           printf("\n Memory could not be reallocated");
           exit(1);
}
printf("\n STR size modified\n");
printf("\n STR = %s\n", str);
strcpy(str,"Hi there");
printf("\n STR = %s", str);
/*freeing memory*/
free(str);
return 0;
}
```

Note With realloc(), you can allocate more bytes without losing your data.

Dynamically Allocating a 2-D Array

We have seen how `malloc()` can be used to allocate a block of memory which can simulate an array. Now we can extend our understanding further to do the same to simulate multidimensional arrays.

If we are not sure of the number of columns that the array will have, then we will first allocate memory for each row by calling `malloc`. Each row will then be represented by a pointer. Look at the code below which illustrates this concept.

```
#include <stdlib.h>
#include <stdio.h>
int main()
{
        int **arr,i,j,ROWS,COLS;
        printf("\n Enter the number of rows and columns in the array: ");
        scanf("%d %d",ROWS,COLS);
        arr = (int **)malloc(ROWS * sizeof(int *));
        if(arr == NULL)
        {
           printf("\n Memory could not be allocated");
           exit(-1);
        }
```

```
    for(i=0; i<ROWS; i++)
    {
        arr[i] = (int *)malloc(COLS * sizeof(int));
        if(arr[i] == NULL)
        {
            printf("\n Memory Allocation Failed");
            exit(-1);
        }
    }
    printf("\n Enter the values of the array: ");
    for(i = 0; i < ROWS; i++)
    {
        for(j = 0; j < COLS; j++)
            scanf("%d",&arr[i][j]);
    }
    printf("\n The array is as follows: ");
    for(i = 0; i < ROWS; i++)
    {
        for(j = 0; j < COLS; j++)
            printf("%d", arr[i][j]);
    }
    for(i = 0; i < ROWS; i++)
        free(arr[i]);
    free(arr);
    return 0;
}
```

Here, arr is a pointer-to-pointer-to-int: at the first level as it points to a block of pointers, one for each row. We first allocate space for rows in the array. The space allocated to each row is big enough to hold a pointer-to-int, or int *. If we successfully allocate it, then this space will be filled with pointers to columns (number of ints). This can be better understood from Fig. A2.

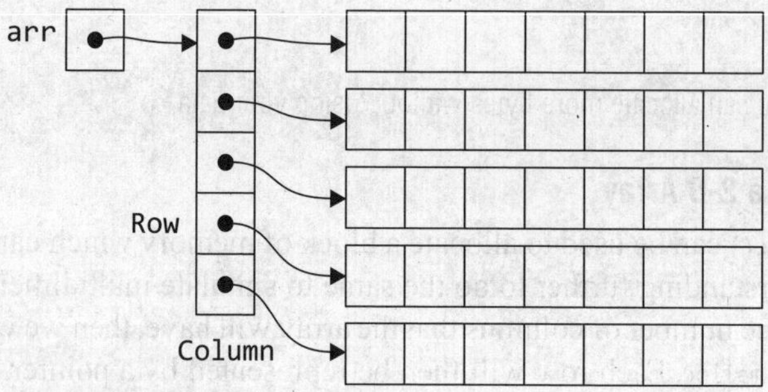

Figure A2 Memory allocation of two-dimensional array

Once the memory is allocated for the two-dimensional array, we can use subscripts to access its elements. When we write, arr[i][j], it means we are looking for the ith pointer pointed to by arr, and then for the jth int pointed to by that inner pointer.

When we have to pass such an array to a function, then the prototype of the function will be written as

func(int **arr, int ROWS, int COLS);

In the above declaration, func accepts a pointer-to-pointer-to-int and the dimensions of the arrays as parameters, so that it will know how many rows and columns are there.

APPENDIX B

Garbage Collection

Garbage collection is a dynamic approach used for automatic memory management to reduce the memory leak problems. The garbage collection process identifies unused memory blocks and reallocates that storage for reuse. Garbage collection is implemented using the following approaches:

Mark-and-sweep In this approach when memory runs out, the garbage collection process locates all accessible memory and then reclaims the available memory.

Reference counting The garbage collection process here maintains a reference count of referencing number for each allocated object. When the memory count becomes zero, the object is marked as garbage and then destroyed by freeing its memory. The freed memory is finally returned to the memory heap.

Copy collection The garbage collection process maintains two memory partitions. When the first partition is full, the garbage collection process identifies all accessible data structures and copies them to the second partition. Then it compacts memory to allow continuous free memory.

Note Some programming languages like Java, C#, .NET, etc., have built-in garbage collection process to self-manage memory leak problem.

Advantages of Garbage Collection

Garbage collection frees the programmer from manually dealing with memory de-allocation, thereby eliminating or substantially reducing following types of programming bugs:

***Dangling pointer* bugs** are often encountered when the memory allocated to a variable (or an object) is freed but there are still pointers pointing to it. If such pointers are de-referenced especially when that memory is re-allocated to another variable or object, then results are simply unpredictable.

Double free bugs occur when the program tries to free a piece of memory that has already been freed. It may be a case that the freed memory has now been re-allocated to some other variable or object of the same or a different program. In such a case, the program will again give erroneous results.

Memory leaks occur when a program is unable to free memory occupied by objects that have become unreachable.

Garbage collection also helps in efficient implementation of persistent data structures.

Disadvantages of Garbage Collection

The typical disadvantages of garbage collection process include:

- Garbage collection consumes computing resources to decide which piece of memory must be freed. This information may already be available with the programmer.

- The time at which the garbage collection process will be executed is unpredictable which may lead to stalls scattered throughout a session. This is unacceptable in real-time environments, transaction processing, or in interactive programs. Although incremental, concurrent, and real-time garbage collectors solve this problem but with some or the other trade-off.
- Some of the bugs addressed by garbage collection can have certain security implications.

Requirements for Automatic Garbage Collection

An effective and efficient garbage collection process must have the following properties:

- Must identify garbage
- The object or variable identified as garbage must actually be garbage.
- Must have less overhead
- During garbage collection, the execution of the program is temporarily delayed. This delay must be minimum.

APPENDIX C

Backtracking

Backtracking is a general algorithm that finds all or some solutions to any computational problem that incrementally builds candidates to the solutions. At each step, while the valid candidates to the solution are extended, the other candidates are discarded. That is, each partial candidate *c* is immediately abandoned after it is determined that *c* cannot be a possible and valid solution to the problem. Hence, the name, backtrack.

The concept of backtracking is applicable only to problems that support partial candidate solutions and a relatively quick test to determine if the partial candidate solution can be completed to a valid solution. Backtracking is extensively used to solve constraint satisfaction problems such as following:

- Puzzles like Sudoku, eight queen's problem, crosswords, verbal arithmetic, Solitaire
- Combinational optimization problem like parsing and Knapsack problem
- Logic programming languages that internally use backtracking include Icon, Planner and Prolog
- *diff* which is a version comparing engine for the MediaWiki software

Backtracking is said to be a meta-heuristic algorithm (in contrast to a specific algorithm) that is guaranteed to find all solutions to a finite problem in a bounded amount of time. The term meta-heuristic implies that the algorithm works based on user-given procedures that define the problem to be solved, the nature of the partial candidates, and how they are extended into complete candidates.

Conceptualizing the backtracking process as potential search tree, the partial candidates of the solution can be viewed as the nodes of the tree. Each partial candidate has child nodes that represent the candidates that differ from it by a single extension step. Of course, the leaf nodes are the partial candidates that cannot be extended further.

The backtracking algorithm recursively traverses the search tree in depth-first order (starting from the root node). At each node *c*, the algorithm checks if *c* can be completed to a valid solution. If it cannot be completed, then the entire sub-tree rooted at *c* is pruned. However, if there is a possibility that *c* may lead to valid solution then the algorithm first checks if *c* itself is a valid solution. If yes, then the algorithm declares *c* as the valid solution otherwise it recursively enumerates all sub-trees of *c*.

Note The tests to determine the valid solution and children of each node are all defined by user-given procedures.

Look at the search tree given below.

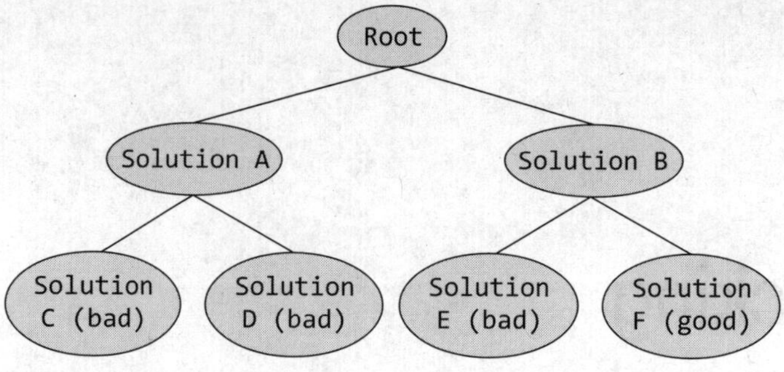

Step 1 Start with the root node. The two available options are—Solution A and Solution B. Select Solution A.

Step 2 At Solution A there are again two options—Solution C and Solution D. Select Solution C.

Step 3 Since Solution C is not a good (valid and possible) candidate, backtrack to Solution A and now select Solution D.

Step 4 Since Solution D is not a good (valid and possible) candidate, backtrack to Solution A. now there are no more options available at Solution A, so select Solution B.

Step 5 At Solution B there are two options—Solution E and Solution F. Select Solution E.

Step 6 Since Solution E is not a good (valid and possible) candidate, backtrack to Solution B and now select Solution F.

Step 7 Solution F is a good (valid and possible) candidate, so the algorithm stops here.

Advantage: By terminating searches and not exploring candidates that cannot lead to valid possible solutions, the backtracking technique reduces the number of nodes examined. The algorithm can be used to solve exponential time problems in a *reasonable* amount of time.

Note Backtracking is not an optimization technique. It just reduces the search space.

APPENDIX D

File Handling in C

1. Write a program to store records of an employee in employee file. The data must be stored using binary file.

```
#include <stdio.h>
int main()
{
        typedef struct employee
        {
            int emp_code;
            char name[20];
        };
        FILE *fp;
        struct employee e[2];
        int i;
        fp = fopen("employee.txt", "wb");
        if(fp==NULL)
        {
            printf("\n Error opening file");
            exit(1);
        }
        printf("\n Enter the details employees");
        for(i = 0;i < 2;i++)
        {
            printf("\n\n Enter the employee code:");
            scanf(„%d", &e[i].emp_code);
            printf("\n\n Enter the name of the employee: ");
            scanf("%s", e[i].name);
            fwrite(&e[i], sizeof(e[i]), 1, fp);
        }
        fclose(fp);
        return 0;
}
```

Output

```
Enter the details of employees
Enter the employee code: 01
Enter the name of the employee: Gargi
Enter the employee code: 02
Enter the name of the employee: Nikita
```

2. Write a program to read the records stored in 'employee.txt' file in binary mode.

```
#include <stdio.h>
int main()
{
        typedef struct employee
```

```
{
    int emp_code;
    char name[20];
};
FILE *fp;
struct employee e;
int i;
fp = fopen("employee.txt", "rb");
if(fp==NULL)
{
    printf("\n Error opening file");
    exit(1);
}
printf("\n THE DETAILS OF THE EMPLOYEES ARE ");
while(1)
{
    fread(&e, sizeof(e), 1, fp);
    if(feof(fp))
    break;
    printf("\n\n Employee Code: %d", e.emp_code);
    printf("\n\n Name: %s", e.name);
}
fclose(fp);
return 0;
```

Output

```
Employee Code: 01
Name: Gargi
Employee Code: 02
Name: Nikita
```

APPENDIX E

Address Calculation Sort

Write a program to sort elements of an array using address calculation sort.

```
#include <stdio.h>
#include <stdlib.h>
#define MAX 5
struct node
{
          int data;
          struct node *next;
}*nodes[10]={NULL};

struct node *insert(struct node *start, int num)
{
          struct node *ptr,*new_node;
          ptr=start;
          new_node = (struct node*)malloc(sizeof(struct node));
          new_node->data=num;
          new_node->next=NULL;
          if(start==NULL)
             start = new_node;
          else
          {
             //insert the new node at its right position
             while((ptr->next->data<=num) && (ptr->next!=NULL))
                ptr=ptr->next;
             if(new_node->data < ptr->data)
             {
                new_node->next=ptr;
                start=new_node;
             }
             else
             {
                new_node->next=ptr->next;
                ptr->next=new_node;
             }
          }
          return start;
}
void addr_calc_sort(int arr[],int n)
{
          int i,j=0,pos;
          for(i=0;i<n;i++)
          {
             pos = arr[i] / 10;
```

```
            nodes[pos]=insert(nodes[pos],arr[i]);
        }
        for(i=0;i<10;i++)
        {
            while(nodes[i]!=NULL)
            {
                arr[j++]=nodes[i]->data;
                nodes[i]=nodes[i]->next;
            }
        }
        printf("\nSorted output is: ");
        for(i=0;i<n;i++)
            printf("%d\t",arr[i]);
}
    void main()
    {
        int arr[MAX],i,n;
        printf("\n Enter the number of elements : ");
        scanf("%d",&n);
        printf("\n Enter the elements : ");
        for(i=0;i<n;i++)
            scanf("%d",&arr[i]);
        addr_calc_sort(arr,n);
    }
```

Output

```
Enter the number of elements : 5
Enter the elements: 23  53  14  78  22
Sorted output is : 14  22  23  53  78
```

APPENDIX F

Program Optimization Techniques

Optimization techniques are used to transform a program to improve the code in such a way that it consumes less resources (i.e., CPU, Memory) and deliver high speed.

During optimization, high-level general programming constructs are replaced by efficient low-level programming codes. However, to optimize the code, certain rules must be followed.

- The output code must not modify the meaning of the program.
- The speed of the program should be enhanced.
- The program should demand less resources.

Optimization can be categorized as machine independent and machine dependent.

MACHINE-INDEPENDENT OPTIMIZATION

Avoid repeated assignment.

```
do                              Item = 10;
{                               do
      tem = 10;                 {
      value = value + item;           value = value + item;
} while(value<100);             } while(value<100);
```

Note that repeated assignment of the identifier (item here), waste CPU cycles on any processor.

MACHINE-DEPENDENT OPTIMIZATION

Machine-dependent optimization is done after the program is written and transformed according to the machine's architecture. But before talking about these techniques, let us first understand the basic concepts.

Basic Blocks: A program may have n number of instructions. These instructions are considered as the basic blocks of the program. Basic blocks do not have any jump statements. All the instructions in the same basic block will be executed sequentially. Examples of basic blocks include, IF-THEN-ELSE, SWITCH-CASE statements and loops like DO-WHILE, FOR, etc.

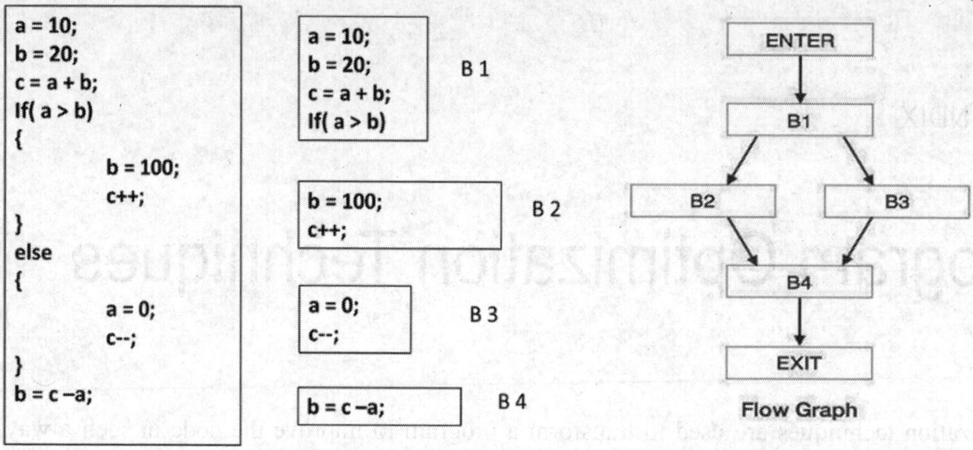

Basic blocks are important for identifying variables. If any variable is being used more than once, the register memory allocated to that variable is not emptied unless the block finishes execution. These blocks can be represented by using control flow graphs. A control flow graph depicts how the program control is being passed among the blocks. It helps the programmer to optimize code by locating any unwanted loops in the program.

Loop Optimization: Most programs have at least one loop. These loop(s) if optimized, help us to save CPU cycles and memory. Loops can be optimized by considering the following points.

- Checking if any code fragment in the loop computes the same value at each iteration. If such code exists, then that code can be moved out of the loop. This would save unnecessary computations with each iteration.
- Replacing expressions that consume more CPU cycles, time, and memory with cheaper ones without compromising the output of expression. For example, replacing multiplication (x * 2) with x << 1. Replacing ** operator with pow() function, x / 2 division operator with x >> 1.

Dead-code Elimination: Dead code refers to program statement(s) which are either never executed or are unreachable. Even if they are executed, their output is never used. This means that dead code does not contribute in program operation and can thus be eliminated.

Let us consider two situations to understand this concept. In graph, value of a is computed inside the loop but never used. Right after the loop, value of a is re-assigned before being used. So, the statement a = x + y can be eliminated.

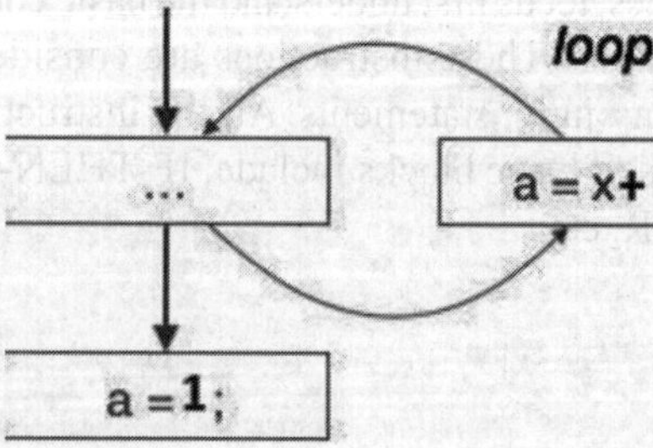

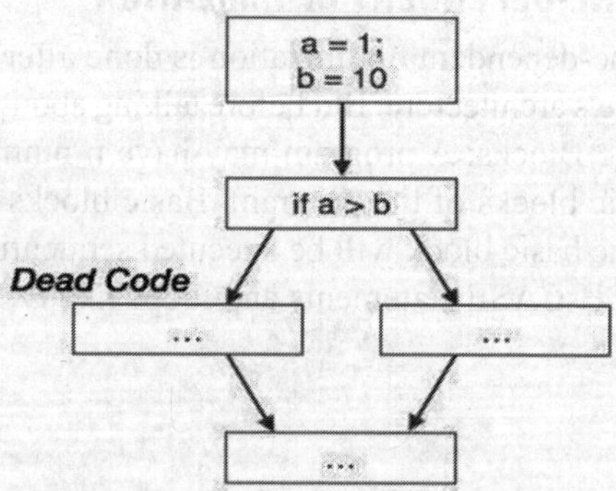

In the second graph, the conditional statement is always false. Any code written in true case, will never be executed, hence it can be removed.

Redundancy: Redundant expressions are computed more than once in parallel path as shown in graph (a). This can be eliminated by using a code-motion technique as shown in figure (b). in the second graph, c + d is performed only once.

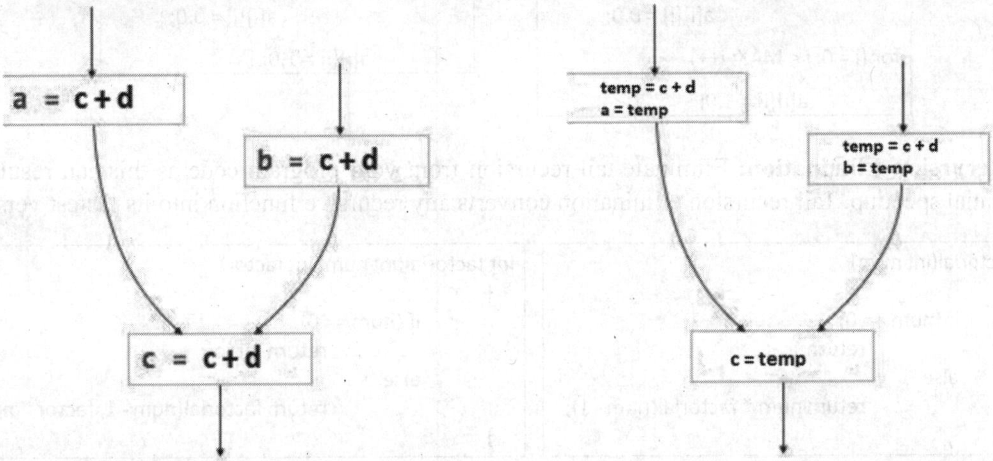

WRITING AN OPTIMIZED CODE

To write an optimized code, you can make small replacements. For example, replace slow sequential search by binary search or hash lookup; replace insertion or bubble sort by quick sort, merge sort, radix sort.

Select an appropriate data structure. A bad choice of data structure will severely impact the performance of the program. For example, if many insertions and deletions are to be done at random places then a linked list would be better than array.

Write clear, simple code because *complicated expressions are harder to optimize. In contrast to this, clean and portable code can easily be deployed on the latest and fastest machine.*

Inlining: Use inline functions to save the overhead of function calls. If the compiler lacks inlining capability then functions can be recoded as macros to obtain similar speedup.

```
Int func(a,b)
{
    a = b + 10;
    ++b;
    return (a * b);
}
```

```
INLINE VERSION
# define func(a,b) (((b) + (10)) * (((b) + 1))
```

However, consider the points given below before using a macro.

1. Macro leads to massive code-bloat and can thus increase the amount of memory space required by the program. So, for large programs, macros are not recommended.
2. Macros in C evaluate their arguments each time the argument is mentioned inside the macro. If the actual argument passed to the macro is a complex expression or function call, then macros will give no performance gains and may even increase CPU time required to execute the program.

Loop Jamming: Adjacent loops can be combined especially those which loops over the same range of the same variable. However, this can be done only when nothing in the second loop indexes forward (for example array[i+3]).

```
for (i = 0; i < MAX; i++)
        for (j = 0; j < MAX; j++)
                a[i][j] = 0.0;
for (i = 0; i < MAX; i++)
        a[i][i] = 1.0;
```

```
for (i = 0; i < MAX; i++)
        for (j = 0; j < MAX; j++)
                a[i][j] = 0.0;
        a[i][i] = 1.0;
```

Tail Recursion Elimination: Eliminate tail recursion from your program code as this can result in a substantial speedup. Tail recursion elimination converts any recursive function into its fastest version.

```
int factorial(int num)
 {
        if (num == 0)
                return 1;
        else
                return num * factorial(num - 1);
 }
```

```
int factorial(int num, int factor)
 {
        if (num == 0)
                return factor;
        else
                return factorial(num - 1, factor * num);
 }
```

The code on the left side has a tail recursion as the returned value is not used directly. It is multiplied by num after the call. To do this, the state of that invocation must be maintained until after the return. The same code has been optimized by eliminating tail recursion (on the right side).

Table Lookup: Prefer using lookup tables if a computation is iterative or recursive. However, calculations that take constant time can often be recomputed faster than they can be retrieved from memory. In this case, lookup table will not be always beneficial.

```
long factorial(int i)
{
   if (i == 0)
     return 1;
   else
     return i * factorial(i - 1);
}
```

```
static long factorial_table[] = {1, 1, 2, 6, 24, 120, 720 };
 long factorial(int i)
 {
   return factorial_table[i];
 }
```

Another way to optimize this code especially in case of a very large table, we can compute all the values on startup and print it.

Sorting: *To gain performance speedup, evaluate the ratio of insertions to lookups.*

- If number of insertions exceeds that of lookups, then sort all the insertions.
- If number of lookups exceed that of insertions, then maintain the array in order by inserting items one-at-a-time in their sorted location to eliminate the need to re-sort the entire data.
- If insertions are expensive, then prefer using merge sort.

Variables: When using variables, avoid referring to global or static variables inside loops.

Do not use the `volatile` qualifier until it is genuinely required.

Avoid passing addresses of the variables to other functions as then the variables can get easily modified.

Function Calls: Though using functions and modularity is a good programming habit, a function call inside a loop is a possible bottleneck due to the following reasons.

- Function calls interrupts the process of optimization. Using references through pointers or global variables makes the code 'dirty'.
- Function call always has an overhead associated with it. Every time a function is called, variables and return addresses are stored and retrieved from the stack.
- If the called function happens to be paged out, then a long delay would be experienced to first read it into memory. On computers with limited virtual memory, repetitive calling other functions may result in thrashing.

Working with Strings: When checking for empty string, instead of writing `strlen(s)` == 0, check for *s == '\0'. This saves the function call overhead plus as now, only the first character has to be checked. This results in substantial improvement especially when the string is fairly long. For the same reason, replace `strcpy(s, "")` with `*s = '\0'`.

Prefer using `strncpy(s, t, n)` than using `memcpy/memmove`. This is because `strncpy` pads short strings with 0›s thereby wasting CPU time. Moreover, `memcpy` is faster than `memmove`. So keep that as your first choice.

```
/* sizeof = 64 bytes */
struct foo {
  float a;
  double b;
  float c;
  double d;
  short e;
  long f;
  short g;
  long h;
  char i;
  int j;
  char k;
  int l;
};
```

```
/* sizeof = 48 bytes */
struct foo {
  double b;
  double d;
  long  f;
  long  h;
  float a;
  float c;
  int   j;
  int   l;
  short e;
  short g;
  char  i;
  char  k;
};
```

Reduce Padding: On machines with alignment restrictions, a small amount of memory can be saved by arranging similarly-typed fields together in a structure. The most restrictively aligned types can be placed prior to less restrictive ones.

Moreover, we often use a `char` or `short` variable to hold a flag. We can instead use bit fields. We can combine several of these flags into one byte using bit-fields and use bitmasks and the & operator to extract the values.

Increase Padding: The variables must begin at even addresses to speedup performance. A variable read from or written to an even address takes lesser CPU cycles than required by those stored at odd addresses. To keep a check on this alignment issue, use malloc instead of a static array. Allocate a block twice as large as you need, then point wherever in it that satisfies the alignment you need. However, always free the memory allocated using free() function to avoid memory leak issues.

Avoid pointer Dereference in loop: Pointer dereferencing should be done outside of any loop. You may assign it to a temporary variable and then use that temporary variable in the loop as shown in the figure.

```
int a = 0;

int* iptr = &a;

// Dereferencing pointer inside loop
for (int i = 1; i < 11; ++i)

        *iptr = *iptr + i;

printf("Value of a : %d", a);
```

```
int a = 0;
int* iptr = &a;
// Dereferencing pointer outside loop
int temp = *iptr;
for (int i = 1; i < 11; ++i)
        temp = temp + i;
// Updating pointer using final value of temp
*iptr = temp;
printf("Value of a : %d", *iptr );
```

```
#include <stdio.h>
int main(void)
{
    register int i = 0;
    register int j = 0;
    int n = 5;
    for (i = 0; i < n; ++i) {
        for (j = 0; j <= i; ++j)
            printf("* ");
        printf("\n");
    }
    return 0;
}
```

Use Register variables as counters of inner loops: Variables stored in registers can be accessed much faster than variables stored in memory.

Fast Mathematics: Avoid unnecessary Integer Division as division operations are slow. Consider the instruction given below.

```
int a = 100, b = 2, c = 5;
int d=a/b/c;    //two division operators
```

We can eliminate one division operation by re-writing this instruction as,

```
int d = a / (b * c); // single division operator
```

As stated earlier, use shift operations to perform multiplication and division. One shift left multiplies a number by 2 and one shift right divides it by 2. For example,

- To multiply by 6, we can write: a= a<<1 + a<<2;
- To multiply by 7, we can write: a= a<<3 - a;
- To divide by 8, we can write: a= a>>3; // division by power of 2

Moreover, expressions can be simplified to reduce the number of operations performed. For example, instruction a*b + a*b*c + a*b*c*d can be simplified by writing it as, (a*b)*(1 + c*(1 + d))

The original instruction had 6 multiplications and 2 additions while the simplified instruction had 3 multiplications and 2 additions.

OPTIMIZATION WITH SWITCH STATEMENT

When defining a switch case statement, keep the most frequently used labels first and the least frequent label at last.

If there are certain statements that are common to more than one label, then combine those labels so that common statements are written only once and every label has only the unique set of statements. For example, in the code on the right side, we have written common statements only once and different statements in related cases using another switch. Common statements are written for cases c, d, e and f. Then another switch-case statement is defined. Once the different statements in case c, d, e, f are specified, we again write common statements for all the cases.

Prefer int to char or short: We should prefer int to char because all operations of char are performed with integral values. So, first char will be converted into integer and after performing the operation, it will again be converted into char. For a single char, this is not a significant issue but if the same operation is performed 100 times in a loop, then it can decrease the efficiency of the program.

Prefer pre-Increment/Decrement to post Increment/Decrement: In pre-increment, first the value is incremented and then copies the value to variable location. But in case of post-increment, the value is copied to a temporary variable, incremented and then new values is copied to the variable location. If post-increment is performed 1000 times in a loop then it will impact the efficiency.

Order of Expression Evaluation: A || B should not evaluate B is A is True. So, put the expression which evaluates to true most of the times, at the A's place.

Similarly, for A && B, B is not evaluated if A is False, so put the expression which evaluates to false most of the times, at the A's place.

```
switch(expression)
{
case a:
    ........
    ........
    break;
case b:
    ........
    ........
    break;
case c:
    common statements;
    different statements;
    common statements;
    break;
case d:
    common statements;
    different statements;
    common statements;
    break;
case e:
    common statements;
    different statements;
    common statements;
    break;
case f:
    common statements;
    different statements;
    common statements;
    break;
default:
    break;
}
```

```
switch(expression)
{
case a:
    ........
    ........
    break;
case b:
    ........
    ........
    break;
case c:
case d:
case e:
case f:
    common statements;
    switch(expression);
    {
    case c:
        different statements;
        break;
    case d:
        different statements;
        break;
    case e:
        different statements;
        break;
    case f:
        different statements;
        break;
    } /*End of switch*/
    common statements;
    break;

default:
    break;
}/*End of switch*/
```

CASE STUDY QUESTIONS

1. Write a program that finds the length of the linked list using iterative approach.
2. Write a program that finds the length of the linked list using recursive approach.
3. Write a program that swap nodes in a linked list without swapping data
4. Write a program that detects and removes Loop in a Linked List.
5. Write a program to rotate a Linked List
6. Write a program that creates a generic Linked List.
7. Write a program that splits a Circular Linked List into two halves
8. Write a program that insert elements in a sorted circular linked list
9. Write a program that implements QuickSort on Doubly Linked List
10. Write a program that implements Merge Sort for Doubly Linked List

11. Write a program that check for Balanced Brackets in an expression using stacks.
12. Write a program that solves The Stock Span Problem using stacks.
13. Write a program to implement Stack using Queues
14. Write a program to implement a stack that allow operations on middle element
15. Write a program to Generate Binary Numbers from 1 to n
16. Write a program to implement Sliding Window Maximum (Maximum of all subarrays of size K)
17. Write a program that finds the first circular tour that visits all petrol pumps
18. Write a program to implement Queue using Stacks
19. Write a program to Find a pair with given sum in a Balanced BST
20. Write a program to check if a given array contains duplicate elements within k distance from each other.
21. Write a program to find number of Employees Under every Manager.
22. Write a program to find the Longest Path in a Directed Acyclic Graph
23. Write a program to check whether a given graph is Bipartite or not.
24. Write a program to solve Snake and Ladder Problem
25. Write a program to minimize Cash Flow among a given set of friends who have borrowed money from each other.
26. Write a program to implement Boggle (Find all possible words in a board of characters).

APPENDIX G

Answers

Chapter 1

Multiple-choice Questions

1. (b) 2. (c) 3. (d) 4. (d) 5. (b) 6. (b) 7. (d)
8. (c) 9. (c) 10. (d) 11. (c) 12. (b) 13. (c) 14. (a)
15. (b)

True or False

1. False 2. True 3. False 4. False 5. True 6. False 7. True
8. False 9. True 10. False 11. False 12. False 13. True 14. True
15. False 16. False 17. True 18. False 19. True 20. False 21. True
22. True 23. True 24. True 25. True

Fill in the Blanks

1. Dennis Ritchie 2. main() 3. ASCII codes
4. Operating system 5. Modulus operator (%) 6. Unary
7. Typecasting 8. Default case 9. printf()
10. Closing bracket 11. \n 12. const
13. sizeof 14. %hd 15. %x
16. – 17. Calling function 18. Calling function
19. Arguments/parameters 20. Function header and function body 21. Call by reference
22. I byte 23. NULL 24. Rvalue
25. *

Chapter 2

Multiple-choice Questions

1. (a) 2. (c) 3. (a) 4. (b) 5. (a) 6. (b) 7. (a)
8. (d) 9. (d) 10. (b) 11. (b) 12. (a) 13. (b)

True or False

1. False 2. True 3. False 4. False 5. False 6. True 7. False
8. False 9. False 10. False 11. False 12. True 13. False 14. False
15. False

Fill in the Blanks

1. Data structures
2. Functions
3. Arrays
4. Data type
5. Root = NULL
6. Considered apart from the detailed specifications or implementation
7. Input size
8. Amortized case
9. Index or subscript
10. Top
11. Peep or peek
12. An attempt is made to insert an element in an array, stack or queue that is already full.
13. Queue
14. Rear, front
15. Linear data structure
16. Program
17. Time complexity
18. Average case running time
19. O(1)
20. Modules
21. Top down
22. Worst
23. Omega
24. Non-asymptotically
25. Is in

Chapter 3

Multiple-choice Questions

1. (b) 2. (b) 3. (d) 4. (b) 5. (b) 6. (d)

True or False

1. True 2. True 3. True 4. False 5. False 6. True 7. True
8. True 9. False 10. True 11. True 12. False 13. False 14. False
15. True

Fill in the Blanks

1. Index or subscript
2. Consecutive
3. *n*
4. Pointer
5. Data type, name, and size
6. Base address
7. The number of elements stored in it
8. Array of arrays
9. Integral value
10. Fourth

Chapter 4

Multiple-choice Questions

1. (b) 2. (c) 3. (a) 4. (c) 5. (d) 6. (a) 7. (c)
8. (b) 9. (b) 10. (b)

True or False

1. False 2. False 3. True 4. True 5. False 6. False 7. True
8. False 9. True 10. False 11. True 12. False 13. True 14. False
15. False

Fill in the Blanks

1. A null-terminated character array
2. Null character
3. 5
4. zero
5. Consecutive
6. 99
7. scanf()
8. 65-97
9. Convert a character into upper case
10. When in dictionary order S1 will come after S2
11. strrev()
12. Morning
13. 15
14. Index operation
15. str2 is less than str1
16. strlen
17. puts

Chapter 5

Multiple-choice Questions

1. (d) 2. (c) 3. (b) 4. (b) 5. (b) 6. (b) 7. (d)

True or False

1. False 2. False 3. True 4. True 5. True 6. False 7. True
8. False 9. False 10. True 11. True 12. True 13. True 14. False

Fill in the Blanks

1. User defined 2. Structure declaration 3. Structure name
4. Typedef 5. Zero 6. Null character
7. Dot operator 8. Nested structure 9. Self-referential
10. We declare a variable of a structure
11. Union 12. Refer to the individual members of structure or union
13. Union

Chapter 6

Multiple-choice Questions

1. (b) 2. (c) 3. (d) 4. (c) 5. (b) 6. (d) 7. (b)

True or False

1. True 2. True 3. False 4. False 5. False 6. False 7. True
8. False 9. True 10. True

Fill in the Blanks

1. AVAIL 2. O(1) 3. O(n) 4. Two 5. One 6. Two 7. Two
8. One 9. Two 10. One 11. Node 12. START 13. Node
14. There is no memory that can be allocated for the new node to be inserted 15. First

Chapter 7

Multiple-choice Questions

1. (a) 2. (b) 3. (a) 4. (c)

True or False

1. False 2. True 3. True 4. True 5. False 6. True 7. False
8. True 9. False 10. True 11. False 12. False

Fill in the Blanks

1. stack 2. stack 3. O(n)
4. We try to delete a node from a stack that is empty 5. Left to right
6. Non-tail 7. Directly

Chapter 8

Multiple-choice Questions

1. (b) 2. (a) 3. (b) 4. (a) 5. (b)

True or False

1. False 2. False 3. False 4. True 5. False 6. True 7. True
8. True

Fill in the Blanks

1. Rear
2. Dequeue
3. O(1)
4. Input restricted dequeue
5. Circular array or a circular doubly linked list
6. Priority queues
7. Queues

Chapter 9

Multiple-choice Questions

1. (a) 2. (a) 3. (d) 4. (a) 5. (c) 6. (d)

True or False

1. True 2. True 3. True 4. False 5. True 6. False 7. True
8. False

Fill in the Blanks

1. Ascendant
2. Nodes
3. 2^{k-1}
4. Two
5. Siblings
6. Structure and contents
7. n and $\log_2(n+1)$.
8. Each node in the tree has either no child or exactly two children
9. Preorder
10. The estimated probability of occurrence for each possible value of the source character.

Chapter 10

Multiple-choice Questions

1. (a) 2. (b) 3. (b) 4. (d) 5. (a)

True or False

1. True 2. False 3. False 4. True 5. True 6. False 7. True
8. False 9. False 10. False

Fill in the Blanks

1. Two way threaded binary tree
2. Right sub tree
3. In-order successor
4. Subtracting the height of its right sub-tree from the height of the left sub-tree.
5. The left sub-tree of the tree is one level lower than that of the right sub-tree.
6. O(log n)
7. LL
8. Black and black
9. P (the parent of n) is the root of the splay tree.
10. Splay

Chapter 11

Multiple-choice Questions

1. (b) 2. (a) 3. (c) 4. (c) 5. (c)

True or False

1. True 2. True 3. False 4. False 5. False 6. True 7. True
8. False 9. False

Fill in the blanks

1. M and M-1
2. m and m-1
3. m/2
4. B tree
5. O(log N)

Chapter 12

Multiple-choice Questions

1. (b) 2. (a) 3. (c) 4. (d) 5. (b) 6. (d) 7. (d)

True or False

1. True 2. False 3. True 4. True 5. False 6. False 7. True
8. False 9. True 10. False 11. False

Fill in the blanks

1. $2i + 1$
2. Priority queues
3. Partially ordered trees
4. Min heap
5. Root
6. i
7. A set of binomial trees that satisfy binomial-heap properties
8. 2^i
9. O(1)
10. Collection of heap-ordered trees
11. Whether node x has lost a child since the last time x was made the child of another node

Chapter 13

Multiple-choice Questions

1. (b) 2. (c) 3. (b) 4. (a) 5. (b) 6. (d) 7. (a)

True or False

1. False 2. False 3. True 4. False 5. True 6. False 7. True
8. True 9. True 10. True

Fill in the Blanks

1. An isolated node
2. Terminate
3. Bit matrix or Boolean matrix
4. Cycle
5. Multi-graph
6. Tree vertices
7. Transitive closure
8. Articulation point
9. bi-connected
10. Bridge

Chapter 14

Multiple-choice Questions

1. (b) 2. (d) 3. (c) 4. (d) 5. (b) 6. (a) 7. (d)
8. (a) 9. (c) 10. (d) 11. (d)

True or False

1. False 2. False 3. False 4. False 5. True 6. False 7. True
8. False 9. True 10. True 11. True

Fill in the Blanks

1. Sorted array
2. O(n)
3. The process of arranging values in a predetermined order.
4. Merge sort / heap sort/ quick sort
5. External sorting
6. Bubble sort
7. $O(n^2)$
8. Merge sort/ quick sort
9. O(n log n)
10. O(n.k)
11. O(n log n)
12. Pivot element

Chapter 15

Multiple-choice Questions

1. (c) 2. (a) 3. (a) 4. (c) 5. (b) 6. (c)

True or False

1. False 2. False 3. False 4. False 5. False 6. True 7. False
8. True 9. True

Fill in the Blanks

1. Hash function
2. Hashing
3. Sentinel value and a data value
4. Collision
5. Probes
6. Quadratic probing

Chapter 16

Multiple-choice Questions

1. (d) 2. (c) 3. (a) 4. (a)

True or False

1. False 2. True 3. True 4. True 5. True 6. False 7. True
8. True

Fill in the Blanks

1. File
2. Type and size
3. Record
4. File position
5. File structure
6. Record number and address
7. Primary
8. Inverted
9. Database

About the Author

Dr Reema Thareja is Assistant Professor in the Department of Computer Science, Shyama Prasad Mukherji College, University of Delhi. In her 18 years of teaching experience, she has taught several courses including BA, BSc, MSc, BBA, MBA, BCA, and MCA.

Dr Thareja has authored several books in Computer Science and her books have been well accepted across the globe. She has published more than 22 research papers in international journals of repute and filed four patents. She also launched a free mobile app, Jruma, for Apple as well Android devices to promote learning through quizzing and excite users by giving them an opportunity to earn while they learn.

Besides being an author, she is an eminent speaker. Dr Thareja has conducted several Faculty Development Programmes, Seminars, Webinars, and Students' Workshops in India, the UAE, and the USA. She was also invited as a speaker for the Global Virtual Summit in New York.

Dr. Thareja is a Board Member of Studies in Computer Science for two eminent colleges in Vijayawada and a member of Technical Advisory Board of Refactor Academy. Being a member of Computer Society of India, Editorial Board and Elite Speakers group of IMRF have added feathers in her cap. She has received multiple awards and recognitions for her immense contributions in the field of education.

Related Titles

FUNDAMENTALS OF COMPUTERS [9780199499274]

- Lab activities – Relevant chapters are followed by lab activities which provide the practical implementation of the concepts covered in the chapter
- Updated version of Windows and MS Office - numerous lab activities based on Windows 10 and MS Office 2013
- Assessment through Oxford Areal – contain numerous MCQs and True/ False questions which help readers to gain immediate feedback on their understanding of the concepts

COURSE ON COMPUTER CONCEPTS [9780199469390]

- The contents of the book completely conform to the latest CCC syllabus prescribed by NIELIT.
- Discusses important topics ranging from basics of computers to applications of MS Word, MS Excel, and MS PowerPoint, and recent technologies (i.e., digital financial services).
- Provides a list of shortcut keys used in MS Word, Excel, and PowerPoint for easy reference.

INTRODUCTION TO C PROGRAMMING [9780199452057]

- Exhaustive coverage of fundamental topics with more than 200 program code examples with outputs
- Chapter on programming languages and the generations through which these languages have evolved, which gives readers an insight into computer software
- More than 700 objective-type questions, including fill-in-the-blanks, MCQS, and true/false questions

PYTHON PROGRAMMING 2E [9789354973765]

- With a comprehensive introduction to computers, problem solving approaches, programming languages, and objectoriented programming, the book goes on to explore Python Programming in detail.
- Separate chapters covering important constructs of Python language such as control statements, functions, strings, files, data structures, classes and objects, inheritance, operator overloading, and exceptions have been added to make learning simpler for readers.
- Plenty of useful chapter-end exercises have also been included on programming and debugging.

PROGRAMMING IN C [9780199492282]

- Employs a very lucid style of presentation which makes the concepts easy to understand
- Provides more than 240 programming examples with outputs to illustrate the concepts
- Includes highly detailed pedagogy entailing examples, figures, algorithms, and programming tips

OBJECT ORIENTED PROGRAMMING WITH C++ [9780199485673]

- Provides plenty of programs executable on Dev C++ and g++ compilers along with their outputs to help readers enhance their programming skills
- Includes Notes and Programming tips to help readers keep in mind the critical concepts and do's and don'ts while developing a program
- Provides case-studies including programs interspersed within the text to demonstrate the implementation of the concepts learnt

COMPUTER FUNDAMENTALS AND PROGRAMMING IN C [9789354977893]

- Provides exhaustive coverage of computer fundamentals, focusing on both the hardware as well as software components
- Offers a detailed coverage of different types of number systems and computer codes
- Covers user-defined data types (arrays, strings, structures, unions) in detail, with each of the operations on these data types implemented using numerous example codes
- Includes case studies after select chapters

Other Related Titles

9780190127275	***Sridhar & Vijayalakshmi:*** Machine Learning
9780199459643	***A. Seth and B.L. Juneja:*** Java: One Step Ahead
9780190124083	***Vasudevan et.al.*** Data Structures Using Python
9780199456666	***H. Bhasin:*** Algorithms: Design and Analysis
9780198093695	***S. Sridhar:*** Design and Analysis of Algorithms